The IDG SECRETS Advantage

Windows 3.1 Configuration SECRETS is part of the SECRETS series of books brought to you by IDG Books Worldwide. The designers of the SECRETS series understand that you appreciate insightful and comprehensive works from computer experts. Authorities in their respective areas, the authors of the SECRETS books have been selected for their ability to enrich your daily computing tasks.

The formula for a book in the SECRETS series is simple: Give an expert author a forum to pass on his or her expertise to readers. A SECRETS author, rather than the publishing company, directs the organization, pace, and treatment of the subject matter. SECRETS authors maintain close contact with end users through column feedback, user group participation, and consulting work. The authors' close contact with the needs of computer users gives the SECRETS books a strategic advantage over most computer books. Our authors do not distance themselves from the reality of daily computing, but rather, our authors are directly tied to the reader response stream.

We believe that the author has the experience to approach a topic in the most efficient manner, and we know that you, the reader, will benefit from a "one-to-one" relationship, through the text, with the author. The author's voice is always present in a SECRETS series book. Some have compared the presentation of a topic in a SECRETS book to sitting at a coffee break with the author and having the author's full attention.

And of course, the author is free to include or recommend useful software, both shareware and proprietary, in a SECRETS series book. The software that accompanies a SECRETS book is not intended as casual filler. The software is strategically linked to the content, theme, or procedures of the book. We expect that you will receive a real and direct benefit from the included software.

You will find this book comprehensive whether you read it cover to cover, section to section, or simply a topic at a time. As a computer user, you deserve a comprehensive and informative resource of answers that *Windows 3.1 Configuration SECRETS* delivers.

David Solomon
Publisher

Windows 3.1 Configuration SECRETS™

by Valda Hilley and James M. Blakely

Foreword by Cheryl Currid

President, Currid & Company

IDG BOOKS

IDG Books Worldwide, Inc.
An International Data Group Company

San Mateo, California◆Indianapolis, Indiana◆Boston, Massachusetts

Windows 3.1 Configuration SECRETS

Published by
IDG Books Worldwide, Inc.
An International Data Group Company
155 Bovet Road, Suite 310
San Mateo, CA 94402

Library of Congress Catalog Card No.: 94-75647

ISBN 1-56884-026-8

Printed in the United States of America

10 9 8 7 6 5 4 3 2 1

1C/QU/RS/ZU

Distributed in the United States by IDG Books Worldwide, Inc.

Distributed in Canada by Macmillan of Canada, a Division of Canada Publishing Corporation; by Computer and Technical Books in Miami, Florida, for South America and the Caribbean; by Longman Singapore in Singapore, Malaysia, Thailand, and Korea; by Toppan Co. Ltd. in Japan; by Asia Computerworld in Hong Kong; by Woodslane Pty. Ltd. in Australia and New Zealand; and by Transword Publishers Ltd. in the U.K. and Europe.

For general information on IDG Books in the U.S., including information on discounts and premiums, contact IDG Books at 800-762-2974 or 415-312-0650.

For information on where to purchase IDG Books outside the U.S., contact Christina Turner at 415-312-0633.

For information on translations, contact Marc Jeffrey Mikulich, Foreign Rights Manager, at IDG Books Worldwide; FAX NUMBER 415-358-1260.

For sales inquiries and special prices for bulk quantities, write to the address above or call IDG Books Worldwide at 415-312-0650.

 is a registered trademark of IDG Books Worldwide, Inc.

 The text in this book is printed on recycled paper.

About the Authors

Valda Hilley is a computer consultant based in Cincinnati, Ohio, specializing in supporting Windows-based installations. Valda, a former engineer and systems designer, has been involved with microcomputers since 1980.

Valda is currently the managing editor of the *Windows Journal* and a sysop on the Windows User Group Network's WINUSER forum on CompuServe. She also serves as a contributing editor to various computing publications.

You can reach Valda on CompuServe by typing GO WINUSER at the CIS prompt, or via CompuServe e-mail at 76711,1205. Internet users can send mail to KODAN!Valda@RYLOS.N2IDF.AMPR.ORG.

James M. Blakely is vice-president of Blakely-Signature Associates, a Microsoft Solution Provider in Bonita Springs, Florida, that specializes in designing and supporting workgroup computing systems. A Microsoft Certified System Engineer, Jim has been involved in the microcomputer field since 1979, and has been installing and designing network-based computer systems for the last ten years.

Jim is a contributing editor to the *Windows Journal* and writes a monthly column in the *Naples PC Business Users Group Newsletter* about Windows issues.

You can reach Jim on CompuServe through the WINUSER Forum, or via CompuServe e-mail at 75665,436. Internet users can send mail to N4ZFD!FRODO@RYLOS.N2IDF.AMPR.ORG.

Contributing Author

Arthur Knowles is the president of Knowles Consulting, based in Woodbridge, Virginia. He is a Microsoft Consulting Channel Partner and Solution Provider, certified in MS-DOS, Windows 3.1, and Windows for Workgroups 3.11. Arthur specializes in support and development for applications running under Microsoft Windows, Windows for Workgroups, Windows NT, Windows NT Advanced Server, and Windows NT SQL Server.

Arthur has been working with computers since 1983. He has written applications in COBOL, FORTRAN, C, C++, Pascal, and assembler languages for use on mainframes (IBM, Honeywell, DEC, and CDC).

Arthur lives in Woodbridge with his cat, CAT. You can reach Arthur on CompuServe through the WINUSER Forum, or via CompuServe e-mail at 71041,2613.

About the Windows User Group Network

Founded in 1988, the Windows User Group Network (WUGNET) was established as an informal network of special interest group leaders, representing the largest PC user groups in the country.

WUGNET was designed from the outset to serve the needs of Windows system developers, programmers, application specialists, and technical experts through a multilevel information delivery system. This system includes a bimonthly publication, the *Windows Journal,* and on-line libraries containing code samples and utilities, trade show activities, professional support, and a forum on CompuServe.

Since opening the CompuServe forum in March of 1993, the forum has rapidly grown in popularity with users all over the world because of the forum's uniquely independent character. The WUGNET Forum is the communications hub of the WUGNET organization.

WUGNET thrives as an independent organization, not formally committed to the ideals of any single vendor or groups of vendors, but positioned as an industry-wide technical resource. WUGNET provides unique resources in the Windows industry through programs and involvement with independent software developers, leading Windows consultants, corporate Windows users. WUGNET's mission is to

- Promote understanding and cooperation among organizations engaged in furthering the progress and application of Windows-based systems.

- Provide an international clearing house for information on Windows-based computing and technology.

- Conduct conferences and exhibitions for the exchange of information.

- Provide document-based information through the publication of a trade journal and reference books.

- Design or develop innovative software tools and utilities to help users manage and optimize the Windows environment.

We invite you to join our membership as we prepare to embark on a new journey into Windows 4.0 (Chicago) and Windows NT (Cairo).

Howard Sobel
Executive Director
The Windows User Group Network

Joel L. Diamond
Technical Director
The Windows User Group Network

About IDG Books Worldwide

Welcome to the world of IDG Books Worldwide.

IDG Books Worldwide, Inc., is a subsidiary of International Data Group, the world's largest publisher of computer-related information and the leading global provider of information services on information technology. International Data Group publishes over 195 computer publications in 62 countries. Forty million people read one or more International Data Group publications each month

If you use personal computers, IDG Books is committed to publishing quality books that meet your needs. We rely on our extensive network of publications, including such leading periodicals as *Macworld, InfoWorld, PC World, Computerworld, Publish, Network World*, and *SunWorld*, to help us make informed and timely decisions in creating useful computer books that meet your needs.

Every IDG book strives to bring extra value and skill-building instructions to the reader. Our books are written by experts, with the backing of IDG periodicals, and with careful thought devoted to issues such as audience, interior design, use of icons, and illustrations. Our editorial staff is a careful mix of high-tech journalists and experienced book people. Our close contact with the makers of computer products helps ensure accuracy and thorough coverage. Our heavy use of personal computers at every step in production means we can deliver books in the most timely manner.

We are delivering books of high quality at competitive prices on topics customers want. At IDG, we believe in quality, and we have been delivering quality for over 25 years. You'll find no better book on a subject than an IDG book.

John Kilcullen
President and CEO
IDG Books Worldwide, Inc.

IDG Books Worldwide, Inc. is a subsidiary of International Data Group. The officers are Patrick J. McGovern, Founder and Board Chairman; Walter Boyd, President. International Data Group's publications include: **ARGENTINA'S** Computerworld Argentina, Infoworld Argentina; **ASIA'S** Computerworld Hong Kong, PC World Hong Kong, Computerworld Southeast Asia, PC World Singapore, Computerworld Malaysia, PC World Malaysia; **AUSTRALIA'S** Computerworld Australia, Australian PC World, Australian Macworld, Network World, Mobile Business Australia, Reseller, IDG Sources; **AUSTRIA'S** Computerwelt Oesterreich, PC Test; **BRAZIL'S** Computerworld, Gamepro, Game Power, Mundo IBM, Mundo Unix, PC World, Super Game; **BELGIUM'S** Data News (CW) **BULGARIA'S** Computerworld Bulgaria, Ediworld, PC & Mac World Bulgaria, Network World Bulgaria; **CANADA'S** CIO Canada, Computerworld Canada, Graduate Computerworld, InfoCanada, Network World Canada; **CHILE'S** Computerworld Chile, Informatica; **COLOMBIA'S** Computerworld Colombia; **CZECH REPUBLIC'S** Computerworld, Elektronika, PC World; **DENMARK'S** CAD/CAM WORLD, Communications World, Computerworld Danmark, LOTUS World, Macintosh Produktkatalog, Macworld Danmark, PC World Produktguide, Windows World; **ECUADOR'S** PC World Ecuador; **EGYPT'S** Computerworld (CW) Middle East, PC World Middle East; **FINLAND'S** MikroPC, Tietoviikko, Tietoverkko; **FRANCE'S** Distributique, GOLDEN MAC, InfoPC, Languages & Systems, Le Guide du Monde Informatique, Le Monde Informatique, Telecoms & Reseaux; **GERMANY'S** Computerwoche, Computerwoche Focus, Computerwoche Extra, Computerwoche Karriere, Information Management, Macwelt, Netzwelt, PC Welt, PC Woche, Publish, Unit; **GREECE'S** Infoworld, PC Games; **HUNGARY'S** Computerworld SZT, PC World; **INDIA'S** Computers & Communications; **IRELAND'S** Computerscope; **ISRAEL'S** Computerworld Israel, PC World Israel; **ITALY'S** Computerworld Italia, Lotus Magazine, Macworld Italia, Networking Italia, PC Shopping Italy, PC World Italia; **JAPAN'S** Computerworld Today, Information Systems World, Macworld Japan, Nikkei Personal Computing, SunWorld Japan, Windows World; **KENYA'S** East African Computer News; **KOREA'S** Computerworld Korea, Macworld Korea, PC World Korea; **MEXICO'S** Compu Edicion, Compu Manufactura, Computacion/ Punto de Venta, Computerworld Mexico, MacWorld, Mundo Unix, PC World, Windows; **THE NETHERLANDS'** Computer! Totaal, Computable (CW), LAN Magazine, MacWorld, Totaal "Windows"; **NEW ZEALAND'S** Computer Listings, Computerworld New Zealand, New Zealand PC World; **NIGERIA'S** PC World Africa; **NORWAY'S** Computerworld Norge, C/World, Lotusworld Norge, Macworld Norge, Networld, PC World Ekspress, PC World Norge, PC World's Produktguide, Publish& Multimedia World, Student Data, Unix World, Windowsworld; IDG Direct Response; **PANAMA'S** PC World Panama; **PERU'S** Computerworld Peru, PC World; **PEOPLE'S REPUBLIC OF CHINA'S** China Computerworld, China Infoworld, PC World China, Electronics International, Electronic Product World, China Network World; IDG HIGH TECH BEIJING'S New Product World; IDG SHENZHEN'S Computer News Digest; **PHILIPPINES'** Computerworld Philippines, PC Digest (PCW); **POLAND'S** Computerworld Poland, PC World/Komputer; **PORTUGAL'S** Cerebro/PC World, Correio Informatico/ Computerworld, MacIn; **ROMANIA'S** Computerworld, PC World; **RUSSIA'S** Computerworld-Moscow, Mir - PC, Sety; **SLOVENIA'S** Monitor Magazine; **SOUTH AFRICA'S** Computer Mail (CIO),Computing S.A.,Network World S.A.; **SPAIN'S** Amiga World, Computerworld Espana, Communicaciones World, Macworld Espana, NeXTWORLD, Super Juegos Magazine (GamePro), PC World Espana, Publish, Sunworld; **SWEDEN'S** Attack, ComputerSweden, Corporate Computing, Lokala Natverk/LAN, Lotus World, MAC&PC, Macworld, Mikrodatorn, PC World, Publishing & Design (CAP), Datalngenjoren, Maxi Data,Windows World; **SWITZERLAND'S** Computerworld Schweiz, Macworld Schweiz, PC Katalog, PC & Workstation; **TAIWAN'S** Computerworld Taiwan, Global Computer Express, PC World Taiwan; **THAILAND'S** Thai Computerworld; **TURKEY'S** Computerworld Monitor, Macworld Turkiye, PC World Turkiye; **UKRAINE'S** Computerworld; **UNITED KINGDOM'S** Computing /Computerworld, Connexion/Network World, Lotus Magazine, Macworld, Open Computing/Sunworld; **UNITED STATES'** AmigaWorld, Cable in the Classroom, CD Review, CIO, Computerworld, Desktop Video World, DOS Resource Guide, Electronic Entertainment Magazine, Federal Computer Week, Federal Integrator, GamePro, IDG Books, Infoworld, Infoworld Direct, Laser Event, Macworld, Multimedia World, Network World, NeXTWORLD, PC Letter, PC World, PlayRight, Power PC World, Publish, SunWorld, SWATPro, Video Event; **VENEZUELA'S** Computerworld Venezuela, MicroComputerworld Venezuela; **VIETNAM'S** PC World Vietnam

Dedication

To my husband Glenn, who stayed up late at night with me as I wrote.

To my daughter Sidney, who waited patiently for me to finish this book.

To my mother, whom I owe a great deal of money for long distance phone calls.

To Judy, my friend and partner, who kept our business afloat while I buried myself in this book.

And to J.L.D., who knows better.

— Valda

Acknowledgments

Jim and Arthur, thanks for taking the plunge with me.

Angela Blakely, Jim's wife, thanks for putting up with all the late night phone calls.

Carole Patton, thank you for your efforts.

Runnoe Connally, thanks for pinch hitting.

My Sysop colleagues on WUGNET's Windows User Forum, thanks for covering for me.

Joel Diamond, Technical Director and co-founder of WUGNET, who developed the concept and original outline for this book: Thanks for introducing me to Jim and Arthur.

Howard Sobel, Executive Director and co-founder of WUGNET, thanks for keeping the wheels rolling and handling administrative stuff behind the scenes.

The authors wish to thank Mary Corder, project editor at IDG for not giving up on us and for turning *Windows 3.1 Configuration SECRETS* into a real book. Also thanks to Mary Bednarek, David Solomon and the IDG Books editorial staff for making us feel like a part of the IDG team.

We'd also like to thank the following companies for their contributions to this book:

Microsoft Corporation

Hewlett Packard, publishers of Dashboard for Windows

Gateway 2000 Computers, we were "Powered by Gateway"

A special thanks to C.E. "Tad" Dekko and Lee Dees at Dri-Dek Corporation, and to Rick Orr at Westinghouse Communities for allowing Jim to experiment with their machines.

ATI Technologies, Inc. for the ATI Ultra Graphics Pro

Delrina, publishers of WinFax Pro and WinComm

Advanced Gravis, Inc. makers of the Gravis UltraSound board.

askSam Systems, publishers of askSam for Windows, used to manage all the research for this book

Ares Software, publishers of Font Minder, Font Monger, and Font Chameleon

Qualitas, Inc. for 386MAX and especially DOSMAX

Quarterdeck Office Systems, for QEMM

Lotus Corporation, for 123 for Windows, and Ami Pro

Stac Electronics, for Stacker for Windows

Supra Corporation, for the Supra Fax Modem V3.2bis a fast and reliable connection for RAS and anything else

Xircom, Inc. for the Xircom Pocket Ethernet Adapter III used to connect my Gateway 2000 notebook to the Windows for Workgroups network

Nomadic Systems, Inc. for developing SmartSync which helped to keep the manuscript files synchronized as I worked from computer to computer

Colorado Memory Systems, Inc. for making the Trakker 250 portable tape back up system. It saved this book manuscript at least twice during the project. I never leave home without it!

On behalf of the Windows User Group Network, I'd like to thank:

Waterside Productions for making this project happen. And Michael Utvich, whose initial vision and effort, made this project a reality.

Greg Russell of CompuServe, for providing the direction and support of the Windows Users Group Network on-line forum, WINUSER, on CompuServe.

System Engineer Development team

Andrew Rowe, the chief programmer of WUGNET's System Engineer. Andrew took ideas, comments and suggestions, and turned them into the highly acclaimed System Engineer.

Jack DeLand, WUGNET's Electronic Publishing Director, who developed the help system for System Engineer and the electronic versions of Microsoft's Windows Resource Kits published by WUGNET.

(The publisher would like to give special thanks to Patrick J. McGovern, without whom this book would not have been possible.)

Credits

VP & Publisher
David Solomon

Managing Editor
Mary Bednarek

Acquisitions Editor
Janna Custer

Production Director
Beth Jenkins

Senior Editors
Tracy L. Barr
Sandy Blackthorn
Diane Graves Steele

Production Coordinator
Cindy L. Phipps

Acquisitions Assistant
Megg Bonar

Editorial Assistant
Darlene Cunningham

Project Editor
Mary Corder

Editors
Barbara L. Potter
Pat Seiler
Shawn MacLaren
abercrombie at random

Technical Reviewer
Daniel J. Willis

Production Staff
Tony Augsburger
Valery Bourke
Mary Breidenbach
Chris Collins
Sherry Gomoll
Drew R. Moore
Kathie Schnorr
Gina Scott

Proofreaders
Betty Kish
Charles A. Hutchinson

Indexer
Sherry Massey

Contents at a Glance

xiv

Table of Contents

xviii

Part IV: Windows for Workgroups Applications 445

Chapter 22: Mail 447

xxviii

xxxii

Part VI: Appendices 665

Appendix A: Troubleshooting Windows 667

xxxiv

xxxviii

xxxix

Foreword

Aah Windows ... clearly the most successful operating environment for computers on planet Earth today. With about 80% of all new Intel-based personal computers coming out with Windows preinstalled, chances are that everyone who uses a computer will someday become a Windows user. And, if you've decided to read this book, you are probably one of the millions of Windows users who has come to know the ups and downs of using Windows.

Luckily, for the most part, using Windows turns into a real treat. It is colorful, consistent, and capable. The Windows environment has become a boon to everyday users because it lets people easily run more than one application at a time, easily exchange information between applications, and easily tap into thousands of exciting software programs.

That's the good news. But, there is another side to the story.

It's no secret that Windows can be tough to configure. Lots of little things can affect how your computer performs. If you know the secrets, you know how to turn an average performing computer into a screamer. But, be warned, the reverse is also true. If you don't pay attention to little configuration tips and techniques, you are likely to take a perfectly apt computer and make it run like snail.

The difference lies in configuration. And that's what this book is all about. Valda Hilley and Jim Blakely uncover the secrets and give you practical advice on how to tune your computer's configuration. You could save thousands of dollars and countless hours of time by reading this book and understanding the tips and techniques contained between these covers.

In clear and precise detail, Valda and Jim unveil the mysteries of setting up the Windows environment. They uncover secrets to help you optimize memory, disk and storage, hardware, video, the keyboard, and even your mouse. They even include secrets for fonts and printing, communications and network configuration. You'll also gain a clear understanding of the basics behind memory and processor architectures.

If you are trying to get the best from the Windows environment, it helps to have some expert advice. And, now you do. Valda and Jim's wisdom are within easy reach – no further away than your bookshelf.

Cheryl Currid
President, Currid & Company
"Windows at Work" columnist for *Windows Magazine*

Introduction

Windows is now the de facto standard for both personal and corporate computing environments. As such, the issues of installing, configuring, optimizing, and
maintaining Windows workstations can seem overwhelming. Our goal for this book
is to provide you with information that will aid you in managing your systems.

In addition to learning about the current state of Windows, we also provide a
few glimpses into the future of Windows. Before you can prepare for the next
generation of Windows, however, you need to understand where we are today
and to take advantage of the tips, workarounds, and secrets available right now.

This book includes coverage on Windows for Workgroups 3.11, whose technology represents a preview of things to come from Bill Gates' vision of "Information at your Fingertips." As early users of Windows for Workgroups 3.11, it
occurred to us that Microsoft misnamed this new version of Windows. It should
have been called "Windows for Networks" or simply "Windows 3.11." *Windows
3.1 Configuration SECRETS* also has a lot to offer you if you're using plain
Windows 3.1. With Windows for Workgroups 3.11, you'll discover major
structural changes to the connectivity components and architecture to the
Windows kernel with new shells, security, extensibility, plus OLE 2.0 and
Microsoft at Work Fax technologies.

This book provides the means for you to maximize the software and hardware
investment you have made in Windows. You will be empowered to take control
of your Windows environment and optimize it to its maximum potential. Your
productivity with any computing task is highly dependent on a solid and well-
tuned configuration, but we have discovered that things don't always work the
way you expect. Turning that situation around and getting Windows to work for
you is the primary theme of this book.

The information in this book was gleaned from our own technical experts on
the WINUSER forum, as well as the other wizards who freely share their knowledge,
workarounds, tips, and some undocumented secrets through CompuServe.

We discovered midway through this project that this book couldn't hold all the
information available to help you with Windows. Not every chapter provides
you with all the secrets, workarounds, tips, and insider information necessary
to solve every potential problem. This book is, however, a focused resource
that provides you with the tools to help you with most of your problems. In
light of the fact that we just couldn't tell you everything, this book comes with its
own technical support system: Join us in the WINUSER forum and in the pages
of the *Windows Journal,* to discover the secrets that overflowed from this book.

How to use this book

This books is designed in manageable sections. As a reference work, we don't expect you to read it from cover to cover. Just use what you need and share the rest. As you get more experience or your computing environment changes, you'll more than likely find yourself coming back to those sections you skipped the first time. Keep this book handy so that you can easily find it when you need it!

We have several suggestions for you to get the most out of this book and WUGNET.

First, after you have read some of the chapters, get the bundled disks out of the back of this book and schedule some uninterrupted time just to experiment with the programs and utilities we have provided you. The authors have put together useful and interesting programs and we hope you take every possible advantage for using them.

These disks include two commercial software products: WUGNET's System Engineer, which is the ultimate enhancement to the Windows Control Panel and configuration management tool, and Hewlett Packard's Dashboard for Windows, a terrific replacement for the Windows Program Manager shell. Each of these programs normally sells for more than the price of this book! And you get them plus many other utilities with this book.

Second, get a CompuServe online membership and log on to the Windows User Group Network (WUGNET) Forum. No book will solve every problem you may have but other WUGNET members in our CompuServe forum would be more than happy to give you helpful (and free) suggestions. (Better than paying for support from some vendors we could mention!) It's a good starting point. Or if the topics covered in this book help you but you discover that you have further questions, you can talk to some of our online experts. In addition, the developers and shareware authors of the software included with *Windows 3.1 Configuration SECRETS* provide support on the WUGNET Forum!

Third, consider becoming a member of the Windows Users Group Network. In addition to the bi-monthly *Windows Journal* packed with technical information, members often get advance product news and discounts on software from WUGNET corporate members. Members also get the latest releases and special upgrade prices for WUGNET'S System Engineer featured in this book.

Fourth, get a copy of Microsoft Windows Resource Kit 3.1 or Windows Resource Kit (WRK). The information contained in the WRK represents a starting point for dealing with many problems and issues in maximizing Windows. Electronic versions of the WRK in Windows HLP format are available exclusively for WUGNET members!

And last but not least, come on-line and share your expertise with us. We're always looking for people who can teach *us* a thing or two!

How This Book Is Organized

Part I: Mastering the Environment Despite the simplicity Windows brings to the user through its colorful interface, Windows is a complex environment. Its operation and performance hinge on the successful interaction of your system's hardware, peripherals, device drivers, and of course, MS-DOS. Part I is designed to give you the underlying fundamentals you need to understand how Windows works and how to manipulate your Windows environment.

Chapter 1, "Understanding Memory" Configuring Windows in many ways is synonymous with configuring memory. Before you can manage memory under Windows you must understand PC memory types. This chapter discusses the five types of memory and how they work so that you can set up MS-DOS and Windows for optimum performance. It also discusses microprocessor types and how each one organizes and uses memory.

Chapter 2, "Optimizing DOS for Windows" Windows 3.11 is essentially a graphical user interface (GUI) with a DOS extender. Windows relies on DOS in order to operate quickly and reliably. This chapter shows you how to optimize your CONFIG.SYS and AUTOEXEC.BAT files and use DOS' memory management capabilities to provide an optimum foundation for Windows.

Chapter 3, "Using Third-Party Memory Managers" There are some advantages to using third-party memory managers over DOS. This chapter examines the characteristics and features of two major products, Quarterdeck's QEMM and Qualitas' 386MAX.

Chapter 4, "Understanding Windows Architecture" This chapter presents an inside look at Windows internal structure and resources. This will enable you to understand the causes and effects of manipulating Windows settings. You'll also understand why Windows has certain limitations and constraints.

Part II: Installing and Setting Up Installing Windows properly requires more than inserting a disk and typing SETUP. Part II is designed to guide you through the installation process by providing you with techniques you can implement in your planning and installation process.

Chapter 5, "Windows for Workgroups 32-Bit Disk Access System" Windows is usually referred to as an operating environment instead of an operating system. With the addition of the 32-bit disk access system, Windows 3.1x is closer to being an operating system. This chapter shows you how to implement 32-bit access on your system, and provides techniques and workarounds to get it working for you.

Chapter 6, "Controlling Windows Environment with Setup" A successful Windows environment usually begins with a well-planned installation strategy. This chapter presents strategies and techniques to ensure a successful Windows installation.

Chapter 7, "Installing Windows on an Existing Network" Windows and Windows for Workgroups 3.1x have been enhanced to coexist with major network operating systems. This chapter discusses topics such as using the SETUP/A administrative feature, installing with SETUP/N, automating installation on multiple workstations, and avoiding installation pitfalls.

Chapter 8, "The Anatomy of a Windows Installation" Windows installs 400 or more files during its installation. This chapter describes the files that Windows places on your hard drive and offers suggestions on ways to decrease the size of the Windows footprint.

Part III: Configuring This part represents the core of the book and is built on what Parts I and II introduce. Part III provides detailed information on configuring Windows through its configuration files, SYSTEM.INI, WIN.INI, and so on.

Chapter 9, "Basic Windows Configuration" This chapter shows you how to modify settings that control your Windows desktop and appearance.

Chapter 10, "Configuring Windows Applets" Windows ships with several applets, Program Manager, Control Panel, and File Manager, all of which have configurable features that give you some degree of control over those aspects of Windows. This chapter shows you how to configure Program Manager, Control Panel, and File Manager.

Chapter 11, "Windows Memory Configuration" Windows is a memory intensive environment and the performance of Windows and Windows applications depends on how well you configure memory under Windows. This chapter provides detailed information, tips, and secrets for configuring memory for Windows.

Chapter 12, "Disk Access and Storage Secrets" The hard disk is an integral component in your Windows workstation. Its speed and reliability impact Windows overall performance, and it provides Windows with virtual memory. This chapter discusses caches, configuring SmartDrive, and disk compression.

Chapter 13, "Hardware Configuration Secrets" Windows wants speed and power. This chapter describes the various hardware that defines the Windows workstation and how to properly configure it for Windows.

Chapter 14, "Video Configuration" With Windows video, the goal is to see more and see it faster. This chapter examines two key issues in improving Windows performance, the video drivers and hardware.

Chapter 15, "Keyboard and Mouse Configuration Secrets" Windows provides many options for using a keyboard and mouse with both Windows and DOS applications under Windows. This chapter tells you how to set up and configure your keyboard and mouse to interact with Windows, including special techniques for accommodating handicapped persons who use Windows.

Chapter 16, "Controlling Fonts and Printing" Windows is known for its abundance of font and type selections, but you pay a price for all these choices. This chapter explains how fonts work under Windows and how to support these fonts with your printer. This chapter also discusses the Windows settings for controlling fonts and printing.

Chapter 17, "Telecommunications Secrets" Windows appears to be the ideal environment for telecommunications because of its multitasking ability. Windows is terrific for telecommunications provided you have Windows configured properly. This chapter shows you how to get the most out of telecommunications under Windows by configuring and optimizing Windows communications settings.

Chapter 18, "Network Configuration Secrets" Although Windows 3.1x was designed to run more efficiently on a network than its predecessor, there are a number of techniques you can use to improve network performance and stability even more. This chapter shows you how to fine tune Windows or Windows for Workgroups on a network.

Chapter 19, "Clipboard, DDE, and OLE Secrets" The way Windows creates synergy between applications often seems mysterious. This chapter examines the functionality within the Clipboard, DDE, and OLE. It shows you how the Clipboard really works, and how you maximize DDE and OLE by configuring your system.

Chapter 20, "Multimedia" Windows puts multimedia within everyone's reach. This chapter explains how Windows handles multimedia information and the hardware you need to take advantage of multimedia. This chapter also discusses how to manipulate Windows settings to accommodate multimedia.

Chapter 21, "Configuring DOS Applications for Windows" Windows is an extremely capable platform when it comes to multitasking both Windows and DOS applications. However, it treats DOS and Windows applications differently. This chapter tells you how to tune Windows to run DOS applications efficiently and reliably.

Part IV: Windows for Workgroups Applications Windows for Workgroups 3.1x has several software options beyond Windows 3.1x. Part IV features Mail, Schedule+, PC FAX, and Remote Access Service components available with Windows for Workgroups.

Chapter 22, "Mail" This chapter describes how to set up, configure, and administer a Windows for Workgroups post office and provides tips and strategies for implementing a post office for your workgroup.

Chapter 23, "Schedule+" Schedule+ is extremely useful for keeping your workgroup personnel in sync. This chapter shows you how set up and customize Schedule+.

Chapter 24, "Extending Windows for Workgroups 3.11 PC Fax" This chapter shows you how to extend the boundaries of your workgroup by using the Microsoft At Work technology that is built into WFW 3.11's PC Fax. It includes detailed information on setup and configuration.

Chapter 25, "Configuring Remote Access Service" Remote Access Service, introduced in Windows for Workgroups 3.11, enables you to make a remote connection to any computer running RAS under WFW 3.11 or Windows NT. This chapter shows you how set up and configure the RAS software, and offers tips and techniques for using RAS.

Part V: Disk Documentation

The disks included in this book are every bit as valuable as the secrets revealed in this book. Our criteria for identifying and selecting the software for this book required the authors to make available commercial, shareware, and public domain software that conformed to innovative and programming excellence. The initial goal was to provide a set of applications, utilities, and tools that represented innovation, problem solving and value that the contributors of this book use daily. The software included in this book is supported 24 hours a day on the CompuServe service on the WUGNET Forum. You will find updates to the shareware, with the entire sysop staff monitoring your questions about any of these utilities.

Part VI: Appendices The appendices contain information offered to supplement what is contained in the rest of this book.

Appendix A, "Troubleshooting Windows" This appendix offers troubleshooting tips specifically for Windows, such as installation troubleshooting.

Appendix B, "Optimizing and Troubleshooting Applications under Windows" This appendix offers troubleshooting tips for running popular applications, such as Excel and Word, under Windows.

Appendix C, "WUGNET Windows Configuration Library" This appendix describes shareware and public domain tools that you can obtain through the WUGNET Forum on CompuServe.

Conventions

To point out special information or information that you might be particularly interested in, this book uses the following conventions:

 This icon points out information that is specific to Windows for Workgroups.

 This icon points to information that gives some special insight into the subject at hand.

 This icon highlights a special point of interest about the topic under discussion.

 This icon points to useful hints that may save you time or trouble.

 This icon alerts you to potential problems.

 This icon references a program that is on the disks bundled with this book.

This icon points to other discussions of the topic at hand found elsewhere in this book.

This icon points out information that is specific to Windows NT.

The following formatting conventions are also used in this book:

- Text that you are asked to type appears in **bold**.
- On-screen messages, prompts, file listings, and programs appear in a special typeface.
- Options that are selected from pull-down menus are shown as File⇨Open.

Part I
Mastering the Environment

In This Part

Chapter 1

Understanding Memory

An optimum Windows configuration is the result of operating synergy between the central processing unit (CPU), random access memory (RAM), and the hard disk drive. Working in concert with these components, Windows surpasses most of the limitations imposed by DOS-based computing.

Windows Supports Different 80x86 Architectures

A close look at Windows 3.1's architecture reveals that two separate products comprise it: standard mode Windows and enhanced mode Windows. Microsoft designed the two modes to accommodate different Intel 80x86 processors, and the underlying architecture of Windows ensures that Windows runs the same under both modes.

An Overview of the Intel CPU

Five classes (8086, 80286, 80386, 80486, and Pentium) of the Intel CPU form the 80x86 family that is used in all IBM PC-compatible computers. These chips differ from each other in several respects. For example, all the microprocessor chips that preceded the 386 were 16-bit chips capable of handling up to 16 bits of data. The 386 and 486, however, are true 32-bit chips that can process up to 32 bits of data internally in a single operation. In discussing the 386 CPU, I need to differentiate between the two variations of this processing unit, the DX and the SX. At this point, it's enough to say that the DX can process 32-bit chunks of data internally and externally, but the SX chip can process them only internally.

The 486 is available as a DX or SX processor. Unlike the 386SX, the 486SX can process 32-bit chunks of information internally and externally. The SX designation on the 486 class also indicates the absence of a floating point processor (math coprocessor).

Of Modes and CPUs

Another limitation of DOS, besides the 640K barrier, is that it supports only one operating mode, real mode. Real mode is a function of the microprocessor and the way it handles memory. *Real mode* operation is characterized by its single-tasking environment, in which programs directly access memory and peripheral devices.

In designing the 286 CPU, Intel implemented two incompatible operating modes in the chip's design. The 286 and later processors can operate in both real mode and protected mode. *Protected mode* operation delivers a multitasking environment, sophisticated memory management, and memory protection. You may ask why Intel didn't do away with real mode altogether, especially because Windows, by virtue of its multitasking ability, runs in protected mode. In short, the answer is that DOS and DOS applications cannot run in protected mode.

Although a CPU can address a large amount of RAM, the amount of RAM that a CPU can actually use depends on whether the CPU is running in real or protected mode. Real mode, the native mode of 8088s and 8086s, relies on a simple memory addressing scheme that sets a limit of 1MB for the amount of RAM that the CPU can address. In contrast, protected mode, which a 286, 386, or 486 can switch to after it powers up in real mode, uses a complex memory addressing scheme that permits the CPU to access larger amounts of RAM.

A 286, 386, or 486 that is running in real mode is limited to 1MB, just like an 8086. In protected mode, a 286, 386, or 486 can use the larger address space. However, increasing the amount of RAM that is available to DOS is not a simple matter of switching from real mode to protected mode. Programs written for DOS do not run in protected mode, so DOS is relegated to running in real mode and is, therefore, subject to the addressing limitations that real mode imposes.

If DOS applications do not run in protected mode, how can you run DOS programs under Windows? The 386, 486, and Pentium CPUs offer a third operating mode called *virtual real mode* or *Virtual-86 mode,* that enables real mode programs to run in a protected mode environment. Intel built Virtual-86 mode into the 386 so that real mode programs could be multitasked in separate Virtual-86 mode sessions (more than one Virtual-86 mode session can be set up and managed concurrently, and each one acts as if it were a separate PC that is running real-mode programs). However, this feature alone doesn't enable DOS to finally break the 640K barrier. Virtual-86 mode tasks are still subject to the real-mode limitation of 1MB of RAM, unless a DPMI or VCPI DOS extender is used.

The SX's interface to the outside world is only 16 bits wide. Therefore, when it sends or receives a 32-bit quantity, it performs the transfer in two consecutive 16-bit operations. This method of operating slightly slows the performance of the chip, but the two CPUs are the same functionally. A 386SX can run anything a 386DX can run.

The various Intel chips also differ in how much memory they can address. Before the 286, the most memory any member of the family could use was 1MB. This limitation was the reason for the DOS 640K barrier; the remaining 384K was reserved for hardware. The 286, however, can address 16MB of memory, and the 386 and 486 can address 4GB.

Inside the Intel CPU

Like most microprocessors, Intel microprocessors contain several internal operating units, and each unit has a specific role that contributes to the overall mission of the CPU. For example, the 386 contains six separate operating units, as follows:

- The *bus interface unit* is the CPU's pathway to its peripherals; all data passes through the bus on its way to or from the microprocessor.

- The *instruction prefetch unit* fetches program instructions from memory, making sure that the 386's 16-byte instruction prefetch queue is filled (or nearly filled) at all times.

- The *instruction decode unit* decodes the bytes coming into the prefetch queue and translates them into instructions that the 386 can understand.

- The *execution unit* executes the instructions.

- The *segmentation and paging units* form actual physical memory addresses from the segmented and paged addresses that the 386 uses internally. (Segmented memory is covered later in this chapter.) These physical memory addresses are what separate the 386 and 486 from the 286.

In configuring and optimizing Windows, you are concerned with three operating units: the bus interface unit, the segmentation unit, and the paging unit. In order to understand the importance of each unit and how they relate to the operation and performance of Windows, you need to look briefly at the progression of the Intel CPUs' architectures, beginning with the 8086.

The 8086 CPU is the minimum unit in CPU compatibility. Even though this CPU cannot execute Windows 3.1 or higher, it can run earlier versions of Windows. Therefore, I consider the 8086 an essential topic in an explanation of memory management. Remember that Intel had to impose some of the 8086's limitations on later generations of CPUs to ensure binary compatibility with DOS programs. These limitations are responsible for the sometimes confusing and frustrating issues in operating systems and memory management techniques.

The 8086

The Intel 8086 CPU is a 16-bit processor that is capable of accessing a maximum of 1024K. This 1024K of memory is not accessible as a single block, because the largest value that a 16-bit register can contain is 65,536, or 64K. Instead, memory is subdivided into 64K sections that are called *segments*.

Segmentation expands the CPU's effective addressing range

When you multiply a 16-bit segment register value by 16, you get a 20-bit value. In a binary numbering system, multiplying by 16 is the same as shifting a number 4 bits to the left. A 20-bit value can hold any number from 0 to 1,048,575. When that value is interpreted as a memory address, it enables the CPU to form a unique address for more than one million different locations in memory.

Segmented Addressing

Segmentation is an important memory addressing concept in the 80x86 microprocessor. Intel implemented segmented addressing on the 8086 to permit the CPU to address or reference 1MB of memory even though its registers are only 16 bits wide.

A 16-bit number can hold values only from 0 to 65,535; without special provisions, a 16-bit CPU can access only 65,536 (64K) different locations in memory. To compensate, Intel designed the 8086 addressing scheme to have two components: a segment and an offset. The *segment address* is the base address of a region of memory, 64K long, that can lie anywhere in the CPU's 1MB address space. The *offset address* specifies the location within the segment (offset from the segment base) of the targeted memory address.

Understanding the difference between a *memory location* and a *memory address* is extremely important. Memory locations are numbered sequentially, starting at 0, and they progress up to the top of addressable memory. Memory locations and actual physical memory have a natural one-to-one correspondence. Memory addresses are just a different way of referring to that same physical memory. They consist of two parts, a 16-bit segment and a 16-bit offset. In real mode, a new segment starts every 10H bytes in memory.

To convert a segment address into a physical address, you multiply by 16. Thus, a segment address of A000H corresponds to the 640K mark because A000H equals 40,960, which, when multiplied by 16, yields 655,360. A typical address is specified as A000:2000, where A000 represents the segment and 2000 represents the offset from the base of the A000 segment. Both numbers are in hexadecimal.

The segment portion of the address is shifted one place left, and a zero is substituted for the empty place on the right (in hex, you can quickly multiply a number by 16 by appending a zero to it, just as adding a zero to a decimal number multiplies it by 10). Then the offset is added in, and the result is an absolute address.

To access a single byte, the CPU combines an offset, or index value, to a segment start value. An interesting property of segment:offset access is that any access beyond the 64K segment limit wraps around to the beginning of the segment. An application can access any address in the system by simply changing the segment start value. Because the Intel 8086 CPU provides no hardware support for memory management or protection, an errant program can quite easily crash the system. Both the 1024K memory limit and the lack of protection led to the development of the next generation of CPU, the 80286.

The 80286

The Intel 80286 can access up to 16M of physical RAM. In order to access memory above 1024K, the CPU must switch to protected mode after it powers up. Protected mode operation replaces the *segment:offset* memory access method with the *selector:offset* method. A *selector* is an index into an internal table of data structures that describes the memory address space. These structures describe the physical starting address, ending address, and flags to limit access to this range of memory. Any illegal access to a memory address generates a general protection fault.

The protection capabilities are provided by the internal architecture and memory management features of the CPU. Protected mode offers four distinct privilege levels as depicted in Figure 1-1. The lowest level is ring 0, often referred to as the *kernel mode,* and the highest level is ring 3, commonly referred to as the *user mode.* A process executing at ring 0 has complete freedom to access any system component, but a process executing at higher levels can access only other system components that are at the same level or above. The current version of Windows uses these features of the CPU to provide a more robust environment by executing the core system components at ring 0 and executing the applications at ring 3. Figure 1-1 illustrates the Intel CPU protection layers.

The 80386

The Intel 80386 CPU, which is a true 32-bit processor, begins the next generation in CPU compatibility. The next generation of operating systems and software will require an 80386 or higher CPU, and the Intel 80286 will eventually follow the Intel 8086 into obscurity. The Intel 80386 provides binary compatibility

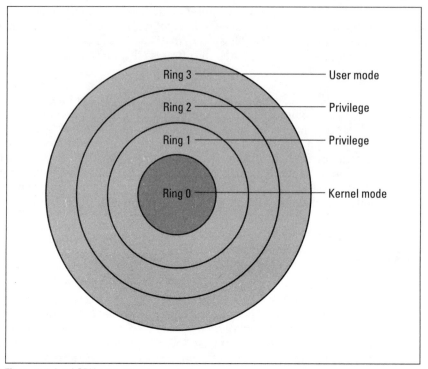

Ring 3 ———————— User mode

Ring 2 ———————— Privilege

Ring 1 ———————— Privilege

Ring 0 ———————— Kernel mode

Figure 1-1: Intel CPU protection layers.

with the Intel 8086 and 80286 CPUs, a higher clock speed, access to 4GB of system RAM, extended memory management, tasking, paging, and memory protection capabilities, and most important, the ability to emulate multiple Intel 8086 virtual machines.

The 80486

There are four different implementations of the Intel 80486 processor: 486SX, 486SL, 486DX, and 486DX2.

The Intel 486DX microprocessor integrates an enhanced version of the Intel 386 integer unit, an optimized Intel 387DX math coprocessor, a cache controller, 8K of cache memory, and a memory management unit.

The Intel 486DX2 microprocessor is the second generation of the Intel 486 microprocessor family. It's designed to run internally at 50 or 66MHz depending on the model. The DX2 processor builds on the basic architecture of the 486DX and incorporates new Intel speed doubler technology. With this technology, the DX2 executes CPU instructions at twice the speed of the external clock. Secondary caches are very important to efficient DX2 operation. Because the external clock speed is half as fast as the internal clock, any memory reference that falls outside of the cache causes additional delays internally.

The Intel 486SX microprocessor is a low level 486 CPU that comes complete with on-chip cache, memory management, and the same one-clock-per-instruction RISC integer core as the Intel 486 DX microprocessor.

The 80486SX is composed of the same integrated units as the DX except that it does not contain the enhanced 80387 (math coprocessor).

The Pentium

The Intel Pentium is the latest generation CPU. Internally, it appears very similar to the Intel 80486, and, of course, it is compatible with all prior generations. Its major difference is that it can execute multiple instructions simultaneously. The Pentium processor is 100 percent code-compatible with previous members of the 80x86 family, preserving the value of users' software investments.

The Intel 486 microprocessor incorporates a single 8K cache, and the Pentium processor features two 8K caches, one for instructions and one for data. These caches act as temporary storage places for instructions and data obtained from slower, main memory; when a system uses data, it will likely use it again, and getting it from an on-chip cache is much faster than getting it from main memory.

The floating point unit in the Pentium processor has been completely redesigned over that in the Intel 486 microprocessor. It incorporates an 8-stage pipeline that can execute one floating-point operation every clock cycle.

Like the 486, the Pentium processor uses a 32-bit bus internally. However, the external data bus to memory is 64-bits wide, doubling the amount of data that may be transferred in a single bus cycle. The 64-bit data bus allows the Pentium processor to transfer data to and from memory at rates up to 528MB/second; this is more than a three-fold increase over the peak transfer rate of the 50MHz Intel 486 (160MB/second).

The bottom line is the Pentium processor's architectural features and enhancements over the 486 architecture improve performance by three to five times (more for math-intensive applications) when compared to a 33MHz 486DX and two and one-half times compared to the 66MHz Intel 486DX2 CPU. Table 1-1 summarizes the features of the 80x86 family of processors.

Table 1-1			Processor Summary		
CPU	Register Size (in bits)	Bus Width (in lines)	Operating Modes	Physical Memory	Virtual Memory
8086	16	16	Real	1MB	N/A
80286	16	16	Real, protected	16MB	N/A*
80386	32	32	Real, protected, V86	4GB	64T
80386SX	32	16	Real, protected, V86	4GB	
80486DX	32	64	Real, protected, V86	4GB	64T
80486SX	32	32	Real, protected, V86	4GB	
Pentium	32	128	Real, protected, V86	4GB	64T

* The 80286

The Intel System Bus

In addition to the characteristics and limitations that I discussed in the preceding section, another aspect of system architecture impacts overall performance. If you think of the CPU as the heart of a PC, then think of the system bus architecture as its arteries.

The *system bus,* a data transfer highway, connects the CPU with different parts of a computer system. The lines on the system bus carry different types of information. For example, several types of lines comprise the system bus: data bus lines, address bus lines, and control bus lines. *Data bus lines* move program instructions and data between RAM and the CPU. *Address bus lines* direct the CPU to specific sections of program instructions or data that is held in memory chips. *Control bus lines* direct the CPU's actions, such as reading information from memory or writing information to memory.

The data bus

Because the data bus lines carry program instructions and data between RAM and the CPU, they impact the system's processing capabilities.

- Each bus line carries one bit at a time.

- The data capacity is determined by the number of bus lines between the CPU and RAM.

- The system bus is wider than the data bus. It is equal to the total number of bus lines, including data, control, and address bus lines.

- The 8088 and 8086 can transfer one byte.

- The 80286 can transfer 16 bits.

- The 80386SX can transfer 16 bits.

- The 80386 and 80486 can transfer 32 bits.

Table 1-2 lists the data bus widths of 80x86 CPUs.

Table 1-2	Data Bus Widths of the 80x86 CPUs		
CPU	8-Bit Processing	16-Bit Processing	32-Bit Processing
8086/8088	Yes	No	No
80286	Yes	Yes	No
80386DX/SX	Yes	Yes	Yes
80486	Yes	Yes	Yes
Pentium	Yes	Yes	Yes

The address bus

Address bus lines direct the CPU to specific memory locations in which program instructions or data are held. How important are address bus lines? Consider these points:

- A processor can access only as much memory as it can address.

- Data and program code can be stored only in the locations that the CPU can address.

- The number of addresses that are available to the CPU depends on the number of address lines that are provided in the system bus.

The Bit, the Byte, and the Word

The 80x86 processors handle data in units that are known as *bits, bytes, words,* and *double words.* A *bit* is a single piece of data that exists in one of two states: on or off. A *byte* is a group of 8 bits; a *word* is 16 bits (two bytes) long; and a *double word* is 32 bits long. The 32-bit micropro- cessors, such as the 386 and higher, generally speak in double-word quantities, and the 16-bit microprocessors speak in words. However, both 32-bit and 16-bit microprocessors can handle smaller units. For example, the 386 can manipu- late bits, bytes, words, and double words.

Using PC Memory

As far as the central processing unit is concerned, memory is just a grid of elec- tronic storage spaces that it uses to locate program instructions and data. Each location has a unique address and stores one byte of data (8 bits). The CPU and memory chips pass memory addresses to one another along the address lines within the system bus.

Addressing Memory

I made some important statements previously in this chapter that I want to reemphasize here. A microprocessor can use only as much memory as it can address. The memory address is merely a pointer to a specific location in memory. And finally, the number of memory address locations that are avail- able to the CPU depends on the number of address lines that the system bus contains.

Computing memory addresses

Think of memory address areas as being similar to post office boxes. Each box location is specified by a unique number and can hold both data and instruc- tions. Like the post office box number, the address number remains the same and is independent of the contents of the box. A post office box can hold many different messages at one time, though an address stores only one item at a time.

Now, each post office box can have as many as 20 digits in its address. How- ever, the digits in the box address are limited to the numbers *0* and *1*. Using this addressing scheme, the post office can have up to 2^{20} or 1,048,576 boxes, so if the system bus has 20 address lines, the CPU can address up to 1,048,576 bytes of storage space.

Table 1-3 gives you a basis for comparing the memory addressing capabilities of the 80x86 series processors. Take a look at the number of address lines that are available to the 8086 and 8088 CPUs. The fact that they can address no more than 1MB is critical to the way that Windows works with DOS applications. Most DOS programs were designed to use the features of the 8086/8088 processor, thereby limiting their operations to the memory capacity of these processors.

Table 1-3   Memory Addressing Capabilities in the 80x86 Series

CPU	Address Lines	Total Addresses
8086 and 8088	16	1,048,576 (1MB)
80286	24	16,777,216 (16MB)
80386SX	24	16,777,216 (16MB)
80386SL	24	16,777,216 (16MB)
80386DX	32	4,294,967,296 (4GB)
80486*	32	4,294,967,296 (4GB)
Pentium	32	4,294,967,296 (4GB)

*Applies to the 80486 DX, SX, and DX2.

Windows 3.1 can work with the 80286, the 80386, and the 80486. It can switch operations to emulate a processor other than the physically installed processor. This emulation capability has profound implications on the way you can use memory under Windows.

Understanding registers

Each of the 80x86 microprocessors contains a set of internal storage locations that are called *registers*. Registers are just like RAM, except that they're internal to the microprocessor, and their storage capacity is significantly smaller. Registers hold data and instructions in the CPU during processing, instead of having the CPU send them to RAM and fetch them from RAM.

What do registers have to do with anything?

When you analyze the processing power of a CPU, you need to consider the size of its general-purpose registers. People base their choice of computers on the processor class and clock speed. Most software packages contain a listing of the recommended hardware configuration for the application, and the listing the recommended hardware configuration for the application, and the listing almost always includes the CPU class and clock speed. What does the speed have to do with registers? Clock speed is a function of the CPU's general-purpose register size.

The CPU has an internal clock that fires pulses at regular intervals. These pulses trigger actions within the CPU in order to carry out a machine instruction. Completing a single machine instruction can require more than one CPU action. To evaluate the system, measure the time between two pulses of the clock, or the *clock cycle*.

When you talk about clock speed, you're actually talking about the pulse rate. A CPU that is operating at 33MHz has a pulse rate of 33 million cycles per second. Breaking the pulse rate down even further, it is the number of clock cycles that occur each second. The clock cycle is the amount of time required to transfer data from one CPU register to another CPU register.

A class divided by registers

Each Intel CPU class has a finite number of general purpose and specialized registers. The size of the general purpose registers separates the CPU classes. The importance of this size difference becomes apparent when you consider how the 80x86 processors calculate memory addresses.

One of the specialized registers, the segment register, or code segment register (CS), specifies the starting location of an area of memory in which the CPU stores program instructions. This area of memory is the *code segment*.

The 80x86 processor calculates a program instruction's memory location by determining how far the instruction is from the start of the code segment. This distance is the *offset*. The offset value is then stored in a general-purpose register. Refer to the previous information on segmentation for a more thorough discussion of this topic.

So why is register size important? Remember that offsets, which are stored in general-purpose registers, represent real memory addresses. The total number of offsets that a 16-bit register can handle is 2^{16}, or 65,536. The implication of this limitation is that the total number of addressable bytes in a code segment is 64K. The largest chunk of a program that can be processed at one time on a 286 processor is 64K. The bottom line is that programs designed for 8- and 16-bit machines can swap no more than 64K in and out of memory.

The 386 began a new ball game, bringing with it 32-bit general registers that are capable of handling up to 2^{32}, or 4GB, of offsets. In theory, code segments can take up 4GB of memory. Think of what this increased capability means for Windows and its multitasking abilities. The handwriting is on the wall. As the time draws nearer for the next release of Windows, users are thinking 32-bit, 32-bit . . . and gigabytes of memory.

Understanding PC Memory

Before you attempt to configure and optimize Windows, you should have a good understanding of PC memory. One of the most intriguing features of Windows is its ability to constantly maneuver portions of programs between different parts of memory (RAM) and the hard disk. During this constant manipulation of program code and memory, Windows works to make sure that different applications and drivers don't try to access the same memory at the same time. Windows achieves this level of protection at the cost of memory optimization. However, if you understand how your hardware and software use memory, you can optimize the performance of Windows by applying memory management techniques.

Memory Types

The amount and types of memory that your system uses significantly affects the performance of Windows. You need to consider five different types of memory in a Windows environment:

- Conventional memory
- Upper memory
- Extended memory
- Expanded memory
- Virtual memory

Figure 1-2 illustrates memory types.

Conventional memory

DOS is still king, no matter what kind of machine Windows is running on. Windows and all other applications have to work together with DOS and its limitations. When you boot your machine, DOS runs the utilities and applications that are listed in the CONFIG.SYS and AUTOEXEC.BAT files. These files often use conventional memory to function and leave the remaining memory available for running other applications, such as Windows.

Conventional memory consists of the first 640K of system memory, and it resides in the system virtual machine. This memory is a finite Windows' system resource. If sufficient free memory is not available in this region, then additional applications cannot load, even if megabytes of free RAM are available in the

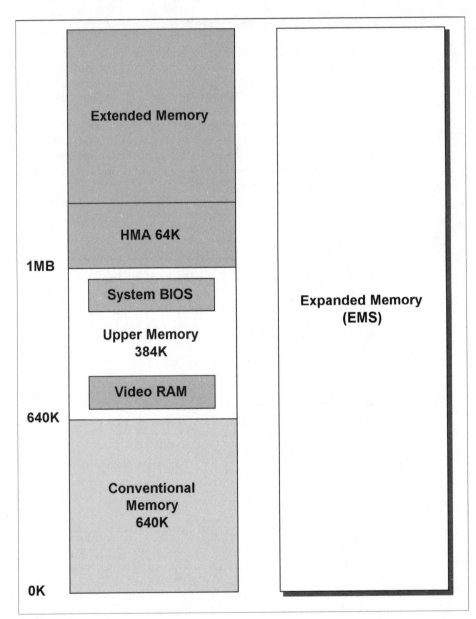

Figure 1-2: Memory types.

global heap (system memory). Windows uses this area to hold various internal data structures as well as *interrupt service routines,* or ISRs. ISRs use memory that is fixed in a single location. By default, Windows places the ISRs as low as possible in memory in order to avoid memory fragmentation.

Upper memory

This region is often referred to as *reserved memory* or the *system adapter segment.* Some peripherals on the system bus, such as a video adapter, will map a local RAM buffer to an address in this range. The CPU can then access this buffer as if it were system memory. Figure 1-3 shows a detailed view of the upper memory area.

Expanded memory

Expanded memory was developed to provide more than 640K of system memory to MS-DOS applications. This memory is not directly accessible by the application. Instead, memory access is limited to a block of data at a time. Memory is mapped to or from this block by an expanded memory manager program, which is responsible for managing all data requests on behalf of the MS-DOS client. The block is called the *page frame.* The page frame is a movable region in the upper memory area that acts as a portal through which the address space in expanded memory is accessed. Figure 1-4 shows the relationship of the 64K page frame to expanded memory.

Expanded memory is of interest to Windows users, but its usefulness is limited because only MS-DOS applications use it and because Windows requires extended, not expanded, memory. In enhanced mode, you can have extended memory converted to expanded memory on a request basis by creating a PIF file for the application.

 Windows comes with its own version of EMM386.SYS, the expanded memory manager, and DOS 5 and 6 ship with a version of EMM386.SYS. You should use the version that is included with Windows because it has been enhanced to work with Windows.

Extended memory

Extended memory consists of all memory above 1024K. It is directly accessible while the CPU is in protected mode. Although the Intel 80286 is still limited to a maximum segment size of 64K, the Intel 80386 and higher CPUs are capable of

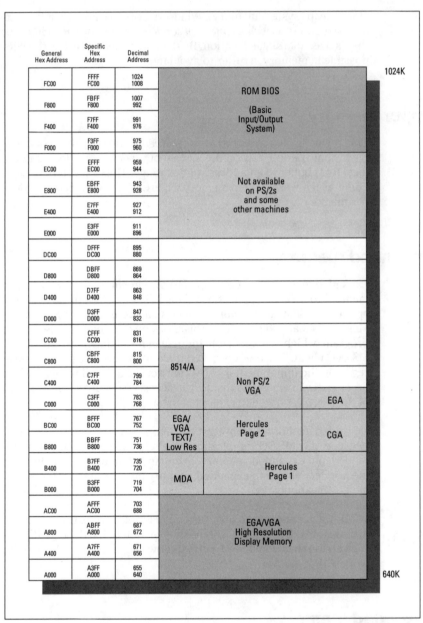

Figure 1-3: A detailed view of the upper memory area.

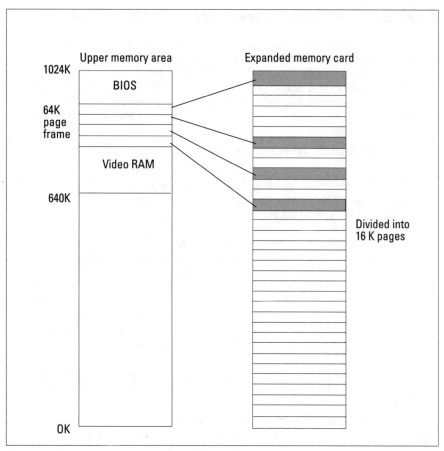

Figure 1-4: Expanded memory requires a 64K page frame in the upper memory area that is composed of four contiguous 16K pages.

accessing a maximum of 4GB per segment. This ability to create and access large memory structures is one of the features that makes the Intel 80386 CPU family so desirable.

Accessing extended memory has been a bit chaotic in the past, but most applications now provide memory access services by using a device driver that is compliant with the extended memory specification, or XMS. The Microsoft HIMEM.SYS or the QEMM386.SYS device drivers, for example, are XMS compliant. Windows comes with its own version of HIMEM.SYS.

Addressing 64K more memory in real mode

I have already said that the largest amount of memory that the Intel 8086 and 8088 microprocessors can address is 1MB. On the basis of that earlier statement, you may conclude that the Intel 80286, 80386, and higher processors, while in real mode, can address only 1MB. On the contrary, because of the architecture of the 80286 and 80386, 80486, and Pentium processors, they can address almost 64K more memory than the 8086 and 8088 can address.

The high memory area

The extra memory space that the 80286 and higher CPUs can address is called the *high memory area (HMA)*. Its maximum size is 64K minus 16 bytes. To access HMA, you need to enable the A20 address line of the 80286 and the 80386 while the system is in real mode.

Normally, for an 80286 to access extended memory, the processer has to switch into protected mode. After accessing extended memory, the processor must then reset so that it returns to real mode. Accessing extended memory in this manner takes time. However, a processor can access the first 64K of extended memory without switching the processor into protected mode. To do so, the processor uses a high memory area provider or an A20 handler to enable access to the first 64K of extended memory. HMA refers to a specific way of accessing the first 64K of extended memory.

Depending on the class of CPU in your system, you can use several device drivers to create the HMA. In 80286-based systems you may use:

- HIMEM.SYS, the extended memory manager that ships with DOS 5.0, 6.x, Windows 3.1, and Windows for Workgroups 3.1x.
- QEXT.SYS, an extended memory manager from Quarterdeck Office Systems.
- MOVEM.MGR, the extended memory manager from Qualitas.

If your system is at least a 386-based system you may use:

- HIMEM.SYS as described in the preceding list.
- QEMM386.SYS, an extended memory manager, designed specifically for 32-bit processors, from Quarterdeck Office Systems.
- 386MAX, the 32-bit extended memory manager from Qualitas. These A20 handlers allow some programs to couple or decouple the addressing between the motherboard and the CPU, thereby allowing that program access to the 64K of memory between 1024K and 1088K without the need to go into protected mode CPU operation.

Unique features of the high memory area

How does the high memory area differ from conventional memory? Several aspects of the HMA distinguish it from normal memory segments. First, conventional memory segments are always available, but a program can access the HMA only while the A20 line is enabled. Second, the HMA does not start at the beginning of a segment; it starts 16 bytes after the beginning of segment FFFFH. Finally, and most important, the high memory area cannot be subdivided. Remember, the high memory area resides entirely inside the highest valid segment, FFFFH; no segment starts inside the HMA. Therefore, the HMA cannot be split up into smaller chunks and cannot be used by more than one program at a time.

DOS uses the high memory area

DOS 5.0 was the first version of DOS to use the HMA for itself. DOS 5.0 and 6.x use HIMEM (or compatible XMS driver) to manage the HMA and load a portion of the DOS system files into this memory. You do this by placing the DOS=HIGH command in the CONFIG.SYS file.

By loading DOS high, a 286 or later PC can gain as much as 46K of free conventional memory because a portion of resident DOS is now using HMA instead of conventional memory. Placing DOS=HIGH in the CONFIG.SYS file also causes BUFFERS to load into the HMA area.

Each computer system may use a different method for activating the A20 handler. Some drivers, such as HIMEM.SYS, require switches in order to accommodate various machines. Check the documentation for your extended memory manager to determine how to configure it for your particular machine. To use the HMA, you must have a 286, 386, or 486 CPU-based PC, an Extended Memory Specification driver, and at least 64K of extended memory.

You can instruct DOS 5.0 and 6.x to load a portion of itself into high memory.

Virtual memory

What is virtual memory, and why is it so important to Windows users? To put it simply, virtual memory is a form of memory that does not physically exist in the system. The system creates virtual memory as needed from the system's hard disk to provide the ability to exceed the physical memory resource limits.

The system creates virtual memory by exchanging physical pages of RAM to a secondary storage media. This secondary storage is often a preallocated portion of the system's hard disk drive. On a Windows system, this preallocated storage exists as a temporary file or a permanent file on the hard disk. The Windows virtual memory manager allocates, deallocates, and moves pages of data to and from this file to accommodate memory allocation requests that exceed the system's physical RAM limit.

Windows Modes and Memory

Windows can use all the different types of memory that I discussed in the preceding section (conventional memory, the 384K UMB, extended memory, expanded memory, and virtual memory). How Windows uses and interacts with a particular type of memory depends on the operating mode in which you start Windows. I begin the discussion of modes and memory with a brief overview of Windows 3.1x's two operating modes (standard mode and enhanced mode), followed by an explanation of how Windows uses the different types of memory in each mode. I don't spend much time discussing expanded memory, except to make a few salient points in case you still have DOS applications in your corral that require expanded memory.

Before elaborating on the what and how of running Windows in standard mode, I need to talk a little bit about real mode. When Microsoft introduced Windows 3.0, it provided support for real mode machines. Many 8086 and 8088 machines were in use at the time, so support for real mode enabled users to run Windows on those machines. Microsoft used its support for real mode as a way of getting everyone hooked on a terrific product!

With Windows 3.0 in high gear, programmers started designing applications to make use of additional registers and processing features that are available in the 286 CPU. The applications had to run in a protected mode environment, Windows standard mode. *Standard mode* is what Windows calls the 286 processor's protected mode.

Running Windows in Standard Mode

Microsoft designed the Windows standard mode to take advantage of the 286 CPU's extended memory addressing and protected mode capabilities. Because standard mode was designed for the 286 CPU, the abilities of this processor determine the abilities of Windows in this mode.

The characteristics and operating parameters of the 286 CPU are described earlier in this chapter. Just to summarize, the 286 can address up to 16MB of memory as follows:

- The first megabyte of addressable memory is the first 640K of conventional memory plus the 384K of reserved or upper memory.

- The remaining 15MB of memory can exist as extended memory or virtual memory (hard disk space).

Standard mode Windows takes advantage of the protected mode capabilities of the 286 and higher processors providing access to as much as 16 MB of memory. Windows runs in protected mode, switching back and forth to DOS for file I/O and various other DOS operations. Because of the limitations imposed by the 286 CPU, standard mode Windows is defined by these characteristics:

- Both the Windows kernel and Windows applications run in 16-bit protected mode.

- DOS applications run in real mode.

- DOS applications cannot multitask. Instead, they are swapped out to disk, with one active DOS application replacing another in memory.

- DOS applications must run full screen; they cannot run in a window.

- Only DOS programs using DPMI can use extended memory.

- The Windows DOS Protected Mode Interface (DPMI) is available to Windows applications.

- When you run a DOS application, Windows swaps most of itself out to disk.

 Contrary to what you may have heard, the 286 processor does support virtual memory. This CPU implements virtual memory through segmentation, breaking programs up into several sections, and then swapping them out to disk.

Because the 286 can handle only code segments that are 64K or smaller, it can swap only one 64K segment at a time to disk. If you consider that Windows applications are usually 640K or larger, you'll realize that this limitation is a serious one.

The 286 processor gets around this limitation by using its addressing capabilities to allow various segments of a program to exist in noncontiguous memory locations in RAM or on disk.

Running Windows applications in standard mode

Currently, most Windows applications are written to support the 286 protected mode.

 Windows 3.1 and Windows for Workgroups 3.1 support 286 protected mode or Windows standard mode. Windows for Workgroups 3.11 does not support standard mode, and future releases of Windows will not support it.

 When running in standard mode, the CPU operates in protected mode and draws from three different areas of memory: conventional memory, extended memory, and high memory. Windows makes no distinction between conventional and extended memory; it sees it all as one large global heap or pool.

Remember the discussion of segmentation earlier in this chapter? Here's where it comes into play. Like DOS applications, Windows applications are divided into segments of 64K or smaller. When you launch an application in Windows, it loads the program code and data segments using memory from the global heap. Because Windows can run more than one application at a time, it needs a way to minimize an application's impact on memory. The 80x86 architecture requires protected mode segments to specify whether they contain code or data. Windows identifies application code by its segment attributes. These attributes fall into four categories:

■ Movable segments

■ Discardable segments

■ Swappable segments

■ Fixed segments

Movable code segments, as the name implies, can be moved from one location in memory to another. Usually, movable code segments are moved between conventional memory and extended memory.

Discardable code segments represent nonessential portions of program code. These code segments are not critical to the program's operation, so they can be thrown away to make room for more important code segments. When the discardable memory is needed again, it is reloaded from disk or recreated.

Swappable code segments can be swapped to disk if physical memory is low and then read back into physical memory as soon as it's available.

Fixed code segments remain at a fixed location in memory. Windows cannot move or discard it. Programmers often use this method to improve a program's speed. Most fixed code segments are used for interrupt service routines (ISRs) to support hardware devices such as a keyboard, mouse, or communications port.

Windows uses the segment attribute information to determine which segments it can rearrange in memory to make room for more applications.

Running DOS applications under standard mode Windows

Windows uses standard mode differently when it is running DOS applications. Because most DOS applications are written to run on 8086 and 8088 processors, they don't use extended memory.

As a rule, DOS and DOS-based programs do not support extended memory or protected mode. In order to get around this restriction, DOS application developers use a programming technology called a DOS extender to take advantage of extended memory. The DOS extender enables the processor to switch to protected mode for memory addressing, and then switch back to real mode to execute program instructions.

The DOS extender is a type of shell that provides the programming support for extended memory. It works like this:

- The program runs in real mode.

- When addressing memory, the processor switches to protected mode.

- File handling and other I/O operations are processed in real mode.

Windows uses a built-in DOS extender technology, HIMEM.SYS, and it can store DOS programs in extended memory only if the application complies with the DOS protected mode interface (DPMI).

Windows and task switching

When you start Windows in standard mode, it loads most of itself into extended memory and then sets up a portion of extended memory that emulates real mode. Because standard mode can hold only one DOS environment at a time, only one DOS application can run in standard mode at a time.

When you run a Windows application in standard mode, Windows uses WSWAP.EXE to swap different code segments between conventional memory, extended memory, and the hard disk.

Each time you start a DOS application, Windows creates a temporary application swap file for that application. When you switch away from the application, Windows moves some or all of that application from memory to the application swap file. When data is moved from memory to the swap file, the memory is then available for use by other applications. When you exit Windows, it deletes any application swap files that it created during that session.

The amount of hard disk space that is available determines how many application swap files Windows can create, and this in turn determines how many DOS applications you can start before running out of memory. Delete unnecessary files from your hard disk to free up space for application swap files. Also scan your disk for extraneous temporary swap files after exiting Windows abruptly such as in a loss of power or accidental shut off.

Use WinZip, which is included on the *Windows 3.1 Configuration SECRETS Disks,* to compress and uncompress files. WinZip brings the convenience of Windows to the use of ZIP files without requiring PKZIP and PKUNZIP. It features an intuitive point-and-click, drag-and-drop interface for viewing, running, extracting, adding, deleting, and testing files in archives. ARJ, LZH, and ARC files are supported via external programs.

Archives are files that contain other files. Typically the files in an archive are compressed. Archives usually have filenames ending with ZIP, LZH, ARJ, or ARC, depending on how they were created. ◘

Unleashing Windows in 386 Enhanced Mode __

As mentioned earlier in the chapter, the 286 CPU can use segmentation to support virtual memory. It watches segment codes as they load into memory to see whether they fit. If it detects that a segment cannot fit into conventional or extended physical memory, the operating environment (Windows in this case) produces a segment fault.

After the segment fault occurs, Windows searches memory for a segment code that it can swap to disk to make room for the new code. Up to this point, Windows handles multiple applications the same way in standard mode and in enhanced mode. What makes the difference is the advanced processing features of the 386 CPU.

The 286 processor implements virtual memory by using segmentation, but the 386 processor uses a more sophisticated technique called *demand paging*. This technique is the foundation for Windows enhanced mode. When running in enhanced mode, Windows offers programs an address space that is larger than the amount of physical memory in the system. The 386 divides virtual address space into 4K blocks that are called *pages* that can reside in memory or on disk. Windows recalls the pages from disk into memory on demand, whenever a program tries to read, write, or execute something on a particular page. In a system without paging, such as a 286 or a system running Windows in standard mode, Windows constantly discards and reloads code segments in an attempt to optimize memory.

Running DOS Applications in Virtual Machines _

I mentioned earlier in the chapter that DOS applications that don't comply with DPMI must run in real mode. Standard mode Windows can set up only one real mode environment at a time, so you can run only one DOS application at a time. However, enhanced mode Windows can use the 386 CPU feature called Virtual-86 mode to set up a real mode environment for each DOS session. Each time you run a DOS application in 386 enhanced mode, the Windows Virtual Machine Manager creates a virtual 8086 machine in which the application runs.

It is a *virtual machine* because DOS thinks the application is running on its own system. The virtual machine emulates a complete 8086 processor, including memory, I/O devices, and any TSRs, device drivers, and network software that were running when you started Windows.

You can save memory by maximizing the amount of memory available to Windows before start up. If you use DOS applications under Windows that require TSRs or device drivers, try loading them along with the DOS application from within Windows. For example, if you normally use a mouse with a DOS application, load the mouse driver and the DOS program from a batch file. Since each DOS application runs in its own virtual machine under enhanced mode Windows, you save memory for the Windows system VM and other DOS VMs.

Which mode to run?

There's a lot of debate as to whether or not you should run Windows applications under standard mode over enhanced mode. The argument is that if you run only Windows programs, you can gain an increase in overall speed by running in standard mode. The justification for this is that you save time by using your machine's physical memory as opposed to waiting for Windows to access virtual memory.

My experience is that this increase in speed is negligible, and when you consider what you give up for an increase in speed that you probably won't even notice, it doesn't make sense. When you run Windows 3.1 or Windows for Workgroups 3.1x in enhanced mode, you take advantage of the full power of Windows.

You can run multiple DOS programs at the same time, each in their own virtual machine, as full screen or windowed applications. Windows uses true virtual memory giving you better protection between programs. You have more control over how DOS programs use memory.

Using 32-bit disk access and Windows for Workgroups 3.11's 32-bit file access, Windows no longer has to depend on DOS for file management. With these features, Windows becomes closer to being an operating system, not just an operating environment.

Summary

This chapter began with an overview of the evolution of the Intel CPU and the various processor memory capabilities. Windows manages multiple programs simultaneously by exploiting the memory addressing capabilities of the 286, 386, 486, and now Pentium microprocessors. Certainly you can use Windows without ever understanding the nuances of how Windows interacts with these CPUs. However, when you want to configure and optimize Windows, you need intimate knowledge of your PC and Windows.

The material in this chapter prepares you for what's ahead in Part II of this book. A firm grasp of PC memory and the Windows operating modes empowers you with the knowledge you need to refine and supercharge Windows. After reading this chapter, you should understand the following aspects of the CPU and memory:

▶ The implications of CPU operating modes and memory addressing capabilities

▶ How system architecture impacts overall performance

▶ How the central processing unit makes use of physical memory

▶ The relationship between a CPU's registers and its processing capabilities

▶ How Windows works within the limitations of DOS

▶ How Windows uses memory in its different operating modes

Chapter 2
Optimizing DOS for Windows

In This Chapter

▶ Optimizing DOS boot-up to benefit Windows

▶ Configuring the DOS environment size

▶ Increasing the size of buffers and files

▶ Understanding whether stacks are really necessary

▶ Setting the path statement to optimize Windows

Many people are surprised to learn that configuring and optimizing memory for Windows begins at the DOS level. Beginning with the release of DOS 5.0, Microsoft went to great lengths to enhance and optimize DOS to make it a solid foundation for Windows 3.1x. This chapter explains the techniques you can use in DOS to optimize memory management for Windows.

The Windows and DOS Partnership

Before the introduction of the 386 CPU, memory managers were concerned only with reorganizing the way system components were loaded into RAM. In an effort to free more conventional memory for DOS applications, memory managers moved components outside the 640K address space into extended memory, expanded memory, and the high memory area (HMA).

The 386 CPU brought enhanced memory-management capabilities with its ability to remap logical memory locations. Drivers and TSRs could be moved outside the physical 640K memory range and still have an address below the 1MB barrier. (Remember that DOS cannot see beyond the 1MB line.) Using the sophisticated memory-management capabilities of 386 and higher CPUs, device drivers and TSRs can move into the extended memory remapped by the 386, filling in gaps in the UMA. The upper memory area, also called HighDOS, has become the most precious real-estate property in the PC.

The term *real mode* refers to the way in which the microprocessor handles memory and is characterized as providing the user with a single-tasking (one program at a time) working environment. In real mode, programs can freely access system memory and input/output devices. Real mode is designed into the 286, 386, and 486 CPU. However, real mode does not provide any memory management or memory protection.

Windows 3.1 introduced a new feature to the memory-management model: protected mode. When operating in protected mode, 80286 and higher processors take advantage of larger address spaces and more advanced features than real mode. When you type **WIN** at the DOS prompt, you launch your 286, 386, or 486 CPU into protected mode, under which you can open and run multiple applications simultaneously, have data security, and use virtual memory.

The problem with this twist in the memory-management model is that MS-DOS was not designed to be a foundation for a protected-mode operating system. Microsoft designed MS-DOS for two fundamental tasks: to serve as a simple program loader and to provide an elementary file system.

When you launch Windows, it assumes command of most PC operations, including I/O and video-related operations. But because Windows is an operating *environment*, as opposed to an operating *system*, it relies on DOS for access to the file allocation table (FAT). That means that whenever you perform disk I/O under Windows, you force DOS to operate in unfamiliar ways.

The enhancements in Windows for Workgroups 3.11 bring Windows closer to becoming an operating system. Windows for Workgroups 3.11 implements 32-bit virtual devices, enabling it to bypass DOS for file and disk I/O operations.

Each time you perform a system-level action, Windows "virtualizes" DOS operations: Windows routes DOS functions or API (application programming interface) calls through protected-mode handling routines so that Windows can control access to DOS features.

The interaction between real-mode DOS and protected-mode Windows is extremely sensitive. When multiple applications are running, there is a potential for simultaneous access to DOS APIs; if more than one application calls an API at the same time, this can yield unpredictable results. As a result, little things, such as not having enough file handles allocated in CONFIG.SYS, can crash DOS and Windows.

Another problem is compatibility between DOS applications and Windows 386 enhanced mode. Although Windows and its native applications run in protected mode and can therefore access up to 512MB of conventional and extended memory, DOS applications under Windows execute within DOS VMs, a feature of the 386 or higher CPU's V86 mode.

Virtual Machines

The 80386 CPU separates each V86 mode task into its own virtual machine. A virtual machine (VM) is supported directly by the Intel 80386 (or higher) CPU and is an executable task consisting of an application, supporting software (such as ROM, BIOS, and MS-DOS), memory, and CPU registers. Windows uses a single virtual machine, called the system VM, in which to run the Windows kernel, other Windows core components and extensions, and all Windows-based applications.

The Virtual Machine Manager (VMM) manages the different VMs running in the Windows environment. The VMM provides the services needed to create and manage the virtual machines where Windows and MS-DOS-based applications run. This allows MS-DOS-based applications to run concurrently with Windows when they are launched by Program Manager or another Windows-based application.

In order to provide support for the Windows environment and for the virtual machines while Windows is running in 386 enhanced mode, Windows uses virtual device drivers to communicate between the system and DOS VMs and hardware devices.

Using the virtual machine manager built into the WIN386.EXE file, 386 and higher chips set up an emulated real-mode environment for each DOS session you start. Windows provides DOS compatibility in the following manner: real-mode instructions and DOS applications execute from within the environment called a *virtual machine* (VM). In effect, DOS thinks that each virtual machine is running on a separate CPU.

One important aspect of a virtual machine is that it inherits the DOS environment set before Windows loaded. Windows takes a snapshot of your DOS configuration before it loads so that it can set up each virtual machine according to that configuration. Each DOS VM contains a copy of DOS and all the TSRs or drivers loaded before Windows loaded, as well as the overhead Windows uses to manage the VM. All this affects the amount of conventional memory free in each DOS VM.

Why Optimize Conventional Memory

Why should you optimize conventional memory? In a word, DOS. If you run DOS applications under Windows, conventional memory is a vital asset. The inherent design of DOS requires that all DOS programs run within the first megabyte of PC address space (actually, within the first 640K). Not even Windows with its multitasking capabilities can change that fundamental law of DOS-based computing.

When you run DOS applications under Windows, each DOS application runs in its own virtual machine. When Windows creates a virtual machine, it uses the conventional memory environment that existed before you launched Windows. For example, if only 436K of conventional memory was free before you started Windows, 436K is the largest amount of conventional memory available to any DOS application running under Windows. This may not sound like a problem at first, but it becomes a problem when you discover that your DOS-based database program requires 480K of conventional memory just to start up.

Every DOS virtual machine inherits the DOS environment that existed in conventional memory before Windows was launched.

Understanding the DOS start-up files

Because the amount of free conventional memory in a DOS virtual machine depends on the configuration of the DOS environment, you need to understand the contents of the system start-up files. Each time you boot your system, DOS looks for two files: CONFIG.SYS and AUTOEXEC.BAT. These two files configure the system. The easiest way to free up conventional memory is by pruning your CONFIG.SYS and AUTOEXEC.BAT files.

Inside the CONFIG.SYS file

The CONFIG.SYS file defines the device drivers and DOS resources that your system uses. This section gives you some suggestions for optimizing your CONFIG.SYS file for Windows.

Before I discuss optimizing the CONFIG.SYS file, I want to explain some of the command lines that might exist in a typical CONFIG.SYS file.

BUFFERS

The BUFFERS command sets the amount of RAM that MS-DOS reserves for information transferred to and from a disk. The syntax for this command is as follows:

```
BUFFERS=n[,m]
```

where n specifies the number of disk buffers. The value of n must range from 1 to 99. The m option specifies the number of buffers in the secondary buffer cache. The value of m must range from one to eight.

Increasing the number of buffers with the CONFIG.SYS BUFFERS command can speed up the transfer of files in memory. However, increasing the number of buffers beyond a certain value only uses more memory without increasing speed. (Each buffer takes up about 500 bytes, which is about the same size as a sector on a disk.) Each buffer can hold a sector of information from a disk.

Buffers hold parts of files that are waiting to be stored or used by a program, in addition to directory and file-table information about the disk.

If you're using SmartDrive (which, of course, you should be), limit the number of buffers to ten. Increasing the number of buffers while using SmartDrive can degrade SmartDrive's performance.

DEVICE

The DEVICE command loads an installable device driver into conventional memory. DEVICE is arguably the most powerful of the CONFIG.SYS directives. With it, you can custom-configure DOS by loading device drivers that serve as low-level interfaces between hardware and software.

DEVICEHIGH

The DEVICEHIGH command loads an installable device driver into upper memory. DEVICEHIGH is just like DEVICE, except that it loads device drivers into upper memory blocks created by EMM386.EXE or other memory managers. If they are loaded into upper memory, device drivers don't reduce the largest executable program size reported by the MEM command.

If your computer is configured to load TSRs and device drivers high, you can optimize RAM usage by replacing all occurrences of DEVICE with DEVICEHIGH. However, you cannot load HIMEM.SYS or EMM386.EXE high. Be sure to have a bootable floppy disk on hand when you experiment with DEVICEHIGH in case loading a driver high locks up your PC.

DOS

The DOS command specifies whether the DOS kernel should be loaded high (in the HMA) or low (in conventional memory), and whether DOS should allocate upper memory blocks (UMBs) created by EMM386.EXE for its own use. The statement DOS=HIGH in CONFIG.SYS saves up to 60K of RAM by transferring DOS from conventional memory to the HMA. You must have at least an 80286 processor to use this command. If you plan to load TSRs and device drivers into upper memory, your CONFIG.SYS file must contain the statement DOS=UMB.

DOS=HIGH and DOS=UMB can be combined into a single statement: DOS=HIGH,UMB. For this statement to be effective, always accompany the DOS=HIGH command with a DEVICE statement that loads HIMEM.SYS. Similarly, accompany DOS=UMB with DEVICE statements loading HIMEM.SYS and EMM386.EXE. It doesn't matter where in CONFIG.SYS the DOS directive appears.

FCBS

The FCBS command sets the number of file-control blocks (FCBs) that MS-DOS can open concurrently. A *file-control block* is a data structure that stores information about a file. The syntax for this command is as follows:

    FCBS=n

where *n* specifies the number of file-control blocks that MS-DOS can have open at one time. Valid values for *n* range from 1 to 255; the default value is 4.

 If a program tries to open more than the specified number of FCBs, DOS might close the files that were opened earlier. Use the FCBS command only if a program requires you to do so. Most newer programs do not require file-control blocks.

FILES

The FILES command sets the number of files that MS-DOS allows to be open at one time. The syntax for this command is as follows:

    FILES=n

where *n* specifies the number of files DOS can access at one time. Valid values for *n* range from 8 to 255; the default value is 8.

STACKS

The STACKS command sets the amount of RAM that MS-DOS reserves for processing hardware interrupts. The syntax for this command is as follows:

    STACKS=n,s

where *n* specifies the number of stacks. Valid values for *n* are 0 and numbers in the range 8 through 64. The *s* option specifies the size (in bytes) of each stack. Valid values for *s* are 0 and numbers in the range 32 through 512.

LASTDRIVE

The LASTDRIVE command specifies the maximum number of drives you can access. The syntax for this command is as follows:

    Lastdrive=x

where *x* is the value representing the last valid drive MS-DOS should recognize. Valid values are A through Z. The minimum value corresponds to the number of drives installed on your system. The default value is the one after the last drive used on your computer.

SHARE

The SHARE command starts the Share program, which installs file-sharing and locking capabilities on the hard disk. You can also execute SHARE from the AUTOEXEC.BAT file. However, when used in the CONFIG.SYS file, the SHARE command should appear as follows:

```
INSTALL=C:\SHARE.EXE [/f:space] [/l:locks]
```

The /f:space option allocates file space (in bytes) for the DOS storage area used to record file-sharing information. The default value is 2048. The /l:locks option sets the number of files that can be locked at one time. The default value is 20.

The INSTALL command causes DOS to load Share as a memory-resident program. Installing Share in the CONFIG.SYS file saves a little bit of memory, because INSTALL does not create an environment to share when loading it.

Typically, SHARE is used in a network or multitasking environment in which programs share files. SHARE loads the code that supports file sharing and locking in these environments. After SHARE is loaded, DOS uses the code to validate all read and write requests from programs.

SHELL

The SHELL command indicates that a command interpreter other than COMMAND.COM should be used or that COMMAND.COM should be set up differently. SHELL specifies the name and location of the command interpreter you want DOS to use. The syntax of this command is as follows:

```
SHELL=[drive:]path filename [parameters]
```

The default command interpreter for MS-DOS is COMMAND.COM. If no SHELL command is entered in the CONFIG.SYS file, DOS searches for COMMAND.COM in the root directory of the start-up drive.

Use the SHELL command if COMMAND.COM is in another drive or directory, or if a different command interpreter is to be used. Also, if you get an error message indicating Out of environment space, use the SHELL command to change the environment space from the default 160 bytes, as follows:

```
SHELL=C:\DOS\COMMAND.COM /E:512
```

Paring down CONFIG.SYS

After reading the previous section, you might conclude that the most obvious way to conserve memory is to convert DEVICE commands to DEVICEHIGH. There are a number of ways to trim down the CONFIG.SYS file and conserve valuable conventional memory.

Stop allocating STACKS

Check your CONFIG.SYS file for a STACKS statement, as described in the previous section. If the statement doesn't exist, you're giving up almost 2K of RAM that DOS reserves to provide additional stack space to hardware interrupt handlers. Most PCs don't need the extra stack space, so you can add almost 2K of RAM to the largest executable program size.

Use STACKS=0,0 to prevent DOS from allocating its interrupt stacks. Interrupt stacks are temporary data structures used by DOS and applications for processing hardware interrupts. Windows automatically chooses a stack for hardware interrupts, so you can save almost 3K of RAM, which increases the largest executable file size.

A special case for stack allocation occurs in the following situation. When DOS receives a hardware interrupt, it allocates one stack from the number specified in the CONFIG.SYS file. When 0 is specified, DOS allocates no stacks, leaving the responsibility to the program currently running. Each program running must then have enough stack space to accommodate the computer's hardware interrupt drivers. Many computers operate correctly, saving some memory for programs. If you get Internal stack overflow messages after changing the STACKS setting, replace the values with the original STACKS setting values.

If you're using EMM386 .EXE, you may receive an Exception error 12 message instead of an Internal stack overflow message.

Make sure your last drive is your last drive

LASTDRIVE reserves space for logical drives up to the specified letter, and each logical drive requires 88 bytes of conventional memory. If you reserve space for more logical drives than you need to, you're throwing away memory.

Check your CONFIG.SYS file for a LASTDRIVE=Z statement. If found, set LASTDRIVE equal to the highest drive letter that you actually use, making sure that all drive letters are contiguous. For example, if your hard disk contains logical drives C and D and you assign a pair of network drives the letters R and S, change R and S to E and F (and set LASTDRIVE=F). This can save almost 1K.

If you're running a Novell network, the network automatically places network drives at the next higher drive letter than your system's logical drives.

Files and buffers can chew up little bits of RAM

Make sure CONFIG.SYS contains a DOS=HIGH statement and a DEVICE= statement, loading HIMEM.SYS so that DOS will be loaded high (in the HMA), and set BUFFERS to 40 or less. Doing so ensures that DOS's disk buffers go in the HMA alongside the DOS kernel. As for FILES, experiment with different settings to determine how little you can get away with. Installing UMBFILES on a PC that uses a setting of FILES=40 adds about 2K to the largest executable program size. If your FILES= setting is larger, you'll save even more by switching to UMBFILES.

Squeezing a few extra bytes by specifying FCBS

Very few DOS programs use file control blocks anymore (data structures used to store information about files in early versions of DOS). You can save a few more bytes of RAM by adding the following statement to CONFIG.SYS:

```
FCBS=1
```

Controlling environment size with SHELL

If you use a SHELL statement to load COMMAND.COM with an /E switch for increasing the environment size, you should grab control of the environment.

Use the SET command to determine how much environment space you really need. At the command prompt, type

SET > ENVSIZE

This directs the current environment variables to print to a file. Then type

DIR ENVSIZE

The file size of ENVSIZE approximates the number of bytes used by the current environment space. (For an exact count, subtract the number of environment variables from the file size and add one.) If the current environment size is substantially less than the amount of space specified with the /E switch, decrease the environment size accordingly. If you receive Out of environment space messages when running batch files, increase the environment size until the messages go away. ◎

I mentioned the INSTALL command in the previous section when discussing Share. DOS 6 has an undocumented feature — the INSTALLHIGH command — which is used to load TSRs into upper memory from CONFIG.SYS on 386 or higher systems. This command is similar to the LOADHIGH command that loads TSRs into upper memory from AUTOEXEC.BAT.

Loading TSRs from CONFIG.SYS allows you to bypass the CONFIG.SYS file entirely or one line at a time during start-up. To implement this feature, use the question mark parameter (?) in the statement and press the F5 and/or F8 keys to bypass CONFIG.SYS completely one line at a time.

With the question mark embedded in a statement that loads a driver or a TSR, DOS prompts you before executing that program. Use this feature when you don't want to waste memory loading a program you don't need at every session. For example, enter this command in CONFIG.SYS to have DOS prompt you with a yes/no query before it attempts to load the program:

```
INSTALLHIGH?=C:\MOUSE\MOUSE.COM
```

Press Y to load the program or N to skip it. To load TSRs and device drivers high, you need to have EMM386.EXE loaded in CONFIG.SYS with INSTALLHIGH commands after it. INSTALLHIGH does not support the LOADHIGH /L switch available in AUTOEXEC.BAT, which allows you to specify the memory region that your program loads. A TSR loaded with INSTALLHIGH is always placed in the largest free upper memory block (UMB).

Inside the AUTOEXEC.BAT file

For the most part, AUTOEXEC.BAT is like any other batch file: it contains a list of DOS commands that execute line by line. The primary difference between AUTOEXEC.BAT and other batch files is that DOS looks for AUTOEXEC.BAT in the root directory of the startup drive every time you start your PC. If found, DOS executes AUTOEXEC.BAT automatically. Obviously, AUTOEXEC.BAT is the ideal place to store commands you want to execute every time you start up the PC.

You can have AUTOEXEC.BAT execute any valid command-line or batch-file command. However, certain commands are commonly associated with the AUTOEXEC.BAT file. For example, nearly every AUTOEXEC.BAT file contains a PATH command that establishes a list of directories that DOS searches for executable files. (When you type an external command, DOS first searches for a file of that name with the extension COM, EXE, or BAT in the current directory; then DOS searches the directories listed in the PATH statement of AUTOEXEC.BAT. In this way, you can execute programs stored in path directories no matter what drive and directory are current.

DOS 6 finally breaks the 127 character command line limit by allowing PATH statements to be created in CONFIG.SYS with a SET command.

To set up a long path statement, open AUTOEXEC.BAT in a text editor, find the PATH statement, and cut and paste it into the CONFIG.SYS file. Insert SET and a space before the PATH statement you just pasted into CONFIG.SYS. For example:

```
SET PATH=C:\!DOS;C:\WIN;C:\UTILS
```

You can add more directories to the end of the statement, separating them with semicolons without worrying about the line's length. Save the edits to the CONFIG.SYS file and reboot the computer to have the changes take effect.

DOS won't show any directories past the 127-character limit when you enter PATH at a DOS prompt.

When setting up your own PATH statement, always include drive letters with the directory names. If you don't, the search path is invalid if you switch to another drive.

In case you're still using DOS 5, you must exercise prudence when specifying a path in AUTOEXEC.BAT. DOS 5 imposes a 127-character limit on commands; if your PATH statement is longer than 127 characters, extra characters are ignored. You can work around this limitation by using the SUBST command to create two-letter drive aliases for path directories. Substitute commands similar to the following in your AUTOEXEC.BAT after including a LASTDRIVE = O statement in CONFIG.SYS:

```
SUBST M: C:\DOS
SUBST N: C:\AMIPRO
SUBST O: C:\EXCEL
PATH M:/;N:/;O:
```

Using the DOS MEM Command in DOS 6.2 _____

You can use the DOS MEM command to analyze your system's memory configuration. In DOS 6, the full syntax for the command is as follows:

```
MEM [/D] [/C] [/F] [/M module] [/P]
```

where D stands for *debug*, MEM /D profiles memory; among other things, it lists the programs that are loaded and the address where they are loaded.

C stands for *classify*, and MEM /C lists all the programs that are loaded and reports their installed sizes.

F stands for *free*, and MEM /F lists all the free spaces in conventional and upper memory.

M stands for *module,* and MEM /M followed by a module name (program name minus extension) lists the memory used by the specified program.

P stands for *page*. The /P switch pauses long listings at the end of each screen, like the DIR command's /P switch.

Running MEM without any command-line switches yields a report similar to this one:

```
655360 bytes total conventional memory
655360 bytes available to MS-DOS
649664 largest executable program size
3489792 bytes total EMS memory
1736704 bytes free EMS memory
3145728 bytes total contiguous extended memory
0 bytes available contiguous extended memory
1736704 bytes available XMS memory
MS-DOS resident in High Memory Area
```

The exact contents of this listing varies, depending on how your PC is configured. This output was taken from a 486 with 4MB of RAM.

You can discern more about the makeup of memory by typing **MEM /D.** In DOS 6, the output looks like the following. *Segment* specifies the segment address of the associated memory block. *Total* specifies the size (in bytes and in kilobytes), and *Name* indicates what is loaded in the memory block. *Type* offers additional information about the block's contents.

Conventional Memory Detail:

Segment	Name	Total	Type
000000		000400	Interrupt Vector
000400		000100	ROM Communication Area
000500		000200	DOS Communication Area
000700	IO	0C88E0	System Data
		QEMM386$	System Device Driver
		EMMXXXX0	System Device Driver
		CON	System Device Driver
		AUX	System Device Driver
		PRN	System Device Driver
		CLOCK$	System Device Driver
		A:-C:	System Device Driver
		COM1	System Device Driver
		LPT1	System Device Driver
		LPT2	System Device Driver
		LPT3	System Device Driver
		COM2	System Device Driver
		COM3	System Device Driver
		COM4	System Device Driver

```
0C8FE0    MSDOS      FFF380      System Data
001060    IO         000310      System Data
          QEMM386    000300      DEVICE=
          QEMM386$   Installed   Device Driver
001380    MSDOS      000000      System Program
001390    MSDOS      000040      System Program
0013E0    LOADHI     000060
001450    COMMAND    000100      Environment
001560    MEM        0000C0
001630    MEM        0176F0
018D30    MSDOS      0872C0      Free
Memory Summary:
655360 bytes total conventional memory
655360 bytes available to MS-DOS
649664 largest executable program size
Handle    EMS        Name        Size
          0                      09C000
          1          HMA         010000
          2          EMB2        100000
3489792 bytes total EMS memory
1736704 bytes free EMS memory
3145728 bytes total contiguous extended memory
0 bytes available contiguous extended memory
1736704 bytes available XMS memory
MS-DOS resident in High Memory Area
```

You can list the memory blocks that belong to a particular program with the /M switch. If memory were structured as shown above, typing **MEM /M COMMAND** would yield the following report:

```
COMMAND is using the following memory:

Segment Region Total Type

00F2D   48      (0K)    Data
00F30   4720    (5K)    Program
0105C   272     (0K)    Environment

Total Size: 5040 (5K)
```

This indicates that COMMAND.COM consumes a total of 5,040 bytes of RAM divided among three memory blocks. You can get a quick reading of the memory consumed by all the programs and device drivers loaded with the /C switch. Finally, you can list all the free memory blocks in the system with the /F switch. Typing **MEM /F** on this system produces the following report:

```
Free Conventional Memory:

Segment              Total

01057 80             (0K)
0106D 144            (0K)
01076 88608          (87K)
02618 499328         (488K)

Total Free: 588160 (574K)

No upper memory available
```

Use the /F switch to analyze upper memory and to determine to what extent it is fragmented.

In DOS 6, you can keep long MEM listings from scrolling off the screen by appending a /P switch, as in MEM /D /P. DOS 5's MEM command supports the /P switch, too, but the switch's meaning is completely different. In DOS 5, the syntax for the MEM command is

```
MEM [/C] [/D] [/P]
```

The /C and /D switches serve the same purpose as the /C and /D switches in DOS 6, although the output is formatted differently. The /P switch produces a report similar to but less detailed than the report produced by the /D switch. To prevent long MEM listings from scrolling off the screen in DOS 5, use the MORE command, as in

```
MEM /D | MORE
```

Be sure that your DOS directory is in the PATH, or else MORE — which is an external command — will result in a Bad command or file name message.

Examining Memory with Microsoft Diagnostics (MSD)

MSD is a useful tool for gathering information about your computer and its hardware/software environment. You can use MSD to help you do the following:

- Check for possible interrupt conflicts
- Check for memory conflicts between the network card and other devices in the system
- Identify hardware that must be reinstalled or reconfigured

For example, you can use MSD to identify how memory is used in the range between 640K and 1MB. Then you can see whether you have free blocks in the upper memory area so that you can avoid conflicts when loading device drivers into this range.

You also can examine the computer's communication ports, memory, type of video card, disk drives installed, and so on. MSD allows you to view the contents of configuration files such as CONFIG.SYS, AUTOEXEC.BAT, and all the Windows initialization (INI) files. In addition, you can print out a report with this information.

 Microsoft ships two Microsoft Diagnostics (MSD) files, MSD.COM and MSD.EXEMS, with DOS 6.2. You need both files to run MSD properly.

MSD versions 2.0, 2.0a, and 2.01 make int 67h EMS calls when interacting with expanded memory services, and pass an incorrect buffer pointer. This causes corrupted memory when int 67h writes information to the invalid buffer.

To work around this problem, MSD.COM loads before MSD.EXE, hooks int 67h, and then monitors for the MSD.EXE int 67h call. MSD.COM patches the buffer pointer to point to the correct MSD.EXE data segment. Doing so prevents the data corruption.

MSD.COM is used rather than making the change in MSD.EXE, because MSD.COM can be used with any 2.x version of MSD.EXE. You can protect against memory corruption by simply placing the MSD.COM file in the directory where MSD.EXE is located.

 This problem was corrected in MSD version 2.1, which is provided with Windows for Workgroups version 3.11.

MSD command-line options

To start the MSD tool, follow these steps:

1. Exit Windows. Because the reports are less accurate when MSD runs within Windows, I don't recommend running MSD.EXE while Windows is running. Run it from DOS instead.

    Both DOS and Windows will install MSD. Check the file dates to determine which is the latest and delete the older one.

2. At the MS-DOS command prompt, type the following line and press Enter:

   ```
   C:\[path]\MSD
   ```

The [*path*] option indicates the directory path to MSD.EXE. Usually, the path is \WINDOWS, unless you removed MSD from the Windows directory. (If you installed Windows for Workgroups in a directory other than \WIN-DOWS or on a drive other than C, make the necessary changes to the [*path*] option.)

MSD also has command-line options you can use when starting the program. The syntax for MSD is as follows:

```
MSD [/b] [/i] [/f <filename> | /p <filename> | /s
[<filename>]] [/?]
```

Table 2-1 explains each of the command-line options.

Table 2-1	Command-Line Options for the MSD Utility
Option	**Description**
/b	Starts MSD in black-and-white mode. Use this option if your computer has a monochrome or LCD monitor.
/i	Specifies that no initial hardware detection be performed. Use this option if MSD fails to start correctly.
/f <filename>	Writes a complete MSD report to the specified *filename*. Requests information such as name, company, address, telephone number, and comments.
/p <filename>	Writes a complete MSD report to the specified *filename* without requesting any information.
/s <filename>	Writes a summary MSD report to the specified *filename*. If no filename is specified, the report is displayed on-screen.
/?	Displays the MSD command options.

Automating memory configuration with MemMaker

MemMaker optimizes your computer's memory by moving device drivers and memory-resident programs to upper memory. To use MemMaker, your computer must have an 80386 or 80486 processor and extended memory.

Do not use this command when you are running Windows.

Following is the syntax for loading the MemMaker utility:

```
MEMMAKER [/b] [/batch] [/session] [/swap:drive] [/t] [/undo]
[/w:n,m]
```

The /b switch displays MemMaker in black and white. Use this option if MemMaker doesn't display correctly on a monochrome monitor.

The /batch switch runs MemMaker in batch (unattended) mode. In batch mode, MemMaker takes the default action at all prompts. If an error occurs, MemMaker restores your previous CONFIG.SYS, AUTOEXEC.BAT and (if necessary) Windows SYSTEM.INI files. After MemMaker has completed, you can review status messages by viewing the contents of the MEMMAKER.STS file. (To view this file, use a text editor such as MS-DOS Editor, or use the DOS TYPE command.)

The /session switch is used exclusively by MemMaker during the optimization process.

The /swap:*drive* switch specifies the letter of the drive that was originally your start-up disk drive. Specify the current drive letter after the colon. This switch is necessary only if the drive letter of your start-up disk drive has changed since your computer started. (The drive letter sometimes changes because of disk swapping performed by some disk-compression programs.) If the drive letter of your start-up drive has changed and you do not specify this switch, MemMaker cannot find your system start-up files.

You do not need to use the /swap:*drive* switch if you are using Stacker 2.0, SuperStor, or Microsoft DoubleSpace.

The /t switch disables the detection of IBM Token-Ring networks. Use this switch if your computer includes such a network and you are having problems running MemMaker.

The /undo switch instructs MemMaker to undo its most recent changes. When MemMaker optimizes your system's memory, it makes changes to the CONFIG.SYS and AUTOEXEC.BAT files (and if necessary, the Windows SYSTEM.INI file). If your system doesn't work properly after MemMaker completes, or if you are not satisfied with your new memory configuration, return to your previous configuration by starting MemMaker with the /undo switch.

The /w:*size1,size2* switch specifies how much upper-memory space to reserve for Windows translation buffers. Windows needs two areas of upper memory for its translation buffers. The *size1* value specifies the size of the first region; *size2* specifies the size of the second region. By default, MemMaker does not reserve upper memory for Windows; this is equivalent to specifying /w:0,0.

The following example runs MemMaker in batch mode and directs it to not reserve any upper memory for Windows translation buffers:

```
MEMMAKER /batch /w:0,0
```

The following example restores your previous system configuration:

```
MEMMAKER /undo
```

Suppose you use a disk-compression program. Your start-up disk is drive C, but after the compression driver starts, drive C becomes your main compressed drive. Your start-up files are now on drive D. Because of this drive-letter swapping, you would start MemMaker by using the following command:

```
MEMMAKER /swap:d
```

This command specifies that the current drive D was originally the start-up drive and contains the CONFIG.SYS and AUTOEXEC.BAT files.

Load DOS high

MemMaker includes DEVICE commands that add HIMEM.SYS and EMM386.EXE to CONFIG.SYS. It also adds the statement DOS=UMB to make the upper memory blocks (UMBs) created by EMM386.EXE available for loading TSRs and device drivers. But MemMaker does not add a DOS=HIGH statement to move DOS to the high memory area (HMA). After you run MemMaker, if your CONFIG.SYS file contains a DOS=UMB command but not a DOS=HIGH command, modify the DOS=UMB line so that it looks like this:

```
DOS=HIGH,UMB
```

You'll gain 45K or more by making this change.

 There is a tradeoff between loading DOS high and specifying too many buffers. Check your buffers setting to make sure that it's set to 40 or less; otherwise, the extra RAM created by loading DOS high is depleted.

Optimize your UMBs

EMM386.EXE and MemMaker convert any unused space between the C600h and F7FFh segments of upper memory to UMB RAM. Although this is an improvement over DOS 5.0, which searched only about half that much space, MemMaker might leave unused space in upper memory.

Use MSD to identify empty regions of upper memory and convert them to usable RAM.

Start MSD and select Memory from the main screen to display a map of upper memory. Check the map to see if the range C000h to C5FFh is free, and add the Include switch, `I=C000-C5FF`, to the end of the EMM386.EXE `DEVICE=` line in CONFIG.SYS. You notice a gain of about 23K.

Don't give up UMBs to get EMS memory

Using EMM386.EXE to emulate expanded (EMS) memory decreases the amount of available UMB RAM by 64K. That 64K belongs to EMS page frame, which serves as a port hole into expanded memory. DOS 6.0 has a feature that allows you to have expanded memory without sacrificing the 64K page frame.

Adding a `FRAME=NONE` switch to EMM386.EXE causes it to emulate expanded memory but without the 64K overhead in UMB RAM. This means that you'll be able to load even more programs high.

If you specify the `FRAME=NONE` switch, you cannot run any EMS applications.

Get every bit of upper memory

Despite all that you may have done thus far, you might still come up short of upper memory when trying to load all your TSRs and device drivers high. Here are a couple of suggestions to squeeze out extra RAM.

Changing the order in which TSRs and device drivers load can sometimes shoehorn more programs into upper memory. This trick often works because some drivers require more memory to load than they need after they're installed. If you used MemMaker, it makes the task of determining the best load order easier. Look for the text file named MEMMAKER.STS in your DOS directory. MemMaker created this file when it analyzed your system configuration. Open it with a text editor and find the `SizeData` section.

Make a note of the `MaxSize` and `FinalSize` listed for each TSR and device driver in this section. Compare the differences between the `MaxSize` and `FinalSize` for TSRs to rank them from the largest difference to the smallest. Try loading the ones with the largest difference first, working your way down to the smallest.

If you're less than 5K short of having enough UMB RAM to load one last TSR or device driver high, add a NOHI switch to the EMM386.EXE command line in CONFIG.SYS. This prevents EMM386.EXE from loading part of itself in upper memory and increases available UMB RAM by about 5K. If the extra 5K allows you to load a 40K TSR high, then your net increase in the largest executable program size is 35K.

Regions scanned by the EMM386.EXE HIGHSCAN switch

The HIGHSCAN switch included in EMM386.EXE version 4.45 allows EMM386.EXE to map expanded memory pages or upper memory blocks (UMBs) over portions of the upper memory area (UMA) used by system read-only memory (ROM).

Choosing Yes in response to the MemMaker prompt Scan the upper memory area aggressively? causes MemMaker to add HIGHSCAN to the EMM386.EXE DEVICE= line.

If you use the HIGHSCAN switch on the DEVICE=C:\DOS\EMM386.EXE line in the CONFIG.SYS file, EMM386.EXE examines the system ROM area starting at memory location F000:0000. If EMM386.EXE determines that ROM is duplicated between F000h-F7FFh and F800h-FFFFh, EMM386.EXE uses the F000h-F7FFh region for expanded memory page mapping or UMB memory. (This adds up to 32 kilobytes to the UMA.)

On Micro Channel (MCA) systems with ROM BASIC (for example, IBM PS/2 systems), the HIGHSCAN switch allows EMM386.EXE to map expanded memory or UMB memory over the ROM BASIC code in the system ROM. Typically, this is the region from F600 to FDFF.

On some systems, EMM386.EXE uses the ROM area and the system does not operate correctly. The symptoms of this condition vary. For example, the system may stop responding (*hang*) or appear to operate normally until you use a floppy disk drive. Because of these potential problems, HIGHSCAN is not used by default.

The Path to an Optimized Windows Workstation

The easiest path to a quick start in Windows is the shortest path. Here's a rule of thumb; keep the DOS search path, as specified in the AUTOEXEC.BAT PATH statement, as short as possible. DOS uses the directories in the PATH statement as pathways to executing programs or commands you invoke at the DOS prompt. In order to execute a program, DOS sifts through each file in the search path until it finds the one you've entered on the command line. A PATH statement with more than two or three subdirectories can slow down your system unnecessarily.

Optimize your PATH statement

Assuming that every subdirectory in the PATH statement is necessary, create a set of batch files to provide access to various directories. First, record your current long path by redirecting the PATH command's output to a file called LONGPATH.BAT. To do this, enter the following command at a DOS prompt:

```
PATH > C: \BATCH\LONGPATH.BAT
```

Open the LONGPATH.BAT file in a text editor and look at its contents. Because the PATH command's output is in the same format as the command itself, the line you see not only describes your path but also resets it when you run it as a batch command. Feel free to remove directories from or add them to the line in LONGPATH.BAT (separating each directory with a semicolon and no spaces), and save it under a different name, such as WINPATH.BAT. You can now load AUTOEXEC.BAT in your text editor and adjust the PATH line to include only DOS program directories. ◎

While you're in the text editor, either load or create a batch file to start Windows. At the beginning of the file, insert two lines, such as the following, that store your current path and load your long path:

```
PATH > C:\BATCH\DOSPATH.BAT
CALL C:\BATCH\LONGPATH.BAT
```

After the lines that load Windows and any other options, reset the path with the following statements:

```
CALL C:\BATCH\DOSPATH.BAT
DEL C:\BATCH\DOSPATH.BAT
```

The first command resets the path; the second is optional and deletes the path-setting file. Experiment with different paths to determine which work best for your favorite applications. Then produce batch files like this one to load the most useful path for your programs.

Protect your AUTOEXEC.BAT file

When you install a program, its installation procedure usually informs you that it's going to modify your AUTOEXEC.BAT file and requests your permission to do so. Some programs make changes to the AUTOEXEC.BAT file secretly — sometimes with disastrous results. Here are strategies you can use to protect AUTOEXEC.BAT from arbitrary edits:

- *Hide the AUTOEXEC.BAT file commands:* Create a batch file called STARTUP.BAT and place all startup commands in it. Edit AUTOEXEC.BAT so that it consists of a single command that invokes STARTUP.BAT. Now if a program alters AUTOEXEC.BAT, the commands in STARTUP.BAT are unaffected.

- *Make your AUTOEXEC.BAT read only:* At the DOS prompt, type **ATTRIB + R AUTOEXEC.BAT** and press Enter. This makes AUTOEXEC.BAT a read-only file and prevents any program from editing the file. Changing this attribute also prevents you from editing the file, however. Remove the read-only attribute before editing AUTOEXEC.BAT (type **ATTRIB -R AUTOEXEC.BAT**) and then replace the read-only attribute when you're done changing the file.

- *Maintain a backup up of your system files:* Store a backup copy of AUTOEXEC.BAT in a remote directory or on a floppy disk. Then, if an installation program modifies the original, you still have the backup.

Use the latest driver versions

Make sure that the most recent versions of HIMEM.SYS, EMM386.EXE, RAMDRIVE.SYS, and SMARTDRV.EXE are stored in the directories specified in the command lines that load these drivers in your CONFIG.SYS and AUTOEXEC.BAT files.

Make sure COMMAND.COM loads correctly

If DOS suddenly begins to ignore your PATH or show a default prompt, check CONFIG.SYS for a SHELL= statement that loads COMMAND.COM. Any such command should end in a /P switch. Without this switch, COMMAND.COM ignores AUTOEXEC.BAT, and worse, leaves your PC susceptible to crashes.

Check the load order of HIMEM.SYS

Load HIMEM.SYS in CONFIG.SYS and make sure the line that loads HIMEM comes *before* commands that load any other applications or drivers that use extended memory.

Load SMARTDRV.EXE in the AUTOEXEC.BAT file

Load SMARTDRV.EXE in AUTOEXEC.BAT and allocate the largest amount of memory possible; the SMARTDrive disk caching driver can produce the biggest Windows 3.1 performance improvement.

Use the correct number of files and buffers

Set FILES=30 in CONFIG.SYS unless you have a software application that requires a higher setting.

Set BUFFERS=10 in CONFIG.SYS if you use SMARTDRV.EXE. Using a higher number of buffers with SMARTDrive decreases efficiency.

If you are not using SMARTDrive, set BUFFERS=20 in CONFIG.SYS. More buffers may improve disk access times, but use more conventional memory.

Create a RAM drive

Install RAMDrive to use as the TEMP environment variable if you have a diskless workstation or if you have limited hard disk space and ample extended memory (more than 8MB). Performance improves for Print Manager and for applications that frequently create TMP files because access is faster for a RAM disk than for a physical disk.

Don't load a mouse driver for Windows

Remove any commands for mouse drivers from your AUTOEXEC.BAT and CONFIG.SYS files if you only use the mouse in Windows and don't want mouse support while running non-Windows applications in 386 enhanced mode.

Summary

This chapter discussed the importance of configuring and optimizing DOS for Windows. This information is particularly useful if you run DOS applications under Windows. In this chapter, you learned:

▶ Tips for optimizing your CONFIG.SYS and AUTOEXEC.BAT files

▶ Command-line options for using HIMEM.SYS

▶ Command-line options for using EMM386.EXE

▶ Command-line options for using DOS 6.x's MemMaker

Chapter 3
Using Third-Party Memory Managers

In This Chapter

▶ How memory managers work

▶ Benefits of third-party memory managers over the Windows-supplied memory managers

▶ Differences between MS-DOS memory managers and QEMM or 386MAX

▶ Using QEMM-386 7.x and 386MAX 7.x to fine-tune your system memory

▶ Using memory manager optimizing routines to find holes in a system's memory

The quest for more memory is a constant one. You need more memory to run larger applications, hold extra drivers and TSRs, work with larger data files, and above all, to work faster. Although MS-DOS and Windows have their own memory managers, EMM386.EXE and HIMEM.SYS, third-party memory managers such as Qualitas' 386MAX and Quarterdeck Office System's QEMM-386 are viable alternatives.

Why Windows Needs a Sophisticated Memory Manager

A look inside your CONFIG.SYS and AUTOEXEC.BAT files would probably show that your DOS-based system is filled with unnecessary items. In addition to the Windows programs you're running, you may be using DOS programs, or your PC may be loaded with peripheral devices that require DOS-based device drivers or TSRs. And if your computer is attached to a network, the network adds even more overhead. To top it off, these items — drivers, TSRs, and so on — may be placed haphazardly in your CONFIG.SYS and AUTOEXEC.BAT files. You need a memory manager to sort and optimize your DOS memory configuration in order to increase Windows' performance.

Chapter 2 stresses the importance of managing conventional memory. A memory manager needs to perform the following two critical tasks:

- First, you want a memory manager to increase the amount of conventional memory available to DOS applications running under Windows (DOS *Virtual Machines*, [VMs]).

- Second, the memory manager should increase Windows overall stability by mapping the upper memory area (UMA), helping to avoid conflicts between Windows and the devices that reside in this region.

Migrating from MS-DOS 5 to MS-DOS 6.2 _____

Because Windows relies on its partnership with MS-DOS, Microsoft made an attempt to solidify that relationship with the release of MS-DOS 5.0. Recognizing extended memory as a critical part of a PC's memory resources, MS-DOS 5 included an extended memory manager (XMS) driver, HIMEM.SYS. It also included a combined expanded memory manager and upper memory block (UMB) driver, EMM386.EXE, enabling you to relocate device drivers and TSRs into UMBs before launching Windows. This reduced the DOS footprint in each DOS VM and allowed DOS to access TSRs and drivers relocated into UMBs.

Another feature introduced in MS-DOS 5 was the ability to move the DOS kernel into the first 64K of extended memory (HMA). With part of DOS residing in extended memory, components running in protected mode can access DOS.

Even with MS-DOS 5's enhanced features, complex memory management issues were still difficult to solve. For starters, you installed and configured EMM386.EXE manually. In addition, MS-DOS 5 is not efficient when managing the UMB space DOS was allotted.

MS-DOS 6: The interim DOS

Microsoft's solution to the memory configuration and management struggle began with MS-DOS 6.0, which includes an automated memory optimization program (MemMaker) and a revamped EMM386.EXE that more aggressively recovers and optimizes DOS memory, especially for use by Windows. MS-DOS 6 divides each UMB into smaller regions and allows you to specify where you want to load a driver or TSR by using the revised Loadhigh function.

You can use MemMaker to automatically reserve UMB space for Windows' translation buffers. Windows uses these buffers when communicating with DOS. See Chapter 2 for more on optimizing DOS for Windows.

Finally, MS-DOS 6.2

Although MS-DOS 6.x memory management prowess satisfies most users, there's still room for third-party memory management tools. If you want total control over your Windows configuration, you can begin with state-of-the-art memory management tools. Refer to Chapter 2 for a thorough discussion of DOS 6.x memory management utilities.

Why not stick with MS-DOS's MemMaker?

Unfortunately DOS was not designed to accommodate all the hefty applications and other memory-grabbing software found on systems today . The software drivers for networks and other expansion cards generally require more RAM than DOS was designed to provide. MS-DOS 5.0 alleviated the problem with the LOADHIGH and DEVICEHIGH commands, when used in conjunction with EMM386.EXE, used to load TSRs and device drivers into unused upper memory blocks. Many people found the LOADHIGH and DEVICEHIGH commands confusing and cumbersome.

MS-DOS 6.x gave us MemMaker to simplify the process of loading drivers and TSRs high. Even so, MemMaker has not accomplished the art of making more upper memory available, so there still may not be enough UMA to quench those memory-gobbling applications.

How Memory Managers Work_____

All memory managers have one function in common: they can free addresses in DOS memory to increase the RAM available to your applications.

DOS memory managers and third-party memory managers free space by moving TSRs and device drivers out of DOS memory. After the memory manager moves the program or driver out of DOS or low memory, it must find address ranges in high memory in which to place the code. Remember that DOS cannot reach beyond the 1MB ceiling, and that the TSR and device driver addresses must remain accessible to real-mode operation.

What sets one memory manager apart from another is its ability to recognize and make use of the addresses in your PC's upper memory area. The idea is simple — the more space the memory manager can find or create, the more TSRs and device drivers you can load high.

Most memory managers, including MS-DOS 5 and 6.x memory managers, let you specify address ranges in which to relocate programs or address ranges to exclude. To specify a certain address range, you have to inform your memory manager that you want to use a specified range. For example, if you know that your hardware doesn't use a certain address range, you can tell EMM386 to map that unused area by specifying that range to include the following:

```
DEVICE=<PATH>EMM386.EXE I=[RANGE][PARAMETER]
```

Several memory managers provide mapping utilities that can find unused address ranges in areas where no memory circuits respond and are therefore not normally detected.

The Making of a Sophisticated Memory Manager

A sophisticated memory manager has automatic installation and optimization routines, and takes into account specific DOS-configuration needs under Windows, such as UMB space for translation buffers. Table 3-1 outlines desirable features in a memory manager.

Table 3-1	Desired Features in a Memory Manager
Feature	**Description**
Support for memory standards	Look for products that support EMS (converted from extended memory) and XMS, as well as products that can create MS-DOS 6.0-compatible upper memory blocks in the UMA. Optional memory standards to look for include VCPI and DPMI.
Memory-mapping utilities	Memory managers that can display a visual or text-based map of your UMA helping you to manually fine-tune your system's memory configuration. A text-based map (a list of available memory) helps you determine the optimal fit for each piece of software you want to move to the upper memory area. A graphics-based map helps you to make quick decisions by showing where available addresses are located.
Windows support	Automatically optimizes Windows components as well as Windows, usually by tweaking the SYSTEM.INI file.
DOS VM support	DOS applications require contiguous memory, so you need a memory manager that can reclaim the unused high-resolution display memory region and free contiguous conventional memory for each DOS VM.

Feature	Description
System resource reports	Effective memory management requires a process of trial and error; when you're tweaking the system, you need all the information you can get. You want a memory manager that provides reports on the memory used by all your system's resources, hardware and software, and also advises you where to relocate programs.
Loads high into unused addresses	Although all memory managers can move memory-resident software to high DOS memory, they differ in the address ranges they can detect. Look for a program with a mapping utility, which will help you locate more addresses without as much trial and error.
Recaptures unused BIOS addresses	Some BIOS routines used by other operating systems are not required by DOS. Look for a memory manager that can free these addresses, which you can then use to relocate your memory-resident programs.
Releases VGA memory	Look for a program that lets you extend the DOS ceiling beyond 640K when you don't need VGA graphics. Some programs automatically use the high DOS area reserved for VGA graphics when there's no EGA or VGA adapter in your system; others let you turn VGA on when you need it and off when you don't.
Remaps all high DOS memory	To extend the DOS addressing range as high as possible, look for a program that lets you move all BIOS, video, and peripheral drivers to the top of high DOS memory. The trade-off to this scheme, however, is you get the most room possible to run applications, but you can't load memory-resident software high.
Automatic memory optimization	The goal of memory optimization is to achieve the best fit for drivers, TSRs, and programs. Finding the best fit requires testing several scenarios or permutations. Advanced memory manager programs automatically shuffle available addresses and software to achieve the best fit. If the memory manager does this work properly, you don't have to examine a memory map.

Inside QEMM and 386MAX

Qualitas' 386MAX and Quarterdeck Office Products' QEMM represent the epitome of sophisticated memory managers. Besides freeing up space below 640K, another measure of a memory manager's success is the amount of upper memory left after it has done its work.

MemMaker is primarily concerned with optimizing low memory instead of being aggressive about freeing upper memory. 386MAX's Maximize and QEMM's Optimize go further in attempts to squeeze every byte of memory, high or low.

Optimize and Maximize features

When you install QEMM-386 or 386MAX, in addition to copying appropriate program files to your system, the installation programs perform the following tasks:

- Evaluate upper memory resources
- Determine memory requirements for drivers and TSRs
- Determine the difference between the initialization and resident sizes of drivers and TSRs
- Identify and configure the system's upper memory
- Examine CONFIG.SYS and AUTOEXEC.BAT files to set up drivers and programs for loading into the UMA

QEMM's Optimize and 386MAX's Maximize are designed to perform just what their names suggest. The optimization routine performs three operations: evaluates the system's available memory resources; analyzes the boot sequence of the DOS configuration; and calculates the best combination of load-order and positioning for each system component.

During optimization, the programs develop a map of your system's memory by locating expansion-board ROM addresses (for video, SCSI, and so forth) and testing the system ROM for unused regions. Optimization is also the stage in which memory managers can make their first mistake. Some regions of the UMA may appear free but are, in fact, reserved by an optional card, possibly as a RAM buffer enabled only when a specific driver is loaded. Such an oversight may cause your system to lock when you boot.

To avoid this problem, intelligent memory managers combine the evaluation phase with a boot-sequence analysis to get a better picture of what the system looks like after everything is loaded. During this phase, the memory manager often installs measuring utilities that monitor each driver and TSR as it loads, and then record the behavior and final, loaded sizes.

Still, you cannot anticipate every scenario (such as the network adapter that doesn't reserve a RAM buffer until the NET START command is issued). Obviously, familiarity with your system's memory layout is desirable. To help, most memory managers include an analysis or reporting program, such as Quarterdeck's Manifest and Qualitas' ASQ, which displays a graphical or text-based map of a system's configuration.

The purpose of the Optimize program is to configure CONFIG.SYS, AUTOEXEC.BAT, and any batch files called by AUTOEXEC.BAT to leave the computer with the most conventional memory possible (the memory below 640K) and the largest possible remaining areas of high RAM. Optimize does nothing permanent to the computer other than edit CONFIG.SYS, AUTOEXEC.BAT, and called batch files. You can manually perform, or reverse, all the work that Optimize does, in whole or in part.

Some QEMM specifics

QEMM employs a technique called *Stealth* that creates imaginary addresses for portions of the video and system BIOS instead of using their conventional addresses in upper memory. This frees those upper-memory addresses for other uses. When an application calls those portions of the BIOS, QEMM intercepts the calls, remaps the BIOS to available addresses, and makes the BIOS functions available to the programs.

This sounds like QEMM is working with smoke and mirrors in the way that it manipulates low-level functions. If you think that the thought of all this shuffling and reshuffling of low-level functions will make your users a little uneasy, then I recommend 386MAX as an alternative because it takes a more conservative approach.

Analysis vs. ROM Search

The difference between QEMM's and 386MAX's approach to memory-management is best illustrated by contrasting QEMM's Analysis and 386MAX's ROM Search.

Analysis is really a tracking mechanism. First, you manually load and exit every program, and access all hardware devices on your computer; when that's done, check the Analysis area in Manifest. It will direct you to add short exclude (X) and include (I) memory statements to the QEMM386.SYS line in your CONFIG.SYS file. A typical example is the following:

```
DEVICE=C:\QEMM\QEMM386.SYS RAM ROM IA X=B000-B7FF I=C000-
C7FF
```

In this preceding line, QEMM is told, in effect, "Hands off grabbing the memory in the B000-B7FF region for EMS swapping; it's in use. But you can allocate the memory C000-C7FF memory region. Nothing's going on there."

Analysis has the advantage of detailed accuracy — of wringing every drop of available memory from your system. It is also time consuming and labor intensive. You will, however, probably want to run Analysis on any programs you subsequently add to your computer, possibly amending your QEMM386.SYS line in response.

ROM Search was introduced in 386MAX 6.0. It circumvents software loading, performing all possible BIOS calls and flipping all access bits in the page table directory. Logic dictates that if a ROM address isn't accessed through these procedures, it can't be touched by any program. The result is memory freed up for 386MAX allocation, within a perfectly stable operating environment.

ROM Search needs to run only once during the Maximize process because it isn't dependent on memory access in programming code. It requires no human interaction — even the changes to the 386MAX.PRO line in your CONFIG.SYS file are automatically added by the memory manager — and it consumes almost no time. You get much gain with no pain.

But if ROM Search effectively ensures an absence of system crashes from memory conflicts, it does so at the expense of some potential memory savings. Analysis examines the memory requirements of your specific applications, which opens up high memory regions that ROM Search cannot recognize.

I should also note that ROM Search arrives at a single conclusion regarding your memory requirements. Because Analysis is application-dependent, you can keep multiple memory configurations with QEMM, optimized for different needs.

Upper Memory Area Configuration

The most critical tasks a memory manager performs are configuring upper memory blocks for use by drivers and TSRs, and loading drivers and TSRs into upper memory. In fact, the primary components of a memory manager package are the UMB provider and the UMB loader.

QEMM-386 and 386MAX use advanced memory optimization routines that automatically determine how to manage and load upper memory blocks. This capability sets them apart from DOS' or Windows' EMM386. To use EMM386 effectively, you have to decide when, where, what, and how to insert `DEVICEHIGH` and `LOADHIGH` commands in your CONFIG.SYS and AUTOEXEC.BAT files. You must manually enter a command for each device driver and TSR that you want to load in upper memory.

The upper memory area (640K to 1MB) is very crowded, though intelligent memory managers know how to recover unused regions. Table 3-2 shows how UMA space is typically used before memory managers fill in the gaps.

Table 3-2	Typical UMA Space Usage
Address	*Description*
A000-AFFF	Reserved for use by EGA and VGA adapters as high-resolution display memory.
B000-B7FF	Used on monochrome systems to emulate the IBM Monochrome Display Adapter; if you're using low-resolution VGA modes, such as 640x480, memory managers can recover this area.
B800-C7FF	Reserved for EGA or VGA ROM BIOS functions.
C800-DFFF	96K is usually unoccupied, though IBM SCSI adapters map on-board BIOS in the C800-CFFF range.
E000-EFFF	Free on most systems, though IBM PS/2s use the range for Advanced BIOS functions, and some PCs (such as Epson) use this range instead of C000-C7FF for VGA BIOS.

Qualitas also has a product called Blue Max, which is designed to reclaim the extended BIOS area on PS/2s.

The 64K range from F000-FFFF is normally reserved by the system's ROM BIOS, though large tracts of this region are unused on many systems after bootup.

Using a Third-Party Memory Manager to Configure the UMA

When you install EMM386, it searches the hex address range C0000 to E0000 for unused memory space. To determine unused space in other address ranges, you must use the DOS MEM command or a memory viewer. After you've made that determination, you have to add the INCLUDE switch in your CONFIG.SYS file for each additional range of addresses that you want to include.

As I discussed previously, QEMM-386 and 386MAX come with their own programs (Optimize and Maximize respectively) that perform memory optimization without any help from you. Optimize and Maximize search the entire 384K upper memory address range to determine unused space and configure them automatically.

QEMM's DOS-UP

Even if you use the DOS=HIGH command in your CONFIG.SYS file, QEMM's DOS-UP moves portions of DOS that DOS=HIGH doesn't move. DOS-UP is a set of utility programs that QEMM and Optimize use to load more of the DOS kernel into upper memory. Obviously, this yields more conventional memory even if you already have everything on your system loading high.

DOS-UP consists of two drivers, DOSDATA.SYS and DOS-UP.SYS. Both are necessary for DOS-UP to work properly.

DOSDATA.SYS must be the very first line in your CONFIG.SYS. Its purpose is to prepare DOS so that it is in the proper place to be loaded into upper memory.

DOS-UP.SYS comes after QEMM loads in the CONFIG.SYS. Its job is to move the pieces of DOS into high RAM and make sure that other programs know about this new location.

DOS-UP can give DOS 5 and 6.x users an additional 7K to 20K of conventional memory, as well as being able to move DOS out of conventional memory without DOS=HIGH, which allows some other HMA user to have the full 64K of HMA instead of only the 35K that DOS=HIGH uses by default.

QEMM and 386MAX Provide Automated UMB Loaders

Unlike EMM386.EXE, both QEMM-386 and 386MAX can determine how to use their UMB provider and loader without your intervention. This is one of the most important benefits of using a third-party memory manager instead of EMM386. When you use EMM386.EXE, you must place DEVICEHIGH and LOADHIGH commands in your CONFIG.SYS and AUTOEXEC.BAT files. As I explained in Chapter 2, you are responsible for determining the configuration, and manually entering a command for each device driver or TSR that you want to load into upper memory.

What Do Third-Party Managers Do while Windows Is Running?

Memory managers, such as EEM386, QEMM-386, and 386MAX, do not run while Windows is running. Windows has its own memory managers. When you launch Windows, any third-party manager that you loaded from within the CONFIG.SYS is suspended, so that Windows drivers can take charge.

Windows' built-in memory managers work similarly to QEMM and 386MAX in that they manage expanded and extended memory and use available upper memory. When you exit Windows or run a virtual DOS machine in enhanced mode, your third-party memory manager awakens to take control.

Because third-party memory managers don't work with Windows applications, you may ask, what good are they if I'm using Windows? Windows' built-in memory managers cannot manage your device drivers and TSRs. You need a package like QEMM or 386MAX if you want to optimize your upper memory area to support virtual DOS machines. Remember that virtual machines inherit the DOS environment that is in effect when you launch Windows. Therefore, any drivers that are loaded from DOS are available in the VM.

386MAX Provides Extra Support for DOS Virtual Machines

386MAX has a unique feature that allows you to configure separate upper memory environments for each DOS session running in a window. Earlier in this chapter, I said that each virtual machine running under Windows enhanced mode inherits the DOS environment that existed prior to starting Windows. This means that if you have DOS programs requiring device drivers or TSRs, when you run such programs under Windows you either had to load them before Windows or load them during the DOS session in Windows. The following two problems occur if you run more than one DOS application and load several different TSRs to work with those applications:

- If you load device drivers and TSRs before starting Windows, you deplete conventional and high DOS memory that Windows uses to load itself.

- If you load the DOS program while in the VM, you can load only one instance of the TSR. You cannot run the same TSR in another VM.

The DOSMAX program enhances each virtual machine by virtualizing and instancing. The virtualized high DOS feature manifests individual copies of upper memory for each virtual machine. What this means is that if you load a TSR into upper memory in one VM it occupies the upper memory of that specific VM only.

The second component of DOSMAX provides *instancing* — allowing you to run one program several times. You can now load the same TSR into several different VMs. Many TSRs can run only one instance at a time; instancing solves this.

Summary

In this chapter, I presented you with some options for choosing and using a third-party memory manager. I discussed:

▶ The common components of third-party memory managers

▶ Basic features of 386MAX and QEMM

▶ How to use third-party memory managers to configure upper memory

▶ How third-party memory managers interact with Windows

Chapter 4
Understanding Windows Architecture

This chapter provides an overview of the architecture that Windows 3.1 and Windows for Workgroups 3.1x uses. Learning about the architecture can help you understand how Windows works so that you can better understand the effects of changing the files and the parameters that control Windows' configuration.

Events Drive Windows

Until you tell Windows to do something, nothing happens. Whenever you press a key or click the mouse, Windows responds to the *event* by shifting into gear and servicing your request. Requesting service is the key to running multiple programs at the same time.

In DOS-based PCs, individual applications control their interactions; but when you load Windows, it manages the events of all programs that are running under it. Each keystroke and mouse movement is passed to Windows as a separate event or message for it to process, and Windows determines how to handle each event. The applications that are running poll Windows to find out whether it has received any events for their use. Figure 4-1 shows how event-driven processing allows several applications to run simultaneously without conflict.

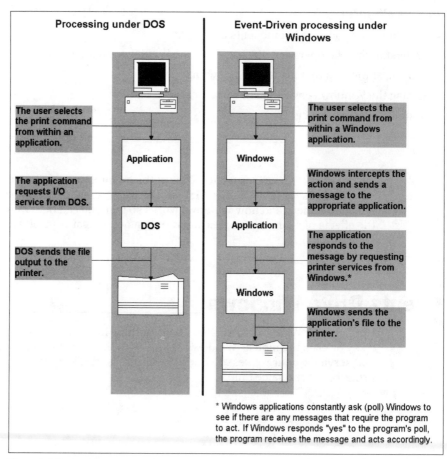

Figure 4-1: Event-driven processing.

Several different applications may poll Windows at any given time. Only the active application polls for keystrokes, and Windows passes events only to the application for which they are intended. Windows does not pass all events and messages to the active application. Instead, Windows evaluates events to determine which events to pass to an application and which ones to use internally. Because Windows can recognize which events are for its own use, you can interact with Windows itself.

You need to understand the event-driven philosophy and the underlying structure of Windows in order to configure and optimize Windows effectively.

Inside Windows

As the preceding section explains, when Windows detects an event, it determines how to handle or process the event. Windows carries out the processing requirements by using several components that are built into its architecture.

The Windows architecture is divided into three primary layers or levels, as illustrated in Figure 4-2:

■ The Windows Application Programming Interface (API)

■ The Windows core and Windows' extensions

■ The Windows drivers

As Figure 4-2 illustrates, no layer is an island. Each layer has a relationship with the other layers; and the relationship is determined by the interaction of components within the layers. Each layer is governed by strict rules that tell it when to pass events to another layer. Figure 4-3 depicts the relationship among the Windows layers and between the layers and other system elements.

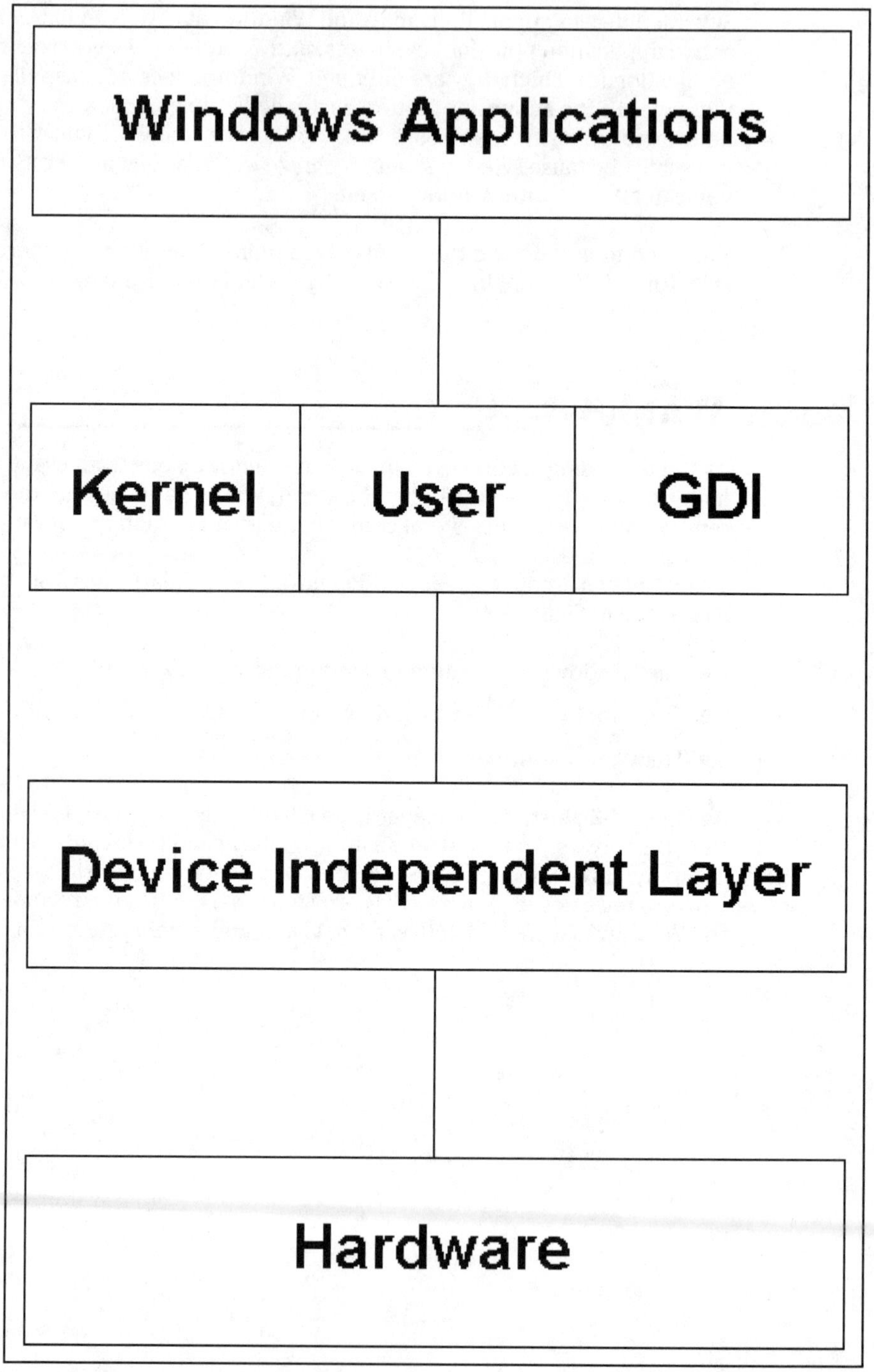

Figure 4-2: The generic Windows architecture.

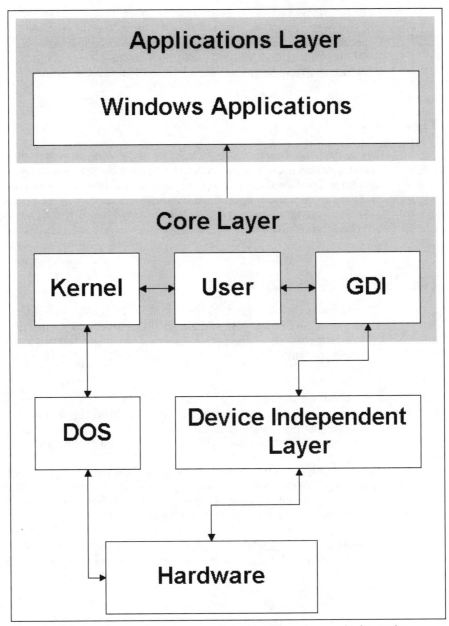

Figure 4-3: Windows is comprised of many components that require complex interactions.

The remaining sections of this chapter explain the event management responsibilities of each Windows layer. They also provide additional information on specific capabilities and limitations of the Windows operating modes. Armed with this information, you can make intelligent decisions about how to use the configuration and optimization techniques that this book presents.

The core

As its name implies, the core is the heart of the Windows environment. This layer contains the operating system kernel and the operating system support routines. The files that make up the core control how Windows handles the millions of events and operations that it processes every day. The core consists of three main components: the kernel, the event handler, and the graphics device interface (GDI).

The kernel is in command

The kernel is the command center of the operating system. In DOS, the kernel consists of the COMMAND.COM file, the ROM BIOS, and some hidden system files, and it controls all the peripherals that are connected to the system. Without the kernel, you cannot use the keyboard, monitor, mouse, or any other device.

The Windows kernel (KRNLX86.EXE), like the DOS kernel, provides the operating system functionality and is responsible for handling file input/output (I/O), managing memory, and performing system task scheduling in the Windows environment. Windows has two kernels, one for each of its operating modes.

The kernel file that Windows uses depends on the type of processor in the computer and the amount of memory you have installed. KRNL286.EXE is the kernel when Windows runs in the standard mode, and KRNL386.EXE is the kernel when Windows runs in 386 enhanced mode.

Each time you launch Windows, its WIN.COM file determines which processor the system has and analyzes the system's basic memory configuration.

When Windows is running in standard mode, it switches the processor into 80286 protected mode, to provide access to extended memory through XMS support. At startup, WIN.COM executes DOSX.EXE, which is the MS-DOS extender for Windows. Then the kernel file, KRNL286.EXE, is loaded and, in turn, it loads the other parts of Windows.

 You can force Windows to start in standard mode by typing **WIN/S** at the DOS prompt. If you have a 286 processor, or if you do not have enough extended memory to support enhanced mode, you do not have to specify the /S switch because Windows automatically starts in the standard mode.

In 386 enhanced mode, Windows can use virtual memory. WIN386.EXE, which is executed by WIN.COM, provides much of the support for virtual memory. When WIN386.EXE begins to load, it looks for the virtual device drivers (VxDs) that are identified in the [386enh] section of SYSTEM.INI. Some of the VxDs are built into WIN386.EXE (these files are designated by an * in SYSTEM.INI entries).

Virtual Device Drivers (VxDs)

By now you're familiar with the term *virtual* as it applies to memory under Windows. In addition to virtual memory, Windows also uses virtual device drivers. Take a look in the Windows/System directory. You'll see a number of files with the .386 extension. These files are virtual device drivers.

A virtual device driver (VxD) is a 32-bit, protected-mode, dynamic link library (DLL) that manages a system resource, such as a hardware device or installed software, so that more than one appli-

cation can use the resource at the same time. The term VxD is used to refer to a general virtual device driver—the x represents the type of device driver. For example, a virtual device driver for a display device is known as a VDD. Windows running in 386 enhanced mode uses virtual devices to support multitasking for MS-DOS-based applications. Virtual devices work in conjunction with Windows to process interrupts and carry out I/O operations for a given application without disrupting how other applications run.

Windows standard virtual device drivers

In 386 enhanced mode, Windows can use virtual memory. Much of the virtual support is provided by WIN386.EXE, which is executed by WIN.COM. When WIN386.EXE begins to load, it looks for the files identified in the [386enh] section of SYSTEM.INI. Some of the standard files are built into WIN386.EXE (designated with the * symbol in SYSTEM.INI entries). The other files that WIN386.EXE loads to support virtual devices are listed in Table 4-1.

Table 4-1   Files Loaded by WIN386.EXE for Virtual Support Device

Filename	Virtual Device Supported
BANINST.386	Banyan VINES 4.0 instancing virtual device
DECNB.386	DEC Pathworks
DECNET.386	
LANMAN10.386	LAN Manager version 1.0 support
HPEBIOS.386	EBIOS virtual device for Hewlett-Packard machines
LVMD.386	Logitech virtual mouse device
MSCVMD.386	Mouse Systems virtual mouse device
V7VDD.386	Video Seven virtual display device
VADLIBD.386	Virtual DMA device for Adlib
VDD8514.386	8514/A virtual display device
VDDCGA.386	CGA virtual display device
VDDCT441.386	82C441 VGA virtual display device
VDDEGA.386	EGA virtual display device
VDDHERC.386	Hercules monochrome virtual display device
VDDTIGA.386	TIGA virtual display device
VDDVGA30.386	VGA virtual display device (version 3.0)
VDDXGA.386	XGA virtual display device
VIPX.386	Novell NetWare virtual IPX support
VNETWARE.386	NetWare virtual support
VPOWERD.386	Advanced Power Management virtual device
VSBD.386	SoundBlaster virtual device
VTDAPI.386	MultiMedia virtual timer device

Filename	Virtual Device Supported
WIN386.PS2	Support for PS/2 architecture
Windows for Workgroups 3.1 adds these VxDs	
MONOUMB2.386	UMB driver for monochrome video space
VCD.386	Virtual communications device
VDMAD.386	Virtual DMA device
VPD.386	Virtual printer device
VPICD.386	Virtual programmable interrupt controller device
VBROWSE.386	WFW virtual network browsing device
VNB.386	WFW virtual NetBEUI device
VNETBIOS.386	WFW virtual NetBIOS device
VNETSUP.386	WFW virtual network support device
VREDIR.386	WFW virtual network redirector device
VSERVER.386	WFW virtual network server device
VSHARE.386	WFW virtual file sharing device
VWC.386	WFW virtual workgroup client device
Windows for Workgroups 3.11 adds these VxDs	
IOS.386	Windows I/O supervisor device
IFSMGR.386	Installable File System Manager
LPT.386	Virtual LPT driver
RMM.D32	Real mode disk driver (used to support VFAT.386)
SERIAL.386	Serial communications driver
VCACHE.386	32-bit cache manager
VCOMM.386	Virtual communications driver
VFAT.386	Virtual 32-bit FAT device driver
VXDLDR.386	Dynamic VxD loader

After you type **WIN** at the MS-DOS prompt, Windows starts in 386 enhanced mode if the system is a 386 or higher and has sufficient extended memory. WIN.COM invokes the MS-DOS EXEC function to load the Windows 386 enhanced mode system kernel (WIN386.EXE). Then WIN386.EXE loads the following:

- The Virtual Machine Manager (VMM), which acts as a traffic director. It creates and manages the resources for Windows virtual machine.

- All virtual device drivers (VxDs) that are specified in the SYSTEM.INI file.

You can load only one kernel file at a time. If you never run Windows in standard mode, delete KRNL286.EXE from the Windows directory.

USER.EXE handles the events

The USER.EXE file is responsible for handling user input and output (which includes managing the keyboard, mouse, sound driver, and timer in addition to managing the communications ports), and for managing and keeping track of elements of the user interface (which includes components such as windows, icons, menus, and dialog boxes).

When you press a key, USER.EXE determines to which application the keystroke applies. USER.EXE surveys the polling requests that it has received from Windows applications that are running.

USER.EXE also manages the way windows are sized and moved on the desktop, as well as tracking and controlling how icons are used. USER.EXE responds to any mouse clicks that you make in any part of a window. Whenever you click the mouse or press a key to change the way one or more windows appear, USER.EXE passes this event to the GDI.EXE file.

GDI.EXE manages the interface

The GDI.EXE file is the Graphics Device Interface, which is responsible for manipulating bitmaps, managing the drawing of graphic primitives, and handling interaction with the device-independent drivers layer (which includes drivers for display and printer output devices).

GDI.EXE responds to requests that USER.EXE makes to modify the way the screen appears. For example, if you resize a window or move an icon, the mouse clicks and movements that you make are events for USER.EXE to process. USER.EXE interprets your actions as an operation for GDI.EXE and passes the event on to it. GDI.EXE redraws the screen according to the instructions provided by your mouse movements. After GDI.EXE redraws the screen, USER.EXE sends data about the revised screen to the Windows kernel, and the new screen description data is stored in memory.

Understanding system resources

Many people think that system resources are a combination of free memory and available hard disk space. Although some Microsoft documentation uses that definition for system resources, it is not correct.

You can divide system resources into two groups. The first group includes the CPU, memory, and hard drive. Within Windows, you are concerned with another kind of system resource — data objects. Data objects are icons, bit-mapped images, dialog boxes, accelerator key tables, some fonts, and more. Each time that you use one of these resources, Windows records it to ensure that the same object is not loaded twice.

Windows stores this information in two memory heaps, or pools of memory, that it reserves for tracking open files and data objects. The first memory heap, which is allocated to USER.EXE, is divided into two parts that are 64K each. This is an improvement over Windows 3.0 which has only one 64K heap. One part manages the menu-related housekeeping chores, and the other part manages open file handles. The second memory heap, which is 64K, is allocated to GDI.EXE.

Here's a common scenario: You're running Windows in enhanced mode on a 386 or 486 system with 8MB of physical RAM and at least 40MB of free hard disk space. You choose About Program Manager from the Program Manager Help menu and learn that you have 11MB of memory free. You plod along, opening several program groups and a few applications. Suddenly, you get a message indicating that you are out of memory.

In Windows, even if you have plenty of physical RAM, you hit a brick wall when the heap memory area fills up. Remember, *system resources* refers to the data objects that are stored in the USER.EXE and GDI.EXE heaps, and you use these data objects to manage the screen, keyboard, and mouse I/O. Also, the contents of the USER.EXE and GDI.EXE heaps represent the amount of system resources that Windows is currently using. The free memory statistic refers to the amount of physical and virtual memory that is available for storing applications and data.

You can use the Program Manager to determine and optimize your system resource usage. Choose About Program Manager from the Program Manager Help menu. If Windows reports that 25 percent or less of the system resources are available, try reorganizing the Program Manager groups by placing the icons in several groups. Also, keep the number of groups that you open to a minimum so that Windows doesn't have to manage information about too many icons at one time.

The Windows driver layer

When you run an application from DOS, the application controls all the devices that are connected to the computer. DOS is not suited to run two or more applications at the same time because each application takes control of the system's devices and DOS has no way to mediate which program gets access to which device and when. To run multiple applications, the operating system or environment has to be able to handle *device contention* — a request by two programs to use the same device at the same time.

Windows provides a separate driver layer that supports a methodology called *device independence.* The driver layer consists of drivers for hardware devices, such as display adapters and printers. This layer enables Windows to directly control the devices that are attached to the system. Device independence means that the devices are independent of the applications, so any program that is written specifically to run under Windows has to request the services of a particular device via the Windows kernel.

Using device drivers

When you install Windows, the Setup program surveys the system to identify what type of keyboard, mouse, monitor, and network are connected to the system. Setup then installs the appropriate drivers for each of these devices.

Each device driver tells Windows how to communicate with a particular hardware device (such as a display adapter, a printer, a network adaptor card, or an audio device). For example, a video display driver tells Windows how to manipulate bits on a video adapter card to display images; a keyboard driver tells Windows how to interpret the signals it receives from the keyboard; and a mouse driver tells Windows how to interact with the mouse so that Windows can detect when you move the mouse and when you press a button on the mouse.

What device independence represents to the user is freedom. Instead of using a different device driver for each application, all Windows applications use the same drivers. For example, if you specify an HP LaserJet III printer as your printer, Windows installs HPPCL5A.DRV to control the operation of the HP printer. No matter what Windows-based program you run — Ami Pro, 1-2-3, Paradox for Windows, and so on — they all use the HPPCL5A.DRV printer driver to print.

Understanding the files that support DOS applications

Windows uses two files to support non-Windows applications that are running under standard or enhanced mode: WINOLDAP and the grabber.

WINOLDAP works with the grabber files to support data exchange between non-Windows applications and Windows. The support for non-Windows applications varies, depending on the capabilities of the system CPU and the mode in which Windows is running.

Windows provides two versions of WINOLDAP for the two Windows operating modes:

■ WINOLDAP.MOD controls the execution of DOS applications that are running in standard mode.

■ WINOA386.MOD for 386 systems controls the execution of DOS applications that are running in enhanced mode.

Windows installs two grabber files, one to support standard mode and the other to support enhanced mode in 386 or 486 systems. Grabber files have the extension 2GR and 3GR respectively. Which grabber file Windows installs depends on the type of display driver on the system (VGA, EGA, and so on).

The *.2GR Grabbers, which are used only for standard mode, enable you to use the Print Screen key to capture the screen and paste the image to the Clipboard. The grabber also works with the Clipboard to copy and paste text between Windows applications and non-Windows applications. The *.3GR grabbers that support Windows 386 enhanced mode provide the following capabilities:

■ Copying text from non-Windows applications

■ Displaying data in a windowed virtual machine

■ Selecting data in a windowed virtual machine

■ Copying graphics to the Windows Clipboard

■ Enabling the Print Screen key

The Windows API

The application programming interface — better known as *API* — refers to a set of functions that belong to one application but are accessible to another application. The Windows API refers to the set of functions within Windows that any Windows application can access. This enables software developers to use Windows APIs to write a Windows-based application without knowing the details of how the Windows core routines work internally. The developer doesn't need to know the implementation details of how Windows device drivers communicate with the hardware either. Likewise, a hardware vendor can write a Windows device driver for communicating with a hardware device by using the published development interfaces; the vendor does not need to know the details of how the Windows core or a Windows-based application functions internally.

For example, the logon dialog box you see when starting a mail-enabled application, such as the Mail or Schedule+ applications provided with Windows for Workgroups, is displayed by the following API call:

```
ulResult = MAPILogon(ulUIParam, lpszProfileName,
lpszPassword,flFlags, ulReserved,
lplhSession)
ULONG          ulUIParam
LPSTR          lpszProfileName
LTSTR          lpszPassword
FLAGS          flFlags
ULONG          ulReserved
LPHANDLE       lplhSession
```

This call, MAPILogon, takes several parameters and returns a result. The parameters include such things as the default user name (lpszProfileName) and the user's password (if in the MSMAIL.INI file). The call also assigns a handle to the mail session that is being started so that the other calls in the API know which mail session they're supposed to be dealing with. (The Extended MAPI system actually allows users to be logged in to mail more than once, and using different accounts.)

Flags tell this API call whether to display the dialog box. The result of the API call is placed in a variable (in this example, ulResult), which indicates whether the call succeeded or whether there was an error.

Notice the funny looking names in the parameter lists. Microsoft recommends the use of *Hungarian notation,* which uses variable naming conventions that indicate the type of variable in the name. For example, flFlags starts with fl because it holds flags. ulReserved starts with ul because it is a ULONG — an unsigned long. lplhSession is a long pointer to a long handle to a Session, and so on.

Windows-based applications use the Windows API to call routines that are present in the Windows core or in Windows extensions. At the Windows application layer, the calls to the Windows core and extension routines are independent of the hardware configuration.

The dynamic link libraries (DLLs)

One of the most appealing aspects of the Windows environment is the extension and flexibility that dynamic link libraries (DLL) provide. A DLL is an executable file that enables applications to share code and other resources that are necessary to perform particular tasks. In fact, Windows itself is a collection of components that are written as dynamic link libraries. This structure opens the environment for software developers to extend Windows by creating a DLL that contains routines for performing operations and then making the DLL available to other Windows-based applications (as well as to internal Windows routines).

Adobe Systems' Adobe Type Manager for Windows is an example of a third-party DLL used to provide greater functionality than the core DLL supplied with Windows.

A DLL lies dormant on the hard disk until an application requests one of its routines. DLLs provide two important benefits:

■ A DLL doesn't take up space in memory until it loads to provide services at the request of another application. When the application that called the DLL function is finished with the function, Windows may remove from memory the components of the DLL that it doesn't need. This setup results in more efficient memory management within the Windows environment.

■ A DLL has to conform to the Windows API conventions, so many applications can use the functions of a specific DLL.

DLL files most often have a DLL filename extension; however, they also may have another filename extension, such as EXE. For example, SHELL.DLL provides the drag-and-drop routines that the Windows File Manager uses, and it has a DLL filename extension. KERNEL.EXE, USER.EXE, and GDI.EXE are examples of DLLs that have EXE extensions.

As things stand, DLLs are more of a concern to a programmer than to an end user. However, many third-party DLLs are available that enable you to configure and customize various aspects of Windows. Also, most of the applications that you install on your system add DLLs of their own. You should be able to identify them so that you can keep track of your software installations.

The Windows Operating Modes

Windows 3.1 and Windows for Workgroups 3.1 support two operating modes — standard mode and 386 enhanced mode. The default operating mode for your computer is determined by the computer's hardware, the amount of memory the computer has, and any startup switches you specify.

Windows for Workgroups 3.11 does not support standard mode. However, you can use the following line to load Windows for Workgroups 3.11 and simulate standard mode; this line starts WFW without loading VxDs:

```
WIN /D:T
```

Before discussing the operating characteristics of each mode, identifying the primary issues that impact the way you work in Windows and distinguishing the two modes is important. Multitasking is not simply the ability to open multiple applications. Multitasking occurs only when at least two applications access the CPU and RAM simultaneously. On the surface, the capability for multitasking is what separates standard mode from enhanced mode. DOS applications cannot run simultaneously under Windows standard mode. Windows applications can multitask in standard mode as long as no DOS application has been set to execute exclusively in the foreground.

Running under standard mode

In Chapter 1, I explain the details of how Windows manages memory in standard mode. In this section, I describe how Windows manages applications in standard mode.

As I pointed out earlier in this chapter, if you're running a 286 system, Windows automatically starts in standard mode. If the system is a 386 or higher, Windows starts in the standard mode only if you type **WIN /S** or if Windows doesn't detect enough extended memory to support enhanced mode.

Standard mode provides access to extended memory for Windows-based applications, but it doesn't use virtual memory.

When you are running Windows in standard mode, Windows acts like a glorified task switcher as far as DOS applications are concerned. In standard mode, Windows does not provide the ability to multitask with MS-DOS-based applications. When you launch a DOS-based application, Windows swaps the portions of itself that reside in conventional memory to disk so that the DOS-based application can run. Windows also suspends any Windows-based applications that are running. After you switch back to the Windows environment (or exit the DOS application), Windows reloads from the disk and resumes any Windows-based applications that were previously running. Figure 4-4 illustrates the memory map when you are running Windows 3.1 or Windows for Workgroups 3.1 in standard mode.

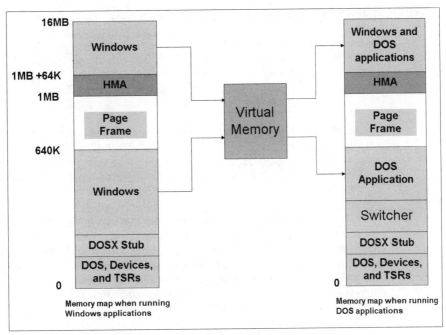

Figure 4-4: The Windows 3.1 standard mode configuration.

A standard mode Windows configuration consists of the extended memory driver (HIMEM.SYS), the extended memory manager for Windows (DOSX.EXE), the kernel (KRNLX86.EXE), and the User (USER.EXE) and GDI (GDI.EXE) functions. You're probably thinking that I've contradicted myself because earlier in the book I said that HIMEM.SYS handles extended memory management. I can clear up this seeming contradiction.

HIMEM.SYS is the DOS memory manager. You configure it at the DOS level and optionally in conjunction with EMM386.EXE. It manipulates the upper memory in which you load TSRs and device drivers. When it comes to Windows, HIMEM.SYS is brain dead. It has no idea how Windows works.

Windows provides its own extended memory manager, DOSX.EXE, when you launch Windows in standard mode. However, don't underestimate the importance of DOS to Windows. You cannot start Windows in either mode unless you've used HIMEM.SYS or a third-party memory manager to configure extended memory at the DOS level. Refer to Chapter 2 and Chapter 3 for a more thorough discussion of Windows, DOS, and extended memory.

Unleashing Windows: 386 enhanced mode

Running Windows in enhanced mode gives you all the features of standard mode to the power of ten. Windows 3.1's 386 enhanced mode, designed for an 80386 or higher processor, provides for the multitasking of DOS and Windows applications and provides more control over those applications than is available in standard mode.

Most important, the 386 enhanced mode supports the virtual 8086 mode (V86) of 80386 (and higher) CPUs. The V86 mode of the 80386 CPU enables an application that is running in this mode to run as if it were on its own self-contained computer, when in fact it may be multitasking with other concurrently running applications.

The 386 enhanced mode Windows configuration consists of the extended memory driver (HIMEM.SYS); the Windows enhanced mode kernel (WIN386.EXE), which provides the virtual machine manager and various internal virtual device drivers; the Windows 386 kernel (KRNL386.EXE); the User (USER.EXE) functions; the GDI (GDI.EXE) functions; and other miscellaneous external virtual device drivers. Figure 4-5 shows the Windows 3.1 386 enhanced mode configuration.

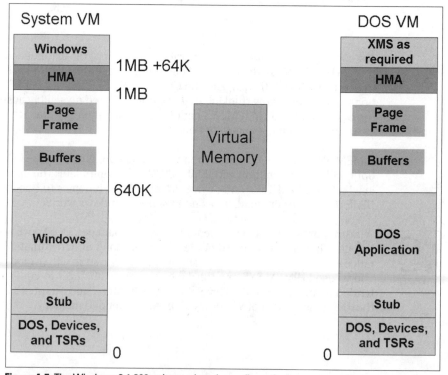

Figure 4-5: The Windows 3.1 386 enhanced mode configuration.

Summary

The Windows environment is extremely powerful and flexible. You can configure it to run various combinations of software and make it run on different hardware configurations. The key to unlocking the power of Windows is understanding and mastering the environment and all of its supporting components, including the system's CPU, memory, DOS, and memory management. Your knowledge of these aspects of your system and how they relate to Windows has an impact on your ability to configure and customize the way Windows works for you.

This chapter explained the foundation and architecture of Windows.

▶ Windows is event driven. Each keystroke or mouse movement is passed to Windows, and Windows determines whether to pass the event to an application or use it internally.

▶ The Windows architecture has three primary layers. The first layer is the Windows application program interface. The second layer consists of the Windows core and extensions. The third layer contains the device drivers.

▶ Windows supports two operating modes — standard mode and enhanced mode. Only enhanced mode supports multitasking of DOS applications, which enables two or more applications to access the CPU and RAM simultaneously.

Part II
Installing and Setting Up

In This Part

Chapter 5

Windows for Workgroups 32-Bit Disk Access System

In This Chapter

▶ How DOS and Windows file I/O work

▶ Understanding 32-bit Disk Access architecture

▶ Enabling the 32-bit Disk Access system

▶ Tips for using 32-bit Disk Access

▶ Decoding 32-bit Disk Access error messages

In Chapters 1 and 2, I pointed out that Windows manages many of the services normally left to DOS, with some exceptions. Despite Windows' device independence, disk I/O operations have been left to DOS and BIOS — until now.

With Windows 3.1, Microsoft introduced a technology called 32-bit Disk Access or Fast Disk. Microsoft has leveraged the 32-bit architecture of the Windows environment by adding 32-bit File Access support to Windows for Workgroups 3.11.

Windows Talks Down to the Hard Disk _____

In the world of DOS, applications communicate with hard disks by requesting interrupt services from DOS or ROM BIOS. The problem for Windows lies with the fact that each hard disk has a separate and often unique controller card for operating the hard drive's mechanical components. The controller card is responsible for activating the read/write heads on the drive each time an application requests part of a program or data stored on the drive. The communication process happens in the following manner:

1. When an application needs data, it pauses long enough to send a special request to DOS to retrieve data that is not in memory. This request is called a *software interrupt*.

2. The software interrupt points to a location in conventional memory where DOS stores the instructions required to carry out a particular I/O service routine.

3. DOS then makes a call to the system's BIOS asking to communicate with the appropriate hardware device, in this case the hard drive controller card.

4. The hard disk controller sends address information back to the ROM BIOS, which then advises DOS where and how to find the requested information.

5. DOS finds and reads the data and finally passes it back to the application.

After reading the description of the communication process, you see that applications depend on DOS, DOS depends on the BIOS, the BIOS depends on the hard disk controller, and the chain of command goes on. What does this mean to Windows? Remember, Windows runs in protected mode, and DOS runs in real mode. Therefore, any time you run a DOS application under Windows, Windows has to switch from protected mode to real mode to allow the DOS application (virtual machine) to access data from the hard disk. Switching modes increases the time needed to access the hard drive.

DOS handles one interrupt request at a time

One of the most significant limitations DOS imposes on Windows is the fact that DOS can handle only one interrupt request at a time. This is an important point to grasp. You're probably thinking that Windows can create several DOS virtual machines at a time, so it ought to be able to pass along interrupt requests from each virtual machine. In fact, either a single DOS VM or the Windows system VM can request DOS or BIOS services at a time.

This all relates to enhanced mode Windows' implementation of the demand paging system. Windows swaps out data to your system's hard disk and stores it in either a temporary or permanent swap file whenever physical memory gets full. DOS, on the other hand, is thoroughly confused at this point.

DOS applications rely on buffers to cache the most recent data read or written from disk. I discussed buffers briefly in Chapter 2, and if you've lived with DOS for any length of time, you're no doubt familiar with them. The problem with buffering and enhanced mode Windows is that Windows does not distinguish between buffers and other types of data that are swapped to disk.

Here's the scenario: You're running a DOS application, and Windows swaps the applications data buffer to disk. The application sends a request to DOS for data to be moved from the disk into the buffer, and in turn, DOS calls the BIOS to access the data. Suddenly, the buffer is nowhere to be found because Windows has swapped it to disk.

Windows is intelligent enough to know that the hard drive controller is seeking buffer space that has been swapped to disk. It makes an attempt to fulfill the application's request by calling a DOS interrupt to page the data back from the hard disk into the application's buffer. The problem is with DOS: DOS and the BIOS are tied up trying to access the hard disk, so DOS obviously cannot respond to Windows' request. Windows and DOS begin an endless loop of calling and searching. The result is a system lockup.

Microsoft built a safeguard into Windows 3.0 by not allowing an active DOS application to swap out to disk. The idea was that if an application's data buffer is always in physical RAM, there's no chance for Windows and DOS to get on that endless loop. Instead of hanging your system, you got an `Out of Memory` message when trying to launch a DOS application, if conventional and extended memory were full. Although this may be better than hanging your system, it's only a partial solution. That's where the benefits of 32-bit Disk Access come in.

32-bit Disk Access bypasses DOS

Windows 3.1 and Windows for Workgroups 3.1x implement 32-bit disk-access capabilities through a set of protected-mode device drivers that work together to enhance your system's BIOS. 32-bit access components filter interrupt calls to the hard disk controller and direct them either through the 32-bit interface with the hard disk controller or through the system BIOS.

Enabling Fast Disk

Microsoft designed 32-bit Disk Access to work directly with the hard disk controller, allowing Windows to bypass DOS and handle disk I/O on its own. Instead of relying on communication with the BIOS, Fast Disk can support any disk controller as long as there is an appropriate virtual device to support that controller.

Windows 3.1 and Windows for Workgroups 3.1x ship with one virtual device — WDCTRL — which supports any disk controller compatible with the Western Digital 1003 controller interface standard.

 WDCTRL does not support SCSI or ESDI drives. If you have one of these drive types in your system, check with the manufacturer for OEM-supplied virtual devices. Several hard disk controller manufacturers provide 32-bit Disk Access drivers for use with hard disk controller adapters.

Because you must have a compatible controller card in your system, the 32-bit Disk Access option is disabled by default when Windows is installed on your system. To enable it, simply turn it on in the Enhanced dialog box in the Windows Control Panel. If 32-bit Disk Access remains disabled, you will not benefit from the hard-disk access performance improvements it provides, but your system remains otherwise unaffected.

During installation, Windows Setup checks to see if your system's hard-disk controller is compatible with the 32-bit Disk Access virtual device driver (WDCTRL). If it is, then Setup automatically installs the proper virtual devices.

Many laptop and notebook computers power down the hard disk to conserve battery life without notifying the system software. In addition, portable computers that conserve power — by using Int 13H to detect Disk Access to power up or power down the hard disk — do not properly identify when the 32-bit Disk Access driver is accessing the hard disk. If the hard disk powers down in the middle of a write or read action, data loss may result.

Due to these situations, 32-bit Disk Access is disabled by default. When the user installs the Windows operating system, 32-bit Disk Access is disabled until the user makes the decision to enable it (through the Control Panel).

Enabling 32-bit Disk Access

You can enable 32-bit Disk Access through the Enhanced section of Control Panel. Double-click the Enhanced icon to display the Windows Enhanced dialog box. Choose the Virtual Memory button to display the Virtual Memory dialog box, which shows the status of the 32-bit Disk Access feature of Windows (whether 32-bit Disk Access is being used or whether communication with the hard disk controller is being handled by the BIOS).

Choose the Change button to display the virtual memory configuration section of the dialog box, which allows 32-bit Disk Access to be enabled. To enable 32-bit Disk Access, select the Use 32-Bit Disk Access check box, as shown in Figure 5-1.

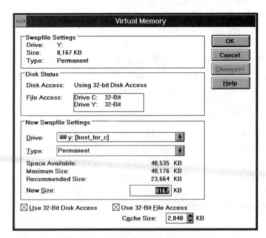

Figure 5-1: The Virtual Memory dialog box is used to enable 32-bit access.

Disk I/O without 32-bit Disk Access

As I mentioned in the preceding section, Windows and Windows for Workgroups do not enable 32-bit Disk Access by default. After the initial setup, the flow of file I/O through the Windows device drivers looks like Figure 5-2.

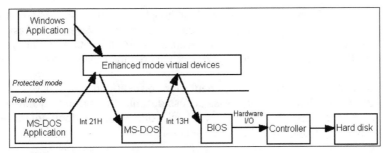

Figure 5-2: The flow of file I/O through the Windows device drivers.

In this scenario, Int 21H calls are processed by MS-DOS and the real mode MS-DOS device drivers. Information on the relevant entries in the [386 Enh] section of SYSTEM.INI is also indicated.

Changing swap file settings

If you want to change only the 32-bit Disk Access entry in the 386 Enhanced section of the Control Panel, it may be necessary to reset the settings for the swap file size and type. When editing the virtual memory settings to change the 32-bit Disk Access entry, the virtual memory settings may also change.

If you want to retain the previous settings, you must enter the virtual memory settings as well as change the setting for the 32-bit Disk Access entry. After all settings are changed, choose OK. Accept the changes and restart Windows when the selection appears.

To prevent the virtual memory settings from changing, you can also change the 32-bit Disk Access setting from outside of the Control Panel. To do this, edit the SYSTEM.INI file and add the following line to the [386 Enh| section:

```
32BitDiskAccess= (ON or OFF)
```

Then restart Windows.

32-bit Disk Access can degrade hard drive performance

Disabling 32-bit Disk Access can improve hard drive performance if you have a system BIOS or hard drive controller designed and optimized specifically for your hard drive.

Some hard drive controllers have built-in optimizing routines that are similar to those that the 32-bit Disk Access system uses. In these cases, 32-bit Disk Access can degrade hard drive performance because some optimization routiness may occur multiple times for each disk operation. This results in slower overall disk access.

Consult your hardware documentation to see if your hard drive controller or BIOS provides any built-in disk access optimizations that may make using the 32-bit Disk Access unnecessary. Check your Windows documentation for the advantages of using 32-bit Disk Access.

Error message: 32-bit disk driver (WDCTRL)

If you run Windows 3.1 in 386 enhanced mode with the 32-bit Disk Access feature enabled, the following error message may appear:

```
The Microsoft Windows 32-bit disk driver (WDCTRL) will not
be loaded because WDCTRLDISABLE=Y is set in this machine's
environment. Remove this environment string and the 32-bit
disk driver will load normally.

To continue starting Windows without using the 32-bit disk
driver, press any key.
```

This error message occurs when there is an environment variable called WDCTRLDISABLE being set at the MS-DOS level before Windows is started.

Use the MS-DOS SET command to check for the existence of WDCTRLDISABLE, and if it exists, type the following at the MS-DOS command prompt to clear it:

```
SET WDCTRLDISABLE=
```

If necessary, edit the AUTOEXEC.BAT file in a text editor such as Notepad or the MS-DOS Editor to remove the WDCTRLDISABLE=Y setting.

32-bit Disk Access compatible disk controllers

Windows and Windows for Workgroups 3.1 ships with one virtual hard-drive controller device: WDCTRL. WDCTRL supports hard-drive controllers that are compatible with the Western Digital WD1003 standard. According to Western Digital, it has two hard-drive controller cards that are compatible with the 32-bit Disk Access feature: WD1006 Controller Card and WD1007A ESDI Controller Card.

The Western Digital WD1006 hard-drive controller is compatible with the WD1003 hard-drive controller in some cases. If the card is configured correctly, it works correctly with the 32-bit Disk Access feature.

WD1006 has a jumper setting to specify whether the drive format is compatible with the WD1003 standard. If the drive has more than eight heads, the drive is slightly incompatible with the WD1003 standard when used with the WD1006 hard-drive controller card. This is due to the way the WD1006 numbers the heads differently than the WD1003. Using a jumper to connect pins seven and eight corrects this problem. This problem does not occur if the hard drive has less than eight heads.

According to Western Digital, the WD1007A ESDI controller card is 100 percent compatible with the WD1003 controller and can be used with the 32-bit Disk Access feature.

Windows for Workgroups 3.11 and 32-Bit File Access

Windows for Workgroups 3.11 builds on the 32-bit Disk Access technology of Windows 3.1 and Windows for Workgroups 3.1 to provide 32-bit File Access. 32-bit File Access uses a 32-bit code path for Windows to access and manipulate data on disk by intercepting DOS interrupt services (Int 21H) in protected mode, instead of leaving them to real mode DOS.

The Int 21H services manipulate the DOS *file allocation table* (FAT), which governs the way information is written to and read from a FAT-based disk volume. In addition to protected-mode Int 21H services, 32-bit File Access also provides a 32-bit protected mode replacement for the MS-DOS–based SmartDrive disk cache program, which features more intelligent disk cache management and results in improved disk I/O performance for the Windows environment. The 32-bit File Access functionality in Windows for Workgroups 3.11 is implemented as two Windows virtual device drivers, VFAT.386 and VCACHE.386.

As with the 32-bit Disk Access feature, the 32-bit File Access feature also is disabled by default when Windows for Workgroups 3.11 is installed. You can enable it through the 386 Enhanced dialog box in the Windows Control Panel.

 If you don't enable 32-bit File Access, be sure to continue using SmartDrive, shipped with Windows for Workgroups 3.11, to provide disk caching functionality.

Enabling 32-bit File Access

Open Control Panel and start the 386 Enhanced applet to view the disk status for 32-bit Disk Access and 32-bit File Access. Choose the Virtual Memory button. The Disk Status section of the Virtual Memory dialog box shows the state of the different drives detected in the system. For the disk volumes on which 32-bit File Access is supported, 32-bit is displayed next to the drive letter (see Figure 5-3). For disk volumes on which 32-bit File Access is not supported, 16-bit is displayed next to the drive letter.

Figure 5-3: The Virtual Memory dialog box shows that 32-bit File Access is supported on drive C.

Choose the Change button to display the virtual memory configuration section of the dialog box, which allows 32-bit File Access to be enabled and configured.

To enable 32-bit File Access, select the Use 32-Bit File Access check box. When enabling 32-bit File Access, you need to set the size of the cache to be used by the 32-bit File Access components. Windows bases the default size on the amount of memory installed in your computer. You should experiment with the size of the cache to provide the best level of disk I/O performance when using 32-bit File Access.

32-bit File Access maximum cache size

The maximum amount of memory that can be set in the 386 Enhanced dialog box in Control Panel is 24MB or 24,576K.

The cache size is limited to the amount of RAM on your computer. Setting the cache size greater than the physical amount of RAM available results in the following error message when reentering the Virtual Memory settings in the 386 Enhanced dialog box:

```
32-bit file access was unable to run. Your hard disk(s) may
not be compatible with 32-bit file access.
```

To manually increase the cache size, do the following:

1. Open the SYSTEM.INI file in a text editor or System Engineer, included on the *Windows 3.1 Configuration SECRETS Disks.*

2. Find the [VCache] section.

3. Change the MinFileCache= setting to the desired value.

The value for this setting is in kilobytes. For example, if you want to create a 50MB cache, the line would be as follows:

```
[VCache] MinFileCache=51200
```

If the 32-bit File Access cache size is greater than 9,984K, the cache size displayed in the Virtual Memory dialog box of Control Panel is truncated. To verify the cache size, choose the 386 Enhanced icon in Control Panel, choose Virtual Memory, and then choose the Change button.

32-bit File Access can slow your system

32-bit File Access can slow your system's performance in a couple of situations.

In the first situation, Windows for Workgroups 3.11 is low on memory after enabling VFAT. If you run VFAT or VCACHE with SmartDrive, Windows for Workgroups may run low on memory because SmartDrive depletes the memory needed by VCACHE.386 and vice versa. Because VCACHE.386 provides the caching on VFAT-enabled drives and network drives (while SmartDrive caches CD-ROM drives and floppy disk drives), it is possible that systems with too large a percentage of memory allocated to caching may have some performance reduction.

If you are running both SmartDrive and VFAT, make sure that the amount of memory allocated to SmartDrive's `WinCacheSize` and the cache size allocated to VCACHE.386 do not exceed roughly 30 percent of total system RAM. For example, on a machine with 4MB RAM, if you have allocated 1024K to VCACHE, set the SmartDrive `WinCacheSize` to 128K as follows:

```
c:\windows\smartdrv.exe <1024> <128>
```

where `<1024>` is the `InitCacheSize` (the cache size at DOS) and `<128>` is the size of the cache in Windows.

In the second situation where 32-bit File Access may slow system performance, VFAT is unable to mount. This can happen as a result of one or more of the following problems:

- The real-mode network redirector has been loaded into memory.
- A TSR or device driver has a file open while Windows loads.
- The drive is involved in a SUBST, ASSIGN, or JOIN action. Because of the way they alter apparent disk characteristics, the SUBST.EXE, ASSIGN.COM, and JOIN.EXE programs are not compatible with *installable file systems* (IFS), such as 32-bit File Access. These utilities can't be used if 32-bit File Access is enabled.
- The cache size selected is too large or invalid.
- Required components are missing, corrupted, or not in the specified directory.

If VFAT is unable to mount, try the following:

- Unload the real-mode network redirector by typing **net stop** at the DOS prompt before starting Windows for Workgroups.
- Check to be sure that no device driver or terminate-and-stay-resident (TSR) program has any files open upon entering Windows for Workgroups.
- Do not use the SUBST, ASSIGN, or JOIN utilities with 32-bit File Access enabled. If you must use one of these utilities, disable 32-bit File Access first.
- Verify that the cache size selected is valid. See the preceding section.

To disable 32-bit File Access and start Windows for Workgroups 3.11, type **win /D:F** at the DOS command prompt. The /D:F diagnostic switch now disables both 32-bit Disk Access and 32-bit File Access.

Requirements for 32-bit File Access

As discussed in the previous section, 32-bit Disk Access implemented in Windows intercepts Int 13H calls destined for the BIOS routines that communicate with the hard disk controller. 32-bit File Access intercepts MS-DOS Int 21H calls that manipulate information stored on a disk device. The VFAT virtual device (VFAT.386) provides support for the protected-mode Int 21H services. When VFAT loads, it identifies the different physical hard disk drives in your system and mounts on hard disk volumes that are supported by 32-bit Disk Access components. As related to 32-bit File Access, *mounting* refers to the process that VFAT goes through to tell the system to pass file I/O calls through VFAT rather than through the MS-DOS device driver chain.

In the same way that DOS uses the real mode BIOS routines to communicate with the hard disk controller, VFAT uses the protected mode 32-bit Disk Access components to read and write information to/from a hard disk. In order for VFAT to mount on a given disk volume, one of the following two conditions is necessary:

■ A 32-bit Disk Access driver is used with a compatible disk controller.

■ The real-mode mapper (described in a later section) is installed to provide a 32-bit Disk Access interface to the DOS device driver chain.

Only one of these conditions must be met to use VFAT. You can use 32-bit File Access without using 32-bit Disk Access.

32-bit File Access is incompatible with DOS SUBST

If you enable 32-bit File Access and you use the DOS substitute command, SUBST, Windows for Workgroups displays the following error message upon starting:

```
The 32-bit file system is incompatible with the SUBST utili-
ity. To use 32-bit File Access, do not use the SUBST utility
before starting Windows for Workgroups.

Press any key to continue.
```

The SUBST command allows you to substitute drive letters for directory names. This method of redirection is incompatible with 32-bit File Access. When IFSMGR.386 detects SUBST, it prevents 32-bit File Access from loading to protect against data loss.

If you use the SUBST command with VFAT enabled, IFSMGR.386 disables 32-bit File Access for all drives, not just the substituted drive. To use the SUBST command, you must first disable 32-bit File Access.

To use 32-bit File Access (VFAT) with DoubleSpace, you must install MS-DOS 6.2. Windows for Workgroups 3.11 does not allow 32-bit File Access on a system that has the DBLSPACE.BIN file from MS-DOS 6.0 loaded. If DBLSPACE.BIN from MS-DOS 6.0 is loaded in memory, the 32-bit File Access option is disabled.

If you are using MS-DOS 6.0 and do not have any compressed drives mounted but DBLSPACE.BIN is loaded in memory, 32-bit File Access is still unavailable. You must unload DBLSPACE.BIN from memory to enable 32-bit File Access. To unload DBLSPACE.BIN, do the following:

1. Remove the system and hidden attributes from the DBLSPACE.INI file in the root directory of your start-up drive by typing the following at the MS-DOS command prompt and then pressing Enter:

```
attrib -s -h -r c:\dblspace.ini
```

2. Rename the DBLSPACE.INI file by typing the following at the MS-DOS command prompt and then pressing Enter:

```
ren c:\dblspace.ini dblspace.ino
```

3. Restart your computer by pressing Ctrl+Alt+Del.

To use any compressed drives on your system, rename the DBLSPACE.INO file to DBLSPACE.INI and restart your computer.

Real-mode mapper

As mentioned in the preceding section, VFAT mounts only on hard disk volumes that have the 32-bit Disk Access components installed. However, some drives may not have a 32-bit Disk Access driver. Even if they do, additional processing may be required after the information is passed off by VFAT towards the disk volume, or before information reaches VFAT from the disk volume.

Many hard disk controllers do not have a compatible 32-bit Disk Access driver to provide 32-bit Disk Access. Typical examples include SCSI and ESDI controllers. To mount VFAT on disk volumes attached to these disk controllers, VFAT must see a 32-bit Disk Access interface for a given disk volume. If no 32-bit Disk Access device driver is available to talk to the controller when 32-bit Disk Access is enabled, the Disk Access interrupt service routine (for Int 13H) must be handled in real mode.

A special virtual device driver called the *real-mode mapper* (RMM.D32) provides a mapping service to take protected mode file I/O calls from VFAT and send them through the MS-DOS device driver chain. The real-mode mapper is installed by the Virtual Memory dialog box automatically when 32-bit File Access is enabled and when either of the following conditions is true:

- 32-bit Disk Access is disabled.

- A compressed disk volume is detected.

The real-mode mapper driver file, RMM.D32, is not explicitly listed in the [386 Enh] section of the SYSTEM.INI file, but it is loaded by the VXDLDR.386 virtual device and supported by the IOS.386 virtual device (there will be a device=vxdldr.386 and a device=ios.386 line in the [386 Enh] section of SYSTEM.INI). You can verify that the real-mode mapper is being used when a drive volume for which 32-bit Disk Access is not supported (for example, 32-bit Disk Access is disabled, or the disk volume is a compressed volume) shows 32-Bit in the Disk Status section of the Virtual Memory dialog box.

To determine if the real-mode mapper is installed, look for the following lines in the [386 Enh] section of SYSTEM.INI (if 32-bit Disk Access is enabled, other entries may also be present):

```
[386 Enh]
device=ifsmgr.386
device=ios.386
device=vxdldr.386
device=vfat.386
device=vcache.386
```

32-bit File Access and disk compression software

Another example of when the real-mode mapper driver is used is when you need VFAT support for a disk volume using a software-based disk compression technique, such as DoubleSpace provided with MS-DOS 6.2 or Stacker from Stac Electronics. Because additional processing of the data is necessary before writing information to the disk controller or after reading information from the disk controller, the 32-bit Disk Access components cannot be used on the compressed volume. In this scenario, it is necessary for VFAT to go through the MS-DOS device driver chain to properly handle Int 21H requests.

The utilities that Stacker 3.1 installs in Windows for Workgroups 3.11 File Manager do not work if 32-bit File Access is enabled.

To work around this problem, disable 32-bit File Access while you are using the utilities. To do this, choose the 386 Enhanced icon in Control Panel, Virtual Memory, and Change, and then clear the 32-Bit File Access check box. You can restore 32-bit File Access after you are finished using the utilities without causing any damage to the disk.

Stacker 3.1 adds the following menu to File Manager:

```
Stacker File Info Disk Info
```

If you try to choose one of these menu items, the following error message is displayed:

```
Stacker not installed
```

The Stacker volume file still functions properly with 32-bit File Access enabled, and all files will be available normally.

Windows hangs on logo screen with 32-bit File Access

If your system hangs at start-up with the Windows logo screen displayed after enabling 32-bit File Access, check to see if the following line is in the [386 Enh] section of your SYSTEM.INI file:

```
NoEMMDriver=ON
```

If you delete the NoEMMDriver=ON entry, your system may be able to start Windows.

This works only if your system configuration requires the RMM.D32 file for 32-bit File Access. The RMM.D32 file is required for 32-bit File Access with MS-DOS 6.2 DoubleSpace, Stacker, and hard drive controllers that are not Int 13 compatible.

The NoEMMDriver= On entry prevents Windows 386 enhanced mode from installing the expanded memory driver. This differs from setting EMMSize=0, which prevents upper memory blocks (UMBs) from being allocated but does not prevent the EMM driver from being loaded.

The default value for NoEMMDriver= is Off.

A number of third-party software applications recommend placing this line in the SYSTEM.INI file to optimize Windows. If you experience any problems with your applications after you remove this entry, contact the manufacturer of the application.

32-bit File Access causes ScanDisk to report error

After you run Windows for Workgroups 3.11 on an MS-DOS 6.2 DoubleSpace-compressed drive with 32-bit File Access enabled, the MS-DOS ScanDisk utility may report the following error when run at the MS-DOS command prompt:

```
ScanDisk found <nnnn> bytes of data on drive <x> that may be
one or more lost files or directories, but which is probably
just taking up space.
```

$<nnnn>$ equals the number of bytes of lost files or directories, and $<x>$ equals the logical drive ScanDisk was scanning.

ScanDisk should not be run from the MS-DOS command prompt in Microsoft Windows or Windows for Workgroups. It should be run directly from MS-DOS. If you must run ScanDisk from within Windows, use the /CHECKONLY switch. This switch prevents ScanDisk from attempting to repair any damage while Windows is running.

This error message is caused by a problem in Windows for Workgroups 3.11. The 32-bit File Access writes buffers in the order they are used, meaning that the first information into the buffer is the first information out. The 32-bit File Access also tries to improve access speed by finding contiguous used buffers and writing them together. If the two optimization schemes both try to clean the buffer simultaneously, an erroneous extra entry in the DoubleSpace file allocation table (MDFAT) may occur.

This problem may also occur when 32-bit File Access flushes the entire volume. Buffers are written sequentially according to their physical location. This optimization has no effect on a compressed volume (because there is no physical-to-logical relationship) and can result in erroneous entries in the MDFAT.

No data loss occurs with this error. If you choose to correct the problem, ScanDisk repairs the volume and creates the standard CHKDSK files (FILE*nnnn*.CHK), which can be deleted. ScanDisk may also report that sections of the DoubleSpace volume are not being used by any files but are marked as unusable; ScanDisk can repair these as well.

Error message: Exit Windows and run MS-DOS

When you run an application (such as Microsoft Undelete) under Windows for Workgroups 3.11, you may receive the following error message:

```
Exit Windows and run the MS-DOS version of this utility. Int 26
(direct sector write) is blocked to preserve volume integrity.
```

If you run Microsoft Undelete and choose Find to search for deleted files, Undelete may display the following error message:

```
System Error Divide by zero or Overflow error
```

This problem occurs when you run any application or utility that calls Int 26 (such as Microsoft Undelete) when 32-bit File Access is enabled.

To work around this problem, do one of the following:

- Disable 32-bit File Access
- Run the MS-DOS-based version of the application that is calling Int 26

Microsoft recommends that you not run MS-DOS-based disk utilities from the Windows for Workgroups MS-DOS prompt. These utilities should be run before or after your Windows for Workgroups session.

IFS Manager

The heart of the file system components provided in Windows for Workgroups 3.11 is the Installable File System (IFS) Manager virtual device driver (IFSMGR.386). IFS Manager maintains a table identifying the type of file system device associated with each connected disk volume and passes the file I/O request to the appropriate device. When an application makes an Int 21H call, IFSMGR intercepts it and checks its table of installed devices. If the Int 21H call is destined for a network drive, it passes the request to the network redirector (VREDIR.386). If the Int 21H call is for a drive mounted by VFAT, it passes the request to VFAT. If the Int 21H call is not passed to one of the other IFS Manager drivers, it is passed to the real-mode MS-DOS device driver chain and handled by MS-DOS.

Any Int 21H calls that are processed by VFAT are handled entirely in protected mode. This results in improved disk I/O performance over previous versions of Windows. With 32-bit File Access installed in addition to 32-Bit Disk Access, the sequence of events to process a file I/O request is shown in Figure 5-4.

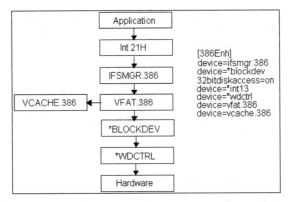

Figure 5-4: The file I/O process with 32-bit access enabled.

With VFAT, there is only one mode transition to process an Int 21H request from an MS-DOS–based application and no mode transitions to process an Int 21H request from a Windows-based application. The remaining calls are processed in protected mode. The performance increase obtained by 32-bit Disk Access by avoiding a processor mode transition is now increased further with 32-bit File Access.

A companion driver to VFAT.386 is VCACHE.386. VCACHE is responsible for providing management routines to handle the cache for both VFAT.386 and VREDIR.386. VCACHE is responsible for the cache operations, including allocating cache memory, freeing cache memory, and managing the algorithm that oversees how data is aged in the cache in case existing data in the cache needs to be replaced with newer incoming data.

32-bit disk cache

In addition to providing Int 21H FAT services in protected mode, VFAT, working in conjunction with VCACHE.386, provides a 32-bit protected-mode replacement for the MS-DOS–based SmartDrive disk cache program. VFAT is responsible for reading and writing information from or to the disk device, while VCACHE is responsible for managing the information VFAT writes to or that is present in the cache. The caching routines provided as part of 32-bit File Access differ from that offered by SmartDrive in the following ways:

■ 32-bit File Access caching routines are implemented as 32-bit protected-mode code.

- 32-bit File Access read-ahead routines work on a per-file basis rather than on a per-sector basis, thus helping to ensure that information read into the disk cache will be used with a higher probability.

- 32-bit File Access caching routines share cache memory with the protected-mode network redirector (VREDIR.386), thus reducing the extra memory overhead for maintaining multiple cache buffers.

- 32-bit File Access caching routines cache information on a per-file basis, providing improved performance over SmartDrive, which caches on a contiguous-sector basis.

A disk cache intercepts system calls

One primary function of a disk cache is to intercept system calls to the device drivers for the hard disk controller to reduce the need for read-write access to the disk. The disk cache routines interpret any calls to the hard disk and load the needed data into a cache in the extended memory portion of RAM.

Subsequent read-write requests to the hard disk are intercepted by the disk cache routines, which search the cache for the requested data. If the data is already present in the cache, the application will access it directly from RAM — which is faster than reading the information from the hard disk. If the data is not in the cache, the disk cache routine accesses the hard disk and loads the necessary data into the cache. The least-recently used data residing in RAM is discarded, unless a change has been made to it that necessitates writing it back to the hard disk, making room for the new data. By loading blocks of data from the hard disk into RAM, the disk cache software helps decrease the number of accesses to the hard disk, which can slow down applications because accessing the hard disk is considerably slower than accessing RAM. Essentially, the disk cache is responsible for maintaining information in RAM that an application may need from the hard disk in the near future.

A technique called *read-ahead caching*, is used by some disk cache software to try to anticipate the information that the system may need next from the disk device and read this information into the cache before the actual request comes from the system to access this information. If the read-ahead cache contains the information that the system needs next, this results in a performance improvement because the system does not need to read the information from disk. However, if the read-ahead cache does not contain the information requested by the system, the information will need to be read from the disk. There are several approaches for basing algorithms for performing read-ahead caching activities. Two such approaches are caching on a contiguous-sector basis and caching on a per-file basis.

Caching on a *contiguous-sector basis* means that a given request results in the cache routines also reading ahead additional contiguous sectors from the disk volume with the assumption that the next request is in the next contiguous group of sectors from the previous sector just read. This type of read-ahead feature works well for some database applications or other types of sequential file access. However, this scenario assumes that a given file is contiguous. For a fragmented file, a read-ahead operation on a contiguous sector basis may read parts of other files into the cache that may never be accessed, resulting in filling the cache with unnecessary information that eventually will be discarded. A cache does not improve performance if information read into the cache is not subsequently accessed from the cache.

Caching on a *per-file basis* means that a given request reads the requested portion (in sectors) of the file and also reads ahead additional sectors of the file with the assumption that the next request is for the next part of the file just read. This type of read-ahead is more efficient because information is read ahead only from within the requested file, and unneeded information from other files is not loaded into the cache due to fragmentation (as with a contiguous sector-based algorithm).

A technique called *write-behind caching*, or *lazy writing*, is also used by some disk cache systems to cache data destined to be written to the disk device, but delays the actual writing of information to the disk device until a time when the computer system is less busy. The time delay can vary, but it is usually no more than a matter of milliseconds or several seconds. When a cache system supports write-behind functionality, control is returned to the application that is writing the data much more quickly because, instead of writing the information out to a disk device, the information is stored temporarily in RAM. Although the use of a write-behind cache can improve the perceived disk I/O performance, it can pose some problems. With the write-behind cache, the information is not written to the disk device until the information from the cache is flushed. Because of this, it is important not to turn off a computer immediately after performing an operation where an application may have written information into the cache, but before it has had a chance to be written to the hard disk.

Using caching and disk compression software

In order for write-behind caching to be safe, it is necessary for the cache routines to be able to reliably know the amount of free disk space left on a given disk volume. Knowing the amount of free disk space on noncompressed disk volumes is pretty straightforward; however, knowing the amount of free disk space on a compressed volume is difficult. The difficulty lies in not knowing exactly how much space the compressed information will use on the disk, given the fact that different types of data compress to different sizes.

By default, write-behind caching is disabled on all compressed disk volumes that VFAT mounts, with the exception of DoubleSpace drives under MS-DOS 6.2. MS-DOS 6.2 features an API mechanism that VFAT can use to query the minimum amount of disk space remaining so that lazy writing can be enabled and used safely. VFAT is unable to reliably determine the minimum amount of free disk space when other disk compression software is installed due to the lack of an API call to obtain this information.

For other disk compression software, lazy writing can be forced by using the ForceLazyOn= switch in the [vcache] section of the SYSTEM.INI file.

 If you force on lazy writing for a compressed disk volume other than DoubleSpace under MS-DOS 6.2, check to make sure that you have sufficient disk space to complete all data writes to the disk. If the disk becomes full and a lazy write occurs, VFAT reports that the disk is full, but the application program that made the original write assumes that the write was completed successfully. Data loss may result in this case.

How to disable write caching for the 32-bit file system

Windows for Workgroups 3.11 caches disk writes by default when the 32-bit file system is enabled. This includes MS-DOS DoubleSpace 6.2 volumes; however, it does not include third-party disk-compression systems.

To disable write caching with the 32-bit file system, add the following line to the [386 Enh] section of the SYSTEM.INI:

```
ForceLazyOff=<drivelist>
```

where <drivelist> is the list of drives in which you want to disable write caching. (Do not use any delimiters or spaces.) For example, the line

```
ForceLazyOff=CDF
```

would disable write caching on drives C, D, and F.

Removing or reconfiguring SmartDrive

With Windows 3.1 and Windows for Workgroups 3.1, it was necessary to use SmartDrive to support disk cache functionality. When 32-bit File Access is enabled, the combination of VFAT and VCACHE replaces the functionality offered by SmartDrive by providing 32-bit protected-mode cache functionality. SmartDrive caching is automatically disabled for drives mounted by VFAT.

You can identify the drives that SmartDrive is caching when running in Windows for Workgroups 3.11 by starting an MS-DOS command prompt and typing **smartdrv**. However, 32-bit File Access does not reclaim the memory used by SmartDrive for its cache.

If you are presently using SmartDrive when 32-bit File Access is enabled, the setup code reconfigures the size of the SmartDrive disk cache to reduce the size of the cache while running in Windows for Workgroups to free up 128K additional memory.

SmartDrive 5.0 offers the ability to cache information on CD-ROM drives and floppy disk drives, while 32-bit File Access does not. If you do not need to cache information on CD-ROM drives or floppy disk drives, you should reduce the size of the cache used by SmartDrive for Windows or remove the SMARTDRV.EXE line from your AUTOEXEC.BAT file. Also, if you are using MS-DOS 6.0 and DoubleSpace, it is necessary to continue to use SmartDrive to provide support for disk caching.

Configuration scenarios

To help further illustrate the interaction of the 32-bit Disk Access and 32-bit File Access drivers here are some other common disk-access scenarios:

- Non-32-bit Disk Access or non-VFAT mounted volume
- WDCTRL 32-bit Disk Access volume
- VFAT mounted on WDCTRL 32-bit Disk Access volume
- VFAT mounted on non-32-bit Disk Access volume
- VFAT mounted on a compressed non-32-bit Disk Access volume
- VFAT mounted on a compressed WDCTRL 32-bit Disk Access volume

Enabling 32-bit Disk Access allows all Int 13H calls to be handled by the 32-bit Disk Access driver. In this case, Int 21H calls are processed by MS-DOS and the real-mode MS-DOS device drivers.

Summary

With the addition of 32-bit File Access to Windows for Workgroups 3.11, Windows grows closer to becoming a true operating system. Using its 32-bit Disk Access architecture, Windows bypasses DOS for file I/O operations, thereby improving its performance. In this chapter, I discuss the following information:

▶ The interaction between DOS and Windows during file I/O operations.

▶ The benefits of the 32-bit Disk Access architecture.

▶ Workarounds for using 32-bit Disk Access and File Access.

▶ Tips for using 32-bit Disk Access.

▶ Recovering from 32-bit Disk Access errors.

Chapter 6

Controlling Windows' Environment with Setup

In This Chapter

▶ Checking your hardware

▶ Preparing for installation

▶ Avoiding installation problems

▶ Installing Windows

▶ Customizing Setup

▶ Installing to several systems

▶ Looking inside Setup information files

I nstalling Windows correctly is the first step to properly configuring your system. In addition, you can customize the setup process so that you can set up identical configurations quickly and easily.

Checking Your Hardware

Before you begin a Windows installation, make certain that the hardware you have is up to the job. Windows can be very demanding on hardware; how demanding depends on what you want to do, and many of today's hardware options were designed specifically with Windows in mind.

To start with, Windows requires a computer with a processor compatible with an Intel 80286 or better microprocessor, 1MB of RAM, and about 7MB of free hard disk space, an EGA or better display adapter — if you're willing to be limited to *standard mode*. To be able to use Windows in *enhanced mode,* you need a computer with an Intel (or compatible) 386 or better processor, 2MB of RAM, 8MB of free hard disk space, and an EGA or better display adapter.

Of course, succeeding versions of Windows have ever greater requirements — Windows for Workgroups 3.11 (WFW), for example, requires a minimum of 3MB of RAM if installed on a network, a VGA or better display, 10.5MB of disk space, and a 386 or better processor — standard mode is a thing of the past.

The above numbers are the facts as published on the box by Microsoft. And, as published numbers tend to be, these numbers are the absolute system minimums. Windows just scrapes by using the minimum hardware requirements as described by Microsoft. In other words, you probably won't be very happy with your system performance if your system matches Microsoft's minimum configuration.

The reality is that Windows and Windows applications are extremely demanding. In addition, applications that require enhanced mode do not work on 286-based computers. Experience shows that the practical minimum configuration for Windows 3.1 is a 386 or better microprocessor, with 4MB of RAM (8MB for a Windows for Workgroups computer that shares its disk or printer), about 30MB of free disk space, and a VGA.

Better performing systems have more RAM (8MB for Windows 3.1, 12MB for Windows for Workgroups), and an accelerated video card. There's a saying among Windows experts that has proven true — "when in doubt, throw more RAM at it."

When you are preparing to install Windows, it's important to know some basic information about the system, particularly if you're installing Windows on a network machine. While the Windows setup program can do an automatic hardware detection, it typically makes low-end choices — such as selecting VGA when the computer actually has an SVGA card.

Fortunately, Microsoft provides a utility that prepares a report containing most of the information needed — the *Microsoft System Diagnostics*, better known as *MSD*. Microsoft shipped MSD with versions of MS-DOS beginning with MS-DOS 5.0. (MSD is also included on the Windows floppy disks in uncompressed form so that you can run it directly from the floppy disks.)

Run MSD, select File➪Print Report, and print an MSD report to your printer. A complete MSD report may be 15 or more pages, but it is worth having on hand if trouble arises.

Preparing for Installation

The first step in preparing for the installation of any software package is to back up the computer. Installing Windows is no exception — because a Windows installation changes many of the system configuration files, such as AUTOEXEC.BAT and CONFIG.SYS, it is very important that you create a new full backup.

There are several methods you can use for backing up a system (which you are probably already familiar with, because you back up your system regularly, right?). The most common method of backup is to a tape drive. Now that the cost of tape drives has fallen below $200, there really is no valid excuse not to get one and use it to back up your system quickly and reliably. Remember, *the cost of doing a good backup is far less than the cost of restoring a system from scratch in the event of problems.*

Of course, you might not have your tape drive yet (but you're still going to run out and buy one tomorrow ...), and you'd like to get on with installing Windows. In that case, you can use the backup software that comes with MS-DOS.

A few words about DOS before I discuss how to back up with DOS Backup. Windows 3.1 requires MS-DOS 3.1 or higher, and Windows for Workgroups requires MS-DOS 3.3 or higher, but a number of features work better if you have the latest revision of MS-DOS, which at this writing was MS-DOS 6.2. Also, Windows for Workgroups 3.11 requires MS-DOS 6.2 or higher if you want to use DoubleSpace and 32-bit File Access together.

If you're using a version of MS-DOS released prior to 6.0, you'll have to use the old character-mode, command line version of DOS backup. You'll also need enough floppy disks to equal the amount of disk space that you've used on your hard drive to store everything. Because Windows is shipped only on high-density floppy disks, I assume that you have either a 1.2MB 5¼" or 1.44MB 3½" floppy disk drive.

The easiest way to figure how many floppy disks you're going to need for backing up a system is to use the MS-DOS CHKDSK command to find out how much space the files are taking up on your hard disk. To do this, type **CHKDSK** at the MS-DOS prompt.

MS-DOS then produces a report that resembles the following:

```
Volume CDRIVE       created 07-07-1993 7:55p
 448167936 bytes total disk space
    204800 bytes in 11 hidden files
   3612672 bytes in 432 directories
 426164224 bytes in 11088 user files
  18186240 bytes available on disk
      8192 bytes in each allocation unit
     54708 total allocation units on disk
      2220 available allocation units on disk
    655360 total bytes memory
    597456 bytes free
```

You can figure the amount of floppy disk space that you need to back up by taking the bytes available on disk number and bytes total disk space number and dropping the last six digits from them. In the preceding example, this means changing 448167936 and 18186240 to 448 and 18, respectively. Subtract the smaller number from the larger number to get the approximate number of floppy disks needed to back up the system. This example requires about 450 floppy disks for a full backup. Now you know why I recommend a tape drive!

The method described in the preceding paragraphs is very rough — it approximates a *maximum* number of floppy disks. You would probably actually need somewhat fewer floppy disks to back up the system, but it's better to have extras than go through the first 40 or 50 floppy disks in a backup only to discover the computer store closed ten minutes ago, and you either have to leave the computer alone until tomorrow, or start all over again.

To actually back up the hard disk to floppy disks using MS-DOS versions prior to 6.0, at the MS-DOS prompt, type the following:

BACKUP C:*.* A: /s /f

MS-DOS responds with

```
Insert backup diskette 01 in drive A:
WARNING! Files in the target drive
A:\ root directory will be erased
Press any key to continue . . .
```

Insert the first floppy disk, press a key, and you're on your way. Remember to label your floppy disks with the appropriate number as you go!

For MS-DOS 6.x, Microsoft provides a new backup utility called MS Backup. You'll really like this utility if you don't have a tape drive, because after Windows is up and running, you can install a Windows version of MS Backup.

First, though, you must back up the current system. Backing up with MS Backup is more straightforward than using the older utility, plus it has the added advantage of compression. MS Backup can, depending on the type of data you have on your disk, back up your disks to as few as half the number of floppy disks you'd need otherwise, with the resulting savings in time and floppy disks.

To back up a system with MS Backup, type:

MSBACKUP

at the MS-DOS prompt.

The very first time you use MS Backup, you are presented with a configuration screen. Follow the directions to insert floppy disks so that the disk drives may be tested. MS Backup does this so that it can directly access the floppy drives rather than going through MS-DOS to do this. The net result is faster backups.

Using the spacebar, or the right mouse button, select the drives that are on your computer (see Figure 6-1). Use the Tab key or mouse to select the Start Backup button to start the backup.

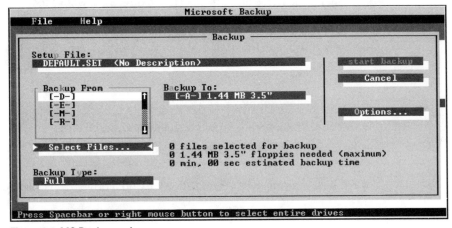

Figure 6-1: MS Backup main screen.

Planning the installation

Before you actually install Windows, it's a good idea to plan the installation process. For all versions and varieties of Windows, some common questions can be asked, as follows:

- Are you doing a full installation of Windows, or do you want to install only the bare minimum required?
- What about the games?
- What printers are you using?
- Is the machine on a network? If it is, are the disk and/or printer being shared with other network users?

Check your path

Be sure the path statement in AUTOEXEC.BAT is as short as possible, and remove any utilities that extend the path beyond MS-DOS's limit of 128 characters. The Windows setup program needs to add the installation directory to the path, so be sure to allow enough room.

That TEMP directory

Windows, MS-DOS, and Windows applications sometimes need a place to store temporary files. These files are placed in a directory, whose location is specified in the MS-DOS TEMP environment variable.

This variable is set in the AUTOEXEC.BAT file with a line such as the following:

```
SET TEMP=C:\DOS
```

General guidelines for picking a TEMP directory are as follows:

- Select a directory that is not on an uncompressed disk.

- Be sure the disk has enough free space for the temporary files — graphics-intensive applications may require 6MB or more.

- For best performance, select a directory on a drive that is cached.

Preparing the hard disk for installation

When you are installing multimegabyte software, such as Windows, you may want to prepare the hard drive for installation by cleaning up the disk. Installing new software creates the opportunity, and reason, to check the disk for unneeded temporary files (such as files with extensions of $$$, TMP, or similar names).

Another good habit to add to your routine for installing new software is to defragment your hard drive. You can use programs such as the Norton Utilities or Central Point PC Tools, or the DEFRAG command of MS-DOS 6.0, for defragging. Although a full defragmentation optimizes the hard disk completely, it is not required. At minimum, you should choose the option in your defragmentor that defragments free disk space. This moves files around the disk in such a way as to create the largest area of contiguous free (unused) disk space. Consolidating free space in this manner ensures that the Windows components are loaded in a nonfragmented manner, and more importantly, maximizes the contiguous space available for a 386 enhanced mode *swap file*.

Check your disk

Another step before any major installation, including setting up Windows, is to make certain that the data and MS-DOS information on all disks are valid. To do this, run CHKDSK for MS-DOS 3.x-5.x, or under MS-DOS 6.x, run SCANDISK, on all disks. If any errors are found, be sure to correct them.

To run SCANDISK, type the following at the DOS prompt:

```
SCANDISK /ALL/SURFACE
```

SCANDISK checks the integrity of all local drives on the system, and then performs a surface scan to ensure that the disks have no undetected bad spots.

If you are using a version of MS-DOS prior to 6.2, then you must run CHKDSK or use a third-party disk utility such as Symantec's Norton Disk Doctor (NDD) or Central Point's PC Tools DISKFIX. CHKDSK does not scan the disk for bad spots; therefore, it misses bad spots on the disk that Norton Disk Doctor or DISKFIX may detect.

To run CHKDSK (which should be in the MS-DOS directory), type

```
CHKDSK/F drive:
```

in which *drive:* is the letter of the drive you wish to check. If the system has more than one drive, you need to run CHKDSK multiple times.

If the disk is compressed with a third-party compression utility, such as Stacker, be sure to run the manufacturer's integrity check utility.

About disk compression

Because of the sheer size of Windows, and the need to put its permanent swap file and temporary directory on an uncompressed drive, you will want to wait to compress the hard disk with Stacker or DoubleSpace until after you have successfully installed Windows.

Compressing after the Windows installation results in optimal file compression, and relocating the permanent swap file is handled automatically. If you can't wait to do the compression because of limited disk space, or because the disk is already compressed, you need to resize the compressed volume to make room for the permanent swap file.

Precautions

When you are preparing to set up Windows, look at the CONFIG.SYS and AUTOEXEC.BAT files. You should remove any virus-protection programs, such as MSAV, VSAFE, and so on, by "Rem'ing them out" — edit CONFIG.SYS and AUTOEXEC.BAT by typing the word **REM** in front of the line, as follows:

```
REM DEVICE=C:\NORTON\N&AV.SYS
```

or

```
REM VSAFE +1
```

Then, when the Windows installation is complete, reedit the file to remove REM and restore the lines to the way they were.

Examples of programs that should be permanently removed include special keyboard handlers (such as SuperKey), caches other than Smartdrive, such as Hyperdisk and non-Microsoft Memory Managers, such as QEMM or 386MAX (reinstall them after Windows setup is completed).

If the system uses the MS-DOS SUBST, APPEND, or JOIN commands you need to permanently remove references to these commands — they interfere with the ability of Windows to create proper pathnames to files and may cause loss of data integrity.

Disable all *multiconfig schemes,* including the MultiConfig feature in MS-DOS versions starting with 6.0. Usually, this means you must rename the CONFIG.SYS file and create a new CONFIG.SYS that contains only the commands that the Windows installation uses. After Windows is set up, you can incorporate the new CONFIG.SYS into the MultiConfig scheme.

Command line editors, such as CED or CMDEDIT, can cause Windows failure. Use only the DOSKEY command line editor, included with versions of MS-DOS starting with MS-DOS 5.0.

The MS-DOS FASTOPEN utility may cause file allocation table problems under certain circumstances. Don't use FASTOPEN with Windows or disk-fragmenting utilities.

I recommend that you not use the MS-DOS GRAPHICS utility if you print from MS-DOS prompts within Windows because you may get unexpected results.

The MS-DOS PRINT utility may also interfere with Windows; Windows Print Manager's functions remove the need for PRINT's background printing.

DOS-based screen savers, such as PYRO!, are incompatible with Windows. Permanently remove them from the system.

Borland SideKick and other TSR programs that are launched via hot-keys from the MS-DOS prompt may cause problems if loaded as a TSR — remove any references to these programs from the AUTOEXEC.BAT file and run them as applications from Windows.

 Microsoft provides a file, SETUP.TXT, on all Windows disks. This file contains the latest known information for troubleshooting Windows installations. Windows Setup may refer you to this file if it detects a potential problem.

Using SETUP options

On most systems, you don't need to set the options available on the SETUP command line. The most common use of SETUP options are for network installations, or when something has gone wrong when using plain SETUP, such as when a system lockup occurs when SETUP is trying to figure out your hardware configuration. Table 6-1 lists the SETUP options.

Table 6-1	SETUP Command Line Options
Option	*Purpose*
SETUP/A	Used for network administrative installations (see Chapter 7).
SETUP/B	Use this option if you're installing Windows on a monochrome monitor, such as a black-and-white VGA.
SETUP/C	Use this option if SETUP hangs when checking for incompatible TSRs. Be sure to manually remove any incompatible TSRs if you need to use this option.
SETUP/H: *filename*	Use this option to automate Windows setup, using a system initialization file (discussed later in this chapter).
SETUP/I	Probably the most important option to be discussed here, use this option to tell SETUP to not try to figure out what hardware the system has, in the event that SETUP hangs as soon as you run it. Only works if Windows 3.1 is not already installed on the system, since SETUP only checks the hardware during the initial installation.
SETUP/O: *filename*	Use this option if you've moved (or modified) the SETUP.INF file.
SETUP/S: *filename*	Use this option to specify the location of the SETUP.INF file, and at the same time, the path to the Windows installation disks. Used if the SETUP.INF is not located in the current directory, or if it is not named SETUP.INF.
SETUP/T	Use this option after Windows has been installed to check for incompatible TSR programs.

Installing Windows

Now that you've planned your installation, it's time to actually type SETUP at the DOS prompt and begin installing Windows. Instead of duplicating the information that you can find in the *User's Guide,* I'll discuss some of the decisions you have to make as you go through the SETUP process. If you're setting up more than one system, you might want to consider creating system initialization files that help automate much of the process by letting you limit or omit many of the choices the user who is running SETUP needs to deal with.

The first choice that you face when running SETUP is *Express vs. Custom Setup.* Most users choose Express, which installs Windows 3.1 or Windows for Workgroups to a default location, normally C:\WINDOWS (Windows NT is installed to C:\WINNT).

 In all cases, if a previous installation of Windows exists, and Express Setup is chosen, Windows attempts to perform an upgrade installation, preserving the configuration of the old version and overwriting the old version with the new. If the old version is in a different directory than C:\WINDOWS, Express Setup upgrades the old version in whatever directory it is installed.

 Upgrading a Windows 3.1 or Windows for Workgroups installation to Windows NT does not remove the old Windows version, even if the new installation is done to the same directory. Although Windows 3.1 or Windows for Workgroups stores many files in the Windows directory, Windows NT stores its files in the WiNDOWS\SySTEM32 directory. Also, an upgrade installation of Windows NT causes existing Program Manager groups to be imported into the Windows NT Program Manager.

If you are using Express Setup for Windows 3.1, the only questions you are asked are to select what type of printer you have and what ports the printers are on.

 Express Setup for Windows for Workgroups asks you for network configuration information in addition to the printer information.

 Express Setup for Windows NT requires you to provide the system administrator's password, and the initial logon account and password.

Custom Setup is for those who like putting Windows files in nonstandard locations (for example, so they can have multiple versions of Windows on a system for testing purposes), or who have special hardware that Windows cannot automatically detect (and who had to use SETUP/I because Windows hangs during installation while trying to determine what hardware is on the system).

As Figure 6-2 illustrates, Custom Setup gives you control over several areas of the computer's configuration.

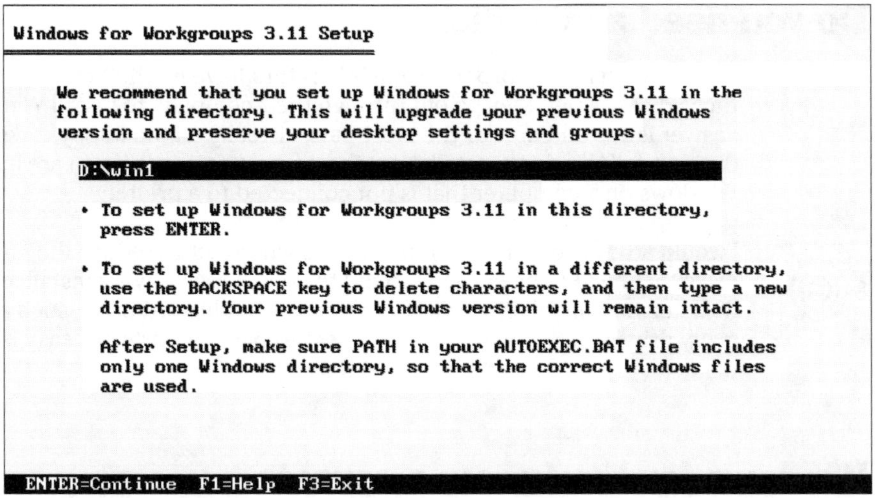

```
Windows for Workgroups 3.11 Setup

    We recommend that you set up Windows for Workgroups 3.11 in the
    following directory. This will upgrade your previous Windows
    version and preserve your desktop settings and groups.

    D:\win1

    • To set up Windows for Workgroups 3.11 in this directory,
      press ENTER.

    • To set up Windows for Workgroups 3.11 in a different directory,
      use the BACKSPACE key to delete characters, and then type a new
      directory. Your previous Windows version will remain intact.

      After Setup, make sure PATH in your AUTOEXEC.BAT file includes
      only one Windows directory, so that the correct Windows files
      are used.

ENTER=Continue   F1=Help   F3=Exit
```

Figure 6-2: Custom Setup screen.

Items that you particularly want to watch for in each of the Custom Setup fields are described in Table 6-2.

Table 6-2	Custom Setup Fields
Field	**Description**
Computer	Several types of computer systems are not 100% IBM PC compatible. Microsoft provides special system drivers for these systems, such as some models of Toshiba laptops. In addition, many new *green* computers, or laptop/notebook computers have circuitry in them that is compatible with the Advanced Power Management specification. If you're using one of these computers, be sure you select MS-DOS system with APC instead of just MS-DOS System.
Display	Windows usually defaults to VGA display, which is the clean choice. That is, if you have any strange problems with running Windows software, one troubleshooting technique is to set the display to VGA even if the system has a fancy Super VGA display. Note the VGA 3.0 setting — this is for use with some computers, such as IBM Thinkpads, that do not run properly with the Windows 3.1 VGA driver.
Mouse	If the mouse came with Windows 3.1 drivers, use the drivers (select unlisted or updated driver). Otherwise, most mice emulate the Microsoft mouse — note that there is only one choice for Microsoft or IBM mice, regardless of whether they are connected to a serial port or via a PS/2-style mouse port.
Keyboard	This option is used mostly outside of the United States because it provides support for international keyboard styles.
Code Page	This option is also for users outside the United States to select their *code page*, which determines the character set that Windows uses. U.S. users normally use code page 437; use 850 for compatibility with multiple languages.

Do you need all the disks?

One concern many corporate administrators have is whether they need "all those disks" when they go out through their company to install Windows. The answer is yes and no. For the most part, virtually all the floppy disks are used during a full Windows installation; the only exception is if you are installing Windows on a computer that is not connected to a printer.

I would advise corporate administrators who want to reduce the number of disks that need to be carried around to consider a network installation. You can do a network installation (SETUP/A) to a portable hard drive, such as one of the many drives on the market that connect to parallel ports, for easy installation in the field.

Windows for Workgroups caveats

Installing Windows for Workgroups requires several considerations that a normal Windows 3.1 installation may not involve.

- Is the installation on a network or stand-alone computer?

- Is remote access to a corporate network needed?

- Will the Microsoft At Work fax capability in Windows for Workgroups 3.11 be used?

- Will the applications that Windows for Workgroups has — Mail and Schedule+ — that plain Windows 3.1 does not have, be used?

Windows NT caveats

A Windows NT installation, as with Windows 3.1 and Windows for Workgroups installations, gives you the choice of Express or Custom Setup. A number of differences exist, however, because Windows NT is a complete operating system, not just an environment running on top of MS-DOS.

First, with Windows NT, you have a choice of installation media — 3½ inch floppies or CD-ROM. You can order 5¼ inch floppies if you need them by using the coupon in the Windows NT System Guide, *but you may have to wait 2-4 weeks for the disks to arrive.*

Three standard methods are used for installing Windows NT. Each method requires you to have a blank floppy disk that is the correct size for drive A . This floppy disk is used to make an "emergency repair" disk. Table 6-3 summarizes Windows NT installation methods.

Table 6-3:	Windows NT Installation Methods
Method	**Description**
Floppy method	Probably the slowest and most inconvenient way to install Windows NT because of the sheer volume of data that has to be installed.
SCSI CD-ROM method	If you have a CD-ROM drive, this is the best route for installation. It requires a SCSI CD-ROM that is on the *Windows NT Hardware Compatibility List (HCL)*, The SCSI ID must not be set to 0 or 1.
Network/Unsupported CD-ROM	Also known as the WINNT method, this method uses a master copy of the Windows NT files on either a network drive or an unsupported CD-ROM. You start this process from MS-DOS. The WINNT.EXE program copies all the Windows NT files over to the installation hard disk, and then begins SETUP.

Installation for Windows 3.1 and Windows for Workgroups

SETUP has two parts, one pertaining to MS-DOS and one pertaining to Windows. This section discusses both portions.

MS-DOS mode SETUP

The primary purpose of the MS-DOS mode portion of SETUP is to put enough Windows files on the hard disk so that Windows can be started and then complete the installation. The MS-DOS mode SETUP encompasses the prompts that I discussed in preceding sections — such as the Express and Custom Setup — and the hardware configuration sections.

One important operation that MS-DOS mode SETUP performs is a check for any TSRs or drivers that are known to interfere with either Windows or SETUP. If you later make changes to the system and you want to check to be sure you haven't changed anything that causes compatibility problems with Windows, SETUP provides such an option, the /t option. If you run SETUP with the /t option from the MS-DOS prompt, it checks for incompatible TSRs and drivers.

After SETUP copies the Windows files over to the hard disk, it builds the WIN.COM startup file. WIN.COM is comprised of a configuration file, the program code that actually loads the Windows components, and the logo bitmap. SETUP then starts Windows by loading WIN.COM.

Windows mode SETUP

Now the drama begins. As soon as SETUP attempts to start the Windows mode portion of SETUP, several things occur that could be failure points for SETUP:

- WIN.COM checks to see if Windows can run in standard mode. To do this, it checks to see if HIMEM.SYS (or another XMS memory manager) is loaded on the system, and if at least 256K conventional memory and 192K extended memory are available on the system. If HIMEM.SYS is not loaded, it also runs XMSMMGR.EXE to act as the XMS memory manager for the duration of SETUP.

- The appropriate Windows kernel and the various device drivers are loaded into memory at this time. This is the most common failure point for Windows SETUP. If the system hangs when SETUP is starting Windows, it is very likely that one of the drivers did not successfully load. Fortunately, SETUP keeps a log file as each driver is loaded so that if you must reboot the system and restart SETUP, SETUP detects a ghost of the previous installation attempt, and tells you which driver did not load.

The most common failure is for a display driver to fail. The best way to work around such a failure is to rerun setup (with the SETUP/I option), but this time, specify the VGA display driver. You can then get a later version of the display driver from your video card's manufacturer after you set up Windows.

Customizing SETUP

The most common reason for customizing setup is to enable corporate administrators to create versions of the Windows disks for field office users who may not be knowledgeable about their hardware and software configurations. The customs disks are then used to simplify the Windows installation.

Windows SETUP provides several ways to create a custom setup: First, through the use of the Batch Mode control file, SETUP.HHH, and second, by directly manipulating SETUP.INF.

The former still allows more sophisticated users to perform normal Express or Custom mode setups because the control file must be invoked using the SETUP /H option.

Most administrators who use this feature copy the template file SETUP.HHH to another file that is dependent upon the various system configurations they have in the field. For example, an administrator might create VGA.HHH, VIPER.HHH, and PARADISE.HHH, for their three standard configurations that have a standard VGA card, a Diamond Viper Accelerator, and a Paradise Accelerator, respectively.

The administrator then sends disks to users with instructions to either type **setup /hvga.hhh**, **setup /hviper.hhh**, or **setup /hparadise.hhh**, or use a batch file that runs the appropriate command for the user's configuration.

The SETUP.SHH file is largely self-documenting. It consists, like other Windows configuration files, of several sections, with keys and values under those sections. Some of the less obvious key values are summarized in Table 6-4.

Table 6-4		SETUP.SHH Key Values	
Section	*Key*	*Values*	*Meaning*
[sysinfo]	sysinfo=	yes | no	If *yes*, the System Information Screen is shown.
[userinfo]			This section can have two lines, the first is the user's name, the second the company name. Both can be up to 30 characters long, and must be enclosed in double quotation marks (" ") if they contain blank spaces.
[dontinstall]	readmes		Don't install README files.
[dontinstall]	accessories		Don't install accessories.
[dontinstall]	games		Don't install games.
[dontinstall]	screensavers		Don't install screen savers.
[dontinstall]	bitmaps		Don't install the wallpapers.
[options]	setupapps		Lets the user choose applications to set up.
[options]	autosetupapps		Sets up all applications found on the user's hard disk.
[options]	tutorial		Runs the tutorial at the end of Setup.
[endinstall]	configfiles=	modify | save	If set to *modify*, SETUP modifies the CONFIG.SYS and AUTOEXEC.BAT files for the user. If set to *save*, SETUP creates alternate files (CONFIG.WIN and AUTOEXEC.WIN) that the user can use as a reference to make changes from.
[endinstall]	endopt=	exit | restart reboot	SETUP's final action — *exit* to MS-DOS, *restart* Windows, or *reboot* the computer.

Modifying INF files

Windows Setup keeps track of drivers, installation options, and so on, in a series of files on its floppy disks (and third-party driver floppy disks), distinguished by the .INF extension. Windows Setup uses several of these files, as follows:

- The SETUP.INF file is the key file to Windows Setup. This file contains instructions about the various options that both the MS-DOS mode and the Windows mode setup presents, what files to copy, the Program Manager groups to create, and so on.

- The APPS.INF file contains information about the application programs that Setup knows how to configure for use with Windows. Corporate administrators may wish to add entries for in-house developed software to this file.

- The CONTROL.INF file contains information about the printers that Windows knows about, what drivers they use, and so on. CONTROL.INF also contains international settings. Corporate administrators may wish to add third-party printer drivers to this file. Setup places CONTROL.INF in the System subdirectory.

- The NETWORK.INF file contains information about network cards and transports. Setup places NETWORK.INF in the System subdirectory.

- The OEMSETUP.INF file contains information about third-party drivers and network transports that are not provided with Windows. OEMSETUP.INF files are included on the driver floppy disks provided by third parties. Setup copies OEMSETUP.INF files to the System directory, renaming them as necessary (to OEM0.INF, OEM1.INF, and so on).

All INF files have a structure similar to that of INI files; they consist of sections, keynames, values, and an optional comment. Sections are preceded by a section header, enclosed in brackets ([ ]). The keyname is followed by an equal sign and then the value. Comments are preceded by a semicolon (;).

Summary

Careful planning is required for a successful Windows installation.

- There is no substitute for making a proper backup.
- Hard drives should be cleaned up, defragmented, and checked for problems before starting setup.
- SETUP/H can be used to control installations when many similar systems need to be set up.
- Setup information files (INF files) can be modified to add or delete options that are available to the user when installing.

Chapter 7
Installing Windows on an Existing Network

A lthough the networking features that are built into Windows for Workgroups and Windows NT enable you to run Windows easily, you can run Windows from an existing network. In fact, this method has several advantages — most notably, the capability to load and run Windows 3.1 completely from a network server, eliminating the need for any disk drives on the workstation, or if the workstation has its own hard drive, a network installation can reduce the amount of hard drive space taken up.

Not having a hard drive on the workstation has a downside, however: storing a swap file on a network drive is much more inefficient. In addition, you cannot have a permanent swap file on a network drive.

Choosing the Administrative Setup

Setting up a shared copy of Windows on a network begins with the *administrative setup*. During the administrative setup, you expand and copy all the files from the Windows setup diskettes to a directory on your network server.

If only a couple of people are going to run Windows, you may use less disk space by installing separate complete copies for each user. Alternatively, you can delete unused files from the shared directory, but this action limits your ability to add more users later.

To begin the administrative setup, at the DOS prompt, type

SETUP /A

DOS prompts you for a directory to which the Windows files should be installed.

Using the MAP ROOT command to install a shared copy of Windows on a Novell server causes some problems. You can work around them by always specifying a subdirectory: that is, if you are going to install the files on the Novell drive SYS: in the Windows directory, which is mapped to the ROOT of J:, install to J:\WINDOWS instead of just J:. This method may create an extra subdirectory level on your server, but you avoid many installation and setup problems with Windows software. These problems are due to the fact that many Windows applications make the assumption that there is always at least one directory level available above the Windows directory.

A complete administrative setup of Windows 3.1 takes 15.3MB; Windows for Workgroups needs 21MB.

Installing from a Shared Copy _____

After you finish the administrative setup, you can install Windows on the rest of the network stations in two ways:

- A standard setup, where Windows is installed on the local hard drive

- A shared network installation, where only some Windows files (mostly individual configuration files) are stored on the local hard drive or on the user's personal, or *home*, directory on the network file server

Standard installation

The standard installation is like a regular installation from floppy disks, except faster: there's no disk swapping, and compressed files are already expanded.

To do a standard installation from a network, go to any workstation, change the DOS prompt to the drive and directory that holds the administrative setup, and type

SETUP

Windows for Workgroup 3.11 contains an administrative utility, ADMINCFG, that enables a network administrator to control a number of different parameters. If you plan to use this utility to create a standard network configuration file, first do a single network installation on any workstation. Then run the ADMINCFG utility and create the configuration file in the shared directory. Of course, full access to the shared directory is needed. After you create this configuration file, the configuration is used for future installations.

See Chapter 18 for more information on ADMINCFG.

Shared network (/N) installation

A shared network installation has some special requirements:

- Users must have access to the directory housing the administrative setup. On a Novell network, this access must include Read and File Scan rights.

- The shared directory should be in the user's path (or on a Novell *search drive*).

- The user needs a private directory — usually a Windows subdirectory off of the network home directory — to store private configuration files (such as INI and GRP files).

- On some networks, the shared files must be flagged as *shareable*.

To begin setup on a workstation that will use the shared network installation, change drive and directory to the location of the shared files created by the Administrative setup. Type

    SETUP /N

to begin the setup procedure.

As previously noted, Windows for Workgroup 3.11 contains an administrative utility, ADMINCFG, that lets a network administrator control a number of different parameters. If the configuration file used by this utility is placed in the shared directory, the configuration set by the administrator is used for the shared network installations.

Remember to specify a directory separate from the shared directory for the user's private initialization files. Setup copies or creates only the files that are needed to personalize the user's installation.

Running from a Shared Copy _____

Running Windows from a shared copy is similar to running Windows from a copy that resides on a local hard drive, except for

- The access constraints created by the need to be logged into the network
- The connection to both the shared administrative directory and the user's private directory

Problems may arise if a user can log into the network from a workstation other than the one that the shared network was installed from.

One way of alleviating these problems is to obtain WinLogin (available only from Microsoft), which enables an administrator to create a central database of computers, users, and their applications: when a user logs in by using WinLogin, the system creates INI and GRP files appropriate to that user's configuration and the particular workstation being used. If necessary, WinLogin not only can perform line-by-line control of initialization files, but it can even copy executable files. In addition, you can administer WinLogin's centralized database of user and workstation settings from a single computer — in other words, all Windows users and workstations on a centralized server-based network can be administered from a single computer.

Installing a Diskless Workstation _____

To install Windows on a diskless workstation, you must do a shared network installation from the diskless workstation and you must install the user's private files to a directory on the network server.

Because Windows for Workgroups 3.11 requires minimal changes to the workstation's CONFIG.SYS and AUTOEXEC.BAT files (one line in each), it is the ideal version of Windows when installing on a diskless workstation. In fact, the AUTOEXEC.BAT file on a diskless workstation is usually replaced by some other batch file on the network server (or by a logon script), so you usually need to make only one change to the *boot image* on the network server. Add the line

```
DEVICE=IFSHLP.SYS
```

to the end of the CONFIG.SYS file. (You also need to copy IFSHLP.SYS from the directory holding the administrative setup to the disk from which the boot image is made.) ◎

Creating Custom Setups

For custom Windows setups, use the SETUP.HHH file and modify the various INF files that control setup.

See Chapter 6 for more information on INF files.

An INF file entry of particular interest to network administrators is the *netsetup=* entry in the [network] section of SETUP.INF. The default for this setting is false, which means that the user can choose any possible Setup type (SETUP/A, SETUP/N, and plain SETUP). In the SETUP.INF created in the shared Windows directory following an administrative installation, network administrators may want to change the line

```
netsetup=false
```

to

```
netsetup=true  ; changed 1-1-94
               ; MJ SMITH
```

Be sure to document the change with a comment in the SETUP.INF file as shown, so that future administrators or users are not frustrated by being unable to do a full installation.

Changing the setting forces all users who use SETUP from the shared directory to perform a shared network installation. As a result, the administrator gains better control of the overall network installation and makes sure that users do not waste local hard disk space.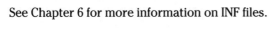

Customizing Program Manager for networks

Network administrators frequently want to limit users' ability to make changes to their Windows setup, Program Manager groups, and programs. In fact, administrators often even want to restrict users from exiting Windows at all.

Program Manager can be configured in a variety of ways to control what a user can do. Simply add a [restrictions] section to the PROGMAN.INI file found in the Windows directory.

Using the settings detailed in the following sections may make it impossible to change anything or add new programs to the system. Always make certain that field technicians can boot systems to the MS-DOS command prompt so that they can temporarily remove the [restrictions] section for configuration purposes (this process can be as simple as booting the system from a plain MS-DOS boot floppy). Of course, the system's users must be prevented from doing the same.

The best way to accomplish both of these goals is to do the following:

1. Use the system's BIOS to password protect its BIOS setup routines.

2. Use the system's BIOS to allow booting only from the system's hard drive (or by using a network remote boot PROM).

3. If using MS-DOS 6.0 or higher, add a line reading

   ```
   SWITCHES=/F /N
   ```

   to the station's CONFIG.SYS file. This line prevents the user from pressing F5 or F8 to bypass the CONFIG.SYS and/or AUTOEXEC.BAT commands.

4. Add the WIN command to the end of the AUTOEXEC.BAT file, forcing the system to load Windows at the end of its boot. 👊

The [restrictions] section can contain the entries listed in the following sections. If neither the [restrictions] section nor any of the possible following settings is present, the restriction does not apply. (Setting a setting to 0 turns the restriction off, too.)

File⇨Run

When you disable the File⇨Run command, the Run command is grayed out; users cannot run applications from Program Manager that have not been set up in a Program group.

Setting: NoRun=1

Default: Not Present

If the Run command in Program Manager is disabled, users can still use the Run command in File Manager. The only way to prevent this workaround is to remove File Manager from the Program Manager's Main group and any other groups it may have been added to.

File⇨Exit Windows

The File⇨Exit Windows command can be disabled, preventing users from exiting Program Manager through the File or Control menus or by using Alt+F4. This restriction shows up most often on publicly accessible workstations, such as store locators in shopping malls, because shutting down Windows without properly exiting can corrupt data.

Setting: `NoClose=1`

Default: Not Present

Options⇨Save Settings on Exit

Disabling the Options⇨Save Settings on Exit command deters users from scrambling the arrangement of their Program Manager groups and icons. Some jumble their screen so much they can no longer find the applications they need.

Setting: `NoSaveSettings=1`

Default: Not Present

 This setting overrides the `SaveSettings=` entry in the `[settings]` section of the PROGMAN.INI file.

File⇨...

Sometimes, you may want to prevent users from using any of the commands on the File menu (New, Open, Move, Delete, Properties, Run, Exit). Adding this restriction prevents users from adding new program icons or groups, modifying or deleting existing ones, running applications that are not already set up in a Program Manager icon, and exiting Program Manager by selecting Exit. Users could still exit Program Manager, however, by choosing Control⇨Close or pressing Alt+F4.

Setting: `NoFileMenu=1`

Default: Not Present

EditLevels

Finally, you also can add `EditLevels` to the `[restrictions]` section. `EditLevels` deal with users' ability to modify various items in Program Manager. Each succeeding `EditLevel` contains all the restrictions of the preceding level (for example, `EditLevel=2` includes the restrictions listed for `EditLevel=1`). Setting `EditLevel=1` disables the New, Move, Copy, and Delete commands on the File menu when a group is selected. `EditLevel=2` also prevents users from creating or deleting program items. `EditLevel=3` also prevents users from changing command lines for program items (this restriction affects the Properties dialog box). `EditLevel=4` also prevents users from changing any program item information (this restriction completely disables the Properties dialog box).

Setting: `EditLevel= 0/1/2/3/4`

Default: Not Present

Customizing File Manager for networks

To restrict users' abilities, administrators also can configure File Manager by including a `[restrictions]` section in WINFILE.INI, File Manager's initialization file.

The version of File Manager provided with Windows for Workgroups recognizes a restriction switch that controls whether Windows displays the file sharing options in the Disk menu. This switch enables the network administrator to control which directories are shared from a user's station.

Setting: `NoShareCommands=1`

Default: Not Present (0).

When testing Program Manager options, it is wise to use an alternate shell, such as HP Dashboard or even File Manager. (A version of HP Dashboard is included on the *Windows 3.1 Configuration SECRETS Disks* accompanying this book.) Then use a copy of Notepad and alter the PROGMAN.INI file as desired. Save the altered file and leave the copy of Notepad open! Using that shell's Run command, execute Program Manager and see whether the appropriate restrictions are in effect.

Using this technique, you can test Program Manager restrictions without restricting your own test system. 🖐🖴

Controlling Control Panel

In addition, you can limit the Control Panel items that are loaded when a user runs Control Panel. Add a `[Don't Load]` section to CONTROL.INI; then add the items you don't want to load to this section. For example, to keep the Network item from loading, add the following to CONTROL.INI:

```
[Don't Load]
NETWORK=1
```

Restricting workgroup choices

One of the most common problems for administrators using Windows for Workgroups 3.10 was the users' ability to arbitrarily change their workgroup. In Windows for Workgroups 3.11, Microsoft added a file called WRKGRP.INI that enables administrators to control the workgroup choices the user (or installer) can select from.

WRKGRP.INI consists of two sections: [Workgroups] and [Options]. The [Workgroups] section consists of the workgroup names that the user can choose from. For example,

```
[Workgroups]
Editorial=
Production=
Marketing=
```

The [Options] section has the following settings:

Setting: ANSI=False | True

Default: False

or

Setting: Required=True | False

Default: False

The former setting indicates whether the workgroup names in the [Workgroups] section are in the ANSI or OEM character set. If set to False (the default), Windows converts the text into ANSI characters.

If the latter setting is False, Windows allows the user to enter anything into the Workgroup box in Network setup. If set to true, only workgroups that appear in the [Workgroups] section are permitted.

Summary

This chapter discussed various issues involved with installing Windows on an existing network:

▶ Use Windows Setup to place all common Windows files in a shared directory, increase administrator control, and make more efficient use of disk space.

▶ Windows for Workgroups 3.11 is a good choice for diskless workstations because it requires minimal modification to the remote boot image file.

▶ Network administrators can customize Program Manager, File Manager, and Control Panel to prevent users from changing system settings.

Chapter 8
The Anatomy of a Windows Installation

In This Chapter
▶ Files that make up Windows

▶ Windows initialization files

▶ Files you can delete after installation

Suppose that after you've completed the Windows installation process, you notice that Windows and its supporting files are taking up 20 to 30MB of hard disk space. This realization may cause great concern if you're installing Windows on a system configured to Microsoft's minimum hardware recommendations. All versions of Windows, from Windows 3.1 to Windows for Workgroups 3.11, install a prolific number of files. As a system administrator — the person responsible for installing, configuring, and maintaining Windows workstations — you may ask yourself repeatedly, "What does this file do? Do I need it, or can I delete it without system-wide repercussions?" This chapter describes the files that comprise a Windows installation and how you can minimize the Windows footprint to ease your configuration burden.

Windows Is a Collection of Files

Windows is a collection of *dynamic-link libraries* (DLLs). The kinds of files that make up Windows 3.1 include the following:

- The WIN.COM file
- The core DLLs (kernel files, USER, and GDI) that contain the code and data for Windows functions
- The font files
- The driver files (for keyboard, display, system, mouse, printers, networks, multimedia, and so on)
- The files that provide MS-DOS support components for Windows

- The Windows applications files and other files such as shells, utilities, and accessories

- The initialization files, which contain the parameters for controlling the Windows environment

Driver files

When you install Windows, the setup program surveys your system to identify the type of monitor, keyboard, mouse, and other peripherals. Setup then installs the appropriate driver files.

 Windows can't determine the type of printer that's attached to your system. As a result, you must tell Windows which printer drivers you want to install.

Device drivers give Windows applications their device independence by providing the hardware-specific interface between the physical devices and Windows. Setup can install several kinds of drivers for Windows, such as:

- Communications drivers
- Mouse drivers
- Printer drivers
- Display drivers
- Multimedia drivers
- Sound drivers
- Keyboard drivers
- Network drivers
- System drivers

The network, multimedia, and printer drivers are optional. Also, drivers can be installed to support virtual machines in 386 enhanced mode.

System support drivers

System drivers provide support for the system timer, information about system disks, and access to OEM-defined system hooks. Two system drivers are shipped with Windows:

- SYSTEM.DRV, the driver for most hardware systems
- HPSYSTEM.DRV, the HP Vectra system driver for standard mode

Keyboard input support drivers

The keyboard drivers shipped with Windows support keyboard input. The Windows keyboard driver is a standard driver for all systems worldwide. Windows also can handle international keyboards, including foreign symbols, by using the keyboard tables to refer to a language library.

KEYBOARD.DRV for standard keyboards is installed by default and KBDHP.DRV is used for all Hewlett-Packard machines.

The keyboard driver is a standard driver for all systems worldwide. Windows for Workgroups is also compatible with international keyboards, including foreign symbols, by using keyboard tables to refer to a language library. Table 8-1 lists keyboard tables and the language that they support.

Table 8-1	Keyboard Table
Keyboard table	*Language Library*
KBDBE.DLL	Belgian keyboard
KBDCA.DLL	French-Canadian keyboard
KBDDA.DLL	Danish keyboard
KBDDV.DLL	U.S.-Dvorak keyboard
KBDFC.DLL	Canadian multilingual keyboard
KBDFI.DLL	Finnish keyboard
KBDFR.DLL	French keyboard
KBDGR.DLL	German keyboard
KBDIC.DLL	Icelandic keyboard
KBDIT.DLL	Italian keyboard
KBDLA.DLL	Latin American keyboard
KBDNE.DLL	Dutch keyboard
KBDNO.DLL	Norwegian keyboard
KBDPO.DLL	Portuguese keyboard
KBDSF.DLL	Swiss-French keyboard
KBDSG.DLL	Swiss-German keyboard
KBDSP.DLL	Spanish keyboard
KBDSW.DLL	Swedish keyboard
KBDUK.DLL	British keyboard
KBDUS.DLL	U.S. keyboard
KBDUSX.DLL	U.S.-International keyboard

Mouse driver files

Table 8-2 lists mouse drivers support pointing devices for use with Windows and Windows applications.

Table 8-2	Mouse Drivers
Driver	*Supported Mouse or Pointing Device*
HPMOUSE.DRV	Hewlett-Packard mouse (HP-HIL)
LMOUSE.DRV	Logitech Serial mouse
MSC3BC2.DRV	Mouse Systems COM2/3 button mouse
MSCMOUSE.DRV	Mouse Systems Serial/Bus mouse
MOUSE.DRV	Logitech Bus or PS/2 style, Microsoft, or IBM PS/2 mouse
NOMOUSE.DRV	No mouse attached to system

Display drivers

Display drivers support the system display and the cursor for the pointing device. The Windows display driver, however, does not support non-Windows applications running in full screen because such applications write directly to video.

Display driver files

The display drivers shipped with Windows for Workgroups support the system display adapter and the cursor for the pointing device. The display driver, however, does not support MS-DOS-based applications running in a full screen, because these applications write directly to video. Table 8-3 lists display drivers.

Table 8-3	Display Drivers
Driver	*Supported Display Adapter*
8514.DRV	8514/A
EGA.DRV	EGA
EGAHIBW.DRV	EGA with 128K RAM
EGAMONO.DRV	EGA monochrome display
HERCULES.DRV	Hercules monochrome display
MMTLLO.DRV	ET4000 (small fonts)
MMTLHI.DRV	ET4000 (large fonts)
OLIBW.DRV	Olivetti/AT&T monochrome or PVC display

Driver	Supported Display Adapter
PLASMA.DRV	COMPAQ Portable plasma
SUPERVGA.DRV	Super VGA (800x600 - 16 colors)
TIGA.DRV	TIGA
VGA.DRV	VGA
VGAMONO.DRV	VGA monochrome display
V7VGA.DRV	Video Seven VGA with 512K (FastWrite, VRAM, 1024i, and compatibles)
XGA.DRV	XGA

Communications drivers

The COMM.DRV communications driver supports serial and parallel device communications.

Advanced Power Management drivers

The Advanced Power Management device driver, POWER.DRV, supports the power management features of laptop and notebook PCs.

Printer support drivers

Printer drivers support output to the printer device. Some of the printer drivers shipped with Windows have a soft font installation utility. The related files also include help files for the printer drivers and soft font installers. In Windows 3.1, many of the dot-matrix drivers have been replaced by a universal printer driver. Other drivers have been updated for performance and to support TrueType fonts.

Network drivers

Network drivers provide a network interface to File Manager, Control Panel, Print Manager, and system utilities. Table 8-4 lists network drivers.

Table 8-4	Network Drivers	
Driver	Support File	Supported Network
WFWNET.DRV	WFWNET.HLP	Microsoft Windows for Workgroups network driver
NETAPI.DLL		Windows for Workgroups network API library
PMSPL.DLL		Windows for Workgroups printer API library

(continued)

Table 8-4 *(continued)*

Driver	Support File	Supported Network
LMSCRIPT.EXE		LAN Manager script support utility
LMSCRIPT.PIF		
MSNET.DRV	Generic network driver*	
NETWARE.DRV	NETWARE.HLP	Novell NetWare 2.10 or above; Novell NetWare386
NWPOPUP.EXE	Supports pop-up messages	
NETX.COM	Workstation shell	
ROUTE.COM		Token Ring IPX source routing support
MSIPX.COM		NDIS-compliant IPX protocol
MSIPX.SYS		NDIS shim for MSIPX.COM to use NDIS drivers

*MSNET.DRV supports 3Com 3+Share, 3Com 3+Open LAN Manager (XMS only), Banyan VINES 4.0, Microsoft LAN Manager 1.x (and compatibles), Microsoft LAN Manager 2.0 Basic (and compatibles), Microsoft Network (and compatibles), and IBM PC LAN Program.

Multimedia support drivers

The drivers listed in Table 8-5 support the multimedia capabilities of Windows 3.1 and Windows for Workgroups 3.1x.

Table 8-5	Multimedia Drivers
Filename	**Purpose**
MCICDA.DRV	MCI CD-audio driver
MCISEQ.DRV	MCI driver for MIDI driver
MCIWAVE.DRV	MCI driver for waveform audio
MIDIMAP.DRV	Driver for MIDI Mapper Control Panel extension
MMSOUND.DRV	Multimedia sound driver
MPU401.DRV	MIDI driver for MPU401 compatibles
MSADLIB.DRV	MIDI driver for Adlib compatibles

Filename	Purpose
SNDBLST.DRV	SoundBlaster 1.5 DSP driver
SNDBLST2.DRV	SoundBlaster 2.0 DSP driver
TIMER.DRV	Multimedia timer driver

Font files

Although font files aren't actually device drivers, they enhance Windows' device independence. Windows has several fonts for supporting the Windows system and Windows applications and for non-Windows applications running in Windows and data copied to the Clipboard from those applications. Font files usually have a .TTF, .FON, or .FOT filename extension.

Raster font files

Windows installs several raster or bitmap font files in the Windows/System directory. Windows comes with six resolutions of raster screen fonts and installs them according to the type of monitor installed on your system. If used for printing, raster fonts print text and graphics as bitmaps or raster lines. The resolutions are identified by a letter added to the filename of the font as described in Table 8-6.

Table 8-6	Raster Font Files Identification			
Letter	**Output Device**	**Resolution**	**x size***	**y size***
A**	CGA display	2:1	96	48
B	EGA display	1.33:1	96	72
C**	Printer	1:1.2	60	72
D**	Printer	1.66:1	120	72
E	VGA display	1:1	96	96
F	8514 display	1:1	120	120

* x,y indicates the height/width aspect ratio, in pixels per inch.

** These fonts are not included on the Windows for Workgroups installation disks.

By appending the letter that identifies the resolution to the raster font filenames, you can see the files that Windows for Workgroups installs for a given display or printer, shown in Table 8-7. For example, the files for the 8514 raster fonts are COURF.FON, SSERIFF.FON, SERIFF.FON, SMALLF.FON, and SYMBOLF.FON.

Table 8-7	Windows for Workgroups Raster Fonts Installed		
Font	*Filename*	*Character Set*	*Font Description*
Courier	COURx.FON	ANSI	Fixed-width with serifs
MS Sans Serif	SSERIFx.FON	ANSI	Proportional-width sans serif
MS Serif	SERIFx.FON	ANSI	Proportional-width serif
Small	SMALLx.FON	ANSI	Proportional small size
Symbol	SYMBOLx.FON	Symbol	Math symbols

 Each raster font is designed for a specific display device, so Windows installs only the font files corresponding to the resolution and aspect ratio of your video card.

Vector font files

Windows provides three vector font files: ROMAN.FON, SCRIPT.FON, and MODERN.FON. Characters in vector fonts are stored as sets of relative coordinate pair points with connecting lines. Vector fonts are fully scalable fonts, so the font can be used in any size desired. Applications or printing devices, however, may have limits on the font sizes they support.

TrueType font files

The TrueType downloadable fonts shipped with Windows 3.1 support the Arial, Courier, Symbol, and Times New Roman font families. Each family requires a TTF file and an FOT file. Table 8-8 lists TrueType filenames and their accompanying font names.

Table 8-8	Windows 3.1 TrueType Fonts Supported
TrueType Filenames	*Font Name*
ARIAL.FOT, ARIAL.TTF	Arial
ARIALBD.FOT, ARIALBD.TTF	Arial Bold
ARIALBI.FOT, ARIALBI.TTF	Arial Bold Italic
ARIALI.FOT, ARIALI.TTF	Arial Italic
COUR.FOT, COUR.TTF	Courier
COURBD.FOT, COURBD.TTF	Courier Bold
COURBI.FOT, COURBI.TTF	Courier Bold Italic
COURI.FOT, COURI.TTF	Courier Italic

TrueType Filenames	Font Name
TIMES.FOT, TIMES.TTF	Times New Roman
TIMESBD.FOT, TIMESBD.TTF	Times New Roman Bold
TIMESBI.FOT, TIMESBI.TTF	Times New Roman Bold Italic
TIMESI.FOT, TIMESI.TTF	Times New Roman Italic
SYMBOL.FOT, SYMBOL.TTF	Symbol
WINGDING.FOT, WINGDING.TTF	Wingding

If the FOT file is deleted, Windows will re-create it.

Fonts that Windows uses internally

Windows installs several font files designed for Windows use only. These fonts support specific display types or screen operations. For example, Windows uses these fonts to display text in standard mode, text for windowed DOS applications, and text used in title bars and menus or in the Clipboard viewer.

System font files

Some of the fonts supplied with Windows support text display on specific types of monitors. Windows ships with three basic fonts, which are designed to support display and output devices, as follows:

Font	Description
System	To draw menus, dialog box controls, and other text in Windows 3.x
Fixed	A fixed-width font included with Windows 3.1 to ensure backward compatibility with Windows 2.x and earlier versions, which used Fixed as the system font
OEM, or Terminal	A fixed-width font used to support the OEM text copied to the Clipboard viewer from Windows and non-Windows applications

Font files for non-Windows applications

Windows also installs fonts for displaying non-Windows applications in a window when Windows is running in 386 enhanced mode. By default, code page 437 (U.S.) fonts are installed.

Other font files, identified by the code page number appended to the filename, are included for international language support.

International support files

Windows provides language libraries to support a number of languages. Table 8-9 lists supported language libraries.

Table 8-9	Windows International Language Support
Filename	*Supported Languages*
LANGDUT.DLL	Dutch language driver
LANGENG.DLL	General international language driver
LANGFRN.DLL	French language driver
LANGGER.DLL	German language driver
LANGSCA.DLL	Finnish/Icelandic/Norwegian/Swedish language driver
LANGSPA.DLL	Spanish language driver

Files used to support MS-DOS

Two kinds of files provide MS-DOS support for Windows: MS-DOS drivers and the grabber files that support data exchange between Windows and non-Windows applications.

MS-DOS Windows for Workgroups driver files

 Several MS-DOS driver files are included with Windows for Workgroups, listed in Table 8-10. The drivers provided with Windows for Workgroups are the recommended versions to use.

Table 8-10	MS-DOS Driver Files Shipped with Windows for Workgroups
Driver	*Purpose*
EGA.SYS	EGA MS-DOS driver
EMM386.EXE	Microsoft MS-DOS 386 EMS manager
HIMEM.SYS	Microsoft MS-DOS XMS manager
RAMDRIVE.SYS	Microsoft MS-DOS RAMDrive utility
SMARTDRV.EXE	Microsoft MS-DOS SMARTDrive 4.0 disk-caching utility

Driver	Purpose
LMOUSE.COM	MS-DOS Level Logitech mouse driver
MOUSE.COM	MS-DOS mouse driver
MOUSE.SYS	MS-DOS mouse driver (installed at MS-DOS boot time)
MOUSEHP.COM	MS-DOS mouse driver for Hewlett-Packard systems
MOUSEHP.SYS	MS-DOS mouse driver for Hewlett-Packard systems
MSCDEX.EXE	Microsoft CD-ROM Extensions 2.21 driver
*.DOS	MS-DOS NDIS network interface card driver(s) include the following
NET.EXE	WFW MS-DOS network redirector
NET.MSG	WFW network redirector message file
NETH.MSG	WFW network redirector help message file
PROTMAN.EXE	WFW protocol manager TSR
WORKGRP.SYS	Real-mode stub for Windows for Workgroups network redirector

Refer to Chapter 4 for a more detailed discussion.

MS-DOS driver files

Several MS-DOS driver files are included with Windows. The following section describes NDIS drivers installed with Windows for Workgroups 3.1 to support network adapter cards.

NDIS network adapter card driver files

Table 8-11 lists the NDIS drivers provided with Windows for Workgroups to support network adapter cards.

Table 8-11	Windows for Workgroups NDIS Drivers
Driver	Related Network Adapter Card
AM2100.DOS	Advanced Micro Devices AM2100/PCnet
DEPCA.DOS	DEC EtherWorks
E20NDIS.DOS	Cabletron E2010-X
E21NDIS.DOS	Cabletron E2112
ELNK16.DOS	3Com EtherLink 16
ELNK3.DOS	3Com EtherLink III

(continued)

Table 8-11 *(continued)*

Driver	Related Network Adapter Card
ELNKII.DOS	3Com EtherLink II
ELNKMC.DOS	3Com EtherLink/MC
ELNKPL.DOS	3Com EtherLink Plus
EVX16.DOS	Everex SpeedLink /PC16 (EV2027)
EXP16.DOS	Intel EtherExpress 16
HPLANB.DOS	HP LAN
I82593.DOS	Intel Motherboard Module
IBMTOK.DOS	IBM Token Ring
MAC586.SYS	DCA 10 Mb
NDIS39XR.DOS	Proteon Token Ring
NE1000.DOS	Novell/Anthem NE1000 (or compatible)
NE2000.DOS	Novell/Anthem NE2000 (or compatible)
NI6510.DOS	Racal-Interlan NI6510
OLITOK.DOS	Intel TokenExpress 16/4
PE2NDIS.DOS	Xircom Pocket Ethernet II
PRO4.DOS	Proteon ISA Token Ring
SMC3000.DOS	SMC 3000 Series
SMCMAC.DOS	SMC (WD) EtherCard PLUS
SMC_ARC.DOS	SMC ARCNET
STRN.DOS	NCR Token Ring
TCCARC.DOS	Thomas Conrad TC6x4x (Enhanced Mode)
TLNK.DOS	3Com TokenLink

Other NDIS drivers are available as part of the Windows Driver Library (WDL).

WinOldAp and the grabber files

Files that provide font support for the grabbers are listed in Table 8-12, with descriptions of the kinds of display drivers that the grabbers support.

Table 8-12	Files that Provide Font Support for Grabbers
File	*Display Drivers*
286 grabber support file	*Display device supported*
CGA.2GR	CGA
EGACOLOR.2GR	EGA
EGAMONO.2GR	EGA monochrome
HERCULES.2GR	Hercules monochrome
OLIGRAB.2GR	Olivetti/AT&T monochrome or PVC
VGACOLOR.2GR	VGA
VGAMONO.2GR	VGA monochrome
386 grabber support file	*Display device supported*
EGA.3GR	EGA 386
HERC.3GR	Hercules monochrome
PLASMA.3GR	Compaq Portable plasma
V7VGA.3GR	Video 7
VGA.3GR	VGA
VGA30.3GR	VGA (version 3.0)
VGADIB.3GR	DIB (8514/A monochrome)

Files for standard mode

When Windows is running in standard mode, the processor is switched into 80286 protected mode, allowing access to extended memory through XMS support. DOSX.EXE, the MS-DOS Extender for Windows, is required for standard mode. When Windows runs in standard mode, WIN.COM executes DOSX.EXE. Then the Kernel file is loaded (KRNL286.EXE for 80286 machines, KRNL386.EXE for 80386 machines), which in turn loads the other parts of Windows. Two more files support task swapping for standard mode:

- WSWAP.EXE supports Windows applications in standard mode.
- DSWAP.EXE supports non-Windows applications in standard mode.

Files for 386 enhanced mode

In 386 enhanced mode, Windows can use virtual memory. Much of the virtual
support is provided by WIN386.EXE, which is executed by WIN.COM. When
WIN386.EXE begins to load, it looks for the files identified in the [386Enh]
section of SYSTEM.INI. Some of the standard files are built into WIN386.EXE
(designated with the * symbol in SYSTEM.INI entries). WIN386.EXE also loads
other files (listed in Table 8-13) to support virtual devices.

Table 8-13   Files Loaded by WIN386.EXE to Support Virtual Devices

Filename	Virtual Device Supported
LANMAN10.386	LAN Manager version 1.0 support
LVMD.386	Logitech virtual mouse device
HPEBIOS.386	EBIOS virtual device for Hewlett-Packard machines
MONOUMB2.386	UMB driver for monochrome video space
MSCVMD.386	Mouse Systems virtual mouse device
V7VDD.386	Video Seven virtual display device
VADLIBD.386	Virtual DMA device for Adlib
VCD.386	Virtual communications device
VDD8514.386	8514/A virtual display device
VDDCGA.DRV	CGA virtual display device
VDDEGA.386	EGA virtual display device
VDDHERC.386	Hercules monochrome virtual display device
VDDTIGA.386	TIGA virtual display device
VDDTLI4.386	Tseng ET4000 Super VGA virtual display device
VDDVGA30.386	VGA virtual display device (version 3.0)
VDDXGA.386	XGA virtual display device
VIPX.386	Novell NetWare virtual IPX support
VDMAD.386	Virtual DMA device
VNETWARE.386	NetWare virtual support
VPD.386	Virtual printer device
VPICD.386	Virtual programmable interrupt controller device
VPOWERD.386	Advanced Power Management virtual device
VSBD.386	SoundBlaster virtual device
VTDAPI.386	Multimedia virtual timer device
WIN386.PS2	Support for PS/2 architecture

Filename	Virtual Device Supported
VBROWSE.386	WFW virtual network browsing device
VNB.386	WFW virtual NetBEUI device
VNETBIOS.386	WFW virtual NetBIOS device
VNETSUP.386	WFW virtual network support device
VREDIR.386	WFW virtual network redirector device
VSERVER.386	WFW virtual network server device
VSHARE.386	WFW virtual file sharing device
VWC.386	WFW virtual workgroup client device

Files for Windows applications

The Windows files also include applications, shells, utilities, accessories, and games. Table 8-14 lists the applications and associated files, with a brief description of each application.

Table 8-14	Windows Applications Files	
Filename	Associated Files	Application Name and Description
CALC.EXE	CALC.HLP	Calculator (general/scientific)
CARDFILE.EXE	CARDFILE.HLP	Cardfile (desktop Rolodex)
CHARMAP.EXE	CHARMAP.HLP	Character Map
CLIPBRD.EXE	CLIPBRD.HLP	ClipBook Viewer
CLIPSRV.EXE		ClipBook DDE server application
CLOCK.EXE		Clock (analog/digital)
CONTROL.EXE	CONTROL.HLP	Control Panel
	CONTROL.INI	Initialization file
	CPWIN386.CPL	386 enhanced mode extension for Control Panel
	DRIVERS.CPL	Installable drivers extension for Control Panel
	LZEXPAND.DLL	File expansion utility for Control Panel
	MAIN.CPL	Main Control Panel extension
	MIDIMAP.CFG	MIDI Mapper extension file for Control Panel
	SND.CPL	Sound extension for Control Panel

(continued)

Table 8-14 (continued)

Filename	Associated Files	Application Name and Description
	WFWSETUP.DLL	WFW network setup extension for Control Panel
DRWATSON.EXE		Windows fault detection utility
MPLAYER.EXE	MPLAYER.HLP	Media Player
	MMSYSTEM.DLL	Multimedia system library
	MMTASK.TSK	Multimedia background task
MSD.EXE	MSD.INI	Microsoft Diagnostics utility and initialization file
MSHEARTS.EXE	MSHEARTS.HLP	Hearts game
	CARDS.DLL	
MSMAIL.EXE	MSMAIL.HLP	Mail Application
	SENDFILE.DLL	File Manager extension to send file as attachment
	AB.DLL	Address Book user interface support functions
	DEMILAYR.DLL	MS WGA System Services layer
	FRAMEWRK.DLL	Microsoft WGA Application Framework layer
	IMPEXP.DLL	Mail message file import utility
	MAILMGR.DLL	Mail Manager API support functions
	MAILSPL.EXE	MS Mail for Windows—Mail spooler
	MAPI.DLL	MS Messaging Applications Programming Interface
	MSSFS.DLL	Microsoft shared file system transport
	STORE.DLL	Message store support functions
	VFORMS.DLL	Mail viewed forms DLL
	WGPOMGR.DLL	Windows for Workgroups Post Office Manager functions
NETDDE.EXE		Network DDE background application
	NDDEAPI.DLL	Network DDE-DDE shares API support
	NDDENB.DLL	Network DDE driver for NetBIOS
NETWATCH.EXE	NETWATCH.HLP	NetWatcher
NOTEPAD.EXE	NOTEPAD.HLP	Notepad (desktop text editor)
PACKAGER.EXE	PACKAGER.HLP	Object Packager
PBRUSH.EXE	PBRUSH.DLL	Paintbrush
	PBRUSH.HLP	
PIFEDIT.EXE	PIFEDIT.HLP	PIF Editor

Filename	Associated Files	Application Name and Description
POWER.HLP	SL.DLL, SL.HLP	Advanced Power Management supporting files
PRINTMAN.EXE	PRINTMAN.HLP	Print Manager (Windows print spooler)
PROGMAN.EXE	PROGMAN.INI	Program Manager (shell)
	PROGMAN.HLP	
RECORDER.EXE	RECORDER.HLP	Recorder (desktop macro recorder)
	RECORDER.DLL	
REGEDIT.EXE	REGEDIT.HLP	Registration Editor and supporting files
	REGEDITV.HLP	
	DDEML.DLL	DDE management library
	OLECLI.DLL	Client library and server
	OLESVR.DLL	For object linking and embedding
SCHDPLUS.EXE	SCHDPLUS.HLP	Schedule+ Application
	SCHDPLUS.INI	
	MSREMIND.EXE	Schedule+ background reminder notification
	SCHEDMSG.DLL	Schedule+ message forms for MS Mail
	TRNSCHED.DLL	Schedule+ shared file system transport
SHELL.DLL		Shell library
SOL.EXE	SOL.HLP	Solitaire game
SMARTDRV.EXE		Disk-caching utility
SOUNDREC.EXE	SOUNDREC.HLP	Sound Recorder
SYSEDIT.EXE		Windows System Editor
TASKMAN.EXE		Task Manager (application switcher)
TERMINAL.EXE	TERMINAL.HLP	Terminal (desktop communications)
TOOLHELP.DLL		Windows Tool Helper library
WINCHAT.EXE	WINCHAT.HLP	Chat
WINFILE.EXE	WINFILE.HLP	File Manager
WINHELP.EXE	WINHELP.HLP	Help (Windows help engine)
	GLOSSARY.HLP	Windows Help glossary
WINMETER.EXE		System performance meter
WINMINE.EXE	WINMINE.HLP	MineSweeper game
WINTUTOR.EXE	WINTUTOR.DAT	Windows Tutorial
WRITE.EXE	WRITE.HLP	Write (desktop word processor)

Control Panel uses LZEXPAND.DLL to expand files from the Windows for Workgroups installation disks. Because most of the files on the Windows for Workgroups installation disks are compressed (except SETUP.INF, SETUP.EXE, and EXPAND.EXE), Control Panel must expand the files to install a new printer or to add fonts. LZEXPAND is a Windows library counterpart to EXPAND.EXE.

Setup-related files

Setup has a number of files for its exclusive use. For example, the *.LGO files contain the code for displaying the opening screen logo, and the *.RLE files contain the actual logo bitmap (in Run Length Encoded [RLE] format). Setup combines the LGO and RLE files with the WIN.CNF file to create WIN.COM.

Files to Control the Windows Environment

Computer systems generally contain *boot files*, or start-up files, that are read when the computer first starts. The CONFIG.SYS file and AUTOEXEC.BAT file are typical examples of boot files on a DOS-based PC. The settings in these two files control how DOS and application software interact with your system. Start-up files enable you to configure software to work together with particular hardware arrangements.

Windows' settings requirements go beyond the setup parameters addressed in the CONFIG.SYS and AUTOEXEC.BAT files. Windows adds its own collection of initialization files. Each time you start Windows, it reads these files and places key pieces of this information into memory during your Windows session. Two of these initialization files, WIN.INI and SYSTEM.INI, are critical to starting and maintaining the Windows environment. Windows and Windows applications use the information in these files to configure themselves to your needs and preferences.

The WIN.INI file contains the settings that let you customize your Windows environment for printers, fonts, ports, and screen colors. The SYSTEM.INI file contains settings that control hardware configuration, device drivers, memory management, the startup shell program and virtual machines. Many Windows programs include their own initialization files, which are read on start-up. Program Manager and File Manager, for example, use PROGMAN.INI and WINFILE.INI respectively, to store their settings.

Control Panel also uses an initialization file, CONTROL.INI, to store settings for printer information, multimedia drivers, desktop patterns and color schemes, and screen saver options. Some applications add their own information to the WIN.INI file during installation. Because INI files cannot exceed 64K, and because the WIN.INI file is usually the largest initialization file, Microsoft recommends that developers create their own application-specific INI files, instead of adding to WIN.INI. If you run a number of Windows applications, you will find several INI files related to these programs on your hard drive.

Your Windows 3.1 directory may include the initialization files listed in Table 8-15.

Table 8-15	Windows 3.1 INI Files
Initialization File	*File Contents*
WIN.INI	Entries that you can use to set up the environment according to your preferences
SYSTEM.INI	Entries that you can use to set up Windows to meet your system's hardware needs
PROGMAN.INI	Entries that define the content of program groups
CONTROL.INI	Entries that describe the color schemes and patterns used, and the settings for printers and installable drivers
WINFILE.INI	Entries that define the appearance and behavior of items in File Manager
PROTOCOL.INI	Entries that define the network protocol and media-access control drivers
MSMAIL.INI	Entries that define the appearance and behavior of Mail
SHARED.INI	Entries that you can use to share Mail custom commands and custom messages with other members of your workgroup
SCHDPLUS.INI	Entries that define the appearance and behavior of Schedule+
EFAXPUMP.INI	Entries used by the Microsoft At Work fax components, provided with Windows for Workgroups 3.11

Formatting initialization files

Windows initialization files are divided into sections that are made up of logical groups. Each section has the following format:

```
[section]
keyname=value
```

in which

- [section] is the section name. The brackets ([ ]) are required, and the left bracket must be in the leftmost column on-screen.

- keyname is the name of an entry, which can consist of any combination of letters and numbers. Most entries require that an equal sign (=) immediately follow the keyname.

- value is an integer, a string, or a quoted string, depending on the entry.

Some entries require a Boolean value. To enable an entry that requires a Boolean value, enter True, Yes, On, or 1. To disable such an entry, you can enter False, No, Off, or 0. Case doesn't matter.

You can include comments in the initialization files by placing a semicolon at the beginning of each line that holds part of a comment.

The order of the sections in an INI file is not important.

Editing INI files

All Windows initialization files follow the same structure. Windows stores the INI files in ASCII format so that you can edit them — just as you can edit the CONFIG.SYS or AUTOEXEC.BAT files.

Exercise extreme caution when editing any of Windows' start-up files; the slightest error can cause Windows to misbehave or crash. Also, do not use Windows Write or another word processor to edit INI files. It's too easy to forget to save the file as an ASCII file.

You can change entries in INI files in several ways:

- Use Program Manager, Control Panel, or File Manager to change entries with menu commands and dialog box options.

- Run Windows Setup again to change system settings, the keyboard or mouse configuration, or network options. Also run Setup again to add or remove printers and fonts.

- Use a text editor, such as Notepad, to edit the file directly.

- Choose a command, such as File⇨Printer Setup in Print Manager, and specify new options.

- Use WUGNET's System Engineer, included on the *Windows 3.1 Configuration SECRETS Disks.*

I recommend using System Engineer, which you can install from this book's companion disks. System Engineer gives Windows professionals a comprehensive set of tools to manage all aspects of Windows configuration on their workstations, whether they stand alone or on networks. System Engineer not only offers a powerful but easy-to-use interface for editing individual sections and statements within Windows configuration files, but also provides a complete librarian for storing, managing, and recovering multiple configurations. Changes to any and all INI files or entries are logged in a master file; as a result, you later can retrace all changes made to configuration files.

System Engineer backs up the WIN.COM, WIN.INI, and SYSTEM.INI files. When the backup option is turned on, System Engineer saves a backup copy of the INI files under the extension .BAK. After saving the backup copy, System Engineer saves the new file with any changes to the current INI file. ▣

Editing the INI source files

If you copy the Windows files to a network server by using the `SETUP /A` option, which installs a shared copy of Windows, Setup uses WIN.SRC, SYSTEM.SRC, and CONTROL.SRC to build WIN.INI, SYSTEM. INI, and CONTROL.INI when a user installs Windows on a workstation with `SETUP /N`. To create custom initialization files for multiple installations, you can change the SRC files.

Before you edit an SRC file, first save a backup copy of the original file. Save the new file with an SRC filename extension in the Windows directory on the network server. And, of course, test the new INI file on a single system before you install Windows on multiple systems.

Initialization file changes from Windows 3.0

If you update to Windows 3.1, Setup automatically updates the INI files (see the following sections). Setup leaves all other sections and entries in your existing WIN.INI and SYSTEM.INI unchanged when you upgrade to Windows 3.1.

Windows 3.1 upgrade changes made to the WIN.INI file

In the `[Windows]` section, Setup adds three new entries:

```
KeyboardDelay=
ScreenSaverTimeout=
DosPrint=
```

Windows 3.1 Setup does not alter any entries left over from the 3.0 version of WIN.INI. If the following entries are not present, Setup adds them:

```
device=
documents=
programs=com exe bat pif
```

In the `[extensions]` section, Setup adds

```
bmp=prush.exe ^.bmp
pcx=pbrush.exe ^.pcx
rec=recorder.exe ^.rec
```

In the [intl] section, Setup changes sLanguage=English (American) to sLanguage=enu.

In the [ports] section, Setup adds

```
LPT1.DOS
LPT2.DOS
```

If the following are not present in WIN.INI, Setup adds these three entries:

```
file:=
com3:=9600,n,8,1,x
com4:=9600,n,8,1,x
```

Setup adds [fontSubstitutes] and [TrueType] to support TrueType fonts. The default [fontSubstitutes] entries are

```
Helv=MS Sans Serif
Tms Rmn=MS Serif
Times=Times New Roman
Helvetica=Arial
```

Setup also adds the [mci extensions] section, with the following entries to support multimedia:

```
wav=waveaudio
mid=sequenccer
rmi=sequencer
```

Setup adds the [sound] section, with the following entries to support multimedia:

```
SystemDefault=ding.wav, Default Beep
SystemExclamation=chord.wav, Exclamation
SystemStart=tada.wav, Windows Start
SystemExit=chimes.wav, Windows Exit
SystemHand=chord.wav, Critical Stop
SystemQuestion=chord.wav, Question
SystemAsterisk=chord.wav, Asterisk
```

Setup also adds the [embedding] section, with the following entries to support object linking and embedding (OLE):

```
SoundRec=Sound,Sound,SoundRec.exe,picture
Package=Package,Package,packager.exe,picture
PBrush=Paintbrush Picture,Paintbrush Picture,pbrush.exe,picture
```

Changes made to the SYSTEM.INI file

In the [386Enh] section, Setup adds device= entries if it encounters Western Digital–compatible protected mode block devices in your system. Many other changes in communications and enhanced mode capabilities for Windows 3.1 have paved the way for new entries in the [386Enh] section.

[drivers], a new section, contains a list of aliases for installable drivers; [mci], another new section, lists the Media Control Interface drivers.

The Windows initialization file

The WIN.INI file contains several sections, each comprising a group of related entries you can use to customize the Windows environment. Your WIN.INI file may not have all these sections or it may have additional sections, depending on your system's hardware and software requirements.

With Windows 3.1, the size of WIN.INI is no longer limited to 32K. The WIN.INI file can now be as large as 64K. But keeping your WIN.INI file lean will help optimize performance, decrease Windows loading time, and possibly save you headaches that are caused by problems like corrupted font files.

The basic sections shown in Table 8-16 can appear in WIN.INI after you first install Windows.

Table 8-16	WIN.INI File Sections
Section	*Purpose*
[Windows]	Affects several elements of the Windows environment
[desktop]	Controls the appearance of the desktop and the position of windows and icons
[extensions]	Associates specified types of files with corresponding applications
[intl]	Describes how to display items for countries other than the United States
[ports]	Lists all available output ports
[fonts]	Describes the screen font files that are loaded by Windows
[fontSubstitutes]	Lists pairs of fonts that are recognized by Windows as interchangeable
[TrueType]	Describes options for using and displaying TrueType fonts
[mci extensions]	Associates specified types of files with Media Control Interface devices
[network]	Describes network settings and previous network connections
[embedding]	Lists the server objects used in OLE

(continued)

Table 8-16 *(continued)*

Section	Purpose
[Windows Help]	Lists settings used to specify the default size, placement, and text colors of the Help window and dialog boxes
[sound]	Lists the sound files assigned to each system event
[printerPorts]	Lists active and inactive output devices to be accessed by Windows
[devices]	Lists active output devices that provide compatibility with earlier versions of Windows applications
[programs]	Lists additional paths that Windows searches to find a program file when you try to open an associated data file
[colors]	Defines colors for the Windows display

The [Windows] section specifies Windows basic configuration

The [Windows] section contains entries that affect the following parts of the Windows environment:

- Applications that start when you start Windows
- Warning beep
- Printing
- Window border width
- Keyboard speed
- Mouse settings
- Definition of files as documents or programs

The system initialization file

When you install Windows, Setup creates the SYSTEM.INI file, which contains global system information that Windows uses when starting up. The sections listed in Table 8-17 can appear in SYSTEM.INI.

Table 8-17	SYSTEM.INI File Sections
Section	**Purpose**
`[boot]`	Lists drivers and Windows modules
`[boot.description]`	Lists the names of devices you can change by using Windows Setup
`[drivers]`	Contains a list of aliases (or names) assigned to installable driver files
`[keyboard]`	Contains information about the keyboard
`[mci]`	Lists Media Control Interface (MCI) drivers
`[NonWindowsApp]`	Contains information used by non-Windows applications
`[standard]`	Contains information used by Windows in standard mode
`[386Enh]`	Contains information used by Windows in 386 enhanced mode

Setup assigns a value to each entry in the `[boot]` and `[keyboard]` sections and to the `Device=` entry and its synonyms in the `[386Enh]` section. These entries must appear in SYSTEM.INI for Windows to function properly. These entries do not have built-in values but have specific values assigned by Setup when you install Windows.

You cannot change most SYSTEM.INI entries through Control Panel, but you can change many settings by running Setup. Other values in SYSTEM.INI can be changed only by opening the file and editing it with a text editor, such as Notepad, or by using System Engineer (included on the *Windows 3.1 Configuration SECRETS* disks).

Any changes you make to the SYSTEM.INI file do not take effect until you restart Windows.

The following sections describe the SYSTEM.INI file's contents and how to change values for entries in it.

[boot] section

The `[boot]` section lists the drivers and Windows modules that Windows uses to configure itself each time you start up.

Windows requires all the entries listed in this section. If you modify or delete any of these entries, Windows may not start or operate properly. Remember that Setup assigns these values based on your system configuration; there are no built-in values for these entries.

[boot.description] section

The [boot.description] section lists the strings used to describe the devices you can change when you run Setup. There is no reason to change these entries. If you do change their values, you cannot use Windows Setup to update drivers to newer versions.

[drivers] section

The [drivers] section contains a list of aliases (or names) assigned to installable driver files.

[keyboard] section

The [keyboard] section provides information about the keyboard. All entries in this section are required. If you modify or delete any of these entries, Windows will not operate properly. There are no built-in default values for these entries; Setup assigns values based on the system configuration.

[mci] section

The [mci] section lists the drivers that use the Media Control Interface (MCI) to play media files. These drivers are installed automatically when you run Setup.

[NonWindowsApp] section

The [NonWindowsApp] section contains entries that affect the performance of non-Windows applications.

[386Enh] section

The [386Enh] section has information specific to running Windows in 386 enhanced mode, including information used for virtual-memory page swapping. For entries that specify virtual devices, the value can appear as either the filename of a specific virtual device driver (with path if necessary) or an asterisk (*) followed immediately by the device name (refers to a virtual device that's built into the WIN386.EXE file).

The Program Manager initialization file

The Program Manager initialization file, PROGMAN.INI, usually has entries for [settings] and [groups], which describe what should appear in the Program Manager window when you run Program Manager. System administrators may choose to add a third section, [restrictions], for custom installations. See Chapter 7 for more information on restrictions.

Control Panel initialization file

The CONTROL.INI file contains sections that specify the options you set by choosing icons in Control Panel. These sections are listed in Table 8-18.

Table 8-18	CONTROL.INI File Sections
Section	**Values Specified**
[Current]	Specifies the current color scheme
[Color Schemes]	Defines the colors for each element of specific color schemes, as set by choosing the Color icon
[Custom Colors]	Defines the custom colors in the color palette, as set by choosing the Color icon
[Patterns]	Defines the color values for the bitmap patterns, as set by choosing the Desktop icon
[MMCPL]	Specifies values related to the multimedia items in Control Panel
[Screen Saver.*]	Specifies the density, warp speed, and password-protection values for the screen saver
[Userinstallable.drivers]	Specifies values related to installable drivers used for multimedia
[Drivers.Desc]	Specifies the MIDI Mapper and Time, the multimedia control devices
[Installed]	Specifies the current version of Windows and the installed printers

The File Manager initialization file

The WINFILE.INI file contains one section, [settings], which specifies the options you set by choosing menu commands in File Manager.

Network Protocol initialization file

The Windows for Workgroups Setup program builds a file called PROTOCOL.INI (located in the Windows directory), which defines the parameters used by the protocol and network adapter drivers supported by Windows for Workgroups. PROTOCOL.INI is created and modified by Setup based on information present in the NETWORK.INF information file or from an OEMSETUP.INF file (if used).

Do not modify the PROTOCOL.INI file by hand unless absolutely necessary. Windows for Workgroups relies on the format and configuration information present in PROTOCOL.INI to execute and install other network components. Inadvertent changes to PROTOCOL.INI may damage the integrity of the Windows for Workgroups environment. To update PROTOCOL.INI, you can change the entry without editing the PROTOCOL.INI file by using the Network icon on Control Panel.

The Protocol Manager (PROTMAN.DOS), used only by Windows for Workgroups 3.1, passes device drivers the information from the PROTOCOL.INI file. PROTOCOL.INI also contains network adapter configuration information, such as the input/output (I/O) address, direct memory access (DMA), and interrupts. The PROTOCOL.INI file contains sections for [network.setup] and [protman] as well as separate sections for each configured network adapter and network protocol.

Windows for Workgroups 3.11 does not use PROTMAN.DOS; it uses IFSHLP.SYS to pass information from the PROTOCOL.INI file.

The following initialization file descriptions are included for reference only. Complete coverage of these files is beyond the scope of this book.

Shared Mail Settings initialization file

The SHARED.INI file permits the sharing of Mail [Custom Commands] and [Custom Messages] with other Windows for Workgroup workstations. The SHARED.INI file and the associated custom commands and custom messages reside on the workgroup post office and are referenced in the MSMAIL.INI file by the SharedExtensionsDir= entry in the [Microsoft Mail] section.

Refer to Chapter 22 for more information concerning the relationship between MSMAIL.INI and SHARED.INI.

SHARED.INI can contain the sections listed in the following table.

Section	Purpose
[Custom Commands]	Specifies a custom command that can be installed in one of the Mail menus at runtime
[Custom Messages]	Specifies a custom message type that's installed into a Mail menu at runtime

Schedule+ initialization file

The SCHDPLUS.INI file is used to define settings used by Schedule+. Schedule+ uses the SCHDPLUS.INI file to track basic information about the user's schedule, such as display and general option settings, current window positions, and printer information. The SCHDPLUS.INI file contains the following sections:

Section	Definition
[Microsoft Schedule]	Defines the appearance and behavior of Schedule+
[Microsoft Schedule+ Appt Books]	Indicates the number and list of other users' Appointment Books that were open when you exited Schedule+
[Microsoft Schedule+ Archives]	Indicates the number and list of Archive files that were open when you exited Schedule+

Microsoft Mail initialization file

MSMAIL.INI is the Microsoft Mail initialization file used by the Mail application provided with Windows for Workgroups. MSMAIL.INI can contain the following sections:

Section	Purpose
[Address Book]	Specifies entries used by the Address Book support functions for the Mail program
[Custom Commands]	Specifies a custom command that can be installed in one of the Mail menus at runtime
[Custom Message]	Specifies a custom message type that's installed in a Mail menu at runtime
[Microsoft Mail]	Defines the configuration of the Mail program as well as the Microsoft Mail transport and name service
[MMF]	Affects the automatic compression of the Mail message file
[EFAX Transport]	Contains information about the state of the EFAX transport when Microsoft At Work fax messaging is installed. (Windows for Workgroups 3.11 only)

Microsoft At Work fax settings initialization file

EFAXPUMP.INI is the initialization file used by the Microsoft At Work fax components provided with Windows for Workgroups. EFAXPUMP.INI may contain the following sections:

Section	Purpose
[COMn]	Specifies the configuration for a fax modem on a given communications port
[EFAX Pump]	Specifies the configuration of the fax message mail pump to send outgoing fax messages
[Message]	Specifies the default values for the options used when sending a fax message
[Modem]	Specifies information for the fax modem to use when sending a fax message
[Network]	Specifies entries used for maintaining information about shared fax modems
[Received]	Contains temporary information about received faxes before they are turned into message attachments and placed in your mail inbox
[Security]	Specifies information about securing fax messages

Getting Rid of Excess Files

Windows ships with a huge number of files. You probably don't use all of Windows' components, especially if you're setting up Windows on a notebook computer. This section can help you tailor Windows' installation according to your computing needs or your system's capacity.

Under no circumstances should you ever delete any of these files while Windows is running. You must exit Windows and delete the files from the DOS command prompt.

Getting rid of the expanded memory manager

When Windows is not running, you can delete EMM386.EXE (expanded memory emulator) — as long as you don't need to provide EMM support for non-Windows applications.

Cleaning up temporary files

When Windows is not running, you can delete

- Any files in the TEMP directory
- Any files that start with the characters ~WOA or ~GRB

Deleting temporary swap files

When Windows is not running, you can delete WIN386.SWP (a temporary Windows swap file).

Do not delete files named 386SPART.PAR or SPART.PAR. These files represent permanent swap files and should not be removed manually. (Use System Engineer or Control Panel to resize or remove the permanent swap file.)

Removing unused components with setup

Choose the Windows Setup icon in Control Panel and then Options⇨Add/Remove Components to remove

- Games
- Screen savers
- Wallpapers (BMP files) and sound files (WAV files)
- Any accessories you do not use (such as Paintbrush, Write, Calendar, Cardfile) along with their related HLP and DLL files

Checking your hard disk for duplicate files

Windows and MS-DOS install different versions of the same programs. Check your hard disk for

- Smartdrive
- MSD
- HIMEM.SYS
- RAMDRIVE
- EMM386

- Unnecessary PIFs
- Help files
- Unnecessary TTF and FOT files

Summary

Windows installs almost 400 files during the installation process. Obviously, Windows is the product of numerous software components.

▶ In this chapter, I described the contents of a Windows installation.

▶ With the information in this chapter, you can determine which file types make Windows operate, determine which files are critical to your Windows' installation and which may be deleted.

▶ You now understand how Windows uses the initialization files that control the environment.

Part III
Configuring

In This Part

Chapter 9
Basic Windows Configuration

In This Chapter
▶ Choosing applications to start automatically
▶ Changing the way Windows looks
▶ Associating documents with applications
▶ Configuring the screen saver
▶ Protecting your Windows session with a password

As a personal computing environment, Windows enables users to make the environment truly their own. It offers bitmapped wallpaper, icons, fonts, colors, sounds, and a host of other customizeable attributes that users can combine and rearrange according to their personal tastes.

Windows stores settings in the WIN.INI file that affect the Windows environment. This chapter is concerned with the settings that control parts of Windows that reflect personal preference.

Most of these settings can be set by one of the applets in Control Panel, in addition to editing the WIN.INI file.

 Chapter 15 covers settings for the keyboard and mouse, and Chapter 16 covers printer configuration.

Configuring the [Windows] Section of the WIN.INI File

The settings in the [Windows] section of WIN.INI control details of Windows operation.

Activating the screen saver

If this setting is set to 1, Windows displays a screen saver when Windows is not actively being used, and the timeout specified by the ScreenSaveTimeOut= setting has elapsed.

Setting: ScreenSaveActive=0 | 1

Default: 0

Setting the screen saver timeout value

When the system is idle for the amount of time specified by this setting, Windows will start the screen saver (if active).

Setting: ScreenSaveTimeOut=seconds

Default: 120

You can create an icon for your favorite screen saver and assign it a hot key for launching. First create a file association in the WIN.INI Programs= line. Add the extension SCR to the line. Exit from the WIN.INI file and restart Windows so that the change takes effect. Next, select a group window in which to place the icon. Choose File ⇨ New from Program Manager's menu. Enter the name of the desired screen saver in the command-line box. If you want the screen saver to activate as soon as you select its icon, add /S to the command line. Then choose an icon to represent the screen saver. Choose OK until you're back to the group window. Double-click the screen-saver icon to launch the screen-saver program. (You can also assign a hot key to the screen saver so that you can quickly activate it when running an application.)

Making a Windows screen saver secure

If the majority of your time is spent in Windows, enable the password protection of the Windows 3.1 screen saver to protect your network files when you're away from your desk or office. In the Windows Control Panel, double-click the Desktop icon to bring up the Desktop dialog box; select the Setup button under Screen Saver. Click the box labeled Password Protected and then click the Set Password button. Passwords can be up to 20 characters long, including punctuation. (Norton Desktop for Windows also provides a screen-saver password and can automatically use your network password as the screen-saver password.) If your screen saver's password protection is enabled, your network files can't be accessed or altered by others. Although an intruder could reboot your machine and sabotage files on your local drive, at least nothing on the network could be changed. Consider setting your screen-saver password to be the same as your network password to reduce the number of passwords you have to remember.

 If you forget your password, edit the CONTROL.INI file, and delete the `Pass-word=` in the `[ScreenSaver]` section. You will still get a password prompt when Windows starts up, but your password will be blank.

Setting the Windows warning beep

When this setting is set to `Yes`, Windows sounds a warning beep if you try to do something that is not allowed.

Setting: `Beep=Yes | No`

Default: `Yes`

Specifying window border width

The width of the borders around all of the windows that have sizeable borders is specified by this setting. This setting can range between 1 and 49.

Setting: `BorderWidth=pixels`

Default: 3

Enabling Alt+Tab fast switching

This setting turns fast task switching on or off. Fast task switching allows the user to switch among the running applications by pressing Alt+Tab. Windows displays the application's icon and title bar text in a box, enabling users to quickly choose the applications they wish to switch to. The default is 1.

Setting: `CoolSwitch=0 | 1`

Default: 1

Controlling the cursor-blink rate

This setting indicates how much time, in milliseconds, elapses between each blink of the selection cursor. The default is 530.

Setting: CursorBlinkRate=*milliseconds*

Default: 530

Identifying document files

Windows considers files that have an extension listed in this setting to be documents. The extensions listed in this setting should not be listed in the [extensions] setting of WIN.INI.

Setting: Documents=*extensions*

Default: Blank

Identifying program files

This setting defines which files Windows regards as applications. The default values are COM, EXE, BAT, and PIF. See the discussion of screen savers earlier in this chapter for a common reason to add an extension to this setting.

Setting: Programs=*extensions*

Default: COM EXE BAT PIF

 Separate the filename extensions with a space and do not include the preceding periods.

Loading a program as an icon

This setting specifies the applications to be run as icons when Windows is started. This setting is a list of application filenames or documents associated with an application. Filenames are separated by spaces. The default is none.

Setting: Load=*filename(s)*

Default: None

Be sure that you specify the path if the file is not located in the Windows directory.

This setting should be located either just before, or just after, the Run= line in WIN.INI for clarity. Use these settings to load programs that must be running at the very start of Windows, such as anti-virus utilities. Use the Program Manager Startup group to load normal applications that you want to be running when you start Windows.

Configuring Windows menus

When this setting is set to 0, menus open so that they are left-aligned with the menu title. Setting this setting to 1 causes menu items to be right-aligned with the menu title.

Setting: `MenuDropAlignment=0 | 1`

Default: 0

Setting menu delay

This setting controls how long Windows waits before displaying a cascading menu.

Setting: `MenuShowDelay=milliseconds`

Default: 0 (on 80386 based computers), 400 (80286 based computers)

Running applications on start-up

This setting tells Windows to run the specified applications when Windows is started. The value of `filename(s)` is a list of application filenames or documents associated with applications. Filenames are separated by spaces. See the description of the `Load=` setting earlier in this chapter for some tips about this setting. The default is none.

Setting: `Run=filename(s)`

Default: None

Be sure that you specify the complete path if the file is not in the Windows directory.

The [desktop] Section

The settings in the [desktop] control the appearance of the screen background and the position of windows and icons on-screen.

 Before changing any of the settings in this section, make a note of the setting's original value so that you can easily change it back if you need to. Many of the settings in this section can make the display difficult to read if set incorrectly.

Setting the invisible grid

When this setting is set to a nonzero value, Windows positions windows on the screen aligned with a grid. The value of this setting is a number between 0 and 49. The number represents eight pixel units on the screen.

Setting: GridGranularity=*number*

Default: 0

Setting horizontal spacing between icons

This setting controls the number of pixels that appear horizontally between icons on the screen.

Setting: IconSpacing=*pixels*

Default: 77

 Set this value with care! An inappropriate value may cause display problems. For example, setting this value too low can cause icons to overlap on the screen.

Specifying icon-title fonts

This setting specifies the name of the font used to display icon titles.

Setting: IconTitleFaceName=*fontname*

Default: MS SansSerif

Any of the fonts listed in the [Fonts] section of WIN.INI can be used.

Set this value with care! Your choice of font may require you to change the IconSpacing= setting to avoid overlapping icons.

Setting icon-title font size

This setting specifies the size of the font Windows uses to display icon titles. If you change this setting, you may need to adjust the IconSpacing= setting to avoid overlap.

Setting: IconTitleSize=*number*

Default: 8

Making icon titles wrap

If this entry is set to 1, icon titles will wordwrap. The icon vertical spacing will automatically be increased if this option is set to 1.

Setting: IconTitleWrap=*0* | *1*

Default: 1

Specifying vertical spacing between icons

This setting controls the vertical spacing (measured in pixels) vertically between icons.

Setting: IconVerticalSpacing=*pixels*

Default: Varies according to font and display driver

Specifying a pattern for the screen background

This entry specifies the pattern used for the screen background. The eight values are decimal equivalents of the binary representation of an 8 pixel wide, 8 pixel high bitmap. In the binary representation, 0 means that the pixel is set to the background color; 1 means set to the foreground color. (Colors are specified in the [colors] section of WIN.INI.)

Setting: Pattern=*b1 b2 b3 b4 b5 b6 b7 b8*

Default: None

Tiling wallpaper

When set to 1, the wallpaper is tiled across the screen. If set to 0, the wallpaper is centered.

Setting: `TileWallpaper=0 | 1`

Default: 0

Do you want to shift your centered wallpaper off-center? Try the following lines:

Setting: `WallPaperOriginX= offset`

Setting: `WallPaperOriginY= offset`

Default: Line not present

These two settings provide an offset to begin either displaying a centered image at a position other than dead center, or to begin tiling at some position other than the top left corner of the screen. Add these lines to the `[desktop]` section. The `offset` value is given in pixels. You need to experiment to find the best values.

Specifying a bitmap as wallpaper

This setting specifies the filename of the bitmap that is used as the Windows wallpaper (screen background). It is necessary to include the pathname if the file does not reside in the Windows directory.

Setting: `Wallpaper=bitmap-filename`

Default: None

The [colors] Section

The `[colors]` section defines the colors for components of the Windows display. To change these entries, choose the Color icon from the Control Panel. This section can contain entries in the following format:

`component=red-value green-value blue-value`

The *component* can be any one of the keynames listed in Table 9-1. The *red-value*, *blue-value*, and *green-value* options are integers that specify the relative intensities of the respective colors. These values can range from 0 (minimum intensity) to 255 (maximum intensity).

The actual screen results depend on your video card and monitor.

Table 9-1	The Components of the Windows Display
Keyname	*Description*
ActiveBorder	The border of the active window
ActiveTitle	The title bar of the active window
AppWorkspace	The application workspace for Windows applications
Background	Refers to the desktop
ButtonFace	The face of dialog box and toolbar buttons
ButtonShadow	The darkened area (shadow) that gives buttons a three-dimensional appearance
ButtonText	Text that appears on a button
GrayText	Text that is dimmed, as in an unavailable command name
Hilight	The background of highlighted text
HilightText	The highlighted text itself
InactiveBorder	The border of an inactive window
InactiveTitle	The title bar of an inactive window
InactiveTitleText	Text in an inactive title bar
Menu	The background of menus
MenuText	Text that makes up the menu options
Scrollbar	The bars that appear at the side or bottom of a window to enable you to scroll through its contents
TitleText	The text in the title bar
Window	The workspace in a window
WindowFrame	The border of a window
WindowText	Text within a window

The [Windows Help] Section

The [Windows Help] section includes settings that specify the size and placement of the Help window and dialog boxes. In addition, you can change the color of text that, when chosen, displays a macro, pop-up window, or new Help window.

Specifying the color of text that leads to a new Help window

This setting controls the color of text that when chosen, causes a hypertext jump to a new window of Help information. The following example indicates black text:

    JumpColor=000 000 000

Setting: JumpColor=*red-value green-value blue-value*

Default: 0,128,0   (green)

The default values for the *red-value, green-value*, and *blue-value* options are 0,128,0. To change this setting, use Notepad to edit the WIN.INI file.

 If no PopupColor value is specified (as described in the following section), the JumpColor setting also applies to text that, when chosen, displays a pop-up window.

Specifying the color of text that leads to a pop-up window

This setting controls the color of text that, when chosen, causes a pop-up window to appear (usually used for glossary definitions).

Setting: PopupColor=*red-value green-value blue-value*

Default: Color specified in JumpColor setting

Specifying the color of text that runs a Help macro

Ths setting sets the color of text that runs a Help macro when chosen.

Setting: MacroColor=*red-value green-value blue-value*

Default: Color set by JumpColor setting

Specifying the color of text that leads to help from a different Help file

This setting sets the color of text that leads to a new Help window that is located in a different Help file.

Setting: `IFJumpColor=red-value green-value blue-value`

Default: Color set by `JumpColor` setting

Specifying the color of text that leads to a pop-up window from a different Help file

This setting controls the color of text that displays a pop-up window that is actually located in a different help file.

Setting: `IFPopupColor=red-value green-value blue-value`

Showing Your Best Colors

Perhaps you have designed the perfect Windows color scheme — and want to make it your company standard. Or maybe you've the colors optimized for laptop use. You can easily distribute your customized color scheme to other Windows users. First, save the color scheme by doing the following: From Control Panel's Color applet, check whether there's a name in the Color Schemes box. If not, click the Color Palette button, click Save Scheme, and enter a name. Then click OK and exit the Control Panel. Use Notepad to open CONTROL.INI from your Windows subdirectory. In the [color schemes] section, find the line that begins with the name of your color scheme and select it along with the lines of any other color schemes you want to share. Then copy and paste the lines into a new text file. Distribute the text file to others so they can use Notepad to copy the lines from this file and paste them into the [color schemes] sections of their CONTROL.INI files. After they save their changes, the new color schemes appear in the Color Schemes box.

Summary

In this chapter, I showed how to configure the personal preference settings in Windows.

▶ I showed how to configure the screen saver.

▶ I showed how to set desktop preferences.

▶ I showed how to set screen colors.

Chapter 10
Configuring Windows Applets

In This Chapter

▶ How to control Program Manager with PROGMAN.INI settings

▶ How to configure and customize Control Panel applets

▶ Adding features to File Manager through DLLs

▶ How to customize File Manager through CONTROL.INI settings

▶ Implementing drag and drop with Program Manager and File Manager

PROGMAN.INI: The Program Manager Initialization File

The Program Manager initialization file, PROGMAN.INI, usually has entries for [settings] and [groups], which describe what should appear in the Program Manager window when you run Program Manager.

A system administrator may also add a third section, [restrictions], for custom installations.

The [settings] section usually has the following entries, which are explained in Table 10-1:

```
[Settings]
Window=60 28 565 388 1
SaveSettings=1
MinOnRun=0
AutoArrange=1
Startup=
```

Table 10-1	The [settings] section of PROGMAN.INI
Entry	**Value**
Window=	Four numbers that indicate the position of the window when you open Program Manager, followed by a 1 if the window is maximized.
SaveSettings=	1 if the Save Settings On Exit option on the Options menu is checked in Program Manager. If so, Program Manager saves the current configuration when you close Windows.
MinOnRun=	1 if the Minimize On Use option is checked on the Options menu in Program Manager. If so, the Program Manager is iconized when you run another application.
AutoArrange=	1 if the AutoArrange option is checked on the Options menu in Program Manager. In this case, the icons in each group are automatically arranged when you run Program Manager.
Startup=	Name of the group that serves as the start-up group. If this entry is blank, the Startup group created in Windows Setup is the start-up group.

The PROGMAN.INI file also has a [groups] section name, which has entries such as the following (described in Table 10-2):

```
[Groups]
Group1=C:\WINDOWS\ACCESSOR.GRP
Group2=C:\WINDOWS\GAMES.GRP
Group3=C:\WINDOWS\ALDUS.GRP
Group5=C:\WINDOWS\WORDFORW.GRP
Group6=C:\WINDOWS\MAIN.GRP
Group7=C:\WINDOWS\STARTUP.GRP
Order= 8 7 2 3 5 1 6
Group8=C:\WINDOWS\APPLICAT.GRP
```

Table 10-2	The [groups] section of PROGMAN.INI
Entry	**Value**
Groupx=	A filename (with full path) for the .GRP file that contains the group created during Setup, created when an application was installed, or that you created in Program Manager.
Order=	A list of numbers separated with spaces, indicating the order in which the groups are drawn in the window.

To change these settings, use the commands on the Program Manager menu.

For network system administration, you can also add a [restrictions] section to PROGMAN.INI to restrict user actions. See Chapters 7 and 18 for more on configuring Windows and networks. The [restrictions] section can have the following entries, which are described in Table 10-3:

```
[restrictions]
NoRun=
NoClose=
NoSaveSettings=
NoFileMenu=
EditLevel=
Entry     Value
```

Table 10-3	The [restrictions] section of PROGMAN.INI
Entry	**Value**
NoRun=	1 disables the Run command on the File menu. The Run command is dimmed on the File menu, and you cannot run applications from Program Manager unless the applications are set up as icons in a section of the PROGMAN.INI file.
NoFileMenu=	1 removes the File menu from Program Manager. All the commands on that menu are unavailable. Users can start the applications in groups by selecting them and pressing Enter or by double-clicking on the icon. Unless you also disable the Exit Windows command, users can still quit Windows by using the Control menu or Alt+F4.
EditLevel=n	Sets restrictions for what users can modify in Program Manager. You can specify one of the following values for n:
	0 allows the user to make any change. (This is the default.)
	1 prevents the user from creating, deleting, or renaming groups. If you specify this value, the New, Move, Copy, and Delete commands on the File menu are not available when a group is selected.
	2 sets all restrictions in EditLevel=1 and prevents the user from creating or deleting program items. If you specify this value, the New, Move, Copy, and Delete commands on the File menu are not available.
	3 sets all restrictions in EditLevel=2 and prevents the user from changing command lines for program items. If you specify this value, the text in the Command Line box in the Properties dialog box cannot be changed.
	4 sets all restrictions in EditLevel=3, plus prevents the user from changing any program item information. If you specify this value, none of the areas in the Properties dialog box can be modified. The user can view the dialog box, but all areas are dimmed.

To enable any of the commands or remove any of the EditLevel= restrictions, remove the entry from the PROGMAN.INI file or set the value to 0.

The Windows Control Panel

The applet you know as the Control Panel, which you use to change colors and to modify hardware settings, is also an interface to program extensions that enable you to control device drivers. Control Panel extensions provide hardware vendors with an easy way to turn control of their specific device drivers over to the end user.

Control Panel extensions are written as add-ins in the form of DLLs with the special extension CPL. When you double-click the Control Panel icon, it loads the CPL files that contain the code for each icon that appears in the Control Panel client area. CONTROL.EXE is actually the launch pad for each of the applets.

When you launch the Control Panel, it begins to populate its window with icons from the available CP extensions. To find these available CP extensions, it loads MAIN.CPL and adds an icon for each applet in the file. Next it loads any installed drivers. Finally, it searches the [MMCPL] section of CONTROL.INI for additonal files that have the CPL extension. (The specific CONTROL.INI file sections and entries are discussed in the next section.)

After you load all the entries in the [MMCPL] section, Control Panel looks for files with the CPL extension in the Windows/System directory. With all the extensions loaded in the client window area, Control Panel waits for you to interact with it, like every other Windows application.

You can automatically load any Control Panel extension by placing its file in the Windows/System directory and then starting Control Panel.

CONTROL.INI: The Control Panel Initialization File

CONTROL.INI has several sections, described in Table 10-4, that specify the options you set by choosing icons in Control Panel.

Table 10-4	CONTROL.INI Sections
Section	*Values specified*
[Current]	Specifies the current color scheme
[Color Schemes]	Defines the colors for each element of specific color schemes, by choosing the Color icon
[Custom Colors]	Defines the custom colors in the color palette, by choosing the Color icon
[Patterns]	Defines the color values for the bitmap patterns, by choosing the Desktop icon
[MMCPL]	Specifies values related to the multimedia items in the Control Panel (see the [MCCPL] settings at the end of this section)
[Screen Saver.*]	Specifies the density, warp speed, and password-protection and any other values you can set for the screen saver
[Userinstallable.drivers]	Specifies values related to installable drivers used for multimedia
[Drivers.Desc]	Specifies the MIDI Mapper and Timer, the multimedia control devices
[Installed]	Specifies the current version of Microsoft Windows and the installed printers

Typical settings in the [MMCPL] section include the following:

```
[MMCPL]
NumApps=15
X=44
Y=44
W=430
H=240
newhotapplet=d:/hotstuff/applet.cpl
End icon secret[drivers.desc]
mciwave.drv=[MCI] Sound
mciseq.drv=[MCI] MIDI Sequencer
timer.drv=Timer
midimap.drv=MIDI Mapper
[InsOuts]
SC1=1
CC1=1
SC2=1
CC2=13
```

```
SC3=1
SC5=1
CC5=1
SC6=1
SC8=1
SC9=1
CC9=5
SC10=1
SC11=1
SC12=1
CC12=10
SC13=1
CC13=3
SC14=1
SC15=1
SC16=1
SC17=1
SC18=1
SO1=1
CO1=5
SO2=1
SO3=1
CO3=3
CO4=14
SO5=1
SO6=1
SO7=1
SO8=1
SO9=1
CO9=15
SO10=1
SO11=1
SO12=1
[installed]
3.1=yes
HPPCL.DRV=yes
FINSTALL.DLL=yes
FINSTALL.HLP=yes
BP1CP2.PCM=yes
DD1CP1.PCM=yes
PANSON24.DRV=yes
DMCOLOR.DLL=yes
```

The X and Y values indicate the position of the Control Panel window and the W and H values indicate its width and height.

The NumApps= line in the [MMCPL] section of CONTROL.INI indicates the number of applets that the Control Panel loaded during its last run. The Control Panel compares this number with the number of applets loaded during each start-up, and if it finds a difference in the count, it resizes the client window so that all icons are visible.

If you want the Control Panel to load an applet that is not located in the Windows/System directory, add a line (usually at the end of the file) that specifies the name and path to the file such as the following:

```
newhotapplet=d:/hotstuff/applet.cpl
```

The [MMCPL] section of the CONTROL.INI file has information that concerns the size and placement of the Control Panel window, the number of iconized applications in the Control Panel, and a path setting for multimedia CPL files residing outside of the Windows System subdirectory. The settings are described in Table 10-5.

Table 10-5	The [MMCPL] Section of CONTROL.INI
Setting	*Description*
x=<number>	Horizontal window coordinate
y=<number>	Vertical window coordinate
h=<number>	Height in pixels
w=<number>	Width in pixels
numapps=<number>	The number of applications in the Control Panel

In addition, Microsoft Windows for Pen Computing might add the following lines to the [MMCPL] file:

```
cppen=c:\windows\cppen.cpl
cphw=c:\windows\cphw.cpl
cprot=c:\windows\cprot.cpl
cpcal=c:\windows\cpcal.cpl
```

These entries allow the Control Panel to find CPL files in subdirectories other than the Windows System subdirectory.

Customizing Icon Displays in the Control Panel

In an earlier section, I described how the Control Panel initializes itself. The Control Panel dynamically loads specific icons based on the equipment installed on your system and the configuration of Windows. For example, the Network icon appears in the Control Panel only if you configure Windows to access a network. Likewise, Control Panel displays the 386 Enhanced icon only when you run Windows in 386 enhanced mode.

You can use the dynamic loading capabilities of the Control Panel to selectively disable any of its icons. If you share a computer with others or want to prevent users from altering certain aspects of the system through Control Panel, you can prevent Control Panel from loading specific components.

When you launch the Control Panel, it reads the settings in its INI (initialization) file, CONTROL.INI, to determine how to configure itself. To configure the Control Panel to disable a specific icon, you add the undocumented section heading [Don't Load] to the CONTROL.INI file. Under this section heading, you add the name of the icon you don't want the Control Panel to display, as in the following line:

```
[Don't Load] Desktop=1
```

If you install Windows on a network, you can restrict which Control Panel functions users have access to by modifying CONTROL.SRC, the master file for CONTROL.INI. After you copy the Windows files to the network server using the SETUP/A option, locate CONTROL.SRC. Add a section called [Don't Load] and list the modules of the Control Panel that you don't want accessible to users. For example, if you want to preserve the look of a standard desktop or if you don't want users to change printers, you could exclude the Desktop and Printers sections.

Description of CPL files

You can add additional icons and functionality to the Control Panel in Windows 3.1 (and to Microsoft Multimedia Extensions for Windows Version 1.0) by adding installable CPL files. These CPL files must be located in the Windows System directory, or the corresponding icon does not appear in the Control Panel. However, you can reference multimedia CPL files in another directory by specifying a new path in the [MMCPL] section of the CONTROL.INI file.

Replacing Control Panel icons

When you run the Control Panel in Windows 3.1, some of the icons may not display if the corresponding .CPL file is corrupt or missing. To correct this problem, you must expand the files from the Windows disks back to the Windows System directory. For example, if you do not install your network properly, the network icon does not display.

Use the following steps to add a missing Control Panel icon:

1. Exit Windows.

2. Copy EXPAND.EXE from the Windows installation disk 3 into your Windows directory.

3. Now put the Windows 3.1 disk with the correct *.CP_ file in your floppy disk drive. Table 10-6 tells you which Windows 3.1 disk to use for the *.CPL files, depending on the disk size you have.

4. Type the following at the MS-DOS command prompt, where *xxxxx* is the name of the file and drive A is the drive containing the floppy disk with the CPL files:

   expand A:*xxxxx*.CP_ C:\\WINDOWS\\SYSTEM

5. Reopen the Control Panel. You do not need to exit Windows because the Control Panel searches for CPL files each time it initializes.

Now put the Windows 3.1 disk with the correct *.CP_ file in your floppy disk drive. Table 10-6 tells you which Windows 3.1 disk to use for the *.CPL files, depending on the disk size you have.

Table 10-6	CPL Files on your Windows 3.1 Disks	
Filename	*3½ Inch Disk*	*5¼ Inch Disk*
CPWIN386.CP_	Disk 1	Disk 1
DRIVERS.CP_	Disk 4	Disk 5
MAIN.CP_	Disk 4	Disk 5
SND.CP_	Disk 4	Disk 6

Default CPL files shipped with Windows 3.1

Windows 3.1 ships with the four installable Control Panel objects described in Table 10-7.

Table 10-7		Installable Control Panel objects		
Compressed Name	**Compressed Size**	**Expanded Name**	**Expanded Size**	**Icon**
CPWIN386.CP_	48841	CPWIN386.CPL	104816	Control Panel's 386 Enhanced mode icon
DRIVERS.CP_	21385	DRIVERS.CPL	41440	Control Panel's Drivers icon for installing and removing Multimedia drivers
MAIN.CP_	89396	MAIN.CPL	148560	Control Panel's Color, Fonts, Ports, Mouse, Desktop, Keyboard, Printers, International Date/Time, Network (if installed) icons
SND.CP_	4986	SND.CPL	8192	Control Panel's Sound icon, which enables you to assign sounds to many system events

The Windows Driver Library disks include an additional .CPL file, SBPMIXER.CPL, (file size 25792, dated 2/1/92) for computers with Creative Labs SoundBlaster Pro sound cards. This icon is an audio-mixing board for the SoundBlaster Pro.

Using a CPL file icon for a program icon

With Windows 3.1, most icons embedded in earlier versions of the CONTROL.EXE file now reside in associated data files located in the System subdirectory. These files include CPWIN386.CPL, DRIVERS.CPL, MAIN.CPL, and SOUND.CPL. To use one of the icons placed in the CPL files for a program item in Windows 3.1, do the following:

1. In Program Manager, select the program item whose icon you want to change.

2. From the File menu, choose Properties to open the Program Item Properties dialog box.

3. Click the Change Icon button.

4. Enter the appropriate CPL filename in the File Name box and then click OK.

GP faults in the Control Panel

If you experience general protection (GP) faults when you open the Control Panel, one of the CPL files is probably corrupted or damaged. Refer to the section on replacing CPL icons for instructions on how to replace a CPL file.

Accessing the Control Panel from the command line

You can spend a great deal of time hunting for program groups. Rather than hunt for the Control Panel group, use Program Manager's command line. Choose File, Run, and enter **CONTROL DESKTOP** in the Command line box to go straight to the Desktop section of the Control Panel. After you make your changes, click OK (or Cancel) to return to the Program Manager. You can quickly get to any of the Control Panel items by specifying the item's title in the command line. For example, type **CONTROL COLOR** for a quick adjustment of your Windows color scheme. Don't worry about mistyping the item's name. Program Manager automatically moves you to the Control Panel's opening menu.

When you exit a Control Panel applet, you also exit Control Panel itself.

The File Manager

Microsoft revamped the Windows File Manager for Windows 3.1 and Windows for Workgroups 3.1x with major improvements in usability and performance. File Manager includes quick format capability, which enables you to format floppy disks in much less time than before, and supports an easier, more intuitive drag-and-drop model for manipulating files.

This section covers just a few of the known enhancements. There are other undocumented features that go untapped by many end users.

Extending the Windows File Manager

Both File Manager in Microsoft Windows 3.1 and File Manager in Microsoft Windows for Workgroups 3.1 support add-on extensions.

Extensions are special dynamic-link libraries (DLLs) that you can add to the Windows 3.1 File Manager menu or the Windows for Workgroups File Manager toolbar. To install an extension, edit the WINFILE.INI file based on the example listed below. The .DLL files normally reside in the \Windows\System subdirectory.

To integrate Mail and File Manager utilities with File Manager, add the `ADDONS=` entry in the `[SETTINGS]` section of the WINFILE.INI. In addition, add a section called `[ADDONS]` and the appropriate extensions to the WINFILE.INI, as follows:

```
[Settings]
Addons=Mail,FMUtils
:
:
[Addons]
Mail Extensions=C:\WINDOWS\SYSTEM\SENDFILE.DLL
FMUtils Extensions=C:\WINDOWS\SYSTEM\FMUTILS.DLL
```

If File Manager cannot load or set up an extension, no error message appears and File Manager removes the extension from the toolbar or menu.

These entries provide additional options on the File Manager menu or toolbar, depending on the version of Windows you use.

The maximum number of DLLs that you can add to File Manager is six; however, one of those DLLs must be the Undelete feature. If you do not add Undelete, the maximum number of DLLs is five.

WizManager, a program included on the *Windows 3.1 Configuration SECRETS Disks*, is an excellent example of using File Manager extensions to enhance File Manager's native capabilities. I encourage you to install WizManager and work with it.

WINFILE.INI: The File Manager Initialization File

The WINFILE.INI file has one section, `[settings]`, that you can use to specify the options you can set by choosing menu commands in File Manager. For example, these settings, explained in Table 10-8, may appear in WINFILE.INI:

```
[Settings]
Window=0,6,800,600, , ,1
dir1=48,7,543,236,-1,-1,3,30,201,1808,150,B:\*.*
Face=Small Fonts
Size=8
LowerCase=1
ConfirmDelete=0
ConfirmSubDel=0
ConfirmReplace=1
ConfirmMouse=1
ConfirmFormat=1
```

Table 10-8	The [settings] section of the WINFILE.INI
Entry	*Option or Value*
Window=	The size and position of the window and whether it is maximized when opened
dir1=	The current directory settings
Face=	The name of the typeface used for desktop items (default is Small Fonts)
Size=	The point size for the typeface (default is 8)
LowerCase=	1 for filenames to appear in lowercase
ConfirmDelete=	1 to prompt the user to confirm file deletion requests
ConfirmSubDel=	1 to prompt the user to confirm subdirectory deletion requests
ConfirmReplace=	1 to prompt the user to confirm file replacement requests
ConfirmMouse=	1 to prompt the user to confirm mouse drag-and-drop requests
ConfirmFormat=	1 to prompt the user to confirm formatting requests

General File Manager Tips

This section contains some general tips that don't have anything to do with configuration per se, but are meant to help you navigate more easily in File Manager and to take full advantage of its features.

Viewing drives in File Manager

To display the contents of more than one drive or directory at once in the new File Manager, double-click the Drive icon to open an additional window for that drive and select the Tile command from the Windows menu.

Customizing fonts in File Manager

To customize the fonts used to display information in a File Manager window, select Font from the Option menu. This opens a dialog box that lists your font display options.

Rearranging directories in File Manager

Drag a directory from File Manager and drop it elsewhere in File Manager. You can make directories into subdirectories by just dropping them in the directory under which you want them to be.

Vertically tiling File Manager windows

By default, Windows tiles the windows in File Manager horizontally. To tile them vertically, hold down the Shift key while you select Window ⇨ Tile.

Selecting contiguous files

To select a block of contiguous files, click the first (or last) file and then hold down the Shift key while clicking the file at the other end of the range.

Moving or copying

If you drag and drop to copy files in File Manager, you often end up moving them instead. This happens because the default setting is to move any file that is dragged onto or within the same drive. To gain control, press Ctrl before and while you drag files when you want to copy (C for copy) and press Alt before and while you drag files to move the file.

Selecting noncontiguous files

To select noncontiguous files in File Manager, click the first file and then press Ctrl while you click any other noncontiguous files.

Implementing Drag and Drop

Drag and drop is referred to as *direct manipulation,* the act of moving an object from one location to another. The object is dragged with the mouse and dropped into the new location. Program Manager and File Manager are just two examples of programs that use or support drag-and-drop features. For example, with File Manager, you can use drag and drop to move files between directories on the same or different disk. Drag and drop can also be interpreted as a copy or link operation, if the context makes those operations more appropriate than a move. For example, in the File Manager, dragging a file icon to a directory on a different disk causes the file to be copied rather than moved. Dropping a file icon from the File Manager into the Program Manager creates a link in the Program Manager. When more than one interpretation of drag and drop is possible for a given context, the application usually provides a way to override the default interpretation by using the Shift or Ctrl keys in conjunction with dragging.

There are other ways to use drag-and-drop features. For example, dragging a file from File Manager onto the Print Manager icon or another Windows application icon, sets up a reaction by the target program. This kind of drag and drop is interpreted as using the drop target to process the item that was dropped. Therefore, dropping a document icon on the minimized Print Manager tells it to print the document. In the File Manager, if you drop a document icon on the associated application icon, this action tells the target application to open with the document ready for editing. Dropping a document icon onto any nondocument area of an open application window, such as on the title bar, menu bar, status bar, application workspace in a multiple-document interface (MDI) application, and so on, is the same as if you had dropped it onto the application's icon.

There is another twist to this drag-and-drop scenario. If you drop a document icon into the document area of an open application window (that is, the text area of Word for Windows), the dropped document is copied (embedded) into the open document and displayed as an icon. The application must support object embedding.

Experiment with These Drag-and-Drop Operations

Using File Manager, drag a document icon into an open document. If the target application supports embedding, the document appears as an icon. What actually happens is that the file represented by the document is encapsulated in a package that in turn is embedded into the open document. As far as the user is concerned, the iconic document simply appears to have been embedded into the open document.

Drag a document icon into the nondocument area of an open application window (for example, title bar, menu bar, status bar, MDI application workspace). If a dropped document is readable by an application, the application opens the document within an application window.

Drag a program or document icon into a Program Manager group window (open or closed) to create a program item in Program Manager that points to the file.

Summary

This chapter presented techniques for configuring and customizing Program Manager, Control Panel, and File Manager. I dicussed the following points:

▶ How to control and maintain Program Manager's settings.

▶ Adding enhancements to File Manager using program extensions.

▶ How to configure and customize the Control Panel.

▶ How to restrict access to Control Panel applets.

▶ How to install missing Control Panel applets.

▶ How Progam Manager and File Manager implement and use drag and drop.

▶ Tips for using Program Manager and File Manager.

Chapter 11
Windows Memory Configuration Secrets

This chapter provides tips and secrets for configuring memory for Windows in standard and enhanced modes and strategies to use in optimizing performance. First, I'll give an overview of Windows memory management, then describe procedures for diagnosing and troubleshooting memory related problems. The chapter finishes with detailed descriptions of the Windows initialization file settings and recommendations for fine-tuning Windows memory usage.

Memory Tuning and Optimization

Optimizing the performance of Windows is not a difficult task, but it can be a bit complex for uninitiated users. In comparison, optimizing other parts of the system is quite simple. For example, faster hardware, such as a faster CPU, disk drive, caching controller, or an accelerated video adapter, always improves performance. However, these options can be expensive and perhaps not as cost effective as other solutions. Memory is the key factor in the general performance of Windows. But how do you know when you have enough memory? Microsoft recommends a minimum of 1MB of memory for Windows 3.1 in standard mode and 2MB in enhanced mode. For Windows for Workgroups 3.1, Microsoft recommends 2MB for standard mode and 3MB for enhanced mode.

For acceptable performance on the average system, I personally recommend a minimum of 4MB of memory for standard mode and 8MB for enhanced mode for Windows 3.1 and Windows for Workgroups 3.1x. If you are running memory intensive applications, such as CAD, graphics, or desktop publishing applications, I recommend a minimum of 16MB of memory — or more if the work load requires it. For example, 16-bit (65,536 colors) and 24-bit (16,777,216 colors) graphics can utilize all the physical memory you can afford. When you cannot afford to purchase additional physical memory, you use virtual memory.

I base my recommendations mainly on a combination of my own experience and the memory requirements recommended by manufacturers for their applications. For example, suppose you plan to use Windows to run Microsoft Word for Windows and link to a spreadsheet or graph in Microsoft Excel via Dynamic Data Exchange (DDE). In order to use DDE, both applications have to execute simultaneously. Microsoft recommends 2MB for Word and 2MB for Excel, for a total of 4MB of RAM. If you do not have enough physical RAM in the system, then either you have to use virtual memory to make up for the lack of available RAM, or Windows discards portions of the applications. Both of these options degrade overall system performance. After all, if the system is swapping to disk or loading discarded resources, then it surely is not performing as well as it could if the additional resources were available.

The first consideration in fine-tuning memory use by Windows is to determine your goals. As the manager or user of the system, you need to identify and prioritize the operating goals for your system. For example, do you want Windows applications to run faster, do you want to increase Windows' capacity for running multiple applications, or do you want to optimize your MS-DOS applications? As you evaluate your system's performance issues, keep in mind that most performance tuning and optimization techniques that relate to memory management trade one aspect of system performance for another.

In this section, I concentrate on memory management options that affect the use of physical and virtual memory by Windows. You can use this section as a reference on how to allocate and control the way Windows accesses different types of memory. Proceed with caution as you explore Windows memory configuration. Manipulating memory management operations is like wielding a double-edged sword. You can significantly enhance or degrade the performance of your system by altering the way that Windows interacts with memory.

Remember to back up all your system files before altering any settings.

Configuring Memory with SYSTEM.INI

I spent a great deal of time in Part I going over PC memory, DOS and memory, memory managers, and Windows' modes and memory. Now comes the payoff. Through the SYSTEM.INI file, you can unlock Windows' memory management secrets and gain control over your system's environment. The `[386Enh]` section of the SYSTEM.INI file is dedicated to enhanced mode configuration options.

Some system administrators use file attributes to hide or prevent files from being deleted inadvertently from a user's hard drive. Be careful about arbitrarily setting Hidden, System, or Read-Only attributes on configuration files. As an example of the problems that can occur, if you mark the SYSTEM.INI file with the System file attribute, the File Manager may cause a general protection fault.

Configuring Conventional Memory

Many people think that because Windows can access and manage megabytes of extended and expanded memory, conventional memory is of little or no consequence to Windows. On the contrary, conventional memory is very important. Remember that WIN.COM is a real mode program that is designed to perform several functions. (Refer to Chapter 4 for more information on WIN.COM and the Windows start-up process.) One of WIN.COM's functions is to provide certain real mode services for Windows. WIN.COM stays in DOS memory (conventional memory) to manage special system buffers and storage. Before tweaking conventional memory settings within Windows, give careful consideration to the TSRs and drivers that you load in DOS.

Specifying buffer size

The following entry specifies the size of a buffer that Windows allocates in conventional memory when it is running in standard mode. The buffer can share information among all non-Windows applications that are started from Windows. This setting has no effect when Windows is running in 386 enhanced mode, and you should never need to change it.

Setting: `GlobalHeapSize=kilobytes`

Default: 0

Chapter 21 covers PIF files in more detail.

Filling holes in conventional memory

In a few configurations, the system may have extended memory but less than 640K of conventional memory. For example, a machine may have 512K of DOS memory and 2MB or more of extended memory. This type of configuration is probably very rare these days. However, Windows automatically checks the amount of existing conventional memory each time it loads.

If Windows determines that the computer has less than 640K of conventional memory, it uses extended memory to backfill or round out the DOS memory to 640K. In the preceding example, Windows uses 128K of extended memory to bring the 512K of memory up to 640K.

Backfilling memory assures that DOS applications have a full complement of memory in which to work. Having sufficient memory is very important if you are loading TSRs and device drivers from DOS.

Setting: PerformBackfill=*Boolean*

Options: PerformBackfill=On

                  PerformBackfill=Off

Default: On

You should never need to change this entry because Windows can automatically detect whether to perform a backfill.

Specifying the minimum conventional memory for starting Windows

Windows can load with as little as 256K of free DOS memory. However, in some situations, you may want to have more conventional memory free. This entry specifies how much conventional memory must be free to start Windows.

Setting: WindowKBRequired=*kilobytes*

Default: 256

In Chapter 1, I mentioned that conventional memory is a limited resource that you need to guard carefully. Even though Windows will start with only 256K of conventional memory free, you need to consider the following:

■ You should load any Windows interrupt service routine (ISR) as low in Windows memory as possible and make sure that it is page locked because the ISR may fail to load if enough memory is not available. If it fails to load, then Windows will not load.

■ When you run DOS applications in enhanced mode, Windows creates translation buffers to communicate with DOS. The only way that Windows can pass data from protected mode to real mode, and vice versa, is by using these buffers. Windows places the translation buffers in conventional or upper memory, depending on available space. The buffers are page locked and loaded as low as possible in memory. MS-DOS cannot access any memory above 1024K, so a failure is probable if Windows loads the buffers in upper memory. If you are on a network, you need to load the translation buffers (24+K) in memory that MS-DOS can access (below 640K).

■ Remember that Windows still lives under DOS's rule. Each task in Windows has a data structure called the Task Database that contains task data. The Task Database is made of two components, one of which contains a DOS Program Segment Prefix (PSP) and is stored in conventional memory. Therefore, each Windows task uses a portion of conventional memory. The implication is that if you need to run a certain number of applications (multitask), Windows cannot load an application if there is insufficient memory for the application after Windows itself loads into memory.

■ You may be using WINSTART.BAT, a batch file that instructs Windows to load terminate-and-stay-resident (TSR) programs when Windows starts in enhanced mode. Using WINSTART.BAT enables you to gain more conventional memory to run DOS applications under Windows. Loading drivers and TSRs in this manner causes Windows to load them into the system VM instead of loading them into each DOS VM. If the system does not have enough conventional memory, you cannot load device drivers and Windows' applications.

■ MS-DOS applications that run under Windows VM inherit the DOS environment and, therefore, the conventional memory limitations. If you do not have enough conventional memory, you cannot run these applications. Consider that most database applications require at least 450K to load.

Limiting Windows' use of conventional memory

This entry limits the amount of conventional memory that Windows can use for itself. The default value indicates that Windows can use as much conventional memory as it needs.

Setting: `WindowMemSize=number | kilobytes`

Default: `-1 (no limit)`

The operating mode determines how much overhead Windows brings to conventional memory. In some instances, Windows 386 enhanced mode may refuse to load because of insufficient memory. Try entering a positive value that is less than 640K if the system does not have enough memory to run Windows in 386 enhanced mode.

Configuring Extended Memory

Windows uses extended memory directly. The settings described in this section allow you to define the way Windows handles extended memory. Manipulating these settings can often improve your system's performance.

Allocating memory

As mentioned in Chapter 1, when you launch Windows, it starts the virtual memory manager (VMM), which in turn virtualizes the system memory. As far as the CPU is concerned, the memory exists as one contiguous block. Even if the system has only 4MB of physical memory, the CPU may manage addresses in the 6 or 8MB ranges.

By default, Windows maps out 16MB of virtual memory when it starts up. The maximum amount of memory that Windows can use equals the amount of RAM installed on your system, rounded to the nearest 4 megabytes multiplied by 4. For example, if you have 3MB of system RAM, you round up to 4MB and then multiply by 4 for a total of 16MB. To determine the virtual memory limit, you subtract the system RAM from the total memory — 16MB total memory, minus 3MB of system RAM, for a result of 13MB of virtual memory.

This entry specifies the multiplier that determines the amount of linear address space that the VMM will create for the system. You compute the amount of linear address space by rounding up the amount of available physical memory to the nearest 4MB and then multiplying that value by the value specified for `PageOverCommit=`. Increasing the `PageOverCommit=` value increases the amount of available linear address space, so the size of data structures increases. You can specify a value between 1 and 20.

Setting: `PageOverCommit=number`

Default: 4

For example, if you want to increase the memory limit to six times the system RAM, you add the setting `PageOverCommit=6` to the `[386Enh]` section. Table 11-1 can help you determine the maximum amount of memory that Windows can access on your system. The amount is based on the value that is assigned to the setting `PageOverCommit=` and the RAM that is currently installed on the system.

Table 11-1	PageOverCommit Values		
System RAM	**PageOverCommit=**		
	4	**5**	**6**
2 – 4MB	16MB	20MB	24MB
5 – 8MB	32MB	40MB	48MB
9 – 12MB	48MB	60MB	72MB
13 – 16MB	64MB	80MB	96MB

Even though you can assign a multiplier between 1 and 20 to the
PageOverCommit= setting, you shouldn't use a multiplier greater than 8. Increasing the value of this setting causes a proportional increase in the amount
of hard disk activity that Windows must perform to access a larger swap file.
Consequently, system performance may suffer if you use a larger multiplier.
When you need more memory than eight times the amount of RAM installed on
your system, you should install additional system RAM instead of increasing
the value of the PageOverCommit= setting.

Although increasing the PageOverCommit= value increases paging activity
proportionately and can slow down the system, you may want to increase this
setting if you have a small amount of memory. Increasing it may enable you to
run Windows applications that you normally couldn't run.

Setting SysVMXMSLimit

This entry specifies the maximum amount of memory that the extended
memory driver will allocate to MS-DOS device drivers and memory-resident
software in the system virtual machine. Set the value to -1 to give an application all the available extended memory that it requests.

Setting: SysVMXMSLimit=*kilobytes*

Default: 2048

Configuring Windows memory for dual displays

Many programmers run Windows workstations with dual monitor setups (VGA
and monochrome). This allows them view code on the monochrome monitor
and run Windows on the VGA monitor. There are several CAD programs that
also allow dual monitor setups.

Because Windows seeks out all unclaimed memory within a system, you need to tell it whether it can use memory that may reside on a second video adapter. The DualDisplay setting is the place to do this. When this setting is On, Windows maps the memory normally reserved for the monochrome display.

Setting: DualDisplay=*Boolean*

Default: Set by Windows SETUP program

Usually, when Windows is running in 386 enhanced mode, the general system uses memory between B000:0000 and B7FF:000F unless a secondary display is detected. If the DualDisplay= entry is set to On, this memory is left unused and is available for display adapters. Or, if you do not have a monochrome display card installed, you can have EMM386.EXE include this address space as an upper memory block (UMB). If this entry is Off, the address range is available on EGA systems but not under VGA systems, because the VGA display device supports monochrome modes, which use this address space.

As a general rule, you should avoid using the memory address range between B000-B7FF. Most video adapters use this range of memory addresses, and you can avoid potential memory conflicts by excluding it from Windows.

Excluding memory addresses

Windows probes every corner of your system for unused memory blocks that it can use for itself, but the technique that Windows uses to scan for unused memory blocks is a problem. The Windows memory probe can disrupt an adapter card by touching all or some portion of the card's memory. Video cards, network cards, and hard disk host adapters are prime candidates for this kind of memory conflict. You can tell Windows what specific address ranges not to scan by using the following setting:

Setting: EMMExclude=*paragraph-range*

Use this setting to exclude a specific address range from being scanned and utilized by the Windows memory manager. This address range must be between 0xA000 and 0xFFFF. The addresses are rounded to the nearest 16K. Multiple occurrences of this setting may occur in the section, and there is no default value.

Starting Windows in enhanced mode with the WIN /D:X switch produces the same result as inserting the EMMExclude=A000-EFFF statement.

Including memory addresses

The opposite of EMMExclude is EMMInclude. Just as Windows may probe your system too thoroughly at times, it may overlook potential memory blocks at times. For example, if you use a dual video display setup (a monochrome card and a graphics card), you may discover that memory is left unused in graphics mode. If you know the address of this memory, you can specify it by using the EMMInclude setting.

Setting: EMMInclude=*paragraph-range*

Use this setting to include a specific address range for the Windows memory manager to scan and utilize. This address range must be between 0xA000 and 0xFFFF. The addresses are rounded to the nearest 16K. Multiple occurrences of this setting can occur in the section, and there is no default value.

Managing Windows use of UMBs

This entry determines how the upper memory blocks are used when Windows is running on MS-DOS 5.0. If this entry is Off, Windows uses all of the upper memory area, leaving no extra UMBs available for virtual machines. If this entry is On, Windows does not use all of the upper memory area, so the UMBs are available locally to each virtual machine.

Setting: LocalLoadHigh=*Boolean*

Default: Off

Specifying virtual memory address space

This setting specifies the address range (in megabytes) in which the memory manager will preallocate physical page-table entries and linear address space. Specifying a large address range enables Windows to manage more virtual memory while minimizing the overhead required to maintain internal tables that Windows needs in order to provide virtual memory services.

Setting: MapPhysAddress

Default: None

Set a value for this entry if you are using an MS-DOS device driver that needs this contiguous memory (such as an older version of RAM drive that uses extended memory). Specifying a large range of addresses implies that Windows should manage all memory in the system as virtual memory.

Specifying the minimum unlocked XMS memory

This entry specifies the amount of memory that must remain unlocked and available for use when switching virtual machines if more than one virtual machine is running. You should never need to change this entry.

Setting:	MinUnlockMem=*kilobytes*
Default:	40

Setting the minimum XMS allocation size

This entry specifies how many kilobytes of extended memory the XMS driver must reserve to use for starting Windows. Leave this value at 0 if no XMS users are in the system virtual machine.

Setting:	SysVMXMSRequired=*kilobytes*
Default:	0

Getting a Handle on Virtual Memory

Virtual memory enables you to run more programs simultaneously than the amount of physical memory installed on your computer would normally allow.

When a program runs in virtual memory, at any given moment, some parts of its code and data may reside in physical memory while Windows swaps the rest of the program to the hard disk. When a reference is made to a memory address, if the information is in physical memory, the information is used without program interruption. However, if the desired information is not in physical memory, a page fault occurs, and the Windows 386 enhanced mode virtual memory manager (VMM) takes control.

The VMM pulls the required code or data physical memory from the hard disk, and if necessary, swaps out other information. Windows swaps out pages according to a least recently used (LRU) algorithm. The pages that have not been accessed for the longest time are the first to be swapped out. All of this swapping is invisible to the user, who sees only a little hard disk activity.

The VMM does not attempt to predict which pages will be needed in the future. The VMM maintains the virtual memory page table that lists which pages are currently in physical memory and which are swapped to disk. Because Windows 386 enhanced mode is a multitasking environment, the VMM page table also contains a list of which memory pages belong to which process. When the VMM needs a page that is not currently in physical memory, it calls the page swap device. The page swap device allocates and deallocates virtual memory and maps pages into and out of physical memory.

Some virtual memory systems rely on program segmentation to do their work. Windows applications are segmented; however, virtual memory under Windows 386 enhanced mode is not related to the segmentation of Windows applications. All memory, virtual and physical, is divided into 4K pages, and the system is managed on this basis. Page mapping starts at 0K and works up. Two kinds of pages can be allocated: physical pages and virtual pages. The number of physical pages is simply the amount of physical memory in the machine divided by 4K. In contrast, memory allocated to an application is made up of virtual pages. At any given time, a virtual page can be in physical memory or swapped to the hard disk.

The benefit of Windows 386 enhanced mode virtual memory support is the ability to run more programs than can be supported by actual physical memory. The drawbacks are the disk space requirement for the virtual memory swap file and a decrease in overall execution speed when swapping is required.

A special feature of enhanced mode Windows 3.1 is that with the help of the WIN32's redistributable dynamic link libraries and virtual device drivers, which provide a flat 32-bit linear address space and enhanced memory management APIs, you can execute many 32-bit Windows NT applications. In order to install WIN32s and execute WIN32 applications under Windows 3.1, you need to enable the virtual memory option.

You change the most common virtual memory settings through the Control Panel applet that is located in the main Program Manager group. To change the virtual memory settings, double-click on the 386 Enhanced icon to bring up the Enhanced dialog box that is shown in Figure 11-1. You use this dialog box to select device contention for the installed serial and parallel ports, Windows foreground and background tasking, the minimum VM time slice (which includes the Windows system VM), and the virtual memory settings.

To view the current virtual memory settings, choose the virtual memory button. You see the Virtual Memory dialog box. Figure 11-2 shows the current swap file and disk status settings. Notice that a permanent swap file, 32-bit disk access, and 32-bit file access are enabled for increased performance. To modify the virtual memory settings, choose the change button. You see an expanded dialog box that displays the modifiable selections. Figure 11-3 displays these user-selectable settings. Notice the check boxes that you can use to enable 32-bit disk and file access. The 32-bit file system also has a user-selectable cache size. If sufficient memory is available, increase this value to increase performance. After you complete the modifications, choose the Change button and restart Windows to enable the modifications.

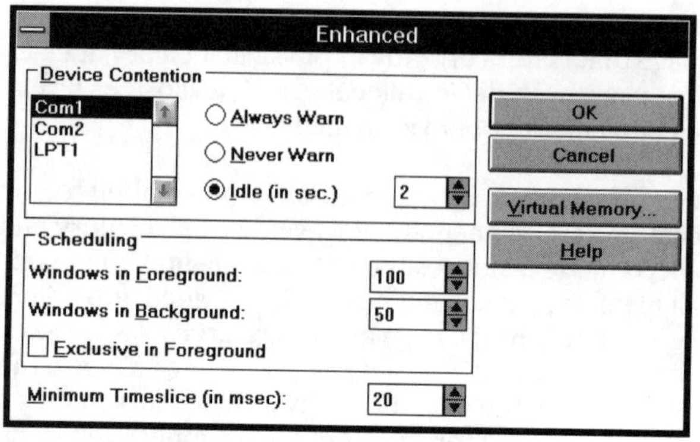

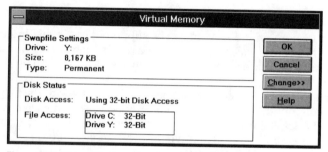

Figure 11-1: Enhanced mode settings.

Figure 11-2: Virtual Memory showing swap file and disk status settings.

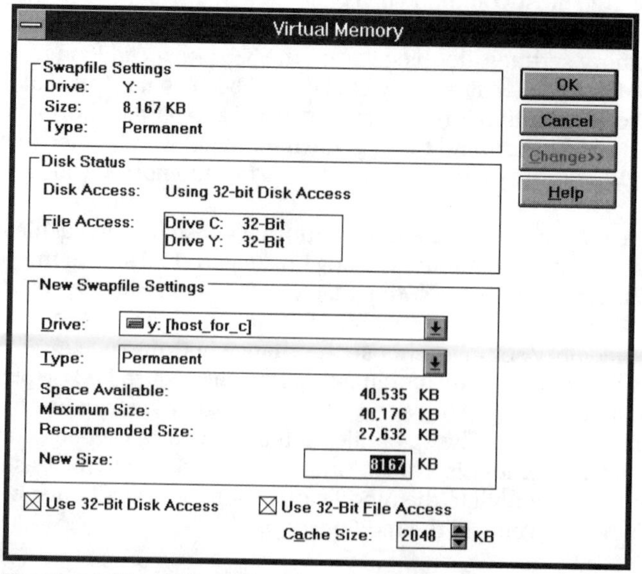

Figure 11-3: Virtual Memory screen showing user-selectable settings.

FastDisk, or 32-bit access if you prefer, offers benefits besides faster disk access. If FastDisk is disabled, all of the VM for the MS-DOS applications must be in physical RAM. As a result, as much as 640K of RAM may be devoted to a single application that may not even be utilizing all of that memory. If FastDisk is enabled, the entire picture changes. The application can, instead, be paged to disk in 4K blocks. Then Windows can manage physical memory more efficiently, and more MS-DOS sessions can be launched.

WDCTRLDRIVEx

is documented in the WDCTRL.386 source code that is provided in the Windows 3.1 Device Driver Kit (DDK). You use WDCTRLDRIVEx to enable FastDisk compatibility for disk controllers that fail the WD1003 compatibility test, yet still work properly with FastDisk. Use it with caution because a complete loss of all data may result. You enable WDCTRLDRIVEx by setting the value to 1. To enable FastDisk support, you set the *x* in *WDCTRLDRIVEx* for the drive, with the first drive being drive 0.

Many virtual memory user-configurable options are stored in the SYSTEM.INI file in the [386Enh] section because not all options are modifiable from the Control Panel. In particular are those options that relate to modifying the Windows virtual memory manager. Although most people have no need to modify the following settings, the adventurous may want to experiment with them.

- MaxPagingFileSize specifies the maximum size of the Windows temporary swap file. The default value is half of the available disk space on the default drive.

- MaxPhysPage informs Windows that additional physical pages of memory are available when the Windows memory management fails to detect all available memory during initialization. The default is auto detected by Windows.

- PageBuffers determines the number of 4K page buffers used to store asynchronous I/O requests. The default is four 4K buffers. Increasing this value can possibly increase performance on systems that utilize 32-bit disk access in combination with a permanent swap file. The maximum value is 32.

Enabling virtual memory

This entry sets demand paging (virtual memory). Set this entry to Off only if you need the disk space that would be used for a temporary swap file.

Setting: Paging=*Boolean*

Default: On

Specifying the virtual memory filename

This entry specifies the path and filename for the temporary swap file that is created when you start Windows in 386 enhanced mode. This file is deleted when you quit Windows. This setting overrides the `PagingDrive=` setting.

Setting: `PagingFile=`*path-and-filename*

Default: `WINDOWS\WIN386.SWP`

Least Recently Used Sweeping

I mentioned earlier that Windows 386 enhanced mode virtual memory management uses the *least recently used* (LRU) page-replacement algorithm. For each page, the virtual page table contains flags that indicate whether the page has been *accessed* and whether the page is *dirty*. *Accessed* means that a process made a reference to the page after it was originally loaded. *Dirty* means that a write was made to the page after it was loaded. Because a memory write qualifies as an access, the dirty attribute implies the accessed attribute.

Here's how it works. Windows 386 enhanced mode runs out of physical memory space, and a process requests additional memory. At this point, Windows has to decide which pages it should swap from physical memory to disk to accommodate the request. Windows uses the following steps to make the decision:

1. The VMM scans the page table, looking for pages without an accessed or a dirty attribute. As it goes through the scanning process, the VMM clears the accessed attribute from all the pages.

2. If the VMM can find enough pages that meet the not accessed/not dirty requirement, it fulfills the request. It swaps the pages to disk and gives the resulting free memory to the process.

3. If the VMM can't find enough pages the first time through, it repeats the scan. This time through, none of the pages has an accessed attribute, because the attribute was cleared by the first scan. Theoretically, therefore, more pages will meet the requirements, and the request can be fulfilled. If the required pages are still not found by the second scan, Windows then swaps out the pages regardless of their attributes.

Six parameters in the `[386Enh]` section of the SYSTEM.INI file impact the way that Windows handles the least recently used list. Exercise care when you alter these settings because they have a significant impact on Windows performance.

LRUSweepLowWater

The `LRUSweepLowWater` entry specifies when Windows should begin the sweeping process. When the number of free pages drops below the set value, the sweeper is turned on.

Setting: `LRUSweepLowWater=number`

Default: 24

LRUSweepFreq

This entry specifies the time between LRU sweep passes.

Setting: `LRUSweepFreq=milliseconds`

Default: 250

LRURateChngTime

This entry specifies the length of time that the VMM stays at high rate with no paging before switching to low rate and the length of time the VMM stays at low rate with no paging before turning the LRU sweep off.

Setting: `LRURateChngTime=milliseconds`

Default: 10000

LRUSweepLen

This entry specifies the length in pages of the region that is swept on each pass. Windows computes this value by dividing the value of `LRUSweepReset=` by the value of `LRUSweepFreq=`. The value must be at least 1.

Setting: `LRUSweepLen=length-in-pages`

Default: 1024

LRUSweepReset

This entry specifies the time desired for an accessed bit reset divided by 4MB of pages. Therefore, the time to reset all accessed bits is number of pages in system + 1023 / 1024, where 1024 pages = 4 MB. The minimum value is 100.

Setting: `LRUSweepReset=milliseconds`

Default: 500

LRULowRateMult

This entry specifies the value that is used to determine the LRU low paging rate sweep frequency, which is computed by multiplying the value for `LRUSweepFreq=` by the value specified for `LRULowRateMult=`. Values between 1 and 65535 can be used.

Setting: `LRULowRateMult=number`

Default: 10

Setting the maximum number of breakpoints

Windows uses system breakpoints to halt program execution and to transfer control from real mode to protected mode (Windows 386 enhanced mode). The breakpoints enable Windows to examine the system status, diagnose problems, and notify the user of critical hardware errors. You can specify the maximum number of breakpoints by using the following setting:

Setting: `MaxBPs=number`

Default: 200

You may need to increase this value if you are using a third-party virtual device driver that requires more breakpoints than the default value.

Setting the maximum temporary swap file size

This entry specifies the maximum size for a temporary swap file. By default, Windows calculates this value as 50 percent of the available disk space. If you find that Windows is not providing enough virtual memory, increase this setting.

Setting: `MaxPagingFileSize=kilobytes`

Setting the maximum virtual memory block address

This entry specifies the maximum physical page number that the VMM can manage as a usable page, so it allows pages to be added at a physical address beyond what the VMM recognized during initialization. If the value specified is less than what the VMM determines, the use of memory is prevented because the VMM will ignore several physical pages that it would normally use. Preventing the use of memory is useful if you are using a hardware device that cannot recognize all of the physical memory in the computer (for example, ISA DMA network cards cannot access physical memory above 16MB). As the default, Windows uses the highest physical page number that the VMM detects during initialization.

Setting: MaxPhysPage=*hexadecimal-page-number*

Setting the permanent swap file drive

This entry specifies the disk drive where Windows in 386 enhanced mode will create a permanent swap file. This setting is ignored if you are using a temporary swap file. The default is none.

Setting: PermSwapDOSDrive=*drive-letter*

Default: none

Setting the permanent swap file size

This entry specifies the desired size of a permanent swap file.

Setting: PermSwapSizeK=*kilobytes*

Default: As set during Windows Setup

Locking DOS session memory

Some applications may misbehave when the program's memory is written to disk. This entry, if set to On, causes the virtual-mode memory that the system virtual machine is using to remain locked in memory instead of being swapped out to disk.

Setting: SysVMV86Locked=*Boolean*

Default: Off

Summary

The settings described in this chapter can affect the way that Windows manages memory. Depending on your machine configuration and the mixture of programs that you run, you probably need to concern yourself with settings that directly affect your particular system.

Most of the time, Windows does a pretty good job of selecting appropriate settings for your hardware configuration. However, the hardware industry is outpacing the software industry. The odds are that if you add new devices and components to your system, you will need to adjust the Windows settings.

You should understand a bit more about how to apply Windows memory management techniques to solve common problems and optimize application performance for Windows systems. Keep the following things in mind when you apply these techniques:

▶ Windows memory management techniques are closely linked to the underlying system hardware. You need to consider the CMOS configuration and system configuration options that are accessed from the computer's setup routine or configuration utility on EISA and MCA machines.

▶ Windows memory management trades one type of memory for another. Performance optimizations that relate to memory management need to be balanced. Always consider general system performance in your optimization plans.

Chapter 12
Disk Access and Storage Secrets

This chapter explains the Windows input/output model and hardware and software caching techniques, and demonstrates several different strategies that you can use to obtain optimal performance in Windows.

The Windows I/O Model

When an MS-DOS application makes a disk request through the Int 21h interface, MS-DOS interprets the service request and then generates an Int 13h call. The Int 13h interface is handled by the system ROM BIOS. The BIOS then programs the hard disk controller to make the actual data transfer from the hard disk. This process becomes a bit more complicated under Windows.

Standard mode

In standard mode, Windows accesses disks by using MS-DOS and the system ROM BIOS.

Enhanced mode

In enhanced mode, Windows uses a mixture of 16-bit real mode code and 32-bit protected mode code for disk I/O. The 16-bit code is contained in the real-mode components of MS-DOS and the system BIOS, and the 32-bit code is contained in the core file WIN386.EXE and various virtual device drivers, or VxDs. Any entry in the SYSTEM.INI file that has an asterisk (*) in front of the device name is contained internally in WIN386.EXE. For example, in the [386 Enh] section, the following entry references the internal VxD.

```
DEVICE=*WDCTRL
```

If your system has a disk controller that does not support the Western Digital 1003 interface and you are fortunate enough to have a disk controller manufacturer such as Ultrastore that provides FastDisk support for their ESDI controllers, the entry may appear in the [386 Enh] section as

```
DEVICE=WDCTRL.386
```

This entry indicates that an external VxD is located in the \Windows\System directory.

These virtual device drivers enable the system to trap an I/O request from an MS-DOS application, interpret the request, and provide the associated service safely in a multitasking environment.

32-Bit enhancements

In addition to I/O trapping, a virtual device driver, or VxD, also can provide a service or extend the Windows operating system. Most often, an extension to the operating system is provided by a mixture of dynamic link libraries and virtual device drivers. A virtual device driver is 32-bit code and can function only in enhanced mode.

Over time, Windows has been extended to provide as much 32-bit functionality as possible to ensure faster response and better protection. The major enhancement to Windows 3.1 is a collection of VxDs that is commonly referred to

as *32-Bit Disk Access* or *FastDisk*. Windows for Workgroups 3.x provided 32-bit networking enhancements, and Windows for Workgroups 3.11 extended the 32-bit I/O model to include 32-Bit File Access, or *VFAT*, and 32-Bit Disk Caching, which is commonly referred to as *VCACHE*.

Disk I/O requests are provided by using one of two methods. The first method employs a task switch to the system virtual memory (VM), which then returns to real mode to process the request though MS-DOS and the system BIOS. The second method uses a VxD to interpret and then process the request directly. This method leads to the next subject, 32-Bit Disk Access. Another name for 32-Bit Disk Access is FastDisk.

32-Bit Disk Access (FastDisk)

FastDisk is one of the most important enhancements to Windows 3.1, and, in my opinion, it has been vastly underrated. FastDisk is composed of four separate VxDs that are included internally in WIN386.EXE. These VxDs are

- `DEVICE=*BLOCKDEV`
- `DEVICE=*PAGEFILE`
- `DEVICE=*INT13`
- `DEVICE=*WDCTRL`

The `DEVICE=*BLOCKDEV` VxD is the heart of the 32-Bit Disk Access system. This VxD manages the I/O request queue and filters all read, write, and cancel requests to the hard disk controller. These I/O requests are processed directly, but all other requests are passed to the hard disk controller BIOS for processing.

The `DEVICE=*PAGEFILE` VxD manages paging requests and utilizes the `BLOCKDEV` VxD to directly access the hard disk controller for paging file access.

The `DEVICE=*INT13` VxD traps and emulates calls that are made to the hard disk controller BIOS through the Int 13h interface. These Int 13h calls are passed to `BLOCKDEV` to be filtered, queued, and eventually processed.

The `DEVICE=*WDCTRL` VxD is installed by Setup only if a Western Digital 1003-compatible (WD1003) or ST-506-compatible controller is detected. The compatible controllers include most MFM, RLL, and IDE drives that are in use today. These controllers provide the communication interface between Windows and the physical hard disk controller.

Working together, these four VxDs provide several performance enhancements to Windows users.

- To provide faster disk access and data transfers for Windows and MS-DOS-based applications, the system BIOS is bypassed for hard disk access.

■ Unlike MS-DOS and the system BIOS, FastDisk is fully reentrant. Reentrancy provides the ability to swap MS-DOS applications to disk in 4K pages instead of swapping the entire 640K that the MS-DOS session may require. Consider the picture without FastDisk in this situation, for example. In order to read a page of the MS-DOS application from the disk, MS-DOS has to service the disk I/O request. Yet how can MS-DOS service the request if the MS-DOS system service has already been paged to disk?

Both MS-DOS and the system BIOS were designed for a single-tasking architecture, rather than the multitasking architecture of Windows. If a system service is requested while the same service is already in use, the internal structures that contain information about the state of the system will be corrupted and probably cause an immediate system crash. This is the case for a nonreentrant system service and one of the problems that FastDisk was designed to solve.

■ The VxDs support overlapped I/O. *Overlapped I/O* simply means that multiple data requests can be made simultaneously. Most old-time programmers would call this ability *asynchronous I/O*. The benefit of this technology to Windows users is that it provides the ability for multiple MS-DOS applications to make simultaneous disk requests without being blocked. In addition, Windows applications can use this facility to provide background I/O processing.

■ The default is to enable `OverlappedIO`:

```
OverlappedIO=True
```

To disable this setting, set the key `OverlappedIO` to `False` in the `[386 Enh]` section of the SYSTEM.INI file. Note that if both the `OverlappedIO` and `InDOSPolling` keys are set to `True` (that is, are enabled), then `OverlappedIO` will be disabled. Most networks (including Windows for Workgroups and Novell NetWare) enable `InDOSPolling`.

The following key is documented in the WDCTRL.386 source code that is provided in the Windows 3.1 Device Driver Kit (DDK):

```
WDCTRLDRIVEx
```

You use this key to enable FastDisk compatibility for disk controllers that fail the WD1003 compatibility test yet still work properly with FastDisk. You should use this key with caution because a complete loss of all data may result. You insert the key in the `[386 Enh]` section of the SYSTEM.INI file. To enable this option, set the value to 1. To enable FastDisk support, you need to set the *x* in *WDCTRLDRIVEx* for the drive; the first drive is drive 0 (zero).

32-Bit File Access and disk caching

Windows for Workgroups 3.11 extends the 32-bit code model to include support for installable file systems (IFSs), including MS-DOS 6.2 compressed drives, virtual file allocation table access (VFAT), and disk caching (VCACHE) services through a collection of five additional virtual device drivers. The IFS, VFAT and VCACHE services are composed of five separate external VxDs:

- `DEVICE=IFSMGR.386`
- `DEVICE=IFSHLP.SYS`
- `DEVICE=VFAT.386`
- `DEVICE=IOS.386`
- `DEVICE=*VCACHE.386`

The `DEVICE=IFSMGR.386` VxD provides the installable file systems manager and the interface to the real-mode device driver.

`DEVICE=IFSHLP.SYS`, which is the real-mode device driver, is loaded in the CONFIG.SYS file.

Windows for Workgroups can be utilized on a standalone (nonnetworked) machine to provide a better platform for power users as well as to benefit users of portable computers.

If you are an MS-DOS 6.x user who is utilizing the multiple boot facility or a user who is utilizing older versions of MS-DOS with third-party selectable boot programs, you may think that the IFSMGR.SYS device driver is required only for network access, and, therefore, you may load this device driver only when you are connected to a network. In reality, the IFSHLP.SYS manager also provides services for VFAT. If this device driver is not loaded, VFAT support is disabled.

To obtain the benefits provided by 32-Bit Disk and File Access, which can make quite a difference in usability, load the IFSHLP.SYS device driver for all Windows for Workgroup configurations.

The `DEVICE=VFAT.386` VxD intercepts the MS-DOS Int 21h service requests. This interception eliminates the real-mode task switch to enable MS-DOS to service the disk I/O requests.

`DEVICE=IOS.386` provides supervisory services for the I/O model.

`DEVICE=VXDLDR.38` is a helper VxD. It loads other virtual device drivers, including the real mode mapper. The real mode mapper provides an interface between VFAT and any real mode device drivers, such as the MS-DOS compression driver DBLSPACE.BIN.

`DEVICE=*VCACHE.386` provides the 32-bit disk caching services. This VxD has its own configuration section in the SYSTEM.INI file.

Direct Memory Access

Direct Memory Access (DMA) under Windows has some unique configuration options. These options are required because a DMA transfer of data from peripheral to computer or vice versa implies access to a physical memory address. These configuration options can be a problem in a multitasking operating system that utilizes logical addressing techniques. The real-mode BIOS and device drivers expect their data buffers to be in specific physical addresses. If the memory manager remaps these physical addresses, however, then when an attempt is made to transfer data, either an access violation (GPF) occurs or the machine locks up. Neither option is very desirable.

During setup, if Windows detects a DMA bus master peripheral, or if it does not detect a WD 1003-compatible controller, then it installs the SMARTDrive double-buffer device driver in the CONFIG.SYS file. Double-buffering provides data transfers to a known physical address from the peripheral to memory, and vice versa. The data is then transferred to the specific application buffer. Although this arrangement slows the system down a bit, it is definitely preferable to the alternative.

If your DMA peripheral is Virtual DMA Specification compliant (VDS compliant), it is aware of the logical addressing scheme that Windows uses, and it does not require double-buffering. However, if it is not VDS-compliant and you are not using SMARTDrive, the following entries that are located in the `[386 Enh]` section of SYSTEM .INI may come in handy:

- `DMABufferIn1MB`. This key informs Windows to allocate the DMA buffer in the first 1024K of system RAM for compatibility with 8-bit DMA bus master peripherals. This buffer will be allocated in the upper memory area if possible. The default value is `NO`; to enable, set to `YES`.

- `DMABufferSize`. This entry specifies the size (in kilobytes) of the DMA buffer to be allocated for DMA transfers. The default value is `16`. The Windows default will allocate a buffer that is of sufficient size to service the transfer.

- `HardDiskDMABuffer`. This entry specifies the size (in kilobytes) of the DMA buffer to be allocated for hard disk DMA transfers. The default values are `0` for AT computers and `64` for microchannel computers or peripherals that utilize DMA channel 3. If SMARTDrive with double-buffering enabled is utilized, the default is `0`.

Troubleshooting

If a problem with any of the 32-bit enhancements prevents Windows from starting after the 32-bit enhancements are enabled, disable the feature and contact the computer or peripheral manufacturer to see whether additional support or a device driver or VxD is available. To disable a feature, utilize a startup command line parameter, edit the SYSTEM.INI file directly, or use a backup version of the SYSTEM.INI file.

Windows for Workgroups 3.11 automatically makes a copy of any SYSTEM.INI file that is modified. This copy has a .CLN extension. If a 32-bit extension option fails, from the MS-DOS command line, copy the SYSTEM.CLN file to SYSTEM.INI, and then restart Windows.

Windows 3.1 and Windows for Workgroups have a command line parameter that disables 32-Bit Disk Access in case of incompatibilities or troubleshooting. Use WIN/D:F to disable 32-Bit Disk Access, or FastDisk.

Windows for Workgroups 3.11 enhances the command line parameter options to include the following:

- WIN/D:C. Disables 32-Bit File Access, or VFAT.
- WIN/D:T. Disables the loading of all 32-Bit VxDs.
- WIN/N. Disables all 32-Bit network drivers. ◎

Caching Techniques

Although keeping current on the latest hardware technology or software techniques is very difficult, it can be well worth the effort if a high-performance system is one of your goals. To achieve a high-performance system, you need to determine where any performance bottlenecks are and what you can do about them. In most cases, maximum performance is limited by the processing capabilities of the CPU, which can cause the system to be *CPU bound,* or by how fast data can be read or written to the hard disk drive, which can cause the system to be *I/O bound.*

The only option for a CPU-bound system is to upgrade the hardware. If the system is I/O bound, you have more choices. One option is to replace various components in the I/O subsystem. For example, you can replace a disk driver that has older and slower technology, such as an MFM disk drive and controller, with a newer and faster IDE or SCSI disk and controller. To make the best of your current hardware investment, you can replace the current disk controller with a caching disk controller or use a software cache.

Both hardware and software caches buffer disk I/O requests. A hardware caching controller uses a dedicated CPU and memory located on the adapter to process I/O requests. A software cache uses the system CPU and system memory that is located on the motherboard. The caching algorithm buffers read requests and may even offer the ability to cache write requests. A caching algorithm that caches write requests is called a _write-back cache;_ one that does not cache write requests is called a _write-thru cache._ A write-back cache offers additional performance gains over a write-thru cache; however, if a power failure occurs while data is still in the cache waiting to be written to disk, data loss can occur.

Hardware vs. Software Caching _____

I am often asked the question, "Which type of caching technique is better, hardware or software?" My answer is always . . . "It depends on the system and your needs." Although that response may sound like a cop-out, in reality it is simply the truth as I see it. A hardware cache can provide additional benefits that a software cache cannot provide, but it may not fulfill everyone's requirements. For example, most hardware caches have a dedicated CPU to process I/O requests and manage the data in the cache; some hardware caches are even bus masters. A bus master controller can directly access the system memory bus and transfer the data without intervention from the host CPU. Some hardware caches even offer battery backed memory that enables you to utilize a write-back cache for maximum performance but offers data integrity in case of a power failure.

However, a hardware caching controller is not an inexpensive choice. First you have to purchase the controller, and then you have to populate the cache. A better choice may be to purchase additional memory for your system and utilize a software cache instead. In many cases, and particularly on fast CPUs, a software cache performs better than a hardware cache. The reason why it performs better is quite simple. A hardware cache has to transfer the data it has collected through the expansion bus, and most expansion bus speeds are slower than the memory bus speed. For example, in an ISA/EISA machine, the bus is generally set to 8MHz, but the memory bus on a 486/33 is 33MHz. So assuming that the required data is in the cache, a software cache can provide faster access to the data.

In my own informal testing, I have found that a hardware cache can provide faster data access than a software cache only on CPUs rated at 20MHz or less. Computers based on the Intel 80286 and 80386 SX CPUs provide the most noticeable difference. On all other CPUs, I recommend that additional system memory be purchased for use in general system services, which includes the software cache. I recommend hardware caching controllers only for systems with limited memory expansion.

Optimizing Disk Throughput

Before discussing how to increase a system's ability to access data on a hard disk, or disk throughput, I want to spend a bit of time on some background information. To start, the physical hardware of a hard disk drive consists of one or more platters that rotate on a single spindle. Each platter is divided into separate tracks, and each track is further divided into individual sectors. Each usable platter has an associated read/write head. Access to a particular bit of data requires knowing which head to access, which track to access, and which sector of the track contains the requested data. This information is written to the disk whenever the unit is low-level formatted. Figure 12-1 illustrates the physical layout of a hard disk.

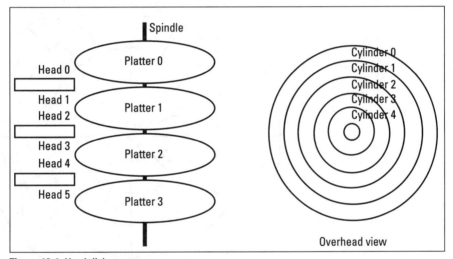

Figure 12-1: Hard disk structure.

One item of concern here is that the sector interleave may be user selectable during a low-level format. The *sector interleave* refers to the way that individual sectors are arranged on the disk track. For example, a standard ST-506-compatible disk drive has 17 sectors per track. With a 1:1 sector interleave, sector 1 is immediately followed by sector 2, sector 2 is followed by sector 3, and so on. For a 2:1 sector interleave, sector 1 is followed by sector 10, sector 10 is followed by sector 2, sector 2 is followed by sector 11, sector 11 is followed by sector 3, and so on. The reason data is interleaved is that not all systems can transfer the first requested sector of data before the second sector of data is under the read/write head. If the computer is not fast enough, then it will have to retrieve the data on the next pass. If your system has to wait for the disk to spin into position to retrieve the data, it is not performing as well as it could.

Interleaving the data provides an additional amount of time for the computer to retrieve data from the current sector and be ready for the next sector. A proper interleave can vastly improve the data transfer rate. Note that most IDE and SCSI drives have a 1:1 interleave, along with an internal buffer on the disk drive, to assure a maximum transfer rate. Figure 12-2 shows the relationship between tracks and sectors and expresses sector interleave.

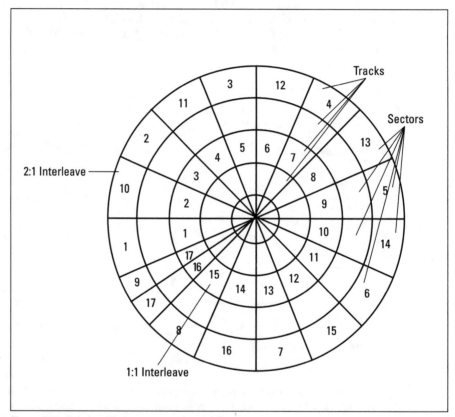

Figure 12-2: Relationship between tracks and sectors.

You can low-level format most hard disk drives, but most IDE drives should be low-level formatted only at the factory. Assuming that your drive may be low-level formatted, you can determine the optimum interleave by utilizing a disk utility. Gibson's SpinRite or Symantec's Calibrate utility can nondestructively do a low-level format of a drive and determine the optimum sector interleave.

As you use a system, the file structure becomes fragmented as new data is added to existing files. Finding and retrieving data from the hard disk requires more head movement because of this fragmented structure. Before you add additional hardware or software to an existing system, you should maximize the system's performance potential by defragmenting the hard disk. A defragmented hard disk has data that is stored in contiguous sectors, which minimizes hard drive head movement, provides improved response for read-ahead caching software, and improves your chances of recovering data with an undelete utility should you mistakenly delete an important file.

For example, suppose you have three newly created files on your hard disk called X, Y, and Z. In the initial state all of the data is stored in a contiguous fashion; see Figure 12-3. However after editing, file Y now spans past the next contiguous sector (where file Z is stored). This state is commonly referred to as fragmentation. To correct the situation, a disk defragmenter would be utilized to physically move the data on the disk until all of the data is stored in contiguous sectors. Of course, this is a very simplistic example. A real-world situation may have hundreds of fragmented files scattered across the disk. Figure 12-3 illustrates fragmentation.

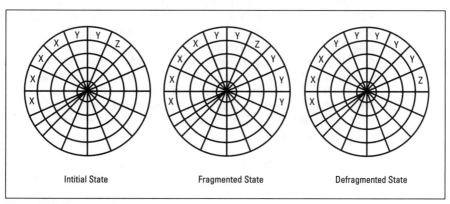

Intitial State   Fragmented State   Defragmented State

Figure 12-3: Fragmentation.

I recommend defragmenting the system once a month, whenever the percentage of fragmented files exceeds 25 percent, or when a significant system degradation occurs. To minimize the time spent in defragmenting a system, I recommend that you divide the drive into two partitions and store the executable files on one partition and the data files on the other partition. Executable files are rarely modified, so only the data partition will need to be defragmented.

Additional Performance Techniques

Depending on your system's configuration, you can choose from several additional techniques to improve the performance of a generic Windows system. Most of these techniques reshuffle system memory from application usage to system usage, and the techniques vary according to the version of Windows that you're using. I first discuss general performance techniques for any version of Windows and then move on to specific techniques for Windows 3.1 when it is operating in standard and enhanced modes. Finally, I discuss Windows for Workgroups 3.11, which executes only in enhanced mode.

If your system has at least 4MB of system RAM, then you should use a disk caching program such as SMARTDrive. SMARTDrive 4.0 is included with Windows 3.1. Different versions of SMARTDrive have slightly different parameters and default actions, so always consult your documentation regarding current functionality. When considering available caching options, keep in mind that a write-back cache will generally outperform a write-thru cache, but a write-thru cache offers peace of mind as well as data integrity.

SMARTDrive 4.0 offers several enhancements over its predecessor, SMARTDrive 3.0, which shipped with Windows 3.0. For example, SMARTDrive 4.0 intercepts MS-DOS block device driver requests instead of intercepting ROM BIOS Int 13h requests. Therefore, SMARTDrive 4.0 can cache any disk device that uses an MS-DOS block device driver. Another significant enhancement of SMARTDrive 4.0 is that it can cache write requests as well as read requests. By default, SMARTDrive 4.0 enables write-back to increase performance. To provide compatibility with disk utilities, data in the cache is flushed to disk whenever a disk reset request is intercepted. Most disk utilities issue a disk reset request when they are directly modifying data on the disk. Data is also written to disk whenever the system is idle or whenever a block of data is older than five seconds.

The syntax to load SMARTDrive is `SMARTDRV.EXE [DriveX [+|-]` `DOSCacheSize WinCacheSize /E:ElementSize /B:BufferSize`.

SMARTDrive 5.0, which is included with Windows for Workgroups 3.11 or MS-DOS 6.2, has been enhanced to provide caching of CD-ROM drives. It also has been modified to disable the write-back caching option by default to provide additional data integrity for users who are unfamiliar with caching technology. SMARTDrive 5.0 has additionally been modified to not return to the command prompt until all data in the cache has been written to disk. I suspect that these modifications are directly related to the number of users who turn off the power to their machines before the cache has been flushed to disk because they mistakenly think that shutting off the machine is safe whenever the command prompt is visible.

For maximum performance, I suggest that you enable the SMARTDrive write-back cache option by specifying the drive to be cached along with the plus sign and that you enable the immediate command prompt return without flushing the cache to disk by specifying the /N switch on the command line. The following entry demonstrates a write-back cache option for drive C:, with an initial cache size of 8MB, a Windows cache size of 4MB, and an immediate command prompt:

```
DEVICE=C:\WINDOWS\SMARTDRV.EXE C+ 8192 4096 /N
```

Windows for Workgroups 3.11 has been enhanced to provide 32-Bit Disk Access compatibility with many popular SCSI adapters. A 32-Bit File Access subsystem and a 32-bit caching subsystem have also been added. These subsystems are referred to as *VFAT* and *VCACHE,* respectively. You can use VCACHE in conjunction with SMARTDrive, but to provide optimum Windows performance, you need to set the Windows cache size for SMARTDrive to the minimum value of 128K.

VFAT can only cache MS-DOS 6.2 compressed drives with the Microsoft-supplied real mode mapper. Therefore, if you are using Windows for Workgroups 3.11 on a machine without MS-DOS 6.2, continue to use SMARTDrive and a larger Windows cache setting. 🎯

If data loss is a concern and you want to make sure that all data in the cache is flushed to disk before you turn off the machine, simply create a batch file called QUIT.BAT, with the following entries, and place the file somewhere in the system path:

```
***ECHO OFF
ECHO One moment while the system writes data to the hard
disk . . .
SMARTDRV/C
ECHO It is now safe to turn the machine off
```

When Windows is installed, it checks the system to see whether the disk subsystem is compatible with the WD1003 standard. If the system fails the compatibility test, a device driver to buffer data is inserted in the CONFIG.SYS file:

```
DEVICE=C:\WINDOWS\SMARTDRV.EXE /DOUBLE_BUFFER
```

To determine whether double-buffering is required, run SMARTDrive at the MS-DOS command line, not from an MS-DOS box that executes under Windows. You see a display such as the following:

```
Microsoft SMARTDrive Disk Cache version 5.0
Copyright 1991,1993 Microsoft Corp.

Cache size: 1,048,576 bytes
Cache size while running Windows:  1,048,576 bytes
```

```
                   Disk Caching Status
      drive   read cache    write cache   buffering
      ─────────────────────────────────────────────
       A:         yes            no           no
       B:         yes            no           no
       C:         yes            no           no
      Write behind data will be committed before command prompt
      returns.
```

```
      For help, type "Smartdrv /?".
```
Carefully check the buffering column for the hard disk drive entries. This column displays one of three values:

■ yes, which indicates that double-buffering is required

■ no, which indicates that double-buffering is not required

■ —, which indicates that SMARTDrive has not yet determined whether double buffering is required

 If you have a bus master controller that supports a device driver for the Virtual DMA Specification, such as an Adaptec SCSI controller, load the driver before you load the expanded memory manager. This setup prevents the memory manager from allocating a buffer to perform double-buffering services, and it increases performance.

If your system has at least 8MB of system RAM, you can use a portion of that RAM to create a RAM drive in which to store temporary files that are generated by Windows applications. You also can use the RAM drive to spool print files, thereby minimizing the time that an application displays the hourglass cursor. In standard mode, you can significantly improve the task-switching response time by using the RAM drive to swap non-Windows applications.

I generally recommend a 1 to 2MB RAM drive in an 8MB system, 4 to 6MB for a 12 to 16MB system, and 8MB for anything with more than 20MB of system RAM. You can create a RAM drive by adding a device driver entry in the CONFIG.SYS file.

The syntax to create a RAM drive is RAMDRIVE.SYS *DiskSize SectorSize NumberOfDirectoryEntries* [/E | /A]. The *DiskSize* parameter can range from 4 to 32767 and is expressed in kilobytes. The *SectorSize* can be 128, 256, or 512 and is expressed in bytes. The *NumberOfDirectoryEntries* can range from 2 to 1024. You create the RAM drive in extended memory by specifying the /E switch and use the /A switch for expanded memory.

The following entry creates an 8MB RAM drive in extended memory with default 512-byte sectors and a default limit of 64 files or directory entries:

```
DEVICE=C:\WINDOWS\RAMDRIVE.SYS 8096 /E
```

This RAM drive will be assigned the next available drive letter, so network users should be aware that their network connections may need to be reassigned. To benefit from this newly created RAM drive, the environment variables TMP and TEMP should be assigned to the RAM drive. To defeat the 64 file/directory root limitation, create a directory on the RAM drive and assign this directory to the TMP and TEMP environment variables in the AUTOEXEC.BAT file. The following example assumes that the RAM drive is drive D and that the temporary directory to be assigned is TEMP:

```
D:
MD TEMP
SET TMP=D:\TEMP
SET TEMP=D:\TEMP
C:
```

Another technique that I use with RAM drives is compression. A compressed RAM drive can offer almost twice the capacity of an uncompressed drive. The compression does not noticeably degrade system performance. Normally, I automate the process of creating the compressed drive and assigning the TEMP environment variables in the AUTOEXEC.BAT file by adding the following entries:

```
C:\DOS\DBLSPACE /CREATE E: /NEWDRIVE I: /RESERVE=.75
I:
MD TEMP
SET TMP=I:\TEMP
SET TEMP=I:\TEMP
C:
```

This example assumes that the drive letter assigned to the RAM drive is E and that the letter I has been reserved for the compressed drive. The only caveat is that you may need to manually modify the /RESERVE switch value because of the size of the RAM disk. This particular example is for an 8MB RAM drive.

Compressed Drives

If you use compression software in conjunction with Windows, you need to apply additional system management techniques. The first order of business is to make sure that the Windows permanent swap file is located on an uncompressed drive. You can assign a temporary file to the compressed drive, but 32-Bit Disk Access to a permanent swap file that is located on a compressed drive requires knowledge of that file system, such as the compression scheme utilized for data access, which, unfortunately, is not available for the current line of Windows products.

MS-DOS 6.2 and Windows for Workgroups 3.11 offer additional support for DoubleSpace compressed drives through VFAT and VCACHE, although support for a permanent swap file is still not available for compressed drives. VFAT Support requires the presence of RMM.D32 in the \Windows\System directory.

The MS-DOS 6.x Applets

MS-DOS 6.x includes both MS-DOS and Windows versions of antivirus, undelete, and floppy-disk-based backup utilities under a license from Symantec and Central Point. Although these utilities work well enough for uninitiated users, advanced users will probably prefer to obtain the expanded versions of these tools from their respective manufacturers.

Configuring Disk Operations with SYSTEM.INI

The SYSTEM.INI file is the collection point for all of the Windows system-specific configuration options. Because this file is only a text file, you can edit it manually. However, I recommend that you use the appropriate Control Panel applets to modify the configuration options so that you will be sure that the modifications are performed properly. These control panel configuration options are discussed in the next section.

You can use the following entries in the [386 Enh] section of SYSTEM.INI to enable/disable 32-Bit Disk Access, as well to as configure some of the paging file options.

- 32BitDiskAccess. This switch enables or disables 32-Bit Disk Access. To enable 32-Bit Disk Access, set this value to on; to disable it, set the value to off.

- MaxPagingFileSize. Use this key to specify the maximum size of the Windows temporary swap file. The default value is half of the available disk space on the default drive.

- PageBuffers. This key determines the number of 4K page buffers that are used to store asynchronous I/O requests. The default is four 4K buffers. Increasing this value can possibly increase performance on systems that utilize 32-Bit Disk Access in combination with a permanent swap file. The maximum value is 32.

■ PageOverCommit. If you need more swap space than the default Control Panel virtual memory settings will allow, increase this key value from the default of 4 to increase the total amount of linear address space that the Windows memory manager can allocate. The linear address space is determined by the amount of physical memory in the system plus 4MB, multiplied by this key value. The value range for this key is from 1 to 20.

■ PagingFile. This key contains the path and filename for the Windows temporary swap file. The default is WINDOWS\WIN386.SWP.

You can use the following SYSTEM.INI entries in the [vcache] section to configure the 32-bit disk caching service:

■ MinFileCache. This key specifies the size (in kilobytes) of the cache. The default is 64.

■ ForceLazyOn. This key enables write-back caching and overrides the default option for specific drives. The drive letters should be concatenated for multiple drives. For example, ForceLazyOn=XYZ enables lazy writes for drives X, Y, and Z.

Enabling the ForceLazyOn switch and overriding the default setting may cause data loss to occur if there is insufficient disk space to store the cached data. Use this switch with extreme caution.

■ ForceLazyOff. This key disables write-back caching and overrides the default option for specific drives. The drive letters should be concatenated for multiple drives. For example, ForceLazyOff=XYZ disables lazy writes for drives X, Y, and Z.

Enabling 32-Bit Support Options from the Control Panel

You use the Control Panel 386 Enhanced applet to configure the paging file, 32-Bit Disk Access, file access, and disk caching options.

After the application is launched, it displays a dialog box that contains the entry point to the virtual memory configuration options.

Choose the Virtual Memory button to see another dialog box that you can use to confirm the paging file size, location, and access method and the disk access method (16-bit or 32-bit). When 32-Bit is displayed for a specific drive, that drive will be accessed by utilizing the 32-Bit File Access services.

Choose the Change button to see the final dialog box. Notice the check boxes that enable 32-Bit Disk and File Access. The 32-bit file system also has a user-selectable cache size. If sufficient memory is available, increase this value to increase performance. After you complete the modifications, choose the Change button and restart Windows to enable the modifications.

Summary

Now that you have gained a better understanding of the Windows I/O model, caching techniques, and applicable performance techniques, here are a few thoughts to keep in mind:

▶ Microsoft is migrating Windows to all 32-bit code to improve system performance and robustness.

▶ As evidence, consider the history of the product (that is, Windows 3.0 and 3.1, and Windows for Workgroups 3.1, and 3.11) as well as the future product (that is, Windows 4.0 or Chicago, and Windows NT).

▶ These improvements are incorporated in virtual device drivers and include FastDisk, VFAT, VCACHE, and the network redirector and transports.

▶ Disk throughput may be increased by utilizing either a software or hardware disk cache and defragmenting as required.

▶ System performance may be increased by utilizing a RAM drive for temporary files. Compressing a RAM drive can also prove beneficial.

Chapter 13
Hardware Configuration Secrets

In This Chapter

▶ Basic configuration issues

▶ BIOS setup optimization

▶ Advanced power management

▶ Hardware peripherals

▶ Default Windows VxDs

▶ Troubleshooting

This chapter provides a basic understanding of the hardware components that make up a working computer system. It also explains how to apply your understanding of the hardware when you are configuring a Windows system.

Basic Configuration Issues

You do not need to understand how your computer works in order to use it daily, but knowing how it works can be extremely helpful when you are troubleshooting, configuring the system, and optimizing performance. The computer system consists of three primary components: the motherboard, the video subsystem, and the disk subsystem. Of these components, the motherboard is the most important, followed by the disk, and then video subsystems. Motherboard assemblies vary from manufacturer to manufacturer; however, all motherboards include at least the following components:

■ System BIOS. The system BIOS, or Basic Input Output System, is the final layer between the operating system and hardware peripherals that are installed in the computer. The system BIOS is read only, and it is located in the last addressable segment of system memory. On an 808x CPU-based system, this segment is the F000 segment. On 20286 or 80386 CPU-based systems, the BIOS is located at the 16MB and 4GB boundaries, respectively, and is remapped to the F000 segment.

An IBM PS/2 Micro Channel or compatible machine has an additional BIOS that is located in the E000 segment. A PS/2 or compatible actually has two system ROMs. One ROM is used for real mode operating systems, and the other ROM is used by protected mode operating systems. Other manufacturers, such as Compaq, may also use the E000 segments for additional ROMs.

■ System memory bus. The system memory bus varies according to the CPU. For Intel 808x, 80286, and 80386SX CPUs, the memory bus is a 16-bit-wide data path. For Intel 80486 CPUs, the data path is 32 bits wide, and the Intel Pentium has a 64-bit-wide data path. The data path is important only when you are considering the maximum performance of a system. Its implementation is transparent to the software that is executing on the system.

The performance factor comes into play when you consider the relationship between data access and the CPU's ability to move the data. For example, assume that you want to search a string for a specific word in your word processor. This procedure is a memory-to-memory comparison, so first the data (your document) has to be read into the CPU's registers, and then it has to be compared. On an 8086, this procedure is a byte-to-byte read and compare, but an 80286 can read and compare two bytes at a time, and an 80386 can read and compare up to four bytes at a time.

When discussing the I/O bus limits, this limitation is the I/O address space limitation, not the memory address limitation. An AT (16-bit) peripheral has only 24 address lines for a maximum access of 16MB; whereas, a 32-bit peripheral may access up to 4 GB.

■ System input/output (I/O) bus. Several different I/O buses are available in today's systems. The first I/O bus that was designed for personal computers is the Industry Standard Architecture (ISA) bus, and it is a 16-bit interface. On an 8086-based system, the I/O bus is limited to accessing 1MB of system RAM, but on an AT class computer, the limit has been expanded to access up to 16MB. This limitation has caused additional I/O buses to be created by manufacturers. The Extended Industry Standard Architecture (EISA) bus and the Micro Channel Architecture (MCA) bus are two such interfaces. The EISA I/O bus is a 32-bit bus that is capable of accessing up to 4GB, and the MCA bus is either a 16-bit or 32-bit interface, depending on the CPU that is installed in the system. All of the MCA computers with a 16-bit CPU, such as the 80286 utilize a 16-bit MCA interface whereas, MCA computers with 80386 or higher CPUs utilize either a mixture of 16-and 32-bit or all 32-bit interfaces. This is similar to an ISA computer utilizing a mixture of 8-bit and 16-bit interfaces on the same motherboard. For example:

Processor	IBM Model	Bus Width
80286	50,60	16
80386	55,70,80	32
80486	76,77,90,95	32

ISA and EISA I/O buses use an 8MHz data transfer clock speed, whereas MCA buses use a 16MHz clock speed. The clock speed determines the maximum rate of data transfer from peripheral to system memory. To increase the data transfer rate, the PC industry created two additional I/O buses, which are known as VL-BUS and PCI.

■ i486 Local-Bus I/O provides an increase in I/O bandwidth by moving the high-performance I/O (like VGA) from the slow I/O bus to the faster processor bus. The VGA controller chip is directly attached to the 132MB/sec i486 processor bus (instead of to the 8MB/sec ISA bus).

■ The VL-Bus or VESA Local bus, is an extension of the local bus design. It is based on a standard developed by the Video Electronics Standards Association. A standard connector is placed on the 486 processor bus, which allows local-bus VGA chips to be mounted on removable cards. Thus, VL-Bus merely refers to the ability to attach I/O devices like VGA to the i486 processor bus via a new kind of add-in I/O card — a VL-Bus card.

■ The PCI Bus (Peripheral Component Interconnect Bus) is based on a standard developed by PCI Special Interest Group, which was formed in 1992. The PCI Bus differs from the local bus in that it is an intermediate bus rather than a local bus. Instead of attaching devices directly to the processor as with the local bus, the PCI Bus is a separate high-performance I/O bus implemented by a memory controller chip that "buffers" the PCI Bus from the processor bus.

■ Peripheral Interrupt Controller. The peripheral interrupt controller (PIC) is the interface between a selected piece of hardware, such as the disk controller, and the operating system. When a peripheral needs to be serviced, it generates a hardware interrupt. The operating system is then responsible for servicing the request. It either handles the service request directly or passes the request to the ROM BIOS. Windows 3.x supports both methods. For example, the Windows 32-bit disk access for WD1003-compatible interfaces directly handles disk I/O requests, and noncompatible interfaces are handled by the disk controller BIOS.

The PIC is programmable. Each device on the system may use a single interrupt that is not sharable on an ISA-based system, but devices on MCA-based systems and EISA-based systems may share interrupts.

An 8086 CPU-based system has a single PIC that can process up to 8 interrupts from 0 to 7, and an AT class system (80286 or higher based CPU) has two PICs and 16 interrupts. The second PIC is accessed through an interrupt on the first PIC. Generally, this interrupt is IRQ 2, and it is often referred to as the *cascade interrupt*, as this interrupt is redirected to interrupt 9 on the second PIC.

■ Keyboard BIOS. The keyboard BIOS is another interrupt service routine, or ISR, that is called each time a key on the keyboard is pressed or released.

The interrupt is generated by the keyboard controller. As each character is serviced, it is placed in a circular buffer to be retrieved by the operating system or application.

■ Keyboard controller. The keyboard controller on IBM AT compatible computers is an Intel 8042 or compatible controller. Of particular interest is the fact that the A20 line which provides access to the extended memory on the system is enabled/disabled by the keyboard controller. On some machines, such as those with an AMI BIOS Fast A20 Gate, the A20 line may be enabled by the chipset on the motherboard providing faster access.

■ CMOS RAM. The AT-based system has a 64-bit storage area that is known as the CMOS RAM. The CMOS RAM is backed up by an external battery, and it is used to store configuration information. This information contains the hard disk configuration, the floppy drive configuration, and so on.

■ Direct memory access controller. A direct memory access (DMA) controller offloads data transfers from a peripheral that is located on the system I/O bus to and from system memory. Each DMA controller has four individual channels. An 8086 CPU-based system has only one DMA controller; 80286 CPU-based systems have two controllers. Channels 0 through 3, which are capable of 8-bit data transfers, have a maximum single access transfer limit of 64K; and channels 4 through 7, which are capable of 16-bit data transfers, have a maximum single access transfer limit of 128K.

■ Interrupts. IBM-compatible computer systems have two types of interrupts: hardware interrupts, which are generated by individual peripherals, and software interrupts, which are generated by the CPU. Interrupts provide a means to service some type of data request, such as a request to read or write data from a hard disk.

ISA peripherals use edge-level interrupts, and EISA and MCA peripherals use trigger-level interrupts. Edge-level interrupts are not sharable. Trigger-level interrupts are priority based and may be shared. Table 13-1 lists the default system interrupts.

Table 13-1	Default System Interrupts	
Interrupt	*Normal Usage*	*Additional Possibilities*
0	Timer (DRAM refresh)	
1	Keyboard	
2	Cascade	Mouse, 8-bit network adapter[1]
3	COM2	COM4
4	COM1	COM3

Interrupt	Normal Usage	Additional Possibilities
5	LPT2	8-bit SCSI, sound card[2]
6	Floppy controller	
7	LPT1	Sound card[3]
8	System clock	
9[4]		
10		Network adapter
11		Adaptec SCSI adapter
12		
13	Math coprocessor	
14	Hard disk controller	
15		

[1]Due to the lack of free low-end IRQs, many 8-bit network adapters use IRQ 2 for network access. However, because IRQ 2 is also the cascade interrupt, network access may be sporadic on some systems.

[2]Future Domain and Trantor SCSI 8-bit SCSI cards are often configured to use IRQ 5 for non-DOS operating systems. Most MS-DOS configurations use I/O polling instead of an IRQ. A peripheral that utilizes I/O polling continually queries the status of an I/O port waiting for an event to be signaled. The Media Vision Pro Audio Spectrum 16 uses IRQ 5 for the Creative Labs Sound Blaster- compatible section of the adapter. Some Sound Blaster compatibles also use this IRQ.

[3]Many sound cards, such as the Creative Labs Sound Blaster and the Media Vision Pro Audio Spectrum series, use IRQ 7. This hardware configuration can cause problems if Windows is configured to use MS-DOS interrupt-driven print services instead of polled I/O-driven services.

[4]If a device such as a serial port or network card is configured to use IRQ 2, in most cases Windows must be configured to use IRQ 9 for the device since IRQ2 is utilized as the cascade interrupt.

■ Input/output address. IBM-compatible systems have 65,536 individual I/O addresses, or ports. These I/O ports can be accessed individually or in series, depending on the CPU used. An 80386, for example, which can read or write 4 bytes to 4 sequential I/O ports in a single access, can provide performance increases over an 80286 that requires two separate read or write requests for the same action.

BIOS setup optimizations

Some system BIOSs are configurable, and some are not configurable. A configurable BIOS enables you to maximize the potential of the system and to maximize compatibility with current and future operating systems.

Many, but not all, computers use a system BIOS that can configure individual system components to optimize the computer system. These configuration options are generally divided into at least two sections. At a minimum, all AT class computers have a CMOS configuration option that is used to select the system date/time, video (monochrome or color), keyboard (installed/not installed), hard disk configuration, floppy drive types, and so on.

Most AMI BIOSs, for example, have three separate sections:

- Standard CMOS Setup. This section configures the default CMOS settings, which include the system date and time, the hard disk drive settings, the floppy drive settings, the video display settings, and the keyboard settings. This information is stored in the 64-bit CMOS RAM area.

- Advanced CMOS Setup. This section configures the advanced CMOS settings, which include selectable keyboard options, memory test options, memory parity options, Num Lock enable/disable, floppy seek enable/disable, Weitech coprocessor support, system boot sequence (A: then C:, or C: then A:, and so on), internal and external CPU cache options, password options, and ROM shadowing options.

- Advanced Chipset Setup. This section is used to configure such motherboard system components as the DRAM speed, the DRAM RAS precharge, the DRAM CAS write pulse width, the DRAM interleave, external cache options, keyboard and I/O bus speeds, and I/O recovery options.

Now that you know all the current BIOS buzzwords, the time has come to find out what some of these options are and when to use them. You first need to consider the memory-specific options. System memory is not accessed as a single block; instead, it is divided into columns and rows. To access a specific byte of memory, the hardware needs to specify the individual column and row. Specifying the column and row, as with all memory access implementations, is transparent to the software that is executing on the system. The *row access strobe* (RAS) and *column access strobe* (CAS) are memory timing options. As you know, Dynamic Random Access Memory (DRAM), must be refreshed at periodic intervals to maintain the state of the stored data. Depending on the clock speed and DRAM speed of the system's CPU, the system may require a faster or slower RAS and CAS.

Another option to consider is the DRAM interleave. When you interleave memory, sequential data access occurs to separate banks of memory. A two-way interleave, for example, separates even address accesses to one bank and odd address accesses to another bank. This arrangement is particularly useful because after the CPU accesses a particular bank of memory, it cannot access that bank again until the DRAM has been refreshed. Interleaving the memory provides for sequential accesses without waiting for the refresh cycle. The system can use slower and, therefore, less expensive memory without a performance penalty.

The next items to consider are the I/O bus speed and I/O recovery select options. The ISA bus design has a maximum clock speed of 8MHz; however, to increase system performance, manufacturers have made modifications that enable users to select the bus speed. The bus speed is generally based on a fraction of the system CPU's clock speed. For example, on a 486/33, a setting of Clk/4 supplies a bus speed of 8.33MHz. Yet some peripherals can handle clock speeds of 12.5 to 16MHz, and such speeds offer significant performance increases. After all, if you can increase the bus speed from 8MHz to 16MHz, you can theoretically double the data transfer rate from the system memory to peripheral devices.

Increasing throughput sounds ideal, but there is a catch. If a device cannot respond quickly enough, either a data loss or a system lockup can occur. The I/O recovery select option can prevent such problems. This option provides a delay between back-to-back I/O requests to a peripheral so that the device can complete its current task before accepting and processing another task.

Advanced power management

Advanced power management (APM) enables you to extend battery life on portable computers by powering down system components that are not used within a specific time frame. These components can include serial ports, parallel ports, hard disk drives, displays, and PCMCIA adapters. The APM 1.0 specification that was introduced with MS-DOS 5.0 and Windows 3.1 is composed of two parts, the vendor-specific device driver APM.SYS and the vendor-independent device driver POWER.EXE. These device drivers are MS-DOS-specific, and Windows 3.x uses them to communicate with the associated hardware. The Windows 3.x-specific components are MMSYSTEM.DLL, POWER.DRV, and the VPOWERDD.386 virtual device driver. Installing APM support for Windows requires that the MS-DOS setup program be executed and either the MS-DOS with APM option or the Intel 386SL Based System with APM option be selected for the system type. The 386SL support option should be used only for Intel 80386SL processors and portables that support the APM features.

The APM.SYS device driver is vendor-specific. You load it in the CONFIG.SYS file before any memory manager. It may not be loaded into upper memory. Refer to your portable computer's documentation for specific parameter options, and if no parameter options are given, use the following syntax to install the device driver:

```
device=[drive:][path]apm.sys
```

You also need to load the POWER.EXE device driver in the CONFIG.SYS file. You may load it into upper memory. Use the following syntax to install it:

```
device=[drive:][path]power.exe [adv[:max|reg|min]|std|off]
[/low]
```

The device driver accepts three different parameters and a single switch for configuring the power management features and device driver installation. The device driver attempts to load into upper memory by default. To make the device driver load into conventional memory, use the /low switch when you install it. The three configuration options are advanced power management for optimum battery life (adv); standard power management (std), which uses only the hardware's power management feature set; and the option to completely disable power management (off). The advanced power management syntax is

```
adv[:max|reg|min]
```

In this syntax, max specifies maximum power conservation at the expense of application performance, reg balances power conservation with application performance, and min minimizes power conservation but provides maximum application performance.

You also can configure the power management driver from the MS-DOS command line. The syntax is

```
power [adv[:max|reg|min]|std|off]
```

To display the current power setting, just execute POWER with no command line arguments.

Hardware Peripherals

A computer system consists of much more than the motherboard. Additional peripherals are required to make a complete system. At a minimum, the system also needs a disk controller to access external storage media, a video adapter and keyboard for user interaction, and an I/O controller that includes serial and parallel ports for accessories such as a modem and a printer.

Disk controllers/adapters

The design of the IBM ROM BIOS disk interface did not anticipate disks with more than 1,024 cylinders. When MS-DOS was first designed, disk drives had certain limitations. To be specific, MS-DOS used a 512-byte sector size and had a limit of 1,024 cylinders, 16 heads, and 64 sectors per track. The maximum physical disk size was 512MB (1024 * 16 * 64 * 512). MS-DOS versions 5.0 and later can use a maximum head limit of 255, which provides for a maximum physical disk limit of 8GB.

- MFM - In the early days of PC computing, disk drives utilized a separate controller conforming to the WD 1003 interface along with a disk drive which utilized a Modified Frequency Modulation encoding method.

- ESDI - Enhanced Small Device Interfaces were developed to increase data transfers and storage capacity and in many cases utilized a WD 1003 compatible interface. Again these systems required a separate controller and disk drive.

- SCSI - The Small Computer System Interface is really another expansion bus that can be utilized to access disk drives, CD-ROM drives, printers, scanners, as well as other types of peripherals. SCSI devices are intelligent peripherals and respond to an established command set and interface with the host computer system through a host adapter.

- IDE - Intelligent Drive Electronics were first introduced by Compaq, and as the name suggests utilize an intelligent disk drive and host adapter. IDE disk drives have become one of the most utilized interfaces in today's market.

Bus-master adapters

Bus-mastering devices do their own direct memory addressing (DMA) without going through the machine's processor. The most common bus-mastering devices are SCSI hard disk controllers, but technically, other types of devices could be bus-mastering devices as well. The problem with bus-mastering devices is that although they are high-performance devices and are quite often found on 80386 and 80486 machines, unfortunately, in their design, they are incompatible with one of the operating modes of the 80386 and 80486 processors — the Virtual 86 mode. See Chapter 12 for a discussion of double buffering and related information.

Specifically, the problem is that the device puts data into absolute memory addresses and assumes that the contents of those memory addresses will always remain constant. However, on a 386 machine with the processor in Virtual 86 mode, this assumption is often incorrect. In Virtual 86 mode, the same physical memory addresses can, at any given moment, hold different data, depending on which virtual machine is current.

If you are using a bus-mastering device on an 80386 or 80486 machine that is in Virtual 86 mode and actual memory paging is occurring (the switching from one virtual machine to another), your machine will probably hang when you use the bus-mastering device.

As an example, Quarterdeck first learned about this problem from customers who had bus-mastering SCSI hard disk controllers. They reported that when they booted their machines and started the multitasking DESQview software, their systems ran fine as long as they ran only one application. As soon as they opened a second application, the system would hang. The problem was also seen by users who were not using DESQview, but who were using the LOADHI feature of QEMM-386.

In this case, the hang occurred because the disk controller would prepare to load some absolute memory addresses with data pertaining to an application that was running; but by the time the data was actually transferred to these addresses, QEMM-386 had switched the memory map. Those absolute memory addresses no longer belonged to the application that could process the data. Instead, they belonged to some other application or process. In theory, this situation could have caused data corruption, but in reality, it never did. The memory corruption was typically so extensive that the systems simply hung as soon as a change in the memory map occurred.

Translating controllers

Many disk drives, such as IDE, ESDI, and SCSI, have more than 1,024 cylinders; in order for MS-DOS to access the additional drive space, the drive must be remapped to fit within the MS-DOS physical limitations. This process of converting the physical disk characteristics to a logical representation is performed by a translating controller. Basically, a translating controller multiplies one drive characteristic while dividing another drive characteristic to fit within the MS-DOS limitations and provide the maximum storage capacity of the drive. For example, a disk drive with physical characteristics of 2,048 cylinders, 8 heads, and 32 sectors per track may be remapped to a logical configuration of either 1,024 cylinders, 16 heads, and 32 sectors per track or 1,024 cylinders, 8 heads, and 64 sectors per track.

After a disk drive has been partitioned with a particular logical configuration, the data on the drive can be accessed only with the same configuration. Make sure that you write down the configuration information and store it in a safe and accessible location so that if you have a CMOS RAM failure, you can restore the original logical configuration and access the data.

When you need BIOS support

If the hard disk does not support the WD1003 or ST506 interface, then Windows will not be able to use the protected mode (FastDisk) support for 32-bit disk access. In such a case, the disk will need to be accessed by the services that are provided by the BIOS that is located on the disk controller if the disk is a boot disk. Otherwise, support may be provided by a device driver.

Virtual HD IRQ

If the disk drive has a nonstandard interface that Windows has trouble supporting, you may need to inform Windows that all disk access should be handled by the disk controller's BIOS. In such a case, add the following line to the [386 Enh] section in SYSTEM.INI:

```
VirtualHDIRQ=OFF
```

Having the disk controller's BIOS handle all disk access will most likely slow down the system but provide better compatibility. After all, a slow system is better than an unreliable system.

Video adapters

There have been various adapters created for the IBM compatible line of computers, starting with the original monochrome text only adapter and ending with various high resolution accelerated graphics adapters. In my opinion, the graphics adapter is one of the most important system components, particularly for a Windows-based system. A slow graphics adapter can make Windows unusable, or at the very least extremely slow. However, a fast graphics adapter can make Windows a joy to use. My personal recommendation is to utilize either a fast frame buffer display adapter, a mild accelerated adapter, or an extremely fast accelerated adapter. This depends on how much money you have to spend on your computer system. When looking at frame buffer display — that is, no acceleration — pick a local bus-based system. As a frame buffer adapter utilizes the system CPU to transfer data from system memory to the video memory buffer, a fast data path can make a significant improvement. Accelerated video adapters utilize either a fixed or programmable controller located on the video adapter to offload processing from the host CPU. To date, these are the fastest type of video display adapters. My personal system utilizes a local bus Diamond Viper, which has the best of both worlds in a fast data path and accelerated graphics. On my 486/66 based system, I generally exceed 50 million WinMarks in 1024x768x256 mode. And faster adapters are on the market!

Upper memory requirements

Every video adapter designed for the IBM compatible computer line utilizes a buffer to store the text or graphics that will be displayed on the system display unit. Table 13-2 shows upper memory buffer address requirements.

Table 16-2	Upper Memory Buffer Address Requirements
Adapter Type	*Buffer Address*
Monochrome Text	B800
Color Graphics Adapter	B800
Enhanced Graphics Adapter	A000
Video Graphics Array	A000
Super Video Graphics Array	A000, B000*
8514/A	C000
XGA	C600*

*Many SVGA adapters utilizing a 256-color mode also utilize this upper memory address space as well as the VGA buffer address space. Some even utilize a 2 to 4MB address space in the 16MB address space for ISA adapters and above the 16MB address space for EISA and MCA adapters.

8-bit and 16-bit video ROM BIOSs

Many of today's video adapters are designed to support both 8-bit and 16-bit I/O slots and can be configured to utilize 8-or 16-bit data access to the video adapter. A 16-bit access is the preferred method, as it provides faster access. However, if the video adapter is followed, in upper memory, by an 8-bit BIOS, then the video BIOS will also be switched in to 8-bit data access. And some adapters will not function correctly in some systems in 16-bit mode. If you encounter a problem on a system with an 8/16-bit BIOS, try configuring the BIOS to function in the 8-bit mode.

Video ROM BIOS shadowing

ROM shadowing is a fairly well-used technique for today's computers. It is utilized to speed up access to the video BIOS functions. However, there can be problems utilizing this technique. The foremost problem I have encountered is that some video BIOSs utilize a page mode access technique which does not work very well when shadowed by the system BIOS shadow options, or by a memory manager. In such a case the BIOS must be shadowed utilizing a device driver from the manufacturer. The other common problem I have encountered with shadowing the video BIOS is that the Windows display driver cannot find the BIOS where it is expected, and will then fail to load. If the video driver fails to load, then Windows will not load as it cannot switch into graphics mode. In such a case, disable all ROM shadowing for the display adapter or utilize the manufacturer's device driver.

Interrupt 2/9 enable

EGA and compatible adapters provide an interrupt, which can be hooked by applications, whenever it is safe to write to the video buffer without causing display related problems. Most VGA and SVGA adapters have a jumper switch to enable/disable support for EGA compatibility. It is very rare to require use of this jumper, except for very old MS-DOS based applications. Wherever possible, I recommend that this jumper be disabled. With the introduction of the VGA adapter, the video buffer can be read and written to without causing a noticeable display problem, hence the need to enable support for the interrupt is no longer needed, except for the case listed above.

Input/output adapters

Two basic I/O adapters that are in use today provide a link to external equipment, such as a modem, mouse, or printer. These adapters are commonly referred to as serial and parallel ports. Universal Asynchronous Receiver/Transmitters (UARTs) are serial devices that control serial ports. A serial port sends and receives data a bit at a time and assembles 8 of these bits into a single byte, whereas a standard parallel port is capable of sending 8 bits at a time but is only capable of receiving 4 bits at a time. The Enhanced Parallel Port (EPP) is capable of sending and receiving up to 8 bits at a time — dramatically enhancing throughput.

UARTs/communication ports

The three common UARTs are the basic model 8250, which was designed for the PC/XT computer; the 16450, which was designed for AT class computers; and the 16550, which was designed to improve high-speed serial communications. You can use any of these UARTs in any IBM-compatible machine because all of them use an 8-bit I/O interface.

- The 8250 is the original UART used in XT computers. Although this chip is very slow, it was more than adequate for the XT's 4.77Mhz bus speed.

- The 16450 UART was designed to accommodate the AT's 8Mhz bus speed.

  The 8250 and the 16450 chips are functionally identical and are pin compatible. In fact, many AT computers have an 8250 UART on their serial ports.

- The 16550 UART is basically a 16450 UART with the addition of a 16-byte FIFO (first in, first out) buffer. Buffering data received or transmitted provides more efficient use of the system's CPU. I consider a 16550 UART necessary (or other intelligent UARTs with a dedicated CPU to offload the workload from the host CPU) for reliable data transmissions at 38400, or higher, bits per second.

 The 16550 can work on any serial port that has an 8250 or 16450. You must have special software to activate the buffer. Otherwise, the 16550 will act like a 16450 without the buffer. Check your communications program to see if it supports the 16550 UART.

There is a program called 16550.EXE which tells the UART to turn on the FIFO buffer, and then the UART is just transparent to whatever communication program you are using.

UARTs can be serviced by interrupt driven service routines (ISRs) or by polled I/O service routines. An interrupt driven service routine is more efficient because it is called only when the complete character assembled in the I/O register is ready to be read or written to memory. A polled I/O service routine must continuously read, or poll, the line status register (LSR) to determine whether the current byte is ready to be received or the next byte is ready to be transmitted. Table 13-3 describes ISA communication ports, and Table 13-4 describes MCA communication ports.

Table 13-3	Communication Ports (ISA)		
I/O Base Address	*Serial Port*	*Default IRQ*	*Recommended IRQ*
03F8H	COM1	4	4
02F8H	COM2	3	3
03E8H	COM3	3	2
02E8H	COM4	4	5

Table 13-4	Communication Ports (MCA)		
I/O Base Address	*Serial Port*	*Default IRQ*	*Recommended IRQ*
03F8H	COM1	4	4
02F8H	COM2	3	3
3220H	COM3	3	3
3228H	COM4	3	3

I/O Base Address	Serial Port	Default IRQ	Recommended IRQ
4220H	COM5	3	3
4228H	COM6	3	3
5220H	COM7	3	3
5228H	COM8	3	3

Configuring COM ports

Communication with various peripherals is considered to be a very important aspect of personal computing, and various INI settings in the [386 Enh] section of SYSTEM.INI provide configuration options for nonstandard hardware in the Windows environment. There are also configuration options for fine-tuning serial port support for non-Windows applications.

- COMxBASE: Windows uses this entry to select the default serial port I/O base address. The default values are determined by the BIOS data areas for COM1 – COM4. Use the Control Panel Ports applet or System Engineer (included on the *Windows 3.1 Configuration SECRETS Disks*) to change the default values.

- COMxFIFO: Windows uses this entry to enable or disable the FIFO buffer on 16550 UARTs. This setting is used only for reception of data, and it applies only to Windows applications. Set this value to 1 to enable the feature or to 0 to disable it. You change the setting by manually editing SYSTEM.INI or by utilizing System Engineer.

- COMxAutoAssign: Windows uses this entry to arbitrate requests for the associated serial port. A value of -1 causes Windows to display a dialog box that lists the applications that are requesting access to the associated port and requires the user to select which application should be granted access to the serial port. A setting of 0 disables all arbitration, and a positive value that is less than 1000 indicates how many seconds the port must be inactive before access is granted to another application. The default setting is 2. For example, to set an inactive time of 5 seconds for serial port 1, the SYSTEM.INI entry would be COM1AutoAssign=5. Use the Control Panel Ports applet or System Engineer to change the default values.

- COMxIRQ: Windows uses this entry to specify the associated interrupt. Use the Control Panel Ports applet or System Engineer to change the default values.

- COMxProtocol: Windows uses this entry to suspend character simulation for virtual machines (that is, MS-DOS applications) when an XOFF character is received during high-speed character reception. Do not modify this entry if the application uses binary data transfers because the application may receive an XOFF character and suspend data reception. Use the Control Panel Ports applet or System Engineer to change the default values.

- COMxBuffer: Windows uses this entry to determine the Windows buffer size for the associated port. The default value is 128 (bytes). Use the Control Panel Ports applet or System Engineer to change the default values if you experience character dropouts with high-speed communications.

- COMBoostTime: Windows uses this entry to specify the time for a virtual machine (that is, an MS-DOS application) to service a serial port interrupt. If the MS-DOS application is dropping characters or having excessive retries on data downloads or uploads, increase this value. The default is 2 (milliseconds). Edit SYSTEM.INI or use System Engineer to change the default values.

- COMxTxFIFO: Windows for Workgroups 3.11 uses this entry to enable or disable the FIFO buffer on 16550 UARTs. This setting is used only for data transmission, and it applies to Windows and MS-DOS applications. You manually edit SYSTEM.INI to set this value to 1 to enable the buffer or 0 to disable it.

Configuring LPT ports

Windows provides the capacity to monitor parallel ports as well as serial ports to prevent multiple applications from overwriting each other's print jobs. These configuration options are located in the [386 Enh] section of SYSTEM.INI.

- LPT1AutoAssign: Windows uses this entry to arbitrate requests for the associated parallel port. A value of -1 causes Windows to display a dialog box that lists the applications that are requesting access to the associated port and requires the user to select which application should be granted access to the parallel port. A setting of 0 disables all arbitration, and a positive value that is less than 1000 indicates how many seconds the port must be inactive before access is granted to another application. The default setting is 2. For example, to set an inactive time of 5 seconds for parallel port 1 the SYSTEM.INI entry would be LPT1AutoAssign=5. Use the Control Panel 386 enhanced applet or manually edit SYSTEM.INI to change the default values.

- SGrabLPT: Windows uses this entry to redirect a virtual machine's parallel port output to the screen. For example, to redirect LPT1 to the screen, specify a value of SGrabLPT=1 in SYSTEM.INI or use System Engineer, included on the *Windows 3.1 Configuration SECRETS Disks.*

Network adapters

If you want to access other systems, you need some type of adapter to provide such access. This can be as simple as a serial port and a modem, or as complex as a dedicated network adapter, associated cables, and device drivers. The two basic types of network adapters are those that utilize I/O port access only and those that also utilize a dedicated buffer located in the upper memory area. Generally speaking, many of the network adapters that contain an upper memory buffer can also contain a dedicated processor to offload processing from the host CPU. Many also utilize DMA to transfer data from the adapter to system memory. As with any adapter that requires an I/O range, dedicated interrupt, or DMA channel, conflicts can occur. To avoid such a conflict, be sure that none of the adapter's I/O, interrupt, upper memory addresses, or DMA channels are shared with any other adapter on the system.

PCMCIA

There are three industry standard, approved Personal Computer Memory Card International Association (PCMCIA) adapter types and one standard, but not industry approved, PCMCIA adapter type. PCMCIA adapters have been designed for the portable computer market, but they are also beginning to penetrate the desktop market. These devices now include fax/modems, network adapters, SCSI adapters, serial ports, flash memory, and hard disk drives. In most instances, these devices perform as well as their full-size counterparts and use 4 – 16K of the upper memory address space that must be excluded from the memory manager.

The PCMCIA specification has the potential to offer several advantages to portable computer users, including such features as hot swapping of PCMCIA adapters, execute-in-place ROM cards, host independence (the ability to use the same adapter on any platform with a PCMCIA expansion slot), and automatic adapter configuration.

PCMCIA adapter types

The four PCMCIA types are as follows:

- The type I slot, which accommodates an adapter that is 54 millimeters wide, 58.6 millimeters deep, and 3.3 millimeters high. The type I adapter is generally used for memory related products.

- The type II slot, which is the most popular expansion slot and can accommodate an adapter with a maximum height of 5 millimeters. All other dimensions are the same. The type II adapter is generally used for network adapters, fax/modems, serial ports, and SCSI adapters.

- The type III slot, which is most commonly used for disk drives and has a maximum height of 10.5 millimeters. All other dimensions are the same as previous PCMCIA type specifications.

■ The type IV PCMCIA slot, which has been introduced by Toshiba and is 16 millimeters high. All other dimensions are the same as previous specifications. This nonstandard expansion slot has been created for manufacturers of PCMCIA adapters to accommodate larger hard drives and fax/modems with built in RJ-11 telephone jacks. Although this card is a nonstandard and nonapproved size, Toshiba does have a considerable market share, so approval will most likely occur in the future.

Socket and card services

PCMCIA adapters use a host I/O chipset, similar to a desktop I/O bus chipset, that interfaces with the installed adapters. Like adapters that are installed on a desktop system, PCMCIA adapters are accessed through device drivers. However, unlike desktop adapters, PCMCIA adapters need to be initialized by either a software enabler or a socket or card service client driver. The host I/O chipset is the interface between the expansion bus and the PCMCIA socket. The socket and card services are layered onto the host I/O chipset. The socket service, which is hardware dependent, configures the adapter by reading the adapter's timing and configuration information from the card information structure (CIS). The socket service is the lowest level interface. Riding on top of the socket service is the card service, which is concerned with system-wide configuration issues.

In theory, PCMCIA adapters are plug-and-play compatible with any PCMCIA expansion slot. In reality, they are not compatible with all manufacturers' PCMCIA chipsets. When you purchase a PCMCIA adapter, always refer to your documentation to find out whether the adapter is supported on your hardware, or at least make sure that the vendor will let you return any PCMCIA adapter that does not function properly in your portable computer.

Hardware Virtualization

In order for Windows to provide multiple MS-DOS sessions, the operating system must simulate individual system components, such as the disk controller, video controller, I/O ports, and so on. This process is known as *hardware virtualization*. Windows provides hardware virtualization only when it is executing in enhanced mode. To provide these services, Windows uses a combination of software and the I/O port trapping that is provided by the 80386 and compatible CPU line. The software components that provide these services are known as *virtual device drivers* (VxDs). These VxDs provide a 32-bit protected mode service and arbitrate hardware software/hardware requests. Because VxDs operate at ring 0 of the Intel 80386 CPU, they have unlimited access to the system and are potentially the most powerful type of software that is written for the Windows environment.

Default [386 Enh] VxDs

Windows 3.x running in enhanced mode is a collection of dynamic link libraries and virtual device drivers. Many of these VxDs are included in KRNL386.EXE and are so noted by a `device=*VxDName` entry in the `[386 Enh]` section of SYSTEM.INI. In addition to these default VxDs, the Windows Setup program installs additional VxDs for certain hardware or software combinations.

Windows 3.1

Windows 3.1 includes the following `[386 Enh]` SYSTEM.INI entries:

- `device=lanman10.386`: This VxD provides CD-ROM support.

- `device=*vmd`: This VxD provides virtual mouse support to multiple virtual machines.

- `network=*dosnet,*vnetbios`: These VxDs translate the NetBIOS APIs for Windows applications in order to provide network access.

- `ebios=*ebios`: This VxD reserves the extended BIOS area for computers that have an extended BIOS.

- `display=*vddvga` for Windows for Workgroups 3.1 and 3.11, and `*vdd` for Windows 3.1: This VxD provides virtual display services for virtual machines. It is display dependent. This particular VxD is for the default VGA driver. It also arbitrates BIOS requests and directs I/O and display buffer requests.

- `keyboard=*vkd`: This VxD provides virtual keyboard services for multiple virtual machines.

- `device=vtdapi.386`: This VxD provides multimedia timer services.

- `device=*vpicd`: This VxD supports other VxDs to process peripheral interrupts.

- `device=*vtd`: This VxD virtualizes the system timer services.

- `device=*reboot`: This VxD installs the Ctrl+Alt+Del handler.

- `device=*vdmad`: This VxD provides direct memory access services that are based on the Microsoft Virtual DMA Services (VDS). It also arbitrates all DMA I/O requests so that multiple virtual machines can use the same DMA channel as well as provide services to bus master I/O controllers, such as SCSI and ESDI disk controllers.

- `device=*vsd`: This VxD arbitrates access to the built-in computer speaker.

- `device=*int13`: This VxD is part of the 32-Bit Disk Access, or FastDisk, services. It intercepts Int13 disk I/O requests, which are then passed to the BLOCKDEV VxD to be queued and serviced.

- device=*wdctrl: This VxD communicates with the physical hard disk controller for WD1003- or ST506-compatible disk controllers.

- device=*v86mmgr: This VxD provides memory management services for virtual machines and other VxDs.

- device=*pageswap: This VxD provides demand page virtual memory services.

- device=*dosmgr: This VxD translates and manages virtual machine MS-DOS application program interface (API) requests.

- device=*vmpoll: This VxD determines when a virtual machine is idle.

- device=*wshell: This VxD manages full-screen error messages, such as the Blue Screen error messages that Windows displays, as well as providing an interface to MS-DOS-based applications.

- device=*BLOCKDEV: This VxD provides developers with an API that services asynchronous read, write, and cancel requests; all other requests are passed to the BIOS for processing. BLOCKDEV queues the requests to be serviced and then passes them to the WDCTRL VxD for processing.

- device=*PAGEFILE: This VxD provides faster and better paging services. When you use it in conjunction with the *int13, *wdctrl, and BLOCKDEV VxDs, MS-DOS is essentially bypassed, and the disk is accessed directly for paging services. This provides the ability to page out portions of virtual machines in 4K pages.

- device=*vfd: The virtual floppy controller VxD provides services to assure that copy protection schemes work as expected for software installations, and it communicates with the virtual DMA VxD for data transfers.

- device=*parity: This VxD installs a handler for nonmaskable interrupts (NMIs); the handler provides a service routine for memory or bus errors to be trapped, and then serviced safely. Generally, this means that once trapped, the system will be shutdown to prevent any further system damage from occurring. Once a memory or bus error has been detected, further processing would most likely be inaccurate.

- device=*biosxlat: This VxD maps the real mode BIOS APIs for protected mode applications that provide support for Windows applications and device drivers to access the BIOS services.

  This VxD supports access to the BIOS services for Windows applications and device drivers by mapping the real mode BIOS APIs for protected mode applications.

- device=*vcd: This VxD provides interrupt services for the COMM.DRV Windows driver, as well as providing virtual COM port arbitration services for multiple virtual machines.

- `device=*vmcpd`: This VxD virtualizes the math coprocessor to arbitrate requests on machines that are equipped with a math coprocessor.

- `device=*combuff`: This VxD provides the buffering services for the communications driver and the physical serial ports that are installed in the system. It also buffers serial I/O requests during task switches.

- `device=*vpd`: This VxD virtualizes the printer or the associated LPT port.

Windows for Workgroups Version 3.1

In addition to the VxDs used by Windows 3.x, Windows for Workgroups includes the following [386 Enh] SYSTEM.INI entries:

- `network=vnetbios.386,vnetsup.386,vredir.386,vserver.386,vbrowse.386,vwc.386`: These VxDs provide network support. They are protected mode drivers that provide NetBIOS, redirector, server, browsing, and workgroup connection services. After Windows for Workgroups is started, the VNETSUP VxD is loaded and, in turn, initializes the NetBEUI (vnb.386) VxD and the NetBIOS VxDs.

- `device=vshare.386`: This VxD provides a protected mode version of file-sharing services.

- `transport=vnb.386`: This VxD provides NetBEUI services.

Windows for Workgroups Version 3.11

In addition to the VxDs used by Windows 3.x and Windows for Workgroups 3.1, Windows for Workgroups 3.11 includes the following [386 Enh] SYSTEM.INI entries:

- `transport=netbeui.386,nwlink.386,nwnblink.386`: These VxDs provide NetBEUI and Novell IPX/SPX services.

- `netmisc=ndis.386,ndis2sup.386`: These VxDs support for real-mode NDIS transport drivers.

- `netcard3=rasmac.386`: This VxD provides Remote Access Services.

- `network=*vnetbios,*vwc,vnetsup.386,vredir.386,vserver.386`

- `device=vrsd.386`: This VxD is a virtual sound driver installed by MS Golf for Windows.

- `device=vpmtd.386`: This VxD is a WIN386.EXE IFAX scheduler device.

- `device=lpt.386`: This VxD provides parallel port arbitration.

- `device=serial.386`: This VxD provides serial port support.

- `device=vcomm.386`: This VxD provides serial port support.

- `device=vcache.386`: This VxD is the 32-bit cache replacement for SmartDrive.

- `device=ifsmgr.386`: This VxD provides Installable File Services support.
- `device=vfat.386`: This VxD supports the 32-bit File Allocation Table (FAT).
- `device=ios.386`: This is the I/O supervisor VxD.
- `device=vxdldr.386`: This is a helper VxD to load additional VxDs.

Additional optional VxDs

A couple of the more common optional VxDs include the following:

- `device=vpowerd.386`: This VxD provides power management services.
- `device=w32s.386`: This VxD provides the WIN32s API for 32-bit applications. This interface includes 32-bit memory management, structured exception handling, floating point emulation, and so on.
- `device=vfintd.386`: This VxD provides services for the MS-DOS 6.x Windows floppy backup utility.

If you utilize a third-party memory manager then perhaps you will see the following Qualitas 386Max support VxDs listed in your SYSTEM.INI file:

- `386MAX.VXD`
- `BLUEMAX.VXD`

Or perhaps you use QEMM386, in which case you may see one or more of the following QuarterDeck support VxDs:

- `STEALTH.VXD`
- `VIDRAM.VXD`
- `ST-ROM.VXD`
- `ST-DBL.VXD`
- `WINHIRAM.VXD`

Troubleshooting

Because MS-DOS is a single-tasking operating system where only one application at a time accesses the system hardware, and Windows is a multitasking operating system where multiple applications access the system hardware, a hardware configuration that works with MS-DOS may not necessarily work reliably with Windows. The three most common causes of system failure or inconsistent hardware functionality are shared interrupts, overlapped I/O addresses, and upper memory conflicts. Several applications can help you diagnose these problems; however, only one method is guaranteed to find and solve such problems. That method is digging out the system documentation, opening the system case, examining each peripheral component, and writing down and comparing each and every system interrupt, I/O port, upper memory address, and DMA channel in use in the system.

Interrupt isolation

Every Windows system includes the Microsoft diagnostic tool, MSD.EXE, which is located in the WINDOWS directory. You can use MSD to help determine what active interrupts are in use. (See Chapter 2 for more on MSD.) An *active interrupt* is an interrupt with an associated interrupt handler, such as the BIOS or device driver. MSD cannot detect interrupts that have been allocated by a peripheral but are not currently in use. Therefore, to gain an accurate IRQ listing, run MSD with a clean boot (that is, no memory manager, no device driver, and so on), then run it with all of the associated device drivers but no memory manager, and finally run it with the memory manager. Compare each listing to gain as accurate a report as possible. As an example, the following listings are from my Toshiba T4600c portable computer. Notice that the clean boot does not list the interrupts in use for the second serial port, mouse, or Xircom CreditCard Ethernet adapter, even though the hardware is installed on the system. Yet after the drivers have been installed, these interrupts are identified.

Clean boot

IRQ	Address	Description	Detected	Handled By
0	1B2C:003C	Timer Click	Yes	Default Handlers
1	1B2C:0045	Keyboard	Yes	Default Handlers
2	1B2C:0057	Second 8259A	Yes	Default Handlers
3	1B2C:006F	COM2: COM4:	No	Default Handlers
4	1B2C:0087	COM1: COM3:	COM1:	Default Handlers
5	1B2C:009F	LPT2:	No	Default Handlers
6	1B2C:00B7	Floppy Disk	Yes	Default Handlers
7	0070:06F4	LPT1:	Yes	System Area
8	1B2C:0052	Real-Time Clock	Yes	Default Handlers Handlers
9	F000:DF4A	Redirected IRQ2	Yes	BIOS
10	1B2C:00CF	(Reserved)		Default Handlers

IRQ	Address	Description	Detected	Handled By
11	1B2C:00E7	(Reserved)		Default Handlers
12	1B2C:00FF	(Reserved)		Default Handlers
13	F000:DF54	Math Coprocessor	Yes	BIOS
14	1B2C:0117	Fixed Disk	Yes	Default Handlers
15	1B2C:012F	(Reserved)		Default Handlers

No memory manager and device drivers loaded

IRQ	Address	Description	Detected	Handled By
0	1EBB:00D2	Timer Click	Yes	MOUSE
1	132D:0045	Keyboard	Yes	Default Handlers
2	132D:0057	Second 8259A	Yes	Default Handlers
3	132D:006F	COM2: COM4:	COM2:	Default Handlers
4	132D:0087	COM1: COM3:	COM1:	Default Handlers
5	24CB:1719	LPT2:	No	XIRCOM$
6	132D:00B7	Floppy Disk	Yes	Default Handlers
7	0070:06F4	LPT1:	Yes	System Area
8	132D:0052	Real-Time Clock	Yes	Default Handlers
9	F000:DF4A	Redirected IRQ2		Yes BIOS
10	132D:00CF	(Reserved)		Default Handlers
11	132D:00E7	(Reserved)		Default Handlers
12	1EBB:02CD	(Reserved)		MOUSE
13	F000:DF54	Math Coprocessor	Yes	BIOS
14	132D:0117	Fixed Disk	Yes	Default Handlers
15	132D:012F	(Reserved)		Default Handlers

Memory manager (EMM386.EXE) and device drivers loaded

IRQ	Address	Description	Detected	Handled By
0	197E:1875	Timer Click	Yes	Block Device
1	197E:1923	Keyboard	Yes	Block Device
2	1318:0057	Second 8259A	Yes	Default Handlers
3	1318:006F	COM2: COM4:	COM2:	Default Handlers
4	1318:0087	COM1: COM3:	COM1:	Default Handlers
5	1DB0:1719	LPT2:	No	XIRCOM$
6	1318:00B7	Floppy Disk	Yes	Default Handlers
7	0070:06F4	LPT1:	Yes	System Area
8	1318:0052	Real-Time Clock	Yes	Default Handlers

IRQ	Address	Description	Detected	Handled By
9	F000:DF4A	Redirected IRQ2	Yes	BIOS
10	1318:00CF	(Reserved)		Default Handlers
11	1318:00E7	(Reserved)		Default Handlers
12	14D3:02CD	(Reserved)		MOUSE
13	F000:DF54	Math Coprocessor	Yes	BIOS
14	1318:0117	Fixed Disk	Yes	Default Handlers
15	1318:012F	(Reserved)		Default Handlers

Memory manager (QEMM386.SYS, No Stealth ROMs) and device drivers loaded

IRQ	Address	Description	Detected	Handled By
0	DC36:1875	Timer Click	Yes	Block Device
1	DC36:1923	Keyboard	Yes	Block Device
2	D8A0:0057	Second 8259A	Yes	
3	D8A0:006F	COM2: COM4:	COM2:	
4	D8A0:0087	COM1: COM3:	COM1:	
5	E425:1719	LPT2:	No	XIRCOM$
6	D8A0:00B7	Floppy Disk	Yes	
7	0070:06F4	LPT1:	Yes	System Area
8	D8A0:0052	Real-Time Clock	Yes	
9	F000:DF4A	Redirected IRQ2	Yes	BIOS
10	D8A0:00CF	(Reserved)		
11	D8A0:00E7	(Reserved)		
12	0FB1:02CD	(Reserved)		MOUSE
13	F000:DF54	Math Coprocessor	Yes	BIOS
14	D8A0:0117	Fixed Disk	Yes	
15	D8A0:012F	(Reserved)		

If you use a third-party memory manager, MSD will not accurately report the interrupt handler for the associated peripheral because in most cases the memory manager will need to hook the associated interrupt to provide proper support.

I/O address conflicts

Determining an I/O conflict in an ISA or mixed EISA/ISA/VL-BUS system can be very difficult, particularly because most manufacturers do not list all of the associated I/O ports that their adapter card uses. MCA-, EISA-, and PCI-based systems can limit some of the problems that are associated with configuring a system and determining I/O port usage. However, the associated data files that these systems use to list the adapter I/O ports may sometimes be incomplete because there is a file size limit. If the listed I/O ports would cause the file size to be exceeded, the manufacturer has to determine which I/O ports to list and which to drop from the list.

When you are attempting to determine an I/O conflict, you need to be aware that most manufacturers list only the starting I/O, or base, address and not the entire range. If the adapter is an 8-bit adapter, then eight I/O ports most likely start from the base address; 16- and 32-bit adapters often function similarly. For example, most 16-bit adapters with a starting I/O address of 0300 actually use the range 0300 to 030F. If another peripheral is configured to use any I/O address in the same range, then an I/O overlap will occur, and the peripheral devices may operate sporadically.

Only one method guarantees that you will find the problem adapter, or at least one method has always worked for me. That method is to build a clean system. A *clean system* is one that has only the video adapter and the disk adapter installed. If the problem still exists after you build a clean system, then swap either the video or disk adapter and try again. If the problem still exists with different video and disk adapters, then perhaps the motherboard is the problem. When the system functions as expected, add each peripheral back into the system, one at a time, to determine the cause of the I/O conflict. You can also use this method to identify interrupt or upper memory problems. After you identify the troublesome peripheral, you should examine the configuration options, modify the peripheral settings, reinstall the peripheral, and then test the system.

One thing to keep in mind is that every system is different. Sometimes, even two supposedly identical systems from the same manufacturer may be slightly different. Do not accept the claims of your friends, acquaintances, or the manufacturer that peripheral X and peripheral Y always work together without incident. Always make sure that you can return a peripheral if it does not function correctly in your system. As an example, I've always liked the ATI series of graphics adapters — especially the ATI Graphics Ultra, which is based on the IBM 8514/A display adapter. I have also been quite fond of the Adaptec line of SCSI controllers. Therefore, when I upgraded my ISA motherboard to an EISA/VL-Bus motherboard, I also purchased an Adaptec 1742a and an ATI Graphics Ultra Pro (EISA version). Unfortunately, this combination would not function in my system. The technical support staffs at ATI and Adaptec were quite responsive to the problem, but they explained that the 8514/A and compatibles use a scattered series of I/O ports, not all of which are listed in the peripheral's configuration file, and that all EISA peripherals use a series of I/O ports that are based on the card slot that the adapter is installed in. The primary suggestion, which worked for other users with EISA and EISA/VL-Bus systems, was to change I/O slots in the hope that a suitable configuration could be found. Unfortunately, this suggestion did not work for me. The Adaptec 1742a would not function in enhanced mode, although it would work in standard mode. My solution was to replace the ATI display adapter with a Diamond Viper VL-Bus and use the Adaptec 1742a in enhanced mode.

Table 13-5 lists some of the more common I/O ports that are defined for IBM-compatible computers.

Table 13-5	Common I/O Ports for IBM-Compatible Computers
Ports	*Description*
0000-000F	DMA controller
0020-002F	Peripheral interrupt controller 1
0030-003F	Peripheral interrupt controller 2
0040-004F	Timer
0050-005F	Timer
0060-006F	Keyboard
0070-007F	Real-time clock
0080-008F	DMA page registers
0090-009F	DMA page registers
00A0-00AF	Peripheral interrupt controller 2
00B0-00BF	Peripheral interrupt controller 2
00C0-00CF	DMA controller 2
00D0-00DF	DMA controller 2
00F0-00FF	Math coprocessor
01F0-01FF	WD1003-compatible fixed disk controller
0200-020F	Game I/O adapter
0270-027F	Parallel port 2
02B0-02BF	Alternate EGA
02C0-02CF	Alternate EGA
02D0-02DF	Alternate EGA
02E0-02EF	Data acquisition GPIB
02F0-02FF	Serial port 2
0300-030F	Prototype adapter card
0310-031F	Prototype adapter card
0360-036F	PC network adapters
0370-037F	Parallel port 1
0380-038F	SDLC or Bisync #2
0390-039F	Cluster adapter
03A0-03AF	Bisync #1

(continued)

Table 13-5 *(continued)*

Ports	Description
03B0-03BF	Monochrome display adapter
03C0-03CF	EGA adapter
03D0-03DF	CGA adapter
03F0-03FF	Floppy disk controller and serial port #1

Upper memory conflicts

The three types of upper memory conflicts are those caused by a memory manager, as explained in previous chapters; those caused by a BIOS-related problem that the peripheral is experiencing; and those caused by a peripheral's upper memory requirements. Once again, the only sure way to isolate an upper memory problem is to open up the system case, get the manufacturer's documentation, and write down all of the peripheral's settings. You also can pull individual peripherals from the system, as mentioned previously, to find the problem adapter. Although many third-party memory managers and diagnostic programs such as MSD and Quarterdeck's Manifest list ROM BIOSs and upper memory regions that have been accessed by the system, these diagnostics rarely catch every address that is in use in the system. Table 13-6 lists common upper memory addresses.

Table 13-6	Common Upper Memory Addresses
Address	**Description**
A000-AFFF	Graphics buffer
B000-B7FF	Sometimes used by SVGA 256-color video modes
B800-BFFF	Text buffer
C000-C7FF	Video BIOS
CC00-CFFF	Generally free
D000-DFFF	Generally free
E000-EFFF	Generally free, on PS/2 computers generally in use for additional ROMs
F000-FFFF	System BIOS

Many portable computers require additional upper memory locations to support various power management features or other special hardware features. For example, my Toshiba T4600c requires the C800–CFFF area to support the battery management services and the E000–E7FF area to support the hard RAM features. Hard RAM is a means of creating a battery-backed, solid-state hard disk by utilizing a portion of system memory.

Summary

In this chapter, I discussed optimizing hardware configuration for Windows:

▶ I covered basic hardware configuration and BIOS setup.

▶ I reviewed power management and hardware peripherals.

▶ Finally, I gave some hardware troubleshooting advice.

Chapter 14
Video Configuration

Windows supports several video display modes and resolutions. As such, the components of a computer's video subsystem come in a variety of configurations. This chapter offers advice on configuring Windows for specific video modes and resolutions, and on using a number of third-party video boards and drivers with Windows.

The Video Connection

For you to understand how Windows interacts with your computer's video components, you need to be familiar with the video subsystem's operation. The video subsystem consists of three basic components: the monitor, the video card or adapter, and the video device driver. How well and how fast Windows applications display data depends on the synergy and operating characteristics of these three components. However, the reliability and stability of your Windows environment is ultimately a function of the video driver.

Windows can use a variety of video displays and adapters. However, Windows is relatively dumb about the differences between hardware devices. Instead of carrying around information about every device on the market, it uses driver programs. All Windows applications use the same video driver.

This brings me to the concept of device independence that I've discussed elsewhere. Just to recap, most DOS applications contain everything they need to know about the computer, the keyboard, the mouse, possible printers, modems, and other hardware devices. In contrast, Windows programs don't know, and don't have to know, about specific hardware devices.

The programs rely on Windows' intelligence in handling all the hardware specifics. Windows is the transmitter and receiver. When you click a mouse button or press a key, Windows tells the application what has occurred. When a Windows application sends output to the screen or to a printer, it sends the data to Windows, which then communicates with the proper device.

Windows ships with standard or generic drivers that allow it to interface with most hardware devices. But if you have a device with specialized features, you may not be able to take advantage of them without proprietary or specialized drivers.

Which Graphics Standard to Use

Windows allows you to choose from a wide variety of video displays and adapters. The video mode you select determines the resolution of the screen and number of colors available. Screen resolution is measured in pixels, which correspond to addressable dots on the screen. The more pixels, the higher the screen resolution and the sharper the image, but you compromise speed. Also, the more colors the board displays, the slower the display because the computer has to process even more data.

When you plan a Windows configuration, consider the kinds of applications that you run and the type of work you do. You may decide that your applications don't need high resolution or numerous colors. You probably won't notice much difference in speed if you go from VGA to Super VGA, but beyond that, there is a drop in speed. Table 14-1 lists various graphics standards and characteristics that you can reference when planning your Windows video configuration.

Table 14-1		PC Graphics Standards	
Standard	*Resolution*	*Colors*	*Windows Support*
CGA	320x200	4	No
	640x200	2	Yes
Hercules	720x348	2	Yes
EGA	640x350	16	Yes
MCGA	640x480	2	Yes
	320x200	256	No
VGA	320x200	256	No
	640x480	16	Yes
Super VGA	800x600	16	Yes

Standard	Resolution	Colors	Windows Support
	800x600	256	Yes
8514/A	1024x768	16	Yes
	1024x768	256	Yes
XGA	1024x768	256	Yes
TIGA	1024x768	16	Yes
	1024x768	256	Yes

Video Board Characteristics

Two points to consider when assessing a video board's color capability are the number of colors the adapter can produce simultaneously on-screen and the size of the palette from which it draws those colors. The memory on the display adapter generally limits the number of colors, while the palette is restricted by the digital-to-analog converter that the board uses.

The reason on-board memory limits resolution is that each pixel needs storage for each of its potential colors. If you divide the amount of memory on the display adapter by the number of pixels on-screen, you get the approximate number of bits available for storing the color of each pixel. For 256 different colors, you need 8 bits per pixel; for 16 different colors, you need only 4 bits per pixel.

For 256 colors drawn from a palette of 256K, you need at least 512K of video memory on a display adapter at either 640x480 or 800x600 pixel resolution. At 1024x768 pixels, you need at least 1MB. True color 800x600 systems need at least 1.5MB; true color 1024x768 systems need at least 2.5MB.

Installing Display Adapters for WFW

The installation procedures that are provided by display-adapter manufacturers may require you to replace or modify the SETUP.INF file in the Windows System directory. This causes problems in Windows for Workgroups.

If your third-party display-adapter installation replaces or modifies the SETUP.INF file, use the following procedure instead.

To install the display-adapter drivers, follow these steps:

1. Rename the SETUP.INF file provided with your display-adapter package to OEMSETUP.INF and place it on the floppy disk or in the directory containing the third-party display-driver files.

2. From the Main group, run Windows Setup.

3. Choose Change System Settings from the Options menu.

4. From the list of Display options, choose Other Display (requires disk from OEM).

5. Insert the disk that contains the OEMSETUP.INF file and the driver files for your display adapter. Or if these files are located on your hard disk, type the path to the directory that contains the files and then choose OK.

6. Select the type of display adapter you want to use and then choose OK.

   Setup copies all necessary files from the driver disk and may request files from the Windows for Workgroups disks.

7. Insert any additional disks that are requested and then choose OK.

If you accidentally overwrite the original SETUP.INF file, you can copy it from Windows for Workgroups 3.11 Disk 1 into your Windows System directory. ■

Installing Display Adapters for Windows

To install Windows drivers, you usually have to rerun Windows' SETUP.EXE from the DOS prompt or copy the supplied files into your \Windows\System directory and run Setup from within Windows. Some video cards come with their own installation programs that modify the Windows initialization files as necessary.

Before installing drivers, make copies of the SYSTEM.INI in the Windows directory and SETUP.INF in Windows\System. This enables you to restore your old setup if you install a driver that renders Windows invisible or unable to start.

When you install a higher-resolution display adapter, there are several things to consider: You must ensure that the upgrade doesn't conflict with any other part of your system, that the upgrade is properly matched to your PC for optimum performance, and that your programs properly recognize the upgrade.

The first step is to check how the new display adapter interacts with the hardware in your PC. Some display adapters duplicate display circuitry already in your PC — the original display adapter, for example, or the display circuitry on your PC's system board. Graphics coprocessors, on the other hand, typically work in cooperation with your current display system.

If you're upgrading to a display adapter with its own VGA circuitry, it's probably best to defeat your old display system so that the new one can take complete control without conflicts. If your PC came with a display adapter in an expansion slot into which you plug your monitor, you can usually just remove the old display adapter and plug in the new one.

If your system has video functions integrated into its system board, however, you have to do a bit of research to eliminate potential conflicts. Most PCs with built-in system-board graphics let you switch off their internal display circuitry with a jumper or dual in-line package (DIP) switch. You have to check your PC owner's manual to find the provision it makes. In most cases, there is an on/off switch labeled VGA. Before installing your new display adapter, switch it off.

It's very important that your monitor be synchronized with the signal your display adapter produces. For the monitor to present a stable image — one that doesn't degenerate into a blur of lines resembling a frenetic zebra — each dot from your display adapter must be precisely synchronized with the sweep of the electron beam across your screen monitor.

The vertical frequency is often called the *refresh* or *frame rate* of the display system. It determines the stability of the on-screen image. The general rule is the higher the frequency, the better. If your display adapter can generate a higher refresh rate and your monitor can accept it, you should set up your system to use the higher rate.

The horizontal frequency, also called the *line rate,* is related to the refresh rate. If you multiply the number of frames appearing each second by the number of lines in the image, you get the approximate line rate. This is an approximation because not all lines used by a display system are visible nor are all of them counted in resolution figures.

To keep the line rate low, some manufacturers of display adapters resort to *interlacing signals,* which break each frame into two fields and alternately display half the lines of the total image in each field. With interlacing, the lines of the two fields alternate — one field shows odd-numbered lines, and the other field shows even-numbered lines — so that the two fields weave together.

With some monitors, interlacing can produce visual problems, such as a pronounced flicker. The key consideration when matching a display adapter to a monitor is that the monitor be able to synchronize to the field rate — twice the frame rate — of the signal. For example, the current IBM XGA system uses a frame rate of 43.5Hz and a field rate of 87Hz. To synchronize with those signals, a monitor must accept a vertical frequency of 87Hz.

The need for stable on-screen images dictates that the frame rate not be too low, and your ability to perceive those images dictates that it not be too high. As a result, the frame rate of any display system falls into a well-defined range. The lowest frame rate you'll find is about 50Hz. The highest in general use is the 87 Hz rate used by the XGA system. Consequently, a monitor with a vertical synchronizing frequency range at least that wide covers the needs of almost any display adapter.

Horizontal synchronizing signals are another matter. The sharper the image, the more lines it needs — practically without limit. An 800x600 pixel image at the VESA standard 72Hz frame rate requires a horizontal frequency of 48kHz; so does a VESA-sanctioned 1024x768 pixel image at a 60Hz frame rate. Raise the refresh rate to 72Hz, and at 1024x768 pixels, you'll need at least 58kHz. The demands of interlaced signals are much lower, however. With its 43.5Hz frame rate and 87Hz field rate, the interlaced XGA requires only 35.5kHz horizontal frequency.

Accessing the Microsoft Windows Driver Library

The Microsoft Windows Driver Library (WDL) contains device drivers for printers, displays, audio devices, and network card adapters. These drivers enable the devices to run with Microsoft Windows 3.1. Microsoft updates this library as new and updated drivers become available. To use these device drivers, do the following:

1. Download WDL.TXT from the Microsoft Software Download Library (GO MSDL) on CompuServe. Locate your device by searching the WDL text file. Note the name of the file listed next to the device. This is the EXE file you need to download; it contains all the files you need to support your device.

2. Download the file to a floppy disk or to a subdirectory you created on your hard disk. If you are downloading to a floppy disk, you need to have a formatted, blank disk. If you are downloading to your hard disk, create a new subdirectory in which you will place the files.

Do not download files directly into your Windows directory. You could inadvertently overwrite files essential to the proper operation of your system.

3. At the MS-DOS prompt, change to the floppy disk drive (or the subdirectory on your hard disk) that contains the EXE file. Type the filename and then press Enter.

When the EXE file finishes running, all the files you need to support your device, such as a DRV file and an OEMSETUP.INF file, are set up. You are also provided with a TXT file that contains instructions for installing the device drivers (or other software) and a licensing agreement.

If you do not have a modem, you can obtain individual Windows drivers on disk by calling Microsoft Product Support Services at 206-637-7098.

Installing drivers from the Windows Driver Library (WDL)

When you install an updated driver from the Windows Driver Library (WDL), the EXE file for the updated driver must be executed in an empty directory before you install the new drivers with the Windows Setup program.

If you obtained updated drivers from the MSDL, they are self extracting. (That is, once the EXE filename is typed, the file extracts the individual files it contains into the current directory.)

The updated video drivers are still compressed after the separate files are extracted from the EXE file. To make them usable, they must be installed using the Windows Setup program.

To install a WDL driver file with Windows Setup, follow these steps:

1. Create a directory in which to expand the individual driver files.

2. Copy the file into the temporary directory and run it by typing its EXE name. For example, to expand the TSENG1.EXE driver, type **TSENG1**. This extracts the individual files from the EXE file.

3. Run Setup from the Windows directory MS-DOS prompt, or while in Windows by executing Setup from the Windows Setup icon in the Main group. For the appropriate hardware setting (such as Display), choose Other (requires disk from manufacturer).

4. Type the name of the directory created in step 1 and press Enter.

5. Select the driver to be installed and press Enter. Doing so expands and copies the updated files to the Windows\System directory.

6. Close and restart Windows.

Why the Video Display Driver Is Crucial

In addition to color support, the video display driver controls the following four aspects of the video picture:

- The resolution or number of pixels displayed

- The size of the screen fonts

- The *logical pixels per inch* (lpi), at which Windows thinks your display runs

- The size of the bitmap resources (icons, buttons, and so on)

VGA runs at 96 logical pixels per inch, so no matter what size monitor you have, Windows concludes that 1 inch equals 96 pixels. As you increase resolution, you increase the logical screen area because Windows still interprets 96 pixels as being equal to 1 inch. More pixels give you more inches so that you need a larger screen.

If you run 1024x768 on a 14-inch monitor, you in effect reduce the physical size of the Windows logical inch. You haven't increased the resolution of the screen display because Windows still believes that 96 pixels is 1 inch. To be consistent, Windows' bitmap VGA screen-font files also assume that the screen is running at 96 lpi.

For comparison, consider IBM's 8514/A standard. In implementing the 8514/A standard, which runs at 1024x768, IBM concluded that 20-inch monitors would not be available to everyone because of their cost, and that the 16-inch monitor fit more in line with a standard system configuration. To prevent text from being too small to read comfortably at 1024x768 on a 16-inch monitor, IBM increased the logical pixels per inch from 96 to 120.

The result is that everything appears about 25 percent larger with the 8514/A standard. For example a 10-point screen font is 25 percent taller than the equivalent screen font under a 96lpi VGA screen driver. What this means in terms of a Windows configuration is that the 8514/A format screen driver has larger system FON files and needs larger bitmap resources. What you gain with this standard is that a 120lpi driver produces cleaner text than a 96lpi driver when you run the text on the same monitor because your 10-point characters are made up of more pixels.

The moral here is that you do not want to mix and match the two formats, using 96lpi VGA FON files with a driver that thinks it's actually running at 120lpi. This creates chaos when running programs such as Adobe Type Manager. One of the first things ATM does is to ask the system what the lpi value is so that it can generate typefaces accordingly. In the above scenario, mixing 96lpi FON files with 120lpi ATM-generated fonts creates a visual mess. Also, if your driver uses the wrong bitmap resources, using the 8514/A resources at 800x600 produces a distorted display, with buttons too big for the display area.

Video Coprocessors

Most video coprocessor cards replace the video adapter in your computer. In DOS mode, they function as a normal VGA or Super VGA adapter. Almost all your present applications and utilities should run flawlessly and perhaps a little faster than they currently do. But when you enter Windows or one of the other supported applications, these cards really crank up the speed.

The default drivers that are shipped with Windows — as well as the drivers supplied with most VGA, SVGA, and other standard video cards — perform all these services in software. They take over the computer's CPU to move and change the bits that turn into screen dots. Consequently, they use a large percentage of your computer's processing power — up to 40 percent, according to some estimates — just to manage the Windows graphical interface. Moving dots around on a PC-compatible video card is difficult and time-consuming, partly because of the necessary organization of the card and partly because the data has to move back and forth on the computer's expansion bus, which runs more slowly than the CPU does itself.

Windows accelerator cards take a different approach. Each is built around a video coprocessor, a special microprocessor that is mounted on the video card. The coprocessor can perform many of the video driver services directly, with little or no intervention from the computer's CPU. For example, the coprocessor may be able to perform BitBlts, draw lines and curves, and fill polygons with a few simple CPU commands. The driver software is written to send these commands to the video coprocessor instead of taking up valuable CPU time.

With an accelerator card installed, your computer can concentrate more of its efforts on what it does best: handling data and responding to your input. The accelerator gives you back much of the processing time and power that Windows graphical interface normally uses for its own management.

Several Windows accelerator cards, based on several different video coprocessor chips, are on the market. Some are bare-bones products; others offer additional features that may make them worthwhile to you.

Almost all the accelerators run Windows at resolutions up to 1024x768 pixels in both interlaced and noninterlaced modes, with either 16 or 256 colors. You will, of course, need a monitor that can match those specifications. If you are planning to upgrade to a new monitor, you probably want to do so at the same time that you install the accelerator card. In any case, make sure that your monitor and the card can work together well. Both the manufacturers and dealers can give you advice.

A few coprocessor cards have a built-in mouse port and mouse. If you buy one of these, make sure it accepts a Microsoft-compatible or Logitech-compatible mouse so that you can replace the mouse in the future without having to replace the entire accelerator card. Mice do wear out eventually.

If you want 256 colors at high resolutions, make sure that the board has 1MB of video RAM (VRAM) installed. If 16 colors satisfies you, 512K is enough. In the near future, if not by the time you read this, some boards will include the Sierra high-color RAMDAC chip that will allow 32,768 colors in 800x600 pixel modes. Most boards have drivers for Windows and for such DOS applications as AutoCAD, GEM Desktop, Generic CADD, Lotus 1-2-3, Ventura Publisher, and WordPerfect. Make sure that the board you want supports the applications you plan to use.

Most boards, especially those built around the popular 86C911 chip from the S3 company, have list prices around $500. All these boards are completely compatible with VGA in DOS mode. Boards built around the Texas Instruments TMS34010, which has long been used for high-power graphics workstations, need a special daughterboard for VGA compatibility and often cost more.

ATI

The ATI Windows display drivers for the Mach32 series of video cards (Graphics Ultra Plus and Graphics Ultra Pro) require that Windows 3.1 or Windows for Workgroups 3.1 be running in 386 enhanced mode. This can cause problems if you run the Windows 3.1 or Windows for Workgroups 3.1 Setup programs to upgrade or reinstall, or if you run Windows in standard mode for testing purposes.

You may encounter the following error message when starting Windows in standard mode or during the graphical portion of the Setup procedure:

```
The ATI FlexDesk drivers require Windows to be running in
386 Enhanced mode.
```

To fix this problem, change the display driver to VGA or 8514/A before running Setup or starting Windows in standard mode. This also means that you cannot install this driver when installing Windows for the first time or to a new directory.

Setting Up Windows to Display Different Resolutions

Running Windows in Super VGA's 800x600 resolution throws more pixels on the screen than you get with VGA alone and shrinks the size of the image to show more of it. This is fine for graphics, but the smaller text and the effects of flicker that higher resolutions bring can lead to eyestrain if the user does much word processing. One solution, which is easier than you may think, is to create batch files to load Windows in either configuration.

First set Windows' display to VGA's standard 640x480 mode. Start Windows Setup, select Options Change System Settings, and change the Display option to your graphics card's VGA mode. This process changes SYSTEM.INI so that when you restart Windows, the new display setting takes effect. Restart Windows to check that the changes work and then use File Manager's File Rename option to duplicate the SYSTEM.INI file under the name SYSTEM.VGA.

Next, invoke Windows Setup and change your display mode to Super VGA. Restart Windows and use File Manager to rename the newly edited file SYSTEM.8X6. Next, open Notepad and create the following pair of DOS batch files that copy one of the backup system files over SYSTEM.INI and start Windows.

Save the first batch file as WINVGA.BAT because it loads Windows in VGA mode:

```
COPY C:/WINDOWS/SYSTEM.VGA C:/WINDOWS/SYSTEM.INI WIN
```

Call the following file WIN8X6.BAT, which starts Windows in Super VGA mode:

```
COPY C:/WINDOWS/SYSTEM.8X6 C:/WINDOWS/SYSTEM.INI WIN
```

To switch display modes, exit Windows and at the DOS prompt, type **WINVGA** (to restart Windows in VGA mode) or **WIN8X6** (to restart in Super VGA mode). Simply typing WIN launches Windows in whichever mode it was last in. Every time you install new software, you must repeat this procedure as the last setup step; otherwise, you lose software settings the next time you switch resolutions.

You can determine the video resolution in *dots per inch* (dpi) for the currently selected video driver by using the Windows Paintbrush application.

To determine the video resolution, follow these steps:

1. Start Paintbrush. From the Options menu, choose Image Attributes.

2. Select Inches and then replace the values for Width and Height with 1.0 (1 inch high by 1 inch wide).

3. Select Pels.

4. The numbers in the Width and Height boxes represent your video resolution in dots per inch or Pels.

You can determine the video resolution in dots for the whole screen for the selected driver as follows:

1. Start Paintbrush. From the options menu choose Image Attributes.

2. Select Pels.

3. Choose Defaults.

The numbers you see in the Width and Height boxes correspond to the resolution of your current video driver.

Common video resolution standards for Windows are EGA, VGA, SVGA, and 8514 Large and Small fonts. The following are examples of these common video resolution standards:

EGA 72 dpi

VGA 96 dpi

SVGA 96 dpi

8514 Large 120 dpi

8514 Small 96 dpi 🖐

Using Self-Configuring Display Adapters

Some display adapters can change their configurations to match what an application tries to do. For example, if an application tries to use a video graphics adapter (VGA) configuration and your display adapter is currently configured as an enhanced graphics adapter (EGA), the adapter can switch from an EGA configuration to a VGA configuration. This type of display adapter makes use of *nonmaskable interrupts* (NMIs) to change its configuration while you work.

To use this type of display adapter, you must disable the NMI (also called self-configuring, auto-switching, or auto-emulating) option after you configure the display adapter. Check the documentation that came with your adapter for instructions on how to disable NMI.

Super VGA VESA Mode 6Ah

Some Super VGA adapters support higher monitor-refresh rates at 800x600 resolution with a special VESA mode. If both your video adapter and monitor support a higher refresh rate and if you are using the Super VGA driver, you may be able to get better video results by including the following setting in the [display] section of the SYSTEM.INI file:

```
svgamode=106
```

If you encounter problems using this mode, delete this setting from the SYSTEM.INI file and then restart Windows.

VGA-compatible

Most VGA-compatible display-adapter cards and main-adapter chips use additional memory to enhance their performance. When Windows is configured for VGA, Windows detects most of these cards and automatically excludes the additional memory.

However, if you have an enhanced VGA that Windows does not recognize, you must exclude the additional memory yourself by adding the following line to the [386 Enh] section of the SYSTEM.INI file:

```
emmexclude=C400-C7FF
```

For more information about modifying the SYSTEM.INI file, see the SYSINI.WRI on-line document.

Video Seven

When you use a Video Seven FastWrite VGA, V-RAM VGA, or VGA 1024i video card in 386 enhanced mode Windows with the Windows VGA driver, the following line must be added to the [386 Enh] section of the SYSTEM.INI file:

```
EMMExclude=C600-C7FF
```

This switch is required because the Video Seven cards use this segment of memory, but the segment appears free to Windows. Thus, Windows may use this segment for its high-memory page mapping and conflict with the Video Seven card.

WinSpeed

The WinSpeed version 1.0 installation program, INSTALL.EXE, does not work properly with Windows for Workgroups. It copies an incompatible version of the SETUP.INF file to your Windows directory. To install WinSpeed for use with Windows for Workgroups, you must get updated installation disks from Panacea.

If you have already used the INSTALL.EXE program to install the WinSpeed drivers on your system, the following message appears when you try to run Windows Setup from the Main group:

```
The SETUP.INF file on your system is not valid for use with
this version of Setup.
```

To correct this problem, perform the following steps:

1. If there is a SETUP.INF file in your Windows directory, delete it. (The SETUP.INF file should never be in your Windows directory.)

2. Copy the SETUP.INF file from Windows for Workgroups 3.11 Disk 1 to your Windows System directory.

3. Contact Panacea, Inc., for updated WinSpeed installation disks that are compatible with Windows for Workgroups and then use these to reinstall WinSpeed.

IBM XGA: Configuring Color and Resolution ___

Windows Setup automatically configures an IBM XGA for 16-color, 640x480 resolution. If your monitor can support 256 colors or higher resolutions, you can configure your XGA to use the color and resolution settings you want. To do the configuration, run Windows Setup from the Main group and then select one of the following drivers from the list of Display options:

- XGA (640x480, 16 colors)

  (This is the default setting and should not be changed if you are using the plasma screen on the PS/2 model 75.)

- XGA (640x480, 256 colors)

- XGA (Small fonts)

- XGA (Large fonts)

Both the Small and Large fonts settings configure the XGA for 1024x786 resolution and 256 colors, if your monitor supports it. Otherwise, these settings configure your display for 640x480 resolution. Select Small Fonts if you have a large monitor (at least 16 inches) or want to fit more information on your screen. Select Large Fonts if you want to improve the readability of text.

Make sure that your monitor supports the XGA configuration you select. If it does not, you will return to the MS-DOS prompt when you try to start Windows for Workgroups.

IBM XGA: Using EMM386 _____

To use the IBM XGA display adapter successfully with the EMM386 expanded-memory emulator, you must manually prevent EMM386 from using the memory address range used by the XGA display. A common range is C600-C7FF.

To prevent the memory manager from using this range, include the X= option on the `device=EMM386.EXE` line in your CONFIG.SYS file, as follows:

```
device=EMM386.EXE  X=C600-C7FF
```

To identify the exact range that your XGA display adapter uses, run the System Configuration Program on the System Reference Disk for your PS/2 and select Display Memory Map.

With some PS/2 model 75 plasma screens or with XGA display adapters configured for 640x480 resolution and 16 colors, you must also include the NOEMS or RAM option on the `device=EMM386.EXE` line in your CONFIG.SYS file. Here is an example:

```
device=EMM386.EXE  NOEMS  X=C600-C7FF
```

Do not include the i=B000-BE00 option on the `device=EMM386.EXE` line in your CONFIG.SYS file. This address range is used by the XGA when running Windows. Therefore, it cannot be used as upper memory area. Windows does not recognize XGA configurations if EMM386 is using this address range.

Summary

This chapter discusses various aspects of configuring video for Windows and Windows for Workgroups and covers the following topics:

▶ The components of video subsystems and how they operate

▶ Installing video drivers

▶ Avoiding contention problems in 386 enhanced mode

Chapter 15

Keyboard and Mouse Configuration Secrets

In This Chapter

▶ Settings in the SYSTEM.INI file that control keyboard and mouse operation

▶ Settings to enable access for individuals with disabilities

Windows is probably known best for its colorful graphical interface, and a pointing device is a natural extension of that interface. Windows 3.1 enables you to choose from a number of different types of pointing devices that range from mice to touch screens. This chapter covers the most common pointing device — the mouse — but many INI file settings that are used by mice are also used by other types of pointing devices.

Although using a mouse may seem like the most natural and obvious way to interact with Windows and Windows applications, in many situations, a keyboard is more natural and more efficient. Windows gives you the best of both worlds. You can use a mouse when you are working with graphical applications and use the keyboard when you are doing word processing, performing data entry, or working with a DOS application under Windows.

The Keyboard Section of the SYSTEM.INI File __

The [keyboard] section enables you to configure and control how the keyboard operates with Windows. These entries do not have built-in default values. When you install Windows, Setup assigns values that are based on the system configuration that is detected during the install process.

Windows requires all the entries that are described in this section. If you modify or delete one of these entries, Windows does not operate properly.

Specifying the keyboard dynamic link library

This setting specifies the name of a dynamic link library that defines the layout for any non-U.S. keyboards and keyboards that are not compatible with IBM-compatible systems.

Setting: `keyboard.dll=filename`

Default: None

This setting is required for all keyboards except the following U.S. keyboards:

- IBM XT, PC/AT, or Enhanced
- AT&T type 301 or 302
- Olivetti 83-key
- Hewlett-Packard Vectra keyboard (DIN)

Choosing character translation

This setting specifies the name of a file that defines OEM/ANSI code page translation tables for systems that do not use code page 437 (the U.S. OEM character set). To change this setting, exit Windows and run Setup from MS-DOS. This setting also changes when you change the Codepage or Display settings.

The code page relates the ANSI character numbers with actual symbols that are displayed or printed. Different code pages are used in different countries. This setting should match your MS-DOS code page. See your MS-DOS documentation for information on setting the proper code page for your location.

Setting: `oemansi.bin=filename`

Setting the type of keyboard

This setting specifies the keyboard type. It can be any one of the values listed in Table 15-1.

Setting: `type=number`

Table 15-1	Settings for Keyboard Types
Value	*Keyboard type*
1	IBM PC- or XT-compatible (83 keys)
2	Olivetti 102-key ICO
3	IBM AT-compatible (84 or 86 keys)
4	IBM-compatible, Enhanced (101 or 102 keys)

If this setting is blank or missing, the driver selects a default type. For IBM-compatible keyboards (using the KEYBOARD.DRV driver), the default type is determined by the BIOS. To change this setting, choose the Windows Setup icon from the Main group window.

Setting the keyboard subtype

For some drivers, this setting distinguishes special features for keyboards that otherwise have identical layouts. Other drivers also can use this value. To change the subtype= setting, choose the Windows Setup icon from the Main group window. See the preceding information on the type= setting for information about type values. The values in Table 15-2 are defined for subtype=.

Setting:　subtype=*number*

Table 15-2		Settings for Keyboard Subtypes
Type	*Subtype Value*	*Keyboard Subtype*
1	2	Olivetti M24 83-key or AT&T 6300 type 301 83-key
1	4	AT&T type 302, sometimes used on the 6300 Plus
2	1	Olivetti 102-key ICO, used on M24 systems

Pausing between pasted keystrokes

This setting specifies the number of times that a read-status Int 16 call sho return a status of empty for the keyboard buffer before pasting another ch ter. When Windows pastes data from the Clipboard to a non-Windows a tion, it pastes the data to the BIOS keyboard buffer before it pastes it ir application. This setting slows down fast pasting from the Clipboard to the keyboard buffer so that the application can handle all incoming characters from the buffer. If you seem to lose characters, or if the screen does not update often enough while you are pasting information from the Clipboard, increase this value. This setting is related to `KeyPasteCRSkipCount=`.

Setting: `KeyPasteSkipCount=number`

Default: `2`

Controlling key paste time-out

This setting specifies how much time to allow an application for making the necessary BIOS calls to read keyboard input before Windows will change from the fast paste (Int 16h) mechanism to the slow paste (Int 9h) mechanism.

Setting: `KeyPasteTimeout=seconds`

Default: `1`

Changing the delay for key paste

This setting specifies how long to wait before pasting any characters after a key has been pasted. Some applications may require more than .003 seconds for recognition of a keystroke.

Setting: `KeyPasteDelay=seconds`

Default: `.003`

Changing the Windows keyboard buffer delay

This setting specifies the time to delay pasting keyboard input after the keyboard buffer is full. Some applications may require more than .2 seconds.

Setting: `KeyBufferDelay=seconds`

Default: `.2`

Changing the idle keyboard delay setting

This setting specifies how long Windows ignores idle calls after simulating a keystroke into a virtual machine. You can set this value to 0 to speed up keyboard input, but some applications may respond sluggishly if you do.

Setting: KeyIdleDelay=*seconds*

Default: 5

Changing the keyboard processing time

This setting specifies how much time an application gets to run with increased priority when it receives a keystroke. Use this setting to increase the response to keystrokes when several background applications are running.

Setting: KeyBoostTime=*seconds*

Default: .001

Other Keyboard Settings _____

In addition to the required keyboard settings listed in the prior section, there are a number of optional settings. These settings control special features that not all users will want (or need) to use to their advantage.

Built-in password security

This setting specifies whether the Virtual Keyboard Device (VKD) should support PS/2 8042 commands that implement password security. This setting applies only to 8042 keyboard controllers that are compatible with the PS/2 computer.

Setting: KybdPasswd=*Boolean*

Default: On (for IBM PS/2 computers)
             Off (for all other computers)

Warm boot

If this setting is On, Windows will attempt to reboot the computer by using a keyboard controller command. On some computers, this method is unreliable. If your computer hangs while rebooting, then set this setting to Off, in which case Windows will quit and display a prompt to press Ctrl+Alt+Del a second time if you attempt to reboot from the keyboard while Windows is running.

Setting: KybdReboot=*Boolean*

Default: On

Local reboot

If this setting is set to On, pressing Ctrl+Alt+Del enables you to quit out of a hung application. If this setting is set to Off, Ctrl+Alt+Delete reboots the computer.

Setting: LocalReboot=*On | Off*

Debug local reboot

If this setting is present, the LocalReboot=On functionality enables forcible quitting from the application that last had the focus, even if Windows doesn't think any application is failing.

Setting: DebugLocalReboot=*On | Off*

Default: Not present 👋

Providing Access for Users Who Have Disabilities

Many individuals who have motion-related disabilities find computer work to be difficult, at best. Microsoft Windows, with its complex use of both the keyboard and the mouse, can make working with computer equipment as difficult for a person who has motion-related disabilities as a flight of stairs is for someone who requires a wheelchair.

The Americans with Disabilities Act requires companies in the United States to remove physical barriers and to provide other reasonable accommodations for workers who have disabilities. In addition, publicly accessible personal computers, which are becoming more and more common, need to be accessible to everyone who needs to use them.

Using the Access Pack for Windows

The Access Pack for Windows provides replacement keyboard and mouse drivers that add features that enable a person with disabilities to use a computer running Windows.

The Access Pack for Windows was written for Microsoft by the Trace Research and Development Center in Madison, Wisconsin. It makes up part of the Microsoft Windows Driver Library, and you can find it as ACCP.EXE in Library 4 of the WinUser Forum on the CompuServe Information Service, as well as on the Microsoft Download System and on the Microsoft Drivers and Patches CD.

The Access Pack was designed so that an individual who needs a feature can turn it on without assistance from others and users who do not need the features don't notice their presence if they are turned off. Because of the Access Pack's design, a computer that has the Access Pack installed can be used by people who do not need the Access Pack's features as well as by people who do need its features.

For this reason, I recommend that you install the Access Pack on all systems that may be used by more than one person, even if no one in your organization currently needs its features. This way, there will be no embarassment when someone who does need it goes to access a system.

The Access Pack consists of three keyboard drivers and a mouse driver that replace the standard Windows drivers. The three keyboard drivers replace the three Microsoft-supplied keyboard drivers — check the `keyboard.drv=` setting in the `[boot]` section of SYSTEM.INI for the driver your system is using. Table 15-3 lists the Windows drivers and their Access Pack replacements.

Table 15-3   Windows and Access Pack Keyboard Drivers

Windows Keyboard Driver	Access Pack Keyboard Driver
KEYBOARD.DRV	AP-KBD.DRV
KBDHP.DRV	AP-KBDHP.DRV
KBDOLI.DRV	AP-KBDOL.DRV

The Access Pack mouse driver, AP-MOU.DRV, works with Microsoft mice and mice that are compatible with Microsoft mice. It is a replacement for MOUSE.DRV.

The Access Pack also includes a control applet called ACCESS.EXE that you can add to the Startup group.

The Access Pack for Windows features function only for Windows applications. If you need similar features for non-Windows Applications, you can obtain AccessDOS free of charge from IBM at 1-800-426-7282.

The Access Pack includes the features that are described in the following sections.

StickyKeys

StickyKeys is a feature that enables people who type with one finger, a mouthstick, or a headstick to be able to use the *modifier keys* on the keyboard (Ctrl, Shift, Alt). You normally use these keys in conjunction with some other key on the keyboard to make the other key do something that it does not do when you press it alone. For example, you usually create uppercase letters by holding down Shift while you press a letter key.

StickyKeys enables you to first press the modifier key and then, as a separate keystroke, press the next key of the combination. You can use the modifier keys alone or in any combination, such as Ctrl+Alt.

StickyKeys has two modes: key latching mode and key locking mode.

- Pressing any modifier key once causes it to go into latched mode. As soon as you press any nonmodifier key, the latched key releases.

- Pressing any modifier key twice causes the key to go into locked mode. In this mode, the key *stays down* until you press it again to release it.

You can turn StickyKeys on by pressing either Shift key five times without disturbing the mouse. You can turn it off in the same way — by pressing a Shift key five times.

For computers that are shared, or publicly accessible, StickyKeys has an *Off when two keys at once* feature. If you use the keyboard in the normal fashion (press and hold a modifier and then press another key), StickyKeys will turn itself off.

On U.S. keyboards (or when the U.S. keyboard DLL is being used), StickyKeys treats both Alt keys as though they were the same. On non-U.S. keyboards, or when one of the international keyboard DLLs is being used, StickyKeys may distinguish between the left and right modifier keys. Many international keyboards use the right Alt key to produce special characters that are peculiar to the given language, and StickyKeys will treat the keys appropriately.

KeyboardResponse

KeyboardResponse is a family of features that are enabled and disabled as a group. These features change the way that individual keys on the keyboard behave or respond when you use them.

Because some users may not be able to use a keyboard at all unless some of the KeyboardResponse features are on, there is an "emergency settings sequence" that involves holding down a single key for about 30 seconds. This sequence turns on a predetermined set of KeyboardResponse features, so that the user can configure the keyboard to his or her needs.

KeyboardResponse can also provide audible *keyboard clicks,* which are particularly useful when the keyboard is slowed. When the keyboard is slowed, the clicks enable the user to know when they've held a key down long enough for it to be recognized.

SlowKeys

SlowKeys can make the keyboard accept characters only if they have been held down for a while. It prevents unwanted characters from being entered when keys are accidentally bumped.

RepeatKeys

RepeatKeys allows adjustment of the rate at which keys repeat when a key is held down. If the rate is set to OFF, keys do not repeat at all.

BounceKeys

BounceKeys is designed for people who tremor or have impaired control of their hands. It prevents extra characters from being generated when the same key is inadvertently pressed more than once. BounceKeys sets a time (up to two seconds) that must elapse between keystrokes in order for the system to recognize a keystroke that is the same as the one that preceded it.

MouseKeys

Some people do not have the physical control that is necessary to use a mouse, yet most Windows software requires you to use one. MouseKeys turns the numeric keypad into a mouse. You press some keys to move the mouse pointer around and others to perform the functions that single clicks and double-clicks of each of the two buttons on a standard mouse perform.

ToggleKeys

ToggleKeys provides sound cues to indicate when the lights on the keyboard that indicate Caps Lock, Num Lock, and Scroll Lock are turned on and off, because some users may not be able to see the lights. ToggleKeys provides a recognizable tone whenever the controlling key is pressed.

SerialKeys

Some people cannot use a keyboard and mouse at all. SerialKeys enables them to use some of the special devices that are available, such as communication aids. These aids connect to the computer via one of the computer's serial ports. Check with the manufacturer of the device for compatibility information and programming instructions.

ShowSounds

Users with a hearing impairment or users who work in a noisy environment can have the ShowSounds feature alert them when the operating system or an application has produced a sound. You can set ShowSounds to either flash the entire Windows screen once or flash the active title bar.

Time-Out

The Time-Out feature enables Access Pack features to disable themselves automatically if the computer is left idle for a configurable length of time. This feature is very helpful on a shared workstation.

Access Pack WIN.INI settings

Access Pack uses several WIN.INI settings to maintain its configuration.

The [FilterKeys] section

This setting specifies whether the KeyboardResponse features are on or off when you start Windows.

Setting: On=*0* | *1*

Default: 0

This setting specifies whether the system should produce a rising or falling audible tone to indicate enabling and disabling of the KeyboardResponse features.

Setting: OnOffFeedback=*0* | *1*

Default: 1

This setting specifies how long you need to hold down a key before it is accepted. The value is in milliseconds.

Setting: DelayBeforeAcceptance=*milliseconds*

Default: 1000

This setting specifies how long you need to hold down a key before it begins auto-repeating. The value is in milliseconds.

Setting: AutoRepeatDelay=*milliseconds*

Default: 1000

This setting specifies the amount of time between automatically repeated keystrokes when a key is held down long enough to activate auto-repeat. The value is in milliseconds; set it to 32760 to turn off auto-repeat.

Setting: AutoRepeatRate=*milliseconds*

Default: 500

This setting specifies the amount of time, in milliseconds, that a key should be ignored after you have pressed it and released it once.

Setting: BounceTime=*milliseconds*

Default: 500

The [StickyKeys] section

If this setting is set to 1, StickyKeys is turned on.

Setting: On=*0* | *1*

Default: 1

If this setting is set to 1, the system produces a rising or falling tone to indicate that you have used the keyboard to turn StickyKeys on or off.

Setting: OnOffFeedback=*0* | *1*

Default: 1

This setting specifies whether pressing a modifier key twice in a row will put it into a locked state. If this setting is set to 0, a second press releases the key.

Setting: TriState=*0* | *1*

Default: 1

When this setting is set to 1, pressing two modifier keys or a modifier key and a regular key at the same time turns off the StickyKeys feature.

Setting: TwoKeysOff=*0* | *1*

Default: 1

If this setting is set to 1, the system generates audible tones to indicate when a modifier key is being latched, locked, or released.

Setting: AudibleFeedback=*0* | *1*

Default: 1

The [MouseKeys] section

If this setting is set to 1, the MouseKeys feature is on when Windows is started.

Setting: On=*0* | *1*

Default: 0

If this setting is set to 1, the system generates a rising or falling audible tone when you use the keyboard to turn the MouseKeys feature on or off.

Setting: OnOffFeedback=*0* | *1*

Default: 1

When you hold down a mouse movement key, the mouse pointer will attain maximum speed after the number of milliseconds specified by this setting has elapsed.

Setting: TimeToMaximumSpeed=*milliseconds*

Default: 3000

This setting specifies the maximum speed, in pixels per second, that the mouse pointer can obtain.

Setting: MaximumSpeed=*pixels per second*

Default: 40

The [ToggleKeys] section

If this setting is set to 1, ToggleKeys is on.

Setting: On=*0* | *1*

Default: 0

If this setting is set to 1, the system produces a rising or falling tone when you enable or disable the ToggleKeys feature from the keyboard.

Setting: OnOffFeedback=*0* | *1*

Default: 1

The [TimeOut] section

If this setting is set to 1, the Time-Out feature is on at startup.

Setting: On=*0* | *1*

Default: 0

If this setting is set to 1, the system produces a falling tone to indicate when the Access Pack features are turned off because of a time-out.

Setting: OnOffFeedback=*0* | *1*

Default: 1

This setting specifies the amount of time that the system must be idle (no mouse or keyboard input) before all Access Pack features are automatically turned off.

Setting: TimeToWait=*minutes*

Default: 5

The [GIDEI] section

If this setting is set to 1, the SerialKeys feature is on when the Access Pack utility is started.

Setting: On=*0* | *1*

Default: 0

This setting specifies the speed that SerialKeys uses to communicate with the input device.

Setting: BaudRate=*bps*

Default: 300

This setting specifies which serial port SerialKeys looks for data on.

Setting: Port=*1* | *2* | *3* | *4*

Default: 1

The [ShowSounds] section

If this setting is set to 1, the screen flashes (if possible on the user's display) when an application generates a sound.

Setting: Screen=*0* | *1*

Default: 0

If this setting is set to 1, the title bar of the foreground window flashes when an application generates a sound.

Setting: Caption=*0* | *1*

Default: 0

Setting the double-click speed

This setting specifies the maximum time between clicks of the mouse button that the system will permit for one double-click. The lower the value of this setting, the less time you have to click twice to make a double-click.

Setting: DoubleClickSpeed=*milliseconds*

Default: 452

Setting the double-click height and width

These entries specify the height and width (in pixels) that the mouse pointer can move between clicks in a double-click. If the mouse pointer is moved farther up or down (or left or right), the two clicks will be treated as separate single clicks. For example, if the setting is `DoubleClickHeight=10`, the mouse pointer cannot move vertically more than 5 pixels in either direction from its starting point between clicks for the two clicks to be recognized as a double-click. If you enter an odd number, it is rounded to the nearest even number.

Setting: `DoubleClickHeight=pixels`

Default: 4

Setting: `DoubleClickWidth=pixels`

Default: 4

Mouse trails

This setting specifies the number of pointers that are shown on the screen when the MouseTrails option is selected in the Mouse dialog box that you access from the Control Panel. You can specify a number between 1 and 7. This setting is supported only if you are using the EGA, VGA, or SuperVGA display driver. To change this setting, choose the Mouse icon from the Control Panel. If the Mouse dialog box does not include the Mouse Trails option, you need to add this setting to WIN.INI to set mouse trails.

Setting: `MouseTrails=number`

Default: None

Mouse acceleration

This setting specifies the relationship between the mouse movement and the pointer movement when the value of either `MouseThreshold1=` or `MouseThreshold2=` is exceeded. When either of them is exceeded, Windows causes the pointer movement to accelerate according to the value of `MouseSpeed=`. If the value is 0, no acceleration occurs. If the value is 1, the pointer moves at twice its normal speed when the mouse movement exceeds the value of `MouseThreshold1=`. If the value is 2, the pointer moves at twice its normal speed when the mouse movement exceeds the value of `MouseThreshold1=` or four times the normal speed if the mouse movement exceeds `MouseThreshold2=`.

Setting: `MouseSpeed=0 | 1 | 2`

Default: 1

Mouse acceleration pixels

These entries set the maximum number of pixels that the mouse can move between mouse interrupts before Windows alters the relationship between mouse movement and mouse pointer movement. If the mouse movement exceeds the threshold defined by `MouseThreshold1=` and if `MouseSpeed=` is greater than 0, Windows moves the pointer at twice the normal speed. If the mouse movement exceeds the threshold defined by `MouseThreshold2=` and if `MouseSpeed=2`, Windows moves the pointer at four times the normal speed.

Setting: `MouseThreshold1=pixels`

Default: *15*

Setting: `MouseThreshold2=pixels`

Default: *10*

Swapping mouse buttons

This setting specifies whether to swap the right and left mouse buttons. If the value is 1, the buttons are swapped. To change this setting, choose the Mouse icon from the Control Panel.

Setting: `SwapMouseButtons=0 | 1`

Default: 0

Specifying a mouse driver

This setting specifies the filename of the mouse driver that you are using. To change the setting, choose the Windows Setup icon from the Main group window and change the setting for the Mouse option.

Setting: `mouse.drv=filename`

Default: None

Mouse Sync Time

This setting affects only Windows in standard mode on computers that have a mouse interface compatible with the IBM PS/2 mouse interface. The setting specifies the number of milliseconds that can elapse between mouse data bytes before Windows assumes that a mouse data packet is complete. It may need to be adjusted if the mouse pointer behaves erratically.

Setting: `MouseSyncTime=milliseconds`

Default: `500`

The mouse virtual device driver

This setting specifies the virtual device driver that handles the mouse hardware in 386 enhanced mode. The setting is a synonym for *Device*. Setup assigns an appropriate value that is based on the system configuration. To change this setting, choose the Windows Setup icon in the Main group window.

Setting: `Mouse=filename | *device name`

Default: None

Mouse initialization

This setting specifies whether Windows should convert Int 33h function 0 hard initialization calls to function 33 soft initialization calls, which do not reset the mouse hardware. Set this setting to `On` if you want to use a mouse with a non-Windows application that is started in a window. Set this setting to `Off` if the mouse pointer and the screen information appear distorted when you are using the mouse with an application. If you set this setting to `Off`, you will not be able to use the mouse with a non-Windows application that is started in a window.

Setting: `MouseSoftInit=Boolean`

Default: `On`

Microsoft Mouse Driver Version 9.0

Microsoft released a new version of the Microsoft Mouse driver when it introduced the new ergonomic Microsoft Mouse Version 2.0. The new kidney-bean shaped mouse is designed to help users avoid health problems that are caused by repetitive motion.

As you use the new mouse, you can hold it in a variety of positions. Its design reflects medical experts' advice that users who change the position of the hand and wrist can avoid the repetition that can be so damaging. In addition, the Version 9.0 driver can alter the mouse pointer's behavior in a number of ways that are beneficial to the user.

Owners of the original Microsoft Mouse can obtain the new mouse driver from Microsoft Sales and take advantage of the new driver's benefits.

The Mouse Manager

Key to the new driver is the Mouse Manager (see Figure 15-1), which replaces the Mouse icon in the Control Panel, performs all of its functions, and controls the new functionality of the driver.

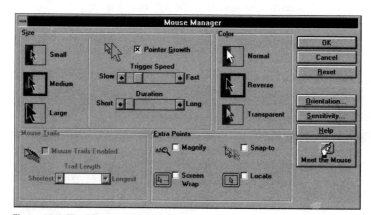

Figure 15-1: The Microsoft Mouse Manager.

Mouse pointer options

The mouse pointer options that are described in the following sections are available with Microsoft Mouse driver Version 9.0.

Size

The size feature enables the user to adjust the size of the mouse pointer for all of the standard pointers that are supplied with Windows. This option is very useful when you are using an LCD screen, where the pointer may be difficult to see.

Pointer growth

If a larger pointer is chosen, this option makes the pointer grow when you move the mouse above a certain speed (*Trigger Speed*). When the mouse stops moving, the pointer returns to the original size after the number of seconds specified (*Duration*).

Color

This feature changes the color of the pointer to improve visibility. You can set the color to normal (white), reverse (black), or transparent (the opposite of whatever it is moving over).

Mouse trails

This feature also improves pointer visibility. It makes the mouse pointer appear somewhat snake-like as it moves across the screen. The faster you move the mouse, the longer the image, so keeping track of the pointer's location is easier. (Mouse trails are also available with other versions of the mouse driver.)

Extra points

You enable these extra settings by using the check boxes in the Mouse Manager's main screen:

■ Magnify. When this check box is checked, you see a drop-down box where you can choose a key-and-click combination (such as Alt+secondary mouse button) that will cause the mouse pointer to turn into a magnifying box to give you finer control of the pointer. This feature is particularly useful for graphics art applications.

■ Snap-to. When this check box is checked, the mouse pointer automatically *snaps* to the default button in any dialog box that comes up. This feature provides a fast way to choose the default action with the mouse.

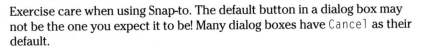
Exercise care when using Snap-to. The default button in a dialog box may not be the one you expect it to be! Many dialog boxes have `Cancel` as their default.

■ Screen Wrap. When this check box is checked, the mouse pointer wraps around the screen — if it moves off the left side of the screen, it automatically comes back from the right. If it moves off the top, it automatically comes back from the bottom.

■ Locate. When this check box is checked, you see a drop-down box open where you can choose a key-and-click combination (such as Ctrl+secondary mouse button) that will cause the mouse pointer to jump to the center of the screen. Again, this feature is intended to help you locate the pointer.

■ Orientation. You can change *which way is up* for the mouse, and which button is primary, by clicking on the Orientation button in the Mouse

Manager. This feature is very important because it enables the user to alter the way he or she holds the mouse.

Figure 15-2 shows the Orientation dialog box. You set the orientation by simply clicking on the Set Orientation button (or pressing Alt+S) while you hold the mouse in the manner you want to and move it upward until the arrow strikes the target.

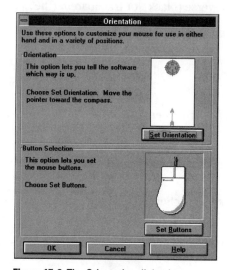

Figure 15-2: The Orientation dialog box.

Changing the primary button is easy. Click the Set Buttons button with the current primary button (or press Alt+B) and follow the instructions on the screen.

Sensitivity

Sensitivity refers to the relationship between how far the mouse pointer travels on-screen and how far you move the mouse. It also refers to how quickly you need to click in order for Windows to recognize a *double-click*, instead of treating it as two separate clicks.

Figure 15-3 shows the Sensitivity dialog box. The new driver enables you to change the relative speed. The horizontal speed is independent of the vertical speed, and, as with the MS-DOS version of the mouse driver, you can set the mouse pointer to accelerate if you move the mouse quickly.

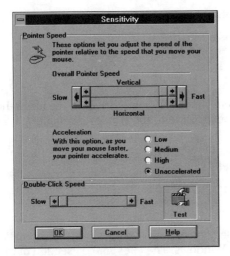

Figure 15-3: The Sensitivity dialog box.

All of the items that are affected by the settings in this dialog box are controlled by the slider bars. You need to use the mouse to alter the settings. You can test the double-click speed by trying to double-click on the test icon. If double-clicking was successful, the icon will change.

System file modifications

The mouse driver stores its settings in the MOUSE.INI file in the directory that the mouse software is stored in.

In addition to these settings, the mouse installation software makes three changes to SYSTEM.INI.

In the [boot] section, it sets

```
mouse.drv=<path>\mouse.drv
```

This setting forces Windows to use the new mouse driver.

In the [boot.description] section, it sets

```
mouse.drv=Microsoft Mouse version 9.00
```

In the [386Enh] section, it sets

```
keyboard=<path>\mousevkd.386
```

and

```
mouse=*vmd
```

These lines change the system virtual keyboard driver to the file in the MOUSE directory, and the virtual mouse driver to the Windows default.

The Mouse Manager also may modify the MouseTrails= setting of WIN.INI, described earlier in this chapter.

Summary

Most of the settings in the SYSTEM.INI file control how Windows pastes information into DOS applications that are running under Windows. The [keyboard] section of the SYSTEM.INI file also contains settings that enable you to configure Windows to a specific foreign language keyboard. This chapter discussed:

▶ How to configure Windows to consistently send data to DOS programs.

▶ How to control rebooting of your system with keystrokes.

▶ How to configure your keyboard and mouse to facilitate usage by persons with disabilities.

Chapter 16

Controlling Fonts and Printing

In This Chapter

▶ Finding corrupted font files

▶ Disabling ATM

▶ Installing and selecting TrueType fonts

▶ Replacing system fonts

The font and printing capabilities in Windows 3.1 offer a number of presentation options. What you see is what you get. Along with this power and flexibility, however, are the complex issues of font management and printing. To understand Windows fonts and printing technology, you must first understand the differences between the three categories of fonts — raster, vector, and TrueType — and how Windows uses them.

Understanding Windows 3.1's Three Font Types

Windows 3.1 provides three basic kinds of fonts, categorized according to how the fonts are rendered for screen or print output:

- *Raster fonts* are stored in files as bitmaps and rendered as an array of dots for displaying on-screen and printing on paper.

- *Vector fonts* are rendered from a mathematical model, where each character is defined as a set of lines drawn between points. Vector fonts can be scaled to any size or aspect ratio. Aspect is the ratio of width to height.

- *TrueType fonts* are outline fonts that use new technology available in Windows 3.1. These fonts can be scaled and rotated.

Besides the font-rendering mechanism, Windows fonts are described according to the output device:

- *Screen fonts* are font descriptions that Windows uses to represent characters on display devices. Windows uses special raster fonts as the system screen fonts for menus, window captions, messages, and other text. A set of system, fixed, and OEM terminal fonts is shipped with Windows 3.1 to match your system's display capabilities (that is, CGA, EGA, VGA, or 8514/A video displays). The default system screen font in Windows 3.1 is System, a proportionally spaced raster font. The installed screen fonts are listed in the [fonts] section of your WIN.INI file.

Some screen fonts are installed for displaying non-Windows applications when Windows is running in 386 enhanced mode. By default, code page 437 (U.S.) fonts are installed. Other screen-font files are included for international language support, identified by the code-page number appended to the filename.

■ *Printer fonts* are the font descriptions used by the printer to create a font. Windows applications can use three kinds of printer fonts: device fonts, downloadable soft fonts, and printable screen fonts.

Windows raster fonts

Raster fonts are bitmaps supplied in different sizes for specific video display resolutions. The Windows MS Serif, MS Sans Serif, Courier, System, and Terminal fonts are raster fonts. A raster-font file contains data that describes all the characters and styles of a typeface for a specific display device. Windows provides several raster-font sizes for various display devices. For example, MS Serif comes in point sizes 8, 10, 12, and 14 for CGA, EGA, VGA, and 8514/A display devices. Windows can scale raster fonts to even multiples of their supplied sizes. This means that MS Serif can be scaled to 16, 20, or 24 points, and so on. Bold, italic, underline, and strikethrough styles can also be generated from a standard raster font.

Normally, Windows Setup installs the correct font sets for your display and printer. Additional raster-font sets can be installed with Control Panel. Table 16-1 lists the raster fonts installed in Windows 3.1.

Table 16-1	Raster Fonts in Windows 3.1	
Font	*Filename*	*Character Set*
Courier	COURIER.FON	ANSI
MS Sans Serif	SSERIF*x*.FON	ANSI
MS Serif	SERIF*x*.FON	ANSI
Small	SMALL*x*.FON	ANSI
Symbol	SYMBOL*x*.FON	SYMBOL

The raster-font sets for different display resolutions are distinguished by a letter suffix on the font name (represented as *x* in Table 16-1). To determine the file that Windows installs for a given display or printer, refer to the Font Set column in Table 16-2 and add the letter that identifies the resolution of the raster font to the character-set filename (from Table 16-1). For example, the resource file for MS Serif fonts for VGA is named SERIFE.FON.

Table 16-2	Raster Font Sets			
Font Set	**Output Device**	**Horiz. Res.**	**Vertical Res.**	**Aspect Ratio H:V**
A	CGA display	96 dpi	48 dpi	2:1
B	EGA display	96 dpi	2 dpi	1.33:1
C	Printer	60 dpi	72 dpi	1:83
D	Printer	120 dpi	72 dpi	1.67:1
E	VGA display	96 dpi	96 dpi	1:1
F	8514/A display	120 dpi	120 dpi	1:1

Raster fonts can also be printed if their resolution and aspect ratio are close to what your printer requires. If you do not see raster fonts for your printer in a fonts dialog box, check your printer's horizontal and vertical resolution and compare it with the preceding chart. If there is a close match, choose the Fonts icon in the Control Panel window and make sure that the appropriate font set is installed. If there is no close match, you cannot print the Windows raster font on your printer. Some printer drivers cannot print raster fonts, regardless of the aspect ratio.

MS Serif and MS Sans Serif in Windows 3.1 replace the identical raster fonts Tms Rmn and Helv installed in earlier versions of Windows. Windows matches MS Serif to Tms Rmn and MS Sans Serif to Helv through the [FontSubstitutes] section of the WIN.INI file.

The new Windows raster font named *Small* was designed for readable, efficient screen display of small fonts. For sizes under 6 points, the Small font is a better choice for screen display than any TrueType font because the Small font is easier to read.

Windows vector fonts

Vector fonts are a set of lines drawn between points, like a pen-plotter drawing a set of characters. Vector fonts can be scaled to virtually any size, but generally they do not look as good as raster fonts in the sizes for which raster fonts are specifically designed. Vector fonts are stored in Windows as collections of graphical-device-interface (GDI) calls and are time consuming to generate but are useful with plotters and other devices for which bitmapped characters can't be used.

Some Windows applications (notably PageMaker) automatically use vector fonts at larger sizes. These applications often allow you to specify the point size at which you want to use vector fonts.

The making of a TrueType font

Each TrueType font is installed in two stages from two different font files. The font file with the .FOT extension is loaded from the Windows System subdirectory at startup. When you apply a TrueType font in your documents, the FOT file loaded at startup points to the rest of the font information — a file with the same name but with the .TTF extension. The TTF file is, in effect, a compiled programming language that contains all the information needed to build any character of a given font at any size.

The principal difference between scalable outline fonts such as TrueType and scalable vector fonts is a technology called *hinting*. In both scalable outline and scalable vector technologies, outlines must be converted to bitmaps before they're sent to printers and monitors — without hinting, the curves and diagonal lines look rough. Fonts look rough because parts of a font outline don't map precisely to a pixel: some parts of a curve are wider than the original outline and some are narrower. The result is uneven curves and serifs, especially at small point sizes and low resolutions.

To solve this problem, hinting algorithms systematically adjust a scaled outline to yield a smoother-looking bitmapped image. Only after hinting does the GDI send the TrueType characters to the screen or to the printer.

TrueType fonts require less disk space. Each TrueType typeface requires only an FOT file and a TTF file to create fonts in all point sizes at all resolutions for all output devices, from video displays to printers.

Understanding Windows Font Technology _____

Because the Windows environment controls your fonts, you need to understand some of the basics about how Windows handles fonts.

Windows uses two separate pieces of information to control screen display: the font metrics or spacing information and the information used to represent the font to your printer together make up a font.

Font metrics files

Printer font metrics files (PFM files) contain information about the relationship between characters in a font, such as spacing attributes, individual character widths, and pair kerning values. Although font metrics don't provide the character shapes displayed on-screen or used by the printer, they do provide the critical link between Windows, the screen font, and the printer font. If font metric information isn't available, Windows won't let you use the font.

When you launch Windows, Windows must determine what fonts are available: Windows looks in the printer driver and in the [Printer, Port] section of the WIN.INI file for the printer you've selected. Any fonts either built into the printer driver or that have their PFM files listed in the [Printer, Port] section of the WIN.INI file for the target printer are available in Windows and Windows applications.

Screen fonts

Screen fonts for both installable and resident fonts are stored as bitmapped information in files with a .FON extension. Windows uses screen fonts to represent the font you've chosen on your computer screen. Because the term *bitmap* can describe both screen fonts and some types of printer fonts, I'll begin by explaining bitmaps.

The word *bitmap* itself refers to a pattern of dots, or bits, mapped to a certain pattern. In other words, the file consists of instructions that say, row by row, "put a dot here, put a dot here, don't put a dot here, put a dot here." When the pixels in your monitor are turned on or off according to these instructions, a character is displayed to your screen.

A single FON file can contain more than one size of a specific font; normally, only a limited number of point sizes are included to maintain your system's efficiency. Windows includes seven screen fonts, discussed in the following section.

Windows and screen fonts

Windows' GDI finds and acts on any installed font on your system, but if it doesn't find the right file, it uses a substitution technique called *font mapping*. A Windows application requests a font from Windows by name and other attributes. If the GDI can't find the font it needs, the font mapper attempts to use a substitute TrueType font so that the characters look good at any point size.

The font mapper uses the other attributes the Windows application requests to substitute a font. For example, if a serif font is requested, the font mapper uses Times New Roman. If it's a sans serif font, Arial is drafted. Courier New stands in for any fixed-pitch font. And for a script or decorative font, the font mapper chooses the best fit from its options.

If both a bitmapped font and a TrueType font exist with the same name, such as Symbol, the bitmapped font is used at sizes for which bitmaps exist, and TrueType is used at all other sizes. To obtain TrueType in all cases, add the following setting to the [TrueType] section of your WIN.INI file:

```
TTifCollisions=1
```

Printer fonts

Printer-font files contain the information that your printer's page-description language uses to actually draw the characters in a font on the printed page. (Information about where to place the characters relative to one another on a line is taken from the PFM file.)

Printer fonts don't have standardized filename extensions, unlike screen-font files and printer-font metrics files that always have the same filename extensions (FON and PFM, respectively). Filenames for printer fonts depend entirely on the font manufacturer and the type of printer you use.

Printer fonts can be *resident* (built into your printer's ROM), read from font cartridges, or downloadable soft fonts. Windows handles each type of font differently. To further complicate matters, printer-font information can be in the form of either premade bitmaps or scalable outlines.

Bitmapped printer fonts are similar in many ways to bitmapped screen fonts and are used by Printer Command Language 4 (PCL 4) and PCL 5 printers (such as the Hewlett-Packard LaserJet Series III and LaserJetIV printers, respectively). Each bitmapped printer-font file contains a description of the character set for that font in a specific point size. If you plan to print the same font in a number of different point sizes, you need a separate printer-font file for each size, which can take up a lot of disk space! If you try to print text in a point size for which you have no printer font, the font your printer considers to be the closest match is substituted.

Scalable printer fonts, also called *outline fonts*, are used by two of the most popular page-description languages (Adobe's PostScript and Hewlett-Packard's PCL 5) to draw the shapes in a particular font when your page is rasterized. When a scalable font is created by the font manufacturer, the shape of each character is carefully drawn in a resolution-independent drawing program and then stored in a file that contains all the shapes (a collection called the *character set*) for the specific font. These shapes are then used by the interpreter to build the bitmap for the printer. One set of outline characters can easily and accurately be resized to any point size because they are stored as resolution-independent shapes rather than resolution-dependent bitmaps.

Understanding How TrueType Works

TrueType fonts are stored as a collection of points and "hints" that define the character outlines. When a Windows application asks for a font, TrueType uses the outline and the hints to render a bitmap in the size requested. *Hints* are the algorithms that distort the scaled-font outlines to improve how the bitmaps look at specific — usually smaller — resolutions.

Each time you run Windows, the first time you select a TrueType font size, TrueType renders a bitmap of the selected characters for display or printing. Because of this, initial font generation may be slower than it is with Windows raster fonts. However, Windows stores the rendered bitmaps in a font cache so that subsequent uses of the font during that Windows session result in display or printing that is just as fast as with a Windows raster font.

The Windows universal printer driver supports TrueType. Any printer that works with the universal printer driver supports TrueType automatically.

Looking at the four levels of font embedding in Windows

TrueType fonts offer another feature: font embedding. Users can create a document containing TrueType fonts, open the document on another machine that does not have that font installed, and use that font within certain limitations.

These limitations are determined by the vendor of the font and are built into the font. Although this technology is built into the font, some users may not be able to use the font because the application must support the ability to embed the fonts when the document is saved. Table 16-3 summarizes the four levels of embedding fonts.

Table 16-3	The Four Levels of Embedding
Embedding Level	*Description*
None	This level of embedding does not allow for embedding. Another font is substituted for the selected font.
Preview & Print	This level of embedding allows the selected font to be seen on-screen and printed from the document in which the font was embedded.
Editable	At this level, the selected font can be seen on-screen, printed, and edited (but only in the host document).
Installable	This level includes the attributes of all preceding levels. The selected fonts can be installed on the computer and used in other documents and applications.

Adding and removing TrueType fonts

Use the Windows Control Panel to add and remove TrueType fonts to and from your system. To add fonts, run Control Panel and select the Fonts icon. Click Add and choose the drive on which the additional fonts are located. Select the fonts you want to install, or choose Select All and click OK. Windows copies the selected font files to your hard drive and makes them available to all your Windows applications.

To remove fonts, highlight them and click Remove. Check the Delete Font File from Disk box if you want the actual fonts files to be cleared from your hard disk; leave the box unchecked if you want to reinstall the fonts more easily later. Finally, choose Yes or Yes to All to remove the fonts.

Installing the maximum number of TrueType fonts

The number of TrueType fonts you can use with Windows 3.1 is limited by the following items:

- *WIN.INI:* The WIN.INI file size is limited to 64K, meaning that you can declare between 500 and 1000 fonts (depending on the length of the filenames and paths).

- *The number of fonts that can be used simultaneously during a Windows session:* The internal tables used by the graphical device interface (GDI) can have no more than 1,600 entries. Limitations are stricter because of the size of the TrueType data segment and the number of selectors available in the system. Between 300 and 800 different fonts can be used simultaneously during a Windows session.

■ The number of fonts that can be printed on the same document.

Understanding the Invalid TrueType Font Detected error message

Windows 3.1 displays the following error message if you use a corrupt TrueType font:

```
Invalid TrueType Font Detected
```

This message means that an application used a TrueType font that caused an error in Windows. You should quit all applications and restart Windows.

As a result of this error, TrueType fonts may no longer be available in your application. This problem occurs because, after Windows detects an invalid TrueType font, it disables the availability of TrueType fonts to maintain the integrity of the system. To enable TrueType fonts again, quit all your applications and restart Windows.

Make sure that you delete and reinstall the corrupt font before using it again. If you don't know which font is causing the error message, follow these steps to determine which font is corrupt:

1. Open the Control Panel and double-click the Fonts icon.

2. Click on each font entry in the Installed Fonts list.

3. Check the line `The size of the font on the disk is: X`. If the size is either 0K or 2K, remove and reinstall that particular font.

If you attempt to reinstall the font without restarting Windows, the following message appears:

```
TrueType fonts are disabled
```

To use TrueType fonts, select the Enable TrueType Fonts check box in the TrueType dialog box and restart Windows before installing TrueType fonts. All you need to do is restart Windows; the TrueType fonts are enabled automatically.

Installing Fonts

In Windows 3.1, you can install fonts on your system in several ways:

- Windows installs TrueType and its screen fonts automatically during installation. When you specify a printer and other options in the Printer Setup dialog box, Windows includes information about font cartridges and built-in fonts for your printer.

- You can install more TrueType fonts from disks by choosing the Add Fonts button in the Font Installer dialog box.

- You can install more HPPCL (Hewlett-Packard Printer Control Language) soft fonts on your hard disk by installing the AutoFont Support files and following the instructions for adding scalable printer fonts. Then choose the Add Fonts button in the Font Installer dialog box to install the fonts in Windows.

- You can install other third-party soft fonts on your hard disk by using the utility supplied by the manufacturer. Then choose the Add Fonts button in the Font Installer dialog box to install the fonts in Windows.

- You can install a new font cartridge in your printer; then choose the Printer icon in the Control Panel window. In the Setup dialog box, select a new item from the Cartridge list.

For more information about using the Font Installer, choose the Help button in the Font Installer dialog box.

How Windows matches fonts

When an application asks for characters to print or display, Windows must find the appropriate font among the fonts installed on your system. Finding the font can be a complex process because, for example, your document may contain fonts not available on the current printer or you may have more than one font with the same name installed on your system.

The basic rules that Windows uses for finding a font are as follows:

- If the font is a TrueType font, TrueType renders the character, and the result is sent to the display or to the printer.

- If the font is not a TrueType font, Windows uses the font-mapping table to determine the most appropriate device font to use.

Before TrueType, when Windows mapped fonts that had the same name, the order of the internal listing of the fonts determined which font was chosen. In Windows 3.1, TrueType fonts are always chosen first; then the internal listing order is followed.

When Windows uses the font-mapping table to match screen fonts to printer fonts, the characteristics used to find the closest match are, in descending order of importance: character set, variable versus fixed pitch, family, typeface name, height, width, weight, slant, underline, and strikethrough.

Table 16-4 shows which types of Windows fonts can be printed on different kinds of printers. Table 16-5 lists the character sets installed with Windows 3.1.

Table 16-4	**Windows Fonts Available by Printer**			
Printer Type	*Device Font*	*Raster Fonts*	*Vector Fonts*	*TrueType Fonts*
Dot matrix	Yes	Yes	No	Yes
HPPCL	Yes	No	Yes	Yes
PostScript	Yes	No	Yes	Yes
Plotter	Yes	No	Yes	No

Table 16-5	**Character Sets Installed with Windows 3.1**		
Font	*Font Type*	*Spacing*	*Default Sizes*
Arial Bold Italic	TrueType	Proportional	Scalable
Arial Bold	TrueType	Proportional	Scalable
Arial Italic	TrueType	Proportional	Scalable
Arial	TrueType	Proportional	Scalable
Courier New Bold Italic	TrueType	Fixed	Scalable
Courier New Bold	TrueType	Fixed	Scalable
Courier New Italic	TrueType	Fixed S	Scalable
Courier New	TrueType	Fixed	Scalable
Courier	Raster	Fixed	10,12,15
Modern	Vector	Proportional	Scalable
MS Sans Serif	Raster	Proportional	8,10,12,14,18,24
MS Serif	Raster	Proportional	8,10,12,14,18,24
Roman	Vector	Proportional	Scalable

(continued)

Table 16-5 *(continued)*

Font	Font Type	Spacing	Default Sizes
Script	Vector	Proportional	2,4,6
Symbol*	Raster	Proportional	8,10,12,14,18,24
Symbol*	TrueType	Proportional	Scalable
System	Raster	Proportional	Display-dependent size
Terminal**	Raster	Fixed	Display-dependent size
Times New Roman Bold Italic	TrueType	Proportional	Scalable
Times New Roman Bold	TrueType	Proportional	Scalable
Times New Roman Italic	TrueType	Proportional	Scalable
Times New Roman	TrueType	Proportional	Scalable

*Symbol, rather than ANSI, character set

**OEM, rather than ANSI, character set

Disk space, memory use, and speed

You may notice a performance decrease if your document uses many fonts in many sizes. Rendering many fonts requires a large font cache, which can force more swapping to the hard disk. This same problem occurs with other fonts in earlier versions of Windows. With TrueType, less memory is used for the cache than is required for corresponding raster fonts, leading to a net performance gain. The font cache uses more memory with TrueType only if multiple logical fonts are mapped to the same raster font. Usually, however, any additional swapping to disk is still faster than discarding the rendered bitmaps.

For TrueType fonts, lack of hard disk space is not the problem it can be for a comparable selection of raster fonts because the font-information files do not contain actual raster images of the fonts, but only outline and hint information. When you install Windows, however, you see that more disk space is used to store fonts. This happens because all Windows raster fonts are still shipped for backward compatibility with earlier applications. Any soft fonts you already have on your hard disk are not affected by the installation of TrueType with Windows 3.1.

Looking at Type Managers

Type managers (such as Adobe Type Manager, Bitstream's Facelift, and Hewlett Packard's Intellifont-for-Windows) are font-enhancement programs designed to change the way Windows displays or prints fonts.

Type managers work by using the information in scalable printer-font files to generate characters for on-screen display. When an application requests a font character be drawn on-screen, the type manager steps in. Rather than using the bitmapped screen font, the type manager uses the scalable outline font in exactly the same way the page-description language interpreter in the printer does: the *glyph* (or character shape) is matched to a grid at the resolution of the screen; pixels covered by the glyph are turned on and bits that the glyph misses are left off.

All three type-manager programs that I mention at the beginning of this section perform well; however, I focus on Adobe Type Manager (ATM) for purposes of this discussion because ATM uses PostScript font technology that makes some PostScript fonts available to non-PostScript printers.

When ATM is installed, you can print Type 1 PostScript fonts on a non-PostScript printer. This makes more flexible printers that could print only bitmapped fonts (for example, non-PostScript printers and PCL printers before PCL 5). If ATM is off, the scalable fonts Roman, Script, and Modern print instead of the chosen bitmap font. If ATM is on, TimesNewRomanPS, GillSans, or Symbol are substituted for your bitmap font. Because ATM treats text as a high-resolution bitmapped graphic, it's possible to bypass any limitations in that printer's handling of fonts. For the same reason, ATM also makes it possible to print reverse text to PCL 4 printers.

If you have a PostScript printer, the only way ATM affects your lifestyle is in the display of Type 1 PostScript screen fonts. But what a difference ATM makes! With ATM installed, you don't need to install any screen fonts, which can save a lot of disk space. You can use any point size of any font for which you have the scalable font outlines and get as perfect a representation of that font as the screen is capable of displaying (usually around 96 pixels per inch; although ATM seems to work magic, it can't improve your screen resolution). Without ATM, you get pretty much the same "perfect" representation of your installed font sizes, but if you use any other size, the screen representation shows jagged type.

How Adobe Type Manager works

The ATM program is composed of PostScript Font Metrics (PFM) files and PostScript Font Binary (PFB) files. The PFB files contain matrices of numbers; the PFM files contain equations.

When you select a font size in any Windows program, ATM sends the appropriate PFB files through the equations in the PFM files. The result of the equation enables the program to draw the selected font on the screen.

Printing to a PostScript device

If you want to print to a PostScript device, the PFM and the PFB filenames must reside in your WIN.INI file as well as in the printer. If the font is resident on the printer, ATM needs to download only the PFM file to the printer. If the font is not available on the PostScript printer, the [PostScript] section of the WIN.INI file must contain both the PFB and PFM files.

Printing to a non-PostScript device

When you print to a non-PostScript printer, ATM *rasters* (creates bitmaps) the fonts down to the printer. This means that the fonts are created like a graph, as opposed to text. The fonts can be printed in either landscape or portrait mode. Any attribute, like bold or italics, can be applied to the font.

You must, however, have the scalable fonts installed on your hard drive if ATM is to have any effect either on-screen or when printing to a non-PostScript printer. You need the scalable font files for all fonts — even the ones you didn't need outline fonts for previously because they were resident in your PostScript printer's ROM.

ATM's only drawbacks are using some of your computer's RAM and slowing down the speed of the screen redraw. The speed of screen redrawing can be improved significantly, however, by assigning more memory to ATM's Font Cache in the ATM Control Panel. The Font Cache is used by ATM to hold the bitmapped images of characters generated on-the-fly for display to the screen; increasing the size of this cache means that ATM can hold more character images in memory and can therefore display your text more quickly.

How to disable Adobe Type Manager

Like most third-party font programs, ATM ties into Windows by replacing the Windows System driver, SYSTEM.DRV, which loads from SYSTEM.INI. Here are the lines that ATM's installation routine changes, both of which are in the [Boot] section of SYSTEM.INI :

```
SYSTEM.DRV=ATMSYS.DRV
ATM.SYSTEM.DRV=SYSTEM.DRV
```

To test Windows without the font manager, open SYSTEM.INI with a text editor and insert semicolons (;) in front of these two lines to comment them out. Then add the following line to the [Boot] section:

```
SYSTEM.DRV=SYSTEM.DRV
```

The next time you load Windows, ATM won't appear on-screen. To reinstate ATM, simply reverse the changes to your SYSTEM.INI file.

How to check for corrupted fonts

Can't get a font to work? The font file may be corrupt. To determine whether this is the case, open Control Panel and choose the Fonts icon; click on the name of the disputed font. If you can't see a preview of the font or if the font file size is listed as 0K, the file is corrupt. Remove the font from your system (select the Remove Font from Disk option) and reinstall it from its original floppies.

Using SYSTEM.INI to Control Fonts

The [TrueType] section

The [TrueType] section of SYSTEM.INI describes options that affect the use and display of TrueType fonts in your Windows applications. The [TrueType] section can contain the entries described in the following sections.

Setting the outline threshold

```
OutlineThreshold=number-of-pels-per-em
```

This entry specifies the number of pels-per-em at which Windows renders TrueType fonts as outline fonts instead of as bitmap fonts. Using bitmap fonts is faster but requires more memory. If your system is low on memory, decrease this value. Do not specify a value over 300 (if you do, you may encounter problems with TrueType fonts). The default is 256. To change this entry, you must edit WIN.INI.

Enabling TrueType fonts

```
TTEnable=0 | 1
```

This entry controls whether TrueType fonts are available. Setting this value to 1 makes TrueType fonts available in your Windows applications. Setting this value to 0 turns off TrueType fonts so that they are unavailable in applications. The default is 1. To change this entry, choose the Fonts icon from Control Panel.

Conflicting font names

```
TTIfCollisions=0 | 1
```

This entry specifies whether to use TrueType fonts in place of other fonts if both types of fonts are installed on your system and have the same font name. If this value is set to 1, the TrueType font is used. For example, Windows provides both a bitmap and a TrueType version of the Symbol font. If you set this value to 0, Windows uses the TrueType version. The default is 0.

Using only TrueType fonts

```
TTOnly=0 | 1
```

This entry specifies whether only TrueType fonts are available in Windows applications. If this value is set to 1, only TrueType fonts are available. If this value is set to 0, all fonts installed on your system are available. The default is 0.

The [FontSubstitutes] section

The [FontSubstitutes] section of SYSTEM.INI describes fonts recognized by Windows as identical to another typeface. This is useful if you want to work on documents that include screen fonts supported by Windows 3.0 but not by Windows 3.1. The [FontSubstitutes] section contains one or more occurrences of the following entry:

```
font-name=font-name
```

These entries specify the font that Windows uses in place of another font only if that font is not installed on your system. For example, if you are viewing a document formatted in Helvetica, but Helvetica is not installed on your system, Windows uses Arial to display the document. To change this entry, you must edit WIN.INI. The default entries for this section are listed here:

Helv=MS Sans Serif

Tms Rmn=MS Serif

Times=Times New Roman

Helvetica=Arial

Understanding Printer Fonts

A *printer font* is any font that can be produced on your printer. The three kinds of printer fonts are as follows:

■ *Device fonts* actually reside in the hardware of the printer. They can be built into the printer itself or provided by a font cartridge or font card.

■ *Printable screen fonts* are Windows screen fonts that can be translated for output to the printer.

■ *Downloadable soft fonts* are fonts that reside on your hard disk and are sent to the printer when needed.

Not all printers can use all three types of printer fonts. Plotters, for example, cannot use downloadable soft fonts. HPPCL printers cannot print Windows screen fonts.

Dot-matrix printer fonts

Dot-matrix printers support device fonts and printable screen fonts. Usually, a dot-matrix printer includes only a limited range of internal device fonts. Typically, fixed-space fonts are supplied in a variety of CPI (characters per inch) sizes. Dot-matrix device fonts are conventionally named *typeface CPI xx*, in which *typeface* is the typeface name and *xx* is the number of characters per inch. Distinguishing a device font for a dot-matrix printer is usually as easy as checking for the CPI designation at the end of the font name, such as Courier CPI 10.

Through the universal printer driver, dot-matrix printers can also support TrueType. When you use TrueType fonts on a dot-matrix printer, Windows sends a rasterized graphics image to the printer. Dot-matrix printers do not provide landscape device fonts, but vector screen fonts can be printed in any resolution or orientation. Dot-matrix device fonts are faster but less flexible than screen fonts.

Some 24-pin dot-matrix printers, such as Epson and NEC printers, also support font cards or cartridges. You can use these printer fonts if the Windows driver for your printer supports them.

HPPCL printer fonts

Printers that use HPPCL can print several different types of fonts. HPPCL printers can use font cartridges, downloadable soft fonts, vector screen fonts, and TrueType fonts. HPPCL printers cannot print Windows raster screen fonts.

When you use TrueType fonts on an HPPCL printer, TrueType performs all the font rendering in the computer and downloads bitmaps of the fonts to the printer. TrueType downloads only the specific characters needed in a document, not the entire font.

If you use an HP LaserJet-compatible printer, be sure to accurately specify the amount of memory installed in your printer. This is important because the Windows HPPCL driver now tracks the available memory in your printer. You may get an out-of-printer-memory or other error if the memory is set incorrectly.

Downloadable fonts

You can get HP LaserJet-compatible downloadable soft fonts from a number of sources, including Hewlett-Packard, Bitstream, SoftCraft, and CompuGraphics. Some downloadable font utilities also generate raster screen fonts for Windows. If an exact screen font match is not available, Windows uses one of its own screen fonts.

Hewlett-Packard downloadable fonts are installed with the Font Installer; third-party HPPCL soft fonts are installed with their own installation utilities. To use the Font Installer, choose the Fonts button in the Printer Setup dialog box.

The Font Installer places soft-font entries in the WIN.INI file under a section specific to a driver and port, such as [HPPCL, LPTx] (where x is the port number), as described later in this section. Because soft fonts are installed for a printer on a specific port, the soft fonts do not appear if you change the printer. To copy the soft-font listings to another port, choose the Copy Fonts To New Port button in the Font Installer dialog box.

HPPCL fonts can be downloaded on either a temporary or a permanent basis. Temporary fonts are downloaded only when the HPPCL driver encounters a particular font while printing. At the end of the print job, the soft font is discarded from the printer's memory. Printers such as the Apricot Laser and Kyocera F-1010, which require temporary soft fonts to be downloaded only at the start of a print job but not during the job, cannot use soft fonts with the Windows HPPCL driver.

HP plotter printer fonts

Because plotters are vector devices, they can print only vector fonts. Plotters cannot print any kind of bitmap, including raster screen fonts and TrueType fonts. HP plotters include one internal vector font called Plotter. However, the Windows vector-screen fonts Modern, Roman, and Script can be printed on HP plotters.

PostScript printer fonts

All PostScript fonts are scalable outlines that can be printed at any size. PostScript outline fonts can also be rotated to any angle and can be printed in both portrait and landscape modes. However, font-size limitations are often imposed by applications. A common PostScript font-size limitation in an application is 127 points.

PostScript soft fonts are installed with utilities provided by soft-font vendors. Because the fonts are scalable, if there is no comparable screen font, mismatches can occur between screen display and printed output.

PostScript printers cannot print Windows raster screen fonts, although they can print vector screen fonts. Printing Windows screen fonts is not usually necessary because of the large selection of resident fonts in a PostScript printer.

Most PostScript printers include either the standard Apple LaserWriter Plus set of 35 scalable fonts or the earlier Apple LaserWriter set of 17 fonts. The LaserWriter Plus standard font set includes 11 typefaces, 8 of which are available in roman, bold, italic, and bold italic (for a total of 35 fonts). The Symbol typeface contains mathematical and scientific symbols; Zapf Chancery is a calligraphic specialty font; Zapf Dingbats contains decorative bullet characters and embellishments. These three typefaces are available only in roman style.

PostScript printers and TrueType

TrueType fonts are treated as downloadable fonts by the PostScript driver. When you use TrueType fonts on a PostScript printer, scaling and hints are always performed in the computer. Scan conversion can be done in the computer or in the printer, depending on the point size. At smaller point sizes, TrueType performs scan conversion in the computer; at larger point sizes, scan conversion is done in the printer.

You can specify how to send TrueType fonts to your printer — for example, as bitmaps or in Adobe Type 1 format. To do this, open the Advanced Options dialog box from the Printer Setup command and select the method you want to use from the Send To Printer As list.

If your PostScript printer supports downloadable fonts, you may want to use printer fonts in place of TrueType fonts to speed up printing and to use less printer memory. To do this, open the Advanced Options dialog box from the Printer Setup command and select the Use Printer Fonts For All TrueType Fonts check box. You can also map a TrueType font to a PostScript font in the [FontSubstitutes] section of the WIN.INI file; although this arrangement increases printing speed, the results on the display may not be exactly the same as the printed output.

If your PostScript printer does not support downloadable fonts, you must use printer fonts to print any TrueType fonts in your documents. There are two ways to do this: allow the PostScript driver to print using the printer fonts that most closely match the TrueType fonts, or edit the Substitution Table to select the printer fonts you want to use.

PostScript downloadable outline fonts

PostScript printers also accept downloadable outline fonts, which can be scaled to any size and printed in both portrait and landscape orientations. Downloadable PostScript fonts are available from several suppliers, including Adobe and Bitstream. Both Adobe and Bitstream supply utilities that install the fonts and add entries to the WIN.INI file. Because the font-installation capability is included with these commercial font products, the Windows PostScript driver does not include a font-installation utility.

Although PostScript downloadable outline fonts can be scaled to any size, Windows screen fonts cannot. You must install specific sizes of Windows screen fonts with the Adobe and Bitstream utilities. Install only the sizes you feel you frequently use. If you specify a PostScript font size that does not have a corresponding screen font, Windows substitutes another screen font. The result is a little loss in display quality but, of course, no loss in print quality.

PostScript cartridges

To use PostScript cartridges with Windows, you must use the PostScript printer driver. Choose the Printer icon in the Control Panel window and follow the steps for installing a printer, selecting the Apple LaserWriter Plus (PostScript) or another PostScript printer from the list in the Printer Setup dialog box.

PostScript cartridges are not supported directly by the Windows PostScript driver.

How to substitute PostScript fonts

You can edit the Substitution Table to specify which PostScript printer fonts you want to print in place of the TrueType fonts in your documents. The changes you make in the Substitution Table affect only the fonts that are printed. The fonts that appear on-screen do not change; the original TrueType fonts are still used to display TrueType text in your document.

To specify which printer fonts to use, choose the Edit Substitution Table button in the Advanced Options dialog box of the Printer Setup command. Then select the TrueType font you want to replace from the For TrueType Font list in the Substitution dialog box. From the Use Printer Font list, select the PostScript printer font you want to use instead of the selected TrueType font.

If your printer supports downloadable fonts, you can select the Download As Soft Font option. In this case, the selected TrueType fonts are sent to the printer using the method you specified in the Send To Printer As list in the Advanced Options dialog box. Repeat these steps until you have selected printer fonts to use in place of all the TrueType fonts in your document.

How to specify virtual memory for PostScript printers

You can change the amount of virtual memory your PostScript printer has available for storing fonts. The PostScript driver uses a default setting for virtual memory (this setting is recommended by the printer manufacturer).

To find out how much virtual memory your printer has, print out the TESTPS.TXT file in the WINDOWS directory. To adjust the amount of virtual memory, open the Advanced Options dialog box from the Printer Setup command and in the Virtual Memory (KB) box, type the amount of virtual memory, in kilobytes, that you want to use.

PostScript drivers

In Windows 3.1, most PostScript printers use the universal PostScript driver, PSCRIPT.DRV. If you install a PostScript printer that does not appear in the List of Printers box in the Printers dialog box, you must install a Windows PostScript Definition (WPD) file for your printer. To do this, choose the Printers icon in the Control Panel window. Then select Install Unlisted or Updated Printer from the List of Printers box in the Printer Setup dialog box.

The WPD file for Windows 3.1 requires a version 3.1 OEMSETUP.INF file. If you have a WPD file for Windows 3.0, you do not need a new OEMSETUP.INF file to install the WPD file.

In Windows 3.1, the PostScript driver can detect certain errors that Print Manager cannot detect. You can specify whether or not to print information about these errors after your document finishes printing. This information may help you or a product-support representative determine what caused the error. To print out PostScript error information, open the Advanced Options dialog box from the Printer Setup command and select the Print PostScript Error Information check box.

Understanding the Importance of Selecting Target Printers

Your choice of a target printer is the single most important factor that determines which fonts are available to you in Windows.

Because the fonts used by printers with different page-description languages are never interchangeable, fonts are considered printer specific rather than part of the Windows environment. Any combination of a device driver (such as Windows' PostScript driver or HP's PCL drivers) and a port (such as COM1, LPT1, or FILE) is considered by Windows to be a printer — whether or not the device actually exists on your system. Just as choosing a printer makes the fonts for that printer available to you, choosing a different kind of printer makes a different set of fonts available. Although conceptually this scheme makes sense, in practice it causes a fair amount of confusion.

Windows gets the information about which fonts are available for any given printer from two places. Printer-resident fonts included in your printer's Read Only Memory (ROM) become available to you in Windows when you target a specific printer driver in either your Windows Control Panel or in an application's printer dialog box. Because the printer-font information is built into the printer, the printer driver simply includes the same information that is otherwise contained in a PFM file.

Soft fonts that either are not built into your printer's ROM or are not included on an installed and selected font cartridge are written into the WIN.INI file into the specific [Printer, Port] sections for the printers for which the fonts were installed. Each time Windows is launched or you target a different printer, Windows checks the printer driver and the [Printer, Port] section of the WIN.INI file for the target printer to see which fonts are available.

Because they're built into the printer driver, Windows' strategy for managing printer-resident fonts is pretty straightforward. The way soft fonts are handled is not. The following sections discuss installing and downloading soft fonts — the two most common problem areas for soft fonts.

How to install soft fonts

The options available to you for installing soft fonts depend on whether you're working with a PostScript or a PCL printer and, to a lesser extent, whether or not you're working with a type manager.

If you're installing PCL fonts, you use a font-creation program such as Adobe's Type Foundry, Bitstream's Fontware, or Hewlett-Packard's Type Director to create the fonts. At a minimum, all three programs generate both PFM files and printer fonts for the fonts you select. If you're using a type manager, you probably don't want to generate screen fonts. If you're using ATM, I recommend that you do not install bitmapped fonts if you have PostScript fonts from the same family available. These font-creation programs automatically install the fonts as they're created by adding information to the appropriate sections of your WIN.INI file and copying the files to a directory on your hard disk. You can also install pregenerated PCL fonts through the PCL printer driver's Font Installer.

You can install PostScript soft fonts with either Adobe Type Manager or the installation program provided with the font. As with PCL fonts, both the scalable printer font files and the PFM files are copied into a directory on your hard drive and references to the names and locations of the files are added to any PostScript-printer sections in your WIN.INI file. Screen fonts are installed independently through the Fonts option in the Windows Control Panel; if you're using ATM, I recommend that you don't install screen fonts at all.

When you install fonts using ATM, they are listed in both the ATM.INI file and the WIN.INI file. ATM uses the ATM.INI file to make fonts available to non-PostScript printers; if the PostScript fonts you install aren't added to the ATM.INI file, they are not available for display or for use with non-PostScript printers. If you're using ATM, I recommend using it to install your Type 1 PostScript fonts.

How to download soft fonts

In addition to letting Windows know what fonts are available, the WIN.INI file also determines whether those fonts are downloaded (or sent) to your printer on a temporary or permanent basis.

Permanent downloading

Permanently downloaded fonts are downloaded to your printer's RAM independent of a specific print job. You use either a batch file run at startup time or a downloading utility such as Adobe's PSDOWN. The term *permanent* may be misleading; permanently downloaded fonts remain in your printer's memory only until the printer is turned off. When the printer is turned back on again, the permanently downloaded fonts are gone until you download them again.

The advantages to permanent downloading are that the fonts are not automatically cleared from memory when a job is completed (beneficial if you are printing several jobs that use the same fonts) and that once you download all the fonts you need, the actual print job goes faster. The disadvantage is that the printer often does not have enough RAM for you to permanently download all the fonts you want. In general, you'll probably want to limit the number of soft fonts you permanently download.

Temporary downloading

Temporarily downloaded fonts are sent to the printer on an as-needed basis and are flushed from the printer's memory when that job is completed.

The advantages to temporary downloading are that it's easier (Windows takes care of it for you) and that the fonts are automatically cleared from memory (beneficial if you are printing several jobs that use different fonts). The disadvantage is that sometimes a font must be repeatedly downloaded after being flushed, making your document take longer to print.

How Windows tells the difference

If you don't tell Windows where to find the printer font by listing it in the WIN.INI file after you list the PFM file, Windows assumes that the font is permanently downloaded and that it needn't worry about it further. If the printer font's location follows the PFM listing in the WIN.INI file, Windows temporarily downloads the font.

This following section of a WIN.INI file (for a PostScript printer on LPT1) shows the difference. The first four fonts listed are temporarily downloaded. Windows assumes that because you haven't told it where to find the printer fonts for the last four, you've already taken care of downloading them.

```
[PostScript,LPT1]
feed1=1
feed15=1
device=15
softfonts=8
softfont1=c:\psfonts\pfm\gn_____.pfm,c:\psfonts\gn_____.pfb
softfont2=c:\psfonts\pfm\gnb_____.pfm,c:\psfonts\gnb_____.pfb
softfont3=c:\psfonts\pfm\gnbi____.pfm,c:\psfonts\gnbi____.pfb
softfont4=c:\psfonts\pfm\gni_____.pfm,c:\psfonts\gni_____.pfb
softfont5=c:\psfonts\pfm\op_____.pfm
softfont6=c:\psfonts\pfm\opb_____.pfm
softfont7=c:\psfonts\pfm\opbo____.pfm
softfont8=c:\psfonts\pfm\opo_____.pfm
```

 If you're working with ATM 1.x, any fonts you install are installed as permanently downloaded; you must modify the WIN.INI file if you want the fonts to be temporarily downloaded.

Understanding Printers, Ports, and Printer Drivers

With Windows, what you see is what you get, and the proof is in the printing. With the wide variety of printers available, the quality of your printout can vary dramatically depending on the type of printer you use.

Why your printer type matters

Although most Windows applications print to any printer for which Windows has a current printer driver, the techniques employed by different printers have their advantages and disadvantages. All printers have two parts: the marking engine and the page-description language that tells the marking engine what to do. The *marking engine* provides the physical mechanism that places the image on the page; most printers are categorized by the type of marking engine they use. The *page-description language* translates an application's description of page objects into commands the printer can execute.

Laser printers

The word *laser* tells you the type of marking engine in your printer — but not the page-description language the printer uses. The two main types of laser printers, PCL and PostScript, are differentiated by their page-description languages.

Printer Command Language (PCL) is the page-description language used by Hewlett-Packard LaserJet printers and those that emulate them. There are two versions of the PCL language: PCL 4 and PCL 5.

PCL 4 was used by the HP LaserJet through HP LaserJet II printers. All PCL 4 printers treat both text and graphics as bitmaps. PCL 4 printers generally don't boast a wide variety of built-in fonts. Bitmapped downloadable soft fonts are supported — but to use these fonts, you have to purchase and install each size, style, and typeface you want to use. Although these fonts print nicely at resolutions up to 300 dpi, it can take some work to get them set up properly.

When a PCL 4 printer prints a page, text and graphics are processed in independent bands. Text comes first; once all the text is processed, all other information is processed and placed on top of it. Although this works fine for most print jobs, it unfortunately means there's no way to print reversed text with these printers. Furthermore, the rigid structure of PCL 4 fonts makes it impossible to print text that has been rotated.

Many type managers make it possible to bypass these limitations and allow PCL 4 printers to print text that has been reversed or rotated or to which "setwidth" commands have been applied. If you're using a type manager, make sure that your "graphics resolution" option is set to 300 dpi.

PCL 5, an updated version of the HP page-description language, solves the problems of reversed and rotated text and offers a great deal of additional flexibility. The PCL 5 language is used by the Hewlett-Packard Laser Jet III printers. PCL 5 printers support scalable fonts, meaning that as long as the scalable font is correctly installed, you can print that font at any point size. Another important advantage offered by PCL 5 printers is that the graphic and text bands are not processed separately, making it possible for these printers to support reversed text. PCL 5 printers are backwards compatible and support all the fonts used by PCL 4 printers.

The *PostScript* page-description language was developed by Adobe Systems. In addition to supporting scalable outline fonts, the PostScript language offers more sophisticated capabilities than other printer-description languages. PostScript supports sophisticated color-separation capabilities and lets you print at resolutions up to 3600 dpi. One of the most widely used graphic formats — on both the Mac and IBM-compatible computer — is EPS, or Encapsulated PostScript. Only PostScript printers can offer full support for this graphic format.

PostScript is considered by most publishing and graphic arts professionals to be the industry standard, in large part because of the flexibility it offers. Your publishing requirements may not demand a PostScript printer, but should you need to produce typeset-quality documents from the desktop, PostScript is an option you should consider.

Jet-type printers

Jet-type printers use small jets to propel ink — black, colored, or a combination — onto paper. Although these printers are generally inexpensive and work reliably with Windows, they can't print EPS graphics and they require soft fonts that can't be used by other printer types (unless a type manager is used).

Dot-matrix printers

Dot-matrix printers have more in common with traditional typewriters than the other printers discussed here. On a dot-matrix printer, a printhead hammers through a ribbon to force a printed dot onto the page. As the printhead moves back and forth across the paper, line by line, the pattern of dots eventually resembles the image of the page displayed on your monitor. Dot-matrix printers don't require printer fonts; when used with a type manager such as ATM, they provide an inexpensive proofing option.

Printer ports

Ports allow you to communicate with peripheral devices — scanners, printers, or modems — by electronically communicating data (in the form of bits and bytes) through a cable. Whenever you print from Windows, you do so through one of the ports on your computer. There are two types of ports: serial and parallel. Understanding how they differ helps you determine which one is most appropriate for the type of communication you plan to do.

Parallel ports use eight separate conductors, or lines, and transmit one bit of data at a time through each of the eight conductors. These eight bits add up to one byte. The fact that data is transmitted over multiple paths makes parallel ports fairly fast, simple, and (electronically speaking) uncomplicated. Most Windows users favor the parallel-port method of communication. Parallel ports are called LPT1, LPT2, and LPT3 and usually have 25-pin connections. Parallel cables can be up to 10 feet long.

Serial ports transfer data sequentially, through a single conductor, bit by bit (literally). Serial ports are slower than parallel ports, but the cabling they require is less expensive. Serial ports are called COM1, COM2, and COM3 and usually have 9-pin connections. Serial cables can be up to 50 feet long.

Although all your physical ports are either parallel or serial, Windows offers the FILE port as an additional option. The FILE port provides an easy way to create files that contain all the data that would have been sent to a printer. Files sent to the FILE port can be taken to another computer (often a service bureau) where they can be printed without worry about font or other system-specific conflicts.

Why ports matter to Windows

Under Windows, a printer selection or target printer can be any printer driver assigned to any port. Because Windows makes it possible for you to work with both hypothetical and real printers and for you to have more than one printer installed for each port (although only one can be active at a time), things can get a little confusing. All you really need to know is that Windows uses ports as a way of organizing the printers you have available. Because fonts are installed for specific printers, keeping track of your ports can help you know where your fonts are.

Your WIN.INI file has a `[ports]` section that lists all the available ports; the list of available ports in the Printers Control Panel is based on this listing. Your WIN.INI file also has a `[Printer, Port]` section for each printer you've installed (you can have as many as 15 printers). These can be different devices, or multiple instances of the same device with various configurations, such as different ports. This flexibility makes it easier to set up your publications without having to constantly reconfigure your printers.

If you change a printer to a different port, a new `[Printer, Port]` section is added to your WIN.INI file. If you have downloadable fonts installed for a PostScript printer on COM1, but you change the printer to another port, you must reinstall your fonts for the new `[Printer, Port]` combination.

Printer drivers

The *printer driver* is the software that serves as the translator or interface between your Windows applications and your printer. Without the right printer driver, Windows can't take advantage of your printer's features (such as built-in fonts).

The driver "translates" the information that makes up a page into signals the printer can understand. The signals are then sent — through a communications port — to the printer, where they're interpreted and turned into marks on paper. The printer driver contains information about the attributes of a printer (such as the sizes of paper it supports, whether the paper feed is automatic or manual, what fonts are resident, what font cartridges are installed, and so forth) so that applications can take advantage of the printer's features.

The [ports] Section of WIN.INI

The [ports] section of WIN.INI lists the available communications and printer ports, defines default values, and lists files to which printer output can be sent. You can specify up to 10 ports. This is similar to the MODE command for MS-DOS.

The [ports] section can contain one or more entries in the following format (explanations of the various options can be found in Table 16-6):

```
portname:=baud-rate, parity, word-length, stop-bits [[, p]]
```

Specify a filename for the *portname* value to direct output to that file. A filename, unlike the other port names, must not be followed by a colon (:). If you specify a value for FILE:=, Windows prompts you to specify an output file each time you print.

To change COM port settings, choose the Ports icon from Control Panel. To change or add other ports, you must edit WIN.INI.

```
LPT1.DOS=path
LPT2.DOS=path
LPT3.DOS=path
LPT4.DOS=path
```

These four settings are used (instead of the corresponding LPT ports) to specify the path of the printer you are using. These settings allow you to print directly to a parallel port. Use these settings to bypass Windows' special handling of parallel-port output. The default *path* value for these settings is none. To change this entry, you must edit WIN.INI.

Table 16-6	Options in the [ports] Section of WIN.INI
Value	*Meaning*
portname	The name of an output port as it is recognized by MS-DOS. This can be one of the following:
	COMx for a serial port, where *x* represents the port number
	LPTx for a parallel port, where *x* represents the port number
	EPT for a specific IBM printer
	FILE for a filename
	LPTx.DOS for a parallel port, where *x* represents the port number. Connecting to LPT2.DOS can bypass Windows handling or print output (choose this option if you have trouble printing).
	Notice that if you specify a *portname* of LPTx, EPT, FILE, or LPTx.DOS, you do not provide any additional parameters. If you specify a portname of COMx, you must provide the baud-rate, parity, word-length, and stop-bits parameters (you may optionally provide the [[,p]] parameter).
baud-rate	Specifies a COM port's baud rate
parity	Specifies the parity setting for a COM port
word-length	Specifies the length of a word (in bits) for a COM port
stop-bits	Specifies the number of stop bits to be used for a COM port
[[,p]]	Specifies that hardware handshaking is in effect

The [devices] section of WIN.INI

The [devices] section of WIN.INI lists the active printers; it is necessary only for compatibility with Windows 2.x applications. The entries in this section are identical to those in the [Printer, Port] section without the timeout values. The [devices] section can contain one or more entries in the following format:

```
device=driver, port [, other ports . . . ]
```

The values specified are identical to the first three items in the [Printer, Port] section. To change these entries, choose the Printers icon from Control Panel.

When changing an entry in the [devices] section of WIN.INI, be sure that it does not conflict with a corresponding entry in the [Printer, Port] section of the file. Problems can occur if a connected device does not appear in the [Printer, Port] section.

Summary

Windows provides many options in terms of fonts and printing. This chapter covered these points:

▶ The three categories of fonts and how Windows uses them

▶ How printers use Windows-specific fonts

▶ Settings in the SYSTEM.INI file you can use to control fonts

▶ Settings in the SYSTEM.INI file you can alter to control printers and ports

Chapter 17

Telecommunications Secrets

In This Chapter

▶ Understanding how Windows communications programs interact with hardware

▶ Knowing how the Windows communications device driver operates in standard and enhanced modes

▶ Using SYSTEM.INI settings to tune communications sessions

▶ Configuring Windows to work with high-speed modems

From a user's standpoint, using a Windows communications program to connect to another computer or service should be as simple as turning on the modem and starting up the program. Instead, electronic communications under Windows is anything but simple. Reliable telecommunications under Windows depends on precise interaction between Windows, the communications program, device drivers, and hardware.

Communications Under Windows _____

As a rule, Windows communications applications speak through a device driver instead of directly manipulating the computer's serial port. In communicating with a serial port, the application follows a logical order. First, the application calls the Windows API, which contains various communications-specific commands. Next, the Windows COMM.DRV interprets the commands, and then it directs the serial port hardware. Communications settings, such as baud rate, parity, and the number of data and stop bits, are all configured through API calls. In the end, all Windows communications programs are at the mercy of the Windows communications driver, COMM.DRV.

COMM.DRV is in control

The Windows communications driver resides in COMM.DRV. Depending on whether Windows is running in standard mode or enhanced mode, COMM.DRV does different things.

In both modes, COMM.DRV implements the device driver calls that the Windows communications API needs to call in order to pass data to and from the COM port. To actually send or receive the characters, COMM.DRV places them in internal queues, where they are transmitted or placed by COMM.DRV's *interrupt service routine* (ISR).

In Windows standard mode, the ISR is located within COMM.DRV itself. When characters need to be sent from the serial port, COMM.DRV places them in a transmit queue and informs its ISR that data is waiting to be sent. The ISR sends a character out the serial port and then returns control to Windows. As the serial port sends the characters out, it signals the ISR with an interrupt to indicate that it is ready for a new character. The ISR continues to send characters in this fashion as long as data is in the queue.

Of course, COMM.DRV can add more characters to the transmit queue while the interrupt-driven transmit is taking place.

In similar fashion, when the serial port receives an incoming character, it sends an interrupt that is serviced by the receive portion of COMM.DRV's ISR. The ISR adds the character to the receive queue and sets a flag that indicates that data is available in the queue.

COMM.DRV then posts a message to the application to let the application know that data is waiting for it. COMM.DRV retrieves the data when the application makes the appropriate API call.

In Windows 386 enhanced mode, this scenario gets a bit more complicated, because 386 enhanced mode is a preemptive multitasking environment in which many *virtual machines* are being preemptively multitasked. Of course, all Windows programs are still being cooperatively multitasked in a single virtual machine, but Windows itself (and COMM.DRV) may not be the currently running process.

To address this need, Windows 386 enhanced mode uses *virtual device drivers* (VxDs). VxDs create a virtual device — a data structure that looks and behaves like the real device but exists only in programming. The VxD controls access to the real device — in this instance, a VxD called *VCD* virtualizes the COM port hardware to arbitrate access among the various virtual machines. In addition, a VxD called COMMBUFF buffers data between the virtual COM port and the physical serial port to avoid data loss when the application is not receiving CPU time.

Facts about electronic communication under Windows

Unlike communications under MS-DOS, where communications programs must interact with the hardware directly, communications under Windows is much better defined.

- Communications programs open and initialize an available communications port through the Windows *application program interface* (API). Windows tracks which ports are being used by other applications. If the requested port is already in use, Windows returns an error code.

- Windows applications rely on the device independence provided by the communications API and driver to access specific types of communications hardware.

- Windows applications use the standard Windows API to send data to the COM port and receive data from the COM port.

- Windows sends application data to the communications driver (COMM.DRV) and receives application data from it. In Windows 3.1, the data is sent and received between Windows and the driver in blocks, rather than as individual characters. This method reduces transmission overhead and improves performance. Windows 3.0 uses individual characters.

- The communications driver sends data to the COM port and receives data from it. The COM driver supports 8250-compatible Universal Asynchronous Receivers/Transmitters (UARTs). Also, the Windows 3.1 COM driver enables the FIFO buffer of 16550A-compatible UARTs in order to reduce interrupt overhead and improve data throughput. To support extra features or a different hardware interface, special communications devices may require a replacement communications driver.

FIFO Buffers

The 16550A UART has 16-byte receive and transmit buffers. These are referred to as *FIFO* (first in, first out) buffers, because the first character into the buffer is the first one transmitted, the second is the second, and so on. Because buffers can hold multiple characters while waiting for the CPU to service communication interrupts, buffers help reduce the load on the CPU and avoid data loss when the CPU is busy.

This behavior is similar to the way guided tours at a local museum occur — people get in line, and when the tour guide is ready, he takes as many people as were in line on the tour. If more than 16 people are waiting, the 17th and on are told to come back later. Of course, in telecommunications, you can't tell a character to come back later, so those characters would be lost.

With this system, people can arrive at any time, but the tour guides can take them on tours on the guide's own schedule, and the museum doesn't need to hire one tour guide for every person who wants to go on the tour.

The behavior of the 16550A is like the queue in the museum. The tour guides represent the interrupts the CPU can handle.

Windows 3.1 does not use the transmit buffer of the 16550A. In addition, it uses only one byte of the receive buffer — so you do not get the full benefit of the 16550A. Many add-on utilities exist, such as KingCom from OTC Corp., that permit full use of the 16550A's buffers.

■ The communications API allows baud rates up to 57.6Kbps.

■ In enhanced mode, the virtual communications device (VCD) virtualizes COM port hardware to moderate access by multiple applications. The VCD notifies virtual machines (VMs) when their COM ports require servicing.

■ In enhanced mode, COMBUFF buffers data between the communications driver and the physical port. Buffering prevents multitasking applications from losing data when they do not currently have CPU time.

■ Finally, the physical COM port receives data from and transmits data to the attached device (for example, modem, a directly connected host computer, fax card, and so on). Some COM ports, such as those using the 16550A UART, have onboard data buffers to improve communications throughput and reduce errors.

Increasing Communications Reliability

Many of the SYSTEM.INI settings discussed in this chapter can be set from the Control Panel. See Chapter 13 for information on how to set Port settings with Control Panel.

These settings specify the number of characters that the device will buffer on the corresponding communications port. Buffering may slow down communications on a port, but buffering may be necessary to prevent some communications applications from losing characters at high baud rates. The size required for the buffer depends on the speed of the machine and the application's needs.

Setting: `COM1Buffer=number`
`COM2Buffer=number`
`COM3Buffer=number`
`COM4Buffer=number`

Default: `128`

Increasing this value may slow down communications a bit, but you'll make up for it with greater reliability. The default setting for these buffers is `128`; try increasing it to `256` and see whether communications reliability increases.

Before changing one of these entries, make sure that the corresponding `COMxProtocol=` setting has the proper value.

Increasing the Time That Windows Gives Communications Programs

This entry specifies the time to allow a virtual machine to process a COM interrupt. If a communications application is losing keyboard characters on the display, try increasing this value.

> Setting: `COMBoostTime=milliseconds`

> Default: `2`

For more efficient background communications under Windows, increase the values of the `COMBoostTime` and `COMxBuffer`. Change the `COMBoostTime` parameter if the characters you type on the keyboard fail to appear on-screen during a communications session.

Using High-Speed Modems

If you are using a 9600 bps modem, or a faster modem, you may experience difficulty when you use a Windows communications program or run a DOS communications program from within Windows. Because Windows is multitasking, it cannot devote continuous resources to one program, and, therefore, it may not be able to keep up with 9600 bps transmissions. As a result, you may find that transmissions are dropping bytes.

You should be able to solve this problem by installing a serial port with a 16-bit UART, such as the 16550. The 16-bit UARTs offer twice the bandwidth of the older 8-bit UARTs and improve performance and reliability by reducing inter-rupt overhead.

Where do you find this UART? If you use an external modem, the UART is in your computer (either on the motherboard or on an I/O card that has the serial port). If you use an internal modem, the UART is on the modem.

If you have a 16550 UART, you need to make sure that your communications software supports it.

Enabling the 16550 UART

These settings specify whether the FIFO buffer of a COM port's 16550 UART should be enabled (`On`) or disabled (`Off`). If a serial port does not have a 16550 UART, this setting is ignored. These values are used by Windows for both standard and enhanced modes.

Setting: COM1FIFO=*Boolean*
COM2FIFO=*Boolean*
COM3FIFO=*Boolean*
COM4FIFO=*Boolean*

Default: On

Enabling the Simultaneous Use of COM Ports

These settings specify which interrupt line a device uses on the specified serial port. Check the hardware documentation for the correct value. If a hardware conflict exists between ports, set a value of –1 to disable input for one of the COM ports.

Setting: COM1Irq=*number*
COM2Irq=*number*
COM3Irq=*number*
COM4Irq=*number*

Default: (for ISA and EISA machines)
COM1Irq=4
COM2Irq=3
COM3Irq=4
COM4Irq=3
(for MCA machines)
COM1Irq=4
COM2Irq=3
COM3Irq=3
COM4Irq=3

Sharing IRQs on EISA and MCA Systems

This setting specifies whether COM interrupt lines will be sharable between multiple serial ports or with other devices. Set this switch if your machine uses the same interrupt for COM3 or COM4 as it does for COM1 or COM2.

Setting: COMIrqSharing=*Boolean*

Default: On (for Micro Channel and EISA machines)
Off (for all other machines)

Fixing SYSTEM.INI

Each COM port needs to have a unique address. Most communications programs, and COMM.DRV, expect COM3 to be at the address 3E8h and COM4 to be at 2E8h. Strangely, though, SYSTEM.INI defaults to the addresses 2E8h and 2E0h, respectively, unless you tell it otherwise. If you plan to use COM3 and COM4, you need to add the following two lines to the [386Enh] section of the SYSTEM.INI file:

```
COM3Base=3E8h
COM4Base=2E8h
```

If you plan to use alternate interrupt numbers, you also need to add the following two lines to the [386Enh] section of SYSTEM.INI:

```
COM3Irq=x
COM4Irq=x
```

where x is the interrupt number that the port is using. Keep in mind that the Windows 3.0 COMM.DRV doesn't recognize this modification; you still need a replacement driver (or possibly Windows 3.1).

Other [386Enh] settings may improve serial communications performance, but these settings are not listed in the Windows manual. They are documented in the SYSINI2.TXT file in the Windows directory.

Before you install a communications program, make backup copies of both the WIN.INI and SYSTEM.INI files so that you can replace them if the third-party communications program changes an existing driver or installs a new driver that conflicts with the system.

Setting the COM Port Base Address

These settings specify the base (first) port for for both standard and 386 enhanced modes for the serial port adapter you are using. Check the hardware documentation for the appropriate value.

```
Setting:  COM1Base=address
          COM2Base=address
          COM3Base=address
          COM4Base=address

Default:  COM3Base=3E8h (and the port address values in the
          BIOS data area for COM1, COM2, and COM4)
```

Resolving Device Contention for COM Ports

These entries indicate the contention detection values for each connected communications port. Windows uses these values to determine how to arbitrate requests for the use of a device by more than one application, at least one of which is a non-Windows application. If the value is -1, Windows displays a warning message that asks you which application should be given control of the port. If the value is 0, any application can use the device at any time. If the value is a positive integer that is less than 1000, this value represents the number of seconds that an application needs to wait to use a device after another application has stopped using it.

Disabling contention checking (by setting this value to 0) can cause problems if two or more applications try to access the COM port at the same time. Also, do not disable contention when using a serial printer — if multiple print jobs attempt to print at the same time, disabling contention causes them to overwrite each other on the printed page.

Setting: `COM1AutoAssign=`*number* | *seconds*
`COM2AutoAssign=`*number* | *seconds*
`COM3AutoAssign=`*number* | *seconds*
`COM4AutoAssign=`*number* | *seconds*

Default: 2

Configuring Windows for a 16550 UART Chip

A 16550 UART chip regulates all data transfers in and out of the computer's serial ports. If the external modem can transmit faster than 9600 bits per second, a 16550 or 16450 UART chip is required for reliable data transfer at this high speed. By design, Windows checks for a high-speed UART port when the program starts, so most switches are not needed.

These entries specify whether Windows 386 enhanced mode should stop simulating characters in a virtual machine after the virtual machine sends an XOFF character. Windows will resume simulating characters when the virtual machine sends another character after the XOFF character. Leave this entry blank if the application does binary data transfers; setting this switch may suspend binary transmissions. Windows will not check for XOFF characters if this entry is blank or set to anything other than XOFF.

Setting: COM1Protocol=XOFF | *blank*
         COM2Protocol=XOFF | *blank*
         COM3Protocol=XOFF | *blank*
         COM4Protocol=XOFF | *blank*

Default: None

If the modem loses some characters at high speeds, set the XON/XOFF protocol for the port. If the application continues to lose characters after you set this entry, try increasing the value in the related COMxBuffer= *value* setting.

Using Other COM Drivers

If this entry is On, it indicates that the Virtual COM Driver (VCD) will use its own copy of the serial communications driver's interrupt handler. Using this interrupt handler improves the performance of COM ports. Set this entry to On if you are using a Windows 3.0 serial communications driver. Set it to Off if you are using the standard Windows 3.1 serial communications driver.

Setting: COMdrv30=*Boolean*

Default: Off

Adding More COM Ports

By using the MaxCOMPort switch, you can increase the number of COM ports that the Windows enhanced mode Virtual Communications Device (VCD) can support. However, you need to use a different communications driver.

Because IBM provided space for only four COM ports in the BIOS port table in its first PC, four is the limit for a default configuration under MS-DOS. In the default configuration, support for more than four ports requires a special MS-DOS device driver that addresses the additional COM ports. However, most MS-DOS communications programs talk directly to the port hardware, so some of them support more than four COM ports without requiring a special MS-DOS device driver.

The Windows communications driver (COMM.DRV) also assumes a limit of four COM ports. COMM.DRV can support more than four ports, but the interface routines in USER.EXE limit the maximum to nine. Although you cannot directly configure COMM.DRV to support more COM ports, several third-party vendors have built new COM drivers that can support more ports by modifying or extending COMM.DRV.

Although you can configure the VCD for 386 enhanced mode to support more than four COM ports, the extra ports are addressable only from MS-DOS applications unless you replace COMM.DRV. The SYSTEM.INI `MaxCOMPort=` switch in the `[386Enh]` section can specify a higher number. This switch assumes that the COM ports are each addressed through separate I/O ports. Some multiport adapters have all of the COM ports share a common set of I/O ports, and then an index value is written to the adapter to indicate which COM port is being addressed. These multiplexed cards are not supported by the VCD.

The VCD under Windows can support up to nine communications ports, and the Windows communications functions also support the use of nine communications ports in a Windows application.

All this information might indicate that you can use a maximum of nine COM ports in a Windows application, but the communications driver (COMM.DRV) that is shipped with Windows 3.1 supports a maximum of only four communications ports.

Setting: `MaxCOMPort=x`

Default: `4`

Running a DOS Communications Program in the Background

To run a DOS-based communications program in the background under Windows, you need to create a program information file (PIF) for that program by using the Windows PIF Editor. Open the PIF Editor (usually found in the Accessories group) and open the PIF for the communications program. Make sure that the Background Execution option box is checked.

If you get errors while you are running the DOS program in the background, increase the program's execution priority and check the Lock Application Memory box in the DOS program's PIF settings. Running the application as a minimized icon during data transfers also can improve its reliability.

To improve data transfer, minimize the DOS-based communications program during sessions.

Using Windows Terminal to Test Your Modem

Windows comes with an applet called *Terminal,* which is a simple terminal emulation program. Although it offers only a small set of communications features, Terminal is satisfactory for many communications needs, such as testing your modem.

Terminal is started by double-clicking on its icon in Program Manager's Accessories group. The first time that Terminal is started, it brings up a dialog box that allows you to set up your communication preferences (speed, parity, COM port, and so on). It then saves this information in the [Terminal] section of WIN.INI so that it does not have to ask you for it again.

Terminal does not provide a method for changing the default communication preferences without editing WIN.INI manually, so make sure that the parameters you enter in the Communication Preferences dialog box are actually the parameters you want for future Terminal sessions.

After clicking OK, you will be looking at Terminal's main screen. At this point, any characters you type are sent to the modem. *Depending on the modem's default configuration, the characters may not be echoed to your screen!*

To check that your modem works, type **ATE1M1V1** and press Enter. Your modem should reply with OK. Then type **ATDT** and press Enter. You should hear the dial tone coming from the modem's speaker. If not, check to make certain that your modem is connected to the wall jack properly, and try again.

If your modem passes the dial tone test, then you can try calling CompuServe's phone number listing to test the rest of the modem. To do this, select Settings⇨Communications and click the Even button in the Parity group. Click OK and select Settings⇨Phone Number.

Terminal translates phone numbers that are spelled out using the letters on the telephone keypad. You can use this feature to dial 555-DATE or other similarly listed numbers without having to figure out what numbers the letters stand for, if you have a telephone on the same phone line as your modem, or plugged into the phone jack on the back of your modem.

When the Phone Number box comes up, enter 1-800-FIND-CIS, and click OK.

Select Phone⇨Dial to make the modem make the call. You should hear dial tone, then the sounds of the modem dialing, followed by some screeching noises, and at last, the word CONNECT should appear on-screen.

Press Enter, and CompuServe's computer should prompt you with Host:. Type **PHONES** and press Enter, and you will be talking to a CompuServe computer that will give you the telephone number of the CompuServe dial-up closest to you.

Select Phone⇨Hangup to hang up the line.

To obtain a CompuServe account, you can call the WUGNET hotline at 1-800-WIN-USER (voice, not with your modem!) and ask for a free CompuServe sign-up kit.

Summary

This chapter described settings that you can modify in the SYSTEM.INI file to configure and optimize communications under Windows.

▶ I showed how to configure Windows for high-speed communications.

▶ I covered methods for increasing communications reliability.

▶ I gave tips for running DOS communications programs.

Chapter 18

Network Configuration Secrets

Running Windows on a network is a daring feat when you stop to consider the implications of having both Windows and the network trying to control the same hardware at the same time. Buried in the SYSTEM.INI file are settings that enable you to modify the way that Windows behaves as it tries to coexist with another network environment.

ADMINCFG — a Tool for Administrators

Windows for Workgroups 3.11 includes a utility called ADMINCFG that enables network administrators to control various aspects of Windows for Workgroups' networking functionality.

ADMINCFG is not installed by SETUP. You need to expand it manually from the last disk in the Windows for Workgroups set. To expand it, choose File⇨Run from the Program Manager or the File Manager and type the following in the command-line box, substituting the actual drive and directory locations:

```
expand a:admincfg.ex_ c:\windows\admincfg.exe
```

You can then run ADMINCFG by choosing File⇨Run, or you can create a Program Manager item for ADMINCFG and run the utility by choosing its icon.

If the network has remote workstations, or if you install local copies of the Windows files, you may want to copy ADMINCFG to a floppy disk so that you can use it on workstations.

ADMINCFG changes settings in the Windows for Workgroups security settings file, WFWSYS.CFG. By default, this file is not password protected, and it does not restrict any functionality.

The WFWSYS.CFG file is not transferable from workstation to workstation. However, if you use ADMINCFG to edit a WFWSYS.CFG file that is located in a shared network directory that was created by using the Administrative Setup (SETUP /A) option, the settings in WFWSYS.CFG file will apply to all workstations that are set up using this directory. To ensure uniformity on the workstations, put common settings in the WFWSYS.CFG file before you set up workstations.

Starting ADMINCFG

Launch ADMINCFG either by double-clicking the Program Manager icon that you created for it or by selecting File⇨Run from the Program Manager and typing **ADMINCFG** in the command line box.

When ADMINCFG starts for the first time, it brings up a common Open dialog box that asks for the location of the WFWSYS.CFG file. If the WFWSYS.CFG file does not already exist, ADMINCFG creates this security file and asks for a password to associate with it. Using a password prevents unauthorized modification of the file.

The Main dialog box

The first dialog box that ADMINCFG presents (Figure 18-1) contains options that enable you to disable peer network sharing options.

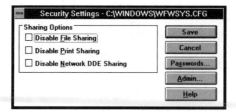

Figure 18-1: Security Settings dialog box.

Disable File Sharing prevents the user from sharing files and directories that are located on this workstation with users of other workstations on the network. It does not affect the user's ability to connect to and use shared directories on other workstations.

Disable Print Sharing prevents the user from sharing his or her printer with other users on the network. It does not affect the user's ability to use network printers connected to other workstations.

Disable Network DDE Sharing prevents users from sharing data by using ClipBook pages, from using Chat, from playing network games, and from using applications that use NETDDE to communicate over the network.

WinPopUp, which does not use NETDDE for its messaging, is not affected by this setting.

The Password Settings dialog box

Clicking on the Passwords button brings up the Password Settings dialog box (Figure 18-2), which includes the following options:

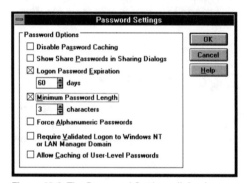

Figure 18-2: The Password Settings dialog box.

- The Disable Password Caching option requires users to provide the password for any shares that they connect to, every time they connect to them, even if the shares are *persistent* (automatically restored at start up). Choosing this option increases the level of security.

- The Show Share Passwords in Sharing Dialogs option removes a level of security. Normally, passwords in the sharing dialog boxes are masked by asterisks. If this box is checked, the actual passwords appear in the dialog boxes.

- The Logon Password Expiration option enables you to set a time when the password will expire. (Most administrators require that passwords be periodically changed.) This setting can range from 1 day to 180 days.

- The Minimum Password Length option enables you to set a minimum password length of from 2 to 8 characters. (Very short passwords are usually not effective in preventing security breaches.)

- The Force Alphanumeric Passwords option is another way to make passwords difficult for unauthorized users to guess. It requires that in addition to letters, the password include at least one numeric character.

- The Require Validated Logon to Windows NT or LAN Manager Domain option allows only valid users of the domain to access *any* shares, even those on other Windows for Workgroups workstations. One of the security limitations of Windows for Workgroups 3.10 is that anyone who knows a share name and password — perhaps on another Windows for Workgroups workstation — can connect to and use the share, even if they are not a user of the LAN Manager or Windows NT Advanced Server domain that the Windows for Workgroups workstations are clients on.

- The Allow Caching of User-Level Passwords option enables Windows for Workgroups to cache passwords that are used to log into servers with user-level security, such as LAN Manager and Windows NT servers. By default, Windows for Workgroups caches only share passwords. This option removes the need for the user to remember any passwords, other than the one the Windows for Workgroups logon dialog box asks for. This password is used to unlock the encrypted file in which Windows for Workgroups stores the cached passwords.

The Administrator Settings dialog box

The Administrator Settings dialog box enables the administrator to change the password on the security file, create a Custom Logon Banner (used in the title bar of the Logon dialog box), and control automatic updating of the security file (Figure 18-3).

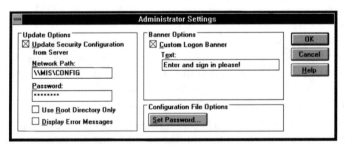

Figure 18-3: Administrator Settings dialog box.

Setting up automatic updating of the security configuration requires the Universal Naming Convention (UNC) path name (and password) to the network share that contains updated configuration files. If the Use Root Directory Only check box is checked, only the security control file in the root directory of the share is used.

If the box is not checked, Windows for Workgroups looks for subdirectories of the specified share whose name matches the computer name of the workstation at start-up time. If it finds one, it uses the security file in that subdirectory — if not, it uses the one in the root directory. This process enables the administrator to administer security files on one computer, have a different security file for each computer on the network, and have a default configuration in the root directory of the share.

The final check box in the dialog box, Display Error Messages, controls whether error messages that relate to the security update are shown to the user. For example, the server may be down, but letting the user know that fact may not be relevant.

Using Net Watcher to Keep an Eye on Things

Net Watcher is found in the Network or Accessories group. It is used most often to view the files and shares that other users are using on the local workstation.

 Windows for Workgroups 3.11 has an added administrative aid called the *Event Log* that is buried in two places. You activate network event auditing by choosing the Network icon in the Control Panel and view the log by using Net Watcher.

As Figure 18-4 shows, the Event Log Viewer can record the times that users connect with and disconnect from the computer, what shares they used, print jobs, and the like. This information can be valuable in tracking the use of network resources.

Date/Time	Computer	User	Share	Type	Access	Document	Event
1/9/94 14:33:56							Windows started
1/9/94 17:43:53	SALEM	ANGIE	CDRIVE	Directory	Full		User connected
1/9/94 17:45:08	SALEM	ANGIE	CDRIVE	Directory	Full		User disconnected
1/9/94 17:46:58	SALEM	ANGIE	WGPO	Directory	Full		User connected
1/9/94 17:48:07	SALEM	ANGIE	CDRIVE	Directory	Full		User connected
1/9/94 17:50:09	SALEM	ANGIE	CDRIVE	Directory	Full		User disconnected
1/9/94 17:50:09	SALEM	ANGIE	WGPO	Directory	Full		User disconnected
1/9/94 17:52:02	SALEM	ANGIE	CDRIVE	Directory	Full		User connected
1/9/94 17:52:59	SALEM	ANGIE	CDRIVE	Directory	Full		User disconnected
1/9/94 17:59:07	SALEM	ANGIE	WGPO	Directory	Full		User connected
1/9/94 18:15:35	SALEM	ANGIE	DIGITAL	Printer	Full		User connected
1/9/94 18:15:46	SALEM	ANGIE	DIGITAL	Printer	Full	Mail Messa	Print job spooled
1/9/94 18:16:19		ANGIE	DIGITAL	Printer	Full	Mail Messa	Print job completed
1/9/94 21:41:45	SALEM	ANGIE	CDRIVE	Directory	Full		User connected

View Event Log on \\BAGEND

Event Log (Begins at 1/9/94 14:33:56):

OK   Clear   Save As...

Figure 18-4: View Event Log window.

Miscellaneous Tidbits

Windows for Workgroups workstations on a Windows NT network are logged into Windows NT servers as *Guest* if they connect to a share on the Windows NT server. You may want to control access to the Windows NT server by restricting the access that the Guest account is permitted or by disabling the Guest account. If so, you need to create a user for the workstation on the Windows NT server and give the user the same name that the workstation uses on the Windows for Workgroups network.

When you are working with applications that use OLE 2.0, or other applications that require the SHARE.EXE TSR that is found in MS-DOS for file-locking on a Novell network, instead of loading SHARE.EXE, load the INT2F.COM utility that is found on the Novell client disk. *Note:* INT2F.COM requires Novell's NETBIOS emulator.

Network .INI File Settings

Windows stores settings that control network behavior and performance in several INI files, including WIN.INI, SYSTEM.INI, and on Windows for Workgroups, PROTOCOL.INI. Some of these settings may be used to tune the network performance, while others should be changed only by using the applets provided with Windows or by using System Engineer (included on the *Windows 3.1 Configuration SECRETS Disks*), because they are dependent upon other settings.

Read this section carefully, and always back up your INI files with System Engineer before making any modifications. 🔒

The [network] section of WIN.INI

The `drive=` entries are created by the Network Connections command on the Disk menu in the File Manager. The drive settings use the actual drive letter, for example: `f=SERVER\SYS:USERS\ANGIE`

Setting: `drive=Server-and-share-name`

Default: None

When you set this entry to 1, Windows reconnects to network servers each time Windows is started. If you set it to 0, reconnection does not occur.

Setting: `InRestoreNetConnect=0 | 1`

Default: 1

Similar to `drive=`, this entry defines the network printer connections that are to be restored each time Windows is started. You replace *port* with the actual name of the port. For example, you use `LPT1=\\PSERVER\PRINTER`. You use the Printers option in the Control Panel to set this entry, or you choose Options⇨Network Connections in the Print Manager.

Setting: *port=*

Default: None

SYSTEM.INI

Most of the Windows system configuration settings are kept in the SYSTEM.INI file, located in the Windows directory. Only the sections and settings that affect network configuration and performance are listed here.

The [boot] section

This setting controls how many files (.EXE and .DLL) Windows keeps open for faster access. However, some networks may have a limit on the number of files that can be open on a server at a time. Lower this number if you have problems running Windows from a network server. The valid range is from 2 to 12.

Setting: `CachedFileHandles=`*number*

Default: `12`

This entry specifies the filename of the network driver. Examples are `netware.drv` (Novell Netware) and `wfwnet.drv` (Windows for Workgroups). SETUP normally provides the filename.

Setting: `network.drv=`*filename*

Default: None

To use Windows for Workgroups 3.10 on a system that is not on a network, make sure that this line reads as follows:

    `network.drv=`

That is, make sure that no filename is specified. 🖌

The [ClipShares] section

This section, which is used only in Windows for Workgroups, is used by the ClipBook Viewer to identify the names of ClipBook pages that have been shared.

 Microsoft has stated that the format and location of the information in the [ClipShares] section is subject to change in a future version of Windows and that you should modify or create these entries only through the ClipBook Viewer and its API.

In Windows for Workgroups 3.1x, this section consists of entries in the following form:

    filename=pagename

In these entries, filename is the name of the file that the ClipBook page is stored in, and pagename is the name that the page is referenced by in the ClipBook Viewer.

The [DDEShares] section

In Windows for Workgroups, this section defines the database of DDE shares for Network DDE.

 Microsoft has stated that the format and location of the information in the [DDEShares] section is subject to change in a future version of Windows and that you should modify or create these entries only through the API calls that are present in the Network DDE API library.

 ### The [net.cfg] section

This section is present only in Windows for Workgroups 3.11, and it contains a single entry:

Setting: path=pathname

This setting specifies the path to the NetWare NET.CFG file that contains Open Datalink Interface (ODI) driver configuration information. This setting is set from the value that the user gives when installing Novell NetWare support with Windows for Workgroups 3.11.■

The [network] section

This section is used in Windows for Workgroups to track network settings.

This setting specifies whether the Event Log has been enabled (see "Using Net Watcher to Keep an Eye on Things" earlier in this chapter).

Setting: `AuditEnabled=`*`Yes | No`*

Default: `No`

This setting identifies the events that are being audited in the Event Log. You set it by selecting the Control Panel's Network icon and using the Event Log button.

Setting: `AuditEvents=`*`hex number`*

Default: None

This setting specifies the maximum size, in kilobytes, that the Audit Log can grow to. After the log is full, no further events are added to the log.

Setting: `AuditLogSize=`*`number`*

This setting instructs Windows for Workgroups to log the user on automatically during startup. If the user's password is blank, no prompt will appear. If the user has a password, a logon dialog box will appear. If a machine must support multiple users, passwords must be used.

Setting: `AutoLogon=`*`Yes | No`*

Default: `Yes`

To set the Title Bar of the Logon dialog box to a message of your choice, use the ADMINCFG utility that is described earlier in this chapter.

This setting specifies the real mode components that are loaded when the NET START command is issued from the command prompt or in AUTOEXEC.BAT.

Setting: `AutoStart=`*`Full | Basic | Popup | Netbind | Netbeui | Workstation [,...]`*

Default: `Netbind`

`Full` results in the full redirector support.

`Basic` loads only basic redirector support.

`Popup` loads the popup interface.

`Netbind` binds protocols and network adapter drivers.

`Netbeui` loads the NetBEUI protocol (which is required, for example, by Delrina's WinFax PRO for Networks).

This setting, when set to `Yes`, causes the Save This Password in Your Password List check box in Enter Password dialog boxes to be checked by default the next time the box is displayed.

Setting: `CacheThisPassword=Yes | No`

Default: `No` (or last value set by user)

This setting provides a description of your computer that appears to other users when they are browsing the network. The description cannot contain commas, and it is limited to 48 characters.

Setting: `Comment=text`

Default: None

This setting sets your computer name on the network. It must be unique, and it can contain letters, numbers, and the following special characters:

   !#$%&( )-.@*_'{}~

The maximum length is 15 characters.

Setting: `ComputerName=text`

Default: Name specified during SETUP

This setting controls whether the browsing of network resources occurs automatically when the Connect dialog boxes are displayed. Set it to `No` if this computer is connected by a slow link or if the network is very large. Base this setting on the Always Browse check box in the Connect dialog boxes.

Setting: `DeferBrowsing=Yes | No`

Default: `No`, unless Remote Access Service is installed

This setting specifies whether direct hosting over IPX is supported. When it is set to `On`, Windows for Workgroups will first try to talk to other computers by using direct hosting, and if the attempt is unsuccessful, it will try hosting over NetBIOS. Configurations that use the NWSUP.386 driver (that is, monolithic IPX and ARCNet configurations) require this setting to be `Off`.

Setting: `DirectHosting=On | Off`

Default: `On`

This setting controls the check box in the Network Settings dialog box in the Control Panel. You should use the Control Panel dialog box to change this entry, because the Control Panel will also remove the appropriate VxD entries from the `[386 Enh]` section of SYSTEM.INI.

Setting: `EnableSharing=0 | 1`

Default: 1

Even if this setting is set to 1 (enabled), a network administrator can disable sharing through the ADMINCFG utility (see "ADMINCFG — a Tool for Administrators," earlier in this chapter).

This setting indicates that Windows for Workgroups should not use the protocols that are represented by the LANA numbers that are specified. This setting is used when a NetBIOS protocol is present, but it cannot be used by Windows for Workgroups network components such as NetWare's NETBIOS.EXE TSR.

Setting: `Exclude=number [,...]`

Default: None (blank)

This setting takes priority over the `LANAs=` or `V86ModeLANAs=` entries.

This setting specifies the number of seconds that Windows for Workgroups waits before it disconnects an implicit connection that is no longer being used. If applications that you use involve pipes, or if the computer runs slowly when you are using implicit connections to perform several directory searches or directory listings, increase this value.

Setting: `KeepConn=number`

Default: 600

This setting limits the automatic detection of protocols to the list of LANA numbers if the network is started before Windows for Workgroups is started. Windows for Workgroups will use only those protocols that are present whose LANA numbers are included in this setting. This setting is useful with NetBIOS protocols that incorrectly identify themselves as being active on LANA numbers other than the numbers that are assigned to them (NetWare's NETBIOS.EXE TSR, for example).

Setting: `LANAs=lana number [,...]`

Default: None (blank)

If this setting is not changed to Yes, Windows for Workgroups workstations will not be visible on the network when LAN Manager users browse the network.

Setting: LMAnnounce=*Yes* | *No*

Default: No

This setting controls whether Windows for Workgroups shows the LAN Manager Logon dialog box at startup. The default value of 0 means that Windows for Workgroups will not log the user onto a domain.

Setting: LMLogon=*0* | *1*

Default: 0

This setting causes real mode network drivers to be loaded into the upper memory area if space is available. If set to No, real mode drivers are loaded into conventional memory.

Setting: LoadHigh=*Yes* | *No*

Default: Yes

This setting specifies whether the Network DDE application (and, hence, NETDDE support) is loaded at startup.

Setting: LoadNetDDE=*Yes* | *No*

Default: Yes

If this setting is set to Yes, the network redirector does not make the physical network connection for persistent connections at startup. As a result, the startup time is shorter. This behavior is known as *ghosted connections*.

Setting: LogonDisconnected=*Yes* | *No*

Default: No

This setting indicates the name of the default LAN Manager domain that validates your password if you choose to log onto a LAN Manager domain when you start Windows for Workgroups.

Setting: LogonDomain=*text*

Default: Designated workgroup for this computer

This entry indicates whether your logon was validated by a LAN Manager server when you last logged on. This setting ensures that you are properly logged off when you end your Windows for Workgroups session.

Setting: LogonValidated=*Yes* | *No*

Default: No

This setting controls whether this computer can be used as the *browsemaster* — the computer that maintains the list of servers that Windows for Workgroups users see when they browse the network. Auto means that this computer is used if necessary. No means that this computer is never used for this function. Yes means that this computer always maintains the list; and if it is not the master, it may step in and become the master if the master goes off-line.

Setting: MaintainServerList=*Yes* | *No* | *Auto*

Default: Auto

Set this setting to No if the computer has very little free memory or if it is connected to the network only via a slow link (such as a telephone line). At least one computer in the workgroup must have a value of Auto or Yes to ensure that a list of workgroups and computers on the network is available.

The actual browsemaster is chosen on the network by an *election* process. If a Windows NT Advanced Server is on the network, it is chosen as browsemaster (unless there are other NT Advanced Servers present, in which case, the one that has been up the longest is designated browsemaster). Similarly, if no Windows NT Advanced Servers are present, the election moves to Windows NT workstations, which elect in the same manner (longest up time). If no Windows NT workstations are present, then a Windows for Workgroups browsemaster is used.

This setting holds the name of any active secondary networks that have had support added on this machine in Windows for Workgroups.

Setting: Multinet=*text [,...]*

Default: None (blank)

This setting disables the Enable Sharing section of the Network Settings dialog box. Set it to 0 to prevent the user from changing the sharing state. This setting does not control sharing; it controls only whether the user can turn sharing on and off.

Setting: NoSharingControl=*0* | *1*

Default: 0

This setting specifies the number of buffers that are used by the protected mode redirector VREDIR.386 to cache data that is read from the network. Increasing this number can improve network operation performance, but it also reduces memory that is available to applications. The default is one-eighth of the available physical memory that is free at load time, so this number defaults to that amount of memory, divided by the size of each buffer (4096 bytes), rounded down. The minimum is 2, and the maximum is 4096.

Setting: `NumBigBuf=number`

Default: Calculated by Windows for Workgroups

This setting specifies the number of seconds of idle printing time that Windows for Workgroups waits before indicating the end of a print job when printing from an MS-DOS application. The time an MS-DOS application is suspended does not count toward this timeout. To make print jobs from MS-DOS applications print sooner, decrease this setting. If long print jobs or graphics are printing incorrectly, try increasing this setting.

Setting: `PrintBufTime=number`

Default: `45`

This setting is analogous to the Novell Netware capture command parameter `Timeout=`.

This setting specifies the relative priority for sharing resources in Windows for Workgroups. The lower the number, the less time is given to sharing resources. This setting is set by the Performance Priority slider bar in the Network dialog of the Control Panel.

Setting: `Priority=number`

Default: `80`

This setting controls the Reconnect At Startup check box in the Connect Network Drive or Connect Network Printer dialog boxes. If `No`, the check box is not selected.

Setting: `reconnect=Yes | No`

Default: `Yes`

This setting controls the default for the Reshare at Startup check box in the Share Directory or Share Printer dialog boxes. If `Yes`, the check box is selected.

Setting: `reshare=Yes | No`

Default: `Yes`

This setting identifies LANA numbers that are slow connections, such as Remote Access Service. This setting will result in changes in packet sizes to avoid timing problems when sending NETBIOS data across the slow link. It also prevents the local computer from becoming a browse server for the given LANA values.

Setting: `SlowLanas=LANA number [,...]`

When this setting is set to `Yes`, the messaging service is started when Windows for Workgroups 3.11 is started, and the WinPopUp application is loaded to send and receive messages and alerts. Also, the Print Manager will send notices of completed print jobs, which is a common reason why users set this setting to `Yes`.

Setting: `StartMessaging=Yes | No`

Default: `No`

This setting specifies the default logon name that is used to log onto Windows for Workgroups. The maximum length is 20 characters.

Setting: `username=text`

Default: Computer name until first logon; then last logon name

This setting specifies the name of the primary Windows network driver. When Microsoft networking is enabled, the setting is `wfwnet`.

Setting: `WinNet=text`

This setting specifies the workgroup that this computer belongs to. The maximum length is 15 characters.

Setting: `WorkGroup=text`

Default: Workgroup name specified during SETUP

The [network drivers] section

This setting sets the pathname to the location of the network device driver files and the PROTOCOL.INI file.

Setting: `devdir=pathname`

Default: The Windows directory

If this setting is set to Yes, real mode NDIS 2.0 drivers are loaded automatically when the NET START command is issued at the MS-DOS command prompt.

Setting: LoadRMDrivers=Yes | No

Default: Yes if NDIS 2.0 drivers are installed; No otherwise

This setting is a comma separated list of the names of NDIS 2.0 network adapter card drivers that are configured for this system. These drivers must be real mode drivers.

Setting: netcard=name [,...]

This setting is a comma separated list of the names of NDIS 2.0 protocol drivers that are configured for the system. These drivers must be real mode NDIS 2.0 drivers.

Setting: transport=pathname [,...]

This setting specifies whether the specified real mode NDIS 2.0 driver will be loaded into the upper memory area (high) or into conventional memory (low).

Setting: <NetworkCardDriver>.DOS=low | high

The [NWNBLink] section

This setting sets the LANA number to assign to the NWNBLink NETBIOS services driver. It is used for the IPX/SPX Compatible Transport with NETBIOS and the IPX Support Driver (Monolithic).

Setting: lanabase=LANA number

The [PasswordLists] section

This section contains settings that specify the location of the password list files. Each user who logs onto a Windows for Workgroups computer has a password list that contains an encrypted list of the passwords that the user has used to connect to password protected resources.

Each entry in this section has the following format:

    username=pathname

In these entries, username is the logon name used, and pathname is the fully qualified path to the password list file.

The [Standard] section

This entry indicates how many Int 28h interrupts are visible to software that is loaded before Windows is loaded. Int 28h interrupts are generated by the system when it is idle, and this setting indicates that Windows should reflect every *n*th interrupt, where *n* is the value of this setting. The default is to reflect every other Int 28h interrupt. Increasing this value may improve Windows performance but also may interfere with some network software.

Setting: `Int28Filter=number`

Default: `2`

This setting controls the size of the buffers that Windows allocates in conventional memory for data transfers over a network that is in standard mode. Some networks may require this number to be increased, at the expense of conventional memory available to applications.

Setting: `NetHeapSize=number`

Default: `8`

The [NonWindowsApp] section

This setting determines whether Windows will permit switching away from an application that is running in standard mode after the application has made an asynchronous NETBIOS call. Switching away from such an application could cause the system to fail. If Windows detects an asynchronous NETBIOS call, it will not allow switching away from the application. If you are sure that your applications will not receive network messages when you are switched away from them, set this setting to `1`.

Setting: `NetAsynchSwitching= 0 | 1`

Default: `0`

The [386 Enh] section

Most of the `[386 Enh]` section consists of these lines, which load VxDs.

Setting: `device=filename`

This setting disables the 32-Bit File System warning screens.

Setting: `DisableVFATWarning=On | Off`

Default: `Off`

If this setting is changed to True, SHARE.EXE sharing violation messages appear when a sharing violation occurs while the system is using the VSHARE.386 device. Set this setting to True if you use MS-DOS applications that rely on the SHARE.EXE messages to inform the user of sharing violations.

Setting: EnableSharingPopUps=*True* | *False*

Default: False

This setting indicates whether Windows should automatically send a message to the File Manager anytime a non-Windows application creates, renames, or deletes a file. If this setting is On, it can cause significant slowdowns in system performance. This setting must be Off for a virtual machine to run exclusively if it modifies files.

Setting: FileSysChange=*On* | *Off*

Default: On in 386 enhanced mode, Off in standard mode

This setting prevents Windows from running other applications when memory-resident software has the InDOS flag set. Some TSRs and network drivers require this setting to be set to On because it needs to be in a critical section to do operations off of an Int 21 hook. If this setting is set to On, system performance will slow slightly.

Setting: InDOSPolling=*On* | *Off*

Default: Off

This setting determines whether a critical section is needed to handle Int 28h interrupts that are used by TSRs. Some network virtual devices use Int 28h interrupts for internal task switching, and they may hang if this setting is set to Off. However, setting this setting to Off may improve Windows' task switching.

Setting: Int28Critical=*On* | *Off*

Default: On

When this setting is set to On, Windows attempts to save a failing NetBIOS request. When an application issues an asynchronous NETBIOS request, Windows attempts to allocate space in its global network buffer for the data. If the global buffer has insufficient space, Windows normally fails the NETBIOS request. When this entry is set to On, Windows attempts to save such requests and allocates a buffer in local memory. It also prevents any other virtual machines from running until the data is received or until the timeout specified by the NetAsynchTimeout= setting expires.

Setting: NetAsynchFallback=*On* | *Off*

Default: Off

This setting is used only when NetAsynchFallback= is set to On, and it specifies the timeout period in seconds. See the preceding information on the NetAsynchFallback= setting for more information on this setting.

Setting: NetAsynchTimeout=*number*

Default: 5.0

This setting is a comma separated list of NDIS 3.0 adapter card drivers that Windows for Workgroups 3.11 loads conditionally — only if NDIS 2.0 network protocols are not loaded on startup.

Setting: Netcard=*drivername [,...]*

This setting specifies NDIS 3.0 network adapter drivers that are always loaded on startup.

Setting: Netcard3=*drivername [,...]*

This setting determines the DMA buffer size (in kilobytes) for NETBIOS transports if a network is installed. The actual buffer size that is used will be the larger of this setting, or DMABufferSize=.

Setting: NetDMASize=*number*

Default: 32 on Micro Channel machines, 0 on others

This setting specifies the size of the buffers that Windows creates in conventional memory for data transfers over a network. The value is in kilobytes, and it is rounded up to the nearest multiple of 4.

Setting: NetHeapSize=*number*

Default: 12

This setting tells Windows to convert synchronous NETBIOS commands to asynchronous commands. This conversion can improve overall system performance when multiple applications are running.

Setting: NoWaitNetIO=*On | Off*

Default: On

This setting, which is ignored if UniqueDosPSP= is set to Off, specifies the amount of additional memory, in 16-byte increments, that Windows reserves in each successive virtual machine. The best value for any given machine varies, depending upon memory configuration and applications that are being used. See the description of the UniqueDOSPSP setting for more information.

Setting: PSPIncrement=*number*

Default: 2

This setting controls Windows' reflection of MS-DOS Int 2A signals. If this value is set to Off, Windows consumes these signals. Setting this value to On may cause Windows to run less efficiently, but some TSRs that rely on detecting Int 2A messages may require that this setting be Off.

Setting: ReflectDOSInt2A=*On* | *Off*

Default: Off

This setting forces Windows into a critical section around all timer interrupt code, ensuring that only one virtual machine at a time receives timer interrupts. Some networks and other global memory-resident software may fail if this entry is not used. This setting can make the system seem to stop for short periods of time. The value is in milliseconds, so setting this entry to 5000 is actually a setting for 5 seconds. This entry is commonly set for Novell Netware.

Setting: TimerCriticalSection=*number*

Default: 0

This setting tells Windows to search for a token ring adapter on machines with IBM PC/AT architecture. You may need to set this value to Off if Windows locks up during startup and the machine does not have a token ring card.

Setting: TokenRingSearch=*On* | *Off*

Default: On

This setting tells Windows to start every new application at a unique address (PSP). The amount of memory that Windows reserves below the application is determined by the PSPIncrement= setting. This setting ensures that applications in different virtual machines start at different addresses. On networks that use the applications' load addresses to identify the different processes, setting this entry to Off can cause an application to fail when another application is exited, because the network sees them as the same application.

Setting: UniqueDOSPSP=*On* | *Off*

Default: On for MS-Net and LAN Manager; Off for all others

PROTOCOL.INI

The PROTOCOL.INI file is used by Windows for Workgroups to specify settings for device drivers and network components. These settings may contain network adapter configuration information, such as I/O address, DMA settings, interrupt settings, and adapter-specific settings — such as transceiver type.

The file contains [network.setup] and [protman] sections, as well as separate sections for each network adapter and protocol.

The details of this file vary widely, according to what protocols and adapter cards the system is using. Describing these details is beyond the scope of this book.

You should never edit PROTOCOL.INI by hand. Always use the Network icon in the Control Panel (Windows for Workgroups 3.10) or Network Setup from the Network group in the Program Manager (Windows for Workgroups 3.11) to change network configuration settings.

When you are using a 3Com 3c509 (Etherlink III) network adapter, problems occur if the card's modem speed parameter in the card's hardware setup is set to a rate that is higher than 9600. Set the rate to 9600, regardless of the actual speed that is used on the serial ports.

When you are using an Intel Etherexpress 16 network adapter, make certain that the Transceiver Type is set to the type of connector (10BaseT, Coax/BNC, AUI) that the network cabling is attached to. You can find out what this setting is by starting Network Setup from the Network Program Manager group, clicking the Drivers button, highlighting the adapter in the list, clicking Setup, clicking Advanced, and choosing Transceiver Type from the list box. Figure 18-5 shows the Network Drivers window with Intel EtherExpress 16 selected.

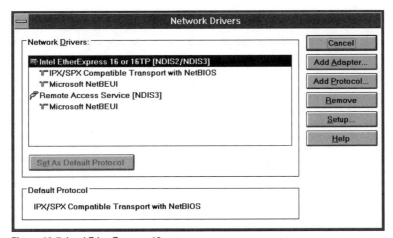

Figure 18-5: Intel EtherExpress 16 setup.

In addition to making sure that Windows for Workgroups knows the correct transceiver type, you also may need to use the SOFTSET utility that comes with the Intel card to set the Connector setting in the EEPROM on the card itself. SOFTSET also can automatically configure the card so that no conflicts occur with other devices in the computer. (See Figure 18-6.)

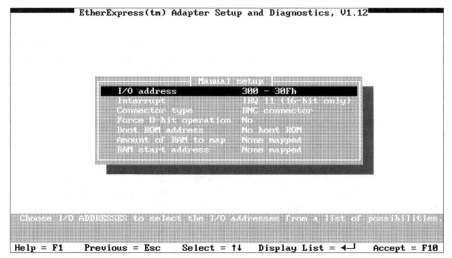

Figure 18-6: SOFTSET Utility.

Microsoft did not deliver the SOFTSET utility in the Windows for Workgroups 3.10 packages that included network hardware. It is available in the Microsoft Software Library and from the Microsoft Download System as WG0760.ZIP.

Summary

This chapter discussed the issues that are involved in running Windows on a network.

▶ Windows provides many INI file settings to control network performance and behavior.

▶ Windows for Workgroups 3.11 contains many enhancements to networking, including better administrator controls.

Chapter 19
Clipboard, DDE, and OLE Secrets

In This Chapter

▶ How the Clipboard uses memory

▶ Understanding and using Clipboard formats

▶ Problems in using the Clipboard

▶ Understanding how DDE works

▶ Using OLE

▶ Using the Object Packager

Most users know the Clipboard as a simple tool that they use for cutting, copying, and pasting information within a document or from one application to another. The Clipboard was designed to be simple to use, and this chapter is designed to show you how powerful it can be.

A Closer Look at the Windows Clipboard _____

The Clipboard's true identity is one of Windows' best kept secrets. People generally associate the Clipboard with the program CLIPBRD.EXE. However, CLIPBRD.EXE isn't really the Clipboard. It's a Clipboard viewer. In reality, the Clipboard is a complex system that lurks deep inside Windows, and the Clipboard program is merely a view port into an area of memory that Windows reserves as a temporary storage area.

The Clipboard is an indexed database of pointers to global memory blocks that includes information about the type of data that is contained in the blocks. It has no inherent abilities for processing or displaying data; it doesn't allocate memory to hold the data; and it doesn't verify the format of incoming data. In fact, the Clipboard is practically brain dead. The Clipboard is totally at the mercy of the applications that are using it. And if these applications misbehave, you end up with corrupted memory, general protection faults, memory overruns, and out-of-memory errors.

At its simplest, the Clipboard enables you to transfer information inside applications. You access the Clipboard through an application's Edit pull-down menu. You use the Cut command to copy a selection to the Clipboard and delete it from the application, the Copy command to copy a selection to the Clipboard, and the Paste command to paste the Clipboard data into the application.

How the Clipboard really works

Here's the sequence of events for a typical Clipboard operation. To place data on the Clipboard, the owner application allocates a global memory block, locks the block so that other applications can't access it, places and formats the desired data in the block, and then unlocks the block to make the data accessible to a target application.

When you invoke the Paste command in the client or target application, that application follows a similar sequence to retrieve data from the Clipboard. First the application opens the Clipboard, gets the handle, and locks the Clipboard memory block. Then it copies the data to its data segment or to another global memory block. Finally, it unlocks the memory block and closes the Clipboard.

All of this activity goes on behind the scenes, and it seems like a very simple give-and-take process. As I mentioned in the preceding section, however, applications that are using the Clipboard rely completely on each other's good behavior.

Problems with Clipboard operations

Copying data to the Clipboard follows one of two scenarios. In the first scenario, the Clipboard is emptied before data is copied to it, ensuring that only the data from the current Copy operation is on the Clipboard. In the second scenario, the Clipboard is not emptied before data is copied to it. Instead, only data of the same format as the data that you are copying is replaced, leaving data in all other formats intact. Most of the time, emptying the Clipboard before new data is copied to it is preferable because that method takes up less memory.

Consider these two important points:

- The Clipboard can transfer only one object at a time. Every time you issue a Cut or Copy command, the data formats that are currently stored in the Clipboard memory area are replaced by the data formats from the new Cut or Copy operation.

- In Windows 3.0, the Clipboard was limited to 64K objects. In Windows 3.1, the Clipboard can handle almost any size object. The amount of memory that is allocated for Clipboard usage is determined by the application that is copying to the Clipboard and the application that is receiving data from the Clipboard. You may receive an application error message if an application does not allocate sufficient memory. The increase in capacity that Windows 3.1 provides can cause problems with low memory or corrupted memory.

The Clipboard and memory conflicts

The Clipboard is a shared system resource. For the Clipboard to function correctly, each application that interacts with the Clipboard must follow protocol to prevent system crashes, endless message loops, and other strange and disturbing events. Because the Clipboard is a shared system resource, its use or misuse has global impact.

- The Clipboard's stability can be impaired, especially when large or complicated formats are manipulated.

- The Clipboard's stability becomes even more sensitive when several large programs are competing for limited system resources.

- When one or more large applications compete for limited resources, system performance rapidly deteriorates. This problem especially occurs when you are working with the Clipboard.

- You can exhaust all available system memory when you are using the Clipboard. If the memory is exhausted, almost any complicated operation will fail.

- Applications sometimes tie up the system for long periods of time during Clipboard operations that require intense computation. For example, to display a large compressed gray-scale TIFF image on a monochrome display, the application must uncompress the image in bands while converting the gray scale to monochrome. Obviously, this process can chew up a considerable amount of the system's resources and take several seconds to complete.

If I pick one recurring theme in this book, it is the idea that *Windows and Windows applications are extremely sensitive to memory conflicts.* Imagine what would happen if two applications tried to access and change the Clipboard at the same time. The concept of ownership comes into play in such a case. Windows enables applications to temporarily block other programs from using the Clipboard while changes are being made. After the changes are completed, the Clipboard is immediately released so that other applications can access it.

Clipboard data formats

The Clipboard appears to contain only one data item at a time. Actually, it can hold a number of different data formats and corresponding data handles, all representing the same data.

Windows defines seven different Clipboard formats that range from standard ASCII text to graphical data in binary form. Table 19-1 describes the common formats.

Table 19-1	Common Clipboard Data Formats
Format	*Description*
BITMAP	Specifies a device-dependent bitmap
DIB	Specifies a device-independent bitmap
DIF	Specifies that the data is in the Software Arts data-interchange format (DIF)
METAFILEPICT	Specifies a metafile-picture structure
OEMTEXT	Specifies null-terminated text in the OEM character set
RIFF	Specifies that the data is in any resource interchange file format (RIFF)
SYLK	Specifies that the data is in the Microsoft symbolic link (SYLK) format
TEXT	Specifies null-terminated text. Windows supports two formats for text: TEXT and OEMTEXT. TEXT is the default Windows Clipboard text format. Windows uses OEMTEXT for text within non-Windows-based applications.
TIFF	Specifies that the data is in the tag image file format (TIFF)
WAVE	Specifies that the data is a RIFF waveform file with form type WAVE

Besides the formats that are listed in Table 19-1, Windows offers a mechanism through which applications can create additional user-defined formats.

 When you paste from the Clipboard, the Paste command is available only if the client application can accept the file format. Use the Display menu of the Clipboard to see the currently available formats. Although you can't control which format is used for pasting, knowing which formats are available and which formats the client application supports enables you to determine whether pasting is supported.

The Clipboard can serve as a file format converter. To convert a TIFF image to a bitmap image, open the TIFF file in a graphics program that supports TIFF formats. Then copy the image to the Clipboard and paste it as a bitmapped image to another program.

Multiple rendering

The Clipboard uses a technique called *multiple rendering* that enables applications to supply the Clipboard with several different formats or representations of the same data each time you perform a Cut or Copy operation. The target application can then choose the best format from the formats that are available on the Clipboard.

For example, the Clipboard may hold a pie chart as both a metafile picture and a bitmap. An application that received the pie chart from the Clipboard would have to choose which representation matched its requirements. In general, the format that provides the most information is the most desirable, as long as the application understands that format.

Delayed rendering

By now you can see that maintaining multiple rendered Clipboard data can use up enormous amounts of system memory. Fortunately, another technique, known as *delayed rendering,* can limit the allocation of memory to only those formats that are actually used. In *delayed rendering,* the server application (copying application) makes a pledge to the Clipboard to provide data for each potential rendering. This pledge remains on the Clipboard until some application requests a particular data item. When the request is received, the server application must make good on its pledge by supplying the data in the client application's desired format, even if the data was copied to the Clipboard some time before. The server allocates data only for those formats that the client actually uses, thereby saving time and resources. Delayed rendering consumes less system memory and eliminates the computation time that is required to produce unwanted formats.

The Clipboard viewer chain

In addition to the multiple and delayed rendering techniques, the Windows Clipboard provides a mechanism, called the *Clipboard viewer chain,* through which it automatically notifies interested applications whenever a Clipboard change occurs. The Clipboard viewer chain works like this: An application receives a message indicating that a Clipboard change has occurred. It processes the message and passes it to the next application in the chain.

A chain is only as strong as its weakest link. In order for the delayed rendering process to be transparent to other applications, the Clipboard owner must handle all interactions correctly. When the Clipboard owner receives a message, it should attempt to render the requested data. If it cannot render the data because of insufficient memory or some other condition, it must notify the system.

Clipmate 2.0 Clipboard Enhancement

ClipMate 2.0, included on the *Windows 3.1 Configuration SECRETS Disks,* is designed to enhance the native capability of the Windows Clipboard. From a functional standpoint, the Windows Clipboard works exactly as it should: allowing the user to transfer an item of data within an application, or between applications. In practice, however, the Clipboard falls short in that it can hold only one item of data at a time — multiple formats yes, but still the same item of data. When you perform a Cut or Paste, the Clipboard is emptied, and your new piece of data is now the sole occupant of the Clipboard. You cannot append new data to the existing Clipboard data nor can you undo, and Clipboard has no long-term memory. That's where ClipMate steps in!

ClipMate adds several value-added enhancements to the operation of the Windows Clipboard. ClipMate enables you to keep many generations of previous Clipboard occupants (Clip Items) for later retrieval. If there is a particular piece of data that you use often, it can be stored indefinitely in ClipMate's Safe List. You can append multiple Clip Items into a single piece of data for pasting into an application, through a process called Gluing. You can browse and edit the Clip Items in ClipMate's Magnification Window. ClipMate has a function to remove unwanted line breaks in your text, and you can print with the press of a button. With ClipMate 2.0, you can collect additional data types, such as bitmap, picture, RTF, and OLE objects. A new PowerPaste feature allows you to paste data into your applications quickly and easily. Once activated, ClipMate enters a kind of "auto pilot," sensing when you've pasted data, and automatically advancing to the next clip item for you. Figure 19-1 shows ClipMate's toolbar and menus.

Figure 19-1: ClipMate.

Here's how ClipMate operates. Desirable Formats are those formats that are supported by ClipMate and the user wants to capture (determined by the filter). ClipMate sits idle most of the time, waiting for any activity in the Windows Clipboard. When you put anything on the Clipboard (by cutting or copying), ClipMate gets a message from Windows. ClipMate checks to see if the Clipboard is holding any desirable formats. If there is, ClipMate automatically makes a copy of the data for itself. It places the new data in one of its lists, creates a title, and displays the title in the text window at the top of the Clip Item Selection List Box. If the Magnification Window is active, the new Clip Item is displayed within it. Access to the ClipMate's data is easily obtained through the use of a drop-down list, or a graphical grid, showing thumbnail sketches of the data. After you make a selection, ClipMate automatically copies that item to the Clipboard. It is then ready for your use in any application that offers Clipboard support for the data formats contained within the item. I usually keep ClipMate running all of the time, as it can't capture data if it isn't running. ClipMate will continue to capture data, even if run as an icon. We suggest placing ClipMate in your Startup group, so that it is always active.

The Windows for Workgroups ClipBook Viewer ___

The ClipBook Viewer, included with Windows for Workgroups, extends the Clipboard functions to the network environment. The ClipBook Viewer enables you to store multiple pages of information and to share stored information with other workgroup members on the network. Information that has been copied to the Clipboard by performing a Cut or Copy operation in an application may be pasted into the ClipBook Viewer to create a new ClipBook page. A ClipBook page represents the contents of a single Copy or Cut operation and is stored in a Clipboard file (with an extension of .CLP). The ClipBook Viewer can hold as many as 127 pages of information. Each page is identified by a name of up to 47 characters, and only the amount of available disk space limits its size.

The ClipBook Viewer stores multiple pages of Clipboard information. When you paste information into the ClipBook Viewer, the ClipBook Viewer displays the Paste dialog box, which prompts you for a name to assign to the ClipBook page. You also can specify whether the information should be shared with other Windows for Workgroups users. After you type a name for the page and choose OK, a new ClipBook page is created (see Figure 19-2).

Figure 19-2: The Clipbook Paste dialog box allows you to name the page.

Sharing a ClipBook page

Sharing a ClipBook page enables a user of another Windows for Workgroups workstation to remotely access the information that is stored in the ClipBook page on your workstation. Windows for Workgroups uses Network DDE to exchange information between two workstations on the network. ClipBook Viewer is the user interface for Network DDE operations that create links between applications, such as word processors or spreadsheets, for information that is stored in a ClipBook page.

The ClipBook Server application (CLIPSRV.EXE) is an invisible Windows application that is loaded by the Windows for Workgroups Winnet driver (WFWNET.DRV) and runs in the background. (You won't see the ClipBook Server program listed in the Windows task list when it is running.) The ClipBook Server is responsible for handling network DDE requests to ClipBook pages when the requests are issued by a ClipBook Viewer that is running on other Windows for Workgroups workstations.

Use System Engineer, included on the *Windows 3.1 Configuration SECRETS Disks*, to view applications in memory at any given time.

If you choose the Share Item Now check box when you create a new ClipBook page, the ClipBook Viewer displays the Share ClipBook Page dialog box shown in Figure 19-3. In the Share ClipBook Page dialog box, you specify how your local Windows for Workgroups workstation behaves when a remote user accesses the shared ClipBook page. If you choose the Start Application On Connect check box, the application that you used to create the information in the shared page automatically starts when the shared page is accessed.

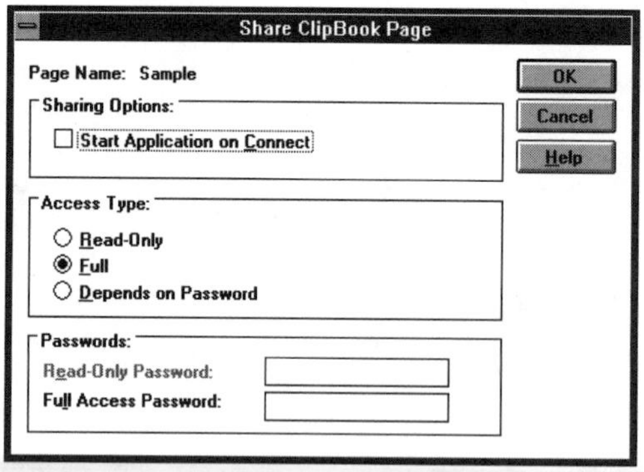

Figure 19-3: Share ClipBook Page dialog box.

Choose the Start Application On Connect option, to allow other Windows for Workgroups users to establish a link to the information.

You use the Access Type option buttons to define the permission level for the operations that another Windows for Workgroups workstation can perform on the shared information. Each access type can be accompanied by a password that is defined by the person who is sharing the ClipBook page so that only users who have the authorized password can access the ClipBook page.

■ A Read-Only access type prevents other Windows for Workgroups users from editing or changing the contents of the shared ClipBook page.

■ The Full access type enables other Windows for Workgroups users to view and edit the information on the shared ClipBook page.

■ The Depends on Password access type enables you to choose which users have which access-permission level and to base their access on the password they supply when they access the shared ClipBook page. A password can be up to 14 characters long, and it is not case sensitive.

Technically, the Read-Only access type tells the ClipBook Server to respond to only the Initiate, Request, Advise, and Terminate DDE messages. This combination of DDE messages doesn't allow the remote Windows for Workgroups workstation to modify the information in the shared ClipBook page.

The Full access type tells the ClipBook Server to respond to all DDE requests, and it thus provides full access to information that is shared in a ClipBook page.

An Example of ClipBook and Net DDE

The ClipBook is a particularly good way to give other workgroup members access to frequently changing information from your computer, without giving them access to the actual files in which the data is stored.

An example of using ClipBook for a workgroup is where detailed information about sales is confidential, but the total sales figure is available to anyone. The sales figures are stored in a Microsoft Excel spreadsheet that is on a nonshared directory. In order to make the total available to everyone, you save the spreadsheet to a file and then you go through basically the same procedure that you use to copy the range to the Clipboard: You select the range for total sales and choose Edit➪Copy.

Press Alt+Tab until you reach the Program Manager. ClipBook is in the Main group. Start ClipBook. Choose Edit➪Paste to paste the contents of the Clipboard onto a ClipBook page. A dialog box pops up, asking for the name of the ClipBook page (make the name descriptive!). Don't forget to check the check box for Share Item Now.

After you click OK, the Share ClipBook Page dialog box opens. This box has options for types of share (just like file shares have) and passwords. For this example, choose a Read Only share.

Also check the Start Application on Connect check box unless the application that created the Clipboard item runs all the time (such as an application that monitors a data collection device).

Click OK, and your work is done.

Anyone who wants to know the total sales figure begins by starting ClipBook and connecting to your ClipBook by using File⇨Connect or the connect button on the toolbar. Sound familiar? That's right, it's just like connecting a drive to a shared directory.

A dialog box opens, showing which computers on the network have ClipBooks. The user selects your computer, and another box opens, showing the list of shared ClipBook pages. The user highlights the one that you shared (you did remember to make the name of the ClipBook page descriptive, right?) and chooses Edit⇨Copy.

Now the range that you copied to your Clipboard is in the user's Clipboard. The user can paste it (or link to it) in applications, just as if everything resided on the user's computer. If the user pastes a link, the latest value from the range always appears in the user's document.

As you can see, ClipBook can be a very powerful feature. In order to accomplish this feat, ClipBook uses a feature of Windows for Workgroups (and Windows NT) called *Net DDE*.

Net DDE is an extension to the DDE interprogram communication that is found in all versions of Windows. It enables programs to directly communicate over the network. Other examples of applications that use Net DDE include Hearts Network and Chat, both of which are included with Windows for Workgroups.

Accessing a shared ClipBook page

A user who wants to access the shared ClipBook information uses the ClipBook Viewer on the workstation to connect to the ClipBook that is stored on the remote workstation. After the user has connected to the remote ClipBook, the names of the shared pages are displayed allowing the user to choose the desired page of information. The user's workstation retrieves a ClipBook page by copying the information to its local Clipboard. If a password has been assigned to the ClipBook page, the user is prompted for the password to gain access to that page.

Sharing information between two workstations

After establishing a link through the ClipBook Viewer to the remote workstation's ClipBook page, the user can copy the information from the remote ClipBook and paste this information into a Windows application on his or her workstation. If the source and target applications support dynamic Data Exchange (DDE) or Object Linking and Embedding (OLE) links, then a Network DDE connection is established between the local workstation and the remote workstation. The selected information may then be dynamically exchanged between the two workstations much like using DDE between two applications on the same workstation.

Understanding Dynamic Data Exchange

Dynamic Data Exchange (DDE) is a message-based protocol that enables two Windows applications to communicate. The two participants in a DDE conversation are the client, the requesting application, and the server, the application providing information. DDE works like this: The client initiates the DDE conversation and then requests data from the server. The server, in turn, responds with the requested data if it is available.

Types of DDE links

DDE conversations, which are also called links, fall into three categories: cold links, warm links, and hot links. The type of link indicates the level of interaction between the client and the server. A cold link occurs when DDE-aware applications exchange data once. If the client needs more data, it has to initiate another DDE conversation. With a warm link, the server informs the client application whenever new data on the topic that is being discussed arrives. In a hot link, the server sends the client all updated data whenever it arrives.

Problems with DDE

As an interprocess communications facility, DDE is adequate. However, it has problems and limitations. At the user level, DDE is fragile and often behaves erratically when the system is heavily loaded.

Another DDE quirk is the *one-way* operation of the DDE linkage. For example, when a user is looking at a piece of Paste-Linked data in a word processing document, absolutely no way exists for the user to determine what application was used to create the data or for the user to load that application in order to change the data.

For a programmer, DDE presents even more obstacles. Because a DDE transaction demands numerous exchanges of special Windows messages, applications must allocate and deallocate and lock and unlock global memory blocks. Any of these operations may fail unexpectedly, leaving the DDE transaction in a void. If one of the applications in the transaction suddenly aborts, the other party to the DDE conversation is left without a clue. As far as the user is concerned, any of these failures may cause a system lockup.

OLE — a Better DDE

Object Linking and Embedding (OLE) is a technology that enables an application to create compound documents that contain information from a number of different sources. For example, a document in an OLE-enabled word processor can accept an embedded spreadsheet object. Unlike traditional cut-and-paste methods, where the receiving application changes the format of the pasted information, embedded documents retain all of their original properties. If the user decides to edit the embedded data, Windows activates the originating application and loads the embedded document.

OLE 1.0 and OLE 2.0

Windows applications can support two kinds of Object Linking and Embedding: OLE 1.0 and OLE 2.0. When you create an OLE object, several dynamic-link library (DLL) files paste a copy of the data or object from the original application into the receiving application.

Connections in OLE 1.0

OLE 1.0 provides two kinds of connections between an object in a file that was created by a client application and the server application that originated the data or another file that contains the original version of the data. An object can be linked, embedded, or both.

Linking objects

A linked object maintains a connection only between the data it displays and the original data in a file that was created by a different program. You set up the link so that when the original data changes, the data in the object is updated in one of two ways. You can choose to update the data automatically whenever you open the file, or you can set up the link so that it's updated only when you select the Update Link menu item.

To choose when the data will be updated, choose Edit⇨Links. You see a dialog box that includes radio buttons that you can use to make a link automatic or manual.

Embedding objects

An embedded object is associated with the program that originally created the data in the object. But, unlike a linked object, an embedded object is not actually linked to a file that contains the original data. In fact, there may be no original file at all — the data lives only in the creating application's data file. When you double-click on the object, however, Windows launches the application that created the object and opens the object file so that you can edit it by using the program that created it.

In OLE 1.0, if the object is linked, hidden instructions tell the original application to contact the OLE libraries and update the source data anytime someone modifies the object. If the object is embedded, when you double-click on it, the hidden instructions launch the native application and send the object to it for editing. You edit the data by using all the tools of the application in which the data was created. When you save your changes, the server application closes and sends the object back to the client.

Deciding whether to link or embed objects

Both object linking and object embedding have advantages and disadvantages. The advantage to linking is that file sizes are smaller than with embedding. The files are smaller because the link consists only of a path to the source file and a pointer to the linked data within the file. Another advantage to linking is that it enables you to make sure that multiple documents all contain the same updated information.

If you link data and then move the source file from the path that is specified in the linked document, you need to specify the new path to make the link current. If you delete the source file, the information embedded in the client document that is linked to that source file can no longer be updated.

The advantage of embedding is that you do not need separate source files in order to pass information among documents or among members of a workgroup. Documents become totally self-contained. But files do get considerably larger when you embed information in them. In addition, information must be updated manually because it's not linked to a source file.

To avoid having to update the data manually, first create an embedded object and then link it.

What's new in OLE 2.0

OLE 2.0 makes the Windows environment even more seamless than OLE 1.0. The most noticeable improvement in OLE 2.0 displays itself when you double-click on an embedded object. Instead of launching the entire server application, OLE 2.0 temporarily replaces the menu and tools in the client application with the menu and tools from the object's native application. For example, you can edit a drawing that is embedded in a word processing document by using the tools supplied by the original graphics application without leaving the context of the word processing document. This type of editing is called *visual editing* or *in-place editing.*

In addition, OLE 2.0 provides for the creation of subobjects within other objects. You can, for example, have a word processing document that includes an embedded illustration that was created in a graphics program. That illustration, in turn, can have an embedded subobject — such as a graph that was created by a spreadsheet program. If you double-click on any of the objects or subobjects, the menus and tools that you need to modify the object appear.

What makes OLE tick?

When an object is incorporated into a document, it maintains an association with the server application that created it. *Linking* and *embedding* are two different ways to associate objects in a compound document with their server applications. The differences between linking and embedding lie in how and where the actual source data that comprises the object is stored; this, in turn, affects the object's portability, its method(s) of activation, and the size of the compound document.

When an object is linked, the source data, or *link source*, continues to physically reside wherever it was initially created, either at another point within the document or within a different document altogether. Only a reference, or *link*, to the object and appropriate presentation data remain with the compound document. Linked objects cannot *travel* with documents to another machine; they must remain within the local file system or be copied explicitly.

Linking is efficient and keeps the size of the compound document small. Users may choose to link when the source object is owned or maintained by someone else because a single instance of the object's data can serve many documents. Any compound documents that have a link to the source object automatically reflect any changes that are made to the source object. From the user's point of view, a linked object appears to be wholly contained within the document.

With an embedded object, a copy of the original object is physically stored in the compound document, as is all of the information that is needed to manage the object. As a result, the object becomes a physical part of the document. A compound document that contains embedded objects is larger than one that contains the same objects as links. However, embedding offers several advantages that may outweigh the disadvantages of the extra storage overhead. For example, you can transfer compound documents with embedded objects to another computer and edit them there. The new user of the document need not know where the original data resides because a copy of the object's source (native) data travels with the compound document.

You can edit embedded objects in place; that is, you can perform all maintenance to the object without ever leaving the compound document. Because each user has a copy of the object's source data, changes that are made by one user do not affect other compound documents that contain an embedding of the same original object. However, if there are links to this object, each document that contains a link reflects changes made to the object.

Object Linking and Embedding (OLE) is a mechanism that enables applications to interoperate more effectively, thereby enabling users to work more productively. End users of OLE container applications create and manage *compound documents*. These documents seamlessly incorporate data, or *objects*, of different formats. Sound clips, spreadsheets, text, and bitmaps are some examples of objects that are commonly found in compound documents. Each object is created and maintained by its server application; but through the use of OLE, the services of the different server applications are integrated. End users feel as if a single application, with all the functionality of each of the server applications, is being used. End users of OLE applications don't need to be concerned with managing and switching between the various server applications; they focus solely on the compound document and the task that is being performed.

OLE registration information

All OLE registration information is stored in the Registration database file, REG.DAT, in the WINDOWS directory. Link information is stored with individual documents that reference information in the Registration database.

You use the information in REG.DAT when you open or print a file from the File Manager, and applications that support OLE also use this information. REG.DAT is set up and maintained by Windows and Windows applications. You should not move or delete this file from the WINDOWS directory. Doing so may result in a loss of functionality in the File Manager, the Program Manager, and applications that support OLE.

Where Windows searches for REG.DAT

Windows searches for the REG.DAT file *only* in the Windows program directory (by default, this directory is WINDOWS). If the file is not found, it will be created whenever an application, the shell (for example, the Program Manager), or the Registration Editor (REGEDIT.EXE) creates a new OLE registration entry.

Any other occurrences of the REG.DAT file on the hard disk will be ignored (for example, in the root directory, on the path, in the SYSTEM directory, and so on).

Because the shell mirrors the OLE server information that is registered in REG.DAT in the WIN.INI file's [embedding] section, the system may be able to correct itself if the REG.DAT file is accidentally deleted. As a result, you should be able to continue editing OLE objects.

If the REG.DAT file is deleted, any data that is registered for opening and printing files in the File Manager or the Program Manager may be lost.

Maintaining OLE functionality when you reinstall Windows 3.1

You can spend a great deal of time setting up OLE information in the Registration database, especially if the only way to reregister an application is to run its setup program again.

This can create a potential problem if you need to reinstall Windows. To preserve the OLE registration data, create a new directory to install Windows 3.1 into and then copy the current REG.DAT file into this directory before you install Windows.

If Windows 3.1 is installed over Windows 3.0 or Windows 3.1, then the REG.DAT file is preserved, and OLE and shell registration information for the Windows 3.1 programs that are packaged with Windows are added to the database.

The same is true if Windows 3.1 is installed to a directory that already has a REG.DAT file in it. Therefore, if you set up a new installation of Windows 3.1 (rather than an upgrade), you should create a new directory to install Windows 3.1 into and copy the current REG.DAT file into this directory before you install Windows.

If Windows 3.1 has already been installed into a new directory, you can copy the REG.DAT file from the old Windows directory to the new Windows directory. Be sure that Windows is not running when you copy the REG.DAT file. Then use the following steps to update the REG.DAT file:

1. Start Windows.

2. Choose File➪Run.

3. Type the following command in the Command Line text box:

   ```
   REGEDIT SETUP.REG
   ```

4. Choose OK.

If you need to merge more .REG files into the database, use the File Manager to search for them and either double-click on each one (or press Enter) or drag and drop all of them (at one time or individually) onto the REGEDIT window.

Do not remove the old Windows 3.1 directory and all subdirectories until Windows 3.1 is reinstalled with OLE information. Applications install OLE servers in the WINDOWS directory tree, and shared DLL files may be in the SYSTEM directory.

Embedding data from a network server

You can share an object (create a link to a piece of data) that is located on a network file server by using OLE 1.0. To do so, both the client application and the server application need to be installed on the same local machine. The interprocess communication that OLE uses (dynamic data exchange) is not supported across the network; it is supported only locally.

In the case of a linked object, the network address for the file that contains the object is stored with the object. When the object is activated, OLE tries to bind to the object. If the network file server is not connected, OLE attempts to make the connection. If the file server has a password, then OLE asks for the password. If the connection cannot be established, or if the file is not found, you see an error message:

```
Linked document is unavailable.
```

The only known limit to the number of connections or links to a network file server is the number of available drive letters.

Although client and server applications need to be on the same PC, an OLE 1.0 object does not have to be on the same PC as either the client or the server. As a result, on a network you can make sure that each person who is using a link is getting the latest version of the data from the same file. Place the source file in a directory on the network server and link all the client documents on all of the systems to it.

Using SETUP.REG to repair REG.DAT

Some OLE servers may provide a text file called SETUP.REG or a similarly named file. This file contains information about the particular server application, and you can use it to repair an application's entry in the Windows REG.DAT file if you think that the entry is incorrect or that the REG.DAT file is corrupted.

The REG.DAT file is the registration database. The database, which is in binary format, is a source of information about server applications. REG.DAT includes the following information:

- Class name, which describes the type of information that an object contains
- The path to the server
- Any verbs that are supported by the server, which include actions that the server can take on the object

SETUP.REG is a text file that contains the same information as REG.DAT, but its format is ASCII instead of binary. You can merge SETUP.REG with an existing REG.DAT file to repair or update an individual entry in the REG.DAT file. If REG.DAT or OLESVR.DLL is damaged or corrupted, you may see the following error message:

```
Failed to register server.
```

Follow these steps to repair REG.DAT with an application's SETUP.REG file:

1. Open the Program Manager and choose File⇨Run.
2. Type **REGEDIT.**
3. Choose OK.
4. Choose File⇨Merge Registration File.
5. Select the REG file that needs to be merged into the existing REG.DAT file.

The Merge Registration File command merges the selected registration (SETUP.REG) file with the currently displayed database (REG.DAT). The merged information is not written to the REG.DAT file until you choose the Save Changes command.

Using the Registration Information Editor (REGEDIT.EXE)

The Registration Information Editor (REGEDIT.EXE) can help to set up shell (for example, Program Manager) and OLE information. This section describes the command line switches for REGEDIT.EXE.

The syntax for REGEDIT.EXE is

```
REGEDIT [/v|-v] [/s|-s] <filename>
```

- `<filename>` is a .REG-formatted file that can be produced with the Save Registration File command in the File menu of REGEDIT.EXE in advanced mode.

- The `[/v|-v]` switch opens REGEDIT.EXE in advanced mode, where the registration database is displayed in a tree structure (similar to the tree window in the Windows 3.1 File Manager). Any part of the database can be edited.

- The `[/s|-s]` switch suppresses any informational dialog boxes that would normally be displayed when a filename is specified on the command line. This switch is useful when you want the Setup program for an application to execute REGEDIT.EXE with a .REG file, but you do not want the user to be confused by any dialog boxes that are displayed.

- You can use either `/` or `-` to signify the optional switches. You can combine the switches (for example, `-vs`) and type them in either uppercase or lowercase. Unrecognized switches are ignored.

The Invalid Link Error message

You may see the following error message after you click on an embedded object:

```
Server failed to open document. Possible invalid link.
```

The most likely reason for any invalid-link message is that the file to which the document is linked has been either renamed or moved to a different directory.

To remedy the situation, look on the Main menu where you find the other linking tools. Click on the various options until you find one that is called *Update Link* or something similar. You can use this option to reestablish the link to the file under its new name or path.

Linking objects within the same application

You can link objects within the same application if the application is both an OLE server and a client. This feature can be helpful if, for example, you have several word processor templates or mail merge documents that include the same return address, position title, part numbers, and so on. Instead of changing the information in each of the documents any time the information changes, create links to another word processing document that contains the information. Then when the data changes, you merely have to change it in the source file.

If you don't know whether an application that you want to link to is an OLE server, you can find out by initiating a link. You will be presented with a dialog box that lists the types of objects that you can link to. From the names of the objects, you can often determine which OLE server they refer to. If you need more information, look in the [Embedding] section of WIN.INI, which lists the names of the objects, along with the pathnames and filenames of the programs with which they are associated.

Using OLE with a DOS program

The Object Packager is an applet in the Program Manager's Accessories group. You use it to create a package that consists of an icon and a path to the server application and the original file. You then use OLE to embed that package in the client document.

A package behaves just as any other embedded object does. When you double-click on the package's icon, the Windows operating system starts the server application, which can display a chart, play a recording, or perform whatever function the application provides. Packages can include whole documents inside other documents, which is helpful when you want to include further help information on a topic or insert DOS command lines.

Using the Object Packager _____

Whenever you install an OLE server, the program adds itself to the OLE registry (which is maintained in REG.DAT) in WIN.INI. If the program that you want to link to appears in the registration database then you're set to use OLE with that program. If it doesn't, you must use the Windows Object Packager utility to link to it.

Creating a packaged object

You can create a packaged object in several different ways, but here is one of the more straightforward methods:

1. In a File Manager window, select the file that you want to package and choose File⇨Copy (or cut to the chase by pressing F8, the keyboard shortcut).

2. In the dialog box that appears, choose the Copy to Clipboard option and click on OK.

3. Start the Object Packager, which is in the Accessories program group by default.

4. The Object Packager has two windows that are named Appearance and Content. Select the Content window and pull down the Edit menu.

5. Use either the Paste command or the Paste Link command to create the package.

The choice between the Paste and Paste Link commands is important. When you transfer the finished package to the client application, you don't link that package; you embed it. That the packages themselves cannot be linked is a given, but what's inside the package can be either embedded data or linked data. If you create the package with the Object Packager's Paste command, you embed it. If you use the Paste Link command, you link it.

When the package is ready, use the Edit menu's Copy Package command to put it on the loading dock — the Windows Clipboard. The rest of the procedure is standard OLE. Just activate the client program and use the appropriate Paste command.

Discovering ways to use the Object Packager

This example shows how the Object Packager can connect an OLE client document to a non-OLE document. But the Object Packager's talents don't end there. You also can use it to embed an iconic representation of data from an OLE server application. This technique annotates compound documents with tidy icons instead of cluttering these documents with visible data. Interested readers can check annotations by clicking on the icons; browsers can skip right over them. You can even create an elaborate hypertext document by embedding additional packages within packaged files.

The Object Packager has another important virtue: You can use this program to embed a Windows command line that is attached to an icon. For example, you can package startup commands for DOS applications, Excel macros, and your favorite games. If the program you use most often is an OLE server, you can use it to create a launch document that is full of program-starter packages. With a little imagination, you'll find that after you get started with the Object Packager, the possibilities are virtually endless.

Summary

This chapter explained some of the virtues and pitfalls of using the Windows Clipboard, DDE, and OLE. In this chapter, I discussed

▶ How the Clipboard really works

▶ Ways to use the Windows for Workgroups Clipbook applet

▶ Strategies for using Object Linking and Embedding

▶ How to maintain the OLE Registration Database

Chapter 20
Multimedia

Until recently, *multimedia* was a catchall term that was often confused with terms such as *hypertext, hypermedia,* and the like. As multimedia technology matures, it can be defined as a technology that encompasses everything from ordinary text to animation, sound, and high-performance video. In short, multimedia breathes life into otherwise ordinary electronic information by integrating sound, animation, photo-quality images, and video with text and graphics.

Multimedia is a complex interaction between hardware and software. This chapter explains the concepts that drive multimedia and offers suggestions on configuring the system, Windows, and the Windows Multimedia Extensions.

An Introduction to Multimedia in Windows

To implement multimedia technology, Windows needs a collection of tools that enable it to control sophisticated audio and video peripherals. Using these tools, Windows can integrate several different data formats in a single system environment. Multimedia in Windows consists of a minimum hardware specification for a Multimedia PC and a set of extensions that are built into Windows and Windows for Workgroups 3.1x. These extensions enable applications to use hardware in a device-independent manner. The Multimedia Extensions are made up of dynamic link libraries (DLLs), device drivers, file formats, and a generalized API that translates programming commands into instructions for any multimedia driver.

Through the Multimedia Extensions, Windows gains enhanced audio capabilities in the form of sampled audio waveforms or MIDI (Musical Instrument Digital Interface) support. These capabilities enable the PC to store voice or music input and play it back. Windows also gains enhanced video, including animation, digital video, or integration with standard television signals (NTSC).

The Making of a Multimedia PC

The Multimedia PC Marketing Council (MPC Council) developed a standard multimedia computer specification known as the Multimedia PC. Building on the standard desktop PC, the Multimedia PC offers an affordable approach to multimedia computing while preserving your investments in PC software.

A Multimedia PC consists of five basic components: a PC, a CD-ROM drive, an audio board, Windows 3.1x, and speakers for audio output. The minimum PC configuration for a Multimedia PC, as defined by the MPC Council, is a system with a 386SX processor and 2MB of RAM, a 30MB hard disk, and a VGA or Super VGA display. Add a CD-ROM drive to this base package to give the Multimedia PC expanded information retrieval capabilities. Adding an audio board and speakers or headphones enables the Multimedia PC to play and manipulate speech, music, and other sounds. This minimum configuration is referred to as a Level 1 MPC.

Hardware evolves so rapidly that the MPC Council released a new specification, known as Level 2, soon after the first specification. Level 2 MPCs meet or exceed the following specifications: a 486SX processor, 4 MB of RAM, a 160MB hard disk, a double-speed CD-ROM drive, and the capability of displaying 65,536 colors at 640 x 480 resolution.

The Level 1 and Level 2 specifications may seem a little weak in terms of hardware performance and power. However, the MPC specification ensures programmers that certain hardware configurations will run the applications they design. Although multimedia application developers usually write their programs for the minimum standard hardware, I recommend building or purchasing an MPC system with a great deal of raw processing power.

Such a system includes an Intel 486DX2/66 with local-bus IDE interface and a high performance video card in the VL-bus slot (such as the ATI Ultra Pro). For expansion, make sure you have at least 4 ISA slots and 1 VL bus slot free, 2 internal drive bays, and 3MB of video memory. For sound, the Sound Blaster 16 with ISA bus, 5kHz-to-45kHz sampling range, MIDI interface, and CD audio is a good choice. I profile the Gravis Ultrasound card in this chapter because that's also worth a look. While dual speed CD-ROMs are the standard right now, that standard is being challenged by triple and quad speed drives. For dual speed drive, lean towards the Toshiba TXM-3401E for its price performance ratio. For triple speed, look at NEC's Multispin 3XE and for quad speed, Pioneer's DRM-1804X is worth a peek. As for the rest, I recommend 16MB of RAM, a 340MB or larger hard drive, and of course Windows for Workgroups 3.11.

How to Upgrade a PC System to Multimedia

You can purchase a Multimedia PC as a complete PC with integrated multimedia hardware, or you can upgrade an existing PC with the appropriate hardware. The first component to consider is the CD-ROM. Multimedia productions are data intensive, requiring access to the hundreds of megabytes of data, graphics, or sound stored on each CD-ROM.

Adding data storage capacity to a standard PC is not enough; you need to add a sound system to bring multimedia to life. A typical PC has a tiny speaker that delivers nothing more than beeps and shrills. Multimedia requires the more refined sound-processing hardware that a sound board provides.

Planning your multimedia upgrade

Before upgrading your PC for multimedia, you need to decide what to add. Choosing a CD-ROM driver and a sound board can be an overwhelming task because of the array of choices that manufacturers offer. In making your evaluation, you need to concern yourself only with the drive's hardware specification, paying particular attention to the drive interface. All CD-ROM drives read standard CD-ROM disks; however, if you later decide that you want to play CD-ROMs that are recorded in the extended architecture (XA) format, you may need to upgrade your interface card.

When you evaluate CD-ROM drives, you should consider two performance aspects: access time, which is the time required to locate a piece of data, and throughput, which is the speed at which the drive transfers data to the PC.

The CD-ROM throughput rate is a function of the hardware standard for audio CD systems. To play back music at the proper speed, CD-ROMs have to deliver data at about 150K per second, excluding housekeeping overhead so most CD-ROM drives send data to a PC at 150K per second. To put that rate in perspective, a color VGA image that is made up of 950K of data takes about 5 seconds to get from the disk surface onto your screen.

Purchase at least a double-speed CD-ROM drive, which cuts transfer time in half by shifting the drive into high gear and doubling the speed at which it spins the disk. These drives can read information twice as fast, thereby increasing the response time of the CD-ROM system.

Choosing a CD-ROM interface

When you compare CD-ROM drive specifications, you'll notice that the interface type and performance ratings vary. Some manufacturers use an industry-standard SCSI adapter interface, but other manufacturers use proprietary interface cards.

How do you decide which interface to go with? For other system components, you might consider speed the determining factor, but for CD-ROMs, interface speed is not an issue. When you compare proprietary and SCSI connections, they generally yield the same performance results. The reason that the results are the same is that the drive interface carries data faster than the disk can read data. A SCSI connection, for example, can move data 20 times faster than a CD-ROM drive can read it. The bottom line is that after you make the connection, distinguishing one interface from the other is difficult as far as performance is concerned.

Base your interface choice on the architecture of the other peripherals in your system. SCSI drives have greater versatility because they enable you to daisy chain other SCSI devices and share their host adapter. For example, if your system has a SCSI hard drive, you can hook an optical disk drive or streaming tape drive into the same host adapter. The advantage of this chaining configuration is that you, in effect, increase the expansion capabilities of a single slot.

In contrast, proprietary interfaces offer plug-and-play installation. While the idea of plug-and-play is appealing, most proprietary interfaces require you to buy a sound board and CD-ROM player as a matched pair. Purchasing them as a set is not a problem until you decide to upgrade one of the components. For example, if you decide to upgrade to a faster CD-ROM drive, you may have to buy a new sound board as well.

Finally, the CD-ROM drive needs to have an extra audio connection to send sound in analog form from the player to the sound board. CD-ROM drives have their own digital-to-analog conversion circuits that turn a digital bitstream read from the disk into CD-quality music.

Gearing up for sound

Multimedia without sound is like a television program with the volume turned off. You miss the nuances of what's going on beyond the pictures. Sound boards expand the bandwidth of multimedia by performing several critical functions:

■ Converting sounds that are stored in the PC from digital to analog form so that you can hear them

■ Recording sounds for playback

■ Creating their own sounds by using built-in synthesizers and mixing the results together

■ Amplifying the final audio product

The Musical Instrument Digital Interface

The Musical Instrument Digital Interface (MIDI) is a protocol that was developed in the early 1980s by several manufacturers of electronic music synthesizers. MIDI connects computers, synthesizers, and human-operated controllers such as keyboards, electronic string and wind instruments, drum pads, dials, foot controllers, and so on.

The components of a MIDI system contain ports for MIDI cables, and the ports are labeled MIDI In, MIDI Out, and MIDI Thru. The components send or receive MIDI messages through the ports. These messages are generally one-, two-, or three-bytes long, but certain *system exclusive* messages can be much longer.

A Multimedia PC requires MIDI In and MIDI Out ports so applications can access the MIDI In port to receive and store messages from keyboards and other MIDI devices. The MIDI Out port can be connected to an external synthesizer for playing music.

A Multimedia PC also must provide an internal MIDI synthesizer. At a minimum, this synthesizer uses channels 13, 14, and 15 for three different voices, each with 6-note polyphony (that is, 6 notes playing at the same time); channel 16 is used for percussion, with 5-note polyphony. The specification also describes a high-end synthesizer that is capable of 9 melodic voices with 16-note polyphony (channels 1 through 9) and 16-note percussion (channel 10).

One problem with MIDI is that the Program Change message is device-dependent. Voice number 1 on one synthesizer may not be the same as voice number 1 on another synthesizer. Windows allows you to control the Program Change message through a utility called the MIDI mapper. You use it to alter the Program Change messages so that they are based on the synthesizer that is being used. The API defines more than 80 standard voice numbers that correspond to different instrument sounds. Applications can use these numbers in a device-independent manner. Once you configure the mapper for the synthesizer you're using, the mapper handles the conversion. Figure 20-1 shows the MIDI Mapper dialog box.

	MIDI Patch Map: 'Ultra'				
		1 based patches			
Src Patch	Src Patch Name	Dest Patch	Volume	Key Map	
0	Acoustic Grand Piano	0	100	[None]	
1	Bright Acoustic Piano	0	100	[None]	
2	Electric Grand Piano	0	100	[None]	
3	Honky-tonk Piano	0	100	[None]	
4	Rhodes Piano	0	100	[None]	
5	Chorused Piano	0	100	[None]	
6	Harpsichord	6	100	[None]	
7	Clavinet	6	100	[None]	
8	Celesta	8	100	[None]	
9	Glockenspiel	8	100	[None]	
10	Music Box	8	100	[None]	
11	Vibraphone	12	100	[None]	
12	Marimba	12	100	[None]	

Figure 20-1: The MIDI Mapper dialog box settings allow you to configure your system for specific synthesizers.

When you play a MIDI file, the computer sends the messages contained in the file to a MIDI instrument, which converts the messages into the sounds of a specific instrument, pitch, and duration. You can also use the MIDI Mapper utility to configure MIDI synthesizers and other devices to conform with either the Standard MIDI or MPC MIDI formats under Windows. Be aware that sound cards supporting MIDI are usually more expensive than those that support just digital audio.

Although MPC standards specify that a Multimedia PC supports MIDI, not all sound boards have ports that enable you to hook up a PC with synthesizers and other MIDI devices. Before buying a sound board, you need to decide how important MIDI compatibility is to you.

Capturing waveform audio

The Windows Sound Recorder sends instructions to the sound card via a software driver. Sound waves that enter the microphone cause a vibration in its diaphragm and induce an electrical current in the diaphragm's electromagnetic components. That electrical current is an analog signal that travels from the microphone into the sound board.

The analog signal enters the mixer chip under instructions from the board's signal processor chip, which has already programmed the mixer to adjust the volume of the incoming sound. The adjusted analog sound passes from the mixer to the ADC (analog-to-digital converter, which is often integrated into the controller chip), where it is converted into the on and off bits of a PC's binary code.

The signal processor sends the digital sound data through the system bus into the PC's memory, where the software driver attaches an identifying header to create a file. The file is then stored on the hard disk.

Playing back waveform audio

To play back a WAV sound file, you either retrieve it in sound software or activate it in another application, often by using Windows' object linking and embedding. The WAV file passes from the hard disk through RAM and the system bus to the signal processor, which sends the file to the DAC (digital-to-analog converter). Here the digital information is converted back into analog form before it travels to the mixer chip.

Most Windows sound files exist as WAV files. However, MIDI files use considerably less disk space, about one-thousandth the disk space of corresponding WAV files. MIDI files conserve disk space because unlike WAV files, they do not contain the sounds themselves; instead MIDI files contain instructions for re-creating music in a synthesizer chip.

When you instruct software to play a WAV file and a MIDI file together, the controller directs the MIDI information to the FM synthesis chip, which reproduces music by using two or more waveforms (called operators) that modulate each other's frequencies to produce musical tones. From the synthesizer, the music is converted to analog sound and sent to the mixer chip, where it is mixed with the WAV file.

The mixed sound moves to the amplifier, which steps up the voltage so that it is strong enough to power the coil in the speakers. Electrical current in the coil induces a magnetic field, which sets a membrane vibrating in reaction to a permanent magnet in the speakers. The vibration produces the sound that comes from the speakers.

The quest for high fidelity

You can use a sound board to reproduce digitized sound or to capture sound. Regardless of how you use the board, its sampling rate and the resolution, or bit depth, of each sample determines the quality that it delivers.

 Sound resolution is measured in bits, typically 8 or 16. However, sound resolution is not related to the bus width of the expansion-slot connection.

The *sampling rate,* the measure of how often the board captures the analog waveform, determines the highest frequencies that the sound board can handle. The physics of digital-to-analog conversion limit the highest frequency that the board can make to slightly less than half the sampling frequency. Filtering brings down the upper limit even more. As a result, a board that uses a 22kHz sampling frequency can't reproduce sounds higher than 11kHz, and its actual upper limit (due to filtering) generally ranges from 7.5kHz to 10kHz. By comparison, audio CDs use 44.1kHz sampling so that they can produce frequencies to the top of the human hearing range, 15kHz to 18kHz.

The bit depth of the sampling determines the dynamic range, or signal-to-noise ratio, of the system. The more bits in each sample, the larger the signal range that can be encoded and the lower the noise level. Today's sound boards typically offer 8-bit or 16-bit resolution. To put those figures in perspective, 8-bit resolution is on a par with AM radio.

 The on-board synthesizer plays an important role in the quality of sounds that a sound board produces. Most sound boards use synthesizer chips that were developed by Yamaha. Inexpensive sound boards usually employ the monophonic 11-voice YM3812 chip; better boards use the stereophonic 20-voice YMF262 or OPL3 chip.

The most _realistic_ sounds are sampled rather than synthesized. Look for sound boards that include their own on-board ROM libraries of sampled sounds. For optimum performance, look for a sound board with Musical Instrument Digital Interface (MIDI) capabilities.

Digital signal processing (DSP) and wave-table synthesis make sound cards sound live. The addition of a DSP chip onboard the sound card enables your system to offload processing of multimedia files directly to the digital signal processing chip. Instead of the CPU decompressing and playing sound files, the DSP, which is programmed to process sound files, handles this chore.

Couple the DSP with an onboard ROM chip that holds prerecorded samples of actual musical instruments, and the sound card creates life-like sounds. Unlike the card with an FM synthesizer that only approximates musical instrument sounds, cards with wave-table synthesis sound like the real thing.

In wave-table synthesis, the sound card's DSP loads an algorithm to read the MIDI file instructions. The instructions define which notes to play, and how to play them. The ROM stores several notes corresponding to each instrument, which the DSP, using another algorithm, manipulates to create additional notes. The sequence flows like this:

- The CPU issues an instruction to the sound card to play a note/s.

- The sound card receives the instruction in its DSP chip. If the DSP knows that there is no corresponding note sample in the sound card ROM, it requests the nearest sample note from which it can adjust to make a C note.

- The ROM chip sends the requested sample note back to the DSP. The DSP transposes the sample note into the desired note, and then passes the note on to the Digital-to-Analog converter (DAC).

- DAC channels the note/s to the card output jacks, and you have music.

The digital processing chip is programmable and fast becoming the specialized processing center in sound cards, modems, video accelerators and even PCs. Without a DSP, your system's CPU must channel a significant amount of its resources toward handling video and other multimedia data types. With the DSP chip, video files are separated from other multimedia and data files so that the DSP is dedicated to video processing and the system CPU continues to process other data.

Some terms to watch for

As you study sound boards, you're bound to encounter some unfamiliar terms. Here are some terms to look for:

- Analog-to-Digital Converter (ADC). A converter that turns sound frequencies into digital information.

- Audio/Video Interleaved (AVI). Microsoft's video standard that will bring digital video that has 160x120-dot-per-inch, 15-frame-per-second resolution to the MPC environment.

- Digital-to-Analog Converter (DAC). A converter that turns digital information into analog sound waves.

- Digital Video Interactive (DVI). A technology from Intel Corp. for compressing and decompressing data, audio, and full-motion video.

- Dynamic Filtering. A technique to help eliminate electronic PC emissions that can show up as noise in the sound board output.

- Musical Instrument Digital Interface (MIDI). A protocol for the interchange of musical information among musical instruments, synthesizers, and sound boards.

- MIDI Synthesizer. Provides for the use of an external MIDI device, such as a musical keyboard, that connects to the sound board so that you can compose music and store it on a PC.

- Pulse Code Modulation (PCM). The process of changing sound waves into digital information and back again.

- Sampling. Recording and playing back sounds.

- Sampling Rate. In a digitizing operation, the frequency with which samples are taken and converted. The higher the sampling rate, the truer the representation in digital form.

- Sequencing Software. Used to handle entire multi-instrument compositions, not just single notes.

Preparing to install a new sound board

Installing any PC peripheral device is never as easy as opening up the PC and popping in the device. Before cranking up for your first multimedia production, you need to properly configure the CD-ROM drive and sound board to work with other peripherals in the PC.

As with installing any expansion card, installing a new sound board may mean selecting IRQs, a base address, or DMA channels that don't conflict with other devices. Even though some manufacturers ship preconfigured boards, problems crop up occasionally. Preconfigured boards are usually set to use settings that most PCs have open, but you may have installed other devices that take up one or more of those settings. Troubleshooting may involve changing board jumpers or switches, or even reconfiguring other installed peripherals. For a more detailed discussion of a sound card installation procedure, read the next section.

CD-ROM installation basics

If your CD-ROM player uses a proprietary interface, then you're almost assured of an easy installation. Manufacturers took most of the guesswork out of installation because the interface design eliminates many variables. On the other hand, SCSI-based CD-ROM drives often require some setup, or at least a check of setup variables.

With a SCSI interface, you need to set a SCSI ID number. Each device connected to a particular SCSI adapter board requires a unique indentifying number. This information should appear in your CD ROM's installation documentation. Next you need to check the termination. Every SCSI chain requires two terminations — in the first and last devices in the chain. Check your documentation to determine how the device should be terminated. If the drive is internal, check for the jumpers or DIP switches that are used to set the ID number. If the drive is preset, jot down the ID number for future reference.

A bundled drive and controller can also simplify the otherwise complex matter of SCSI termination. Because most CD-ROM drives are the only SCSI devices that are connected to their host adapters, they should be terminated. But most CD-ROM drives arrive with terminations already in place, so ordinarily, you don't have to make any adjustments to your drive.

When connecting more than one SCSI device to your host adapter, you should remove the terminations from the devices in the middle of the SCSI chain. Leave the terminations on your host adapter and on the last drive in the chain. Most internal SCSI drives use a set of three resistor packs to supply their terminations. Leave the packs in place to maintain the termination of your drive; remove them if you do not want the drive to be terminated. ◎

Installing Advanced Gravis UltraSound

The *Advanced Gravis UltraSound,* or *GUS,* as it's known to its fans, is an advanced but affordable 16-bit sound card. Its distinguishing feature is its use of wavetable synthesis for its MIDI synthesizer. *Wavetable synthesis* means that instead of manipulating a few oscillators, as do simpler cards, such as the FM synthesizer-based Sound Blaster cards, the GUS synthesizes the instrument sounds from actual digital recordings of the instrument. As a result, a trumpet sounds like a trumpet, not like some kind of electronic buzzer.

Another feature that sets the GUS apart from other wavetable cards, such as the Turtle Beach Multisound, is its use of onboard RAM to store the digital samples from which it creates the sounds. (In musician's parlance, these samples are called *patches.*) The GUS comes with 256K of RAM, but most users upgrade the card immediately to its full complement of 1MB of RAM. The GUS uses 256K x 4 RAM chips, similar to those that are used by video cards.

The GUS is almost completely software-configurable. The only settings that you cannot set through software are the Base Port (I/O address) and the Game Port. You can disable the Game Port by simply removing the board's jumper that is marked *GAME.* You can set the Base Port to one of six addresses by using the jumpers on the pins marked *4, 5, 6,* and *7.* Table 20-1 lists the possible Base Port settings.

Table 20-1	Possible Base Port Settings for the GUS			
Address	*4*	*5*	*6*	*7*
210	off	on	on	on
220	on	off	on	on
230	off	off	on	on
240	on	on	off	on
250	off	on	off	on
260	on	off	off	on

Outside of Windows, one GUS feature that is of interest to users is its Sound Blaster compatibility mode. If you want to use the GUS outside of Windows (for MS-DOS based games, for example), you should set the Base Port only to 220 or 240.

For the rest of the GUS configuration, you use a device driver called *ULTRINIT* that loads in the CONFIG.SYS file. It's not a real device driver (it doesn't take up any RAM after it loads). The format of the ULTRINIT line is as follows:

```
DEVICE=C:\ULTRASND\ULTRINIT.SYS ULTRASND=220,5,5,12,7
```

where 220 is Base Port;

5 is Playback DMA Channel;

5 is Record DMA Channel;

12 is UltraSound IRQ; and

7 is MIDI IRQ.

The Base Port has already been discussed. Playback and Recording use separate channels so that both operations can take place simultaneously. As with most 16-bit sound cards, you can achieve the best results on the GUS by using one of the 16-bit DMA channels (5, 6, or 7) that are available in most computers. Note that some bad runs occurred on the Opti and UMC 386 system chipsets that have faulty DMA controllers and cannot handle 16-bit DMA. On these systems, the choice is limited to DMA 1 or DMA 3. DMA 1 is usually the best choice.

The UltraSound card uses two different interrupts (IRQs). Because it is a full 16-bit card, it can use one of the *extended* interrupts (11, 12, and 15) as the *UltraSound* interrupt, which is used for the actual sound generation by the card. The other interrupt, which is used for the MIDI output port and the Sound Blaster compatibility function, should normally be set to IRQ 7, where it will be shared with LPT1.

Because the UltraSound stores its patches in RAM, instead of using the more limited ROM method, it requires approximately 6MB of hard disk space to store the patch files. In addition, some multimedia applications do not completely adhere to the MPC Council's Multimedia PC (MPC) specification, which requires support for patch caching.

Patch caching, which is built into the multimedia drivers, provides a means for a multimedia program to keep track of which patches are currently loaded into a sound card. Patch caching also ensures that new patches are loaded when they are needed. Most MPC-compatible applications (for example, the Windows Media Player and Microsoft Home applications such as Microsoft Bookshelf and Encarta) support patch caching. When GUS owners use these MPC-compatible applications, they do not have to give any further thought to patch caching.

However, some multimedia software (such as Space Quest 4 by Sierra Online) does not properly support patch caching. As a result, some patches need to be loaded into the GUS manually. In addition, you need to use the MIDI Mapper to establish a new MIDI setup so that the full range of MIDI instruments can be represented with a minimal number of patches.

To change the MIDI setup, start Control Panel, and double-click the MIDI Mapper icon. The dialog box shown in Figure 20-2 appears.

Figure 20-2: The MIDI Mapper dialog box.

Make sure that the UltraSound setup for the amount of memory that is installed on the UltraSound card is selected. Then start Media Player and load the patches into the card by playing the appropriate MIDI file for the amount of memory that is installed on the card. The files are in the ULTRASND\MIDI directory.

When you install the UltraSound multimedia drivers, the installation program should pick up the configuration automatically for the card's port address, interrupt, and so on. Under Windows, several additional configuration parameters are available in the MIDI Synth dialog box, which is shown in Figure 20-3. You access this box by choosing Control Panel⇨Drivers⇨UltraWave⇨MIDI Synth.

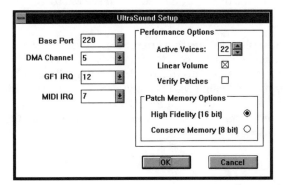

Figure 20-3: The MIDI Synth dialog box used to configure sound board features.

The additional options in this dialog box control some special features of the GUS. First, the Patch Memory Options settings control whether the UltraSound Windows drivers load 16- or 8- bit patches. Choosing the patch size involves a tradeoff between size and sound quality. If you use patch-cache aware applications, use the High Fidelity setting to get the best sound. If you are using the nonpatch-cache workaround, then you need to use the smaller 8-bit patches so that all the patches that need to be loaded can fit on the card.

Next is the Linear Volume box. Always leave this box checked. It exists only for compatibility with software that was written for early versions of the GUS Windows drivers.

Finally, you need to choose the Active Voices number. This number determines how many simultaneous voices the card can generate. In theory, the GUS is capable of generating 32 simultaneous sounds; however, a hardware constraint on the card causes sound quality to diminish noticeably if this number is set to more than 22. If you are using a 386SX-based system, you should always set this option to 14.

Getting the CD-ROM Up and Running

Getting a CD-ROM installed and configured begins at the DOS level, so you first need to understand how a CD-ROM drive works under DOS. To bring a CD-ROM player to life, you need to add a device driver to the system's CONFIG.SYS file. The device driver enables the PC to recognize the CD-ROM driver. After you install the low-level device driver, you need to run the Microsoft CD-ROM Extensions program so the computer knows how to manage the CD-ROM.

Today's CD-ROM drives are for the most part SCSI devices. SCSI is not directly supported by most system BIOSs, so a CD-ROM drive relies on device drivers and TSR programs to trick DOS into thinking it's dealing with another disk drive. At this level, you're dealing with two software components: low-level drivers, which control the hardware of the SCSI adapter, and high-level redirectors, which redirects the disk I/O interface and monitors DOS drivers for calls to the CD-ROM drive.

Check the DOS drivers

If the CD-ROM drive is part of a shared *SCSI chain,* a configuration consisting of other SCSI devices that share the same host card, several low-level drivers work in concert with a driver manager. Driver managers typically conform to the Advanced SCSI Programming Interface (ASPI) specification, and the CD-ROM's driver relies on the ASPI to communicate with the drive. If the CD-ROM drive doesn't share a SCSI adapter with other devices, it may use only a single low-level driver that controls the entire adapter.

The high-level redirector that is used under DOS is a TSR program called the Microsoft CD-ROM Extensions (MSCDEX.EXE). When MSCDEX loads, it extends the logical drive lettering scheme to make the CD-ROM drive available as a DOS mass-storage device. If the last physical drive is a hard disk, drive C, then the CD-ROM drive appears as drive D.

You need to use the latest versions of both the SCSI drivers and the MSCDEX TSR and make sure that you have installed these drivers properly. MSCDEX is discussed in detail in the next section.

SCSI device drivers vary from adapter to adapter; check with the manufacturer of your SCSI adapter to ensure that the versions you have are up to date. All SCSI adapters have an on-board BIOS. Check for BIOS upgrades from the manufacturer of your SCSI adapter.

Configuring Microsoft CD-ROM Extensions

Microsoft CD-ROM Extensions provides an interface between MS-DOS and the CD-ROM's individual driver. You normally load this TSR in the AUTOEXEC.BAT file.

Starting with MS-DOS 6.0, Microsoft began including MSCDEX.EXE with versions of MS-DOS. As of this writing, Version 2.23 of MSCDEX is being used.

The latest version is normally available from the Microsoft Download Service BBS (206-936-6735) or the Microsoft Software Library on CompuServe (GO MSL). To share a CD-ROM drive under Windows for Workgroups, you need Version 2.22 or later.

Before looking at the various configuration options, I want to take a moment to talk about versions. If you haven't upgraded to MS-DOS 6.2 and you have a CD-ROM (why else would you be reading this section?), now is the time to run out and buy that upgrade. Why? Because the version of Smart Drive that's provided with MS-DOS 6.2 provides markedly improved performance by caching CD-ROMs.

MS-DOS 6.2 also includes Version 2.23 of MSCDEX. This version, like version 2.22, which came with Windows for Workgroups 3.10 and MS-DOS 6.0, allows sharing of your CD-ROM as a network drive in Windows for Workgroups or other compatible MS-NET networks.

Command line options

MSCDEX.EXE offers the command line options that are described in this section. (The CD-ROM's device driver should already be loaded in the CONFIG.SYS file.)

/D:

This option specifies the signature that is associated with the CD-ROM's device driver entry in CONFIG.SYS. If you have more than one CD-ROM device, the order in which the /D: options appear determines which drive letter is associated with which CD-ROM drive:

```
/D:driver1 [/D:driver2... ]
```

If the system has more than one CD-ROM drive, you need to use different *signatures* for the device driver for each of the drives. For example, if you have two CD-ROM drives, the following lines may be in the CONFIG.SYS file:

```
DEVICE=C:\SCSI\NECCDR.SYS /D:CD001 /V

DEVICE=C:\SCSI\NECCDR.SYS /D:CD002 /V
```

This configuration has two drives. The first drive's signature is CD001, and the second drive's signature is CD002.

/E

If expanded memory is available on the system, this option enables MSCDEX to store buffers in it.

/K

This option enables the use of Kanji (Japanese) encoded CD-ROMs.

/S

This option permits sharing of the CD-ROM on Windows for Workgroups or compatible MS-NET networks.

/V

This option enables *verbose* mode, which displays memory statistics upon start up.

/L:letter

This option specifies the drive letter to assign to the first drive. If you have used the /D: option to specify more than one drive, this option specifies the first drive letter, and others are added in sequence. You can use additional /L: commands to set the letters of additional drives.

In this example, the user has two drives with the signatures CD001 and CD002. The following MSCDEX line assigns drive letter F: to CD001 and drive letter H: to CD002:

```
MSCDEX /D:CD001 /L:F /D:CD002 /L:H
```

 If you specify a high drive letter (R:, for example), you will have room for other drive letters if you add more hard drives to the system, and you will avoid having to reconfigure software.

 You may need to adjust the LASTDRIVE= entry in the CONFIG.SYS file to allow enough drive letters for your CD-ROM. For example, to set LASTDRIVE= to allow for drive letters from A: to R:, put the following line in CONFIG.SYS:

```
LASTDRIVE=R:
```

/M:number

This option sets the number of buffers that are available to MSCDEX.

 If a large number of buffers is specified and MSCDEX (Version 2.21 or later) is being loaded high, then, for maximum efficiency, MSCDEX will silently adjust the number of buffers it uses so as to take all of high memory.

If a large number of buffers is specified and MSCDEX is not being loaded high, MSCDEX will use all available memory except for 48K.

Sharing a CD-ROM Under Windows for Workgroups

Wanting to share a CD-ROM drive is only natural, especially under a peer-to-peer network such as Windows for Workgroups. Here's a typical situation: You share the drive by using the File Manager and its Share-As functions, but for some strange reason, other workgroup users can't attach to it. Or users may be able to attach to the drive only to have the server system (with the CD-ROM) suddenly reboot for no apparent reason. The following sections offer some suggestions for sharing a CD-ROM drive.

Change the load order for NetWare drivers

Windows for Workgroup's Novell NetWare support can bring a functional CD-ROM sharing system to its knees. When you install NetWare support under Windows for Workgroups 3.1, Windows for Workgroups arbitrarily places references to MSIPX.COM and NETX.COM (the NetWare protocol stack and shell) into the AUTOEXEC.BAT file. If these components load before MSCDEX, users can connect to the shared CD-ROM drive, but if they try to view the directory, they get the following message:

```
NO FILES FOUND
```

This error message indicates that MSCDEX has loaded after MSIPX or NETX. If you see this error message, check the load order of those files in AUTOEXEC.BAT, and if necessary, move MSCDEX to a position before MSIPX and NETX. Also, check the MSCDEX command line to ensure that the /S parameter is present.

Get rid of LANMAN10.386

If you've installed Windows for Workgroups as an upgrade over an existing Windows 3.1 installation that had a CD-ROM drive, an old VxD may be clinging to the system. In the [386 Enh] section of SYSTEM.INI, Windows 3.1 requires an entry for the LANMAN 10.386 virtual device driver (VxD). This driver enables a CD-ROM drive to work in Windows 3.1's Enhanced mode when you are using an older version of MSCDEX (versions earlier than 2.2). Microsoft incorporated this functionality in Windows for Workgroups' core operating system, and leaving the older, external VxD in place causes a conflict. The Windows for Workgroups setup program doesn't automatically remove the entry. Check the SYSTEM.INI file's [386 Enh] section and remove any references to LANMAN10.386.

Keep an eye on upper memory blocks

If you're running DOS 5.0 or higher, you're probably using a memory manager (EMM386.EXE, QEMM, or 386MAX, for example) to create upper memory blocks (UMBs). If so, note that the CD-ROM host adapter usually has an on-board ROM BIOS and that a portion of the BIOS code is mapped into a UMB region, usually D000-DCFF, on boot-up. Most memory managers do an acceptable job of detecting reserved regions of upper memory and excluding them from the optimization process.

If you're experiencing intermittent CD-ROM problems, check the memory manager's command-line parameters to make sure that the adapter's ROM BIOS is not being overwritten with backfilled UMB space.

After you have properly configured the CD-ROM drive at the DOS level, you should be able to share it just as you share any other logical drive.

Windows 3.1x Multimedia Support

Microsoft implemented multimedia support in Windows 3.0 through an add-on called Multimedia Extensions 1.0. In Windows 3.1x, those extensions are built into the operating environment. Windows 3.1x fulfills its multimedia capabilities as follows:

- Windows provides multimedia device independence in the same manner in which it provides device independence for printers.
- The Windows Media Control Interface (MCI) links the environment with generic multimedia devices.
- Windows communicates with each device via a multimedia device driver.

The Media Control Interface

Multimedia has finally overcome the initial barriers of the high cost of multimedia hardware and the raw CPU power that is required to drive it. The final hurdle, the lack of a device-independent platform on which to build the applications, was overcome when Microsoft introduced the Media Control Interface as part of Multimedia Extensions 1.0 for Windows.

The *Media Control Interface* is a device-independent layer that enables applications to control both audio and visual peripherals. MCI was originally designed to work with CD-ROMs, Digital Audio Tapes (DAT), video overlay adapters, image scanners, MIDI sequencers, VCRs, LaserDisc players, and audio digitizers.

The MCI software layer insulates multimedia applications from having to know the complex details of each actual device interface. This isolating layer consists of device drivers that respond to MCI commands that the application issues.

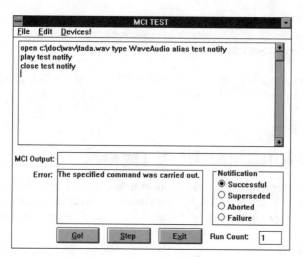

Figure 20-4 The MCI tool in the MS software developer's kit allows you to directly input commands to the device drivers.

The device type name consists of the device type and the unit number. For example, the first CD-ROM player is addressed as cdaudio1, the second CD-ROM as cdaudio2, and so on. The unit number is omitted when only one physical device is present (for example, cdaudio). You need to define the entire listing of logical names in the [mci] section of the SYSTEM.INI file.

RIFF and other file formats

A multimedia presentation can use many different information components: waveform audio, MIDI data, bitmaps, metafiles, and so forth. To store this information logically, the Resource Interchange File Format (RIFF) has been defined.

RIFF is a tagged file structure that incorporates other file formats that may exist independently of RIFF. The RIFF format is composed of chunks. Each chunk begins with a 4-character text string that identifies the chunk, followed by a 32-bit size of the chunk and the chunk data. In many cases, these chunks are in other file formats that may exist independently of the RIFF file.

The device-independent bitmap (DIB) file format was introduced in Windows 3.0. This file format contains header information concerning the size and color format of the bitmap, color data, and the bitmap data, which has possibly been compressed by using a run-length-encoded (RLE) algorithm.

The RDIB file format (which is how a DIB appears in a RIFF file) can be as simple as a DIB prefixed with the identifying text string RDIB and a chunk size. An extended RDIB format has also been defined to incorporate additional compression schemes and color use.

For the MIDI interface, Multimedia Windows adopted the standard file format defined by the International MIDI Association (IMA). These files may be used directly in MCI strings. MIDI data appears in a RIFF file in the RMID format, which is simply the text string "RMID" and a chunk size prefixed to a standard MIDI file.

The WAVE format is used for storing waveform data.

Configuring Multimedia in Windows

Settings in the Windows initialization files specify the interaction between Windows, the device drivers, and the Media Control Interface. This section gives you the information that you need to edit those settings.

Multimedia settings in the SYSTEM.INI file

When you install Windows 3.1, it automatically adds the following sections to the SYSTEM.INI file:

```
[drivers] Section
```

This section contains a list of aliases (or names) assigned to installable driver files. The [drivers] section can contain this entry:

```
alias=driver filename[parameters]
```

This entry assigns an alias name to an installable driver and specifies any parameters used by the driver. This entry is associated with the drivers= entry in the [boot] section of SYSTEM.INI. If the driver includes parameters, you must assign an alias to it and then specify the driver by alias name in the [boot] section. You can define multiple aliases by specifying multiple alias lines in this entry. The default is none. Most Setup programs for Windows applications add these settings to SYSTEM.INI when installing drivers, so you shouldn't need to change the values.

The drivers listed in Table 20-2 support the multimedia capabilities of Windows 3.1x.

Table 20-2	Multimedia Driver Files
Filename	*Purpose*
MCICDA.DRV	MCI CD-audio driver
MCISEQ.DRV	MCI driver for MIDI driver
MCIWAVE.DRV	MCI driver for waveform audio
MIDIMAP.DRV	Driver for MIDI Mapper Control Panel extension
MPU401.DRV	MIDI driver for MPU401 compatibles
MMSOUND.DRV	Multimedia sound driver
MSADLIB.DRV	MIDI driver for Adlib compatibles
SNDBLST.DRV	Sound Blaster 1.5 DSP driver
SNDBLST2.DRV	Sound Blaster 2.0 DSP driver
TIMER.DRV	Multimedia timer driver

[mci extensions] section

The [mci extensions] section contains entries that associate different types of media files with Media Control Interface drivers. Whenever a media file is selected, Windows will use the associated driver to play it.

[mmsystem]

Lists options that control the stack used by MMSYSTEM.DLL at interrupt time.

[Multimedia.Setup]

Lists audio and display drivers selected during setup of Windows with Multimedia Extensions for use by the Setup program and the Display application in the Control Panel.

[sound] section

The [sound] section lists the system events that support sound and the sound files that are assigned to each event. The [sound] section can contain one or more occurrences of the following entry:

```
system event=filename,description
```

This entry specifies the sound file assigned to and a description of a *system event*. The *filename* keyname is the name of the sound file. The *description* keyname is a text string that describes the system or application event.

Choosing a sound driver

The [boot] section of the SYSTEM.INI file contains a list of drivers and Windows modules that Windows uses to configure itself each time you start it. This is where you'll find the default sound driver for your system. Depending on the type of sound board in the system, you may need to select or install the correct driver for your board.

Setting: `sound.drv=filename`

Default: `sound.drv=mmsound.drv`

where `<filename>` is `Drivers=`.

Linking MCI devices with drivers

The [drivers] section lists installable device drivers for Windows with Multimedia Extensions. These drivers do not include Media Control Interface (MCI) device drivers, which are listed in the [mci] section of the file.

Entries in this section have the following format:

```
device_type=driver_name [parameters]
```

where `device_type` is the type of device and the `driver_name` is the filename for the device driver installed for that device type.

Parameters that are specific to a device driver may follow the `driver_name`. Alternatively, the following parameters may be given in a section with the same name as the device driver:

```
joystick=<filename>
```

Windows with Multimedia provides: IBMJOY.DRV

Purpose: This setting specifies the joystick device driver.

```
midi=<filename>
```

Purpose: This setting specifies the MIDI device driver.

```
timer=<filename>
```

Windows with Multimedia provides: TIMER.DRV

Purpose: This setting specifies the timer device driver.

```
wave=<filename>
```

Purpose: This setting specifies waveform-audio device driver.

Associating files with multimedia applications

Windows keeps a list of multimedia application file associations just as it does with document file associations. Edit the [mci extensions] section of the WIN.INI file to add or change the file associations.

Setting: `extension=mcidevice type`

Defaults: `wav=waveaudio`
             `mid=sequencer`
             `rmi=sequencer`

Disabling sounds

Not all system sound events are disabled when the Enable System Sounds check box is cleared. This option only enables or disables the Default Beep event. (The Enable System Sounds check box is accessed by choosing the Sounds icon from Control Panel.)

To disable an individual system sound in Control Panel, the event's sound should be assigned to <none> in the Files list.

The Enable System Sounds option can be changed manually by editing the WIN.INI file and changing the Beep= line in the [windows] section to yes or no.

Assigning sounds

The [sound] section of the WIN.INI file contains a list of sounds associated with system events. You can specify the events and their corresponding sounds as desired by editing this section of the WIN.INI file. The syntax is as follows:

```
System event=filename,description
```

The default sounds are as follows:

```
SystemDefault=ding.wav, Default Beep
SystemExclamation=chord.wav, Exclamation
SystemStart=tada.wav, Windows Start
SystemExit=chimes.wav, Windows Exit
SystemHand=chord.wav, Critical Stop
SystemQuestion=chord.wav, Question
SystemAsterisk=chord.wav, Asterisk
```

You can add sounds to your system by copying WAV files to your Windows directory. Check CompuServe and other bulletin board services for collections of WAV files.

[mci] section

The [mci] section lists MCI device drivers for Windows with Multimedia Extensions. If more than one device of a given type is installed, the keyname has a number as its last character.

Windows with Multimedia adds the following settings to the [mci] section:

```
CDAudio=<filename>
```

Windows with Multimedia settings: MCICDA.DRV

Purpose: This setting specifies the filename of the MCI driver used to control audio compact-disc (CD) players.

To change: Select the Drivers icon from the Control Panel. Choose Add to add a new videodisc driver, or select CDAudio from the Installed Drivers list to modify the current driver. Click Setup to select options for the device driver (for example, the device number for the CD player). Then choose OK.

```
Sequencer=<filename>
```

Windows with Multimedia settings: MCISEQ.DRV

Purpose: This setting specifies the filename of the MCI driver used to control playback of MIDI sequences.

To change: Select the Drivers icon from the Control Panel. Choose Add to add a new driver, or select Sequencer from the Installed Drivers list to modify the current driver. Click Setup to select options (if any) for the device driver. Then choose OK.

```
Videodisc=<filename> [<com-port>]
```

Windows with Multimedia settings: MCIPIONR.DRV COM1

Purpose: This setting specifies the filename of the MCI driver used to control external videodisc players.

To change: Select the Drivers icon from the Control Panel. Choose Add to add a new videodisc driver, or select Videodisc from the Installed Drivers list to modify the current driver. Click Setup to select a COM port for the videodisc player. Then choose OK.

Specifying the amount of Audio Data Buffer memory

Alternately, modify the size of the buffer in the SYSTEM.INI file. The numeric parameter on the WaveAudio line in the [mci] section specifies the size of the buffer:

```
WaveAudio=<filename> [<buffer-size>]
```

Windows with Multimedia settings: MCISEQ.DRV 4

Purpose: This setting specifies the filename of the MCI driver used to control recording and playback of waveform audio files. It may optionally specify the number of seconds (an integer in the range 2 to 9 seconds) of audio that the driver should buffer during playback or recording.

To change: Select the Drivers icon from the Control Panel. Choose Add to add a new driver, or select WaveAudio from the Installed Drivers list to modify the current driver. Click Setup to select options (for example, buffer size). Then choose OK.

The following is a sample of the SYSTEM.INI file:

```
[mci]
WaveAudio=mciwave.drv 4
```

where 4 is the buffer setting in seconds. 4 is the default.

[mmsystem] section

The [mmsystem] section includes options used by MMSYSTEM.DLL. Windows with Multimedia puts the following settings in the [mmsystem] section:

```
StackFrames=<number>
```

Defaults: 3

Purpose: This setting specifies the number of stack frames used when new instances of MMSYSTEM.DLL are called.

To change: Use Notepad to edit the SYSTEM.INI file.

```
StackSize=<number>
```

Defaults: 1536

Purpose: This setting specifies the number of bytes in each stack frame used when new instances of MMSYSTEM.DLL are called.

To change: Use Notepad to edit the SYSTEM.INI file.

[Multimedia.Setup] section

The [Multimedia.Setup] section records information about the currently installed audio and video hardware from your input during setup. Anytime you run Setup after the initial setup, and anytime you select the Display application from the Control Panel, these programs use the information given in this section.

Windows with Multimedia adds the following settings to the [Multimedia.Setup] section:

```
audio=<filename>,<port>,<interrupt>,<dsp-version>
```

Windows with Multimedia uses: SNDBLST.DRV,210,3,none

Purpose: This setting specifies the device driver for the audio device you specified when setting up Windows with Multimedia.

To change: Rerun Setup.

```
display=<filename>
```

Windows with Multimedia uses: MMV7VGA.DRV

Purpose: Specifies the device driver for the video card you specified when setting up Windows with Multimedia.

To change: Rerun Setup.

Configuring installable device drivers

To support various types of hardware, Windows with Multimedia Extensions uses installable device drivers. This adds another set of conventions to the standard device entries in the SYSTEM.INI file. Now you need to be concerned about driver-specific parameters listed on the driver entry lines.

For example, an entry in the SYSTEM.INI file might look like the following:

```
[mci] cdaudio=mcicda.drv waveaudio=mciwave.drv 4
```

The `waveaudio=` entry has both the driver name, `MCIWAVE.DRV`, and an extra parameter that is specific to the MCIWAVE.DRV driver (4). In this example, 4 is the number of seconds of wave data the MCIWAVE.DRV should buffer.

Because this parameter can be stored here, MCIWAVE.DRV is not required to add another section to the SYSTEM.INI file to store the number of seconds to buffer.

This parameter can be changed through the Drivers application in the Control Panel by choosing Setup for the MCIWAVE.DRV driver (in the Control Panel window, select the Drivers icon, select the MCIWAVE.DRV driver, then choose the Setup button).

[ibmjoy.drv] [sndblst.drv]

Next, I describe the entries that may appear in the `[ibmjoy.drv]` and `[sndblst.drv]` sections. (Additional sections may appear for other audio, video, or peripheral devices installed on the system.)

```
[ibmjoy.drv] axes=<2-or-3> timeout=<hex-number>
```

Defaults: `axes=2 timeout=0x3000`

Purpose: The axes option specifies whether the joystick is two-dimensional (2) or three-dimensional (3). The timeout option is a hexadecimal value specifying how many times the joystick driver is polled before the system determines that a joystick is not installed on the system.

To change: Use Notepad to edit the SYSTEM.INI file.

```
[sndblst.drv] port=<hex-number> interrupt=<number>
DisableWarning=<Boolean>
```

Defaults: None

Purpose: The port option specifies the port number for the Sound Blaster audio card. This is the port where the jumper on the card is set. The interrupt option specifies which interrupt the Sound Blaster uses. The DisableWarning option, if enabled, displays a warning message if a DOS application running from the Windows DOS prompt tries to access the Sound Blaster port given in the port option or the interrupt given in the interrupt option. This option is enabled by default.

Summary

In this chapter, you've learned:

▶ How to specify and upgrade a PC system to a multimedia system.

▶ How to configure Microsoft CD-ROM extensions.

▶ How Windows supports multimedia.

▶ How to configure Windows for multimedia.

Chapter 21

Configuring DOS Applications for Windows

Before there was Windows, there was MS-DOS. Many programs were written to run under MS-DOS, and as a result, one of the design requirements for Windows was that it be able to run MS-DOS applications.

Resource Contention

Perhaps the most significant difference between the MS-DOS environment and the Windows environment, from an application's point of view, is that Windows is a multitasking environment and MS-DOS is a single-tasking environment.

In MS-DOS, a single program controls the entire machine and its resources, such as the display, keyboard, mouse, hard disk, and so on. Under Windows, these resources are managed cooperatively. Each program can use only the devices and resources that Windows specifically allocates to it. This is known as *resource contention*, referring to the fact that programs must contend, or compete, for resources.

Before the 80386 was invented, using the virtual 8086 mode (which lets an operating system create virtual machines for applications to run in), required you to disable multitasking if you wanted to run an MS-DOS program under Windows because Windows could not control the program's behavior. This means that when Windows is running in standard mode, an MS-DOS program is suspended if it is not in the foreground. In enhanced mode, with its virtual 8086 mode, MS-DOS programs can run concurrently with Windows programs and other MS-DOS programs.

Fonts in DOS and Windows

MS-DOS programs are generally text-based, and normally rely on the character-generating ROM built into the video display adapter to create the images of the characters that appear on the display, which limits DOS-based programs to a handful of fonts.

When you run MS-DOS programs full-screen in Windows, the hardware handles the fonts as if Windows was not running. When you run a compatible MS-DOS program in a Windows window, however, Windows simulates the hardware actions.

When you run MS-DOS applications in a window in 386 enhanced mode, Windows uses one of several font files that SETUP installs specifically for this purpose.

Windows SETUP installs the fonts listed in Table 21-1 to use when Windows runs an MS-DOS program in a window. The table shows the name of the file the font resides in, the translation table (if applicable), what code page the font is used with, and which configurations the font is installed with.

Windows needs to use a *translation table* to translate the ASCII values an MS-DOS application may use into the equivalent characters in an international font.

Table 21-1   Non-Windows Fonts Installed by Windows for MS-DOS

Filename	Translation Table	Code page	Configuration
APP850.FON		850	U.S., 386 enhanced mode
DOSAPP.FON		437	U.S., 386 enhanced mode
CGA40850.FON	XLAT850.BIN	850	Multilingual
CGA40WOA.FON		437	U.S.
CGA80850.FON	XLAT850.BIN	850	Multilingual
CGA80WOA.FON		437	U.S.
EGA40850.FON	XLAT850.BIN	850	Multilingual
EGA40WOA.FON		437	U.S.
EGA80850.FON	XLAT850.BIN	850	Multilingual
EGA80WOA.FON		437	U.S.

Filename	Translation Table	Code page	Configuration
HERC850.FON	XLAT850.BIN	850	Multilingual
HERCWOA.FON		437	U.S.
VGA850.FON	XLAT850.BIN	850	Multilingual
VGA860.FON	XLAT860.BIN	860	Portuguese
VGA861.FON	XLAT861.BIN	861	Icelandic
VGA863.FON	XLAT863.BIN	863	French Canadian
VGA865.FON	XLAT865.BIN	865	Norwegian/Danish

Full-Screen and Windowed Display Mode

Full-screen mode is rather limited. In this mode, which is available in standard mode and 386 enhanced mode, applications run as though they were at an MS-DOS prompt. None of Windows' advanced features, such as cut and paste, are available from full-screen mode. You can, however, use the Clipboard to pass information from an application that is running in full-screen mode to Windows.

In windowed display mode, available only in 386 enhanced mode, you can resize the window, shrink it to an icon, and perform cut and paste operations. MS-DOS applications in 386 enhanced mode are also preemptively multitasked.

Using the Clipboard

In standard mode, the only way to pass information from an MS-DOS program back to Windows programs is to use the Print Screen key, which essentially prints the screen to the Clipboard.

In enhanced mode, an option is available from the Control menu of a windowed MS-DOS application that aids cutting and pasting. To choose an area of the window to copy to the Clipboard, choose Edit⇨Select from the Control menu.

To paste from the Clipboard to a windowed MS-DOS application, choose Edit⇨Paste from the Control menu.

If you have trouble pasting to a windowed MS-DOS application, see "Tips for taming unruly DOS applications" later in this chapter.

The [NonWindowsApp] Section of SYSTEM.INI _

The [NonWindowsApp] section contains entries that affect the performance of non-Windows applications.

Setting the DOS environment size

Setting: CommandEnvSize=*bytes*

Default: 0 with MS-DOS versions prior to 3.2; size of MS-DOS environment otherwise

The CommandEnvSize option specifies the size of the COMMAND.COM environment for MS-DOS prompts and batch files under Windows. It must be 0 or between 160 and 32768. If you specify the environment size in a .PIF file, the size specified in the PIF file takes precedence.

An Out of Environment Space error message when running DOS under Windows doesn't force you to exit Windows and edit your CONFIG.SYS file's SHELL= line before you can get things working. All you need to do is open DOSPRMPT.PIF with the PIF Editor. Insert /E:900 in the Optional Parameters box, then save your changes and exit. This expands the environment space for your DOS session to 900 bytes. If you continue to get Out of Environment Space messages, increase the number, within the aforementioned setting limitations until the errors go away. If you reach the maximum environment size, and the Out of Environment Space messages don't go away, contact the developer of the application you're trying to use.

Controlling fonts and positions

The DisablePositionSave= setting disables the saving of positions and fonts for an MS-DOS application in the DOSAPP.INI file when the application is exited. If this setting is 1, any settings not saved previously are not saved. If this entry is 1, you can override the setting for each non-Windows application by selecting the Save Settings On Exit check box in the Fonts dialog box. Figure 21-1 shows the Font Selection dialog box.

Setting: DisablePositionSave=*Boolean*

Default: 0

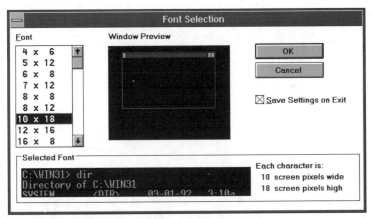

Figure 21-1: The Font Selection dialog box.

Font changing capability for old drivers

This setting provides the capability to change the fonts when running MS-DOS based applications in a window.

Use this setting if you run Windows 3.0 video drivers under Windows 3.1.

Setting: `FontChangeEnable=Boolean`

Default: 1 on systems with Windows 3.1 grabbers, 0 on systems with Windows 3.0 grabbers.

For more discussion on grabbers, see Chapter 4.

Listing local TSRs

This is a list of TSRs that work properly if you copy them to each virtual machine, rather than have one global copy for the entire system. Use this setting only if you know for certain that the TSR is compatible.

Setting: `LocalTSRs=list`

Default: `dosedit,ced`

Limiting scroll lines

This setting tells Windows how many lines it can scroll in an MS-DOS based application that is running in a window, before the display is updated.

Setting: ScrollFrequency=*number*

Default: 2

Using a mouse in a DOS box

Change this setting to 1 if you use a Windows version 3.0 grabber and you want mouse support. Windows 3.1 grabbers handle this automatically if you have a mouse driver loaded.

Setting: MouseInDosBox=*Boolean*

Default: 1 (if an MS-DOS mouse driver is loaded and has the extension .COM or .SYS, and supports using a mouse with an MS-DOS application)

Instead of using Ctrl+S or Ctrl+P to pause rapidly scrolling screens in a DOS window, freeze scrolling text by setting MouseInDosBox=0. Then exit and restart Windows. Now when you have scrolling text in a DOS window, just click the left mouse button anywhere on the screen to freeze it. Windows stops the scrolling and adds the word Select to the DOS window's title bar. Click the right mouse button to unfreeze the DOS window.

The disappearing mouse

If you use a serial mouse, you may encounter problems with the mouse pointer disappearing when you switch between Windows and DOS applications in enhanced mode. Usually, you can correct this problem by changing the device contention setting for the COM port that your mouse uses.

Double-click on the 386 Enhanced icon in the Control Panel, then select the Never Warn radio button. Click OK to save your settings and restart Windows.

Switching and NetBIOS calls

If you change this setting to 1, you can switch away from an application running in standard mode after it makes an asynchronous NetBIOS call. NetBIOS applications usually communicate with other NetBIOS applications over the network using asynchronous NetBIOS calls.

Setting: NetAsynchSwitching=*Boolean*

Default: 0

 Setting this to 1 can cause your system to fail because the application's code may not be available to service the response from the asynchronous NetBIOS call.

Setting the number of lines per screen

This setting controls the number of lines that appear on the screen when you run an MS-DOS application.

Setting: ScreenLines=*number*

Default: 25

To display more lines in your DOS sessions under Windows, change this setting to ScreenLines=50. Most VGA and better adapters support a 50-line mode under Windows. ScreenLines=43 also works with most video adapters.

Changing standard mode DOS swap directory

Standard mode Windows swaps DOS applications to a file when you switch windows. Use the setting to specify the directory to which Windows swaps MS-DOS based applications.

Setting: SwapDisk=*directory*

Default: TEMP directory

Improve Your DOS Applications with Custom PIFs

Although DOS applications can't take advantage of Windows directly, they can benefit from running under Windows. Windows exploits 386 and higher processors to provide DOS applications with new capabilities, such as multitasking and the capability to integrate DOS and Windows applications.

In standard mode Windows, DOS applications run in full-screen only, not inside a window. You can start several DOS applications when running in standard mode, however only one application — the one on which you're currently working — can run at a time. As soon as you switch from one DOS application, it's swapped out to a file, where it remains idle until you return to it.

On the other hand, Windows 386 enhanced mode runs several DOS applications simultaneously, enabling you to switch between applications. DOS applications can also run in individual windows that you can move, resize, and shrink to an icon. Furthermore, Windows 386 enhanced can create virtual DOS machines (VDM), each one simulating a PC that has its own memory, hardware devices, and software configuration.

By learning how to tune program information files (PIFs), along with INI file settings and batch files, you can run a variety of DOS applications that perform as if they are in their own custom-configured machine. Each custom VDM needs only the drivers and TSRs required by a single application, leaving more conventional memory free for the program. Finally, virtual DOS machines can take advantage of Windows components, such as SmartDrive and FastDisk.

Creating Virtual DOS Machines _____

To create a virtual DOS machine, Windows uses a *program information file (PIF)*, which defines the way a virtual machine can use the system resources. A PIF is critical for preventing memory conflicts between DOS and Windows, so Windows supplies a default PIF for any DOS application that lacks a corresponding PIF. Every time you run a DOS program, Windows searches for a PIF that has the same name (with a PIF extension) as the file you attempt to run. If it doesn't find one, it uses the _DEFAULT.PIF file.

Many DOS programs work well with the default PIF, but you can usually resolve compatibility problems and improve performance of the DOS application by learning to create and tune PIFs.

To create and edit PIF files, Windows provides the PIF Editor utility, which enables you to define a custom PIF that has the settings required to run a particular DOS application.

PIF Editor enables you to set parameters that provide the DOS application with the system resources it needs to be able to run and avoid conflicts with Windows. For example, one application might require a serial port. Another application might need extended memory or require a keystroke combination usually reserved for Windows. The PIF also provides Windows with information about how to manage multiple DOS programs in 386 enhanced mode and enables you to adjust settings that control each program's use of CPU time.

DOS in a Window

When you install Windows, Setup creates a Program Manager icon called MS-DOS Prompt, which runs COMMAND.COM in full-screen mode using the file DOSPRMPT.PIF. To get a DOS session to run in a window, open DOSPRMPT.PIF using PIF Editor, click on the Windowed button, and use Save As to save the PIF under a different name. Create a program item icon for the new PIF.

The Anatomy of a PIF

Most of the settings in the [NonWindowsApps] section of SYSTEM.INI have a global effect on DOS applications that run under Windows. Sometimes you want to configure a certain DOS program in a specific way. This is why PIFs were designed.

You use PIFs to override global settings, and to control the way a DOS program behaves. Figure 21-2 shows the PIF Editor dialog box. You can use PIF files to:

■ Specify startup parameters

■ Configure video memory and RAM requirements

■ Control background execution

■ Set up full-screen or windowed modes

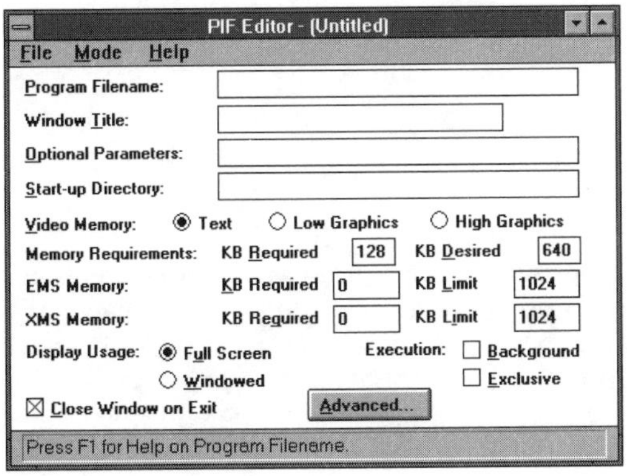

![PIF Editor dialog box]

Figure 21-2: The PIF Editor dialog box allows you to specify settings to control DOS individual applications.

If you run Windows in 386 enhanced mode, you can specify the following advanced options (see Figure 21-3):

- Multitasking options
- Memory configuration options
- Display setting options
- Hot keys or shortcut keys

You create PIFs by using the PIF Editor applet.

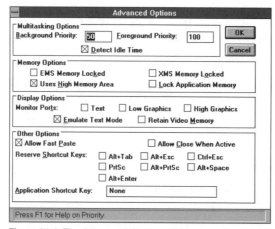

Figure 21-3: The Advanced Options dialog box allows you to control advanced settings for individual DOS applications.

Creating PIFs

When you use the Setup program or Program Manager to create a program item for a non-Windows application, Windows automatically creates a PIF. When you start a non-Windows application, Windows looks for a PIF to use with that application. If there is no PIF for the application, Windows uses a default PIF. If your application doesn't work using the default PIF, you can create a new PIF.

Use the following steps to create a PIF:

1. Select File⇨New.

2. From the Mode menu, choose the mode the application runs in (standard or 386 enhanced).

If you choose the mode in which you are not currently running, a message appears. To continue setting options for the mode you selected, choose OK.

3. Specify the options that apply to the application.

4. If you plan to run the application in standard and 386 enhanced modes, use the Mode menu to switch to the other mode, and then specify the options for that mode.

5. Select File⇨Save As.

6. In the Filename box, type the name of the application's program file with .PIF as the extension.

7. Choose OK.

Editing PIFs

When an application doesn't run properly, you can try editing its PIF. For example, you might want to try the following:

■ Specify a new path for your application.

■ Specify a program parameter or change the default directory that contains your application's files.

■ Allocate more memory or all available memory to the application.

Use the following steps to edit a PIF:

1. Select File⇨Open.

2. Type or select a filename, and then choose OK.

3. Change any options that you want to change.

4. Select File⇨Save.

Modifying the default PIF

When you start a non-Windows application that doesn't have a PIF, Windows uses a default PIF named _DEFAULT.PIF. While the settings in this file work with many applications, you may need to modify this PIF to get it to run properly or to configure it to your preferences.

 Windows uses the default PIF for other applications for which no PIF is defined. Do not modify the default PIF; use the default file as a starting point and then save the file using a new filename.

To change the default PIF, follow these steps:

1. In the Program Filename box, type **_DEFAULT.COM**.

2. Leave the Window Title box blank.

3. Change any other settings as appropriate. If Windows uses _DEFAULT.PIF to start an application, it does not use some settings, such as the start-up directory and optional parameters settings. However, because PIF Editor verifies the contents of these fields, you should provide complete valid settings.

4. Select File⇨Save As.

5. Type the filename **_DEFAULT.PIF**.

6. Choose OK.

Close window on exit

Clear the Close window on exit check box if you want the window (or screen) to remain open when you quit the application. This is especially useful if you run a command or application that displays output on-screen. If the window closes too quickly, you can't see the output. By default, the window closes when you quit the application.

Display usage

Use these options to control the way the application initially appears.

Option	Purpose
Full Screen	Start the application in a full screen.
	Running an application in a full screen saves memory. You switch between a full-screen application and the Windows desktop by pressing Alt+Tab.
Windowed	Start the application in a window. Running an application in a window uses more memory. However, you gain the advantages of running in a window, including sharing information between applications easily.

To switch an application from a full screen to a window, or vice versa, press Alt+Enter. Some applications can run only in a full screen because they display graphics or have direct access to the part of memory used by the screen. In these cases, a message appears when you try to switch from a full screen to a window.

Similarly, to access the Control menu of an MS-DOS application, press Alt+Spacebar. If the application was running in full-screen mode, it is reduced to an icon and the Control menu opens.

EMS memory

When you run in 386 enhanced mode, Windows simulates expanded memory for applications that use 386 enhanced mode. Use EMS Memory options to specify the amount of expanded memory to allocate to an application.

Option	Specifies
KB Required	The minimum amount of expanded memory in kilobytes (KB) that your application requires. Check the requirements for your application. If you don't know the required EMS memory, leave the setting unchanged.
	If you run other applications and Windows cannot provide the specified amount of memory, a message appears. You might need to free some memory before you can continue. Use a setting of 0 for applications that do not require expanded memory.
KB Limit	The maximum amount of expanded memory that can be allocated for your application. This option prevents an application from taking more expanded memory than it needs.
	The default setting is 1024. A setting of –1 allocates as much expanded memory to an application as it requests, up to the KB Limit, which can greatly slow your system. A setting of 0 prevents the application from using EMS memory.

You can also use System Engineer to change these settings. System Engineer is included on the *Windows 3.1 Configuration SECRETS Disks*.

Execution background

Select the Execution background check box if you want the application to be able to run when it is not the active application. If you select this option, the application runs in the background (calculating numbers, for example) while you work in another application. Other applications run more slowly if they have to share resources with background applications. If you don't select this option, the application runs only when active.

Execution Exclusive

Select this check box for the application to have exclusive use of resources when active. No other applications, including those with the Background option set, can run when the application is active. You can select this option both for applications that run in a window and in a full screen. However, an application running in a window does not receive all the computer's resources. Windows reserves some resources for itself and for running Windows applications.

Background and Foreground Priority

When you specify Background and Foreground Priority, you determine the way CPU resources are allocated to the applications. The numbers you specify set the priority of the application relative to the other applications that are running. (Therefore, these numbers cannot be translated into a fixed percentage of CPU time.)

The higher the priority of an application, the more CPU resources are allocated to it. Priorities range from 0 to 10000. Default Foreground Priority is 100. Default Background Priority is 50.

The Foreground Priority is the application's priority when active. For example, to ensure that an application receives all the processing time it needs without interruption, set this option to 10000. The Background Priority is the application's priority when it is not the active application.

 When you run a DOS application in a window, you can also change its priorities by using the Settings command on the Control menu.

Timeslicing

When running in 386 enhanced mode, Windows remains in memory and active while running DOS applications. Windows considers each DOS application as a multitasking "task" for which it manages timeslicing and device contention. To administer services to the DOS applications, Windows uses preemptive scheduling as compared to nonpreemptive scheduling with Windows applications. Remember that Windows and all Windows applications run in the System VM and are considered as a single preemptive task. You assign the priority for Windows in the 386 Enhanced dialog box in Control Panel as shown in Figure 21-4. Windows treats each DOS application as a separate task, and you assign their priorities in their PIFs.

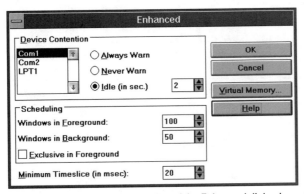

Figure 21-4: The Scheduling section of the Enhanced dialog box allows you to specify Windows timeslicing.

How to compute the timeslice

The percentage of time spent on an application is its assigned priority divided by the sum of all priorities for Windows and all non-Windows applications currently running.

Table 21-2 shows how timeslicing is allocated between Windows and non-Windows applications.

Table 21-2	Timeslicing Allocation	
Windows in the foreground, with two non-Windows applications running		
Virtual machine	*Setting*	*Processor time*
System virtual machine	100	50%
MS-DOS VM #1	50	25%
MS-DOS VM #2	50	25%
Total value:	200	100%
Windows in the foreground, with four non-Windows applications running		
Virtual machine	*Setting*	*Processor time*
System virtual machine	100	32%
MS-DOS VM #1	50	17%
MS-DOS VM #2	50	17%
MS-DOS VM #3	50	17%
MS-DOS VM #4	50	17%
Total value:	300	100%

(continued)

Table 21-2 *(continued)*

Non-Windows application in foreground, with Windows and another non-Windows application running in the background

Virtual machine	Setting	Processor time
System virtual machine	50	25%
MS-DOS VM #1	100	50%
MS-DOS VM #2	50	25%
Total value:	200	100%

The files that support non-Windows applications in 386 enhanced mode are the .3GR grabber file for your display device and WINOA386.MOD (WinOldApp).

Memory requirements for 386 enhanced mode

Use these settings to allocate conventional memory to the application.

Option	Specifies
KB Required	The minimum amount of memory in kilobytes (KB) that your application requires. Check the system requirements of your application. If you don't know how much is required, leave the setting as it is.
	If you run other applications and Windows cannot provide the specified amount of memory when you start the application, a message appears. You might need to quit some applications or specify a smaller number before you can continue. You might also need to free memory before you can start Windows. Specify 0 to indicate that the application has no minimum memory requirement; Windows allocates whatever memory is available, up to the limit set using the KB Desired option. Specify -1 to allocate the maximum amount of memory possible.
KB Desired	The maximum amount of memory that your application can use. Some applications run better if more than minimal memory is provided. The limit is 640K.
	Specify -1 to allocate as much memory as possible to the application.

Do not use the memory requirements listed in the application's documentation, which usually are an estimate of the total amount of memory your system should have, not the amount of memory that must be free for the application to run.

Optional parameters

Type parameters that your application uses, the same parameters you would type after the application's filename if you started the application from the MS-DOS command prompt. For example, to run Microsoft Word in character mode, type **/c**. If your application doesn't require parameters or you don't want to use them, enter nothing. See the application's documentation for valid parameters.

If you want Windows to prompt you for parameters when you start the application, type a question mark (**?**). If you start the application by using File⇨Run in Program Manager or File Manager, you can override the parameters specified in the PIF by typing parameters after the application's name in the Run dialog box. You can also specify optional parameters by using the Properties command on the File menu in Program Manager. Settings made in Program Manager override settings made in PIF Editor.

You can also specify an environment variable in the optional parameters field. By using an environment variable, you can place a variable name in the PIF and assign it a value by using the set command in the AUTOEXEC.BAT file. When you type the variable name, enclose it in percent signs (**%**).

Program filename

Type the name of the file that starts the application. If necessary, include the drive, directory, and the filename extension. Make sure the PIF filename matches the program filename. For example, if the program filename is MP.COM (Microsoft Multiplan), the PIF filename should be MP.PIF. If you start your application from a batch program, you can specify its filename in this box. You can also specify an environment variable in this field. By using an environment variable, you can place a variable name in the PIF and assign it a value by using the set command in the AUTOEXEC.BAT file. When you type the variable name, enclose it in percent signs (**%**).

Start-up directory

Type the drive and directory you want Windows to use as a *start-up directory* (or *working directory*). This is usually the location of the application's program file, but can be any directory where you want the application to save files. This entry is optional. If you want Windows to determine the start-up directory, leave this box blank. You can also specify a start-up directory by using the Properties command on the File menu in Program Manager. Settings made in Program Manager override PIF settings.

You can also specify an environment variable in this field. By using an environment variable, you can place a variable name in the PIF and assign it a value by using the set command in the AUTOEXEC.BAT file. When you type the variable name, enclose it in percent signs (**%**).

Video memory

You use this option to specify the video mode in which you want the application to start. Windows allocates system memory to display the application depending on the video mode you specify. Text mode uses the least amount of memory, and High (resolution) Graphics mode uses the most. If you specify a mode that allocates too little memory, you can't start the application. A message appears that says there is insufficient memory to run the application. Some applications can run in several modes. If you switch to a mode that requires less memory or if you run an application in a full screen, Windows frees the extra memory for use by other applications. If you switch back to a mode that requires more memory for video display, the memory might not be available, and display information might be partially or totally lost. To prevent this loss from occurring when you switch modes, you can select both the High Graphics and (in the Advanced dialog box) Retain Video Memory settings. This way, you always have the memory needed to display the application, regardless of the mode in which the application is running. However, the memory is not available to run other applications, even when the memory is not in use.

Some display adapters, such as Hercules and color graphics adapters (CHIS), have only one graphics mode, so there is no difference between the Low Graphics and High Graphics options.

Window title

Type a descriptive name for your application. This description appears in the window's title bar when you run the application. If you leave this box blank, the title bar displays the name of the application without an extension.

 You can also specify a window title by using the Properties command on the File menu in Program Manager. Settings made in Program Manager override settings made in PIF Editor. You can also specify an environment variable in this field. By using an environment variable, you can place a variable name in the PIF and assign it a value by using the set command in the AUTOEXEC.BAT file. When you type the variable name, enclose it in percent signs (%).

XMS memory for 386 enhanced mode

Use the XMS memory options to specify the amount of extended memory available to your application. Because few applications require extended memory, you can usually leave these options at their default settings.

Option	Specifies
KB Required	The minimum amount of extended memory in kilobytes (KB) required by your application. Check the system requirements for your application. If you don't know how much is required, leave the setting unchanged.
	If you run other applications and Windows cannot provide the specified amount of memory when you start the application, a message appears. You might need to free some memory before you can continue. Use a setting of 0 for applications that do not require extended memory.
KB Limit	The maximum amount of extended memory in kilobytes that can be allocated to the application.
	Use this setting to prevent an application from reserving all available extended memory blocks. The default setting is 1024. A setting of –1 allocates as much extended memory to an application as it requests, up to the limit of system memory. This can greatly slow the rest of your system. A setting of 0 prevents the application from using extended memory, except the high memory area (HMA).

Controlling How DOS and Windows Programs Work Together

Windows multitasks both Windows and DOS applications when running in 386 enhanced mode. It manages this by dividing CPU time between programs. Settings in the 386 enhanced section of the SYSTEM.INI file affect the way Windows determines the amount of time to allot to each program.

Giving Windows applications exclusive access

When this setting is on, Windows obtains exclusive use of the CPU time when a Windows application is in the foreground. This essentially suspends background MS-DOS applications.

Setting: WinExclusive=*Boolean*

Default: Off

Setting timeslice priorities

This setting enables you to give Windows applications priority over non-Windows applications. The first number is the relative processing time (based on MinTimeSlice=) that all Windows-based applications running in the foreground have, relative to the time allocated to all MS-DOS applications running in the foreground.

The second number is similar, only it is for applications running in the background.

Setting: WinTimeSlice=*number, number*

Default: 100,50

Tips for multitasking with DOS applications

To speed up your applications, increase the ratio of time devoted to Windows in the foreground or background, depending on where your program is running. These settings are found under the 386 Enhanced icon in Control Panel.

To speed up a DOS application's performance in the foreground or background, increase either the Foreground Priority value or the Background Priority value in the program's PIF. You can also modify this value on the fly by opening the application's Control menu and selecting the Settings item.

Adjust the PIF settings for your DOS programs. Make sure that the Monitor Ports settings are all unchecked unless you really need them.

 Check to be sure that the configuration statement `FileSysChange=Off` appears in the `[386 Enh]` section of SYSTEM.INI. This particular setting has the side effect of preventing Windows from updating an open File Manager window automatically, so you have to do it manually by pressing F5.

Minimum virtual machine timeslice

This controls the amount of time a virtual machine can run before another machine takes over. Measured in milliseconds.

Setting: `MinTimeSlice=number`

Default: 20

Sleep idle setting

This setting sets timer interrupts to periodically wake up virtual machines after the specified number of seconds elapses.

Setting: `IdleVMWakeUpTime=seconds`

Default: 8

Window update time

Specifies the time Windows takes between updates of the display for an MS-DOS based application running in a window.

Setting: `WindowUpdateTime=milliseconds`

Default: 50

To accelerate the refresh rate, set a higher value — from 100 to 200.

Video ROM soft font

When On, Windows uses the soft font stored in the video ROM for displaying messages in full screen. Set to Off if random dots and shapes appear on your screen.

Setting: UseROMFont=*Boolean*

Default: On

Setup DOS Applications in Windows

Use Windows' Setup program to install DOS programs to Program Manager. Run Windows Setup and choose Setup Applications from the Options menu. Specify the application to add and click OK. In the dialog box, you can type in the program name or use the Browse facility to search your hard drive for the program you want to add. After you specify a program and select a group file, click OK, and Setup adds the item to the group you choose. If you name a DOS program that's included in the Windows applications database, Windows even constructs a PIF for you.

The APPS.INF file in the Windows directory is an ASCII text file that contains information that Windows Setup uses to create the PIFs for DOS applications. You can view this file to see which applications are included and to determine which PIF settings to use. You can add new applications to this file or change the PIF values for the applications already listed. The APPS.INF file has hints that might help you figure out how to modify the file.

Reserving Expanded Memory for a DOS Application

Create a PIF for the DOS program by using Windows' PIF Editor. To do this, load PIF Editor, and enter the number of kilobytes of EMS RAM that you want to reserve for that program in the box labeled EMS Memory. For example, if you need 2M of expanded RAM, enter **2048**.

Preventing Out of Memory Errors While in DOS Applications

An `Out of Memory` error in a DOS application indicates that Windows is out of conventional or expanded memory to allocate for the application. The following is a list of some suggestions you might try:

- Minimize open applications.

- Turn off desktop wallpaper.

- Increase the size of your permanent swap file (this is especially useful with FastDisk's 32-bit access).

- Remove unnecessary drivers and TSRs from your CONFIG.SYS and AUTOEXEC.BAT files.

- Load DOS and other drivers and programs into upper memory in your CONFIG.SYS and AUTOEXEC.BAT files.

- If you run multiple DOS applications, configure some or all of them to run in the foreground only.

- Adjust the PIF settings for your DOS programs. Make sure that your memory-related settings don't specify more memory than a program actually needs to run.

- Run your DOS applications before running your Windows applications. Windows programs can configure themselves to run in a limited-memory environment; DOS programs cannot.

Loading a Problem DOS Application

If you try to load a problem DOS application, first in a full-screen window, you may be able to load your other programs subsequently. Clearing the Retain Video Memory and Lock Application Memory options from the PIFs of other programs also releases memory to the system.

"File not found" When Running a DOS Program

One of the most common causes of this error message is multiple PIFs in the program's directory. Watch for programs that install their own default PIFs. If you install the program in a different directory or create a second PIF, File Manager tries to start the application using the default values for the first PIF.

Gaining Access to Floppy Drives While in a DOS Program

If you encounter problems when you try to access a floppy drive while running a DOS program under Windows, try setting IRQ9Global=Yes in the [386 Enh] section of SYSTEM.INI. If this doesn't work, try to disable the Monitor Ports option and set Video Memory to Text instead of High Graphics in the Advanced options for the application's PIF.

Keeping a DOS Prompt Window

Sometimes you need to run a batch file to set up certain parameters in a DOS session under Windows. This might pose a problem because the DOS session closes after the batch file runs. To keep the DOS window open, add one line to your batch file: add **%COMSPEC%** as the last line. The environmental variable COMSPEC, framed by percent signs, represents the location of your command interpreter, COMMAND.COM. Placing this command in your batch file starts another instance of COMMAND.COM at the end of your batch file, so the DOS session remains on-screen until you type **EXIT**.

Eliminate DOS Session Instructions

Add the following line: **DOSPromptExitInstruc=no** to SYSTEM.INI. Save your changes, then exit and restart Windows. When you shell out to DOS, the instructions no longer clutter your screen. All you see is Microsoft's copyright message and then the DOS prompt.

DOS Session Reminder

It's easy to forget that you're running Windows during full-screen DOS sessions. Here's an easy fix. Open your AUTOEXEC.BAT file and find the PROMPT statement that defines your DOS prompt. Add this line after it: **SET WINPMT=You're running DOS under Windows.PG**. You can change the text that follows WINPMT= to any prompt you want, and you can use any of the special characters allowed in normal PROMPT statements. Reboot your computer and start Windows.

DOS Commands to Avoid While Running Windows

You can run most standard DOS commands such as COMPARE, COPY, FIND, MEM, MODE, and XCOPY in a DOS window, just like from DOS. Avoid commands that modify disk structural information, such as UNDELETE, APPEND, ASSIGN, CHKDSK /F, FDISK, JOIN, RECOVER, and SUBST. Windows and DOS handle disk access differently and therefore these commands are incompatible under Windows.

Making a Quick Exit from a DOS Program

If you keep a DOS window open while you work in Windows, you can't exit Windows unless you switch to and close the DOS window. To change this, launch the PIF Editor and open DOSPRMPT.PIF, the program information file that Windows creates for the DOS prompt. Click the Advanced button, then select the Allow Close When Active box. Windows displays a warning. Double-click OK, then close the PIF Editor and save your changes.

If you try to exit Windows while the DOS command-line window is open, Windows reminds you that a program is still running. Click OK to exit Windows anyway, or click Cancel to return to Windows.

The Allow Close When Active setting works for any DOS applications controlled by a PIF. A DOS application has no clue that Windows is about to shut down, so be sure you saved all your work before you exit the application. Otherwise, you lose any unsaved data.

Tips for Taming Unruly DOS Applications

Many MS-DOS applications were written before Windows was on the market, and many of them were written with the assumption that they would have full control of the computer. As a result, some DOS applications may require special attention.

If you can't paste text from the Clipboard into a DOS application

Open the program's PIF file. Click Advanced, and in the Advanced Options dialog box, uncheck Enable Fast Paste (386 enhanced mode only).

DOS programs stop running when you switch out

If the application stops running until you switch back to it when you switch out of a DOS application by using Alt+Tab, Alt+Esc, or Ctrl+Esc, open the applications PIF and check the Execution: Background box (386 enhanced mode only).

Windows responds with "You cannot run this program in a window or in the background"

When switching out of any DOS program using the Alt+Tab, Alt+Esc, or Ctrl+Esc, Windows responds with, `You cannot run this program in a window or in the background,` or `You cannot run this application while other high-resolution applications are running full-screen.` This usually happens when running Windows and/or a DOS application in Super VGA mode. Try switching to the standard VGA driver in Windows Setup and using the standard VGA driver in the DOS application. Or try another compatible Super VGA driver, such as the generic one that ships with Windows.

Windows hangs when you switch from a DOS application back to Windows

Watch out for older versions of Logitech drivers. LMOUSE.DRV 5.0 and earlier versions are not compatible with Windows 3.1. Switch to the driver that came with Windows, instead of the one that came with your mouse.

Windows says you're "Out of environment space" when starting a DOS application

If you get this error message, do the following:

1. Edit the program's PIF. (If there is no PIF, use Windows Setup to create one.)

2. Double-click the Program Filename box to highlight its contents.

3. Press Ctrl+X to cut the filename, and type `COMMAND.COM`.

4. Position the insertion point at the beginning of the Optional Parameters field.

5. Type `/E:2048  /C` and a space, press Ctrl+V to paste the program filename, insert a space, and save the PIF.

If you still get the `Out of environment space error`, increase the `/E:`xxxx value by 512 and try again. Repeat until you can start the application successfully.

Summary

This chapter covered how to fine tune Windows 3.1 to work with DOS applications.

▶ I discussed how to allocate CPU time between foreground and background applications.

▶ I explained the difference between timeslicing for Windows applications and DOS applications.

▶ I described how to create PIF files.

▶ I told you what parameters you can modify to affect the way DOS programs appear under Windows.

Part IV
Windows for Workgroups Applications

In This Part

Chapter 22
Mail

In This Chapter

▶ Setting up Mail on a workgroup

▶ Locating the post office on a NetWare server

▶ Administrating a workgroup Mail system

▶ Using Microsoft At Work Fax to send mail outside your workgroup

▶ Reaching beyond the workgroup with the post office extensions

▶ The MSMAIL.INI demystified

▶ Using Windows for Workgroups clients in enterprise-wide Mail system

---

Setting Up Mail

The Mail system included with Windows for Workgroups is comprised of two main parts: the *Mail client software*, which installs in your network group, and the *post office*, which is created the first time Mail is run.

Planning the post office

Before you create a Mail system, you should decide where to locate the post office. Because the post office is a simple directory tree, you can locate it just about anywhere in the network, provided that the following guidelines are followed:

- The post office directory must be accessible by all users.

- You must provide enough free space to hold at least all users' unreceived mail — if Mail files are stored on the users' local drives. Users also have the option of storing their Mail files in the post office, which increases the free-space requirement for the post office. An empty post office requires 360K of disk space plus 16K for each user's account.

- Users must have read, write, create, erase, and modify permissions for the directory that contains the post office. (See "Sharing the post office," later in this chapter.)

For consistency with the Microsoft documentation, name the workgroup post office directory WGPO.

Setting up the post office

Once the location of the post office has been determined, start the Mail client by double-clicking on its icon in the Network group in Program Manager. Figure 22-1 shows the Welcome to Mail dialog box.

Figure 22-1: Welcome to Mail dialog box.

Select the Create a New Workgroup Post Office button and click OK. A message box confirming that you want to create a new post office appears. Click Yes; a dialog box opens that asks you to specify the location of the post office.

You can create the post office on a local hard drive or select a location for the post office on a network drive by using the Network button.

Although the Windows for Workgroups Mail system allows you to create multiple post offices on your network, users must have accounts in the same post office if they are to send messages to each other. Because the choice of post office is made the first time Mail is run, exercise caution when making this choice.

If you actually need multiple post offices, you need the "full" MS Mail package. See "Reaching beyond the workgroup with the Post Office Upgrade" and "Understanding Windows for Workgroups in the Enterprise" later in this chapter for more information on the "full" MS Mail package.

One approach to ensuring that the Mail system is set up properly is to set up the computer that will contain the post office before Windows for Workgroups is installed on the other computers on the network. Then go to the other computers and set up Windows for Workgroups on them and immediately return to the Mail system and select the post office that you created. In this way, users do not have an opportunity to accidentally create a new post office.

Restarting the Mail initialization procedure

The first time you run the Windows for Workgroups Mail system, you are presented with two options: to connect to an existing post office or to create a new post office. After you make your selection, you cannot go back and change it. To change your initial selection, you must reinitialize Mail or trick it into thinking it's performing a new installation and then select the option that you want.

The Mail initialization procedure is controlled by the `CustomInitHandler=` setting in the MSMAIL.INI file, which looks like this:

```
CustomInitHandler=WGPOMGR.DLL,<procedure #>
```

The MSMAIL.INI file is described in detail later in this chapter.

Each time you launch Mail, it checks the MSMAIL.INI file for the `CustomInitHandler=` setting. If it finds this setting, Mail begins executing the procedure defined by the setting's parameters.

The file named WGPOMGR.DLL, in this case, contains a procedure that displays the Connect Or Create dialog box, which allows you to either connect to an existing remote post office or create a new workgroup post office. Choosing the Cancel button causes WGPOMGR.DLL to close Mail. If you choose OK, WGPOMGR.DLL removes the `CustomInitHandler=` line from the MSMAIL.INI file and returns to Mail, automatically signing you in to the post office.

If you need to reinitialize Mail without reinstalling the product, follow these steps:

1. Open the MSMAIL.INI file using System Engineer or an ASCII editor such as Microsoft Windows Notepad.

2. Locate the `ServerPath=` and the `login=` lines and comment them out by typing a semicolon (`;`) at the beginning of each line.

3. Look for the `CustomInitHandler=` line and modify it as follows:

   ```
   CustomInitHandler=WGPOMGR .DLL,10
   ```

   If this lines does not exist in your MSMAIL.INI file, add it to the `[Microsoft Mail]` section of the file.

4. Start Mail; the initialization procedure begins.

Setting up a post office across a network

You can set up the workgroup post office from one computer to another computer across the network. Suppose that you set up and administer the post office from computer A, a Windows for Workgroups machine. Also suppose that the post office files are located on computer B, which has server/sharing capabilities provided by a Windows for Workgroups machine, a LAN Manager 2.x server, or a Novell server.

To set up your post office across such a network, follow these steps:

1. After setting up Windows for Workgroups on computer A, start Mail by clicking the Mail icon in the Network group in Program Manager.

2. Choose Create A New Workgroup Post Office from the dialog box that pops up.

3. Connect to computer B by choosing the Network button. If computer B is running Windows for Workgroups or LAN Manager 2.1 server, enter the server name and share name (<*server**share*>) to indicate where you want the post office created; then select OK.

You must have access rights to the server and the share.

If computer B is a Novell server, you must log on to the Novell server and have the correct permissions before connecting to the server. Use the following naming convention:

```
server/share:directory \\server\share\directory remapped
drive:\directory
```

If you are installing the post office on a Novell NetWare server, make sure that you are logged in as the supervisor, not as a user with supervisor equivalence. The files and directories in the post office must be owned by the supervisor for proper operation to occur.

Sharing the post office

The final step in setting up your workgroup Mail system is to make the directory tree containing the post office available for other users. The way this task is done varies according to the type of network server on which the post office is located.

Microsoft networks

To share the workgroup post office on a Windows for Workgroups server or a Windows NT server, start File Manager, highlight the post office directory, and select Disk⇨Share As. Make certain that WGPO is chosen as the share name.

All users of the post office need full access to the directory, so select the Full Access button and specify a Full Access password if you want to prevent some network users from accessing the post office.

Windows NT has user-level security. In place of the Full Access button, Windows NT provides a Permissions button. After clicking on the Permissions button, give Full Access permissions to all the users who need access to the post office. (On most networks, you can give the group "Everyone" Full Access.)

Novell NetWare

Novell NetWare is a server-based network operating system. Instead of sharing the post office directory, you give the users of the post office read, write, create, erase, and modify *rights* to the directory. Do this with the NetWare SYSCON or FILER utilities.

NetWare makes post office connections to the workgroup post office with the `ServerPath=` entry in the MSMAIL.INI file, which indicates the appropriate NetWare Workgroup post office location. You cannot share a redirected network drive in Windows for Workgroups.

Creating the administrator account

After properly setting up the post office, a dialog box opens that lets you specify the details of the administrator account (see Table 22-1 for account detail entries). If you follow the guidelines for allowing multiple Mail users on one computer (presented later in this chapter), the administrator can be named something like *Administrator*; otherwise, the administrator account should have the same account name as the user of the computer (see the next section for suggested account name conventions).

The computer from which you set up the post office becomes the *administrator computer*. All administrative tasks (described later in this chapter) must be done from this computer. The post office does *not* have to be located on the administrator computer.

Setting up users

After the post office is set up and the Administrator account created, the next step is to create the users' accounts.

Naming user accounts

There are a number of naming conventions for computer accounts in use. One of the most popular conventions, and in my opinion the best one, takes the user's first name and last initial as his or her mailbox name. If another user already has this mailbox name, additional letters from the last name are added until a unique mailbox name is created.

For example, using this convention, the mailbox names for the authors of this book are VALDAH and JAMESB. If JAMESB already exists, the next candidate would be JAMESBL, and so on.

One of the ways a user's mailbox can be created is through the Post Office Manager, which is installed on the administrator's computer when the post office is created. By creating user mailboxes with the Post Office Manager, the administrator can ensure that naming conventions are followed. In addition, it may be easier and more efficient to set up mailboxes for the entire company at once rather than one user at a time in the field. For more information on the Post Office Manager, see "Administrative Tasks," later in this chapter.

Connecting to the post office

Setting up a user's Mail client starts by double-clicking the Mail icon in the Network group in Program Manager. The Welcome to Mail dialog box appears (which Figure 22-1 shows). Choose the Connect to an existing post office option. Mail asks whether you already have an account. If the administrator has already created a mailbox for you, select Yes and enter your mailbox name and password.

If you need to set up your own mailbox, select No when Mail asks whether you already have an account. An Account Details dialog box appears. Table 22-1 describes the information necessary to define a Mail account.

Table 22-1	Mail Account Details
Item	*Description*
Name	The user's full name. This is the name that appears in the address book.
Mailbox	The mailbox name used to log in to Mail.
Password	The user's mailbox password. The password does not have to be the same as the user's network password.
Phone #1	(Optional) The user's phone number.
Phone #2	(Optional) If the user has a second phone number, put it here.
Office	(Optional) The user's office location.
Department	(Optional) The user's department's name.
Notes	(Optional) Any notes or comments about this account.

Administrating a Workgroup Mail System

The administrator of a workgroup Mail system has several tasks to perform on a regular basis:

- Adding new users
- Removing old users

- Maintaining existing users
- Managing disk space used by the post office

In addition, a number of other tasks may need to be performed occasionally.

Administrative Tasks

The administrator is responsible for performing a number of administrative tasks. To perform adminstrative tasks, start the Mail client on the adminstrative computer and select Mail⇨Post Office Manager.

Adding new users

To add a new user, click the Add User button. The User Details dialog box opens. See Table 22-1 for a description of the entries in this dialog box.

Removing old users

To remove an existing Mail user, highlight that user in the Post Office Manager and click the Remove User button. You are asked to confirm that you actually want to delete the user.

Removing a user permanently deletes the user's mailbox from the system.

Maintaining existing users

Sometimes users forget their passwords or change their names, jobs, or locations. To change a user's account, click the Details button in Post Office Manager. You can change any of the account details listed in Table 22-1.

Managing disk space

Any Mail user can create *shared folders:* Mail folders stored in the post office and available to all users. When messages in shared folders are deleted, the disk space used by the messages is not automatically recovered. Instead, the administrator must *compress* the folders using the Post Office Manager.

A shared folder must not be in use while being compressed. Always ask all users to close all shared folders before starting the compress function.

To compress a shared folder, start the Post Office Manager and click the Shared Folders button. A dialog box opens showing the status of all shared folders on the system. Select the Compress button to recover all recoverable space in the shared folders.

One of the improvements Microsoft made to Mail in Windows for Workgroups 3.11 was to give the option of storing mail files on the post office. A side effect of storing the mail file on the post office is that multiple mail users can share the same computer.

See "Storing mail in the post office" later in this chapter for details of how to set this option.

Handling administrative problems

In addition to the day-to-day administrative tasks described in the preceding sections, you may have other administrative tasks. Some are described in the following sections.

Resolving local post office connection problems

Remember that the post office can reside on any appropriate computer designated by the administrator during set up. If a Windows for Workgroups Mail administrator sets up the post office on another workgroup user's computer, that user cannot connect to the post office. When the local user attempts to connect to the post office, Mail responds with one of the following error messages:

```
The selected network path cannot be found
This operation is not supported on this machine
```

You may think that this problem is merely a browsing problem and that all you need to do is insert the local path to specify the post office location. Indeed, Windows for Workgroups Mail uses uniform naming conventions (UNC) to specify the location of the post office. However, you cannot use UNC to connect users to a share on their local machine.

You can get around this problem if you edit or create a new MSMAIL.INI file for the local user's computer:

1. Copy the MSMAIL.INI file from any computer that is already connected to the post office.

2. Edit the MSMAIL.INI file for the local user's computer. Look for (or add) the following line in the [MSMail] section of MSMAIL.INI:

```
ServerPath= "local path"
```

Insert the name of the local path that hosts the post office, as set up by the Mail administrator:

```
login= "local user's mailbox"
```

3. Copy the newly edited MSMAIL.INI file to the WINDOWS directory on the local user's computer.

You can use the Mail administrator's MSMAIL.INI file as the source for the MSMAIL.INI file for the local user's computer. Just remember to remove all references to the WGPOMGR.DLL file.

Moving a post office from one machine to another

If you are upgrading equipment and want to transfer a post office from one server to another without changing administrators, you can do so. Follow these steps:

1. Make sure that you have full access to the new post office share.

2. Using File Manager, drag the post office directory to the target shared directory. (Pay careful attention to make sure that you select all the post office subdirectories.)

3. Edit the MSMAIL.INI files for each user, including the administrator. Change the ServerPath= line to point to the new server location:

```
ServerPath=\\newservr\wgpo
```

Changing the post office administrator

Although you perform all administrative tasks on the computer from which you set up the post office, there may be instances in which you want to transfer administrator responsibilities from one person to another. If computer A is the current post office administrator and you want computer B to become the new post office administrator, follow these steps:

Name: Mailbox: Password: (You must know the passwords for Admin1 and Admin2.)

1. Make a copy the MSMAIL.INI file located on computer A to a floppy disk. You use this copy to establish the administrator account on computer B.

2. From computer A, log on to Mail, select the Mail option, and then select Post Office Manager.

3. Select the Details option and write down the required information for Admin1 and Admin2 (obtain the passwords from the administrators; passwords don't appear in the Details dialog box).

4. If the administrator on computer A no longer needs a Mail account, delete the user account for Admin2 and edit the details of the computer A account to match the new post office administrator's account on computer B.

5. Edit the MSMAIL.INI file on computer A, removing the following lines from the [Custom Commands] section:

```
WGPOMgr1=3.0;Mail;;13 WGPOMgr2=3.0;Mail;&Post office
Manager...;14;WGPOMGR.DLL;0;;Manage Workgroup Post
office;MSMAIL.HLP;2870
```

6. Exit and sign out of Mail on computer A.

7. On computer B, open the MSMAIL.INI file you copied to the floppy disk. Using a text editor, cut the following lines from this file:

```
WGPOMgr1=3.0;Mail;;13 WGPOMgr2=3.0;Mail;&Post office
Manager...;14;WGPOMGR.DLL;0;;Manage Workgroup Post
office;MSMAIL.HLP;2870
```

Although the line mentioned above has been split into multiple lines so that I can show you all of the line, the entire line must appear on a single line in your MSMAIL.INI file.

8. Paste these lines into the [Custom Commands] section of computer B's MSMAIL.INI file, making sure that these lines are the last two lines in the [Custom Commands] section.

9. Save the changes to computer B's MSMAIL.INI file and start Mail.

A message may appear, stating that Mail was unable to find your MMF file. A dialog box then appears, displaying the MMF file that was detected. Select that MMF and choose OK to select the MMF file found on the hard disk drive.

10. Select the Mail option to verify that the post office administrator option is now available on computer B.

11. If desired or necessary, create a user account for computer B.

Setting User Preferences

Figure 22-2 shows the Mail Options dialog box. You access it by selecting Mail⇨Options from the Mail client. Table 22-2 summarizes the configurable settings in this dialog box.

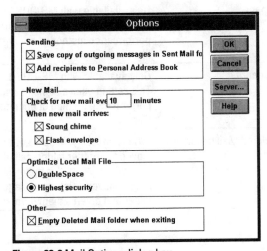

Figure 22-2: Mail Options dialog box.

Table 22-2	Mail Options	
Section	*Item*	*Description*
Sending	Save copy of outgoing messages in Sent Mail folder	Automatically keeps a copy of outgoing messages.
	Add recipients to Personal Address Book	Every user can have a private Personal Address Book. This option automatically adds the recipients of mail sent by you to your Personal Address Book.
New Mail	Check for new mail every *x* minutes	This option specifies how often Mail should check for new messages. This option also controls when Mail sends messages you have written.
	Sound chime	If this box is checked, Mail plays the sound associated with the MailBeep item in the Sound item in the Control Panel.

(continued)

Section	Item	Description
	Flash envelope	If this box is checked, the mouse pointer briefly becomes an image of an envelope when new mail is received.
Optimize Local Mail File	DoubleSpace	Only available with MS-DOS 6.0 or later. This setting uses a lower-security, higher-performance method of encrypting the Mail file.
	Highest security	Only available with MS-DOS 6.0 or later. This setting uses a higher-security, lower-performance method of encrypting the Mail file.
Other	Empty deleted Mail folder when exiting	When a message is deleted, it is actually moved to another folder, called the Deleted Mail folder. When this option is checked, Mail removes deleted messages from this folder and deletes them permanently.

Table 22-2 (continued)

Storing Mail files

Clicking on the Server button brings up a dialog box that lets you pick where you want the file that holds your mail stored. There are two possibilities: storing the Mail file in the post office or storing it on the user's local hard drive.

Storing mail in the post office

Give strong consideration to the location in which you store Mail files. There are advantages to storing your Mail file in the post office:

■ Storing mail in the post office enables centralized backup of the Mail files. Many network administrators only back up data on servers, meaning that a locally stored Mail file — and any mail stored in it — could be lost if the local hard drive fails.

■ Storing the Mail file on the server means that more than one Mail user can use a given computer. This also means that any given user can access his or her mail from any computer that also is set to store Mail files in the post office.

Storing mail in a local file

In highly decentralized networks in which there is no central server with a large disk, it may make sense to store Mail files on local hard drives. In these types of networks, each computer usually has a single user who is responsible for maintaining his or her own resources, including backup.

If the user needs the ability to work *offline* (by taking the computer off of the network), the Mail file must be stored locally.

Many companies have notebook computers that different staff members take with them out of the office. For example, a notebook might be shared by the company's executives when they take business trips.

Because different users need to access Mail on this computer, set up the Mail system on the executives' workstations and on the notebook to store mail in the post office. When someone takes the notebook out of the office, he or she first logs into Mail on the notebook and sets the Mail file to a local file. Mail automatically moves the user's mailbox and Personal Address Book to the notebook.

When the user is on the road, disconnected from the network, Mail detects the lack of a network and goes into offline mode. In offline mode, the user can read the messages stored in the local file, and even send messages (although they won't actually be transmitted until the user has reconnected to the network). If the user needs to be able to transmit messages while on the road, the Microsoft Remote Mail client for Windows can be used if the post office has been upgraded with the Microsoft Post Office Upgrade package.

Once the computer is hooked back up to the network, the user goes into Mail; the user's notebook mailbox is merged with the mailbox on the network. Then the user can set his or her Mail file to store in the post office and go back to working on their other workstation. 👋

Keeping copies of mail in both places

When a user reads his or her mail, Mail takes messages out of the *mailbag* in the post office and moves them into the user's Mail file. If the user needs the ability to dial into the Mail system (using the full Microsoft Mail system, as described later in this chapter), the user should mark the Copy Inbox on Post Office for Dialing Access check box in the Mail⇨Options⇨Server dialog box.

Sending electronic mail via Microsoft At Work Fax

If you have personnel in remote offices and want to include them in your e-mail system, one cost-effective way is to use the Microsoft At Work Fax capabilities included in Windows for Workgroups 3.11.

Using Microsoft at Work Fax, you can send binary files and e-mail over a fax connection, provided that both ends have EIA Class 1 fax modems. Microsoft At Work Fax includes the ability to send mail from Mail-aware applications (using MAPI) and lets you imbed objects and binary attachments.

See Chapter 25, "Microsoft at Work Fax" for more information.

Reaching beyond the workgroup with the Post Office Upgrade

The Microsoft Post Office Upgrade package (also known as the Mail and Schedule+ Extensions for Windows for Workgroups) provides the tools to upgrade a workgroup post office to a full Microsoft Mail 3.x post office. The upgrade package gives you the ability to send mail between multiple workgroups, to use gateways to other mail systems, and provides a means for remote users to dial in and access their mail.

Controlling Mail Configurations with MSMAIL.INI

All forms of Microsoft Mail, including the workgroup version of Mail included with Windows for Workgroups, store user settings in the MSMAIL.INI file, located in the WINDOWS directory.

Settings that apply to the Mail system as a whole, such as specialized forms created with the Microsoft Electronic Forms Designer, can be stored in a file in the post office called SHARED.INI. SHARED.INI can contain two sections: [Custom Commands] and [Custom Messages], which are identical to their MSMAIL.INI counterparts described in this part of the chapter. For more information on the MS Electronic Forms Designer, see *Windows 3.1 Connectivity SECRETS,* also published by IDG Books Worldwide.

[Address Book] section

The entries in this section contain settings concerning Mail's address books.

The entries in this section are created and modified by the Mail client software. Some of these entries are duplicated, or linked, to entries that Mail makes in the user's Mail file (the file with the extension MMF). For this reason, you should never change anything in this section.

NSID length

This setting holds the length of the default directory Name Service Identifier entry.

Setting: `Default ID Data=bytes`

NSID ID

This setting is the value of the NSID for the directory the user has chosen as the default.

Setting: `Directory ID=string of hex bytes`

NSID name

This is the name of the directory displayed when the Address Book dialog box opens.

Setting: `Directory Name=name`

[Custom Commands] section

The settings in this section specify custom commands that are made part of the Mail menus. Each entry must be on a single line in the file. Each of the lines has the following format:

```
tag=version;menu;name;position;DLL name;command;event
map;status text; help file;help context;
```

Many of the items are optional. If one is omitted, the semicolon used to separate the items must be included as a placeholder. See Table 22-3 for information on the items that make up the entries in this section.

Table 22-3	Custom Command Items
Item	**Description**
tag	Identifies the command to someone reading the MSMAIL.INI file.
version	The version number of Mail with which the command is compatible.
menu	The Mail menu to which the custom command is added.
name	The command name that appears on the menu. An ampersand (&) can be placed just before the letter to be used as an Alt+key shortcut.

(continued)

Table 22-3 (continued)

Item	Description
position	The position within the menu at which the command appears. The first position is number 0; the second, number 1, and so on.; the end of the menu is -1.
DLL name	The path name of the Dynamic Link Library (DLL) that provides the custom command.
command	The string passed as a parameter to the DLL.
event map	A sequence of up to 16 digits, each a 0 or a 1, representing 16 individual events. Each digit indicates whether the DLL should be called for a specific event (a 1 indicates that the DLL should be called). In Windows for Workgroups 3.11, only the first three events are defined — the rest of the digits must be 0.
	If the first digit is set to 1, the DLL is called at Mail start-up; if the second digit is set to 1, the DLL is called at Mail exit; if the third digit is set to 1, the DLL is called at the arrival of a new message.
status text	The text displayed on the status bar when the user points to the command in the menu.
help file	The Windows help file invoked when the user presses F1 when the command is selected.
help context	The parameter passed to the Windows Help program along with the help filename. The help context value indicates the entry in the help file for this command. Use -1 if there is no specific entry in the help file.

[Custom Messages] section

Custom messages are used by Mail-aware and Mail-enabled applications to send information to other instances of themselves, to implement special forms, and so on.

Similar to the [Custom Commands] section, the [Custom Messages] section is made up of entries, each of which must be on a single line. The entries have the following form:

```
class=version;menu;name;position;DLL name;command;operation
map;status text;help file;help context
```

Many of the items are optional. If one is omitted, the semicolon used to separate the items must be included as a place holder. See Table 22-4 for information on the items that make up the entries in this section.

Table 22-4	Custom Messages Items
Item	**Description**
class	The unique identifier for the message type. Mail places this string in messages and uses it to call custom-message DLLs based on its value.
version	The version of Mail with which the custom message is compatible.
menu	The menu to which the compose command for the message type is added.
name	The command name that appears on the menu. An ampersand (&) can be placed just before the letter to be used as an Alt+key shortcut.
position	The position in the menu at which the command appears. The first item is number 0; the second, number 1, and so on; use -1 to place the command at the end of the menu.
DLL name	The path name to the command's Dynamic Link Library (DLL).
command	The string passed as a parameter to the DLL.
operation map	A sequence of up to 16 digits, each can be a 0, 1 or 2. A 0 means that Mail should perform its usual operation on the custom message. A 1 means that the DLL should be called to handle the operation. A 2 means that the operation should be completely disabled. The meaning of the digit positions, starting from the left, are listed in Table 22-5.
status text	The text displayed on the status line when the user points to the command in the menu.
help file	The Windows help file invoked when the user presses F1 when the command is selected.
help context	The parameter passed to the Windows Help program along with the help filename. If there is no specific entry in the help file for this command, set this item to -1.

Table 22-5	Operation Map Digits
Position (from left)	**Operation**
0	Compose
1	File.Open
2	Mail.Reply
3	Mail.Reply to All
4	Mail.Forward
5	File.Print
6	File.Save as
7	Arrival of new mail

[Mac FileTypes] section

The entries in this section are used to map Macintosh file-type and creator tags to MS-DOS file extensions so that Mail can launch the appropriate application to handle an attachment sent from a Macintosh Mail client. This section is normally used only with the full (nonworkgroup) Mail client.

The entries in this section are of one of two forms:

```
creator:type=.extension
:type=.extension
```

Both *creator* and *type* are sequences of four characters, possibly including blanks.

[MS Proofing Tools] section

This section is used by the spelling checker that comes with the full version of MS Mail.

Setting the custom dictionary

Setting: `CustomDict=keyname`

This setting is the name of an entry in the `[MS Proofing Tools]` section of the WIN.INI file that specifies the path to the custom dictionary.

Specifying a spelling checker

Setting: `Spelling=keyname`

This entry lets Mail use a spelling checker that you may be using with another Microsoft application. It is the name of an entry in the `[MS Proofing Tools]` section of WIN.INI.

[Custom Menus] section

This section consists of entries that specify menu names to be added to the Mail menu bar. The Windows for Workgroups 3.11 implementation of Microsoft At Work Fax uses an entry in this section, for example, to add a fax item to the menu bar.

Each entry must be on a single line with the following format. Table 22-6 lists the details of the items in each line.

```
tag=version;name;name to follow;status text
```

Table 22-6	Custom Menu Items
Item	**Description**
tag	Identifies the command to someone reading the INI file.
version	The version of Mail with which the commands to be added to this menu are compatible.
name	The command name that appears on the menu. An ampersand (&) can be placed just before the letter to be used as an Alt+key shortcut.
name to follow	The name of an existing menu after which this menu is to be added.
status text	The text to be displayed in the status bar when the user points to this menu.

[Microsoft Mail] section

The behavior of the Mail program and the Microsoft Mail transport and name service is controlled by the entries in this section. Many of these entries are present only if the full Microsoft Mail system is installed.

Spooler latency interval

Setting: CheckLatencyInterval=*seconds*

Default: 30

This setting sets the length of time the spooler is to wait without work before it reinitializes its latency algorithm.

Exported folder location

Setting: ExportMmfFile=*pathname*

This setting is the path name of the MMF file that was the last file to which a Mail folder was exported. It is used as the default value in the Export Folders dialog box.

Alternate (fixed) font

Setting: FixedFont=*facename, size*, 0 | 1, 0 | 1

This entry identifies a fixed font used as an alternative to the standard proportional font when reading messages. The third and fourth parameters are flags for bold and italic, respectively.

Although Mail intends that a fixed-pitch font be used for displaying Mail messages of a tabular nature (so that columns line up), any font name can actually be used.

Spooler scan interval

Setting: `ForceScanInterval=seconds`

Default: 300 (5 minutes)

This setting sets the length of time that the spooler, when it has outstanding work to do, waits before it begins to ask for idle time more frequently.

Global address list only

Setting: `GALOnly= 0 | 1`

Default: 0

When this setting is set to 1, the Mail address book displays only the Global Address List (GAL) and the Personal Address Book. This setting is valid only with post offices that are Mail for PC Networks V3.0, 3.0b, or 3.2 with GAL support enabled — including workgroup post offices upgraded with the Post Office Upgrade.

Spooler idle interval

Setting: `IdleRequiredInterval=seconds`

Default: 2

This entry causes the spooler to defer its work temporarily if the system has serviced an interactive request within the specified interval.

Local MMF file

Setting: `LocalMMF=0 | 1`

Default: 0

If this entry is 1, the Mail file is created in the WINDOWS directory rather than in the post office.

Mailbox login name

Setting: `Login=name`

This entry specifies the default mailbox name that appears in the Login dialog box.

New mail chime

Setting: MailBeep=*pathname*

Default: Blank (Mail beeps twice)

This entry sets the path to a Windows WAV file to be used as the mail chime when the Sound Chime option in the Mail Options dialog is checked.

Temporary file location

Setting: MailTmp=*pathname*

Default: Value of the TEMP environment variable; if none, the Windows directory

This is the directory in which Mail places temporary copies of attached files.

MAPI help file

Setting: MAPIHelp=*pathname*

Default: MSMAIL.HLP in the WINDOWS directory

This setting is the location of the MAPI help file used to provide help when it is requested from any of the dialog boxes displayed by the MAPI support functions.

Print multiple notes on a page

Setting: Multi-Message=0 | 1

Default: 1

This entry is the default for the Print multiple notes on a page option in the Mail Print dialog box. When set to 1, the option is checked.

NetBIOS usage

Setting: 1

If this entry is set to 1, the Mail transport uses NetBIOS to notify users of the arrival of new mail from users in the local post office.

If this entry is set to 1 and Mail is open when you exit Windows for Workgroups, you see the following error message:

```
Application was sending on network
```

To avoid this error, set this item to 0 with Windows for Workgroups.

Download new messages at startup

Setting: NewMsgsAtStartup=0 | 1

Default: 0

If this entry is set to 1, Mail downloads new messages as quickly as possible at startup (but you have to wait for it to finish before you can do anything else in Mail). When set to 0, new mail comes in, but more slowly than if it's set to 1.

Automatically open the next message

Setting: NextOnMoveDelete=0 | 1 | -1

Default: 1

When this setting is set to 1, Mail automatically opens the next message in a folder when the current message is deleted or moved. When set to -1, the previous message is opened. If set to 0, Mail just closes the Read Note window.

Disable Check for New Mail option in Mail⇨Options dialog box

Setting: NoCheckInterval=0 | 1

Default: 0

If this entry is set to 1, the Check for new mail every *x* minutes field in the Mail⇨Options dialog box is disabled, preventing the user from changing the setting.

Normal mail font

Setting: NormalFont=*facename, size*, 0 | 1, 0 | 1

Default: Helv, 10, 0, 0

This entry sets the font Mail normally uses to display messages. It is usually a proportionally spaced font. The third and fourth parameters are flags for bold and italic respectively.

Disable the Server button

Setting: NoServerOptions=0 | 1

Default: 0

When this entry is set to 1, the Server button in the Mail⇨Options dialog box is disabled, preventing the user from moving his or her message file.

Location of the local Mail file

Setting: OfflineMessages=*pathname*

This entry is created and removed by Mail when you choose to store your Mail file off the post office.

Old location of the Mail file

Setting: OldStorePath=*pathname*

This entry is written by Mail while it moves the message file (in response to a change in the Mail⇨Options⇨Server dialog box). It contains the original path to the file if the file was originally stored off the post office. This entry is removed once the move is successfully completed. The line is visible only if a system crash occurs during a move.

Automatically supply the password

Setting: Password=*password*

Default: (item omitted)

This entry, in conjunction with the Login entry, tells Mail your account login information without your having to type it into the dialog box.

If this entry is omitted, Mail always asks for your password, even if your password is blank.

Use the Remember Password check box in the Mail Login screen when running Windows for Workgroups 3.11. Instead of storing the password in this entry, Mail adds it to the user's encrypted password list file.

Mail polling interval

Setting: PollingInterval=*minutes*

Default: (item omitted; Mail uses 10 minutes as default)

This setting is the default value for the Check for new mail every *x* minutes option. It is intended for use by administrators to provide a uniform initial polling interval. Once the Mail client has been run, the polling value is stored in the MMF file and can be changed only through the Mail client.

Default printer

Setting: `Printer=printer name, driver name, port`

Default: Windows default printer

This is the default printer Mail uses to print messages.

Font used to print messages

Setting: `PrintFont=points`

Default: 10

This entry sets the default point size for the font used by Mail to print Mail messages. The actual font used to print the message is the font used to display the message (as specified by either the `FixedFont` or the `NormalFont` setting described earlier in this chapter).

Spooler cycle interval

Setting: `PumpCycleInterval=seconds`

Default: 60, or the value specified in the Check for new mail every *x* minutes item in the Mail⇨Options dialog box

This entry is intended for use only by transport implementers. Changing this value has a significant effect on system performance; the entry should be used only for debugging.

Changes the intervals at which the spooler checks for new mail, and so on.

Reply prefix

Setting: `ReplyPrefix="string"`

Default: Empty

This string is used to distinguish comments from the original message when replying to Mail. Both the greater-than symbol (>) and the vertical bar (I), followed by a space, are popular choices. The string must be enclosed in quotation marks.

Spooler system availability check

Setting: ScanAgainInterval=*seconds*

Default: 2

This setting controls how often the spooler checks the availability of the system when it defers work because of higher-priority interactive tasks.

Prompt for password when restore from icon state

Setting: Security=0 | 1

Default: 0

When this entry is set to 1, Mail prompts for your password when its window is restored from the icon state. This setting prevents others from seeing your messages if you minimize Mail before leaving your terminal.

Post office drive

Setting: ServerDrive=*drive letter*

Default: M

This entry, when present, causes Mail to look for the post office in the default directory on the specified drive. The MAIL.DAT file (when present) and ServerPath entry take precedence over this entry.

Server share password

Setting: ServerPassword=*password*

This entry is the password needed to connect to the server specified by the ServerPath entry.

Post office location

Setting: ServerPath=*pathname* | ServerPath=*server**share**path password*

This entry tells Mail where to look for the post office. It has two forms: a normal path name and a UNC format, with the password separated from the UNC path name by a space. If the UNC path name contains spaces, the password must be specified in the ServerPassword entry.

If the UNC form is used, Mail connects to the file server dynamically, without using a drive letter.

SHARED.INI path

Setting: SharedExtensionsDir=*path* |
            SharedExtensionsDir=*server**share**path password*

This entry tells Mail the directory in which SHARED.INI is located. SHARED.INI is described earlier in this chapter.

Enable shared folders

Setting: SharedFolders=0 | 1

Default: 1 if the Logon entry in the [Providers] section is MSSFS, 0
            otherwise

This entry enables the use of Mail shared folders.

Spooler transient-error retry time

Setting: SpoolerBackoffInterval=*milliseconds*

Default: 2000

This entry specifies how long the spooler waits before retrying an operation that has failed because of a Mail server error classified as transient (for example, if the Mail file is locked).

Spooler fatal-error retry time

Setting: SpoolerReconnectInterval=*seconds*

Default: 60

This entry specifies how long the Mail spooler waits before retrying an operation that has failed because of an error considered fatal (for example, a lost network connection).

Gateway header handling

Setting: StripGatewayHeaders=0 | 1

Default: 1

When this entry is set to 1, message headers (above the dashed line) are stripped from Mail messages that arrive through a gateway. Setting this entry to 0 allows you to see the extended information supplied by the gateways, such as routing information, and so on.

MSMAIL.EXE version information

Setting: `WG=0 | 1`

This entry is set to 1 if MSMAIL.EXE detects it is the Windows for Workgroups version. It determines this by checking the copyright information stamped into the MSMAIL.EXE file. This setting determines whether the title bar reads `Mail` or `Microsoft Mail`.

Main window coordinate

Setting: `Window=left right top bottom zoom toolbar statusbar scrollbars`

Default: Window position determined by Windows; zoom normal; toolbar on; status bar on; scroll bars on

The first four numbers of this entry are pixel coordinates of the four sides of the main window: left, right, top, and bottom. The fifth number is 1 if the main window is in a normal state, 2 if it is maximized, and 3 if it is minimized. The last three numbers determine whether the toolbar, status bar, and scroll bars are displayed (if these options are set to 1, the item is displayed).

[MMF] section

Most of the entries in this section control the automatic compression of Mail message files. When enabled, automatic compression uses idle time on your computer to recover disk space freed by deleting messages.

Automatic file-close time

Setting: `AutoDisconnectInterval=minutes`

Default: `60`

This entry controls the amount of system idle time that must occur before a Mail file not stored locally is closed. Any system activity automatically reopens the file. This entry ensures that your Mail file can be backed up when the administrator backs up the Mail server. If the Mail file is stored locally, it must be backed up by the user.

When this entry is set to 0, the Mail file is closed only when the user exits and signs out of Mail. This setting should be larger than the `Secs_Till_Fast_Compress` setting so that Mail has time to compress the file before it is closed.

Free kilobyte count to start compression

Setting: `Kb_Free_Start_Compress=number of kilobytes`

Default: 300

The background-compression algorithm starts when it detects at least this much recoverable space in the message file.

Free kilobyte compression stop

Setting: `Kb_Free_Stop_Compress=kilobytes`

Default: 100

This entry indicates the point at which automatic compression should shut down. This entry prevents the background algorithm from wasting resources trying to recover every bit of space.

Disable compression

Setting: `No_Compress=0 | 1`

Default: 0

If this entry is set to 1, background compression of the message file is disabled.

Free space percentage to start compression

Setting: `Percent_Free_Start_compress=percentage`

Default: 10

This entry specifies that background compression should start when the amount of recoverable space rises above the percentage of the message-file size indicated by this setting.

Free space percentage to stop compression

Setting: `Percent_Free_Stop_Compress=percentage`

Default: 5

Background compression of the Mail file stops when the amount of recoverable space drops below this percentage.

Time to switch to fast compression

Setting: Secs_Till_Fast_Compress=*seconds*

Default: 600

The background-compression algorithm has two modes: fast and slow. Compression begins in a slow mode to avoid impacting system performance. After a period of system inactivity longer than this entry, compression switches to fast mode until some user activity occurs.

[Providers] section

This section specifies the components that provide the various services of Mail.

Logon and session management

Setting: Logon=*DLL path name*

Default: MSSFS

This entry is the name of a single DLL (without the DLL extension) that handles logon and session management. Use a full path name if the file is not in a directory in your MS-DOS path or in the Mail executable directory.

System and personal user list handlers

Setting: name=DLL [DLL] ...

Default: MSSFS PABNSP

The DLLs listed in this entry contain functions required for browsing user lists. The order is significant to ambiguous name resolution — once a name is found in a DLL listed, the system does not query the rest. Values are separated by blanks.

Ambiguous name resolution is the process that Mail goes through to turn a name that a user has typed in an address field into a valid mail address. For example, typing "Jim" when the user's name in Mail is actually "Jim Blakely".

Shared folder handler

Setting: SharedFolders=*DLL name*

Default: MSSFS

This entry specifies the single DLL used to read and write shared folders.

Mail transport

Setting: Transport=*DLL name*

Default: MSSFS

The single DLL specified by this setting contains the functions needed for sending and receiving mail.

Understanding Windows for Workgroups in the Enterprise

One of the advantages of using Windows for Workgroups rather than plain Windows 3.1x as the clients for an enterprise-wide Microsoft Mail system is that Windows for Workgroups automatically includes a license for the Mail client software.

Looking at differences between Windows for Workgroups and enterprise Mail

The primary difference between the workgroup version of Mail included with Windows for Workgroups and the enterprise version included with the Microsoft Mail for PC Networks package concerns the post office: Messages in a workgroup post office can be to and from users of that post office only.

In the enterprise (or "full") version of Microsoft Mail, a Mail transfer agent (MTA) can be defined to move messages destined for users whose accounts reside on another post office to that post office. *Gateways* also can be used to connect the Mail system to other types of mail systems such as MCI Mail or the Internet.

Moving messages between post offices

Movement of messages between post offices is accomplished by using one of two external message transfer agents (MTAs). The first, EXTERNAL.EXE, runs on a dedicated MS-DOS workstation and can transfer messages between post offices using network connections or using modems or serial connections.

The second type of MTA is known as the multitasking MTA (MMTA), a specialized version of the MTA that runs on OS/2 version 1.3 (a copy of OS/2 version 1.3 is included in the box). The MMTA is most often used on busy mail systems where a single MTA is not enough. MMTA is also used to provide multiple dial-in connections for other MTAs or remote Mail users.

Looking at gateways to other mail systems

Gateways enable Microsoft Mail post offices to transfer mail to and from other mail systems. As of this writing, gateways between Microsoft Mail and other mail systems generally run on dedicated computers that use MS-DOS and a gateway software. However, Microsoft is in the process of changing Microsoft Mail to a new version that uses Extended MAPI instead of MS-DOS-based transports.

The new MAPI-based version of Microsoft Mail will bring a new level of flexibility to mail systems because users will be able to choose the Mail client they like best and couple it with messaging services that provide the connections they need. Users will also stay compatible with the MAPI-based Mail-aware applications that they currently use.

Summary

Electronic mail is the lifeblood of many organizations. By using this communication medium, you can create what's known as the *virtual office*. The virtual office enables company personnel to share and communicate files and messages. Windows for Workgroups provides many options for connecting team personnel and entire teams. This chapter described the following aspects of the Microsoft Mail system:

▶ Setting up the Windows for Workgroups post office connection.

▶ Strategies and tips for administrating workgroup post offices.

▶ Tips for using Microsoft At Work Fax to reach remote workgroup members.

▶ How to use the MAIL.INI file to control your Mail configuration.

▶ How to integrate workgroup post offices throughout your enterprise.

Chapter 23
Schedule+

S chedule+ is one of the workgroup applications provided with Windows for Workgroups. It is probably one of the easiest-to-use scheduling applications available.

Because of this ease of use, Schedule+ is often the reason network users choose Windows for Workgroups. Because of its tight integration with Mail, Schedule+ brings true workgroup scheduling to Windows.

Workgroup Scheduling means that the members of a workgroup can share scheduling information with other members of the workgroup. With Schedule+, a user can view times that other users are free or busy, and automatically schedule meetings for times when all of the attendees are free.

Schedule+ automatically sends invitations via Mail, and Mail users can automatically accept or decline invitations by pressing a button in a dialog box.

Extending Schedule+ with the Post Office Upgrade

When a Windows for Workgroups post office is upgraded to the full Microsoft Mail post office (using the Post Office Upgrade), the workgroup version of Schedule+ is also upgraded to the full version.

This upgrade adds the ability to do the following:

- Share busy/free information with users of other post offices

- Change the default archival reminder period

- Export schedules to a Sharp Wizard

- Utilize training demos that are included with the upgrade

Accessing Schedule+ Information from Another Application

One of the strengths of Schedule+ is that it uses MAPI to interface with Microsoft Mail and sends invitations via Mail. In addition, Microsoft has published the Schedule+ Access Libraries for C and Visual Basic, which allows developers to access Schedule+ data from within their applications.

One example is the workgroup extensions to Microsoft Project, which are also available as part of the Microsoft Workgroup Templates. These extensions allow a project manager to assign tasks to workers in Microsoft Project, have the workers be informed of their assignments via Mail, and have the tasks automatically added to their Schedule+ task list.

 For more information on the workgroup features of Microsoft applications, including Project, see *Windows 3.1 Connectivity SECRETS,* also published by IDG Books Worldwide.

SCHDPLUS.INI

 Schedule+ uses two Windows INI files to store its configuration information. MSMAIL.INI is used as a source of information about the user, such as Login name. See Chapter 22 for more information on the contents of the MSMAIL.INI file.

The bulk of Schedule+'s configuration information is stored in the SCHDPLUS.INI file, located in the Windows directory. Configuration information that does not appear in either of the MSMAIL.INI or SCHDPLUS.INI files, such as the access privileges that other users have been granted, is stored in the calendar (CAL) file on the post office so that other users may access the information.

[Microsoft Schedule] section

The [Microsoft Schedule] section of SCHDPLUS.INI contains settings that affect the behavior and appearance of Schedule+. These settings affect items such as color and display order.

Schedule+ program location

The program location setting specifies the directory that Schedule+ and its executable files reside in. The setting is used by Mail to find Schedule+ when you receive a meeting-request message.

Setting: AppPath=*path*

Default: Windows directory

Local calendar file path

This local calendar setting points to the location of the last user's local calendar file.

Setting: LocalPath=*path*

Last user

The last user setting is the name of the last user to use Schedule+ on this computer.

Setting: LocalUser=*username*

Current printer

This setting indicates the current printer. The default is the printer the user has selected as the Windows default printer.

Setting: DefaultPrinter=*name, driver, port*

Font Size

The font size setting determines the font size in the Appointment Book and Planner. If this entry is 1, the font is 10 points. If the entry is 2, the font is 8 points.

Setting: LargeFont=*1 | 2*

Default: 2

Appointment Book position

This setting indicates the position of the Appointment Book window on-screen. The numbers represent the coordinates of the sides of the Appointment Book window in the following order: left, right, top, bottom.

Setting: AppointmentView=*left right top bottom*

Schedule+ window location

This setting is the location of the main Schedule+ window. The settings are the pixel coordinates of the edges of the window.

Setting: MainWindow=*left right top bottom*

Status bar

The status bar setting indicates whether the status bar is displayed. If this entry is 1, the status bar is not displayed; if the entry is 0, the status bar is displayed.

Setting: NoStatusBar=*0* | *1*

Default: 0

Messages window position

The Messages setting establishes the coordinates for the Messages window.

Setting: RequestSummary=*left right top bottom*

Appointment Book background color

This background color setting indicates the user's preference for the background color of the Appointment Book. The color numbers correspond to the colors shown in the Options ⇨ Display dialog box, in order.

Setting: ApptBookColor=*color number*

Default: Yellow

Color of lines in Appointment Book

This line color setting indicates the user's preference for the line color of the Appointment Book. The color numbers correspond to the colors shown in the Options ⇨ Display dialog box, in order.

Setting: ApptBookLinesColor=*color number*

Default: Black

Appointment color

This color setting determines the color of your appointments in the Planner. The color numbers correspond to the colors shown in the Options ⇨ Display dialog box, in order.

Setting: UserColor=*colornumber*

Default: Blue

Appointment color for other users

This color setting specifies the color in the Planner for the appointments of other users. The color numbers correspond to the colors shown in the Options ⇨ Display dialog box, in order.

Setting: `OtherColor=colornumber`

Default: Red

Page color

The page color setting indicates the color of the background of the Schedule+ window. The color numbers correspond to the colors shown in the Options ⇨ Display dialog box, in order.

Setting: `PageBackgroundColor= colornumber`

Default: Gray

Planner background color

This color setting indicates the color of the background of the Planner window. The color numbers correspond to the colors shown in the Options ⇨ Display dialog box, in order.

Setting: `PlannerColor=colornumber`

Default: White

Planner Line Color

This color setting indicates the color of the lines in the planner. The color numbers correspond to the colors shown in the Options ⇨ Display dialog box, in order.

Setting: `PlannerLinesColor=colornumber`

Default: Black

First time behavior

The first time setting determines whether an on-line CAL file is created on the post office the first time a Schedule+ user signs on. If the setting is 1, the CAL file is created; if 0, the CAL file is not created.

Setting: `CreateFileFirstTime=0 | 1`

Default: 1

Reminder behavior

This reminder setting controls the Remind Again check box (when the user is reminded of an appointment). If this entry is 1, the user is reminded of appointments at the requested intervals. If set to 0, the user will be reminded of the appointment only once.

Setting: `DefaultRemindAgain=0 | 1`

Default: 0

Reminder interval

This reminder setting controls the number of time units to wait before reminding the user of an appointment after the first reminder.

Setting: `DefaultRemindAgainAmount=timeunits`

Default: 5

Reminder Time Units

This reminder setting determines the type of time units the reminder is using.

Setting: `DefaultRemindAgainUnits=minutes | hours | days | weeks | months`

Default: `minutes`

Demos available

The demos setting indicates whether the demos, which are shipped as part of the Post Office Upgrade, are present. If set to 1, the Help ➪ Demos option is shown. The default is to not show the demos option.

Setting: `DemosEnabled=0 | 1`

Default: 0

Exporting notes

The exporting notes setting indicates whether the user wants to export notes. If set to 0, notes are exported. The default is to export notes.

Setting: `ExportNoNotes=0 | 1`

Default: 0

Exported range

The exported range indicates the range of information to export. If 0, the entire file is exported. If set to one, only a certain range of dates is exported. The default depends upon the driver that actually saves the Schedule+ information in the exported file format.

Setting: ExportRange=0 | 1

Default: Driver dependent

Export file type

The export file type setting indicates the current default file type for exporting. If 0, the schedule information is exported in Schedule+ format; if 1, the information is exported in Text format.

Setting: ExportType=0 | 1

Default: 0

Duplicate appointment handling

The duplicate appointment setting indicates the user's choice about importing duplicate appointments. If this is set to 0, duplicate appointments are imported; if 1, they are not imported.

Setting: ImportDoNotAddDuplicates=0 | 1

Default: 0

Asking about conflicts

This setting determines whether conflicting appointments are added automatically. If this setting is set to 1, the conflicting appointments are added; if 0, the user is asked what to do.

Setting: ImportDoNotAskAboutConflicts=0 | 1

Default: 0

Import file type

The import file type setting determines the format of the import files. If this setting is set to 0, import files are assumed to be in Schedule+ format; if 1, the files are in Windows calendar format.

Setting: ImportType=0 | 1

Default: 0

Start-up setting

The start-up setting determines whether Schedule+ starts up on-line or off-line. If this setting is 0, Schedule+ starts up on-line; if 1, Schedule+ starts up off-line.

Setting: `StartupOffline=0 | 1`

Default: 0

Tasks normally private

When this item is 1, the Private check box in the Task dialog box is automatically checked when creating new tasks. Checking the Private check box prevents other users to whom you have given access to your schedule from seeing the task you are creating. When set to 0, the box is unchecked by default.

Setting: `DefaultPrivateTask=0 | 1`

Default: 1

Sort order for tasks

The sort order for tasks setting determines whether the tasks are sorted by priority, due date, or description. If this setting is 0, tasks are sorted by priority; if 1, by due date; if 2, by description.

Setting: `TaskSortOrder=0 | 1 | 2`

Default: 0

Secondary sort order

This setting indicates whether the secondary sort order is by priority, due date, or description. If this setting is 0, the secondary sort order is by priority; if 1, by due date; if 2, by description.

Setting: `TaskSortSecond=0 | 1 | 2`

Default: 0

Window display order

The window display setting indicates which window appears on top of the display. In this setting, the Schedule+ window is represented by 0, and the Messages window by 1. The first value is the window that is on top; the second value is the window behind the top window.

Setting: `WindowOrder=0 | 1  1 | 0`

Show task list setting

This task list setting controls whether the task list shows all tasks or only the active tasks. If it is set at 1, only the active tasks are displayed; if it is set at 0, all tasks are displayed.

Setting: `ShowActiveTasks=0 | 1`

Default: 0

Task project view

This task setting determines how the tasks are displayed. If this setting is 0, tasks are displayed by project. If set to 1, tasks are not grouped by project.

Setting: `ViewNotByProject=0 | 1`

Default: 0

Screen update frequency

The screen update setting indicates the frequency at which the screen is updated, in centiseconds. A centisecond is one one-hundredth of a second.

Setting: `PollTime=centiseconds`

Default: 6000 (one minute)

Alarm change detection time

The alarm setting controls how often Schedule+ checks for alarm changes.

Setting: `ReminderPollTime=minutes`

Default: 15

CAL file update time

The CAL file update time indicates the time interval in which Schedule+ copies the CAL file from the server to the local workstation.

Setting: `CopyTime=minutes`

Default: 15

Post office update frequency

The post office update frequency setting indicates the time interval that the post office is updated after a change is made.

Setting: `UpdatePostOfficeTime=`*centiseconds*

Default: 6000

[Microsoft Schedule+ Appt Books] section

The `[Microsoft Schedule+ Appt Books]` section of SCHDPLUS.INI tracks other users' Appointment Books that you had open when you last exited Schedule+.

Number of other users' books

This appointment setting indicates the number of other users' Appointment Books you had open when you last exited Schedule+.

Setting: `Count=`*number*

[Microsoft Schedule+ Archives]

The `[Microsoft Schedule+ Archives]` section of SCHDPLUS.INI tracks the open Archive files you had open when you last exited Schedule+.

Open archive file count

This archive setting indicates the number of open Archive files you had open when you last exited Schedule+.

Setting: `Count=`*number*

Summary

In this chapter, I discussed how to optimally configure the Windows for Workgroups Schedule+ application and covered the following:

▶ How to set different color options to change the appearance of Schedule+ windows

▶ How to change the positions of Schedule+ windows

▶ How to set various alarms and timers

▶ How upgrading the post office affects Schedule+

Chapter 24

Extending Windows for Workgroups 3.11 with PC Fax

In This Chapter

▶ Overview of Microsoft At Work technology

▶ Using the Windows for Workgroups PC Fax component to reach beyond your workgroup

▶ Installing and configuring PC Fax

▶ Configuring Microsoft At Work Fax features of PC Fax

▶ Inside the EFAXPUMP.INI file that controls PC Fax

▶ Overcoming the limitations of PC Fax with Delrina WinFax PRO 4.0

This chapter describes the capabilities offered by PC Fax software included with Windows for Workgroups 3.11. PC Fax software is the first implementation of the Microsoft At Work architecture.

The Microsoft At Work Fax architecture provides a set of specifications for sending and receiving messages comprised of binary file attachments or Group-3 facsimiles. The Microsoft At Work architecture also provides for secure messaging through the use of public key encryption and digital signature technology.

With Windows for Workgroups PC Fax and a compatible fax modem, stand-alone and networked computers can take full advantage of the Microsoft At Work Fax features by using the Microsoft Mail client or a mail-enabled application.

PC Fax is the correct name of the fax software included in Windows for Workgroups 3.11. The specification it is written to is the Microsoft At Work Fax specification. Because the implementation in Windows for Workgroups 3.11 is the first commercially available implementation of Microsoft At Work Fax, many writers and publications in the computer industry have mistakenly referred to the PC Fax software as Microsoft At Work Fax; this mistake creates the impression that the limitations of PC Fax are limitations of the Microsoft At Work specification. This is not the case.

To avoid this confusion, we will use the term *PC Fax* to refer to the *implementation* in Windows for Workgroups 3.11 and *Microsoft At Work Fax* to refer to the specification.

Overview of Microsoft At Work Fax Software __

In June 1993, Microsoft unveiled a new software architecture that would make a wide range of office tasks easier to perform and more cost-effective to accomplish. Microsoft At Work represents Microsoft's vision of the components necessary to tie together the digital office. Building on the existing business and technical infrastructure, the Microsoft At Work architecture focuses on creating digital connections between machines to allow information to flow freely throughout the workplace.

Windows for Workgroups 3.11 features the first PC-based implementation of the Microsoft At Work Fax technology. The PC Fax software simplifies and improves communications for fax messaging. PC Fax is integrated with the Windows environment and allows users to send fax messages from within Windows–based applications as easily as printing a document to a printer or sending an e-mail message.

Microsoft At Work Fax provides many benefits over standard fax messaging, including the following:

- Extends fax technology capabilities by enabling the transmission of richer document formats: Microsoft At Work Fax allows users to send binary files, such as word processor files and spreadsheets, as easily as they send them with e-mail today. This feature extends the workgroup to include anyone with Windows and a fax card. For example, Microsoft At Work Fax can enable geographically separated groups to coauthor and edit documents or roll up financial statements. Companies can use Microsoft At Work Fax to automate mission-critical tasks, such as automating the purchase order and billing processes with subsidiaries. Although a data communications package can be used to send binary information point-to-point, Microsoft At Work Fax simplifies the exchange of information by using a familiar e-mail interface rather than a complex communications application. Figure 24-1 shows the Default Fax Options dialog box.

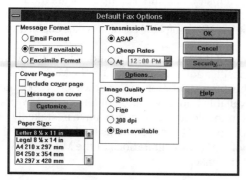

Figure 24-1: Fax options that can be configured include the time of transmission, cover page options, image quality, and security settings.

Microsoft At Work Fax allows users to send messages with editable files, quality images, cover pages, and a certain time of transmission.

■ Integrates fax into e-mail to create a single focal point for desktop messaging: PC Fax is fully integrated with the Windows for Workgroups Mail client, and other implementations of Microsoft At Work Fax will also tie into the Mail system. This integration allows users to send documents either from Mail or from any Mail-enabled application (one that uses the MAPI or CMC APIs). Windows for Workgroups users can use PC Fax as a stand-alone fax application or combine it with e-mail by using the workgroup post office. Anyone using the workgroup post office or Microsoft Mail can send information to e-mail users and fax users simultaneously. Fax addresses can be entered into the Personal Address Book. These addresses can be for users with fax addresses and members of group aliases, along with users of other types of e-mail addresses.

Received faxes go directly into the user's mailbox. For messages that contain regular faxes, double-clicking the message brings up the fax viewer, with which the user can view the fax, copy its contents to the Clipboard, or print it out. The user can save received messages in private Mail folders and then share the messages or route them to shared folders in the post office. Users also can reply to received messages or forward messages to both e-mail and fax recipients.

■ Enables sharing fax boards in a workgroup environment: Users of Windows for Workgroups can send messages through a fax board in their own computer. Multiple users can share a single fax board in one workstation on the network. Outbound faxes are automatically routed to the designated shared fax board. Inbound faxes are received by the machine with the shared fax board and automatically routed to the correct recipient's PC. Group-3 messages (those from a standard fax machine or most other types of PC fax software) are placed into the shared fax attendant's inbox, who must then forward the message to the designated recipient.

Windows for Workgroups users can share a fax modem for both sending and receiving fax messages.

■ Includes tight security features so that users can confidently fax sensitive information: Microsoft At Work Fax compliant fax systems, including PC Fax, include a full security system. Users can encrypt documents to prevent others from reading them. Users can require authentication of recipients before a message is delivered. They can also include a digital document signature that guarantees the contents of a document have not been altered.

■ Has complete compatibility with existing industry-standard facsimile services: Microsoft At Work Fax is completely compatible with the 21 million installed Group-3 fax machines. Note that the advanced services (binary file transfer and security) are not available when communicating with Group-3 fax machines.

■ Provides compatibility with office equipment based on the Microsoft At Work architecture: Microsoft At Work Fax messaging allows users to communicate directly with office devices, such as fax machines, servers, and multifunctional peripherals that utilize the Microsoft At Work software. For example, from a Windows for Workgroups-based PC, a user can send a binary file to a Microsoft At Work-based fax machine, which in turn can automatically forward the file to the appropriate recipient through the LAN.

Sharing a Fax Modem Over the Network

With PC Fax, you can install a fax modem in one computer and share it with other computers on the same network. Individual computers can have their own fax modems installed and still use the shared fax modem.

To share a fax modem with others on a network, follow these steps:

1. From the Main group, choose the Control Panel icon and then choose the Fax icon. The Fax Modems dialog box appears.

2. In the Fax Modems dialog box, verify that the modem you want to share with other users on the network is set as the active modem. Then choose the Share button. The Share Local Fax Modem dialog box appears.

   Note that the Share button changes to Stop Sharing when the default modem is shared.

3. In the Share Local Fax Modem dialog box, type the path of the empty shared directory you want to use for the fax modem (see Figure 24-2).

Figure 24-2: The Share Local Fax Modem dialog box, used to create the directory in which the fax queue will reside.

4. If you have not already created the shared directory, choose the Create Directory button to create the directory you have typed in the Directory box.

5. If you have not already shared the directory, choose the Create Share button and refer to the procedure following these steps for information on creating a share.

If you are unable to create a share at this point, see your network documentation.

6. In the Fax Modems dialog box, choose the OK button. The active modem is now shared.

 If you change your shared active modem by selecting a modem on a different COM port, the new active modem becomes the shared modem. If you change your shared active modem by selecting a shared network fax modem, your new active modem is not a shared modem.

To create a share, follow these steps:

1. In the Share Local Fax Modem dialog box, choose the Create Share button. The Share Directory dialog box appears (see Figure 24-3).

Figure 24-3: Use the Share Directory dialog box to share the directory in which the fax queue will reside on the network.

2. In the Share Directory dialog box, type a name for the share in the Share Name box; alternatively, press Tab to accept the name of the directory as the share name.

3. The path of the directory you will be sharing appears in the Path box. Type the path of a different directory or press Tab to move to the Comment field.

4. In the Comment field, type an optional description of the shared directory.

5. If you want the modem to be shared after you restart your computer, select the Re-share At Startup check box.

6. Select either Full or Depends On Password for the Access Type.

 You must change the Access Type from Read-Only to Full when sharing the directory. If you leave the Access Type as Read-Only, other users cannot use your shared modem.

7. If you select Depends On Password, type the password you want to use for the shared directory in the Full Access Password box. Click the OK button twice.

Using the Advanced Dialing Feature

By using the Advanced Dialing feature, you can enter a fax number into your Personal Address Book that can be used from anywhere in the world without requiring you to change any prefixes. Microsoft At Work Fax uses this fax number to identify to whom you may send messages, for recipients who have been digitally signed or encrypted for the purpose of security.

Three components make up the Advanced Dialing feature:

- Your fax modem number, including country and area codes
- The Advanced Dialing prefixes
- The names and fax numbers of recipients in your Personal Address Book, entered in international format

Enter your fax modem number and the Advanced Dialing prefixes when you configure your fax modem, as described in the following section.

Entering your fax modem number and Advanced Dialing prefixes

Whenever you select a recipient with an internationally formatted fax number from your Personal Address Book, Microsoft At Work Fax reads your fax modem number and the Advanced Dialing prefixes to determine which numbers it must dial to connect. You entered your fax number and Advanced Dialing prefixes when you set up your modem. You can change this information at any time.

To change your fax modem number and add Advanced Dialing prefixes, follow these steps:

1. From the Main group in Program Manager, choose the Control Panel icon and then choose the Fax icon. The Fax Modems dialog box appears.

2. In the Fax Modems dialog box, choose the Setup button to open the Fax Setup dialog box.

3. Type your complete fax modem number, including country code and area code.

4. Choose the Dialing button to open the Modem Dialing Options dialog box (see Figure 24-4).

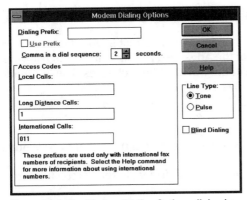

Figure 24-4: The Modem Dialing Options dialog box.

5. Type the appropriate Advanced Dialing prefixes:

Dialing Prefix: If you must dial a number to reach an outside line, type that number in this field. For example, many business systems require that you dial *9* to reach an outside line.

Local Calls: In this field, type any numbers required for local calls within your phone system. Most often, this setting is left blank.

Long Distance Calls: In this field, type all the numbers required to access a long-distance line from your fax modem. For example, you may have to dial a *1*.

International Calls: In this field, type all the numbers required to reach an international line from your fax modem. For example, you may have to dial *9*, plus *011*.

6. Click OK three times to close all open dialog boxes.

If you want to use a telephone calling card with the prefix settings, enter the entire calling-card number in the Dialing Prefix setting using the following syntax:

```
9,<number to access long distance company>,,,,<calling card
number>,,,,<destination number>
```

Many modems have limited space for long telephone numbers. Avoid putting in extraneous characters, such as dashes or spaces, when entering phone numbers.

To increase the length of the pauses between numbers, increase the number of commas.

Entering fax numbers in the Personal Address Book

By entering fax numbers in international format in your Personal Address Book, you can take advantage of the Advanced Dialing feature and use your Personal Address Book anywhere in the world without changes. The international format for fax numbers is as follows:

```
recipient name@+countrycode-areacode-phonenumber
```

Be sure to include the plus sign (+) in front of the *countrycode* number.

To enter a fax number in international format in the Personal Address Book, follow these steps:

1. Access the Address Book dialog by selecting Mail⇨Address Book from the Mail menu bar.
2. In the Address Book dialog box, choose the Blank Card button.
3. In the New dialog box, select Microsoft At Work Fax.
4. In the Fax Number box, type the fax number in international format.

When you select a recipient whose fax number is in international format, Microsoft At Work Fax uses your fax modem number and the Advanced Dialing prefixes to determine what digits must be dialed to complete the call.

For example, if you send a fax to a local recipient, Microsoft At Work Fax determines that the country code and area code aren't required, so it doesn't dial them. But suppose that you take your Personal Address Book to another country, connect to a new modem, and enter that modem's fax number and the Advanced Dialing prefixes. If you send a fax to the same recipient, Microsoft At Work Fax determines that it now needs to dial the access code for an international line and then the country code, area code, and the number.

With Microsoft At Work Fax, you can ensure the security of the faxes you send by encrypting them. An encrypted fax cannot be read by anyone except the intended recipient. You can also send a fax with a digital signature to assure all recipients that only you could have sent it. Encryption is selected by clicking Options⇨Fax when composing a fax in Mail.

There are two ways to encrypt a fax: password encryption and key encryption. When you use *password encryption*, you type a password that locks the fax and then tell the recipient what the password is. This method is less secure than key encryption (described in the following section), but it is sufficient for many situations.

Protecting messages with key encryption

When you establish security, Microsoft At Work Fax assigns two security keys to you, a *private* key and a *public* key. You can exchange public keys with anyone you choose. When you send a key-encrypted message, Microsoft At Work Fax uses the recipient's public key and your private key to encrypt the message. When the message is received, Microsoft At Work Fax uses your public key and the recipient's private key to decrypt it. Using your own private key ensures that the message could have been sent only by you. Using the recipient's public key ensures that only the recipient can unlock the message. (Both sender and recipient must be using Microsoft At Work Fax software.)

You can send a fax that is both digitally signed and encrypted.

Establishing and maintaining security

In order to send and receive secured faxes, you must exchange public keys with your correspondents. You and your correspondents must all use Microsoft At Work Fax, must type your fax phone numbers in the Fax Setup dialog box in international format, and must enable security.

You should disable security whenever you are not sending or reading secured faxes. The security system is password protected; by disabling security, you eliminate the possibility of someone using your private key either to read your encrypted messages or to send messages digitally signed by you.

A digital signature is legally binding. Protect yourself from fraudulent use of your digital signature by disabling security when you are not using it. Never leave your computer unattended while security is enabled.

Establishing security

To establish security, follow these steps:

1. In Mail, choose Advanced Security from the Fax menu. The Fax Security dialog box opens (see Figure 24-5).

2. In the Fax Security dialog box, choose the Enable Security button.

3. Microsoft At Work Fax displays a message that you do not have an account and asks whether you want to establish one. Choose the Yes button.

4. In the Password box, carefully type a password. The characters you type do not appear on screen.

5. In the Verify box, carefully type the password again; then choose the OK button.

6. In the Fax Security dialog box, choose the Close button.

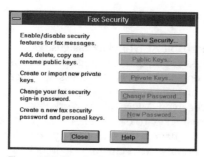

Figure 24-5: Use the Fax Security dialog box to configure Microsoft At Work Fax security options.

To enhance security, change your password periodically, using the Change Password button.

Disabling security

To disable security, follow these steps:

1. In Mail, choose Advanced Security from the Fax menu. The Fax Security dialog box appears.

2. In the Fax Security dialog box, choose the Disable Security button and then choose the Close button.

Enabling security

To enable security, follow these steps:

1. In Mail, choose Advanced Security from the Fax menu. The Fax Security dialog box opens.

2. In the Fax Security dialog box, choose the Enable Security button. The Login dialog box opens.

3. In the Login dialog box, type your password and choose the OK button. All the buttons except the New Password button are now available.

4. In the Fax Security dialog box, choose the Close button.

For information about sending a secured fax, see "Sending and receiving secured faxes," later in this chapter.

Changing your password

To change your password, follow these steps:

1. Make sure that security is active; then choose the Change Password button in the Fax Security dialog box.

2. In the Change Password dialog box, type your existing password in the Old Password box. The characters you type do not appear on-screen.

3. In the New Password box, carefully type your new password.

4. In the Verify Password box, carefully type the new password again and then choose the OK button.

   The purpose of verifying your password is to reduce the possibility of misspelling the password and locking yourself out of your own fax security.

5. When the Fax Security dialog box reappears, choose the Close button.

Creating a new password and changing personal keys

If you forget your password or suspect that your security has been breached, you can create a new password and change your personal keys to prevent the misuse of them by someone else. Changing your personal keys requires that you distribute your new public key to everyone who has your old one.

To create a new password and change your personal keys, follow these steps:

1. In Mail, choose Advanced Security from the Fax menu.

2. When security is disabled, choose the New Password button in the Fax Security dialog box. Microsoft At Work Fax displays a warning. Choose the Yes button.

3. Carefully type the new password in the Password box.

4. Carefully type the password again in the Verify Password box.

5. Choose the OK button.

Managing personal keys

The easiest way to exchange public keys is by exporting them to a floppy disk and then exchanging disks with your correspondents. You can then import other people's public keys from the disks. You are safest if you accept public keys directly from the only owner, through registered mail, or from a third party who is well known and trusted by you. Otherwise, you may receive a "signed" fax from an impostor or you may send a secured fax that can be read by someone other than the intended recipient. If you receive a public key through registered mail, you can call the sender on the telephone to verify the contents.

You should always back up both of your personal keys so that you can restore them in the event of a computer failure. You should export the keys to a floppy disk and then lock the disk in a safe place. If you need to restore your personal keys, you can import them from the floppy disk.

 The keys for security are stored in the file KEYFILE.DAT in your Windows directory.

Using signed keys

If you want a more secure method for exchanging public keys, you can create digitally signed keys. Use this method to specify that all public keys imported by the users of your system must have the valid digital signature of a specified person. The owner of that signature verifies each public key before distributing the digitally signed key among users (through electronic mail or a network share, for instance). Each user then verifies the signature of the certifying person when using the Import Public Keys dialog box to import the public key.

To create a signed key, first verify the authenticity of the key using the methods described earlier. Import the public key into your public key database and then use the Export Public Keys dialog box to export it as a signed key. To export the key as signed, specify an extension of AWS for the name of the exported key file. Users who already have received your public key can verify your signature on the key file and will feel confident that it contains valid public keys.

Not only do signed keys provide a more secure method of key distribution, but they also make it easier to distribute keys to a large number of people. However, you should accept a key that has been signed by its owner only if you receive it directly from the owner or view the key and verify its contents with the owner. You can also use a trusted third party to physically carry the key on diskette from the owner to you.

Exporting your private key

To export your private key to floppy disk, follow these steps:

1. Insert a floppy disk into the disk drive.

2. Make sure that security is active; choose the Private Keys button from the Fax Security dialog box. The Private Key Management dialog box opens.

3. In the Private Key Management dialog box, choose the Export button.

4. In the File Name box, type a name for the private key file. Assign a filename extension of AWR.

5. Choose the floppy disk drive to which you want to export the key file from the Drives list and choose OK.

6. In the Private Key Management dialog box, choose the Close button.

Store your private key backup disk in a secure location, such as a locked file cabinet, a safe deposit box, or a safe.

Importing your private key

To import your private key from floppy disk, follow these steps:

1. Insert the floppy disk containing your private key into the disk drive.

2. Make sure that security is active; choose the Private Keys button in the Fax Security dialog box. The Private Key Management dialog box opens.

3. In the Private Key Management dialog box, choose the Import button.

4. From the Drives list, choose the floppy disk drive in which the floppy disk containing your private key is located.

5. Select the AWR file containing your private key from the list of files (or type the filename in the File Name box) and choose OK.

6. In the Import Private Keys dialog box, type your password and choose OK.

7. In the Private Key Management dialog box, choose the Close button.

Exporting and importing a public key

To export and import a public key, follow the procedures for exporting and importing private keys but choose the Public Keys button in the Fax Security dialog box.

If someone gives you his or her public key on paper, you can enter the key into your system by simply typing it in.

To type a public key into your system, follow these steps:

1. Make sure that security is active; choose the Public Keys button.

2. In the Public Keys dialog box, choose the Type In button. The Enter Public Key dialog box appears (see Figure 24-6).

Figure 24-6: The Enter Public Key dialog box.

3. In the Name@Number box, type the recipient's name and fax number, using the international format.

You must type the recipient's fax phone number in international format, which is as follows:

recipient name@+countrycode-areacode-phonenumber

Be sure that you include the + sign in front of the *countrycode* entry.

4. Carefully type the contents of the key in the boxes and then choose the OK button.

When security is enabled, you can view your public key or someone else's public key by choosing the View button in the Public Keys dialog box and then selecting the key you want to view. To rename a public key, choose the Rename button. To copy a public key, choose the Copy button.

Microsoft At Work Fax uses the fax number included in the recipient's address to find the correct public key for that recipient. You should make certain that the fax number information included in the recipient's address is identical to the name of the key as it appears in the Public Keys dialog box.

Sending and receiving secured faxes

When security is active, you can send a key-encrypted or digitally signed fax. You can also read a secured fax you have received. You can set the key-encrypt and sign options as global fax options.

You do not need to start security to send or read a password-encrypted fax; however, you must select the password-encrypt option for each password-encrypted fax you send.

Sending a password-encrypted fax

To send a password-encrypted fax, follow these steps:

1. In Mail, choose the Compose button.

2. Choose the Options button on the toolbar and then choose the Fax button.

3. In the Fax Message Options dialog box, choose the Security button.

4. Under the Encrypt heading, choose the Password check box.

5. Carefully type the password in the Password box. Carefully type the password again in the Verify Password box.

6. Choose OK in the Fax Security dialog box; the dialog box closes. Choose OK in the Options dialog box; that dialog box closes.

7. Address and send the fax as usual.

8. Notify the recipient of the password.

Sending a key-encrypted or digitally signed fax

To send a key-encrypted or digitally signed fax, follow these steps:

1. In Mail, choose Options from the Fax menu.

2. In the Default Fax Options dialog box, choose the Security button.

3. In the Fax Security dialog box, select the option you want. Then choose OK.

4. In the Options dialog box, choose OK.

5. Send your fax as usual.

Reading a secured fax

With security active, you read a secured fax exactly as you would any other fax or mail message. If you have not enabled security, Microsoft At Work Fax notifies you that you must do so before you can read a secured fax.

 When you are finished sending or reading secured faxes, disable security to avoid the possibility of someone else using your terminal to send faxes with your identification.

The EFAXPUMP.INI File

The PC Fax software uses the EFAXPUMP.INI file to store its settings. This file can be found in your WINDOWS directory.

The [EFAXPump] section

The entries in this section of the EFAXPUMP.INI file are used to configure the fax message mail pump to send outgoing fax messages. The fax message mail pump is the part of the software that takes mail messages and turns them into faxes, and vice versa.

The `MaxRetries=`*n* entry specifies the maximum number of attempts that are made to send an outgoing fax message before failing.

The `SpoolDirectory=`*path name* entry specifies a path name to which fax messages are spooled while they reside in the outgoing queue. By default, fax messages are spooled to the directory identified by the TEMP environment variable.

The [Message] section

The entries in this section of the EFAXPUMP.INI file identify the default values for the options used when sending a fax message.

The `CheapTimeEnds=`*n* entry specifies the time when cheap phone times end, using a 24-hour clock. The default value for this entry is `600` (6 AM).

The `CheapTimeStarts=`*n* entry specifies the time when cheap phone times start, using a 24-hour clock. The default value for this entry is `1800` (6 PM).

The `DeliveryFormat=`*n* entry specifies the default delivery format for sending an outgoing fax message. A value of `0` indicates that the fax message should be sent as a binary message. A value of `1` indicates that the fax message should be sent as a rendered Group-3 facsimile transmission. A value of `2` indicates that the fax message should be sent as e-mail if the destination machine supports that type of message; otherwise, a Group-3 facsimile will be transmitted. The default value is `2`.

A *rendered* fax is one in which the message is sent as a graphics image of the page. If a fax message is sent as e-mail, the receiver will receive the actual characters in the message and can edit or paste the characters of the message into other programs. A rendered file will exist only as a picture of the printed page and cannot be edited with a text editor or word processor.

The `ImageQuality=`*n* entry specifies the default image quality rendered for an outgoing fax message. A value of `0` indicates standard resolution. A value of `1` indicates fine resolution. A value of `2` indicates 300 dots per inch (dpi). A value of `3` indicates that the best image quality supported by the destination machine is used. The default is `3`.

The `IncludeCover=`*n* entry specifies whether a cover page should be included with the fax message. A value of `0` indicates that the cover page should not be included; any other value indicates that a cover page should be used. The default is `0`.

The next several entries provide the choices of cover page logos that the user is presented with in the Fax Options dialog.

The `LastLogoFile1=`*path name* entry specifies the pathname to a previously used bitmap for the logo on a cover page. The pathname must be a fully qualified pathname that references the given bitmap image.

The `LastLogoFile2=`*path name* entry specifies the pathname to a previously used bitmap for the logo on a cover page. The pathname must be a fully qualified pathname that references the given bitmap image.

The `LastLogoFile3=`*path name* entry specifies the pathname to a previously used bitmap for the logo on a cover page. The pathname must be a fully qualified pathname that references the given bitmap image.

The `LastLogoFile4=`*path name* entry specifies the pathname to a previously used bitmap for the logo on a cover page. The pathname must be a fully qualified pathname that references the given bitmap image.

The `LastLogoFile5=`*path name* entry specifies the pathname to a previously used bitmap for the logo on a cover page. The pathname must be a fully qualified pathname that references the given bitmap image.

The `LogoFile=`*path name* entry specifies the default bitmap for the logo for the cover page. The pathname must be a fully qualified pathname that references the bitmap image.

The `MinutesBetweenRetries=`*n* entry specifies the number of minutes to wait before retrying the attempt to send the fax message after a send fails. The default is 10 minutes.

The `PaperSize=`*n* entry specifies the default paper size to use when rendering the fax message image. Valid setting values include: 0 (letter), 1 (legal), 2 (A4), 3 (B4), and 4 (A3). The default is 0.

The `ScheduledTransmitTime=`*n* entry specifies the default transmit time for an outgoing fax message when a specific time is wanted, using the 24-hour clock. The default is 1200 (12 PM).

The `TransmitPriority=`*n* entry specifies the default priority to use when sending a fax message. A value of 0 indicates ASAP, a value of 1 indicates cheap, and a value of 2 indicates at a specified transmit time. The default is 0.

The [Modem] section

The switches in this section identify information the fax modem uses when sending a fax message.

The `DefaultFax=`*n* entry specifies the default fax device to use. A value of 0 is undefined or no default; values in the range 1 through 4 indicate COM ports 1 through 4; values in the range 6 through 21 are the allowable 16 network connections; a value of 38 indicates a Communications Application Specification (CAS) modem. The value of 5 is not used. There is no default.

The ValidPorts=*n* entry specifies the valid communication ports (1 through 4) available in the system using a four-bit map. The low-order bit means that COM1 is valid; the second lowest bit means that COM2 is valid; and so on. This setting is determined at the time the fax components are installed.

The CasModem=*n* entry specifies whether or not a CAS modem is installed. A value of 0 specifies that no CAS modem is installed. A value of 1 indicates that a modem is installed. The default value is 0.

The [Network] section

Entries in this section of the EFAXPUMP.INI file are used for maintaining information about shared fax modems.

The NetworkName*nn*=*string* entry specifies the share name and type of fax modem configured on the given share. The valid range for *nn* is 00 through 15 and identifies the 16 possible network shares. The *string* identifies the name of a share serving as the fax modem queue.

The ValidNetConns=*n* entry specifies which of the NetworkName*nn*= entries are actually installed. A 16-bit map is used to represent the existence of the NetworkName*nn*= present, with the low-order bit representing 00, and the high-order bit representing 15.

The [security] section

Entries in this section are used for maintaining information about fax message security.

The AlwaysEncrypt= 0 | 1 entry specifies whether fax messages sent in e-mail format should be key-encrypted by default. A value of 1 enables the encrypting of each of these messages. The default setting is 0, which disables this feature.

The AlwaysLogin= 0 | 1 entry specifies whether fax advanced security is enabled. A value of 0 means that advanced security features are disabled. A value of 1 means they the features will be enabled the next time the user starts the Microsoft At Work Fax transport. The user will be required to enter his or her fax security password at that time.

The AlwaysSign= 0 | 1 entry specifies whether attachments of fax messages sent in e-mail format should be digitally signed by default. A value of 1 enables the digital signing of each of these attachments. This setting defaults to 0, which disables this feature.

Overcoming the Limitations of PC Fax with WinFax PRO 4.0

As this book was going to press, Delrina Corporation was putting the finishing touches on a new version of their popular WinFax PRO 4.0 fax software.

This new version will be the second implementation of Microsoft At Work Fax compatible fax software available on the PC, and it addresses many of the limitations of PC Fax. WinFax PRO 4.0's features include:

- Full coverpage library support

- Fax broadcast capabilities

- Full logging of both incoming and outgoing faxes, as well as archival features

- OCR capabilities to turn incoming rendered Group III facsimiles into editable text

- Full support for all Microsoft At Work features, including encryption, digital signatures, sending and receiving e-mail

- Fax Forwarding — sending received faxes on to another location (with optional Microsoft At Work Fax encryption)

- Fax Polling — queuing faxes until another WinFax PRO 4.0 system calls and requests them

- Phonebooks stored in DBF files, with the ability to import phonebooks from ASCII, CAS, dBASE or Lotus Organizer files

- Full DDE support, including the ability to use phonebooks in a PIM, such as Packrat or ACT! for Windows

- Can be used as your mail client by sending and receiving e-mail from workgroup users from inside Winfax

- TWAIN compliant scanners fully supported

The authors were able to send and receive e-mail with embedded Microsoft Word documents between PC Fax and the beta version of WinFax PRO 4.0, using the Microsoft At Work Fax features of both. The only drawback is that the Microsoft At Work Fax compliant version of WinFax PRO 4.0 does not currently support shared fax modems; however, this functionality will be added in a future version of WinFax PRO for Networks.

Summary

This chapter discussed Microsoft At Work Fax, along with its implementation in Windows for Workgroups 3.11 PC Fax, and Delrina WinFax PRO 4.0.

▶ You examined the difference between the Microsoft At Work Fax specifications and its implementations.

▶ Procedures for installing and configuring Windows for Workgroups 3.11 PC Fax were discussed.

▶ Microsoft At Work Fax features, such as encryption, were examined.

▶ The settings in the EFAXPUMP.INI file were discussed.

Chapter 25

Configuring Remote Access Service

In This Chapter

▶ Using Remote Access to extend your workgroup

▶ Installing and configuring Windows for Workgroups 3.11 Point-to-Point Server

▶ Setting up modems for RAS

▶ Modifying the MODEM.INF file to configure unsupported modems

▶ Error messages you may encounter

▶ Using RAS to network two computers using serial ports

▶ Using Remote Access features to extend your workgroup environment

▶ Installing and configuring Remote Access

▶ Installing and configuring the Remote Access client

▶ Using the Remote Access Point-to-Point Server

Until the advent of Windows for Workgroups 3.11, Remote Access was exclusively the province of users of larger networks—typically a LAN Manager or Windows NT-based network. With ordinary modems, users of these networks could dial into their corporate network and participate as though they were connected to the network.

Remote Access has a number of advantages and disadvantages; because the remote workstation is logically connected to the network, you can achieve true client/server computing. On the other hand, because data transfer rates are limited to what is possible with serial devices, large amounts of data take a long time to move over the connection.

In Remote Control, the user of one workstation takes control of another, like a puppeteer controls a marionette. Remote Control provides faster response with nonclient/server applications because only screen images and keyboard/mouse movement information must travel across the modem connection.

Remote Control requires the use of third-party software, such as CloseUp or Carbon Copy for Windows. These utilities can be difficult to set up and may restrict the host computer's configuration (such as requiring that the user run Windows in VGA mode, rather than using advanced features of the users' hardware).

 Microsoft's Remote Access Service (RAS) supports ISDN adapters. If ISDN is available in your area, its high speeds and relatively low cost make it a cost-effective way to obtain good performance with Remote Access Service.

Remote Access Service consists of two parts: the client (which runs on the remote computer) and the server (which runs on a computer attached to the network). Until recently, the only Remote Access servers that were available ran on LAN Manager or Windows NT servers. RAS servers are full featured—that is, they provide access to all resources on the network (subject to the network's security controls, of course).

Understanding the Remote Access Service Client

The Remote Access Service (RAS) client enables a remote computer running Windows for Workgroups 3.11 to dial in to a Windows NT or Windows NT Advanced Server RAS to gain seamless access to network resources. The connection works the same as if the user were sitting at a workstation attached to the physical network.

Microsoft released a Remote Access Service upgrade for Windows for Workgroups 3.11 workstations during the writing of this book, which adds point-to-point RAS server capabilities to Windows for Workgroups 3.11. The Windows for Workgroups 3.11 Point-to-Point Server enables a Windows for Workgroups 3.11 system to accept incoming calls from other Remote Access clients. There is one major difference between the Point-to-Point Server and the Windows NT or Windows NT Advanced Server RAS: when using the Point-to-Point Server, you have access only to the resources shared on the machine you dial in to.

If you need access to all shared network resources (such as shared files and printers located on the network), the computer on the server side must be running Microsoft Windows NT, Windows NT Advanced Server, or Microsoft LAN Manager in addition to Remote Access Service. Windows for Workgroups 3.11 Point-to-Point Server does not have the security features built in to Windows NT and Windows NT Advanced Server. Obviously, you do not want to expose your entire network to Remote Access without having enhanced security features.

Network users, however, aren't the only ones to benefit from the Point-to-Point Server. Anyone who has ever left files on his or her work computer and gone on the road or who has a notebook computer and a desktop computer can benefit—because the Point-to-Point Server makes it possible for you to have a two-station network just by connecting an inexpensive null-modem serial cable between them. See "Making direct serial connections with a NULL modem" later in this chapter for details.

As of this writing, the Windows for Workgroups Point-to-Point Remote Access Server was available from the Microsoft Download System and the Microsoft Workgroup (MSWRKGRP) Forum on CompuServe. The filename is WFWPTP.EXE.

Installing the Remote Access client

You install the Windows for Workgroups 3.11 RAS client after Windows for Workgroups 3.11 is completely set up and operating.

Windows for Workgroups 3.11 was released with a slight but annoying anomaly in its RAS client. When following the installation procedure, you may see a dialog box that states that various parts of the RAS client are already on your system. The dialog box asks whether you want to replace the currently installed version of certain files with "the version you are installing." Always choose the Yes to All button. If you tell Windows to keep the existing version, you usually are caught in an infinite loop in the RAS setup program.

To install the Windows for Workgroups 3.11 RAS client, double-click on the Remote Access icon in Program Manager. RAS detects that it has not been set up yet and begins installing itself automatically.

Installing the Point-to-Point Remote Access Server

To install the Windows for Workgroups Point-to-Point Remote Access Server from the downloadable file, you must first set up the RAS client that comes with Windows for Workgroups, as explained in the preceding section. Then download the WFWPTP.EXE file from CompuServe and copy it to an empty temporary directory on your system. Exit Windows for Workgroups and change your current directory to the directory containing the WFWPTP.EXE file. At the MS-DOS prompt, extract the RAS files from the WFWPTP.EXE file by typing **WFWPTP**.

After extracting the files, install the Point-to-Point Server update by typing **COPYPTP C:\WINDOWS** and pressing Enter.

If you installed Windows for Workgroups in a directory other than C:\WINDOWS, substitute the name of that directory for C:\WINDOWS in the preceding command line.

After completing the update, you can delete the original files from the temporary directory.

Configuring RAS

When RAS starts, Windows presents you with a simple dialog box, in which you can specify the communication port and type of connection you will use. Figure 25-1 shows the RAS Configuration dialog box.

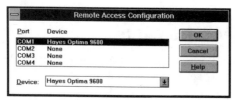

Figure 25-1: Use the Configuration dialog box to specify an RAS connection type.

Setting up a modem for RAS

If you specify a modem as the connection type for an RAS session, you can choose a supported modem from the list of modems in the Remote Access Setup dialog box.

In an ideal situation, use matching modems on the client and server ends for better compatibility. If the modems are not the same type, choose for the client the same brand of modem as the one connected to the Remote Access server, select the same initial speed, and enable the same features. In cases where the modem brands are different, make sure that the client uses a modem with the same CCITT standard as the server's modem.

Enabling your Windows for Workgroups 3.11 workstation to accept calls

If you installed the Windows For Workgroups Point-to-Point Server, it adds another set of options in the Configuration dialog box. To allow your system to receive calls from remote workstations, check the Allow Incoming Calls to this Computer check box in the Configuration dialog box. Then specify the port and a password.

If you do not enter a password in the Password box in the Configuration dialog box, anyone can connect to shared directories on your computer.

Connecting to the network

After installing RAS, you may want to test its operation before configuring and optimizing your connection device. First, you add the appropriate dialing information and then initiate dialing. Use the following instructions to accomplish these tasks:

1. Double-click on an entry to dial. RAS displays the Authentication dialog box shown in Figure 25-2.

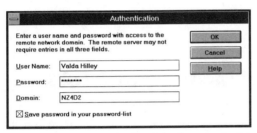

Figure 25-2: The Authentication dialog box contains information required to validate your connection to a remote server.

2. Type your user name, your password, and the domain of the Remote Access server into which you are dialing.

Make sure that you have the correct user name, password, and domain name for the server into which you are dialing. Otherwise, you are not allowed to connect.

Once connected to the network, you can minimize the Remote Access Phone Book and work with your computer as though it were connected directly to the LAN. You can send and receive e-mail, access servers, copy files through File Manager, and so on, as though you were in the office.

You can access servers or other shared resources on attached machines only if the server side is running Microsoft Windows NT, Windows NT Advanced Server, or Microsoft LAN Manager in addition to Remote Access Service.

Browsing a domain over a remote connection takes a long time, depending on the number of servers in the domain. Often, it's more convenient to turn browsing off by default.

To turn off domain browsing from the File Manager, follow these steps:

1. From the Main group, double-click on the File Manager.

2. From the Disk menu, choose Connect Network Drive.

3. In the Connect Network Drive dialog box, clear the Always Browse check box.

4. Choose OK.

To turn off domain browsing from Print Manager, follow these steps:

1. From the Main group, double-click on Print Manager.

2. From the Printer menu, choose Connect Network Printer.

3. In the Connect Network Printer dialog box, clear the Always Browse check box.

4. Choose OK.

Using Unsupported Modems with RAS _____

Each time you start the Remote Access Service program, it reads a file named MODEM.INF to determine the type of modem and the parameters it should use. If your modem is an unsupported modem (that is, one that hasn't been tested and isn't listed in the Configuration dialog box), you must edit the modem script file, MODEM.INF.

Configuring an unlisted modem for RAS

If your modem is not listed among the supported modems in the RAS Configuration dialog box, use the following procedures to configure and test the modem for compatibility. You have to select from the list of supported modems a modem that matches yours as closely as possible. For best results, make your choice by first comparing entries in the MODEM.INF file with commands for your modem. You can find these commands in your modem's documentation.

To configure an unsupported modem, follow these steps:

1. Start Remote Access Service.

2. Select Configure from the Setup menu and choose a modem from the list of modems that is most similar to your unsupported modem. Click OK to accept the choice. Try making a trial run by following the steps in the next section.

 If you select and configure a new port for the unsupported modem, restart your computer. If you reconfigure a port already in use, you don't have to restart your computer but you *do* need to restart the Remote Access Service.

Testing a modem for compatibility with RAS

If you have trouble connecting through an unsupported modem, test the modem's compatibility. Follow these steps to make a trial run with the unsupported modem:

1. Check the modem's documentation to make sure that you have installed and configured the modem correctly.

2. Make sure that your modem is connected to a serial communications (COM) port on your computer.

3. Turn on your modem.

4. Start the Windows Terminal program by double-clicking on its icon in the Program Manager Accessories group and select Communications from the Settings menu.

5. In the Communications dialog box, select the bps at which your modem sends and receives data; then select the COM port to which your modem is connected. Choose OK.

6. On the Terminal screen, type **at** and press Enter.

Your modem should return OK, which is echoed on the screen. Some modems return 0, depending on their result-code settings. If your modem doesn't respond in Terminal, it is probably malfunctioning.

If the modem still does not work with RAS after you have verified that it works with Windows Terminal, you have two options: contact your modem's manufacturer and request a modem command file compatible with the Remote Access Service MODEM.INF file or modify the MODEM.INF file. The MODEM.INF file is described in the following section.

Looking at the Modem Script File, MODEM.INF _

The MODEM.INF file lists all the modems supported by the Remote Access Service, along with the command and response strings each modem needs for correct operation. When you select a modem during Remote Access installation, the setup program associates the selected modem with the specified communications port. Remote Access connection utilities read MODEM.INF to obtain the command strings for the modem associated with each communications port.

The MODEM.INF file consists of two main parts:

■ A global [Responses] section. This section contains common result strings returned by a variety of modems.

■ Individual sections for each supported modem that contains initialization, dial, and listen command strings.

The syntax for MODEM.INF

If you study the MODEM.INF file, you'll find that it contains the following components.

- Section header: Identifies the specific device to which the section applies. In MODEM.INF, the section header is normally a name that identifies the modem make and model. A section header is a string of up to 32 characters between square brackets; it occupies the first line in each section.

- Configuration parameters: Remote Access works with the modem through these parameters. They take the following form:

  parameter_name=value_string

  For example:

  ```
  MAXCARRIERBPS=9600

  CALLBACKTIME=8
  ```

- Substitution macros: *Substitution macros* are place holders that are replaced by their values in command strings. Macros follow these rules:

  - In the MODEM.INF file, macros must come before the first command and, by convention, after the configuration parameters.

  - Macro names must be enclosed in angle brackets (< >).

  For example:

  ```
  <reset>=&F <speaker_on>=M1 <speaker_off>=M0
  ```

- Commands: *Commands* are strings of characters sent to the modem. These strings can contain macros and take the following form:

  command_keyword=value_string

- Comment lines: *Comment lines* begin with a semicolon (;) and can appear anywhere in the file. Comment lines convey important information to those who maintain INF files. Here is a sample comment line:

  ```
  ; Explanation of modem commands
  ```

The first four components of the MODEM.INF file appear in the order given. Comment lines can appear anywhere in the file.

Line continuation

A backslash (\) signals a line continuation. This mark indicates that commands or responses are continued on the next line, making files more legible.

The backslash (\) character is interpreted as a line continuation except when it is preceded by another backslash. If your modem uses commands that include a backslash, be sure that you use double backslashes (\\) when entering these commands. For example, the AT&T Comsphere 3820 modem enables error control with the \N5 command. Be sure to enter **\\N5** in the initialization string for this modem instead of \N5 or Remote Access will report a hardware error when trying to dial.

Aliases

If a modem's command strings are identical to those already listed for another modem, the name of the latter modem can be used as an alias for the former.

For example:

```
[AT&T Comsphere 3810] ALIAS=AT&T Comsphere 3820
```

In this example, the AT&T Comsphere 3810 is set up to use the command strings of the AT&T Comsphere 3820. Note that aliases cannot be nested. Therefore, in addition to the preceding statement, you could have the following statement:

```
[AT&T Comsphere 3811] ALIAS=AT&T Comsphere 3820
```

However, the following statement is not acceptable:

```
[AT&T Comsphere 3811] ALIAS=AT&T Comsphere 3810
```

How to modify MODEM.INF

If you decide to modify your MODEM.INF file, use the following procedure:

Remember to back up your existing MODEM.INF file before making any changes.

1. Make a template by copying an existing modem section to the end of MODEM.INF and rename the section header of the copy to the name of your modem. You will create a new entry by editing this template.

2. The section header with your new modem name cannot exceed 33 characters, including the square brackets, otherwise an error results.

3. Provide the following strings:

Initialization string which specifies the following:

Recall factory settings.

Track the presence of data-carrier-detect (DCD) (high when a carrier is detected).

Hang up and disable auto-answer when data terminal ready (DTR) goes from ON to OFF (high to low).

Return result codes.

Return verbose codes.

Enable character echo in command state.

Wait about 55 seconds for a carrier.

Disable the +++ escape sequence.

Dial string containing go off hook and dial.

Listen string containing answer after one ring.

Check your modem's documentation to see whether the modem's responses (its result strings) are already included in the global section of MODEM.INF. If they are, you don't need to make any changes for the responses. If they are not, you can create private responses in your modem's section.

To avoid unexpected consequences, do not add responses to or delete any from the global response section in MODEM.INF.

Multiple command strings

Because most modems accept strings of only about 50 characters, Remote Access supports multiple command strings. You can break up long commands into shorter strings that the modem can accept. For example, many of the modems included in the MODEM.INF file have more than one COMMAND_INIT command string, each of which is sent to the modem one at a time, in order.

Responses

A command-response set consists of one command followed by zero or more responses. *Responses* are strings that your workstation expects to receive from the device; responses can contain macros. Responses take the following form:

```
keyword=value_string
```

The MODEM.INF file contains two types of responses:

■ Global: Responses used by most modems are in the global [Responses] section of MODEM.INF.

■ Private: Individual modem sections in MODEM.INF can contain private response strings. Remote Access checks for private responses first. If it doesn't find a response string to match the actual string returned by the modem, it continues its search in the global [Responses] section.

There is one exception, however. If the first part of a string containing an <append> macro is matched in the private section, the global section is not searched. Instead, Remote Access waits a few seconds for the rest of the string to arrive from the modem.

Requirements for advanced modem features

In creating a new modem section for an unsupported modem, be sure to set the following requirements in the MODEM.INF file to enable the advanced modem features:

■ Hardware (CTS/RTS) flow control ON

■ Hardware (CTS/RTS) flow control OFF

■ Error Control Protocol ON

■ Error Control Protocol OFF

■ Compression ON

■ Compression OFF

Setting advanced modem features

Modem features are associated with an entry in the Phone Book. With this arrangement, you can control the connection to specific server workstations according to the type of modem used by the server.

To set modem features, follow these steps:

1. Create, edit, or clone a Phone Book entry to access the Phone Book Entry dialog box.

2. In the Phone Book Entry dialog box, select Advanced. The Phone Book Entry dialog box expands as shown in Figure 25-3.

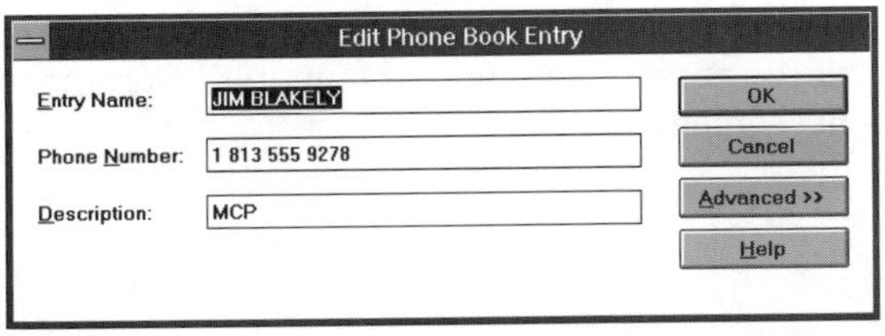

Figure 25-3: Accessing the Advanced Settings area in the Phone Book Entry dialog box.

3. Click on the Modem button at the bottom of the Advanced Phone Book Entry dialog box. The fields in the resulting Modem Settings dialog box are described in Table 25-1.

Table 25-1	Advanced Modem Settings
Setting Name	*Setting Description*
Modem	Displays the modem you've chosen.
Remote Access Initial speed (bps)	Changes the speed at which your modem begins to negotiate with the Remote Access Server's modem. The speed, in bits per second (bps), may increase or decrease during negotiation.
Hardware Flow Control	Enables hardware handshaking. This feature allows the modem to tell Remote Access software when the line is congested or clear so that the Remote Access software can temporarily stop transmitting data when necessary. Handshaking streamlines data transmission, prevents overrun errors, and improves overall data throughput.
Modem Error Control	Checks errors on blocks of data through cyclic redundancy checks (CRCs). Modem error control causes the modem to retransmit garbled data, ensuring that only error-free data passes through the modem.
Modem Compression	Compresses the modem-to-modem data stream, reducing the number of bytes transmitted and therefore reducing the transmission time. The reduction achieved depends on the amount of redundancy in the transmitted data.
Enter Modem Commands Manually	Lets you enter AT commands to the modem manually when dialing rather than executing scripted commands. Enable this feature when you are testing modem strings for new entries in the modem script file (MODEM.INF) and for unusual situations in which interaction is required midway through the dialing sequence.

Understanding compression

Software compression is more effective than hardware compression because a much larger pattern buffer is available on the computer than on the modem. In addition, modem (hardware) compression delays the first transmission while the modem's pattern buffer is filled at computer-to-modem speed. Software compression accomplishes this task at faster memory speed and transmits compressed data over the entire computer-to-computer link rather than just the modem-to-modem segment.

In general, do not enable modem compression and software compression at the same time; there is no benefit from compressing precompressed data. In fact, enabling modem compression and software compression at the same time may actually increase the size of the transmitted data, depending on the algorithm used by the modem.

 Do not enable the manual-commands setting when dialing with the telephone keypad (to connect through a switch controlled by a human operator, for example).

Known problems with supported modems

Although the supported modems listed in the Configuration dialog box have been tested for compatibility, many of the modems have their own idiosyncrasies. Modems that Remote Access supports do not necessarily work in all modes with other modems listed in the Remote Access setup dialog box. For example, some V.32bis modems do not work with port speeds of 14,400 bps, although they communicate at a modem-to-modem speed of 14,400 bps. So if your V.32bis modem does not work at an initial speed of 14,400 bps, change the speed to 19,200 bps.

The following sections describe the known problems that you may experience if you use these modems.

Codex 326x Series

If you are connecting through a Codex 3260, 3261, 3262, 3263, 3264, or 3265, turn off flow control if:

- You're connecting at 2400 or 9600 bps.
- The modem negotiates down to 9600 or 2400 bps from an initial speed of 19,200 or 38,400 bps.

If you are connecting with a Codex V.FAST (3260, 3261, 3262, 3263, 3264, or 3265) to a Remote Access Server that also has a Codex V.FAST, make sure that hardware flow control is enabled. Otherwise, you do not connect and you see the following error message: The device has switched to an unsupported baud rate.

Hayes V-Series 9600

The Hayes V-Series 9600 modem connects at 9600 bps only with another Hayes V-Series 9600 modem. Before you install this modem on your computer, make sure that the Remote Access Server also has a Hayes V-Series 9600 modem. Otherwise, connections are probably made at 2400 bps.

US Robotics HST

US Robotics HST modems use a proprietary protocol that cannot negotiate connection speeds greater than 2400 bps with modems that do not support this protocol.

Even if you have HST-compatible modems on both the remote client and server, Microsoft does not recommend connecting at 14,400 bps with these modems. The HST protocol is not a full-duplex 14,400 bps protocol. In other words, data transmitted in one direction travels at 14,400 bps but data traveling in the opposite direction travels at a much slower rate. This results in a low throughput because the Remote Access Service depends on the same speed for transferring data in both directions.

VenTel 14400

Because the VenTel 14400 fax modem does not detect when a client hangs up, it ties up the line until the timeout period has expired. Therefore, you should not use this modem as a server modem unless you don't mind having the lines tied up for long periods. However, this modem works fine as a client modem.

Configuring Serial Ports

COM1 and COM3 share interrupt (IRQ) level 4. COM2 and COM4 share interrupt (IRQ) level 3. As a result, you cannot use COM1 and COM3 simultaneously or COM2 and COM4 simultaneously. For example, you cannot run serial communications with Remote Access on COM1 and Terminal on COM3.

This rule applies if you are using the mouse in addition to other serial communications programs such as Remote Access or the Windows for Workgroups Terminal program. However, the rule does not apply if you are using intelligent serial adapter cards such as the DigiBoard serial cards.

 To share COM ports under Windows, you need a third-party product such as OTC's KingCOM.

Understanding cabling requirements

The Remote Access Service requires the following pins on the RS-232 (serial) cable:

Pin	Description
Rx	Receive
Tx	Transmit
CTS	Clear to Send
RTS	Request to Send
DTR	Data Terminal Ready
DSR	Data Set Ready
DCD	Data Carrier Detected

The RS-232 cable must have all seven pins listed here. The Remote Access Service does not work if any of these pins is missing. If any pins are not present or not working, the Remote Access Service reports a hardware error.

Most ISA and EISA computers have one of the following types of serial port connectors:

■ 25-pin male D-shell connectors

■ 9-pin male connectors

Most off-the-shelf cables work with your modems, but not all. Some cables do not have all the pins connected as shown in the tables for 25-pin, 9-pin, and NULL modem cabling.

Do not use the 9-to-25-pin converters that come with most mouse hardware; some of these converters do not carry modem signals.

Making direct serial connections with a NULL modem

You can select a NULL modem to establish a direct serial connection between two computers. Although a direct serial connection eliminates the need for a network adapter card, it is a slow link. With a NULL modem connection, password authentication is still required. A NULL modem configuration works well only for computers physically located near each other. The RS-232C specification allows for a maximum distance of about 100 feet, with shielded cable — at those lengths, using network cards and cabling can actually be less expensive.

Configuring your system for a direct serial connection

If you want to configure your COM ports for a direct serial connection, select a NULL modem from the list of modems during RAS setup. You must configure a null modem for this connection on both the client and the server. See "Configuring RAS" earlier in this chapter for details.

Wiring a cable for a NULL modem connection

If you are using a NULL modem to make a direct serial connection between two computers, your cable must be wired as shown in Tables 25-2 or 25-3.

Off-the-shelf NULL modem cables may not be wired properly. Be sure to tell your dealer that your NULL modem cables must be wired as shown in the 9-pin or 25-pin NULL modem table.

Table 25-2	9-Pin NULL Modem Cabling	
Remote Host Serial Port Connector	**Calling System Serial Port Connector**	**Signal**
3	2	Transmit Data
2	3	Receive Data
7	8	Request to Send
8	7	Clear to Send
6, 1	4	Data Set Ready and Data Carrier Detect
5	5	Signal Ground
4	6, 1	Data Terminal Ready

Table 25-3	25-Pin NULL Modem Cabling	
Remote Host Serial Port Connector	**Calling System Serial Port Connector**	**Signal**
2	3	Transmit Data
3	2	Receive Data
4	5	Request to Send
5	4	Clear to Send
6, 8	20	Data Set Ready and Data Carrier Detect
7	7	Signal Ground
20	6, 8	Data Terminal Ready

Using alternative communication methods

In addition to the more traditional methods of remote communication (modems and serial cables), which are relatively limited in their transfer rate capabilities, Remote Access Service supports *ISDN* and *X.25* communication adapters. Both of these communication methods are fully digital — unlike modems, which must change the computers' digital signals into analog tones and back because of the requirements of the voice-grade telephone system.

Integrated Services Digital Network (ISDN)

ISDN service is available from most of the regional telephone companies in the United States. With ISDN, you can achieve data rates of up to 128kbps, and ISDN lines usually do not cost much more than adding a second voice phone line.

To make use of ISDN, you must have an ISDN adapter card in both computers. They are available from companies such as Digiboard, Hayes, or Link Technologies for prices ranging from about $350 to $1,200.

Wide Area Networks — X.25

X.25 is an international protocol used for wide-area networks. If you've ever called in to CompuServe or Delphi, or any of the other online services, chances are that the computer you actually connected to was talking to the service's main computers through an X.25 network.

You can hook your computer into an X.25 network by using an X.25 Smartcard. For more information, contact X.25 service vendors such as SprintNet or Tymnet.

Error Messages

600 An operation is pending.

601 The port handle is invalid.

602 The port is already open.

603 Caller's buffer is too small.

604 Wrong information specified.

605 Cannot set port information.

606 The port is not connected.

607 The event is invalid.

608 The device does not exist.

609 The device type does not exist.

610 The buffer is invalid.

611 The route is not available.

612 The route is not allocated.

613 Invalid compression specified.

614 Out of buffers.

615 The port was not found.

616 An asynchronous request is pending.

617 The port or device is already disconnecting.

618 The port is not open.

619 The port is disconnected.

620 There are no endpoints.

621 Cannot open the phone book file.

622 Cannot load the phone book file.

623 Cannot find the phone book entry.

624 Cannot write the phone book file.

625 Invalid information found in the phone book.

626 Cannot load a string.

627 Cannot find key.

628 The port was disconnected.

629 The port was disconnected by the remote machine.

630 The port was disconnected due to hardware failure.

631 The port was disconnected by the user.

632 The structure size is incorrect.

633 The port is already in use or is not configured for Remote Access dialout.

634 Cannot register your computer on the remote network.

635 Unknown error.

636 The wrong device is attached to the port.

637 The string could not be converted.

638 The request has timed out.

639 No asynchronous net available.

640 A NetBIOS error has occurred.

641 The server cannot allocate NetBIOS resources needed to support the client.

642 One of your NetBIOS names is already registered on the remote network.

643 A network adapter at the server failed.

644 You will not receive network message popups.

645 Internal authentication error.

646 The account is not permitted to log on at this time of day.

647 The account is disabled.

648 The password has expired.

649 The account does not have Remote Access permission.

650 The Remote Access server is not responding.

651 Your modem (or other connecting device) has reported an error.

652 Unrecognized response from the device.

653 A macro required by the device was not found in the device .INF file section.

654 A command or response in the device .INF file section refers to an unde
fined macro.

655 The <message> macro was not found in the device .INF file section.

656 The <defaultoff> macro in the device .INF file section contains an unde
fined macro.

657 The device .INF file could not be opened.

658 The device name in the device .INF or media .INI file is too long.

659 The media .INI file refers to an unknown device name.

660 The device .INF file contains no responses for the command.

661 The device .INF file is missing a command.

662 Attempted to set a macro not listed in device .INF file section.

663 The media .INI file refers to an unknown device type.

664 Cannot allocate memory.

665 The port is not configured for Remote Access.

666 Your modem (or other connecting device) is not functioning.

667 Cannot read the media .INI file.

668 The connection dropped.

669 The usage parameter in the media .INI file is invalid.

670 Cannot read the section name from the media .INI file.

671 Cannot read the device type from the media .INI file.

672 Cannot read the device name from the media .INI file.

673 Cannot read the usage from the media .INI file.

674 Cannot read the maximum connection BPS rate from the media .INI file.

675 Cannot read the maximum carrier BPS rate from the media .INI file.

676 The line is busy.

677 A person answered instead of a modem.

678 There is no answer.

679 Cannot detect carrier.

680 There is no dial tone.

681 General error reported by device.

682 ERROR_WRITING_SECTIONNAME

683 ERROR_WRITING_DEVICETYPE

684 ERROR_WRITING_DEVICENAME

685 ERROR_WRITING_MAXCONNECTBPS

686 ERROR_WRITING_MAXCARRIERBPS

687 ERROR_WRITING_USAGE

688 ERROR_WRITING_DEFAULTOFF

689 ERROR_READING_DEFAULTOFF

690 ERROR_EMPTY_INI_FILE

691 Access denied because username and/or password is invalid on the domain.

692 Hardware failure in port or attached device.

693 ERROR_NOT_BINARY_MACRO

694 ERROR_DCB_NOT_FOUND

695 ERROR STATE MACHINES NOT STARTED

696 ERROR STATE MACHINES ALREADY STARTED

697 ERROR PARTIAL RESPONSE LOOPING

698 A response keyname in the device .INF file is not in the expected format.

699 The device response caused buffer overflow.

700 The expanded command in the device .INF file is too long.

701 The device moved to a BPS rate not supported by the COM driver.

702 Device response received when none expected.

703 ERROR_INTERACTIVE_MODE

704 ERROR_BAD_CALLBACK_NUMBER

705 ERROR_INVALID_AUTH_STATE

706 ERROR_WRITING_INITBPS

707 ERROR_INVALID_WIN_HANDLE

708 ERROR_NO_PASSWORD

709 ERROR_NO_USERNAME

710 ERROR CANNOT START STATE MACHINE

711 Cannot get communications port status.

712 Cannot set communications port status.

713 Cannot enable communications port notifications.

714 Configuration error. Make sure you logged on from Windows and not from MS-DOS.

715 X.25 diagnostic indication.

716 Too many errors occurred because of poor phone line quality.

717 Serial overrun errors were detected while communicating with your modem.

718 The account has expired.

719 Error changing password on domain.

720 No active ISDN lines are available.

721 No ISDN channels are available to make the call.

Summary

This chapter covered a variety of issues in configuring Remote Access Service:

▶ Installing and configuring RAS, and setting up a modem for RAS.

▶ Using unsupported modems with RAS.

▶ Configuring serial ports.

▶ Understanding RAS error messages.

Part V
Disk Documentation

Disk Documentation

This section is the documentation for all the programs and utilities bundled with this book. The disks contain both commercial software and shareware. The commercial software are programs and utilities that usually require payment upfront before you are allowed to look at it. The commercial software contained in these disks were "paid for" when you bought this book. No further charge is expected. The shareware contained here gives you the chance to examine software free of charge during your evaluation of it. If you don't decide to use and keep it, you don't owe anyone anything at all. However, if you decide the shareware is something you want to keep and use, then you are on your honor to send the requested fee to the shareware author. The shareware author keeps the entire fee. It is not shared with either the book authors or publisher. Please print out and use the registration forms found on the disks.

Configuring Windows with System Engineer Version 1.3

Computer systems generally have *boot files* that are read when the computer is first started. CONFIG.SYS and AUTOEXEC.BAT files are typical examples of boot or start-up files on a DOS-based PC. The settings in these two files control how DOS and application software interact with your system. Start-up files enable you to configure your software to work together with your particular hardware configuration.

Windows settings requirements go beyond the setup parameters addressed in the CONFIG.SYS and AUTOEXEC.BAT files. Windows adds its own collection of initialization files. Each time you start Windows, it reads these files and places key pieces of this information into memory during your Windows session.

Two Windows initialization files, WIN.INI and SYSTEM.INI, are critical to starting and maintaining the Windows environment. Windows and Windows applications use the information in these files to configure themselves to your needs and preferences.

The WIN.INI file contains the settings that enable you to customize your Windows environment for printers, fonts, ports, and screen colors. The SYSTEM.INI file contains settings that control hardware configuration, device drivers, memory management, and virtual machines.

Many Windows programs include their own initialization files that the program reads on start-up. Program Manager and File Manager, for example, use PROGMAN.INI and WINFILE.INI, respectively, to store their settings. Control Panel also uses an initialization file, CONTROL.INI, to store settings for printer information, multimedia drivers, desktop patterns and color schemes, and screen saver options.

Some applications add their own information to the WIN.INI file during installation. Because INI files cannot exceed 64K, and because the WIN.INI file is usually the largest initialization file, Microsoft recommends that developers create their own application-specific INI files rather than append to the WIN.INI. If you run a number of Windows applications, you will find several INI files related to these programs on your hard drive.

Introducing System Engineer

The structure for all INI files is essentially the same, and the technique for editing INI files is essentially the same for all INI files. Windows stores the INI files in ASCII format so that you can edit them just as you edit MS-DOS CONFIG.SYS and AUTOEXEC.BAT files. You must be extremely careful when editing any Windows start-up files, however; the slightest error may cause Windows to misbehave or crash.

Until recently, the tools available for editing initialization files were merely text editors. You must have intimate knowledge of the organization, syntax, and setting functions to edit the INI files safely and accurately with a text editor.

System Engineer (Figure 1) provides Windows professionals with a comprehensive set of tools to manage all aspects of Windows configuration on the workstation, whether stand-alone or on networks. In addition to its powerful but easy-to-use interface for editing individual sections and statements within Windows configuration files, System Engineer provides a complete library for storing, managing, and recovering multiple configurations. Changes to any and all INI files or entries are logged in a master file, which creates an audit system that enables users to retrace specific changes made to configuration files.

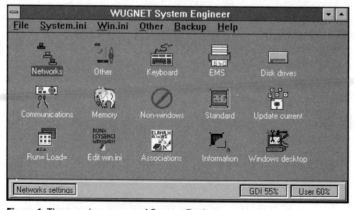

Figure 1: The opening screen of System Engineer.

Unlocking the Windows environment

System Engineer provides access to every SYSTEM.INI and WIN.INI parameter, including

- Undocumented parameters for managing memory
- Undocumented parameters supporting the Windows keyboard interface
- Network setting options, including support for Windows-specific Novell NetWare
- Configuration settings for managing all asynchronous communications ports
- Parameters for setting Windows EMS memory and virtual memory management
- Parameter settings for Windows operation of disk storage devices
- Parameter settings supporting DOS applications running under Windows
- Parameter settings exclusive to Windows standard mode
- System fonts used by Windows

Using real-time monitoring capabilities

System Engineer introduces easy-to-use, real-time monitoring facilities for both expert and nonexpert Windows users.

The *Task Monitor* provides a real-time data window displaying all active tasks with their task handles.

The *File I/O Monitor* enables users to track what files and devices are currently open and determine read/write privileges. This facility also supports monitoring of open data files and Windows-supported devices that are shared, protected, or read-only in nature. This information can then be used by general users in determining the optimum files, buffers, and cache settings for particular tasks in Windows.

The *Memory Monitor* is not just a viewer but a comprehensive statistical monitor reporting the memory use of active module components in six specific memory classes including fonts and dynamic-link libraries (DLLs). Use the monitor snapshots to analyze application-specific GDI and USER system resource memory heaps and to determine what discardable and nondiscardable portions of memory a particular Windows 3.1 module or application is utilizing.

Examining the System Engineer Interface

The anatomy of System Engineer includes an application window title bar, a menu bar, an application workspace, a window control menu button, a status bar, and four tabular panels or *panes*: CONTROL, SYSTEM.INI, WIN.INI, INFORMATION, and BACKUP.

Menus contain all the major commands in System Engineer. You can issue any command simply by making a menu selection. The following sections describe each of System Engineer's menus.

Using the File menu

The File menu (Figure 2) has commands that enable you to carry out the following operations:

- Edit any INI file
- Change a variety of preferred settings
- Access the Windows Control Panel
- Access Windows Setup
- Exit System Engineer

Figure 2: The File menu.

Opening an INI file

Use the Open INI File option to load any compatible Windows 3.x INI file in the System Engineer INI editor (Figure 3).

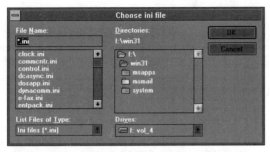

Figure 3: The Choose INI File dialog box.

Choosing preferences to configure System Engineer

You choose File⇨Preferences to display the Preferences dialog box (Figure 4) in which you can set a variety of configuration options, altering the preferences that System Engineer uses. Before you use System Engineer for the first time, you should configure this feature. Double-click the System Engineer icon to load System Engineer, and choose File⇨Preferences. The following paragraphs describe the options you find in the Preferences dialog box.

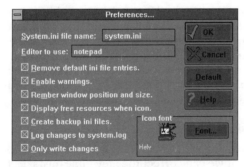

Figure 4: The Preferences dialog box.

SYSTEM.INI File Name

The SYSTEM.INI File Name setting defaults to SYSTEM.INI. You can alter the name of the SYSTEM.INI file to experiment with Windows settings. System Engineer searches the Windows directory for this file. Do not include a path specification with the SYSTEM.INI filename; System Engineer creates or edits the file in the Windows directory automatically. If you maintain several configurations for Windows, specify the name of the SYSTEM.INI file to which you want System Engineer to default.

Editor To Use

The default Editor To Use setting is NOTEPAD.EXE. This option specifies the default editor System Engineer uses to edit files. You can enter a name for a different editor if you prefer (Brief, for example). If you choose another Windows editor, it must be located in a directory specified in the PATH statement in your AUTOEXEC.BAT file.

Remove Default .INI Entries

The Remove Default .INI Entries default setting is Yes (turned on). If you are not familiar with the default WIN.INI and SYSTEM.INI entries, turn off this switch by clearing the check box. If you enable this option, then only entries that differ from the default values are written to system files. Each INI file entry that matches the default value is deleted from the INI file to keep your system file sizes to a minimum.

Enable Warnings

Because changing the SYSTEM.INI file can make Windows unstable or unusable, System Engineer warns you before you try to change SYSTEM.INI. (System Engineer warns you even if the particular set of changes proposed may not make Windows unstable.) To turn off the warning, uncheck the Enable Warnings option.

Remembering Window Position and Size

Use the Remember Window Position and Size option to make System Engineer remember its last window position and use it the next time you start the program. If you have a preferred size and positioning for System Engineer, and you have set this switch to On, System Engineer records this position to SYSENG.INI. Each time you load System Engineer, it opens to the size and position it recorded at the close of the previous session. Setting this switch to Off causes System Engineer to open at the default size the next time it's started.

Create Backup .INI Files

Creating backups when working with critical files is absolutely standard operating procedure (SOP) so that we can correct the inevitable mistakes that we all make. System Engineer backs up the WIN.COM, WIN.INI, and SYSTEM.INI files. When you check the Create Backup .INI Files option, System Engineer saves a backup copy of the INI file under the extension BAK. After saving the backup copy, System Engineer saves the new file with any changes to the current INI filename.

Log Changes to SYSENG.LOG

Enable the Log Changes to SYSENG.LOG option so that most of your changes are logged in the SYSENG.LOG file. You can edit the log, but only changes that you made to SYSTEM.INI and WIN.INI, by using System Engineer, can be undone with the View Syseng Log option on the Other menu.

The default setting for Log Changes to SYSENG.LOG is on. With this setting, System Engineer logs each change to SYSTEM.INI or WIN.INI. The log file shows the last 100 changes made to the system, but only if you've selected Preferences⇨Log Changes to System File. Use this dialog box to view and/or change the settings that System Engineer has made to your Windows system. To undo a change that you have made, select an item in the scrollable list and then click Undo.

Only Write Changes

The Only Write Changes option gives you three iconized view options:

- Icon: When this radio button is active, System Engineer displays as a static icon while minimized.

- Resources: This option tells System Engineer to display free system resources when it is running as an icon. Check this radio button if you want to monitor system resources while using other applications.

- Swapping: Select this option to have System Engineer display the percentage of memory that is being swapped out to disk.

Icon Font

The Icon Font option controls the typeface and point size for the System Engineer's interface. Select the Font button to choose the font from a list of fonts available on your system.

Setting Print Options

Use the Print Options command to change or adjust the font that System Engineer uses to print. To change from the default font, check the Select Printer Font radio button in the Print Options dialog box (Figure 5). Then select the Choose Font button. The Font dialog box appears. Choose the font from the list box, and select a point size. Click OK to complete the command.

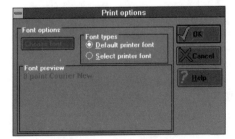

Figure 5: The Print Options dialog box.

Restarting Windows, quitting Windows, quitting and rebooting Windows

Some changes take effect only after you have restarted Windows. Use this command to restart Windows so that the settings you have changed take effect. If you have active programs with unsaved files, the command asks those programs to close the files before restarting Windows. Windows does not restart if any DOS (non-Windows) programs are active.

Viewing SYSTEM.LOG

Select the View SYSTEM.LOG command to view the log file of changes made using System Engineer (Figure 6). This file is available only if you have checked the Log Changes to SYSTEM.LOG option in the Preferences dialog box.

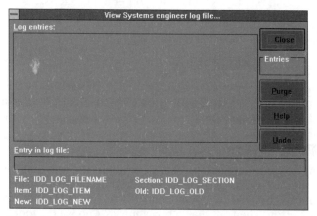

Figure 6: The View System Engineer Log File dialog box.

Accessing the Control Panel

Use the Control Panel command to access the standard Windows Control Panel. The Control Panel displays icons representing the controls for various features and options offered by Windows. The Control Panel enables you to establish settings to customize many aspects of your Windows environment.

Using the Setup program

You can run Windows' Setup program from within Windows to easily change common device drivers: Display, Keyboard, Mouse, and Network. To change any of these device drivers, select File⇨System Setup.

Exiting System Engineer

Choose the Exit option to exit System Engineer.

Using the SYSTEM.INI menu

The SYSTEM.INI menu (Figure 7) includes all the commands that you use to adjust the Windows system settings. After configuring System Engineer, you're ready to raise the hood on Windows and get inside Windows with System Engineer.

Figure 7: The SYSTEM.INI menu.

Looking at SYSTEM.INI: Windows system file

The SYSTEM.INI file, along with the WIN.INI file, is one of the two primary initialization files used by Windows. Most of the information in SYSTEM.INI describes your hardware configuration to Windows.

The SYSTEM.INI file is created by the Windows Setup program during installation. The settings contained in the SYSTEM.INI file after initial installation represent the hardware information specified in Setup during the installation process. Although you can change some of the settings through the Setup program, most of the settings must be edited or added manually.

The SYSTEM.INI file contains several sections, which define groups of related settings. The sections and settings are listed in the SYSTEM.INI file as follows:

Section	Purpose
[boot]	Lists drivers and Windows modules
[boot.description]	Lists the names of devices you can change using Windows Setup
[drivers]	Contains a list of aliases (or names) assigned to installable driver files
[keyboard]	Contains information about the keyboard
[mci]	Lists Media Control Interface (MCI) drivers
[NonWindowsApp]	Contains information used by non-Windows applications
[standard]	Contains information used by Windows in standard mode
[386 Enh]	Contains information used by Windows in 386 enhanced mode

Most of these settings have a built-in default value that is present whether or not the setting appears in SYSTEM.INI. You might need to change one or more of these values to improve the performance of Windows or applications with your system. System Engineer is the tool that enables you to edit Windows initialization files quickly, easily, and accurately.

The following paragraphs take an in-depth look at the SYSTEM.INI settings and tell you how to alter the settings using System Engineer.

Select SYSTEM.INI from the menu bar. The drop-down menu presents you with a list of command options. Each command is listed and its usage explained in this section.

Configuring Windows for non-Windows applications

The NonWindowsApps command enables you to alter the system file settings that affect the performance of non-Windows applications while running under Windows. The [NonWindowsApp] section may contain the following statements:

```
CommandEnvSize=
DisablePositSave=
FontChangeEnable=
GlobalHeapSize=
LocalTSRs=
MouseInDOSBox=
NetAsynchSwitching
ScreenLines=
SwapDisk=
```

System Engineer enables you to edit the entries, described in the following sections, in the Non Windows Application dialog box (Figure 8).

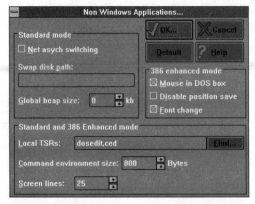

Figure 8: The Non Windows Applications dialog box.

GlobalHeapSize=

This entry specifies the size of a buffer in conventional memory that Windows allocates when running in standard mode. You can use this buffer to share information among all non-Windows applications that are started from Windows. The Global Heap Size setting has no effect when Windows is running in 386 enhanced mode. The default is 0. (You should never need to change this setting.)

MouseInDOSBox=

This entry specifies whether the mouse is supported when you're running a non-Windows application in a window. Mouse support for non-Windows applications running in a window is available automatically if you are using a Windows 3.1 version of the grabbers. If you are using a Windows 3.0 version of the grabbers, and you want mouse support, enable this setting. If you do not want mouse support, disable this setting. The default is 1 if an MS-DOS mouse driver is loaded that has the extension of COM or SYS and that supports using a mouse with a non-Windows application. Otherwise, the default is 0.

DisablePositSave=

When this entry is 0, the position and font used in a non-Windows application is saved in the DOSAPP.INI file when you quit the application. If this entry is 1, any settings that weren't saved previously in DOSAPP.INI are not saved. If this entry is 1, you can override the setting for each non-Windows application by selecting the Save Settings On Exit check box in the Fonts dialog box. The default is 0.

FontChangeEnable=

This entry, if 1, gives you the ability to change the fonts when you're running non-Windows applications in a window on systems that use version 3.0 of the grabbers (usually in version 3.0 display drivers). Windows version 3.1 video grabbers (used in version 3.1 display drivers) include built-in support for changing fonts when running non-Windows applications in a window. If you are using a 3.0 grabber that has not been updated to include the capability to change fonts, and you want to use this feature, set this value to 1. When the Font Change entry is 1, however, your screen might lose characters, and the cursor might change size and position slightly. The default is 1 on systems that use Windows 3.1 grabbers, and 0 on systems that use Windows 3.0 grabbers.

LocalTSRs=

This entry specifies which terminate-and-stay-resident (TSR) programs work properly if they are copied to each instance of a virtual machine. When you start Windows, it detects any TSR programs that are currently running. If the TSR is on the LocalTSRs= list, Windows places a copy of the TSR in each virtual machine you run. Many TSRs do not run properly if they are added to this list. Make sure that your TSR is fully compatible with Windows and can be copied to a virtual machine before you add the TSR to the list. The default is `dosedit, pced, ced`.

CommandEnvSize=

This entry specifies the size of the COMMAND.COM environment. Because running batch files with the extension BAT starts COMMAND.COM, this setting also applies to batch files. The value for this setting must be either 0 or between 160 and 32768. A value of 0 disables the setting. If the value is not valid, it is rounded up to 160 or down to 32768. If the value is less than the current size of the actual environment, the setting is disabled as if it were set to 0. If you specified the environment size in a PIF for COMMAND.COM, the PIF setting overrides this setting. The default is 0 with MS-DOS versions earlier than 3.2. Otherwise, the value is the /e: parameter in the `shell=` line in CONFIG.SYS. To change this value, you must edit SYSTEM.INI.

ScreenLines=

This entry specifies the number of lines displayed on-screen when a non-Windows application runs. An application that specifies a different screen mode can override this entry. The default is 25.

Configuring Windows for standard mode operation

The commands you access when you choose Standard from the SYSTEM.INI menu enable you to alter the system file settings used that affect Windows' operation when it's running in the standard mode. When you choose Standard, the Standard settings dialog box appears (Figure 9).

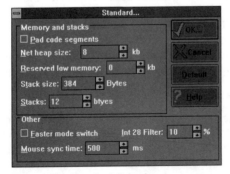

Figure 9: The Standard dialog box.

In the Standard dialog box, you can access the statements contained in the
[Standard] section of the SYSTEM.INI file. The [Standard] section can contain the following statements:

```
FasterModeSwitch
Int28Filter=
MouseSyncTime=
NetHeapSize=
PadCodeSegments=
Stacks=
StackSize=
```

The following paragraphs explain how to use these statements.

PadCodeSegments=

Setting this value to 1 tells Windows to pad code segments with 16 bytes of
additional memory. You might need this padding with some 286 processors.
Padding prevents the last instruction in the segment from being too close to the
segment limit for 80286 C2 stepping. Set this value to 1 only for this 80286 stepping. To determine whether your processor requires stepping, try setting this
value to 1 if your 80286 system hangs in standard mode. The default setting is 0.
(The best option is to get rid of your 286 and get a decent computer!)

NetHeapSize=

This entry specifies the size of the data-transfer buffers that Windows standard
mode creates in conventional 640K memory for transferring data over a network. If an application is not running correctly, your network might require a
larger buffer than the default. Increasing this value decreases the amount of
memory available to applications. If no network software is running, this entry
is ignored, and no memory is allocated. The default value is 8, which specifies
8K buffers for network data transfers.

StackSize=

This entry specifies the size of the interrupt reflector stacks used by DOS.EXE,
the standard mode MS-DOS Extender. The default is 384, which means that
each interrupt reflector stack specified in the stacks statement is 384 bytes in
size. (You should never need to change this entry.)

Stacks=

This entry specifies the number of interrupt reflector stacks used by the standard mode MS-DOS Extender (DOSX) to translate an MS-DOS or BIOS API from
real mode to protected mode. You can specify a number between 8 and 64. The
default is 12. If you receive a Standard Mode: Stack Overflow message, try
increasing this number.

FasterModeSwitch=

This entry, which is used for 286 computers only, tells Windows standard mode to use a faster method of switching from protected to real mode. When this entry is 1, Windows responds more quickly to hardware interrupts, enabling better throughput for interrupt-intensive applications, such as communications applications. The default is 0.

You should set this entry to 1 if you are using a Zenith Z-248 system and are losing characters while typing, or if you are using an Olivetti M-250-E and lose control of the mouse.

Int28Filter=

This entry specifies the percentage of Int 28h interrupts, generated when the system is idle, that are visible to software loaded before Windows. Windows reflects every nth interrupt, where n is the value of this entry. A value of 1, for example, reflects every Int 28h interrupt, a value of 2 reflects every second Int 28h interrupt, a value of 3 reflects every third Int 28h interrupt, and so on. Increasing this value might improve Windows performance but might interfere with some memory-resident software such as a network.

Set this value to 0 to prevent Int 28h interrupts. Keep in mind, however, that setting this value too low adds to system overhead that might interfere with communications applications. The default is 10.

MouseSyncTime=

This entry specifies the number of milliseconds that can elapse between mouse data bytes before Windows running in standard mode assumes that a mouse data packet is complete. This setting affects only Windows standard mode on computers with an IBM PS/2 mouse interface. The default is 500. To change this value, you must edit SYSTEM.INI.

NetWare

This section describes System Engineer's support for Windows-specific Novell NetWare. Figure 10 sows the NetWare dialog box.

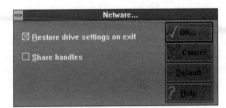

Figure 10: The NetWare dialog box.

Restore Drive Settings on Exit

Check box checked equals `true`.

Normally, when you exit Windows, all your drive mappings are restored to the way they were before you started Windows, and all changes you made inside Windows are lost.

If you set the `RestoreDrives` value to `false`, the mappings you made inside Windows remain when you exit Windows.

Share Handles

Check box checked equals `true`.

Makes drive mappings global.

Normally, each virtual machine you start from Windows has its own set of drive mappings. Changes you make in one virtual machine do not affect another.

If you set the `NWShareHandles` value to `true`, drive mappings are instead global, and changes made in one virtual machine affect all other applications.

386 Enhanced

Use this dialog box to alter the system file settings that are used when Windows is running in 386 enhanced mode. Figure 11 shows the 386 Enhanced submenu.

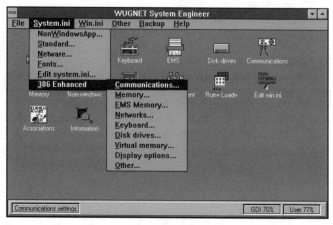

Figure 11: The 386 Enhanced nested submenu.

386 Enhanced, Communications

The [386Enh] section of SYSTEM.INI gives Windows information on running in 386 enhanced mode. If you are running a 286-based system, you can skip this section. If you are running a 386 chip or higher, you should be running Windows in the enhanced mode.

The [386Enh] section contains the most diverse variety of statements compared to any other section in the Windows initialization files. The [386Enh] settings enable you to optimize Windows performance when operating in 386 enhanced mode. These are the settings you manipulate to fine-tune Windows, resolve compatibility issues, and handle other problems related to running DOS applications or hardware configurations. Figure 12 illustrates settings you can make via the 386 Enhanced, communications window.

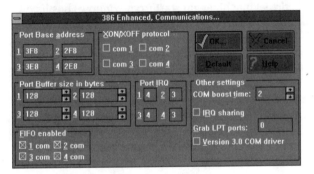

Figure 12: 386 Enhanced, Communications.

Port Base Address

The following port base address entries specify the base (first) port for the serial port adapter you are using for both standard mode and 386 enhanced mode. Check your hardware documentation for the appropriate value. The defaults are COM3Base=3E8h, and the port address values in the BIOS data area for COM1, COM2, and COM4. To change this entry, choose the Ports icon in Control Panel, and click the Advanced button for the selected COM port.

```
COM1Base=address
COM2Base=address
COM3Base=address
COM4Base=address
```

Port IRQ

These entries specify which interrupt line is used by the device on the specified serial port. Check your hardware documentation for the correct value. If a hardware conflict exists between ports, set a value of -1 to disable input for that COM port. The defaults for ISA and EISA machines are COM1Irq=4, COM2Irq=3, COM3Irq=4, and COM4Irq=3; for MCA machines, the defaults are COM1Irq=4, COM2Irq=3, COM3Irq=3, and COM4Irq=3. To change this entry, choose the Ports icon in Control Panel, and click the Advanced button.

```
COM1Irq=number
COM2Irq=number
COM3Irq=number
COM4Irq=number
```

FIFO Enabled

These entries specify whether the FIFO buffer of a COM port's 16550 Universal Asynchronous Receiver Transmitter (UART) should be enabled (On) or disabled (Off). If a serial port does not have a 16550 UART, this setting is ignored. These values are used by Windows for both standard and enhanced modes. The default is On.

```
COM1FIFO=Boolean
COM2FIFO=Boolean
COM3FIFO=Boolean
COM4FIFO=Boolean
```

COM Boost Time

This entry specifies the time to allow a virtual machine to process a COM interrupt. If a communications application is losing keyboard characters on the display, you can try increasing this value. The default is 2.

```
COM1Buffer=number
COM2Buffer=number
COM3Buffer=number
COM4Buffer=number
```

These entries specify the number of characters that the device will buffer on the corresponding communications port. Before changing one of these entries, make sure that the corresponding COMxProtocol= entry has the proper value. Buffering might slow down communications on a port but might be necessary to prevent some communications applications from losing characters at high baud rates. The size of the buffer required depends on the speed of the machine and the application's needs. The default is 128. Before increasing this value, see COMxProtocol=.

IRQ Sharing

This entry specifies whether COM interrupt lines are shared among multiple serial ports or with other devices. Set this switch if your machine uses the same interrupt for COM3 or COM4 as it does for COM1 or COM2. The default is On for Micro Channel and EISA machines; Off for all other machines.

```
COM1Protocol=XOFF | blank
COM2Protocol=XOFF | blank
COM3Protocol=XOFF | blank
COM4Protocol=XOFF | blank
```

These entries specify whether Windows 386 enhanced mode should stop simulating characters in a virtual machine after the virtual machine sends an XOFF character. Set the value for a port to XOFF if a communications application using that port is losing characters while doing text transfers at high baud rates. Windows resumes simulating characters when the virtual machine sends another character after the XOFF character.

Leave this entry blank if the application does binary data transfers; setting this switch might suspend binary transmissions. The default is no entry, which is the same as any entry other than XOFF. Windows does not check for XOFF characters if this entry is blank or set to anything other than XOFF. If the application continues to lose characters after this entry is set, try increasing the related COMxBuffer= value.

Version 3 COM Driver

This entry, if On, indicates that the Virtual COM Driver (VCD) will use its own copy of the serial communications driver's interrupt handler, which improves the performance of COM ports. Set this entry to On if you are using a Windows 3.0 serial communications driver. Set this entry to Off if you are using the standard Windows 3.1 serial communications driver. The default is Off.

Memory

Use this dialog box to adjust the memory settings that Windows uses in 386 enhanced mode (Figure 13).

In the Memory Manager group box, you find the following options:

Local Load High (into UMB)

This entry determines how the upper memory blocks (UMBs) are used when Windows is running on MS-DOS version 5.0. If this entry is Off, Windows uses the entire upper memory area, leaving no extra UMBs available for virtual machines. If this entry is On, Windows does not use all the upper memory area, so the UMBs are available locally to each virtual machine. The default is Off.

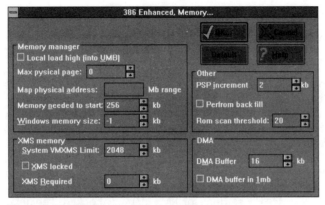

Figure 13: The 386 Enhanced Memory dialog box.

Max Physical Page

This entry specifies the maximum physical page number that the Virtual Machine Manager (VMM) can manage as a usable page, allowing pages to be added at a physical address beyond what the VMM recognized during initialization. If the value specified is less than what the VMM determines, the VMM ignores several physical pages that it would usually use, preventing the use of memory. This feature is useful if you are using a hardware device that cannot recognize all the physical memory in your computer. (ISA DMA network cards, for example, cannot access physical memory above 16MB). The default is determined by Windows, based on the highest physical page number detected by the VMM during initialization.

Map Physical Address

This entry specifies the address range (in megabytes) in which the memory manager preallocates physical page-table entries and linear address space. Set a value for this entry if you are using an MS-DOS device driver that needs this contiguous memory (such as an older version of RAMDrive that uses extended memory). The default is none.

Memory Needed To Start

This entry specifies how much conventional memory must be free to start Windows. The default is 256.

Windows Memory Size

This entry limits the amount of conventional memory Windows can use for itself. The default value indicates that Windows can use as much conventional memory as it needs. Try entering a positive value less than 640 if you don't have enough memory to run Windows in 386 enhanced mode. The default is –1.

In the XMS Memory group box, you find the following options:

System VMXMS Limit

This entry specifies the maximum amount of memory the extended memory driver allocates to MS-DOS device drivers and memory-resident software in the system virtual machine. Set the value to –1 to give an application all the available extended memory that it requests. The default is 2048.

XMS Locked

This entry, if On, locks the contents of the extended memory used by all Windows and non-Windows applications into memory (instead of swapping it to disk), and overrides PIF settings for XMS Memory Locked. The default is Off. (You should never need to change this entry).

XMS Required

This entry specifies how many kilobytes of extended memory must be reserved by the XMS driver to start Windows. Leave this value at 0 if no XMS users are in the system virtual machine. The default is 0.

In the Other group box, you find the following options:

PSP Increment

This entry specifies the amount of additional memory, in 16-byte increments, that Windows should reserve in each successive virtual machine when `UniqueDosPSP=on`. The value that works best for your machine might vary depending on the memory configuration and the applications you are running. Valid values are 2 through 64. The default is 2. See `UniqueDosPSP=` for more information.

Perform Backfill

This entry specifies whether to allocate a full 640K of memory to a computer that has less than 640K of base conventional memory. Setting this entry overrides the automatic checking done by Windows. The default is On. (Windows automatically checks to see whether it needs to fill in memory based on how MS-DOS is occupying memory.) (You should never need to change this entry because Windows can automatically detect whether to perform a backfill.)

ROM Scan Threshold

This entry specifies a parameter used to determine whether an area of memory in the adapter area (usually between C000-EFFF) is ROM when the area has no ROM header or incorrect header information. The number for this entry specifies how many transitions (value changes) must occur within the memory area to determine whether it is ROM. If the number of transitions is greater than the value for this entry, Windows recognizes the memory as ROM. If the number of transitions is less than the value, Windows recognizes the memory as usable memory. Specifying 0 causes Windows to recognize the memory area as ROM and then reserve it as unusable. The default is 20. (You should never need to change this entry.)

In the DMA group box, you find the following options:

DMA Buffer

This entry specifies the amount of memory to be reserved for the Direct Memory Access (DMA) buffer. This memory is allocated above 640K, if possible. Windows 386 enhanced mode defaults to a DMA buffer size that handles disk access. The default is 16.

DMA Buffer in 1 MB

This entry, if set to On, indicates that the DMA buffer memory should be in the first 1MB of memory (above 640K, if possible) to be compatible with 8-bit bus master cards. The default is Off.

EMS Memory

Use this dialog box (Figure 14) to adjust the EMS memory settings that Windows uses in 386 enhanced mode.

Don't use Windows EMS driver.

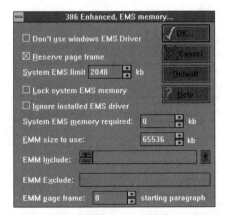

Figure 14: The 386 Enhanced, EMS Memory dialog box.

This entry, if set to `On`, prevents Windows 386 enhanced mode from installing the expanded memory driver. This setting differs from setting `EMMSize=0`, which prevents UMBs from being allocated but does not prevent the EMS driver from being loaded. The default is `Off`.

Reserve Page Frame

This entry tells Windows whether to give preference to EMS page frame space or conventional memory when it has to use one of them to allocate MS-DOS transfer buffers. This choice is necessary when Windows cannot find space between 640K and 1MB other than EMS page frame space. If set to `On`, this entry preserves EMS page frame space at the expense of conventional memory. If you are not going to run non-Windows applications that use expanded memory, set this entry to `Off` to give non-Windows applications more conventional memory. The default is `On`.

System EMS Limit

This entry specifies how many kilobytes of expanded memory Windows should be permitted to use. Setting this value to `0` prevents Windows from gaining access to any expanded memory. Setting it to `-1` gives Windows all the available expanded memory that it requests. The default is `2048`.

Lock System EMS Memory

This entry, if On, locks the contents of expanded memory used by all Windows and non-Windows applications into memory (instead of swapping it to disk) and overrides PIF settings for EMS Memory Locked. Set this value to `On` if you are using a disk cache program that uses expanded memory. The default is `Off`.

Ignore Installed Driver?

This entry, if set to `On`, enables Windows to start in 386 enhanced mode even when an unknown expanded memory manager (EMM) is running. Starting Windows with an unknown EMM running can cause the system to fail if memory-resident software was using expanded memory before Windows started. Set this entry only if no such software is installed, or you are sure that it will not be active when you run Windows. This entry applies only to EMMs servicing physical EMS hardware; Windows will not disable unrecognized 80386 expanded memory emulators. The default is `Off`.

System EMS Memory Required

This entry specifies how much expanded memory must be free to start Windows. Leave this value at `0` if no non-Windows application running under Windows will require expanded memory. The default is `0`.

EMM Size To Use

This entry specifies the total amount of memory to be made available for mapping as expanded memory. The default allocates the maximum possible amount of system memory as expanded memory. Specify a value for this entry if you run an application that allocates all the available expanded memory. You can tell that you are running such an application if, when you run the application, you can never create any new virtual machine. If the EMM Size To Use value is 0, no expanded memory is allocated. This entry does not prevent the EMS driver from being loaded; use NoEMMDriver=on to turn off EMS. The default is 65536.

Networks

Use this dialog box (Figure 15) to adjust the network settings that Windows uses in 386 enhanced mode.

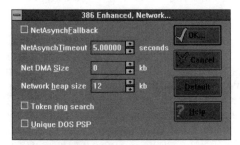

Figure 15: 386 Enhanced, Network.

Net Asynch Fallback

This entry, if set to On, tells Windows to attempt to save a failing NetBIOS request. When an application issues an asynchronous NetBIOS request, Windows attempts to allocate space in its global network buffer to receive the data. If the global buffer has insufficient space, Windows usually fails the NetBIOS request. If this entry is On, Windows attempts to save such a request by allocating a buffer in local memory and preventing any other virtual machines from running until the data is received and the timeout period specified by NetAsynchTimeout= expires. The default is Off.

Net Asynch Timeout

This entry specifies the timeout period when Windows needs to enter a critical section to service an asynchronous NetBIOS request. This value is used only when NetAsynchFallback= is set. This value can include a decimal, such as 0.5. The default is 5.0.

Net DMA Size

This entry specifies the DMA buffer size for NetBIOS transport software if a network has been installed. In this case, the buffer size is the larger value between this value and the value of DMABufferSize=. The default is 32 on Micro Channel machines, and 0 on non-Micro Channel machines.

Network Heap Size

This entry specifies the size, in 4K increments, of the data-transfer buffers that Windows 386 enhanced mode allocates in conventional memory for transferring data over a network. All values are rounded up to the nearest 4K. The default is 12.

Token Ring Search

This entry, if On, tells Windows whether to search for a token ring network adapter on machines with IBM PC/AT architecture. Set this entry to Off if you are not using a token ring card and the search interferes with another device. The default is On.

Unique DOS PSP

This entry, if set to On, tells Windows to start every application at a unique address (PSP). Each time Windows creates a new virtual machine to start a new application, Windows reserves a unique amount of memory (*i* bytes) below the application. For example, the first application would be loaded at address M, the second at address M+*i*, the third at M+2*i*, and so forth. The amount of memory (*i*) is determined by PSPIncrement=. These entries ensure that applications in different virtual machines all start at different addresses. Some networks use applications' load addresses to identify the different processes using the network. On such networks, setting this entry to Off might cause one application to fail when you exit another because the network interprets them as the same application. But setting this entry leaves slightly less memory for non-Windows applications. The default is On if you are running a network based on Microsoft Network (MS-Net) or LAN Manager; Off for all other networks.

Keyboard

Use this dialog box (Figure 16) to adjust the keyboard settings that Windows uses in 386 enhanced mode.

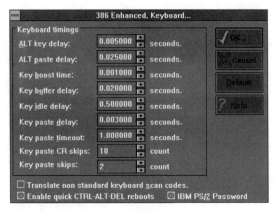

Figure 16: 386 Enhanced, Keyboard.

KeyBoostTime

This entry specifies how much time an application gets to run with increased priority when it receives a keystroke. Use this entry to increase the response to keystrokes when several background applications are running. The default is .001.

KeyBufferDelay

This entry specifies the time to delay pasting keyboard input after the keyboard buffer is full. Some applications might require more than .2 seconds. The default is .2.

KeyIdleDelay

This entry specifies how long Windows ignores idle calls after simulating a keystroke into a virtual machine. You can set this value to 0 to speed up keyboard input, but some applications might respond sluggishly if you do. The default is .5.

KeyPasteDelay

This entry specifies how long to wait before pasting any characters after a key has been pressed. Some applications might require more time than .003 seconds for recognition of a keystroke. The default is .003.

KeyPasteTimeout

This entry specifies how much time to allow an application to make the necessary BIOS calls for reading keyboard input before Windows changes from the fast paste (Int 16h) to the slow paste (Int 9h) mechanism. The default is 1.

KeyPasteCRSkipCount

This entry specifies the number of times that a read-status Int 16 call should return a status of `empty` for the keyboard buffer after pasting a carriage return and before pasting another character. When pasting data from the Clipboard to a non-Windows application, Windows must first paste the data to the BIOS keyboard buffer before pasting it into the application. This setting is used to slow down fast pasting from the Clipboard to the keyboard buffer so that the application can handle all incoming characters from the buffer. If you seem to lose characters, or if the screen does not update often enough while pasting information from the Clipboard, increase this value. This setting is related to `KeyPasteSkipCount=`. The default is `10`.

KeyPasteSkipCount

This entry specifies the number of times that a read-status Int 16 call should return a status of `empty` for the keyboard buffer before pasting another character. When Windows pastes data from the Clipboard to a non-Windows application, it must first paste the data to the BIOS keyboard buffer before pasting it into the application. This setting is used to slow down fast pasting from the Clipboard to the keyboard buffer so that the application can handle all incoming characters from the buffer. If you seem to lose characters, or if the screen does not update often enough while pasting information from the Clipboard, increase this value. The default is `2`. This setting is related to `KeyPasteCRSkipCount=`.

KybdPasswd

This entry specifies whether the Virtual Keyboard Device (VKD) should support PS/2 8042 commands that implement password security. This entry applies only to 8042 keyboard controllers that are compatible with the PS/2 computer. The default is `On` for IBM PS/2 computers; `Off` for all other computers.

KybdReboot

If this entry is `On`, Windows attempts to reboot the computer by using a keyboard controller command. On some computers this method is unreliable. If your computer hangs while rebooting, set this entry to `Off`, in which case Windows quits and displays a prompt to press Ctrl+Alt+Del a second time if you attempt to reboot from the keyboard while Windows is running. The default is `On`.

Disk Drives

Use this dialog box (Figure 17) to adjust the disk settings that Windows uses in 386 enhanced mode.

Figure 17: 386 Enhanced, Disk Drives.

File System Change Notification

This entry indicates whether File Manager automatically receives messages anytime a non-Windows application creates, renames, or deletes a file. When this entry is Off, you can run a virtual machine exclusively even when it modifies files. Setting this entry to On can slow down system performance significantly. The default is On for 386 enhanced mode; Off in standard mode.

Minimum User Disk Space Free

This entry tells Windows how much disk space to leave free when creating a temporary swap file. Use this entry if your system's paging drive has less available space than Windows can use for paging. This entry has no effect if a permanent swap file exists. The default is 500.

Virtual Hard Drive Interrupt

This entry enables Windows 386 enhanced mode to terminate interrupts from the hard disk controller, bypassing the ROM routine that handles these interrupts. Some hard drives might require that this entry be set to Off for interrupts to be processed correctly. If this entry is set to Off, the ROM routine handles the interrupts, which slows the system's performance. The default is On for AT-compatible computers; Off for other computers.

Virtual Memory

In the Other group box (Figure 18), you find the following options:

System VMV86 Locked

This entry, if set to On, causes the virtual-mode memory being used in the system virtual machine to remain locked in memory rather than being swappable out to disk. Because Windows handles this process, there is no known reason to set this entry. The default is Off.

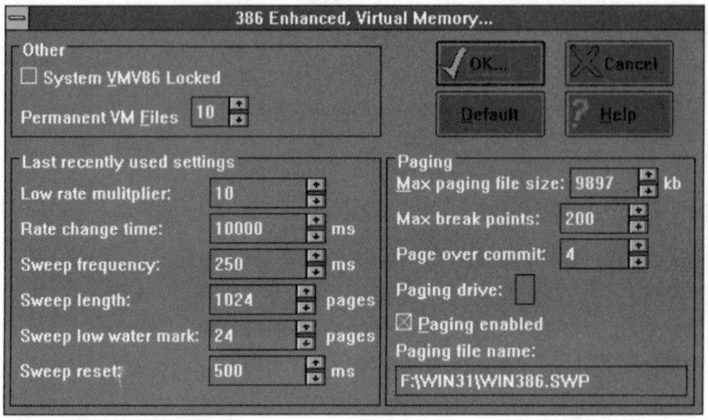

Figure 18: 386 Enhanced, Virtual Memory.

Permanent VM Files

This entry specifies the number of private file handles Windows should allocate to each virtual machine. Increase this value if an application does not have enough file handles to run. The total number of file handles, including the global handles specified in the `files=` statement in CONFIG.SYS, cannot exceed 255. If it does exceed 255, this value is rounded down. Set this value to `0` to prevent the allocation of any private file handles. The default is `10`; if the MS-DOS Share utility is installed, this setting in SYSTEM.INI is ignored.

In the Last Recently Used Settings group box, you find the following options:

Low Rate Multiplier

This entry specifies the value used to determine the Least Recently Used (LRU) low paging rate sweep frequency, which is computed by multiplying the value for `LRUSweepFreq=` by the value specified for `LRULowRateMult=`. You can use a value between `1` and `65535`. The default is `10`. (You should never need to change this entry.)

Rate Change Time

This entry specifies the length of time that the Virtual Memory Manager (VMM) stays at high rate with no paging before switching to low rate, and the length of time the VMM stays at low rate with no paging before turning the LRU sweep off. The default is `10000`. (You should never need to change this entry.)

Sweep Frequency

This entry specifies the time between LRU sweep passes, which is also the high paging rate sweep frequency. The default is `250`. (You should never need to change this entry.)

Sweep Length

This entry specifies the length in pages of the region swept on each pass. Windows computes this value by dividing the value of `LRUSweepReset=` by the value of `LRUSweepFreq=`. The value must be at least 1. The default is 1024. (You should never need to change this entry.)

Sweep Low Water Mark

This entry specifies when the LRU sweeper should be turned on. When the number of free pages drops below this value, the sweeper is turned on. The default is 24. (You should never need to change this entry.)

Sweep Reset

This entry specifies the time desired for an ACC bit reset divided by 4MB of pages. Therefore, the time to reset all ACC bits is the number of pages in the system plus 1023 divided by 1024, where 1024 pages equals 4MB. The minimum value is 100. The default is 500. (You should never need to change this entry.)

In the Paging group box, you find the following options:

Max Paging File Size

This entry specifies the maximum size for a temporary swap file. The default is 50 percent of the available disk space.

Max Break Points

This entry specifies the maximum number of break points (a method for transferring control to Windows 386 enhanced mode) that can be used by the VMM. You might need to increase this value if you are using a third-party virtual device driver that requires more break points than the default value. The default is 200.

Page Over Commit

This entry specifies the multiplier that determines the amount of linear address space the VMM creates for the system, which is computed by rounding up the amount of available physical memory to the nearest 4MB and then multiplying that value by the value specified for `PageOverCommit=`. Increasing this value increases the amount of available linear address space, causing the size of data structures to increase. A higher value also increases paging activity proportionately and can slow down the system. You can specify a value between 1 and 20. The default is 4.

Paging Drive

This entry specifies the disk drive where Windows 386 enhanced mode allocates a temporary swap file. This entry is ignored if you have a permanent swap file. If you don't have a permanent swap file and no drive is specified or the specified drive does not exist, Windows attempts to put the temporary swap file on the drive containing the SYSTEM.INI file. If the specified drive is full, paging is turned off. The default is none.

Paging Enabled

This entry sets demand paging (virtual memory). Set this entry to Off only if you need the disk space that would be used for a temporary swap file. The default is On.

Paging File Name

This entry specifies the path and file name for the temporary swap file that is created when you start Windows in 386 enhanced mode. This file is deleted when you quit Windows. This setting overrides the PagingDrive= setting. The default is WINDOWS\WIN386.SWP.

Display options

A number of different statements in the SYSTEM.INI file affect your display. The display driver and grabber files are listed in the [boot] section, usually the first section in the SYSTEM.INI file. Use this dialog box (Figure 19) to adjust display settings.

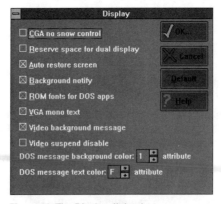

Figure 19: The Display dialog box.

CGA No Snow

This entry, when On, causes Windows to do special handling to avoid snow appearing on an IBM CGA display device. The default is Off.

Auto Restore

This entry specifies whether the display for non-Windows applications should be restored by Windows or by the applications themselves when they become active. If this entry is On, Windows saves the display information for a non-Windows application in memory when you switch away from the application. When you switch back to the application, Windows restores the screen. If this entry is Off, the application must restore its own display by repainting the screen. This action requires less memory but can slow down performance because Windows can usually restore the screen faster. This entry applies only to VGA displays and affects only applications that notify Windows that they can update their screens automatically when Windows sends a display update call. The default is On.

Background Notify

This entry specifies when a notification should be sent to a non-Windows application or to Windows to prevent the application from attempting to access the display (which might corrupt the display of a different application). This notification can be sent while switching to a different application or when attempting to access the actual display. If this entry is Off, Windows sends a notification when switching between applications. Set this entry to Off if you are using a display that has special hardware (for example, 8514 and TIGA). If you are using a VGA display, setting this entry to On should work in most cases. The default is On for VGA displays; Off for 8514 displays.

VGA Mono Text

This entry tells Windows to ignore the video memory address space in VGA displays, usually used for monochrome adapters. When this entry is Off, Windows can use the B000h through B7FF range in upper memory if no hardware device is using these addresses and other applications do not use the monochrome display mode of the VGA adapter. This entry applies only to VGA displays. The default is On.

Video Background Message

This entry, if On, causes Windows to display a message when a background application is suspended or if its display cannot be updated properly because video memory is low. Setting this entry to Off turns off the warning message.

This entry affects all non-Windows applications currently running. The default is `On`.

Video Suspend Disable

This entry specifies whether to suspend an application running in the background if its display becomes corrupted. If this entry is `On`, the application continues running. If it is `Off`, the application is suspended, and a warning message appears if the `VideoBackgroundMsg=On`. This entry applies only to VGA displays. The default is `Off`.

DOS Message Background Color

This entry specifies the background color of message screens, such as the screen that appears when you press Ctrl+Alt+Del. The default is `1` (for blue).

DOS Message Text Color

This entry specifies the color used to display text in message screens, such as the screen that appears when you press Ctrl+Alt+Del. The default is F (for white).

Other

Use this dialog box (Figure 20) to adjust all the other settings (i.e., those not covered in the topics on memory, EMS memory, keyboard, etc.) that Windows uses in 386 enhanced mode.

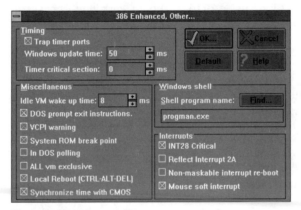

Figure 20: 386 Enhanced, Other.

In the Timing group box, you find the following options:

Trap Timer Ports

If this entry is set to Off, Windows enables applications to read from and write to the system timer ports. In this case, Windows can usually detect when an application has changed the timer interrupt interval and then make any adjustments to the time. Some applications, however, might prevent Windows from keeping accurate time. If your system's time appears to be running fast or slow, set this entry to On so that Windows denies access to the timer ports. An On setting ensures that the system time is accurate but might cause applications that frequently access the timer ports to run slowly. If you do not want to set this entry to On, set SyncTime=On, which causes Windows to restore the correct time periodically regardless of whether applications access the timer ports. The default is On.

Windows Update Time

This entry specifies the time Windows takes between updates of the display for a non-Windows application running in a window. The default is 50.

Timer Critical Section

This entry instructs Windows to go into a critical section around all timer interrupt code and specifies a timeout period. Specifying a positive value ensures that only one virtual machine at a time receives timer interrupts. Some networks and other global memory-resident software might fail unless you use this entry. Using this entry, however, does slow down performance and can make the system sluggish or seem to stop for short periods of time. The default is 0.

In the Miscellaneous group box, you find the following options:

Idle VM Wake Up Time

This entry causes timer interrupts to periodically "wake up" idle virtual machines after the specified number of seconds has elapsed. If a virtual machine does not use timer interrupts (Int 8 or Int 1Ch), Windows does not usually force timer interrupts into a virtual machine unless it is active. This entry forces the timer interrupts to occur. The value for this entry is rounded down to the lowest power of 2 (for example, 1, 2, 4, 8, 16, 32, 64). The default is 8.

DOS Prompt Exit Instructions

This entry, if On, causes a message box to appear when you start the MS-DOS Prompt, displaying instructions on how to exit and switch away from the MS-DOS Prompt. Set this entry to Off if you do not want to see the message. The default is On.

System ROM Break Point

This entry specifies whether Windows should use ROM address space between F000:0000 and 1MB for a break point. Windows 386 enhanced mode usually searches this space to find a special instruction that is used as a system break point. If this address space contains something other than permanently available ROM, set this entry to Off. The default is On if Windows is started in real mode of the 80386/486 CPU; Off if Windows is started in virtual mode of the 80386/486 CPU. Most 386 memory managers, such as QEMM and 386MAX, require this value to be set to Off. If a 386 memory manager is running, Windows is started in virtual mode. Otherwise, Windows is started in real mode.

In DOS Polling

This entry, if set to On, prevents Windows from running other applications when memory-resident software has the InDOS flag set. Setting this entry to On is necessary if the memory-resident software needs to be in a critical section to do operations off an Int 21 hook. Setting this entry to On slows down system performance slightly. The default is Off.

All VM Exclusive

This entry, when On, forces all applications to run in exclusive full-screen mode, overriding all other settings in the application PIFs. Setting AllVMsExclusive=on might help avoid UAEs when you are running network or memory-resident software that is not compatible with Windows. The default is Off.

Local Reboot

This entry specifies whether you can press Ctrl+Alt+Del to quit applications that cause an unrecoverable error in 386 enhanced mode, without restarting Windows. If this setting is On, you can quit the application. If this setting is Off, pressing Ctrl+Alt+Del restarts your entire system (as it usually does).

Synchronize Time with CMOS

This entry, if On, causes Windows to synchronize its time periodically with the computer's CMOS clock. If this entry is Off, Windows usually maintains the correct time, unless TrapTimerPorts=off when you are running applications that can cause the system time to run faster or slower than the actual time. The default is On.

In the Windows Shell group box, you find the following option:

Shell Program Name

This entry specifies the Windows shell program that runs when you start Windows. Unless you change this entry, Program Manager runs when you start Windows. The default is none (blank). Setup initializes this value as PROGMAN.EXE.

In the Interrupts group box, you find the following options:

INT28 Critical

This entry specifies whether a critical section is needed to handle Int 28h interrupts used by memory-resident software. Some network virtual devices do internal task switching on Int 28h interrupts. These interrupts might hang some network software, indicating the need to add an INT28hCritical= entry. If you are not using such software, setting this entry to Off might improve Windows task switching. The default is On.

Reflect Interrupt 2A

This entry indicates whether Windows should consume or reflect MS-DOS Int 2A signals. If the value is Off, Windows consumes these signals and therefore runs more efficiently. Set this entry to On if you are running memory-resident software that relies on detecting Int 2A messages. The default is Off.

Non-maskable Interrupt Reboot

This entry, if set to On, causes a reboot to occur when a nonmaskable interrupt is received. The default is Off.

Mouse Soft Interrupt

This entry specifies whether Windows should convert Int 33h function 0 hard initialization calls to function 33 soft initialization calls, which do not reset the mouse hardware. Set this entry to On if you want to use a mouse with a non-Windows application started in a window. Set this entry to Off if the cursor and screen information appear distorted when you are using the mouse with an application. If you set this entry to Off, you are not able to use the mouse with a non-Windows application started in a window. The default is On.

Using the WIN.INI menu

Use the WIN.INI menu (Figure 21) to

- Specify programs to run or load at Windows start-up
- Alter menus and icon fonts

- Change colors for different kinds of Help text
- Edit WIN.INI sections
- Flush the WIN.INI internal file cache
- Associate data files with EXE files

Figure 21: The WIN.INI menu.

Looking at WIN.INI: Windows initialization file

The WIN.INI file contains several sections, each of which consists of a group of related entries that you can use to customize the Windows environment. A specific WIN.INI file might not have all these sections, or it might have additional sections, depending on your system's hardware and software requirements. For example, many Windows applications add entries in WIN.INI to define user preferences and other items. These basic sections can appear in WIN.INI after you first install Windows.

Section	Purpose
[Windows]	Affects several elements of the Windows environment.
[desktop]	Controls the appearance of the desktop and the position of windows and icons.
[extensions]	Associates specified types of files with corresponding applications.
[intl]	Describes how to display items for countries other than the United States.
[ports]	Lists all available output ports.
[fonts]	Describes the screen font files that are loaded by Windows.
[fontSubstitutes]	Lists pairs of fonts that are recognized by Windows as interchangeable.
[TrueType]	Describes options for using and displaying TrueType fonts.
[mci extensions]	Associates specified types of files with Media Control Interface devices.

Section	Purpose
[network]	Describes network settings and previous network connections.
[embedding]	Lists the server objects used in Object Linking and Embedding (OLE).
[Windows Help]	Lists settings used to specify the default size, placement, and text colors of the Help window and dialog boxes.
[sound]	Lists the sound files assigned to each system event.
[printerPorts]	Lists active and inactive output devices to be accessed by Windows.
[devices]	Lists active output devices that provide compatibility with earlier versions of Windows applications.
[programs]	Lists additional paths that Windows searches to find a program file when you try to open an associated data file.
[colors]	Defines colors for the Windows display.

More sections can be inserted in WIN.INI by other Windows applications, although some applications set up their own INI files. For information about those sections, see the application's documentation.

Specifying start-up programs

Select this command from the WIN.INI menu or an icon to change the programs that Windows loads or runs at start-up. Programs specified on the RUN= and LOAD= line can be separated by a comma (,), tab (\t), or space. Figure 22 shows the dialog box used for these settings.

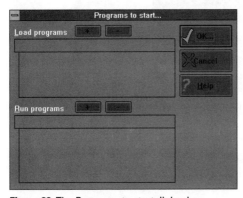

Figure 22: The Programs to start dialog box.

To add a start-up program, follow these steps:

1. Click in either the Load Programs or Run Programs list.

2. Click the + button and use the dialog box to find a program name.

To remove a start-up program, follow these steps:

1. Select a program in either the Load Programs or Run Programs list.

2. Click the - button.

System Engineer verifies whether the program is in the path. If true, System Engineer removes the path specifier from the filename and removes any EXE, BAT, or COM filename extensions.

To save start-up program changes, choose the OK button.

Modifying the desktop display

Select this command from the menu, or double-click the Windows Desktop icon. In the Desktop dialog box (Figure 23), you can change a variety of Windows menu and icon features. You can change the appearance of the icon title font that all Windows applications use when minimized. A sample of the font is displayed at the bottom of the dialog box. This sample icon shows what the new icon title font might look like. When you choose the OK button, the changes are saved to WIN.INI and made to all programs currently running.

Figure 23: The Desktop dialog box.

Right Menu Drop Alignment

Check the check box to align drop-down menus on the right (rather than the left).

Menu Show Delay

Specify a value in milliseconds for the delay before menus drop down.

Icon Vertical Spacing

Use the scroll bar to adjust the value in pixels.

Size of Icon Title Font

Adjust the value by using the scroll bars or clicking Find.

Font Name

Type a new name in the edit box, or click the Find button.

Find Font

Scroll the list to find a font for the dialog title.

Bold Icon Title Text

Check the check box to change the icon text to bold. Choose a font from the scrollable list.

Word Wrap Titles of Icons

Check the Word Wrap Titles of Icons check box.

Apply

Click the Apply button to apply the font changes to the sample icon.

Changing Help Colors

Use the Help Colors dialog box (Figure 24) to make a global change to colors for the links used in all Windows Help programs running on your machine. Using different colors helps you identify what sort of topic links are in use.

Click a button and then use the scroll bars to adjust the red, green, and blue (RGB) values.

The colors for System Engineer Help are hard-coded and unchangeable.

Figure 24: The Help Colors dialog box.

Jump

Jumps to another topic in the current Help file.

Popup

Displays a Help topic from the current Help file within a pop-up box.

Macro

Executes a WinHelp macro.

If Jump

Jumps to another Help topic in a different Help file.

If Popup

Displays a box of Help text from a topic in a different Help file.

Find

Displays a color palette so that you can choose a premixed color.

Editing WIN.INI

Use the Edit WIN.INI command to edit a Windows INI file. You can archive and unarchive several versions of one file for experimentation. See the Options command on the Backup menu.

System Engineer uses the same dialog box (with a different title) to edit both SYSTEM.INI and WIN.INI. Only WIN.INI is shown in Figure 25.

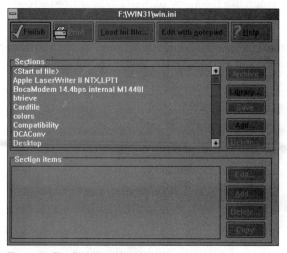

Figure 25: The F:\WIN31\WIN.INI dialog box.

Finish

Use this option to leave the dialog box. If you haven't saved a changed section, System Engineer asks for confirmation.

Print

Use this option to print only the current section of the INI file.

Load .INI File

Use this option to load a different INI file into the INI editor.

Edit with Notepad

Choose this option to load the current INI file into your editor. You can use any editor, not just Windows Notepad. Use File⇨Preferences to change editors.

Archive

Use this option to archive the current section to the specified INI archive backup file.

Library

Use this option to retrieve and manage archived sections.

Save

Use this option to save to the INI file only the section currently being edited.

Add

Use this option to add a section to the current INI file. System Engineer presents a dialog box for you to complete.

Delete

Use this option to remove the selected section from the INI file.

Edit

Choose this option if you want to edit the highlighted section item. You also can double-click the item to begin editing.

Add

Use this option to add an item to the current section. System Engineer presents a dialog box for you to complete.

Delete

Choose this option to remove the selected item from the section.

Sections

Click a section of the INI file here. System Engineer then presents the section items in the Section Items scrollable list. Use the buttons to the right of the Sections scrollable list to modify entire sections.

Section Items

Click an item from the INI file section here. Use the buttons to the right of the scrollable list to modify only section items.

Flushing the WIN.INI cache

Windows stores WIN.INI settings in an internal cache to speed up the reading and setting of these options. Often when you change an option in the WIN.INI file, some applications seem to take no notice of these changes. The reason is that the settings have been stored in the cache, and Windows has not reread the WIN.INI file.

Use the Flush Cache command to flush the WIN.INI cache, and Windows reads from the (updated) WIN.INI file the next time you ask it to read an option.

The command also sends a message to all applications telling them that the WIN.INI file has changed and to reread stored WIN.INI file options.

Editing Associations

Use the Associations command to edit the file extension associations stored in WIN.INI. Figure 26 shows the dialog box used to accomplish this.

Figure 26: The Associations dialog box.

To edit an existing association, follow these steps:

 1. Select the association from the list of associations.

2. Edit the association extension or program by using the edit windows. Choose a new program to associate with the extension by clicking the Find Program button.

3. Click the Update Association button to save your changes.

To delete an existing association, follow these steps:

1. Select the association from the list of associations.

2. Click the Delete Association button. The association you deleted shows as =*delete* in the Associations list box.

3. Choose the OK button to remove the association permanently.

To create a new association, follow these steps:

1. Type the new association information into the edit windows. Choose a new program to associate with the extension by clicking the Find Program button.

2. Click the New Association button.

3. Click the OK button to save the changes to the association information.

Configuring Program Manager

The last command in the WIN.INI menu, Program Manager Restrictions (Figure 27), bears a little more discussion. This command enables you to configure characteristics for Windows' Program Manager. Because this command manipulates entries in the PROGRAM.INI file, I'll discuss it in a separate section that follows.

Figure 27: The Program Manager Restrictions dialog box.

Setting up System Engineer for drag-and-drop support

System Engineer is a drag-and-drop–aware utility, but to use drag and drop, you need to modify the Associations section of your WIN.INI. All files with the INI extension are listed in the [Associations] section of WIN.INI like this:

```
[Associations]
*.ini=Notepad.exe ^.INI
```

Use an editor, such as Notepad, to change this line to

```
*.ini=syseng.exe ^.INI.
```

Save your WIN.INI file, and launch System Engineer. Open the WIN.INI menu, and choose Flush.WIN.INI.Cache. This command forces Windows 3.1 to reread your edited WIN.INI from the disk.

Looking at PROGMAN.INI: the Program Manager initialization file

The Program Manager initialization file, PROGMAN.INI, usually has entries for [settings] and [groups], which describe what should appear in the Program Manager window when you run Program Manager. The [settings] section usually has these entries:

```
[Settings]
Window=60 28 565 388 1
SaveSettings=1
MinOnRun=0
AutoArrange=1
Startup=
```

Entry	Value
Window=	Four numbers that indicate the position of the window when Program Manager is opened, followed by a 1 if the window is maximized.
SaveSettings=	1 if the Save Settings on Exit command on the Options menu is checked in Program Manager. In this case, Program Manager saves the current configuration when you close Windows.
MinOnRun=	1 if the Minimize on Use command is checked on the Options menu in Program Manager. In this case, the Program Manager is iconized when you run another application.
AutoArrange=	1 if the AutoArrange command is checked on the Options menu in Program Manager. In this case, the icons in each group are automatically arranged when you run Program Manager.
Startup=	Name of the group that serves as the start-up group. If this entry is blank, the Startup group created in Windows Setup is the start-up group.

The PROGMAN.INI file also has a section named [groups], which has entries such as these:

```
[Groups]
Group1= C:\WINDOWS\ACCESSOR.GRP
Group2= C:\WINDOWS\GAMES.GRP
Group3= C:\WINDOWS\ALDUS.GRP
Group5= C:\WINDOWS\WORDFORW.GRP
Group6= C:\WINDOWS\MAIN.GRP
Group7= C:\WINDOWS\STARTUP.GRP
Order=  8 7 2 3 5 1 6
Group8= C:\WINDOWS\APPLICAT.GRP
```

Entry Value

Group*x*=	A filename (with full path) for the GRP file that contains the group created during Setup, created when an application was installed, or that you created in Program Manager.
Order=	A list of numbers separated with spaces, indicating the order in which the groups are drawn in the window.

Using the Program Manager Restrictions command

A system administrator might use the Program Manager Restrictions command to add or adjust the restrictions placed on users accessing Program Manager, for custom installations. System Engineer provides direct access to the settings that control the access level.

```
[restrictions]
NoRun=
NoClose=
NoSaveSettings=
NoFileMenu=
EditLevel=
```

Entry	Value
The File⇨Disable Run command keeps the user from running programs.	
NoRun=	1 disables the File⇨Run command. The Run command appears dimmed on the File menu, and the user cannot run applications from Program Manager unless the applications are set up as icons in a group.
The File⇨Disable Exit Windows command keeps the user in Windows.	
NoClose=	1 disables the File ⇨Exit Windows command. Users then cannot quit Program Manager through the File menu or the Control menu (the Exit Windows and Close commands are dimmed) or by using Alt+F4.

The Disable Save Settings command keeps the user from changing settings.

NoSaveSettings= — 1 disables the Options⇨Save Settings on Exit command. The Save Settings command appears dimmed on the Options menu, and any changes that the user makes to the arrangement of windows and icons are not saved when Windows is restarted. This setting overrides the SaveSettings= entry in the [Settings] section of the PROGMAN.INI file.

The Remove File Menu from Program Manager command deletes the File menu from Program Manager.

NoFileMenu= — 1 removes the File menu from Program Manager. All the commands on that menu become unavailable. Users can start the applications in groups by selecting them and pressing Enter or by double-clicking the icon. Unless you have also disabled the Exit Windows command, users can still quit Windows by using the Control menu or Alt+F4.

The Edit Level on Program Manager Groups command assigns the level of control (from 1 to 4) the user can have in changing Program Manager groups.

EditLevel=*n* — Sets restrictions for what users can modify in Program Manager. You can specify one of the following values for *n:*

- 0 enables the user to make any change. (This setting is the default value.)

- 1 prevents the user from creating, deleting, or renaming groups. If you specify this value, the New, Move, Copy, and Delete commands on the File menu are not available when a group is selected.

- 2 sets all restrictions in EditLevel=1, plus prevents the user from creating or deleting program items. If you specify this value, the New, Move, Copy, and Delete commands on the File menu are not available at all.

- 3 sets all restrictions in EditLevel=2, plus prevents the user from changing command lines for program items. If you specify this value, the text in the Command Line box in the Properties dialog box cannot be changed.

- 4 sets all restrictions in EditLevel=3, plus prevents the user from changing any program item information. If you specify this value, none of the areas in the Properties dialog box can be modified. The user can view the dialog box, but all the areas are dimmed.

The Other menu

Use the Other (Figure 28) menu to

- Get real-time information on the current window (such as task number, class name, hWnd)
- Restart Windows
- Get real-time information on how Windows is performing (such as resources, drivers, and free memory values)
- Open the System Engineer log file
- Get lists of currently open files, running tasks, and memory usage by module
- Change restrictions on Program Manager (especially handy for network management)

Figure 28: The Other menu.

Obtaining window information

The Window Information dialog box (Figure 29) displays information on the window underneath the mouse pointer. If you move the mouse pointer over the Window Information dialog box, the box moves to the other half of the screen away from the mouse pointer. To stop the display, press Esc or click the right mouse button. To see a menu of actions you can take on a window, click the left mouse button. As well as the usual Windows functions, you also can use the menu to change the caption or text held in the window (Set Window Text) and show the window's memory settings and usage (Memory).

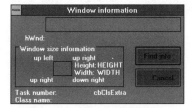

Figure 29: The Window Information dialog box.

Listing tasks

The List Task command displays the number of different Windows programs currently running on your system. Figure 30 illustrates this.

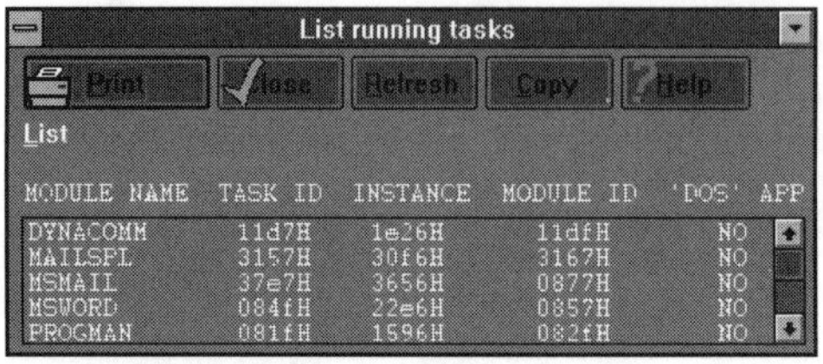

Figure 30: The List running tasks dialog box.

Listing Memory

The List Memory command (illustrated in Figure 31) displays the number of total bytes free and the largest free block of memory.

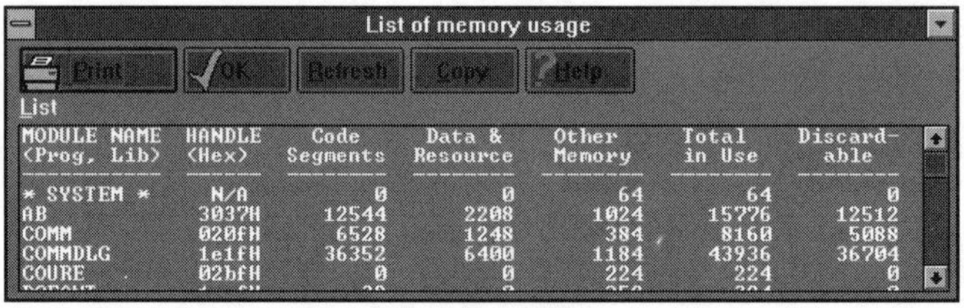

Figure 31: The List of memory usage dialog box.

Examining system resources

The System Resources command displays a percentage representation of the amount of free resources available for Windows programs (Figure 32). GDI is the amount of free memory in the Windows Graphical Device Interface segment, which contains all of Windows' graphical objects (such as icons). User is the amount of free memory in the User segment of Windows, which contains all the information used to maintain windows.

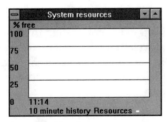

Figure 32: The System Resources graph.

Displaying the Memory Free Graph

The Memory Free Graph command maintains Windows configurations (Figure 33).

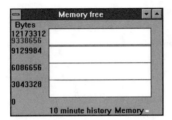

Figure 33: The Memory Free graph.

The Backup menu

Use the Backup menu (Figure 34) to

- Set backup parameters for system files and groups
- Update the current backup (ACV) file
- Restore previously backed up files
- Modify the file structure of existing backups

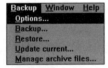

Figure 34: The Backup menu.

Using the Options command

Configuring System Engineer's backup system is explained in this section. System Engineer has an array of backup features that help you maintain your Windows configuration files. You use the Backup⇨Options command to set System Engineer's backup preferences. Selecting the Options command brings up the Configure Backup dialog box (Figure 35).

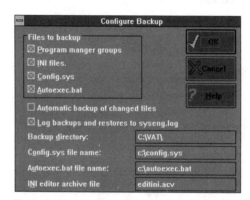

Figure 35: The Configure Backup dialog box.

Specifying types of files to back up

System Engineer archives four types of files: Program Manager GRP files, CONFIG.SYS, AUTOEXEC.BAT, and all files with the extension INI. You can specify the types of files for which you want System Engineer to maintain backups.

Select the types of files that you want to archive. System Engineer searches the WINDOWS directory for the GRP and INI files. It looks for CONFIG.SYS and AUTOEXEC.BAT with the names you've entered.

The icon bitmaps used in GRP files create large archive files. If you are archiving for the first time, you should archive your GRP files. Otherwise, I recommend that you set this default option off, especially if you will be creating custom archived Windows setups. Text-based INI files are relatively small.

Automatic Backup of Changed Files option

Enabling this option backs up all changed and new files to the special archive file CURRENT.ACV each time you start System Engineer.

Backups and restores to SYSENG.LOG

Select this check box to enable System Engineer's change log. Remember that SYSENG.LOG can retain only the last 100 records of editing and backup operations.

Specifying a backup directory

Use the Backup Directory edit window to define the path for a backup directory; the default path is the directory in which System Engineer is located. You might want to create a backup subdirectory in the System Engineer directory—for example, \WINDOWS\SYSENG\BACK.

Specifying AUTOEXEC.BAT and CONFIG.SYS filenames

If your workstation is configured with various CONFIG.SYS and AUTOEXEC.BAT files, you might want to include these files in your backup archives. If you plan to maintain different AUTOEXEC.BAT and CONFIG.SYS files and customized WIN.INI and SYSTEM.INI configurations, you have to reboot your computer after any restoration process. If you maintain just INI files in your archive files, you can restart Windows directly from System Engineer (provided that you do not have any unsaved Windows application data files open). You can rename these files to experiment safely with different configurations.

Archiving files with the INI editor

System Engineer enables you to archive selectively a specific INI file section in an archive file named EDITINI.ACV while using its INI editor.

If you click the Archive button while in the INI editor, that section is archived to SYSENG.ACR. The default location for the saved file is your backup directory. You also can change the name and maintain specific INI topic and/or section archives.

Viewing the Completion Status

This shows percent complete for entire backup. This is the first item in Figure 36.

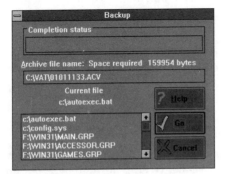

Figure 36: The Backup dialog box.

Archive File Name

System Engineer suggests a unique filename by concatenating the following components:

- Full path to the file
- Current day/month/hour/minute
- Archive file extension (ACV)

To change the archive filename, retype in the edit box.

Current File

The file being backed up now.

Scrollable List

You can choose from the list to create a selected backup. To back up one or more items, select them first. To back up all the items on the list, make sure that no items are selected.

Go

Choose this option to begin the backup process.

Restore

Use this command to restore your backed up system files from an archive file.

To restore a file, follow these steps:

1. Select the backup archive file by using the File Open dialog box that is shown when you first select this command.

2. Select in the Multiple Selection list box the files that you want to restore.

3. If you want to restore them to their saved filenames, choose the Restore button.

4. If you want to restore the files to a different name, then choose the Restore As button. You are asked for a new filename for each file that is being restored. If a named file exists, you are asked for confirmation before it is overwritten.

Update Current option

Use the Update Current option to back up various changed and new system files to the current backup archive file. To stop the automatic backup, click the Cancel button.

Managing backup archives

Use the Manage Backup Archives option to handle all your archive file management tasks. If no other dialog box is active, you can start this dialog box by dragging a file from File Manager onto System Engineer. Figure 37 shows the Choose active file for restore dialog box.

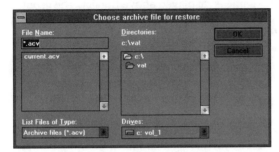

Figure 37: Choosing an archive file to restore.

1. Open a backup archive.

2. Load a different archive file into the dialog box.

3. Delete backup archive.

4. Delete the current archive file.

5. Add a file.

6. Add an archive version of the file to the current archive. Clicking here presents a scrollable list of INI files currently on your hard disk.

7. Freshen the file.

8. Replace the archived version of the selected file with the current one on the disk drive.

9. Remove the file.

10. Remove the archived version of the selected file from the current archive file.

11. Restore As.

12. Restore the selected file from the archive to the disk drive. A confirmation dialog box appears, displaying the name for the selected file. To overwrite the current version with the archive version, click the OK button. To keep both versions, type a different name in the dialog box.

13. Delete the file.

14. Delete the selected file from the archive file.

This procedure does not delete the current version on your hard disk.

This box provides a description of the contents of the archived file. You can enter your own comments when archiving files; otherwise, System Engineer can do it for you.

Scrollable List

The current archive filename is displayed above the list. The group files and system files shown in the illustration are all archived within the sample file, named C:\SYSENG\08211211.ACV. Select a file and then click a button to perform an action on the selected archive file.

Using the Help menu

Use this menu (Figure 38) to access the System Engineer Help system. Figure 39 shows the About WUGNET System Engineer dialog box.

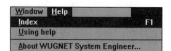

Figure 38: The Help menu.

If you've never used System Engineer before, take the hypergraphic tour to familiarize yourself with the menus and dialog boxes. For help on complete procedures (such as editing files, archiving, etc.), use the How To section. For help in a hurry, or to make hard copy printouts of just System Engineer topic text (no graphics), use the Quick Reference section. To access Microsoft's troubleshooting charts in an interactive sequence, use TroubleShooter. You also can print the original flow chart graphics in hard copy.

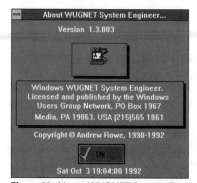

Figure 39: About WUGNET System Engineer.

Summary

I have now finished covering System Engineer version 1.3 in considerable detail. For many of you, this information is all you need. For power users, however (you know who you are!), an advanced version is available: System Engineer 2.0. Information on this version is given in the following paragraphs, and a coupon for upgrading is included in the back of this book as well.

Looking at System Engineer 2.0 for Windows

New features and capabilities result in the ultimate control panel for Windows users. The Windows User Group Network (WUGNET) has available System Engineer version 2.0. This package enables you to fine-tune, optimize, and customize your Windows environment. The latest version, which includes KingCom technology, enables you to have a fax program, communications program, or dialer software all minimized simultaneously on your Windows desktop, thereby solving a common problem called "device contention."

Version 2.0 also includes full drag-and-drop support for Windows File Manager (or PC Tools for Windows or Norton Desktop), enabling you to select an INI file, drag it to the System Engineer icon, and immediately have the INI editor with the INI loaded. System Engineer 2.0 provides access to the Windows Control Panel and also offers an enhanced Control Panel.

System Engineer gives you a comprehensive set of timesaving tools to manage all aspects of Windows' configuration on your workstation, whether stand-alone or on networks. In addition to its powerful but easy-to-use interface for editing individual sections and statements within Windows configuration files, System Engineer provides a complete archival system for storing, managing, and recovering multiple configurations. Changes to any INI files or entries are logged in a master file, which creates an audit system that enables you to retrace specific changes made to configuration files, including support for installation and deinstallation of Windows applications and supporting system enhancements.

Unlocking the Windows environment

System Engineer provides access to every SYSTEM.INI and WIN.INI parameter, including the following:

- Undocumented parameters for managing memory
- Undocumented parameters supporting the Windows keyboard interface
- Network setting options, including support for Windows-specific Novell Netware
- Configuration settings for managing all asynchronous communications ports

- Parameters for setting Windows EMS memory and virtual memory management
- Parameter settings for Windows operation of disk storage devices
- Parameter settings supporting DOS applications running under Windows
- Parameter settings exclusive to Windows standard mode
- System fonts used by Windows

Obtaining real-time information

This release of System Engineer introduces easy-to-use real-time monitoring facilities for both expert and non-expert Windows users.

- The Task Monitor provides a real-time data window displaying all active tasks with their task handles.

- The File I/O Monitor enables you to track which files and devices are currently open and to determine read/write privileges. You also can monitor open data files and Windows-supported devices that are shared, protected, or read-only in nature. You then can use this information to determine the optimum files, buffers, and cache settings for particular tasks in Windows.

- The Memory Monitor is a comprehensive statistical monitor reporting the memory use of active module components in six specific memory classes, including fonts and dynamic-link libraries (DLLs). Use the monitor snapshots to analyze application-specific GDI and USER system resource memory heaps and determine what discardable and nondiscardable portions of memory a particular Windows 3.1 module or application is utilizing.

New System Engineer features with 2.0

New features in System Engineer 2.0 solve Windows' most complex user issues. System Engineer's new interface now includes separate panels for all the configuration management tasks in Windows. Windows SETUP.EXE and Control Panel are incorporated into the interface, with additional tabular windows for SYSTEM, WIN.INI, INFORMATION, and BACKUP support.

System Engineer 2.0 now includes OTC Corporation's KINGCOM COM port driver, an enhanced communications port driver and configuration tool enabling System Engineer to manage all data/fax traffic and eliminate conflicts that develop when multiple applications access the same fax/modem hardware.

The Windows COM driver is limited to two active serial devices, but multiple applications can support the active port. For example, when a fax application attempts to access a modem while a terminal communications package is loaded, the result is an error message. System Engineer's inclusion of KingCom, developed by OTC Corporation, solves this problem. By creating a "virtual" COM port driver, users can designate all their software to a specific COM port.

Looking at advanced configuration tools and features

The System Engineer INI editing system includes support for archiving, library, backup (full and selected), and restoration for Windows INI files and Windows applications INI files. Any INI topic or parameter, for example, can include specific comments, deleted, archived into the system engineer archive.

The INI editor archive capability enables you to select a topic and store it in the active archive. After the topic is archived, you can selectively restore it to another INI file or use the archived library for network system maintenance of other user INI files. Any modification through the INI editor is also maintained in an active log, providing insurance and complete Undo support. You can use the Log Browser to monitor changes to all INI files made through System Engineer.

The system configuration backup and restore support has been expanded to include Windows GRP, AUTOEXEC.BAT, and CONFIG.SYS files. A complete backup archive can be restored, enabling you to maintain multiple configurations as well as share custom configuration files on individual workstations or through central server or peer networks.

Finally, System Engineer 2.0 has expanded its system exit and restart support. Now you can make changes to your system files and choose either to restart or restart/reboot. A DOS unarchive utility is provided to make backup archives both portable and recoverable through DOS.

Analyzing support, price, and availability

System Engineer is supported by a team of professionals 24 hours a day on the forum. Upgrades for WUGNET members are $19.95 plus $5.00 shipping; upgrades for System Engineer 1.4 users are $29.95 plus $5.00 shipping. New orders are $49.95 plus $5 shipping. Orders are being taken now at 800 WINUSER (946-8737) or Fax (215) 565 7106. Allow ten business days for delivery.

For more information, contact:

Windows Users Group Network
126 E. State St.
Media, PA 19063
(215) 565-1861
Fax (215) 565-7106
CompuServe 76702,1023

Hewlett-Packard's Dashboard 1.0 _____

Dashboard for Windows (Figure 40) is the convenient push-button utility which gives you quick access to and maximum control over your Windows programs. Dashboard includes these features (and many more):

- Convenient menus and buttons for launching programs.

- Drag-and-drop support for printing, plotting, and faxing.

- Miniature screens that make it easy to work with several full-screen programs at once.

- An alarm clock with a built-in snooze alarm.

- "At a glance" feedback to let you know which programs are running and how much memory you are using.

Figure 40: The Dashboard main screen.

Dashboard Panels

About button

The About button shows information about Dashboard, including the product number, product version number, and copyright information.

Alarm Clock

The Alarm Clock shows the date and time set on your computer. Double-click to add or edit an alarm and to configure the way the clock looks. You can customize the clock face to be analog or digital. You can also display the clock's date and time information on the Dashboard title bar.

Customize button

Use the Customize button to personalize different features of Dashboard and set the preferences for different items on Dashboard. You can use the Customize dialog box (Figure 41) to change the positions of items on Dashboard, and you can choose whether to show or hide particular items. You can also set Dashboard to always be displayed in front of the Program Manager. You can save specific configurations of Dashboard in files and load those configurations as needed. Figure 41 shows the Customize dialog box.

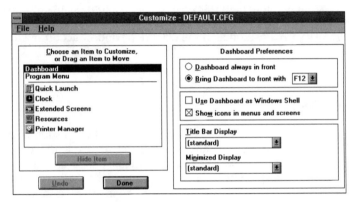

Figure 41: Customize dialog box.

Extended Screens

Use Extended Screens to position currently active program windows on Dashboard's extended screens. The extended screens area contains miniature windows corresponding to the open program windows, displaying the icons and titles of programs in those windows. The extended screens and their program windows are interactive. For example, if you change the size or position of a program window, the extended screen in Dashboard is updated automatically. Resize or move items on the extended screens, and their corresponding program windows change too.

To switch back and forth among different screens, click the selector button under the extended screen. To move open windows among the extended screens, drag the mini-windows in the Dashboard extended windows, or move the full-sized windows by dragging on the title bar.

Help button

Use the Help button to find the help you need. Click on the Help button and the cursor becomes a question mark. Put the question mark on any item on Dashboard and click there to see specific help for that item. Double-click the Help button to see an index of help topics. Click a topic to see the instructions you want or click the Search button to locate a particular word or phrase.

Layout menu

Use the Layout Menu to name, save, and load custom Dashboard layouts or to edit existing layouts. You use Dashboard layouts to open all the programs you want to work with, positioned in the extended window according to your specifications.

Maximize button

The Maximize button extends Dashboard horizontally to its full width. When you click the Maximize button, any panels which are expandable increase in size to use more space in Dashboard. Expandable panels are displayed with scroll arrow buttons to indicate that more items exist than are currently shown. If none of the current Dashboard panels are expandable, Dashboard does not change its size. If Dashboard is already maximized, this button returns it to its previous width.

You cannot resize Dashboard if it is maximized. You need to click the Restore button to return Dashboard to its original size.

Minimize button

The Minimize button reduces Dashboard to an icon. You can customize the minimized icon using the Customize dialog box. You can choose between the standard Dashboard icon, a clock icon, and an extended screen icon.

Printer Manager

The Printer Manager controls printers, fax machines, and plotters. To print or fax a file, drag and drop the file from the File Manager or a program group window onto the desired printer icon. Click a printer icon to see the full name and description. Double-click to see the Printer Configuration box. Change the necessary configuration settings; then click OK to save the changes.

Choosing a default printer

The green light (or "on" light if you don't have a color monitor) denotes the default printer. To choose a different default printer, click the default printer light.

Scrolling in the Dashboard to see other printers

If Dashboard is not wide enough to display all printers, the Print Manager portion of Dashboard will include scroll arrows. Click the scroll arrows to see printers that aren't currently visible.

Installing new printers

The Printer Manager offers a quick and easy way to handle all your installed printers. However, the Printer Manager does not install printers. To install a new printer, use the Windows Control Panel. Refer to your Windows documentation for more information.

The printer icon on Dashboard reflects the orientation of the printer (portrait or landscape). If you change the orientation setting in the Printer Configuration box, the icon will change also.

Program menu

The Program menu lists the program groups in the Windows Program Manager. Click a program menu button on the Program Menu to see an alphabetical list of programs. Click the program item on the list to launch the program. You can choose the order in which groups appear in the Program Menu, and you can also add new groups, modify and delete selected groups, and open a program window for a group.

Quick Launch buttons

You can create a set of Quick Launch buttons for the programs you use most often. Once a program has been assigned to a Quick Launch button, just click that button to run the program. To change Quick Launch preferences in the Customize dialog box, double-click the right mouse button on any of the Quick Launch buttons. With the Quick Launch Preferences, you can create new Quick Launch buttons, modify or delete existing buttons, and change the position of the buttons on Dashboard.

Resource Gauge

The Resource Gauge (shown in the Resource dialog box, Figure 42) shows the level of Windows System Resources currently available. As your System Resources get low, the needle drops toward Empty, and you may not be able to open new programs. The Warning Indicator blinks and sounds an alarm as you reach the alarm level for available total free memory or Windows System Memory. Double-click to see a list of all programs currently running. Try closing programs if you are running out of memory.

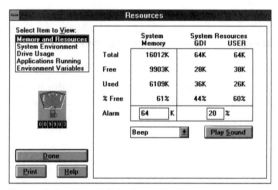

Figure 42: Resources dialog box.

The Memory Meter shows the amount of free system memory. The numbers are in kilobytes. You can see more detailed resource information by double-clicking the Resource Gauge or the Memory Meter.

Show Program Menu button

Click this button to show or hide the Dashboard Program Menu, which lists program groups.

Sizing bar

With the cursor placed over the Sizing bar, you can click and drag to change the width of Dashboard. There are Sizing bars along the left and right edges of Dashboard. When the cursor is placed over a Sizing bar, the cursor becomes a double-headed arrow. The size of Dashboard is limited by the number of items on Dashboard that can be expanded or hidden from view. For example, if the Dashboard window only has one printer icon and one Quick Launch button, there's probably no reason to resize. But if your computer has multiple printers, you may have to resize it accordingly. You cannot make Dashboard bigger than is necessary to display all items adequately.

Enlarging Dashboard may cause some of its panels (such as the panels for the printers or the Quick Launch buttons) to be too big to show all of their items. When that happens, panels on the left will have priority over panels on the right. For example, if the Quick Launch panel is to the left of the printers' panel, more Quick Launch buttons will be visible than printers. Scroll arrows will be next to the printers so you can scroll to see the other printers. To take advantage of this feature, rearrange the panels that you work with most often to be on the left side.

System menu

The System menu includes standard Windows System menu commands for working with the window, plus extra Dashboard commands to switch to other menus and features.

Task menu

The Task menu switches among currently open programs. You can also use the Task menu to display an open program on the current full-screen view, run new programs, and close all programs other than Dashboard, the Program Manager, and DOS applications. If you make changes to program windows, you can update your extended screens to correspond to these program windows by using the Update command on the Task menu.

Title bar

The Title bar displays the window caption and can also show date and time, depending on the option you choose in the Customize dialog box. Click and drag the title bar to move the entire Dashboard.

Launching Programs with the Program Menu __

1. Select a program group from the Program menu listed across the top of Dashboard. Click to see the program items listed on a menu, or double-click to see the items displayed as icons in the program window. If all the Program Menu buttons are not displayed on Dashboard, click the scroll arrows to display them.

2. Select the program you want to run by clicking the item in the menu or double-clicking the icon in the program window. If the list of programs is too long to fit on the menu, click the More command on the menu. The program group window opens, and you can scroll through the window to see all the items.

Launching Programs with the Layout Menu _____

1. Click the Layout Menu button (the third button on the left side of the Title bar) or choose Layout menu from the System menu.

2. Click the Load Layout command. A cascading menu of previously saved layouts appears.

3. Click the layout that you want to load in the cascading menu. All the programs associated with the selected layout are launched. The programs are displayed on the extended screens according to the layout you saved.

Launching Programs with the Run Command

1. Click the Task Menu button (the second button on the left side of the Title bar) or choose Task menu from the System menu.

2. Choose Run.

3. Enter the command line for the program to run. Use the Browse button to find the program's location and enter the information in the command line. Choose the Run Minimized option if you want the program to be minimized when you open it. The Command History list shows the last 20 commands that have been entered. If the command you want to enter is already listed, you don't have to type it or browse to find it. Simply double-click it to enter the information in the command line.

4. Click OK.

Launching Programs with Quick Launch Buttons

You can create a set of Quick Launch buttons for the programs you use most often. Once a program has been assigned to a Quick Launch button, just click that button to run the program. If there are more Quick Launch buttons than can be shown at one time, use the scroll arrows to display buttons not currently in view.

Creating Quick Launch buttons

Use Quick Launch buttons on Dashboard to launch any program directly from Dashboard with a single click.

Creating a Quick Launch button by dragging a program

Drag the program from the File Manager or program window to a Quick Launch panel on the Dashboard.

Creating a Quick Launch button with the Customize dialog box

1. Double-click the right mouse button on one of the Quick Launch buttons to open the Customize dialog box with Quick Launch preferences.

2. Click New.

3. Enter a title for the button.

4. Enter the correct command line (path name and filename) and working directory for the program. Click Browse if you don't know the path name for the program.

5. Choose the Run Minimized option if you want the program to be minimized when you open it.

6. If the program includes an icon file, its icon appears on the Quick Launch button. If the program does not have an icon, Dashboard will display a default icon. Click Change Icon to change the displayed icon.

7. To save the changes and close the dialog box, click Done. If you don't want to keep the changes, click Undo.

Customizing the Alarm Clock

You can customize the alarm clock to change its appearance and to set the interval for the snooze button.

1. Double-click the right mouse button on the clock.

2. Click a Clock Type option. Analog clocks show time with minute and second hands pointing to numbers, and digital clocks represent time as a number.

3. Click to open the Clock Face drop-down list, and choose an option to specify the appearance of the clock you want.

4. Next to Snooze Interval, type the number of minutes in which you want the alarm to reappear after you click the Snooze button in an alarm message.

5. Click Alarms to set an alarm. If you did not install the Sound Driver for PC-Speaker during the Dashboard installation procedure, you cannot hear sound with the alarm. For instructions on installing the driver, see your Dashboard Owner's Handbook.

6. To save the changes and close the dialog box, click Done. If you don't want to keep the changes, click Undo.

Resetting the Date and Time

The Alarm Clock displays the date and time as set on your computer. To reset the date and time, use the Windows Control Panel.

Customizing the Printer Manager

You can customize Dashboard Printer Manager to choose which print devices (printers, plotters, and fax machines) you want to appear in Dashboard, the order in which they appear, and which printer should be the default printer and to specify the icons and descriptions for each printer.

1. Double-click the right mouse button on one of the printer icons.

2. Select a printer device you want to work with from the list on the right.

3. Use the Hide Printer and Show Printer buttons to choose whether the selected device should appear in Dashboard.

4. The order in which printer devices are listed indicates the order in which they will appear, left-to-right, in Dashboard. To move a printer to its new position on Dashboard, click it in the list and drag it to its new position in the list.

5. Use the Description text area to enter a title for the selected printer. This title will appear on the printer icon in Dashboard.

6. Click the Change Icon button to change the displayed icon for the device.

7. Click the Set As Default button to select a default device.

8. Click the Setup button to display the Printer Configuration dialog box for the selected printer. Refer to Windows or your printer documentation for more information.

9. To save the changes and close the dialog box, click Done. If you don't want to keep the changes, click Undo.

Installing a new printer, plotter, or fax machine

Dashboard's Printer Manager includes devices that have been installed in Windows. To install new devices, use the Windows Control Panel.

Customizing the Resource Gauge _____

Dashboard includes an alarm that warns you when the total free memory or your Windows System Resources are getting low. You can determine the levels at which you want Dashboard to sound an alarm when either total free memory or Windows System Resources reaches a certain point.

1. Double-click the right mouse button on the Resource Gauge.

2. Enter exact kilobytes to set an alarm level for free System Memory.

3. Enter a percentage to set an alarm level for available System Resources (memory set aside for Windows).

4. Click Alarm Sound to choose a sound for the alarm. If you did not install the Sound Driver for PC-Speaker during the Dashboard installation procedure, you cannot hear sound with the alarm. For instructions on installing the driver, see your Dashboard Owner's Handbook.

5. To save the changes and close the dialog box, click Done. If you don't want to keep the changes, click Undo.

Customizing Extended Screens _____

The extended screens feature allows you to create and switch back and forth between as many as nine full-sized screens containing different program windows. You can choose the maximum number of extended screens you want up to nine, depending on the available space on Dashboard and the resolution of your monitor.

1. Double-click the right mouse button on one of the extended screens to open the Customize dialog box with the Extended Screens preferences.

2. Click an option to choose the number of extended screens. If a number is grayed out, there is not enough room on Dashboard for that many extended screens. To make more room on Dashboard, remove items from Dashboard by clicking one of the Dashboard items listed in the Customize dialog box and selecting Hide Item. You can then select a larger number of extended screens to display.

   If you decrease the number of extended screens on Dashboard, any applications contained in the removed extended screens (the left or right screens) are moved into the closest extended screen remaining on Dashboard.

3. Click the background options to select a different background for your extended screens.

4. To save the changes and close the dialog box, click Done. If you don't want to keep the changes, click Undo.

Rearranging Items on Dashboard

1. Click the Customize button.

2. Click the item you want to move in the list and drag it to its new position in the list. As you drag the item, the cursor changes to a two-headed arrow pointing up and down. The top-to-bottom sequence in the list corresponds to how items are arranged from left to right on Dashboard. For example, if you want the clock to be on the far right, drag it to the bottom of the list.

3. To save the changes and close the dialog box, click Done. If you don't want to keep the changes, click Undo.

Setting an Alarm

You can set alarms to display a message, set off an alarm sound, or launch a program automatically.

1. Double-click the Alarm Clock on Dashboard.

2. In the Clock Alarms dialog box, click the Add button.

3. Specify a time for the alarm. Enter the hour and minutes or click the up and down arrows to change the setting. Select AM or PM from the drop-down list.

4. Choose the One Time Only option if the alarm should occur only once. Otherwise, it will occur each day at the same time.

5. Next to Alarm Text, type the text you want displayed in the alarm message.

6. If the alarm is to launch a program automatically, enter the path of the program and the working directory under Optional Alarm Actions. Use the Browse button to help locate the program and its command line, and choose the Run Minimized option if you want the program to be minimized when you open it.

7. Choose the alarm's sound from the Sound drop-down list. To hear a sound, select it and click Play Sound. If you did not install the Sound Driver for PC-Speaker during the Dashboard installation procedure, you cannot hear sound with the alarm. For instructions on installing the driver, see your Dashboard Owner's Handbook.

8. Click OK.

Setting Dashboard Preferences

1. Click the Customize button.

2. Under Dashboard Preferences, choose the Dashboard always in front option if you want the Dashboard window in front of all other windows at all times.

3. If you don't choose to have Dashboard always on top, you can set an F-key to bring it to the top when you need it.

4. Choose the Show Icons in Menus option if you want to display mini program icons on the extended screens, Program menu list, and the Task Menu.

5. Make a choice from the drop-down list under Title Bar Display to customize the appearance of the Dashboard Title bar. You can choose the standard Dashboard display or the clock display, which shows the current date and time.

6. Make a choice from the drop-down list under Minimized Display to change the icon displayed when Dashboard is minimized. You can choose the standard Dashboard icon, the clock icon, or the extended screens icon. If you choose the extended screens icon, you can switch screens by clicking the little boxes in the minimized icon.

7. To save the changes and close the dialog box, click Done. If you don't want to keep the changes, click Undo.

Using Custom Dashboard Configurations

1. Make all the changes you want in the Customize dialog box.

2. Choose Save or Save As from the File menu. Save saves the current configuration into the configuration file currently being used. The caption of the Customize dialog box shows the name of the current file. Use Save As to save to a different filename.

3. In the Save As dialog box, enter the path and filename for the file in the edit box. A CFG extension is automatically added to the new filename and the current configuration file now changes to the new filename.

4. Click OK and then click Done in the Customize dialog box. If you don't want to keep the changes, click Undo.

Managing Extended Screens _____

Dashboard's extended screens make it possible to work with your computer as if it had several screens attached to it. Each extended screen on Dashboard represents a full-screen view. The extended screens and their corresponding full-screen views are interactive. For example, if you change a full-screen view by closing a window or running a new program, the extended screen in Dashboard is updated automatically. Move items on the extended screens, and their corresponding full-screen views change too. If you change the size of the original program window, the size of the mini-window on the extended screen will change accordingly.

To switch back and forth among different programs, click the selector button under the extended screen showing the window you want to view. To move open windows among the extended screens, drag the mini-windows in the Dashboard extended screens, or move the full-sized windows by dragging on the title bar.

Managing Program Groups with the Program Menu _____

The row of Program Menu buttons under Dashboard's title bar lists the program groups in Windows' Program Manager. Click any program group to see a list of programs contained in it. When Dashboard is the shell, you can create a program group within another group. If a program group contains another group, the items in that group are listed in a cascading menu. You can also double-click a program group to see its group window.

If there are more program groups in the Program Manager than fit on Dashboard, use the scroll arrows on the right side of the Program Menu to scroll through the groups. If Dashboard is the shell and Program Manager is not running, you can perform the following functions:

Adding a new program menu button

1. Double-click with the right mouse button one of the Program Menu buttons to go into Program Menu Preferences.

2. Click the New button.

3. At the New Program Group dialog box, enter the name of the new group and select a color key setting. You can also enter the name of the group file if you want. Do not use an existing group file to create a new group.

4. Click OK.

Changing the position of a group on Dashboard

1. Double-click with the right mouse button on one of the Program Menu buttons to go to into Program Menu Preferences.

2. Click the program group you want to move in the list and drag it to its new position in the list. The top-to-bottom sequence in the list corresponds to how program buttons are arranged from left to right on Dashboard. For example, if you want the Main button to be on the far left, drag it to the beginning of the list.

Deleting a group from Dashboard

1. Double-click with the right mouse button on one of the Program Menu buttons to go into Program Menu Preferences.

2. Click the program group you want to delete from the list of program groups.

3. Click Delete. Dashboard no longer displays the program group.

Modifying a program group's color key or description

1. Double-click with the right mouse button on one of the Program Menu buttons to go into Program Menu Preferences.

2. Click a group in the Program Groups list.

3. Click Modify.

4. Enter a new group description or select a new color key setting. The group description you enter will appear on the Dashboard Program Menu button.

Regardless of whether Dashboard is the shell or not, you can do the following operations.

Specifying a height for the Program menu

1. Double-click with the right mouse button on one of the Program Menu buttons to go into Program Menu Preferences.

2. Use the Show 2nd row of text option to display two rows of text on the Program Menu buttons.

Choosing whether to display colors in the Program menu

1. Double-click with the right mouse button on one of the Program Menu buttons to go into Program Menu Preferences.

2. Use the Show Color Keys option to add color tabs on the Program Menu buttons.

Updating Dashboard with changes made in Program Manager

1. Double-click with the right mouse button on one of the Program Menu buttons to go into Program Menu Preferences.

2. Click the Reread from Program Manager button.

Managing Program Groups with Program Windows

When you double-click a program group in the Program Menu, the Dashboard program group window opens and displays program items as icons. If Dashboard is the shell, you can click and drag programs into other group windows, and even create groups within groups. These functions are disabled if Program Manager is running. If Dashboard is the shell, you can perform the following in Program Windows:

Moving and copying a program from one group to another by dragging the icon

1. Open both group windows by double-clicking in the Dashboard Program Menu.

2. Click and drag the program item icon from one window to the next to move the item. To copy a program, hold the Control key and click to drag the program item to another window.

Moving a program from one group to another using the Move command

1. Open the group window from which you want to move the program.

2. Select the program item you want to move.

3. Choose Move from the File menu.

4. Enter the name of the group to which you want to move the program.

5. Click OK.

Copying a program from one group to another

1. Open the group window from which you want to copy the program.

2. Choose Copy from the File menu.

3. Enter the name of the group to which you want to copy the program.

4. Click OK.

Creating a new program group within an existing program group

1. Open the existing group window by double-clicking in the Dashboard Program Menu.

2. Choose New Group from the File menu.

3. Type a name for the group and click OK. Enter a group file name as an option. Do not use an existing group file name. The new group is displayed as an icon.

4. Double-click the icon to open the new group window.

Creating a new program item

1. Open the group window by double-clicking in the Dashboard Program menu.

2. Choose New Item from the File menu.

3. Enter a title for the program item.

4. Enter the correct command line (path name and filename) and working directory for the program. Click Browse if you don't know the path name for the program.

5. Choose the Run Minimized option if you want the program to be minimized when you open it.

6. Click OK.

Changing a program item's properties

1. Open the group window by double-clicking in the Dashboard Program menu.

2. Click the program item for which you want to change the properties.

3. Choose Properties from the File menu.

4. Enter the new information in the Program Item Properties dialog box.

5. Click OK.

Deleting a program item or program group

1. Open the group window by double-clicking in the Dashboard Program Menu.

2. Click the program item or program group you want to delete.

3. Choose Delete from the File menu. Deleting a program group will delete all of the items and groups contained within it.

If Dashboard is not the shell, you can use the Properties command to view the properties of a program item or program menu. However, the information within it can not be edited.

Moving and Resizing Dashboard _____

1. Put the cursor on the Title bar.

2. Click and drag to move.

Resizing

1. Put the cursor on the sizing border on the left or right edge of Dashboard. The cursor becomes a double-headed sizing arrow.

2. Click and drag to resize. The size of Dashboard is limited by the number of items on Dashboard that can be expended or hidden from view. For example, if the Dashboard window only has one printer icon and one Quick Launch button, there's probably no reason to resize. But if your computer has multiple printers, you may have to resize it accordingly. You cannot make Dashboard bigger than is necessary to display all items adequately.

Enlarging Dashboard may cause some of its panels (such as the panels for the printers or the Quick Launch buttons) to be too big to show all of their items. When that happens, panels on the left will have priority over panels on the right. For example, if the Quick Launch panel is to the left of the printers' panel, more Quick Launch buttons will be visible than printers. Scroll arrows will be next to the printers so you can scroll to see the other printers. To take advantage of this feature, rearrange the panels that you work with most often to be on the left side.

Printing and faxing

The Printer Manager controls all of the printers, fax machines, and plotters you have installed and configured in Windows.

Printing from Dashboard

1. Open the File Manager and select a file to print or open a Dashboard program group window.

2. Click and drag the file to the appropriate printer icon on Dashboard. If the printer is not currently displayed on Dashboard, use the scroll arrows on Dashboard to display it. If the application with which the file was created is not registered properly with Windows, you cannot print the file by dragging it to Dashboard. You can check the Windows Registration Info Editor to see whether your application is registered. For instructions on opening the Windows Registration Info Editor and for registering an application, see the README.TXT file that came with your Dashboard program.

Choosing a default printer

The green light denotes the default printer. To choose a different default printer, click the default printer button.

Scrolling in Dashboard to see other printers

If Dashboard is not wide enough to display all printers, the Print Manager portion of Dashboard will include scroll arrows. Click the scroll arrows to see printers that aren't currently visible.

Displaying a printer's full name and description

Click a printer icon to see the full name and description.

Working with the printer's configuration

Double-click to see the Printer Configuration box, and change the appropriate settings.

Installing new printers

The Printer Manager offers a quick and easy way to handle all your installed printers. However, the Printer Manager does not install printers. To install a new printer, use the Windows Control Panel. Refer to your Windows documentation for more information.

Removing Dashboard

If you want to remove Dashboard from your system, you can do so by using the Remove Dashboard icon in your Dashboard program group.

1. Double-click the Remove Dashboard icon. Dashboard displays a message asking if you want to remove Dashboard for Windows from your system.

2. If you don't want to remove Dashboard, click Cancel. If you want to remove Dashboard, click Remove. Dashboard displays the Remove Dashboard dialog box containing the path for the Dashboard program.

3. If you don't want to remove Dashboard, click Cancel. If you want to remove Dashboard, click OK. Dashboard is removed from your system.

Running Dashboard as a Shell

If you run Dashboard as a shell program, Dashboard will be the first program to run when you start Windows, instead of the Program Manager. Running Dashboard as a shell lets you control Windows with Dashboard only.

1. Click the Customize button.

2. Under Dashboard Preferences, check the Use Dashboard as Windows Shell box.

3. Click Done. Dashboard displays a message saying you need to restart Windows to implement the change.

4. Click Yes to restart Windows immediately or click No to remain in Windows and continue to work with Dashboard. If you click No, the next time you restart Windows, Dashboard will be displayed as the shell.

When Dashboard is the shell, you can edit, move, create and delete groups, as well as reorder the groups on Dashboard's Program menu.

Using Dashboard with a Grayscale Monitor

If you want to use Dashboard with a grayscale monitor, such as the monitor on a laptop computer, you can change the DASH.INI file to improve the grayscale rendition of certain Dashboard features. For example, the default printer light on the Dashboard will be displayed as black, as will some of the other Dashboard colors.

In the Monitor paragraph, the possible settings are:

`GrayScale=0` not set to grayscale

`GrayScale=1` set to grayscale

To set the monitor to grayscale:

1. Double-click the DASH.INI file to open it as a Notepad file.

2. In the Monitor section of the .INI file, change the setting to `GrayScale=1`.

3. Choose Save from the Notepad File menu.

4. Choose Exit from the Notepad File menu.

The Dashboard will now appear in grayscale. To change the monitor back later, reset the Monitor paragraph to `GrayScale=0`.

Using Dashboard with a Keyboard _____

You can use certain keys to work with Dashboard. The information in this section explains what you can do with each key.

Bring the Dashboard window to the front of other windows. (You can change to some other F-key using the Customize button.)

Alt+(character)	Choose a button or menu command that has its selection character underlined. For example, if a button is labeled Add, the letter A is the letter for selecting the Add key, and pressing Alt+A is equivalent to clicking the button.
Alt+Spacebar	Show the System Menu.
Alt+Tab	Cycle through the open programs running under Windows. Use this option to bring the Dashboard window into focus.
Ctrl+Alt+Cursor	Keys Move (reorder) items on a list in the Customize dialog box.
Cursor Keys (up/down/left/right)	Select items from menus and from groups within a dialog box. If you use Tab to select an item on the Dashboard window, using the cursor keys will cycle through individual components of the items.
End	Move to last item on a list.
Enter	Equivalent to double-clicking the mouse on the selected item. In a dialog box, equivalent to clicking OK.
Esc	Exit a menu. Cancel out of a dialog box.
Home	Move to first item in a list.
Shift+Tab	Tab key functions in reverse.
Spacebar	Selects chosen items on the Dashboard window. Equivalent to clicking the mouse.
Tab	When the Dashboard window has the focus, use the Tab key to cycle through and change the keyboard focus on different sections of it. When a dialog box is active, the Tab key cycles through groups in it. (Use cursor keys to choose items within a group.)

Creating Layouts

You can use Dashboard layouts to open all the programs you want to work with, already positioned in the extended screens and ready to go. For instance, if you want to work with WinWord on extended screen 1, Paintbrush on extended screen 2, and the File Manager minimized on extended screen 3, you can save that arrangement as a layout. Then, when you open that layout, all of those programs will automatically open in the same screen location. If you have another project that requires working with some other programs in a different arrangement, you can save them as another layout and reload them with a single command when you need to work on this project.

1. Open all the programs you want to include in the layout.

2. Arrange the programs on the extended screens.

3. Choose Save Layout from the Layout menu.

4. Enter a name for the layout.

5. Click OK.

Editing layouts

1. At the Save Layout dialog box, select a program from the programs list and then click Edit. The Edit Layout dialog box appears. The dialog box contains the command line and working directory for the selected program.

2. To change the command line or working directory, enter the new information in the appropriate field.

3. Enter a name for the program in the Application Name box. This name is a descriptive name, not a filename.

4. Enter the correct command line and working directory in the Command Line box.

   If you want a particular file instead of just the program to open as part of a layout, enter the command line for loading the file here.

5. Choose a size for the program window from the Window Size pull-down menu.

6. To exit the Edit Layout dialog box and save any changes, click OK.

7. To exit the Edit Layout dialog box without saving changes, click Cancel.

Loading layouts

1. Click the Layout button (the third button on the left side of the Title bar) or choose Layout menu from the System menu.

2. Choose Load Layout from the Layout menu. A cascading menu of previously saved layouts appears.

3. Click the layout that you want to load in the cascading menu. All the programs associated with the selected layout are launched.

Managing layouts

To change the program information in a layout, choose Manage Layouts from the Layout Menu. The Manage Layouts dialog box opens. Use the Manage Layouts dialog box to make any of the following changes to your layout.

Removing a layout

1. Select the layout in the Layout list.

2. Click Delete Layout.

Changing the name of a layout

1. Select the layout in the Layout list.

2. Click Rename.

3. Enter the new name in the Rename dialog box and click OK.

Removing a program from a layout

1. Select the program in the Applications for Layout list.

2. Click Delete.

Editing a program's specifics

1. Select the program in the Applications for Layout list.

2. Click Edit.

3. Enter the appropriate information in the Edit Layout dialog box.

Exiting the Manage Layouts dialog box

1. To exit the Manage Layouts dialog box and save any changes made, click Save Changes.

2. To exit the Manage Layouts dialog box without saving changes, click Cancel.

Changing the Program Menu _____

The Program menu displays a list of program groups you can work with from Dashboard. These groups are the same as those you see in the Program Manager. If Dashboard is configured as the shell, then you can make changes to these groups and to the Program menu itself using the Customize dialog box. You can modify, add, and delete groups using Dashboard and change the order of the Program Menu buttons. If Program Manager is running as the shell, these functions are disabled.

When you modify program groups or add a new group in Program Manager, these changes will not be reflected in the Dashboard groups until you click the Reread from Program Manager button in the Program Menu preferences. If you close Dashboard and then run it again, the changes will also take effect. If Dashboard is the shell, you can manage groups directly from the Dashboard Customize dialog box.

1. To open the Customize dialog box with the Program Menu preferences displayed, double-click the right mouse button on one of the Program Menu buttons.

2. To make a change to a program group, click that program group in the list, and then click one of the following buttons to choose which task you want to perform on the selected program group.

   Modify: Changes the color of the key on the program group button, or enters a new description for the program group.

   Open: Opens the program group.

   Delete: Deletes the program group from Dashboard and the Program Manager.

   New: Creates a new program group.

To change the position of a program group on Dashboard, click the group in the list and drag it to its new position in the list. The position of the program group's button on Dashboard is changed appropriately.

Regardless of whether Dashboard is the shell or not, you can perform the following:

1. Choose the Show 2nd row of text option if you want the Program Menu buttons to be full size. If this option is not checked, the buttons will show only a single row of text.

2. Choose the Show Color Keys option if you want color keys for each program group to be displayed in the Program Menu.

3. To update Dashboard with changes made using the Program Manager, click the Reread from Program Manager button.

Checking Your Resources

To help you check your total free memory and Windows System Resources, Dashboard includes these tools:

The Resource Gauge shows the level of Windows System Resources currently available. As it gets closer to E (empty), you may not be able to open new programs.

The Warning Indicator blinks and sounds an alarm as you reach the alarm level for either available free system memory or system resources. Double-click to see a list of all programs currently running. Try closing programs if you are running out of memory.

The Memory Meter shows the total amount of free system memory. The numbers are in kilobytes. You can see more detailed information about your resources and system by double-clicking the Resource Gauge on Dashboard.

Using Help

Use the Dashboard Help button to find the help you need.

Index Help

1. Double-click the Help button to see an index of help topics.
2. Click Introducing Dashboard to see a brief explanation of Dashboard.
3. Click a topic from the How To list to see instructions for that task.

Context Help

1. Click the Help button and the cursor becomes a question mark.
2. Put the question mark on any item on Dashboard and click there to see specific help for that item.

GoCIS

GoCIS is a Windows interface for automating CompuServe operations. How does it work?

Before you go online, you specify the CompuServe actions to be performed. Then you select a type of online processing. Finally, GoCIS automatically calls CompuServe, logs on to the system by using your ID, and performs all your requested actions.

■ GoCIS automatically checks for mail in your CompuServe mailbox every time you access CompuServe. If you have mail waiting, GoCIS retrieves it into a mailbox where you can read and respond to it at your convenience.

■ GoCIS maintains a CompuServe address book for easy access and selection of user names for sending data.

■ GoCIS provides automated reading, composing, and sending of all forum messages.

■ GoCIS stores all message information in forum message databases so that you can easily access messages later.

■ GoCIS optionally keeps forum library download indexes for all files available in forum libraries. GoCIS automatically retrieves selected files to your PC during its next online session.

Typical GoCIS operation accesses CompuServe in two stages:

1. Start GoCIS, and press the MESSAGES or MAIL button. GoCIS logs on to CompuServe. For all forums you have selected, GoCIS reads outstanding messages or e-mail created since your last online session. If you have set up forum processing to access message download lists, GoCIS creates the lists during this access of CompuServe. You then have e-mail, messages, and download lists in GoCIS databases ready to be read.

2. You can review the lists of files and messages available and mark those you want to download from CompuServe. You also can read and respond to your e-mail and forum messages. Then press the ACTIONS button to go back online to CompuServe to send mail, read marked messages, and download files.

Getting Started with GoCIS

To start GoCIS, double-click the GoCIS icon; or use the Program Manager's File⇨Run menu item to run GoCIS.EXE.

When you start GoCIS for the first time, you are asked if you want to configure GoCIS for your use. Choose the OK button; GoCIS displays configuration windows into which you must enter the following information:

(You must fill in proper values in each of the configuration windows to enable GoCIS to connect to CompuServe.)

CompuServe User ID.	Enter the name, user ID, and password that you currently use in accessing CompuServe.
Processing Options.	Set processing options that are used to control mail and message processing with CompuServe.
Default Directories.	Change the default directories that are used by GoCIS for saving files.
Phone Number.	Change the phone number that will be dialed by GoCIS when you press any of the Automated processing buttons on the Main Processing window.
Communications Port.	Set up the modem commands and parameters. Change port number, baud rate, etc.
Modem Menu Items.	Select predefined modem settings, or define or change modem settings. To select a predefined modem, click the pull-down arrow to pull down a list of predefined modems. Then click the modem type that matches the modem you will use to connect with CompuServe.

If you don't see your modem type, try selecting the Hayes Compatible modem.

After you enter the configuration information, GoCIS displays the Main Processing window. You use this window to start all GoCIS processing.

Testing CompuServe Access

To make sure that you have successfully set up the GoCIS parameters for accessing CompuServe, follow these steps:

1. Choose the Interactive button on the Main Processing window.

   If you have configured GoCIS with the correct modem parameters and specified the correct CompuServe logon user ID and password, GoCIS calls CompuServe and initiates interactive command mode.

   The GoCIS Terminal window appears, displaying a series of modem commands being sent, followed by your user ID, and finally messages from CompuServe indicating that you have been successfully logged on.

2. Type **OFF** and press Enter.

3. Select File⇨Exit from the Terminal window to exit this window and display the Main Processing window again.

Using the Address Book

To add your CompuServe user ID to the GoCIS Address Book, perform the following steps:

1. Select EMail⇨Edit Address Book from the Main Processing window.

2. Press the ADD button in the Address Book window.

3. Enter your name, CompuServe ID, and any optional notes in the Add to Address Book window.

4. Choose the OK button on the Add to Address Book window. You then see that your name has been added to the Address Book.

5. Choose OK on the Address Book window to return to the Main Processing window.

Sending and Reading E-Mail Messages

To send yourself an e-mail message and then use GoCIS to read that message, perform the following steps:

1. Select EMail⇨Create Mail from the Main Processing window. GoCIS displays a window where you can enter routing information.

2. Choose the Browse button in the Mail Send To? window. The Address Book window appears; you can browse through and select a name and address for your e-mail message.

3. Click your name in the Address Book window, and choose the Select button to enter your name and address as the recipient of the message.

4. Enter **GoCIS EMail** in the Subject area of the Mail Send To? window, and choose the OK button in this window. You then see the EMail window with a Compose To area where you can start entering your e-mail message.

5. Enter anything you want in the Compose window, and then select Send⇨Standard. This menu choice schedules the message you just entered for sending to CompuServe and returns you to the Main Processing window.

6. At the Main Processing window, choose the Mail button to have GoCIS log on to CompuServe and send your e-mail message. You should see GoCIS successfully dial CompuServe, enter your name and user ID, Go Mail, compose your message, and log off. GoCIS reads your mail message the next time you log on to CompuServe to process mail.

7. To have GoCIS read your e-mail message, choose the Mail button again. GoCIS logs on to CompuServe, notices that you have electronic mail waiting, and reads your mail message, saving it on your PC for you to read at your leisure.

   After GoCIS logs off, you can browse through any mail messages that have been read by selecting EMail⇨Latest EMail Received from the Main Processing window. This menu option displays your e-mail messages. After reading your e-mail message, select File⇨Exit to return to the Main Processing window.

Joining and Getting Section Names

When you add a forum to GoCIS, GoCIS goes online to get detailed forum information (section names, message areas, etc.) from CompuServe. The Practice forum and Help forum have already been added to the initial version of GoCIS that you install, so you can practice joining these forums and getting section information.

To add a forum, follow these steps:

1. Under the Do View or Forum? question on the Main Processing window, click the View radio button. This action tells GoCIS to perform any scheduled automatic actions for the forums that are currently listed on the right side of the window. Scheduled actions for each forum are listed next to the forum name, right after the ellipsis (. . .).

2. Choose the Actions button to log on to CompuServe and perform the scheduled actions of automatically updating Forum(Sections). GoCIS goes to the Practice and Help forums, joins them (if you are not already a member), and retrieves their section names.

Reading Messages

1. Double-click the left mouse button on the Practice forum name to display the Practice Processing Options window.

2. Choose the Browse button in the upper part of this window, following Scan New Message Headers in Section. This action displays a list of section names; you can select one or more names from which to scan for new messages.

3. Click the General Information section name in this list, and choose the OK button. GoCIS enters a 1 (the number assigned to the General Information section) to indicate that it will scan for all message headers in this section.

4. Choose the OK button in the upper right corner of the Practice Processing Options window to return to the Main Processing window.

5. Highlight the Practice forum name in the Forum List box by clicking the name.

6. Under the Do View or Forum? question on the Main Processing window, click the Forum radio button. This action tells GoCIS to perform automatic processing for Practice only, the currently highlighted forum.

7. Press the Messages button bar to log on to CompuServe and obtain message headers for the General Information section of the Practice forum.

8. When GoCIS logs off CompuServe and displays the Main Processing window, choose the Headers button located on the button bar to display the Practice Forum Message Headers window. The window contains a short "header" for each message currently in the General Information section of the Practice forum.

9. Click selected headers to highlight the messages for reading during your next GoCIS processing session.

10. Choose the OK button in this window and the OK button in the Processing Options window to return to the Main Processing window. The message Message(Read) should appear after the ellipsis (. . .) next to the Practice forum in the Forum List box.

11. Choose the Actions button to log on to CompuServe and read the selected messages (perform the Message(Read) action) for the Practice forum.

12. When GoCIS logs off CompuServe and displays the Main Processing window, select Forum⇨Messages from the Main Processing window. GoCIS displays the Practice Message window.

13. You can browse through messages in this window by pressing the down-arrow button.

14. After browsing through the messages, select File⇨Exit from the Practice Message window; then choose the OK button in the Practice Processing Options window to return to the Main Processing window.

Sending Messages to a Forum

You can create a message to send to a forum while reading messages, or you can initiate the create process from the Main Processing window.

To send a new message to the My TEST Message section of the Practice forum, perform the following steps:

1. Click the right mouse button on the Practice forum to display a menu; from this menu, select Messages⇨Create New Message. The Send To? window appears.

2. Choose the Browse button in the Send To? window, and double-click the SysOp entry in the address book.

3. Enter **Test message** in the Subject text area, and then choose the pull-down arrow at the bottom of the Send To? window.

4. Use the scroll bar to find the My TEST Message entry in the pull-down list, and click that entry to select it as the section to which you want to send the message. You can then choose the OK button in this window.

5. Enter any message you want into the Compose window that appears. When you have entered your message, select Send⇨Standard to indicate that you are done entering your message. GoCIS returns to the Main Processing window with an action of Message(Send) scheduled for the Practice forum.

6. Choose the Action button to log on to CompuServe and send your message to the Practice forum.

Searching for a File to Download from a Forum

To use GoCIS to download a file from a forum's libraries, you must first create a Catalog of Files. This Catalog contains information about all the files that match search criteria you specify for each forum. To create a Catalog of Files, perform the following steps:

1. Click the left mouse button on the Practice forum name to select the forum.

2. Select Forum⇨Library⇨Search Patterns from the Main Processing window to indicate that you want to define and/or select search patterns to use in building a Catalog of Files.

   GoCIS displays a Search Criteria window for you to use in defining the first pattern for this forum.

   To define a pattern, perform the following steps.

3. Enter **Recent files** in the Pattern Name/Name text entry area.

4. Enter –1 in the Days text entry area. GoCIS searches for all files since the last scan. Because no scans have yet been performed, entering –1 retrieves all files.

5. Choose the Browse button to display a list of library sections for this forum. Click the first one in the list, and choose the OK button in the Practice Library(s) window and the OK button in the Search Criteria window.

6. Choose the Mark All button at the bottom of the Library Search Patterns window to select all the patterns for use in searching the Practice forum libraries for files to include in the Catalog of Files.

7. Choose the OK button in this window and the OK button in the Practice Processing Options window to return to the Main Processing window. You should have a Library(Scan) action now scheduled for the Practice forum.

8. Choose the Action button to have GoCIS log on to CompuServe and scan the Practice forum libraries for files that match your selected search patterns.

Downloading a File from a Forum

If you have performed the steps defined in the previous section ("Searching for a File to Download from a Forum"), you have a Catalog of Files to browse. From this Catalog, you can select files to be downloaded to your computer.

To select and download a file, follow these steps:

1. Click on the Practice forum in the Forum List box to select that forum for processing. Then select Forum⇨Libraries⇨Catalog of Files to display the Practice Catalog of Files window. This window contains a list of the files that match the search criteria defined and selected (see the previous section).

2. You can display information in the Catalog of Files in one of two ways. Select Options⇨Show Full Description or Show FileList Only to change the format of the display between the two display types.

3. Click a filename in the displayed list to mark a file to be downloaded to your computer. When you have marked at least one file, choose the OK button in this window. GoCIS returns to the Main Processing window with an action of Library(Download) scheduled for the Practice forum.

4. Choose the Action button to log on to CompuServe and download (perform the scheduled Download action) for the file you marked.

5. During the download, GoCIS displays a window to inform you of the current processing status. After the download is complete for all files you marked, GoCIS logs off and displays the Main Processing window.

ClipMate

ClipMate adds several value-added enhancements to the operation of the Windows Clipboard. It enables you to keep many generations of previous Clipboard occupants (clip items) for later retrieval. If you use a particular piece of data often, you can store it indefinitely in ClipMate's safe list. You can append multiple clip items into a single piece of data for pasting into an application, through a process called Gluing. You can browse and edit the clip items in ClipMate's Magnification window. ClipMate also includes a function to remove unwanted line breaks in your text, and you can print with the press of a button.

You can use ClipMate to collect additional data types, such as bitmap, picture, RTF, and OLE objects. The new PowerPaste feature enables you to paste data into your applications quickly and easily. When activated, ClipMate enters a kind of "auto pilot," sensing when you've pasted data, and automatically advancing to the next clip item for you.

Understanding How ClipMate Operates

When you put anything on the Clipboard (by cutting or copying), ClipMate gets a message from Windows. ClipMate checks to see if the Clipboard is holding any *desirable formats* (those formats supported by ClipMate that the user wants to capture, as determined by the filter). If desirable formats are present, ClipMate automatically makes a copy of the data for itself. It places the new data in one of its lists, creates a title, and displays the title in the text window at the top of the Clip Item Selection list box. If the Magnification window is active, the new clip item is displayed within it.

You can access ClipMate's data by using a drop-down list or a graphical grid that shows thumbnail sketches of the data. After you make a selection, ClipMate automatically copies the selected item to the Clipboard. It is then ready for your use in any application that offers Clipboard support for the item's data formats.

Having ClipMate running all the time is generally advisable. ClipMate continues to capture data, even if run as an icon. I suggest placing ClipMate in your Startup group so that it is always active.

Advanced Installation

Windows 3.1 users can take advantage of the hot key, the Run Minimized, and the Startup group methods of installation.

Using a hot key

You can set a hot key combination to activate ClipMate (after it's running) and bring it to the top of all other windows. To use this method, highlight the ClipMate icon in the Program Manager (the one that's actually on the Program Manager, NOT the one that represents the running application). Select File⇨Properties from the Program Manager's menu. You are presented with the Properties dialog box for ClipMate. Click your mouse in the Hotkey field. Give it a hot key, probably some combination of Ctrl+Alt+ whatever you want. The default is Ctrl+Alt+C.

Using the Run Minimized method

If you normally want ClipMate to be iconified when run, you can set the properties of the ClipMate icon to cause ClipMate to start as an icon. To use this method, highlight the ClipMate icon in the Program Manager (the one that's actually on the Program Manager, NOT the one that represents the running application). Select File⇨Properties from the Program Manager's menu. You are presented with the Properties dialog box for ClipMate. Check the Run Minimized check box. That's it!

Putting ClipMate in your Startup group

The Startup group is a Windows 3.1 feature that enables you to determine easily which programs automatically execute when Windows is loaded. You probably want to put ClipMate in your Startup group.

Specifying Data Files

If you want to use a filename other than DEFAULT.CLM for your data, you can specify your filename as a parameter to ClipMate. In this case, the command line in the Program Manager should be

```
C:\CLIPMATE\CLIPMATE.EXE MYFILE.CLM
```

Uninstalling ClipMate

If you need to uninstall ClipMate, a short write-up is included in the CLMREAD.TXT file.

Examining the Main Window

ClipMate's main window contains a drop-down combo box, showing the title of the currently selected clip item, a toolbar, and pull-down menus. Buttons and menus provide access to other ClipMate windows and functions. Often, the buttons change their appearance to indicate a particular mode of operation, or they might be grayed out to indicate the inability to access a particular function.

Controlling the layout: full vs. brief

ClipMate gives you the option of displaying all its graphical controls, along with the menu (Full Layout), or just showing some of the graphical controls, with no menu, to save space (Brief Layout). The brief layout gives you the PowerPaste, Delete, Print, Glue, and Magnify buttons, along with the Config, Multi Select, and About buttons.

In the brief layout, not all features are accessible. In particular, you lose the ability to switch back and forth between the recyclable list and the safe list. In the full layout, you have access to all features, but ClipMate takes up more screen space.

Using the Clip Item Selection list box

The Clip Item Selection list box is your primary method for recalling data back onto the Clipboard. You use the mouse to activate the list box and then make your selection from its scrolling list of clip item titles. After you've made your selection, the selected clip item is copied onto the Clipboard.

Using the mouse

The Clip Item Selection list copies clip items from one of the clip item lists back onto the Clipboard. You can accomplish this task by selecting the title of a stored clip item from the Clip Item Selection list. When you click the down-arrow icon to the right of the text window, you see a scrolling list, by title, of the clip items in the active list. When you have made your selection, the list goes away, the title of the selected clip item appears in the text window, and the item is copied to the Clipboard.

Using the keyboard

Alternatively, you can use the up and down arrows on the keyboard to make the selection. This method sometimes has an advantage, such as when you are browsing the list through the Magnification window. Sequentially zipping through each clip item by pressing the down-arrow key is very easy. To use the cursor key, you must first give input focus to the list box or the text window at the top of the list box. To do so, simply click the text window itself with the mouse, and it appears in reverse video, indicating that it has the input focus. You should learn to use both methods because they each have advantages.

Some rules of thumb

■ Whenever either of the clip item lists becomes active, the top entry of the active list is shown in the text window and therefore is also copied to the Clipboard. This rule includes the initial activation of the recyclable list, upon start-up.

■ Whenever the Clipboard contents are erased by an application, or it contains only formats that are filtered out by the user-definable filter, the selection list displays a message stating that the Clipboard is empty or invalid.

■ During certain operations where no single current selection is made, such as Multi-Select, the selection list box might display messages stating that such an operation is taking place.

Using the toolbar

Toolbar buttons appear across the top of the main Clipmate window.

Using the Multiple Selection dialog box

This dialog box enables you to select several clip items at a time. Several operations take advantage of the multiple selection, such as Delete, Print, Glue, and Copy to Safe List. The dialog box consists of two list boxes: the selection list on the left and the confirmation list on the right.

Follow these steps to use the Multiple Selection dialog box:

1. If you need to see the Magnification window, activate it before opening the Multiple Selection dialog box. Use of the Magnification window is highly recommended because it enables you to see easily what you are selecting.

2. Choose the MS button to bring up the dialog box. When the dialog box is displayed, you can't go back to the rest of ClipMate without choosing either OK or Cancel.

3. If necessary, move and/or resize the Magnification window.

4. The selection list appears in the list box on the left. With the mouse or spacebar, select the titles of the clip items with which you want to work. As you make each selection, the clip item you select is displayed in the Magnification window. The Magnification window holds only one clip item at a time, so only the most recent selection is shown.

In the confirmation list (on the right), your selections appear in the order that you selected them. This read-only window provides visual confirmation that you have selected the items in the order that you intended. It is especially helpful when you're gluing clip items because it gives an outline of what you are composing. For the Copy to Safe List operation, the order also comes into play. The items are copied to the safe list in the order in which you selected them and therefore the order in which they appear in the confirmation window.

5. If you change your mind about a particular item, just click it again. The highlighting disappears and is removed from the confirmation list on the right. You can select and deselect as many times as you want.

6. When you are done with your selections, choose OK.

The Delete, Print, Glue, and possibly Copy to Safe List buttons (depending upon what list is currently active) are now enabled. You can perform any of these functions using the multiple selection.

Using the ThumbNail Select button

This button is available only in the full layout. You use the Thumbnail Select button to open or close the Graphic Selection window.

Using the PowerPaste button

This button is available in both the full layout and the brief layout. When activated, PowerPaste enables you to paste multiple items into an application, without having to access ClipMate continuously to select the next item. This feature gives ClipMate a "hands-off" mode and makes it quick and easy to use ClipMate's data.

As you paste data into an application, ClipMate senses that you've pasted the current item, and *automatically* advances to the next item. Paste again, and you get the second item. Paste once more, and you get the third item. This process continues until you deactivate PowerPaste or reach the end of the clip list (in the chosen direction).

As it advances its way through the current clip list, PowerPaste can either work its way up (toward newer data) or down (toward older data). After you activate PowerPaste, you can keep pasting until you encounter either the top or bottom of the current list. You select the direction by choosing one of the two "outlets" that form the PowerPaste button.

Note that when you're PowerPasting, nothing prevents you from copying new data into ClipMate. The new data appears on top of the list and not at the location of the PowerPaste pointer. So, if you're PowerPasting up, you can encounter this new data if you continue far enough.

The direction of PowerPaste determines whether you get the data in the order in which you copied it or in reverse. PowerPasting up preserves the order; down reverses it.

PowerPaste begins with the currently selected clip item, which is visible in the Clip Item Selection list box. If you have made no selections, PowerPaste begins at the top of the current list, by default. This setting is often suitable for PowerPasting down. If you want to PowerPaste up, however, you don't get very far unless you select a starting point farther down in the list. Of course, if you plan on copying more data to ClipMate, the top might be a fine place to start.

The PowerPaste button is actually two buttons: an upper outlet and a lower outlet, which correspond to the PowerPaste (up) and PowerPaste (down) options from the Edit menu.

When you choose either outlet, it "glows" to show you that it is active. If you choose the other outlet, it glows, and the other one returns to normal. In this way, the outlets work much like a pair of radio buttons because they are mutually exclusive.

Click the active outlet, and the operation ends. Note that if you reach either end of the list, the operation automatically terminates, with an audible beep.

In the previous example, I used the Tab key frequently. This choice has nothing to do with ClipMate or PowerPaste. It is just used to navigate from one field to another in my order-entry screen.

You can encounter problems PowerPasting into certain applications that hold the Clipboard open too long when pasting. You get a message from ClipMate saying that an `Error Opening Clipboard` has occurred. A possible workaround is to slow down the PowerPaste action by adding the following line to the \WINDOWS\CLIPMATE.INI file, under the `[CLIPMATE]` heading:

```
PPDELAY=500
```

The delay interval is in milliseconds (1000 ms = 1 second). The default is `100`, which is nearly instantaneous. Slowing it down gives your application more time to paste its data, but you need to keep this delay in mind when pasting because you can get ahead of PowerPaste.

Using the Delete button

This button is available in both the full layout and the brief layout. Delete works with single or multiple selections to delete the currently selected clip item or items from the active list. The next item in line is then copied to the Clipboard and shown in the Clip Item Selection list box.

Printing Text Items

The Print Text Item button is available in both the full layout and the brief layout. This button works with single or multiple selections to print the currently selected clip item or items. This function works only with text. Its keyboard shortcut is Ctrl+P.

Printer support is generic. Output appears in a font, such as Courier that is supported by your printer. No options are available for fonts, margins, or such. The purpose of this setup is to enable ClipMate to give basic printer services to as many printers as possible. Now, you can print any text that you can get into the Clipboard—with only a mouse click! If you need more sophisticated printing, just paste your data to any application that meets your needs.

Items are printed to the default Windows printer, unless you have specified a printer by using the Print Setup option, found on the File menu. After you have chosen a printer with Print Setup, that setting remains until you change it to something else. It is not reset upon shutdown. This way, if you have more than one printer, you can conveniently and routinely always use a different printer for ClipMate output. Many ClipMate users direct their ClipMate output to their desktop (dot-matrix) printer, leaving their shared network (laser) printer for other tasks, such as word processing.

The notion of retaining a printer selection from session to session is not typical practice in Windows. But it makes sense in this case. If you use ClipMate to make 3270 emulation more bearable, I'm sure you'll agree. A potential pitfall could arise if you were to delete the printer definition for the printer that you have chosen as ClipMate's printer. If you do delete the definition, just select another printer by using File⇨Print Setup.

Gluing Text

The Glue Text button is available in both the full layout and the brief layout. This button operates on text items only. If you glue several items that contain multiple formats, only the text component is glued.

The Glue function concatenates (appends together) selected clip items into one big clip item. The resulting item is then copied back onto the Clipboard for use by other applications.

You can use this feature in two ways.

The first method (Auto-Glue) turns on the glue mode and then copies data to the Clipboard. This mode is a special mode of operation, where ClipMate appends each new text item directly to the end of its predecessor instead of creating new clip items for each new piece of text. If you turn on the glue mode and then copy ten paragraphs to the Clipboard from other applications, for example, you end up with one clip item that is ten paragraphs long. In addition, the resulting clip item is always on the Clipboard and is up-to-date (as long as Auto-Glue is still on). You don't even have to interact with ClipMate at all to use this new item.

To use this method, just click the Glue button, or select Edit⇨Glue Together. You should NOT perform a multiple selection prior to entering glue mode. Doing so invokes a Manual Glue (the second type of gluing method).

When you enter glue mode, a fresh, empty clip item is created. It initially has a title stating <<Glue In Process. . .>>. As you copy text from other applications, the title changes to indicate the number of items that have been glued together. To finish, click the Glue button again. The title changes to <<Glue Finished, (x) Items>>, and ClipMate exits Glue mode. At any time during the glue operation, you can utilize the new item in its current state.

The Auto-Glue feature ends automatically if you try to use other ClipMate functions while it is active. You can open or close the Magnification window, but only to browse the data. Any other action terminates the current glue operation, as if you had chosen the Glue button to turn off the glue mode. After it's stopped, you can't restart a glue. You can, however, perform a multiple selection and use the Manual Glue method to put several glues (or single items) together.

The second method (Manual Glue) glues existing clip items together within ClipMate. This operation requires you to have previously performed a multiple selection.

Manual Glue is useful for making one large clip item from several smaller items. You select the items that you want by performing a multiple selection, and then choose the Glue button (or select Edit⇨Glue Together).

One advantage that manual gluing has over auto gluing is that you don't have to plan it in advance. Another is that you can easily change the order of the result because the multiple selection gives you the ability to select items in any order that you want.

Using the Magnify button

This button is available in both the full layout and the brief layout and is also accessible from the View menu. The Magnify button opens or closes the Magnification window.

When the Magnification window is open, the Magnify button appears to be checked. In this way, it functions like a standard Windows check box. When you choose the button again, it pops up, and the Magnification window closes.

Copying to a safe list

The Copy to a Safe List button is not available in the brief layout. You use this button to copy selected clip items to the safe list; the button is available only when the recyclable list is the active list. Copy to a Safe List works with single or multiple selections.

Activating the recyclable list

The Activate the Recyclable List button is not available in the brief layout but is accessible from the View menu. This button causes the recyclable list to become the active list.

The Recyclable button and Safe button are bound together and act like radio buttons. When you press one, it takes on a depressed appearance, and the other button pops out. This way, you can easily see which list you're using.

Activating the safe list

The Activate the Safe List button is not available in the brief layout but is accessible from the View menu. This button causes the safe list to become the active list.

The Recyclable button and Safe button are bound together and act like radio buttons. When you press one, it takes on a depressed appearance, and the other button pops out. This way, you can easily see which list you're using.

For information about using ClipMate menus and working with Clipboard formats, please refer to ClipMate Help.

WizManager

WizManager is a powerful add-on or extension to the Windows File Manager. It appends many features missing in File Manager and enhances your power to manage your disks and files. WizManager is automatically loaded when File Manager starts and is removed from memory when the latter closes. You do not have to intervene—after it is installed, WizManager becomes entirely part of File Manager, just like standard features.

WizManager additions belong to three main groups: the Fast Access button bar, the Command Line box, and utilities that you can place in a pull-down menu.

Using the Fast Access button bar

The Fast Access button bar accelerates the application and facilitates access to WizManager's functionalities. Instead of browsing through the menus, you can activate a command by clicking the appropriate button.

Using the Command Line box

The Command Line box is not the simple Run command found in the File menu. It is for File Manager users who want sometimes to be able to type DOS commands like DEL or COPY, or start a program or open a file by typing its name instead of using a mouse and menus. All WizManager DOS commands are executed in Windows, without shelling out to DOS.

Using the utilities

You can place frequently used functions or applications in a customizable Launch pull-down menu for fast and easy access.

- Clicking the right mouse button anywhere on File Manager displays a pop-up menu listing all the currently active applications in Windows and enabling you to switch quickly to any of them.

- You can use a specified association (for example, a program associated with the TXT extension) or a specified program name (browse to find the application path, or enter it directly). You also can send all the files to the same application.

- With the Print Directory utility, you can print the displayed File Manager directory listing. You can either print File Manager selected files, entire directory listings, or Search Result lists. A Print Tree utility is available as well.

- Many other functionalities are available, such as exiting or restarting Windows, rebooting the system, accessing the different Control Panel functions directly, creating Script files, File Viewer access, etc.

Configuring WizManager

Through the Preferences dialog box, you can customize WizManager and specify how you want to work with its various components. The following tables describe the areas of the dialog box you use to specify your configuration settings.

Using the General Setup check boxes

The General Setup check boxes are described in the following table:

Check Box	Check this box to:
Activate Right Mouse Button	Display the WizManager pop-up menu when you click the right mouse button anywhere on File Manager.
Move to Command Line Box at Startup	Make the Command Line box active and ready for command entries when File Manager is started.
Include Hidden Tasks in Task List	Include hidden tasks in WizManager pop-up menu Task List.
Beep on Error	Tell WizManager to emit a beep when an error is detected.
Display Button Info	Display a help window when the mouse cursor is positioned over a button on the button bar.
Force Refresh	Force File Manager to refresh its Status bar and its Directory window each time WizManager performs a COPY, MOVE, or DELETE command.

Using the Confirm On check boxes

The Confirm On check boxes are described in the following table:

Check Box	Check this box to:
File Copy	Have a confirmation dialog box displayed each time WizManager's COPY command is used.
File Move	Have a confirmation dialog box displayed each time WizManager's MOVE command is used.
File Replace	Have a confirmation dialog box displayed before a WizManager's command is executed when a file declared in the source parameter has the same file name as an existing file in the target directory.
File Delete	Have a confirmation dialog box displayed each time WizManager's DELETE command is used.
File Rename	Have a confirmation dialog box displayed each time WizManager's RENAME or REN command is used.
Directory Remove	Have a confirmation dialog box displayed each time WizManager's RMDIR or RD command is used.

Using the Include check boxes

The Include check boxes are described in the following table:

Check Box	Check this box to:
Hidden Files	Have WizManager's commands always include hidden files.
System Files	Have WizManager's commands always include system files.

Setting Up the System

The following paragraphs describe how you use the buttons in the System Setup group of the Preferences dialog box to set up the system the way you want it.

Setting a password

The Password dialog box enables you to assign a password that you (or another user) must enter in order to unlock WizManager's Lock feature. Lock minimizes all running applications and locks Windows until you enter your password in the displayed Unlock dialog box.

To enter a (new) password, select Preferences from the WizManager menu; then select the Password button in the System Setup group. The Password dialog box appears, enabling you to enter the password to unlock your system. Entering a new password erases any previously saved password. (You also can type **password** in the Command Line box to access the Password dialog box directly.)

A password can be any combination of letters, numbers, and/or punctuation. Spaces (spacebar spaces) are accepted. For maximum security, I strongly suggest that you NOT use passwords shorter than four characters. Neither should you use passwords such as birthdays or first names. These are often the first ones tried by anyone who would try to break into your system.

Designating the start-up directory

The Startup Directory dialog box enables you to assign the Command Line box current directory when WizManager's button bar is displayed (either at WizManager's start-up or later when you choose to display the button bar).

To enter a new start-up directory or to modify an existing one, select Preferences from the WizManager menu, and then select the Startup Directory button in the System Setup group.

In the Startup Directory dialog box that appears, select to use the directory that is current when the button bar is displayed as the Command Line box current directory, or enter a start-up directory in the dialog box's edit field.

Setting the additional path

In addition to the DOS search PATH, WizManager searches the path set in the Additional Path dialog box for commands, programs, files, or scripts not found in the current directory.

To enter an additional path or to modify an existing one, select Preferences from the WizManager menu, and then select the Additional Path button in the System Setup group.

In the Additional Path dialog box that appears, select no additional path, or enter a path or set of paths in the dialog box's edit field. To specify a set of paths to search, separate the entries with a semicolon (;).

Selecting a path shortcut symbol

The path shortcut symbol represents the path of the active File Manager directory window. The path shortcut symbol (character) is a command parameter prefix that is useful when the current Command Line box directory differs from the active File Manager directory window directory. The path shortcut symbol represents the full path of the active File Manager directory. Using this symbol enables you to work on the files displayed in the active File Manager directory window from the Command Line box with a minimum of keystrokes. To specify a file displayed in the active File Manager window, simply enter the path shortcut symbol followed by the filename.

To select a path shortcut symbol, select Preferences from the WizManager menu, and then select the Path Shortcut button in the System Setup group.

The path shortcut symbol can be one of these characters:

  ; (a semicolon)

  + (a plus sign)

  @ (the at character)

(Or you can choose to activate no path shortcut symbol.) The default path shortcut symbol is the semicolon character (;). You can change the path shortcut symbol by selecting another dialog option in the Select a Path Shortcut Symbol group.

Specifying the DOS PIF file

When opening a DOS Prompt session, WizManager executes the program named COMMAND.COM through a PIF configuration file specified in the DOS PIF File Preferences.

DOSPRMPT.PIF is the default configuration file that is installed in your Windows directory when Windows is installed. DOSPRMPT.PIF is also the default configuration file preset by WizManager. To enter the path and filename of a different configuration file, select Preferences from the WizManager menu, and then select the DOS PIF File button in the System Setup group. Enter the PIF path and filename in the edit field, or select Browse to browse through your drives and directories and find the appropriate PIF file.

The DOS PIF configuration file controls several facets of the way COMMAND.COM is launched from the DOS Prompt command. You can set or modify a PIF file by using the Windows application PIFEDIT.EXE. Refer to the "PIF Editor" chapter of your *Windows User's Guide* for detailed information on how to customize a PIF file.

Setting the Fast Open applications

The Set Fast Open feature enables you to designate two applications that you can access quickly to open or use to work on the selected files in File Manager. When a Fast Open application is executed, the Open Files dialog box is not displayed.

To set the Fast Open application paths and filenames, select Preferences from the WizManager menu, and then select the Set Fast Open button in the System Setup group.

Enter the path and filename of each Fast Open applications in the respective edit fields; or select the corresponding Browse button, browse through your drives and directories, and set the appropriate Fast Open application.

The application specified in the upper edit field is launched and opens the selected files in File Manager when you hold down the Ctrl key while selecting Open Files from the WizManager menu or the Open Files button in the button bar. The second application is selected and launched when you hold down the Ctrl+Shift keys while selecting Open Files from the WizManager menu or the Open Files button in the button bar.

Setting the File Viewer application

The Set Viewer button enables you to set the path and filename of a file viewer application. After you have set the viewer application, clicking the button bar's Viewer button or selecting View Files from WizManager's menu starts the viewer application and displays the files selected in File Manager.

A file viewer is a program that enables you to view the contents of a file. Notepad, the text editor provided with Windows, is probably the simplest file viewer, although its viewing capabilities are limited to small text files. More elaborated file viewers are available, such as Drag And View by Canyon Software (shareware) or Norton Viewer, the viewer included in the Norton Desktop for Windows. These file viewers are able to display the file contents not only of text files but also of formatted files created with word processors, spreadsheets, databases, drawing programs, etc.

To set the viewer application path and filename, select Preferences from the WizManager menu, and then select the Set Viewer button in the System Setup group. Enter the path and filename in the dialog box's edit field; or select the Browse button, browse through your drives and directories, and set the appropriate file viewer application.

Check Start Only One Viewer Instance in the dialog box if you want to start only one copy of the viewer application to display all the files selected in File Manager. Be aware that many file viewers are not able to display multiple files or generate an error message with this option checked.

Customize ButtonBar

The Customize Buttonbar dialog box enables you to reorganize the button bar's button order. To optimize your work with the button bar, move the most often used buttons to the top of the list and the least often used to the bottom.

To reorganize your button bar, follow these steps:

1. Select the entry in the button list that represents the button you want to move.

2. Select the Move Up or Move Down button to move the button towards the top or the bottom of the button list.

3. Repeat Move Up or Move Down until the button's position in the button list is as you want it.

4. Repeat steps 1 through 3 for each button you want to move.

5. Choose OK to save the changes and rebuild the button bar.

The button bar now displays the buttons in the order you specified. If you want to reset the button order on the button bar back to the default order, select the Reset button.

Using the Command Line Box Commands and Switches

Command	Definition
386	Optimizes Windows for 386 enhanced mode.
About	Displays WizManager About dialog box.
Associate	Associates a file with an application.
Attrib or AttribQ	Changes or displays file attributes.

Command	Definition
Cascade	Overlaps File Manager directory windows.
ChDir or CD	Changes the current directory.
Close	Closes running applications.
CloseBar	Closes the WizManager button bar.
Color	Changes the Windows screen colors.
Copy or CopyQ	Copies one or more files to another location.
CustBar	Customizes the WizManager button bar.
CustLnch	Enables you to customize your Launch menu.
Date	Changes the date of your computer's clock.
Del or DelQ	Deletes one or more files.
Desktop	Changes the look of your desktop.
Dir	Displays a directory of files and subdirectories.
DiskCopy	Copies one floppy disk's content to another.
DiskFree or DF	Displays disk free space.
DiskInfo or DI	Displays disk information.
DOS	Starts a DOS Prompt session.
Drivers	Sets up optional drivers.
Erase or EraseQ	Erases one or more files.
Exit	Exits File Manager.
ExitWin	Exits Windows.
FDetails	Displays all information on files and directories.
FileType	Displays a specified group of files.
FName	Displays file and directory names only.
Fonts	Adds and removes fonts.
Format	Formats a floppy disk.
Help	Displays WizManager Help contents.
Indicate	Indicates expandable branches in directory tree.
Interntl	Specifies international settings.
Keyboard	Specifies keyboard repeat rate and delay.
Lock	Locks Windows (safety feature).
MaxFM	Enlarges File Manager to its maximum size.
Mem	Displays free memory (RAM) and resources.

Command	Definition
MinApp	Reduces all running applications to icons.
MinFM	Reduces File Manager to an icon.
MinWin	Reduces all directory windows to icons.
MkDir or MD	Creates a directory.
Mouse	Changes your mouse settings.
Move or MoveQ	Moves one or more files to another location.
NetCon	Connects to a network drive.
NetDis or NetDel	Disconnects from a network drive.
Network	Specifies settings for your network connections.
NewWin	Opens a new File Manager directory window.
Open	Opens selected files in File Manager.
Password	Sets or changes the Unlock password.
Path	Displays the search path.
PDetails	Displays partial information on files and directories.
Ports	Specifies serial ports communication settings.
Pref	Sets or changes WizManager preferences.
Print	Prints a file.
PrintDir	Prints a File Manager directory listing.
Printers	Sets up printers.
PrnTree	Prints a disk directory structure.
Reboot	Exits Windows and reboots system.
Refresh	Updates the active File Manager directory window.
Ren or RenQ	Renames a file or files.
Rename or RenameQ	Renames a file or files.
RestApp	Restores all applications to their original sizes.
Restart	Exits and restarts Windows.
RestWin	Restores all directory windows.
RmDir or RD	Removes a directory.
SaveNow	Saves positions and views of open directory windows.
Search	Searches for files and directories.
SelDrive	Selects disk drive.

Command	Definition
Select	Selects files and directories in a directory window.
ShDir or SD	Shares directory on network.
SortDate	Sorts directory window files by last modification date.
SortName	Sorts directory window files and directories by name.
SortSize	Sorts directory window files by size.
SortType	Sorts directory window files and directories by type.
Sound	Assigns sounds to system events.
StopSh or SS	Stops sharing directory on network.
Sys	Copies DOS operating-system files onto a floppy disk.
SysInfo	Displays system information.
Task	Displays WizManager Task menu.
TileH	Arranges directory windows horizontally.
TileV	Arranges directory windows vertically.
Time	Changes the time of your computer's clock.
Type	Displays the contents of a text file.
Ver	Displays WizManager, DOS, and Windows versions.
Verify	Sets or displays file write verify status.
Vol	Displays a disk volume label.

You can customize the execution of any program or the opening of any file (from the Command Line Box or from the Launch menus) by using the following switches placed at the end of the command:

Switch	Action
/+	Opens maximized.
/-	Opens minimized.
/=	Opens restored (normal size).
/H	Opens and hides.
/@	Makes the directory where the application (or file) resides the working directory.
/;	Makes the active File Manager directory the working directory.

Examining Commands Added to the Options Menu

Selecting the Save Settings Now menu item from the Window menu saves the positions and views of all open File Manager directory windows.

Save Settings Now enables you to save immediately the positions and views of open File Manager directory windows. When you restart File Manager, the open directory windows are in the same positions and have the same View menu settings as they had at the time you used the Save Settings Now command. With Save Settings Now, you don't have to set the Save Settings on Exit menu command and close File Manager to keep the directory windows' layout. It is saved at the time you select the Save Settings Now command.

Holding down the Shift key while selecting File⇨Exit has the same effect as selecting the Save Settings Now command.

Understanding the Shareware Concept

Contrary to popular belief, shareware is not a type of software but a method of marketing software. It is a marketing plan based entirely on trust between the creator of the shareware program and you, the user. Shareware is copyrighted software that you can try before buying. This great concept enables you to use the program during a limited time (21 days for Mijenix WizManager) and evaluate its features on your terms. In many cases, shareware programs are as good as, or even better than, software available only through normal retail channels. Because shareware is distributed at minimal cost, buying shareware programs enables you to save money and helps shareware authors continue providing innovative, affordable programs.

Shareware authors release programs with an element of trust, expecting payment if a program is used past the evaluation period. When users register shareware programs they find useful, they receive in return the right to use the program. When registering Mijenix WizManager, you receive the latest version and full-featured WizManager. In addition, you receive an in-depth user's manual, new release information, the newsletter *TIPS and TRICKS for File Manager*, and free technical support.

WinSince

WinSince is a list-oriented file manager that builds a list of files based on your selection criteria. From the list, you can

- Execute DOS commands and run DOS and Windows programs.

- Set up an icon that automatically performs a file task (such as finding all files with a BAK extension, for example).

- Sort the list of files in a lot of ways, such as by filename, extension, date, and size.

- Search for files created since a particular date or for files created a specified amount of time before the current time.

- Create a text file that logs all the files WinSince finds and records the actions it takes.

- Perform repetitive or time-dependent activities, based on a built-in timer.

With its customizable DOS and Windows actions and definable file type buttons, WinSince is a flexible utility construction set that enables you to automate many file-related tasks. You can have as many copies of WinSince running as you have tasks for it to do.

Examining the Main WinSince Screen

When you double-click the WinSince icon, the main WinSince screen (Figure 43) appears.

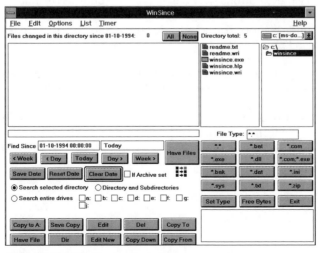

Figure 43: The WinSince main screen.

When WinSince starts, the three list boxes in the top half of the screen default to the following settings:

- The current drive and directory designations (in the list box on the right side of the screen). To change the directory, double-click the root directory, scroll through the directory list, and double-click the selected subdirectory name.

- A list of all files in the current directory (in the center list box).

- A list of all the current directory files that have been changed today (in the main file list on the left side of the screen).

Working with the drive, directory, and file lists

The file details shown in the main file list are the name of the file, its creation date (in MM-DD-YYYY HH:MM:SS format), its size in bytes, any attributes (such as a for archive, or r for read-only), and the full path of the file. When you select one of the files by clicking it, it appears in reverse video.

You can change the drive, directory, and files shown in the list boxes by using the File buttons and controls immediately above and below the list boxes to specify file search criteria.

Using the file buttons and controls

The Find Since line below the main file list shows the WinSince search date and time. The default is today at midnight (00:00:00).

The Directory radio buttons (just below the Date buttons) enable you to choose whether to search for files in the selected directory (Search Selected Directory), down into subdirectories (Directory and Subdirectories), or across entire drives (Search Entire Drives).

The Files Changed line above the main file list box (top left) shows the number of files found, the date being checked, and the type of search.

The file type button section (beneath the list boxes on the right side of the screen) has 12 buttons. *.* is the default file type criterion.

Using the Action buttons

The main screen has 14 action buttons:

- The ten buttons in the bottom left of the screen are user-definable action keys.

- The Have/Get Files button (above the colorful WinSince icon in the middle of the screen) displays Get Files when you have defined a new file search. When you click Get Files, WinSince finds the specified files and lists them in the main file list box. The button changes to display Have Files to indicate that the search is complete.

- Three action buttons beneath the file type buttons enable you to define the file type buttons (Set Type), determine the amount of free disk space on a selected drive (Free Bytes), and exit WinSince (Exit).

Examining the Edit Screen

When you click the Edit menu item, WinSince displays the Edit screen (Figure 44), where you can examine existing action definitions and invent your own.

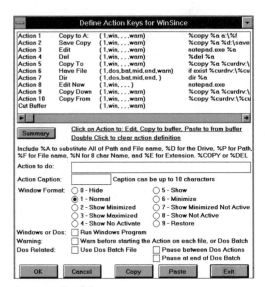

Figure 44: The Edit screen.

At the top of the two-part Edit screen, WinSince displays a list of summarized actions. The lower half of the screen is the editing area. When you first display the Edit screen, the top half lists the default definitions for the ten user-definable action keys that appear at the bottom of the main screen. For a discussion of the meaning of the supplied actions and the cut buffer, look up Actions in WinSince Help.

When you select a numbered action by clicking it, it appears in reverse video, and the lower editing area changes to reflect the components of the selected action in the lower-screen Summary fields. Later sections in these instructions tell you how to use the Edit screen fields and buttons to change the default action button definitions.

To return to the main WinSince screen, click the Exit button in the lower right corner of the Edit screen.

Finding Files

When WinSince starts, it defaults to finding all files changed today in the current directory.

You can use the Add Files control immediately above the Get Files button to add to the file list with each file search; then, when you click Get Files or Have Files, WinSince does not clear the file list. Add Files is useful for creating lists of many types of files or files from many different directory areas. It is equivalent to the /Add command line option.

You can select three file search options:

1. Search Selected Directory (the default mode): Searches only the directory you select by using the drive and directory selection controls.

2. Directory and Subdirectories: Begins the file search in the current directory and includes any subdirectories under the current directory.

3. Search Entire Drives: Enables you to select one or more hard drives to search. Next to the radio button is a listing of the drives that are available to you, such as a:, b:, c:. You also can check the total disk space available on the selected drive. Click the box to the left of your hard drive's letter, and then click the Free Bytes button on the lower right of the screen. In the box below, you then see the number of bytes free on this disk and the percent free.

The drive and subdirectory selection controls operate in the standard Windows manner. The Directory Total file list box shows the names of files matching the file type in the current directory. Clicking a file in this list shows the file details of the file below the main file details list box.

Under the subdirectory control is the File Type text box. You can enter the file type here, such as HELLO.*, or you can click one of the 12 file type buttons. WinSince accepts the DOS * (multiple-character wild card) and ? (single-character wild card) symbols. You also can separate the file types with a semicolon to search for multiple file types (*.EXE;*.TXT;*.RPT, for example).

Defining the File Type buttons

To define your own file type button, click the Set Type button (located just below the file type buttons). A small form (Set File Button) overlays the existing file buttons. Enter the file type designation (*.eco or *.wks, for example) in the blank. Then click one of the 12 file buttons; WinSince assigns the entered value to the button you clicked. Click the OK button to accept the file button assignments, click Cancel to return without changes, or click Reset to reset the file buttons to their original values.

Dragging and dropping a file into the file list

You can drag and drop a file from the directory control into the file list without using the Get File button. When the new file is dropped onto the list, WinSince adds it to the beginning of the file list and updates the total size of the file list.

Selecting the file date

Next to the Find Since prompt is the Date text box. You can enter the date here in MM-DD-YYYY HH:MM:SS format, or use the VCR controls to move forward or backward by a day or week at a time. The adjacent text box shows the date offset, relative to today (for example, Yesterday). To select files created since January 20, 1993, the Date field appears as 01-20-1993 00:00:00. The time defaults to midnight so that files created any time during the selected date are found.

For more specific searches, you can set the time in 24-hour format. To find files changed or created since noon on January 20, 1993, the Date field appears as 01-20-1993 12:00:00. Note that only a single space appears between the date and the time portions.

The time portion remains the same when you change the date portion with the VCR Date controls. You can reset the time to midnight by double-clicking anywhere in the Date field.

The Clear Date button enables you to look for files without regard to their creation date.

The Save Date button stores the current date for later retrieval with the Reset Date button.

WinSince also allows relative date searching for finding files created some amount of time before Now. The relative date format is -DDD:HH:MM:SS; it starts with a minus sign (–) followed by any number of days. The number of hours can be from 00 to 23, the minutes and seconds from 00 to 59.

For example, to select files created in the last hour, the date field would appear as `-0:01:00:00`. When you press Enter, WinSince converts the relative date (such as Today) to an absolute date in the text field to the right of the Find Since Date field.

You can drag and drop a file from the directory control onto the Find Since date. This action sets the file search date to that of the file dropped.

Sorting the file list

You can use the List menu to sort the file list in a variety of ways: by File Name, by Full Path, by Extension, by Creation Date, by Size, and by File Attributes. For sorts other than by File Name and Full Path, the list is sorted secondarily by File Name.

When you sort a list, WinSince deselects any selected files. When you perform a new search, files in the new file list appear in the order in which they were found. When you drag and drop a file from the directory list into the file list, the new file appears at the top of the file list.

Defining the Action Buttons

Two rows of definable action buttons (10 in all) are located along the bottom left of the main WinSince screen. Each button specifies an action to be performed on a file selected from the main file list. To view the current set of action button definitions, select Edit to display the Edit screen. To select an action from the list, click it.

The ten default action definitions provided by WinSince are defined in WinSince Help, under Actions in the Distribution Kit. You can redefine any of the default actions to suit your own file management requirements.

The Action to Do box holds a DOS command or program (such as COPY or FOX.EXE) or a Windows program (such as EXCEL.EXE) up to 100 characters long. Special substitution symbols (defined in WinSince Help under Editing and Using the Action Buttons) enable you to pass the selected files to the action in very flexible ways.

For example:

Selected file:	C:\WINDOWS\FILE.TXT
Selected action:	COPY %A A:\%N_2.%E
Resulting command:	COPY C:\WINDOWS\FILE.TXT A:\FILE_2.TXT
Explanation:	%A is C:\WINDOWS\FILE.TXT; %D is C (you add ":\"); %P is WINDOWS (note how there is no "\" at front or back); %F is FILE.TXT; %N is FILE; and %E is TXT.

Two file tokens point to the current drive and directory: %CurDrv substitutes the drive letter of the current directory, and %CurDir substitutes the current directory. If the current directory (within WinSince) is C:\WINDOWS\SYSTEM, then %CurDrv is C, and %CurDir is WINDOWS\SYSTEM. (Note that the : and starting and ending \ are not included; this is the general rule when creating WinSince actions.) For more examples, please refer to the SINCE.INI file.

WinSince has four built-in functions: %Copy (copy a file to another location), %Del (delete a file), %Attrib (modify file attributes), and %Action (combine actions). For more information about %Copy and %Del, please refer to Copying and Deleting Files in WinSince Help. For more information about %Attrib, please refer to Setting File Attributes in WinSince Help. %Action is discussed later in this section (see "%Action: combining actions").

The Window Format setting is usually Normal, Show Minimized, or Show Maximized. For %Copy and %Del actions the format is always Normal.

To run a Windows program, select the Run Windows Program check box. For DOS commands and programs, leave this box unchecked.

If you check Warn before Starting, WinSince displays a message box before performing an action on a selected file. On the message box, No presents the next selected file; Cancel ends the action for all selected files; Yes executes the action on the selected file; and Yes to All executes the action on all selected files. (For DOS batch file actions, a single warning appears before the batch file is started, showing a sample action contained in the batch file.)

Checking the Warn before Starting box for all %Copy and %Del actions gives you a chance to verify that the action is what you intend.

To run DOS actions, select Use DOS Batch File, which uses the SINCECLS.PIF file to run the action in a windowed DOS box and close the window when done. If you do not use the Use DOS Batch File option, each iteration of the action on a list of files creates a new DOS box under Windows, usually causing you to run out of memory.

If you check Pause between DOS Actions, WinSince inserts a DOS Pause command between each action in the batch file.

If you check Pause at End of DOS Batch, WinSince inserts a DOS Pause command after the last action in the batch file. If you do not specify Pause, the window closes when the action is completed.

For Windows actions, no direct parallel to the Pause ability of the DOS batch file exists. To insert a pause between or after Windows actions, check the Warn before Starting box. Before executing the action on the next file, WinSince displays the warning box. Ignore the warning box, and click the Windows application. When you finish the application, the warning box is still on-screen. You can then progress to the next file or cancel subsequent actions.

To make your action button changes permanent, select File⇨Save Actions. WinSince warns you if you are about to exit without saving new actions.

If you make an error while editing an action, you can start fresh by exiting and reentering the Edit screen or by exiting WinSince without saving the changed action definitions. If you ever need to, you can get the original WinSince actions and file types back by reinstalling WinSince.

The other buttons perform the following functions:

Button	Function
OK	Saves the changes and displays them in the Action list box. The action caption on the corresponding action button in the main WinSince window changes to match the new definition.
Cancel	Cancels the changes if you have not yet clicked on the OK button.
Copy	Copies a selected action to the cut buffer.
Paste	Copies the contents of the cut buffer to a selected action.
Exit	Displays the main WinSince screen. Note that WinSince does some checking of the action contents when you choose OK, to try to determine whether the action is incomplete.
Preview	Shows how the command will appear when it is run on a file, performing the filename substitutions on a sample filename. This button is useful for verifying your action to do entries.

Selecting files

Click a filename to select a single file. To select additional files, hold down the Ctrl key and click the other files to be selected. To select all files up to the file clicked, hold down the Shift key. To select all files, click the All button. To unselect all files, click the None button.

You also can drag and drop a file from the directory control onto an action button. The same action warnings are in effect.

Double-clicking to start a program

You can start any executable program (.EXE, .COM, .BAT, .PIF) by double-clicking its name in either the directory file list or the selected files list box. You also can start a program by double-clicking a data filename with an associated extension (such as starting NOTEPAD.EXE when you double-click README.TXT). Your WIN.INI file describes your current file associations.

Select Options⇨Warn before Run Double Click to verify what program will be run when you double-click a particular file type. When you are confident that clicking a file type runs the right program, you can reset this option.

%Action: combining actions

You can use the %Action command to run multiple actions on the list of files with a single button click. (You also can run the same combined actions from the start-up command line with the /Action qualifier.) You can add up to nine actions together. WinSince executes actions in the order of their appearance in the action definition.

The format for a combined action is

```
%Action1+%Action4+%Action3
```

WinSince executes Action1, then Action4, and finally Action3. The %Action command requires that you combine at least two actions. One %Action command cannot point to another action that contains a %Action command, and it cannot point to itself.

On the Edit screen, the portions important to the %Action command are the Action to Do, the Action Caption, and the Warning before Start. If the warning is set, WinSince warns you that the proposed action is a combined action before beginning execution. This setting is independent of the warning for each of the combined actions, which you can set or reset in the Edit screen. You also can use the Option menu to suppress action warnings.

Using Batch Mode and Command Line Qualifiers

One of the strengths of WinSince is its capability to be customized with the command line used to start it. By combining WinSince start-up switches (such as /FILETYPE=*.BAT), you can set up multiple WinSince icons to automate your file management or customize your interactive WinSince session. WinSince can run minimized in batch mode, logging files found, performing an action on the files found, and then exiting when done (if requested).

The 23 start-up commands are described fully in the online help and in the WINSINCE.WRI file.

You can create as many WinSince icons as you need, and have as many versions running at once as you need to perform your file tasks. You also can set up WinSince to use the command line switches. Both options are defined in WinSince Help under Batch Mode and Command Line Qualifiers.

Using the Options Menu

The ten options for WinSince are

1. Get File Information when Start Up

2. Warn before Run Double Click

3. Warn before Clear File List

4. Run Program on Own when Double Click

   When you exit WinSince, the preceeding four options are saved. Six other options are not saved because of their batch orientation. You can set the following six options in the Options menu or specify them on the start-up command line:

5. Suppress Warning before Action (!)

6. All Files Selected after Each Search

7. Ignore Non-fatal File Copying Errors

8. Copy Only if Different Date or Size

9. Copy Only if Source File Is Newer

10. Ignore Attribute Setting Errors

Please refer to Options Menu in WinSince Help for more information.

Using the Timer

The timer enables you to trigger a file search and action at regular intervals. For example, you can keep a background copy of WinSince running, deleting BAK files or copying new files to a safe area once an hour.

You also can use the timer without an action. You can audit activity on your system, for example, by using the log file to track which files have been created in the last hour.

Starting and stopping the timer

The Start or Stop Timer menu item toggles the timer on or off. Before starting the timer the first time, you need to set up the interval between timer events by using the second menu item, Set Up Timer and Action (see the next section, "Setting up the timer and action").

When the timer is running, WinSince displays the word `Running` beside the Timer menu heading on the main screen. The Timer History form is also displayed, showing a summary of timer information.

You can stop the timer by using the Start or Stop Timer menu item or by clicking the Stop button on the Timer History form.

While the timer is running, controls on the WinSince screen are disabled. If you need to do some interactive work while the timer is running, you can start another copy of WinSince.

You can minimize the timer copy of WinSince while it runs by using the /MIN command line switch or by clicking the minimize buttons.

Setting up the timer and action

The Set Up Timer and Action item on the Timer menu tells WinSince how often the timer should go off, how many times to run the timer, and what (if any) actions to execute. Timer menu options are defined in WinSince Help under Using the Timer.

Displaying the Timer History form

Choosing the Timer History menu item pops up the Timer History form, the same form displayed when you start the timer. This form summarizes timer values and shows the ending values from the previous timer session, if one exists. Fields on the Timer History form are defined in WinSince Help, under Using the Timer.

An example: using the timer from the command line

To look for all new files created in the C:\WORK directory every hour, and copy them to a safe directory, set up the following command line for the WinSince icon:

```
WINSINCE.EXE /FILETYPE=*.* /DIR=C:\WORK /SINCE=-0:01:02:00
/TIMER=0:01:00:00 /IFDIFFERENT/NOWARN /ACTION=2
```

The /SINCE switch is set to look for files created in the last 62 minutes rather than 60 minutes, but the /TIMER switch is set to 1 hour (60 minutes). These settings are made for two reasons: The /TIMER value is the time between the end of the previous timer event and the start of the next, and the event of searching for files and copying them might take a minute. Also, under Windows, a timer might not get a chance to be activated if another program is not releasing the CPU. The /IFDIFFERENT switch offsets this situation by not copying a file of the same size and date previously copied. You could even set /SINCE to be a longer time, such as /SINCE=-0:02:00:00 (the last 2 hours) to be sure. The /NOWARN switch prevents the timer from being interrupted by confirmation warning messages.

Using unique log files

When using the timer, you can create a log file to keep an audit trail of what was done. When the timer is used minimized in the background, a log file is a good source of information about what files WinSince found, whether any errors occurred, and at what time.

Each WinSince timer icon you set up can have a unique name to distinguish it from the usual interactive log file (often set to /LOG=C:\WINSINCE.LOG). For example, you might use /LOG=C:\WSTIMER1.LOG or /LOG=C:\WSTIMER.log. This method prevents an error if a timer version of WinSince tries to open the locked log file. It also provides the audit trail of what happened.

As a reminder, you can use /LOG=C:\%DATE to have WinSince generate a unique log filename, though you might want to create these in a separate subdirectory, such as /LOG=C:\LOG\%DATE.

WinZip

WinZip features an intuitive point-and-click interface for viewing, running, extracting, adding, deleting, and testing files in archives. Optional virus scanning support is included.

Archives are files that contain other files. Typically the files in an archive are compressed. Archives usually have file names ending with ZIP, LZH, ARJ, or ARC, depending on how they were created. Archives make grouping files easy and make transporting and copying these files faster.

To open an archive, double-click an archive listed in the File Manager, drag and drop an archive onto WinZip, or use the standard Open dialog box. The main WinZip window features a list box with the names, sizes, and date/time stamps of all files in the open archive. You can scroll this list and sort it on any field. A toolbar provides fast access to commonly used actions. You can save and restore all options (including window size and position). Extensive context-sensitive help is always available.

Double-clicking a file in the main WinZip window has the same effect as double-clicking in the File Manager. First, the file is extracted from the archive. If the file is executable, it is run. Otherwise, the file is opened by the appropriate application (for example, Windows Write for *.WRI files) based on standard Windows associations.

The Windows 3.1 drag-and-drop interface is fully supported. You can drag and drop files from WinZip to other applications. WinZip extracts the files before dropping them on the target application. The target application treats the files as if they had been dropped by the File Manager. You also can drop archives on WinZip to open them, or drop files on WinZip to add them to the open archive.

WinZip's unique CheckOut facility enables you to install files in archives quickly and easily. Click the CheckOut button to extract all files and create a Program Manager group for all files in the archive. This group contains one icon for each file. Double-click an icon to view the corresponding file with the appropriate application. WinZip optionally deletes the CheckOut files and Program Manager group.

Examining the System Requirements

ZIP files are the most common archive format. WinZip does not require external programs for basic archive operations. PKZIP and PKUNZIP from PKWARE, Inc. are, however, required for two advanced options: disk spanning and encryption. You also need PKZIP and PKUNZIP from PKWARE, Inc to create ZIPs that span multiple disks, create self-extracting ZIP files, or access password-protected ZIPs.

To access LZH files, you need the LHA.EXE program from Haruyasu Yoshizaki.

To access ARJ files, you need the ARJ program from Robert Jung.

To access ARC files, you need one of the following programs: ARCE.COM and ARC-E.COM version 4.0e, PKXARC.COM version 3.5, PKXARC.EXE version 3.6, PKUNPAK.EXE version 3.61, or ARC.EXE version 5.20 or 6.0.

WinZip automatically detects the following virus scanners: NAVW and NAV, WNAPVIR and CPAV, MSAV, and SCAN.

For additional information about external file requirements and virus scanners, please refer to WinZip Help.

Uninstalling WinZip

You can uninstall WinZip by following these steps:

1. Delete the WinZip-related files listed above. If you installed these files in a directory containing no unrelated files, you can delete the entire directory.

2. Delete the WinZip icon from your Program Manager group(s). Click the icon once, and press the Del key. When asked whether you want to delete the icon, choose Yes.

3. Delete the file WINZIP.INI from your Windows directory.

4. Optionally delete the WinZip entries from your WIN.INI file. This deletion saves less than 1K of disk space, so do not perform this step unless you are comfortable modifying your Windows configuration files.

Working through a Brief Tutorial

This section is a brief tutorial for basic WinZip operations. The tutorial assumes the following:

- Your system meets the requirements described in the section titled "Examining the System Requirements."

- You know how to use standard Windows features, such as dialog boxes, menus, and the drag-and-drop interface. If you are not familiar with these features, please consult your Windows documentation.

- You are familiar with the concept of archives.

Remember that context-sensitive help is always available. Press the F1 key at any time to access the full documentation.

Working with existing archives

The first step is to open an archive. You can do so in several ways:

- Double-click the archive in the File Manager.
- Drag the archive from the File Manager, and drop it on the WinZip window.
- Select Open from the WinZip File pull-down menu, or choose the Open button on the toolbar, and select an archive from the standard Open dialog box.

After an archive is open, you can select from the operations in the Actions pull-down menu. To extract files from the archive, for example, select Actions⇨Extract, or choose the Extract button on the toolbar. This step activates the Extract dialog box. For complete documentation on these actions, click the appropriate entry in the Commands and Procedures section in the Table of Contents.

Creating archives

To create a new archive, select New from the WinZip File pull-down menu, or choose the New button on the toolbar. This step activates the New dialog box. Enter the name of the archive you want to create (not the names of the files you want to compress). You can use the Drives and Directories list boxes to choose the drive and directory where you want to create the archive. The names of any existing archives on the selected drive and directory are listed to help you choose a name that is not already in use. Choose the OK button to complete your selection.

Normally the Add dialog box is displayed automatically. Simply type the name(s) of the files you want to add to the new archive, and choose the Add button. Alternatively, you can add files to an archive by dragging the files you want to add from the File Manager and dropping them on the WinZip window.

Using the Drag-and-Drop Interface

The drag-and-drop interface provides a convenient way to extract files from an archive; add, freshen, move, and update files in an archive; and open an archive.

Extracting files from an archive with the drag-and-drop interface

You can drag and drop files from WinZip to other applications. WinZip extracts the files before dropping them on the target application. The target application treats the files as if they had been dropped by the File Manager.

To extract a file from an archive with the drag-and-drop interface, follow these steps:

1. Click a file in the main WinZip window.

2. While holding down the mouse button, drag (move) the mouse pointer to a window that accepts dropped files (the mouse pointer indicates whether the target window accepts dropped files).

3. Release the mouse button to drop the file. The Extract dialog box appears. After the files have been extracted from the archive, the target window processes the file you dropped.

To extract multiple files from an archive, using the drag-and-drop interface, select the files before beginning the drag operation.

You also can extract files by choosing the Extract push button or selecting Actions⇔Extract.

You can move or copy files from one archive to another by opening multiple copies of WinZip, one for each archive, and dragging files from one to the other.

Different applications handle dropped files in different ways. When you drop a file on the Write application distributed with Windows, for example, Write embeds the file as an OLE object, but when you drop a file on the Notepad application, it opens the file. You might need to experiment with drag and drop before relying on it.

The Windows File Manager does NOT accept files dropped by other applications. This limitation is not a bug; it is the result of a design decision made by Microsoft.

The Windows Program Manager adds dropped files to the group on which the files are dropped, providing a convenient way for you to add files in an archive to a Program Manager group. Unfortunately, many people (particularly those who have used OS/2 1.3) would rather drop files on an icon in the Program Manager to start the program associated with the icon, passing the dropped file as a parameter. But WinZip can do nothing about this problem. Again, this situation is not a bug, but the result of a design decision made by Microsoft.

Adding a file to an archive with the drag-and-drop interface

To add a file to an archive, using the drag- and-drop interface, follow these steps:

1. Click a file in the Windows 3.1 File Manager or an NDW 2.0 drive window.

2. While holding down the mouse button, drag (move) the mouse pointer to a WinZip window. If you've minimized WinZip, you can drag the files to the minimized icon. If you're using NDW 2.0, you also can drag files to inactive WinZip icons.

3. Release the mouse button to drop the file. The Drop dialog box appears.

To add multiple files to an archive by using the drag-and-drop interface, select the files in the File Manager before dragging them to WinZip.

You also can add files to an archive by using the Add dialog box.

You cannot use the drag-and-drop interface to add files with an extension of ZIP, LZH, ARJ, or ARC (use the Add dialog box instead).

Opening an archive with the drag-and-drop interface

To open an archive with the drag-and-drop interface, follow these steps:

1. Click an archive in the Windows 3.1 File Manager or an NDW 2.0 drive window.

2. While holding down the mouse button, move (drag) the mouse pointer over a WinZip window. If you've minimized WinZip, you can drag the files to the minimized icon. If you're using NDW 2.0, you can also drag files to inactive WinZip icons.

3. Release the mouse button to open the selected archive.

You also can open archives by double-clicking the name of an archive in the File Manager, by clicking the Open button in the main WinZip window, or by selecting File⇨Open.

Using the Drop dialog box

The Drop dialog box appears when you use the drag-and-drop interface to add files to an archive. In the Drop dialog box, you can change the name of the open archive in one of two ways:

■ Type the name of the archive in the Add to Archive edit field.

■ Click the New or Open button to activate the standard New and Open dialog boxes, respectively. These shortcuts provide a quick way to add files to a different archive without going through the File pull-down menu.

Please refer to WinZip Help (under Adding Files To Archives) for a description of the options available in this dialog box.

Menu Tree

File Menu

Option	Function
New Archive	Open a new archive
Open Archive	Open an existing archive
Close Archive	Close the open archive
Select All	Select all files in an archive
Deselect All	Deselect all files in an archive
Exit	Exit WinZip

Actions Menu

Option	Function
Add	Add files to the open archive
Delete	Delete files from the open archive
Extract	Extract files from the open archive
View	View files in the open archive
Virus Scan	Run a virus scan program against archive contents
Make .EXE File	Create a self-extracting archive
Test	Test integrity of an archive
CheckOut	Examine and/or run programs in an archive

Options Menu

Option	*Function*
Configuration	Modify configuration options
Directories	Specify default directories
Font	Specify font for main window
Password	Set password for subsequent archive operations
Program Locations	Specify program names and paths
Sort	Specify sort order for list of files in archive
Save Settings on Exit	Control whether options are saved when WinZip is closed
Save Settings Now	Save configuration settings immediately
View Last Output	View output from the last DOS command issued by WinZip

Help Menu

Option	*Function*
Contents	Start Help and display topics in WinZip Help file
Brief Tutorial	Display brief WinZip tutorial
Search for Help On	Open Search dialog box for WinZip Help
How To Use Help	Display instructions for using Help system
Copyright/License Agreement/Warranty	Display license agreement
Ordering Information	Display order form
About WinZip	Display copyright notice

Please refer to WinZip Help for detailed instructions on using each menu option.

WinMap

by Olaf Hess

CompuServe: 10031,3536

Copyright © 1993 Olaf Hess

WinMap displays how much memory your drivers, programs and fonts are using. WinMap will allow you to free memory that is marked as *discardable* if Windows is low on memory.

Mark Gambor Color Palette Utilities

by Mark Gambor

Copyright © 1992 Barbarsoft

Palette Dialog and Palette Loader

These two utilities work together to give you control over the hardware palette of a VGA adapter. Palette Dialog creates an icon in Control Panel that is used to change the colors in the hardware palette, independent of the settings Windows is using.

Palette Loader will automatically load a palette that you have chosen and saved whenever you start Windows.

Instant File Access

by Alexoft

Copyright © 1993 Alexoft

Instant File Access creates a floating list of recently used files that can be accessed with any application that uses the Windows common Open File dialog box. Enables you to open a file you worked with earlier.

DosBar — Toolbar for MS-DOS Prompts

Copyright © 1993 Andreas Furrer

DosBar adds a toolbar to MS-DOS prompts, making it easy to cut and paste, or even scroll back.

Rosenthal WinLite™

Compresses Windows programs and their resources to reduce size on disk. Makes programs smaller and more efficient. The compression process is totally automatic, requiring no special drivers, and uses documented Windows functions, so there's no danger. Programs can be made inherently anti-virus if the additional Virus Armor is licensed from the devloper.

The Dieter Utilities

by Dieter Prifling

DlgDrop, MySound, ShowPar, WWaitNGo, DirAll, FMExtend, FMView

Dialog Drop gives you the ability to drag and drop to any edit box in any dialog. MySound gives you control over what sound file Windows applications use for their various beeps and whistles.

ShowPar shows various file parameters. WWaitNGo gives control over whether or not to load something at start-up time.

DirAll will create text files listing the full directory of disks, sorted on any of many different criteria (even several disks). Useful for hunting down duplicate files.

FMExtend is an add-on to File Manager that allows you to get around the four add-on limit of File Manager. In addition, it can put menu items in a submenu, cleaning up the File Manager menu.

FMView will display the current selected file in File Manager on-screen in an appropriate format automatically. Understands over 20 different file formats.

Uninstall

Tracks your Windows installations and allows you to quickly uninstall Windows programs, getting all of the DLLs, INIs, and other files that they install.

MaintINI

An MS-DOS program that lets you modify any Windows INI file from the MS-DOS command line in an easy-to-use fashion.

WIN GDI — GDI Monitor

by Russell E. Holcomb

CompuServe: 70062,2236

Gives a detailed listing of current GDI resources. Useful for determining what applications do not release their resources.

InfoSpy

Shows Heap, Windows, Tasks, and Modules in a window and shows their relation to each other. Can unload modules, save memory dumps, terminate tasks, and more.

Part VI
Appendices

Appendix A
Troubleshooting Windows

This appendix provides information about troubleshooting Microsoft Windows. If you have trouble installing Windows, or if Windows doesn't run as well as you expect it to, this appendix can help you find out why and show you how to isolate and solve common problems.

Creating a Clean Boot Disk

A *clean boot* disk helps you pin down the source of problems. The technique is simple: Take out all extraneous drivers, TSRs, and so on, and then add them back one by one until the source of the trouble becomes apparent.

When you are using MS-DOS 6.x, a *clean boot* can be a Multi-config entry.

To create a *clean boot* disk for troubleshooting, first do the following:

1. Back up the hard disk before you make any configuration changes.

2. Minimize the configuration in CONFIG.SYS and AUTOEXEC.BAT so that these files include only the drivers and programs that are necessary for the computer to boot and run Windows. Remove all other TSRs or drivers.

For testing purposes, reduce the CONFIG.SYS file to the following:

```
files=40
buffers=20
device=c:\windows\himem.sys
device=c:\windows\ega.sys    ; if you have an EGA
                                        monitor
stacks=9,256   ; if MS-DOS 3.3 or later
shell=c:\dos\command.com c:\dos /p /e:256
```

Make sure that COMMAND.COM is in the C:\DOS directory.

```
[plus any network command lines]
```

Reduce the AUTOEXEC.BAT file to the following:

```
path=c:\;c:\dos;c:\windows
set temp=c:\windows\temp
```

TEMP must point to a valid directory on an uncompressed drive.

```
prompt $p$g
[plus any network command lines]
```

3. Make a boot disk by placing a blank disk in drive A: and typing the following command at the command prompt:

```
format a:/S
```

4. Copy the configuration files to this disk by typing the following commands at the command prompt:

```
copy \config.sys a:
copy \autoexec.bat a:
```

5. Save the current initialization files on the floppy disk by typing the following commands at the command prompt:

```
copy \windows\win.ini a:
copy \windows\system.ini a:
copy \windows\progman.ini a:
```

To make troubleshooting easier, make one change at a time to the configuration files. Always test with the standard Windows and MS-DOS drivers first, rather than with third-party drivers, and then add the third-party drivers later.

Troubleshooting Setup

Many Setup-related problems are caused by TSRs, memory conflicts, or problems with drivers in the system. Typically, failure occurs at one of three points:

■ During the initial detection of TSRs in the system

■ During hardware auto-detection in MS-DOS Mode Setup

■ During the initial loading of Windows

A Setup failure at any of these points may display an error message or even cause the system to lock up.

Type **SETUP /?** to see a list of command line options for the Setup program.

Troubleshooting TSRs that conflict with Setup

To check for TSRs that conflict with Setup, type the following:

```
SETUP /T
```

If you receive a message that incompatible TSRs or drivers are present when you try to run Setup, follow these steps:

1. Check the SETUP.TXT file on Windows Disk #1 for instructions about the particular TSR that is on the system. Some TSRs interfere with Setup but can be used with Windows; some should not be used at all with Windows.

2. Uninstall the TSR by following the instructions in the program's documentation or by removing the filename from the AUTOEXEC.BAT or CONFIG.SYS files.

3. Reboot the computer and start Windows Setup again.

4. After Windows has been successfully installed, follow the instructions in the SETUP.TXT file to determine whether you can use the TSR with Windows.

Troubleshooting MS-DOS mode Setup

If MS-DOS mode Setup hangs the system or drops out to the command prompt immediately after you start Setup, a problem probably exists with Setup's automatic hardware detection. To work around this problem, start Setup by typing the following:

```
SETUP/I
```

Setup will use default settings, which may or may not match the actual hardware. Be sure to verify that the proper choices are made.

One common source of problems is computer systems that have special requirements. Check the Computer: choice in Setup to see whether your machine is among the systems listed.

The following machines can be specifically selected during Setup:

- MS-DOS System
- AST: All 80386- and 80486-based machines
- AT&T PC
- AT&T NSX 20: Safari Notebook

- Everex Step 386/25

- Hewlett-Packard (all machines)

- IBM PS/2 model L40SX

- IBM PS/2 model P70

- Intel 386 SL-based system with APM

- MS-DOS system with APM

- NCR: All 80386- and 80486-based machines

- NEC PowerMate SX Plus

- NEC ProSpeed 386

- Toshiba 1200XE

- Toshiba 1600

- Toshiba 5200

- Zenith: All 80386-based machines

The following networks (and specific versions of most networks) can be specifically selected during Setup:

- No Network Installed

- 3Com 3+Open

- 3Com 3+Share

- Artisoft LANtastic

- Banyan VINES

- DEC Pathworks

- IBM OS/2 LAN Server

- IBM PC LAN Program

- Invisible Software Invisible Network 2.21

- Microsoft LAN Manager

- Microsoft Network (or 100 percent-compatible)

- Novell Netware

- TCS 10Net

Troubleshooting Windows mode Setup

After MS-DOS mode Setup completes, it starts Windows to complete the installation process. When Windows starts, it loads the following files in this order:

1. WIN.COM

2. KRNL286.EXE or KRNL386.EXE

3. SYSTEM.DRV

4. MOUSE.DRV

5. DISPLAY.DRV

6. SOUND.DRV

7. COMM.DRV

8. GDI.EXE

9. USER.EXE

10. NETWORK.DRV

11. SETUP.EXE

Setup hangs when starting Windows

If Setup hangs when first starting Windows mode, one of the files was probably unable to load. A file may be corrupted (a bad disk, a network problem — if loading from the network — or an incorrect hardware choice). When Setup is restarted, it gives an indication of what failed to load.

This problem commonly occurs with display drivers. If Setup indicates that the display driver failed to load, choose one of the basic Windows drivers (EGA or VGA).

Error message: Bad fault in MS-DOS extender

This error message is generated if DOSX.EXE encounters another memory error when it is already processing an exception. The cause is usually one of the following:

- HIMEM.SYS is unable to control the A20 line. (See "Troubleshooting Windows Running in Standard Mode," later in the appendix, for a discussion of the A20 line.)

- DOS=HIGH is not functioning properly (related to HIMEM.SYS control).

- A problem exists with the memory hardware on the computer.

■ You are running DR DOS.

■ The third-party memory manager is not configured correctly.

■ You have an old, out-of-date ROM BIOS.

■ The CMOS settings are incorrect.

■ The Windows files are old or corrupt.

■ Disks are corrupt.

■ The system is infected with the Yankee Doodle virus.

Troubleshooting the desktop configuration

When you start Windows, you may get an error message that indicates that a group (.GRP) file is invalid or damaged and instructs you to reconstruct the group. This error occurs because of one of the following reasons:

■ A GRP file has been deleted or damaged.

■ The files were moved into another directory, but the PROGMAN.INI file was not updated to reflect this change.

You also may need to rebuild groups if no group windows or icons appear when you enter Program Manager after starting Windows. To rebuild the groups that were created when Windows was installed, choose File⇨Run in the Program Manager and type **SETUP /P** in the box that comes up.

This error can also be caused by an invalid shell= in SYSTEM.INI. Make certain there are no extraneous spaces on the line. Also make certain that the file specified as your shell is actually the correct shell (it may have been damaged, either accidentally or intentionally).

Troubleshooting TSR compatibility problems

Although Setup can warn you about TSRs that it knows about, other TSRs may cause Windows to crash or behave erratically. To troubleshoot these problems, start MS-DOS from the *clean boot* and then run one TSR. Start Windows and try to do your usual tasks. If the system functions normally, exit Windows, load another TSR, and test again. Repeat these steps until the trouble returns. The last TSR that you loaded is the source of the trouble.

Disabling Norton Desktop and PC Tools

Using an alternate shell, such as Norton Desktop or Central Point PC Tools Desktop, is a common source of problems for both the Windows Setup and application Setups. These shells do not always handle the commands that some setup programs use to add Program Manager groups and icons. Setting the Program Manager as your shell is always a good idea. Make certain that the `shell=` line in SYSTEM.INI reads as follows:

```
shell=progman.exe
```

TSRs that cause problems with Windows Setup

The following TSRs cause problems with Setup, and you should remove them prior to running Setup. However, they should work with Windows after its installation:

- ASP Integrity Toolkit 3.7 causes various problems with Setup.

- Data Physician Plus 2.0 (VirAlert) causes problems during Setup. Version 3.0 does not appear to cause problems.

- Norton Anti-Virus 1.0 can cause Setup to crash. This problem appears to have been corrected in Version 1.5.

- PC-Kwik 1.59 may cause Setup to crash. Version 2.0 does not appear to cause this problem.

- SoftIce Debugger causes Windows Mode Setup to crash.

- Vaccine causes Setup to hang.

- VDefend, a PC-Tools Deluxe TSR, should not be in use during installation, but you can run it with Windows after Setup is complete.

- Virex-PC 1.11 causes Setup to crash.

- ViruSafe 4.0 causes Setup to crash. Version 4.5 does not appear to cause this problem, but its authors recommend that you run ViruSafe with the `/C-` switch with Windows.

TSRs that cause problems with Windows 3.1

The following programs cause problems when you run them with Windows 3.1. You need to remove them.

- ANARKEY 4.00 may prevent Windows 3.1 from loading under certain circumstances. Version 4.01 does not appear to cause this problem.

- APPEND, an MS-DOS utility, interferes with the ability of Windows and Windows applications to build valid paths for files that they want to access. Do not use APPEND with Windows 3.1.

- DOSCUE, a command line editor, produces unreliable results with Windows 3.1. I recommend that you do not use this program with Windows 3.1.

- GRAPHICS, an MS-DOS utility, is loaded into all virtual machines (VMs) for non-Windows applications that run under Windows 3.1. Printing from those VMs can be unpredictable because the VM that has the focus sends its output to the printer, and printing becomes intermixed if you switch between non-Windows applications.

- JOIN, an MS-DOS utility, works fine with Windows 3.1 if you do not change the state of the joined drives during a Windows 3.1 session. Such changes include adding or removing joined drives from within Windows. I recommend that you do not use JOIN when you are running Windows Setup or Windows 3.1.

- LanSight 2.0 is a utility for controlling and monitoring workstations that are attached to a Novell network, and it requires TSRs to be loaded on the workstations before Windows is started. If a message that requests permission to view the screen is sent from the supervisor workstation to a workstation that is running Windows 3.1, the workstation that is running Windows may require rebooting.

- Lockit 3.3 (PC Vault, Secure It) strips spaces out of the load= entry in WIN.INI. Version 3.3+ does not appear to have this problem.

- MIRROR, an MS-DOS utility, cannot be removed from memory with the MIRROR /U command if it is loaded from Windows standard mode by using the File⇨Run command.

- Newspace 1.07, a disk-compression utility, is not compatible with Windows 3.1.

- Diskreet and Ncache, which are Norton Utilities 5.0 programs, are not compatible with Windows 3.1, and they can cause the system to hang. Most of the problems have been corrected in Version 6.01.

- DiskMon, the Norton Utilities 6.01 disk-monitoring program, may cause inconsistent results under Windows 3.1 if you try to access files in a directory that DiskMon is monitoring. I do not recommend that you use this TSR with Windows 3.1.

- Printer Assistant is a TSR that enables workstations on Netware 286 and 386 to share a printer. Some Windows applications mix garbage with correct printer output when you use this TSR.

- XGAAIDOS.SYS causes Windows 3.1 in standard mode to freeze at the opening logo.

TSRs that need special consideration

The following programs will run with Windows if you take special action to make them work together:

- BOOT.SYS, a power user's tool for booting under multiple configurations from a menu, creates several sections in CONFIG.SYS and AUTOEXEC.BAT. Windows Setup modifies only the first section in CONFIG.SYS and AUTOEXEC.BAT. You need to manually modify the other sections to use Windows 3.1 with the alternate configurations.

- Doubledisk 2.5, from Vertisoft, creates *phantom* disk drives that Windows 3.1 may try to access. Vertisoft has a DRVOFF utility to make these phantom drives invisible to Windows 3.1. Contact Vertisoft to get this utility if you want to run Doubledisk with Windows.

- LaserTools Control Panel 2.2 may cause the system to hang in both standard and 386 enhanced modes if you load this TSR from within Windows 3.1. If you use this product, load it before you start Windows 3.1.

- The LANtastic KBFLOW TSR should not be loaded before you start Windows 3.1. To use KBFLOW, start Windows 3.1 and then run the TSR from within Windows.

- Le Menu 1.0 can cause the loss of environment information, such as PATH, PROMPT, and WINDIR, when you run a non-Windows application under Windows. If you want to start Windows 3.1 from a menu option in Le Menu, set up Windows 3.1 as a batch file menu option so that COMMAND.COM can be loaded before Windows 3.1 is loaded. (See the Le Menu documentation.)

- Logitech Mouse Software 5.0 and 6.0 must be loaded from within a non-Windows application after the application is launched in Windows if you want to use the Click and Logimenu TSRs. You need to load this software from within the application even if the TSRs were loaded before Windows 3.1 was started. After exiting Windows 3.1, reload these TSRs to make them function from the command prompt.

- The Norton Utilities 6.01 Ncache program prevents you from creating a permanent swap file if this caching program is on a disk drive. Windows 3.1 will work with this program, however. The optimal solution is to disable the Ncache program and use SMARTDrive instead.

- PC Tools Deluxe 6.0 (Desktop) may cause the machine to hang if you launch it from a non-Windows application that is running under standard mode Windows. In 386 enhanced mode, it may cause the machine to reboot. Version 7.0 of PC Tools does not appear to have these problems. Even with Version 7.0, however, you should not run Desktop from within a non-Windows application if the TSR was loaded prior to Windows 3.1. I recommend that you run Desktop from a PIF.

- Pyro! 1.0, a screen saver, blanks the screen after the delay period has expired if it is loaded before Windows is started. Restoring the Windows screen is impossible.

- SideKick 1.0 and 2.0 and SideKick Plus cause several problems with Windows 3.1. I recommend that you run SideKick from within Windows by using a PIF, instead of loading it as a memory-resident program.

- SPEEDFXR is not compatible with Windows 3.1 as a TSR. Running SPEEDFXR -X appears to work better with Windows 3.1 because it does not remain in memory.

- SUBST, an MS-DOS utility, works fine with Windows 3.1 if you do not change the state of the substituted drives while you are running Windows. Such changes include adding and removing substituted drives from within Windows.

- Trantor T100 Host Adapter Driver (TSCSI.SYS) identifies the SCSI hard disk drive as a removable drive, so the system may crash if you try to access this drive through the File Manager. Other unexpected results can occur while you are deleting files through the File Manager.

For information about running network drivers with Windows, see "Troubleshooting Networks" later in this appendix.

Troubleshooting Display Adapters

Display drivers are responsible for more Windows problems than any other component. Always make certain that you have the latest version of the display driver for your video card.

Never manually install one of the files from a display driver floppy disk. Display drivers actually comprise several related and interdependent files. Always install the drivers by starting Setup or the video card manufacturer's utility for changing video drivers.

Try the following solutions for typical display-related problems:

- **Problem:** Windows or Windows applications are not displayed correctly.

  Solution: Reinstall the correct display driver.

- **Problem:** You can't copy and paste data between non-Windows applications and Windows, you can't start non-Windows applications, or an error message identifies an incompatible display adapter.

Solution: Usually, these problems indicate that the *grabber,* which is the part of the display driver that deals with non-Windows applications, does not match the rest of the display driver. Try reinstalling the driver or obtaining a new driver version from the hardware manufacturer. If all else fails, install one of the standard Windows drivers, such as the VGA driver.

■ **Problem:** In 386 enhanced mode, the Windows logo appears and then disappears, leaving the screen blank.

Solution: A handful of video display adapters (such as some ATI adapters) use the *nonmaskable interrupt (NMI)* to change video modes. Check the manual that came with the adapter to find out how to turn off the NMI operation.

■ **Problem:** An incorrect-system-version error message appears when you try to run a non-Windows application in 386 enhanced mode.

Solution: This problem is another case of mismatched grabber and driver. Reinstall the driver.

■ **Problem:** The system has a VGA display adapter, and you experience problems when you are running Windows in 386 enhanced mode.

Solution: Some VGA-compatible cards (especially SuperVGA cards) use additional memory to speed up video accesses. Although Windows usually detects these cards, under some conditions it may not detect them. Add the following to the `[386Enh]` section of SYSTEM.INI:

```
EmmExclude=C400-C7FF
```

■ **Problem:** The system has a VGA adapter, and an application does not display properly.

Solution: The digital-to-analog converter (DAC) on the VGA card may need to be updated. Contact the display adapter manufacturer for an upgrade.

■ **Problem:** The system has a SuperVGA adapter, and you experience display problems.

Solution: Make sure that you are using the latest version of the manufacturer's drivers for the adapter or one of the standard Windows SVGA drivers.

■ **Problem:** You experience specific display problems with the PS/2, Toshiba plasma display, Video Seven 256-color adapter, or other hardware.

Solution: Always check the README.WRI file that is installed in the WINDOWS directory for additional information about specific display adapters.

■ **Problem:** You experience problems when you are running Microsoft Multimedia applications with an ATI graphics card.

Solution: Turn off the DeviceBitmap option in the ATI control panel.

Troubleshooting MS-DOS Configuration Problems

Some Windows problems are caused by MS-DOS configuration problems.

Using APPEND with Windows

When you run the MS-DOS APPEND utility with Windows, you get a cannot-find-file error message that looks similar to the following:

```
Change Disk
Cannot find WINWORD.EXE, Please insert in drive A:
```

This message occurs because using APPEND causes Windows to form incorrect path names to files. The solution is to not use APPEND with Windows.

Troubleshooting EMS memory problems

MS-DOS configuration problems also can cause problems with Windows in memory management, especially when you use the expanded memory emulator, EMM386.EXE.

■ **Problem:** You get an error message that says that the path for EMM386 is invalid when you start Windows in 386 enhanced mode.

Solution: Specify the path to EMM386.EXE by adding the /Y=PATH switch to the line that loads EMM386.EXE:

```
device=c:\dos\emm386.exe /y=c:\dos\emm386.exe
```

To ensure that HIMEM.SYS and EMM386.EXE are functioning correctly on the computer, create a boot disk that has a CONFIG.SYS that consists of the following:

```
device=c:\dos\himem.sys
device=c:\dos\emm386.exe noems x=a000-efff
```

In the disk's AUTOEXEC.BAT file, place the following lines:

```
path=c:\dos
prompt $p$g
set TEMP=C:\
```

If the computer fails after you make these changes, a problem exists in HIMEM.SYS or EMM386.EXE on the computer. If the computer works properly, then HIMEM.SYS and EMM386.EXE are functioning correctly.

■ **Problem:** Some other programs conflict with EMM386.

Solution: Disk caches other than SMARTDrive may interfere with EMM386. To test, remove the other disk cache and add a line to AUTOEXEC.BAT that loads SMARTDrive.

■ **Problem:** Another program uses the same upper memory block (UMB) space that EMM386 uses.

Solution: If the computer fails, the problem may be that another program or an adapter card is using UMB memory that EMM386 is trying to use. Check for TSRs that are being loaded by the LOADHIGH command in MS-DOS. You may be able to resolve the problem by removing the LOADHIGH command so that the TSR loads in conventional memory.

Adapter cards can cause conflicts with EMM386 if they use portions of the upper memory address space for RAM of their own. For example, many network cards and all video cards use some area of upper memory.

Check the documentation that came with the adapters in the computer or contact the manufacturer. Cards that use upper memory may refer to it as *shared RAM, shared memory, video memory,* or *adapter RAM.* Use the X= switch to keep EMM386 from trying to use the space (referred to as *excluding* the region).

For example, if a network card uses the C800h -CFFFh range of addresses, the line in CONFIG.SYS that loads EMM386.EXE would look like this:

```
device=c:\dos\emm386.exe x=c800-cfff
```

Also exclude the region in the SYSTEM.INI file by adding the range to the EMMExclude= line in the [386 Enh] section.

You can exclude multiple regions by including multiple X= switches on the command line.

■ **Problem:** Microsoft Windows 3.1 does not provide expanded memory after EMM386 is installed.

Solution: This problem's symptoms vary, but they usually have to do with seeing out-of-memory messages when you start non-Windows applications or with the system's stopping when certain non-Windows applications are started.

Try changing the line in CONFIG.SYS that loads EMM386.EXE so that it includes the RAM switch, and not the NOEMS switch. The line would then resemble the following:

```
device=c:\dos\emm386.exe RAM
```

Of course, exclusions may still be required.

Troubleshooting Windows Running in Standard Mode

If you have successfully installed Windows, then using the `WIN /S` switch should force Windows to start in standard mode if the following conditions are met:

- The machine has an 80286 or higher processor.
- At least 256K of conventional memory is free.
- HIMEM.SYS or another XMS driver is installed.
- At least 192K of extended memory is free.
- Windows for Workgroups 3.11 is not being used.

Problems with starting Windows in standard mode are usually related to the XMS driver (HIMEM.SYS) or to a lack of available extended memory.

- **Problem:** RAMDrive or other resident software may be using extended memory and preventing Windows from accessing that memory.

  Solution: Decrease the size of the RAM drive or do not load the memory-resident software. Do not use IBM's VDISK.SYS.

- **Problem:** The XMS driver is out of date or incompatible with Windows 3.1.

  Solution: If your version of MS-DOS is earlier than 6.0, replace the XMS driver with the one in the WINDOWS directory.

- **Problem:** HIMEM.SYS may be incorrectly identifying the machine type.

  Solution: HIMEM tries to detect the machine type and use a routine that is appropriate to the machine that it is running on to access extended memory. The way that HIMEM accesses extended memory involves address line 20 on the CPU, hence the name *A20 handler* for this routine. When HIMEM is loaded, it displays a message to indicate which routine it is using:

```
Installed A20 handler number x.
```

The x in the preceding line is replaced by the number of the routine that HIMEM is using. On some machines, HIMEM picks an incorrect routine, and you need to use the /M switch on the line in CONFIG.SYS that loads HIMEM.SYS to specify which routine from the following table should be used.

Table A-1	A20 Handlers	
Name	*Number*	*Computer Type*
at	1	IBM PC/AT
ps2	2	IBM PS/2
pt1cascade	3	Phoenix Cascade BIOS
hpvectra	4	HP Vectra (A and A+)
att6300plus	5	AT&T 6300 Plus
acer1100	6	Acer 1100
toshiba	7	Toshiba 1600 and 1200XE
wyse	8	Wyse 12.5 Mhz 286
tulip	9	Tulip SX
zenith	10	Zenith ZBIOS
at1	11	IBM PC/AT
at2 delay)	12	IBM PC/AT (alternative
css	12	CSS Labs
at3 delay)	13	IBM PC/AT (alternative
philips	13	Philips
fasthp	14	HP Vectra

The version of HIMEM.SYS that comes with Windows 3.1 recognizes only machine types 1 – 8 in the table. The version of HIMEM.SYS that comes with MS-DOS 6.2 recognizes the 14 types that are listed.

HIMEM.SYS with a /M parameter would resemble the following:

```
device=c:\dos\himem.sys /m:1
```

■ **Problem:** The system doesn't have enough extended memory.

Solution: To make more extended memory available, remove any unnecessary programs that use extended memory from CONFIG.SYS or AUTOEXEC.BAT (RAMDrive, for example). Make sure that the physical memory in the machine is enough for the program's needs or use 386 enhanced mode if possible.

Troubleshooting Windows Running in 386 Enhanced Mode

If you have successfully installed Windows, Windows will start automatically in 386 enhanced mode if the following conditions are met:

- The machine has an 80386 or higher processor.
- 256K of conventional memory is free.
- An XMS driver such as HIMEM.SYS is already loaded.
- 1024K of extended memory is free.

Problems with 386 enhanced mode usually relate to the interaction of Windows with hardware:

- **Problem:** The system crashes when you run Windows in 386 enhanced mode.

  Solution: The first step in troubleshooting when Windows crashes or will not start in 386 enhanced mode is to check whether it will run in standard mode. To test it, type **WIN /S** or, if using Windows for Workgroups 3.11, **WIN /D:T.**

  If Windows fails to run in standard mode, troubleshoot standard mode first (see the preceding section). If it runs successfully in standard mode, try the next solution.

- **Problem:** You can run Windows in standard mode but not in 386 enhanced mode.

  Solution: When Windows runs only in standard mode, a conflict may exist in an upper memory block (UMB). Perhaps a network card or other adapter has undetected shared RAM in this region.

  To check whether a UMB conflict is the problem, start Windows with the `/D:X` command line option. For example, type **WIN /D:X.**

  Using this option is equivalent to adding the following line to the `[386Enh]` section of SYSTEM.INI:

  ```
  EmmExclude=A000-FFFF
  ```

  If Windows runs successfully after you add this option, a conflict existed. Check the hardware manuals for the adapter cards that are in the system to find out what upper memory addresses they use. Then, similarly to adding the EMM386 line that is mentioned in "Troubleshooting EMS memory problems," earlier in this appendix, add an appropriate `EmmExclude=` line to exclude the region that Windows should not use.

Avoid excluding extra regions of memory. Doing so can prevent Windows from placing its translation buffers and page frame in the upper memory area. Instead, Windows has to place these structures in conventional memory, thus reducing memory that is available to non-Windows programs that you want to run.

Use MSD to see which memory regions the programs and drivers are using. Always run MSD from the MS-DOS prompt to get an accurate reading of the actual system.

■ **Problem:** You experience hard disk problems when you are running Windows in 386 enhanced mode.

Solution: Disk controllers other than standard ST506 and ESDI controllers, such as SCSI controllers, may need the double-buffering features of SMARTDrive in order to work with Windows.

Even if SMARTDrive is loaded, you may experience hard disk access errors such as the following in some configurations:

```
Cannot Read from Drive C:
Cannot Write to Drive C:
Drive C: Not Ready Error
```

If you receive one of these errors, add the entry `VirtualHDirq=off` in the `[386enh]` section of SYSTEM.INI. Also, you must have SMARTDrive installed without the `/B-` switch. For example, add the `VirtualHDirq=off` entry to SYSTEM.INI if you use a Plus Hardcard or a SCSI hard disk drive that uses direct memory access (DMA).

`VirtualHDIrq=off` is the highest level of compatibility that is available with Windows. If you still have disk errors after setting this option, contact the manufacturer of the disk or controller.

■ **Problem:** You get an internal stack overflow message while you are running Windows in 386 enhanced mode.

Solution: If you receive this message and the computer uses MS-DOS 3.2, add the following line to CONFIG.SYS:

```
STACKS=9,192
```

If the system uses MS-DOS 3.3 or higher, add the following line to CONFIG.SYS:

```
STACKS=9,256
```

■ **Problem:** Typing slows down when you run more than one application, but the system seems to have plenty of memory.

Solution: The time slice for multitasking is taking processing time away from the foreground application. You can increase the foreground application's priority in the 386 Enhanced dialog box in the Control Panel or in the application's PIF. Better still, you can increase the priority of the foreground application only when it receives a keystroke by adding the entry `KeyBoostTime=.005` (or use a larger increment) in the `[386enh]` section of SYSTEM.INI.

Troubleshooting for Non-Windows Applications

You can find up-to-date information on running Windows with specific applications in the README.WRI file in the WINDOWS directory. This section contains additional information on some of the problems that you may experience when you run non-Windows programs under Windows.

■ **Problem:** You receive an `Unexpected MS-DOS Error #11` message.

Solution: This error indicates that Windows has attempted to run an executable file that has an invalid format. Windows uses a special Windows program to run a non-Windows program. This error pertains to the special Windows program.

If Windows is in standard mode, then either the WINOLDAP.MOD file or the 286 grabber is corrupted. If it is in 386 enhanced mode, then either the 386 grabber or the WINOA386.MOD file is corrupted.

To solve this problem, expand the WINOLDAP.MOD file or the WINOA386.MOD file from the Windows installation disks. To fix a corrupted grabber, reinstall the video driver.

■ **Problem:** You experience problems when you are running non-Windows applications in standard mode.

Solution: The application may not run in the directory that is specified in its PIF file. Check the Working Directory that is specified in the Properties box for the application's Program Manager icon. The setting in the Properties box supersedes the PIF file.

Lost or garbled data can mean that the non-Windows program uses system resources, such as directly talking to the keyboard or modifying the system's COM ports. Verify that its PIF file settings indicate the hardware that it accesses directly. Also make certain that the No Save Screen option is not checked.

The No Screen Exchange setting in the PIF file will prevent pasting of screen images.

The Prevent Program Switch option will keep a non-Windows application from switching to Windows while the application is running. Also, the Directly Modifies Keyboard option will prevent the application from switching to Windows because the application may not let Windows take keyboard control.

■ **Problem:** You experience problems when you are running non-Windows applications in 386 enhanced mode.

Solution: To fix out-of-memory errors when you are running high-resolution graphics applications, check High Graphics in the Video Memory option and check Retain Video Memory in the Advanced section of the PIF editor.

Also try choosing the Full Screen option if the system is running out of memory.

If the mouse doesn't work when you run the application in full-screen mode, make sure that an MS-DOS mouse driver is installed.

If a non-Windows application doesn't display properly, verify that the Monitor Ports options in PIF Editor are checked. Garbled text or a misplaced cursor may mean that Emulate Text Mode is improperly checked. Uncheck it.

Some non-Windows applications are not compatible with Fast Paste. If you have problems pasting into a non-Windows application, try unchecking Allow Fast Paste in the Advanced section of PIF Editor.

■ **Problem:** Performance problems occur when you run some non-Windows applications with others, but each application works when you run it by itself.

Solution: One of the applications requires expanded or extended memory, but another application has Lock EMS or Lock XMS checked.

■ **Problem:** Lotus 1-2-3 Release 3.1 will not start or does not run properly.

Solutions: This problem can have several causes.

The system may not have enough XMS memory available. Lotus 1-2-3 needs at least 384K.

The PIF file for Lotus 1-2-3 may have been modified. Verify that the PIF file indicates that 384K of XMS memory is required.

EMM386 may not provide a page frame for 1-2-3 to use. When you are using 1-2-3 Release 3.1, make certain that the line that loads EMM386 does not include the `noems` parameter.

Troubleshooting TrueType Fonts

You can experience several problems with TrueType fonts, especially if you are not using the correct drivers.

- **Problem:** The display driver causes problems with displaying TrueType fonts.

  Solution: Check with the display adapter manufacturer for updated display drivers.

- **Problem:** Old printer drivers cause problems with TrueType fonts.

  Solution: Always use a Windows 3.1 printer driver.

- **Problem:** Some font converters are not completely compatible with TrueType fonts and cause system crashes or other problems.

  Solution: Do not use the font converter and contact the manufacturer for an update.

- **Problem:** TrueType fonts do not work well on systems with less than 2MB of memory.

  Solution: Increase system memory or avoid using TrueType fonts.

Troubleshooting Printing

Many printing problems in Windows are not Windows problems per se. They are often related to other hardware or system configuration difficulties.

Troubleshooting printing difficulties begins by trying to eliminate as many variables as possible:

- Always check the PRINTERS.WRI file in the WINDOWS directory for up-to-date information about printing and printers.

- Next, make certain that you can print from MS-DOS. Copy a file directly to the printer port to verify that the communication path (computer port, cable, printer port) operates correctly.

  To check the communication path for a non-PostScript printer that is connected to a parallel port, type **DIR > LPT***x***,** where *x* is the number of the port that the printer is on.

  Similarly, for a printer that is attached to a serial port, type **DIR > COMx.**

  To check a PostScript printer, copy the file TESTPS.TXT from the WINDOWS\SYSTEM directory to the printer port by typing **COPY \WINDOWS\SYSTEM\TESTPS.TXT PRN**.

■ Check that the printer's cable connections are tight. Verify that the printer is turned on, that it is on-line, and that it has paper and toner.

■ Make certain that you have a SET TEMP= statement in AUTOEXEC.BAT and that the statement points to an existing directory on an uncompressed drive with sufficient disk space to hold the temporary files that Windows generates. The temporary files may require as much as 6MB or more. If the SET TEMP= entry points to a network drive, make certain that the user has read, create, and write access.

■ Verify that you are using the correct printer driver for the printer. Check the driver by selecting the Printers icon in the Control Panel and looking at the list of printers in the Printers dialog box.

Resolving serial port problems

The following information is useful if you experience problems when you are using a serial printer.

■ Verify that the port settings that you see when you select the Ports icon in the Control Panel match the printer's settings. Almost all serial printers, such as Hewlett-Packard plotters and most PostScript printers, use the settings of 9600 baud, no parity, 8 bits, 1 stop bit, and hardware handshaking.

■ To make sure that the printer has the same settings as Windows, use the printer's interactive front panel or DIP switches.

■ To set handshaking on PostScript printers, choose Printer Setup from any application or choose it by selecting the Control Panel's Printer icon. The PostScript driver will send a program that sets the desired handshaking settings to the printer.

■ The Print Direct to Port setting that you access by selecting the Printers icon in the Control Panel and then choosing Connect can cause problems with some printers. Turn this setting off for testing purposes.

■ If you have problems such as garbled printing when you are printing on a network that redirects the printer port (that is, it logically connects an LPT port to a network printer queue), try printing to the LPTx.DOS port rather than to the LPTx port.

■ If you are printing on a network printer, also make certain that you have the latest version of the network drivers.

Resolving specific printing problems

You may experience some of the following printing related problems.

■ **Problem:** You get a cannot-print error message.

Solution: You can get this error message when you are printing on a network or on a physical parallel port. On a network, this can be due to the wrong network driver or a network that Windows does not support. Try printing to the LPTx.DOS port rather than to the LPTx port.

If you are using a physical port, typically, one of the following is true: the printer is off-line, out of paper, or jammed; the printer has faulty cabling; or the printer uses an incompatible print-sharing device, switch box, or buffer.

For testing purposes, remove any print-sharing devices and buffers and connect the printer directly to the computer's parallel port with a single cable that meets the Centronics parallel specification (a cable of 10 feet or less).

Check the TEMP variable in the AUTOEXEC.BAT file. Verify that sufficient disk space is available.

■ **Problem:** You get a printer error message in the middle of printing a document.

Solution: Set the Windows printer time-outs for each individual printer in the Printers section of the Control Panel. The time-out options are Device Not Selected and Transmission Retry. The Device Not Selected option indicates how long Windows will wait for the printer to be on-line before it gives an error message. The Transmission Retry option sets the time that the printer will stay busy before Windows gives an error message. Increasing the Transmission Retry setting should help.

■ **Problem:** PostScript print jobs are incomplete or missing.

Solution: A problem may exist in the communications settings, the cable, or the PostScript code. If the problem is intermittent or can be traced to a given application, download the PostScript error handler to the printer by performing the following steps:

1. Select the Printer icon in the Control Panel and then choose the Options button in the Printer Setup dialog box.

2. Choose the Advanced button. In the Advanced Options dialog box, check the Print PostScript Error Information option, specify any other options that you want, and then choose the OK button.

3. Repeat the procedure that resulted in the problem.

If you see a PostScript error message, the problem is being caused by the application or by the degree of compatibility of your PostScript printer.

If you don't see a PostScript error message, recheck the solutions that are described in the preceding section.

Troubleshooting Networks

While it is beyond the scope of this book to give detailed instructions on how to troubleshoot the many networks that are available, the following are some general tips for network troubleshooting.

Memory conflicts

Many problems with networks and Windows are caused by shared memory conflicts. These can range from GPFs to random system lockups. Always make certain that you have excluded any memory addresses that your network card uses on both the line that loads EMM386.EXE (in CONFIG.SYS) and on the `EMMExclude=` line in the `[396Enh]` section of SYSTEM.INI.

Also shadow RAM can cause memory conflicts — you might need to disable shadow RAM on your system by using your computer's SETUP utility.

Interrupt conflicts

Another source of common problems in Windows is interrupt (IRQ) conflicts between your network adapter and another device in your system. Table A-2 lists common IRQs used by devices that may be present in your system. Check your network card's documentation for how to set the IRQ it uses.

 Choose a network card that can be set up by software, rather than by setting switches or jumpers on the card itself. Examples include the Intel Etherexpress series and the 3Com Etherlink III series. By choosing this type of adapter, you don't just avoid having to open your system back up in the event of a wrong choice. These cards can be completely automatically configured by the software that comes with them, resolving any conflicts in one step.

Table A-2	Interrupts (IRQs) Used by Standard Devices
IRQ	**Device**
1	System timer (motherboard)
2	Cascade to second interrupt controller
3	COM2,COM4
4	COM1,COM3
5	LPT2 — also commonly used by add-on cards, such as sound cards
6	Floppy disk controller
7	LPT1 — sometimes shared with add-on cards, such as sound cards
8	Real-Time Clock
9	Cascade to IRQ 2 (the motherboard redirects IRQ2 to IRQ9 so that a device that uses IRQ2 is seen as IRQ9. Commonly used for network cards, although some EGA/VGA cards also use IRQ 2/9)
10	Available (Intel Etherexpress 16 and the 3COM Etherlink III use IRQ 10 by default)
11	Available
12	PS/2 Mouse Port
13	Math Coprocessor
14	Hard Disk Controller
15	Available

Many network cards do not work properly with Windows for Workgroups 3.11 and may cause mysterious lockups if set to IRQ 15.

Network driver problems

Make certain that the network you've told Windows (in Windows Setup) matches the network you're actually using. Be particularly sure of versions — there are at least three choices for Novell Netware, depending on the version of the Novell shell that you're using.

Refer to the NETWORKS.WRI file, found in your WINDOWS directory, for information that may be specific to your particular network. To read this file, you can select File⇨Run from Program Manager and type **NETWORKS.WRI** in the Command Line box. Windows will automatically recognize it as a Windows Write document and start Windows Write for you.

Detailed information about troubleshooting Windows on Novell NetWare networks can be found in *Windows 3.1 Connectivity SECRETS*, also published by IDG Books Worldwide.

Other Sources of Troubleshooting Information

There are quite a number of sources for help troubleshooting Windows problems. The following sections name but a few.

WUGNET membership

Membership in WUGNET (the Windows User Group Network) is an ideal source of topical, up-to-date information about Windows. See the special WUGNET offer elsewhere in this book for more details.

Resource kits

Microsoft no longer publishes technical material in the User's Guides that come in the package with Microsoft Software, including Windows, Windows for Workgroups, and other products. Instead, they publish this material in *Resource Kits*, which are the authoritative source for technical information about Microsoft Products. The Windows, Windows for Workgroups 3.10, and Windows for Workgroups 3.11 Resource Kits are available in print from Microsoft directly or at your favorite book or computer store, or you can obtain an electronic version, in Windows Help format, from WUGNET as a membership bonus.

On-line help

One of the best sources of help from experts (including the authors of this book!) are the electronic forums on CompuServe and Delphi. In addition, Internet users have access to the Microsoft FTP server.

Windows User Forum on CompuServe

Hosted by the Windows Users Group Network (WUGNET), the Windows User Forum on CompuServe is the electronic home to a network of experts who can provide assistance on any subject related to Windows. The leading Windows shareware can also be found here.

The Windows User Forum can be accessed by typing **GO WINUSER** at any CompuServe ! prompt. If you do not already have a CompuServe account, call WUGNET at 1-800-WIN USER and ask for a free CompuServe sign-up kit (including your $15 usage credit).

Windows Users Forum on Delphi

Hosted by the authors of this book, the Windows Users Forum on Delphi is a source for help and advice on Windows and Windows configuration, as well as the latest news that affects Windows users.

The Windows Users Forum can be accessed by typing **GO CUSTOM 151** at any Delphi prompt. If you don't already have a Delphi account, you can obtain one (and five hours free usage) by following the following instructions:

- Dial with your modem 1-800-695-4002, or, if you're already on the Internet, telnet to delphi.com
- After connection, press Return once or twice.
- At the Username: prompt, type **JOINDELPHI.**
- At the Password: prompt, type **CUSTOM151.**

You can also participate in the Internet Usenet Windows discussion lists through the Delphi Windows Users Forum. These discussion lists put you in touch with other Windows users around the world.

Microsoft FTP Server

Internet users, including Delphi users, can access the Microsoft FTP server and download patches, updates, network drivers, network clients, and technical information, including Microsoft Knowledge Base articles. To do so, follow the instructions for your particular Internet access site and FTP to ftp.microsoft.com.

Knowledge Base on CompuServe

The Microsoft Knowledge Base, the database of technical data, problem resolutions, and so on, that Microsoft Support Technicians use to answer your questions, can be accessed on CompuServe by typing **GO MSKB** at any CompuServe ! prompt.

Microsoft Solution Providers

Microsoft Solution Providers are independent organizations that are qualified to offer a full range of services that meet the varying needs of customers that use Microsoft products. Solution Providers provide vertical and horizontal solutions, line-of-business applications, and expanded services, including multivendor expertise and local assistance.

Services available include integration, custom development, end-user and technical professional training, and technical support. Solution Providers apply and qualify for the program based on proven expertise in technology services and Microsoft products.

In addition, Microsoft Solution Providers are required to have Microsoft Certified Professionals onstaff. These are individuals who have demonstrated, through standardized testing the knowledge and skills needed to plan, implement, or support solutions with Microsoft products.

To locate a Microsoft Solution Provider near you, call Microsoft at 800-426-9400.

Microsoft Support Network

Microsoft has changed its support policies to provide a limited amount of free technical support via a toll-call telephone number. In addition, they offer a number of fee-based support programs as part of the Microsoft Support Network.

As part of the Microsoft Support Network, Microsoft has made available several CD-ROM subscriptions: Microsoft TechNet, Microsoft Development Library, and Microsoft Development Platform.

Microsoft TechNet provides a monthly CD-ROM containing the Knowledge Base, technical articles, strategy papers, resource kits, and other information of interest to support personnel. In addition, a TechNet subscription includes the quarterly Drivers and Patches CD-ROM, containing the contents of the Microsoft Software Library, and any patches or drivers that have been released. To subscribe to TechNet, call 800-334-2121.

The Microsoft Development Library, formerly known as the Microsoft Developer Network CD, provides the Developer's Knowledge Base, documentation for the various Microsoft Software Development Kits (SDKs) and Driver Development Kits (DDKs), technical information, Microsoft Systems Journal articles, and so on. It is the definitive source of information for the Windows Developer.

The Microsoft Developer Platform, also known as the Microsoft Developer Network CD, Level II, contains all Microsoft SDKs, DDKs, and operating systems for use by software developers. A Microsoft Developer Platform membership is a must for a serious software developer because there will be no other way to obtain the SDKs and DDKs. This membership also includes the Microsoft Developer Library CD.

To subscribe to either the Microsoft Developer Library or Platform, call 800-759-5474.

Appendix B

Troubleshooting Applications under Windows

Many applications that you might want to use that run under Windows have their own peculiarities that may cause problems. This section includes tips for optimizing and troubleshooting some of the most common Windows applications.

Troubleshooting Lotus 1-2-3 Release 4 for Windows

This section explains some of the problems you may encounter in using Lotus 1-2-3 and offers some solutions.

Network setups

For Database Manager access to an OS/2 2.0 server, you need the Local Area Network Support Program Version 1.3. Lotus 1-2-3 Release 4 does not use the LOTUSBCF environment variable; it reads only records that are listed in the LOTUS.BCF file that is located in \LOTUSAPPS\DATALENS.

If you are using Version Manager with Lotus Notes Release 3, start SHARE.EXE before you start Windows. To start SHARE.EXE before every Windows session, add the following line to AUTOEXEC.BAT:

```
C:\DOS\SHARE
```

When you use shared files, Lotus Notes displays messages in a special untitled error window during the 1-2-3 session. Closing this window ends communication with the Notes server for the rest of the 1-2-3 session.

If you delete all versions from a range in a shared file (.NS4), you will be unable to create any more versions in that range. Do not delete all versions from a range unless you are sure that you no longer want to share it.

Printing

Lotus 1-2-3 Release 4 for Windows supports the following printer drivers:

- HP DeskJet Family Version 3 or higher
- HP LaserJet III Versions 2 and 2.1 (newer than 31.3.89)
- HP LaserJet IV Version 31.V1.18 or higher
- IBM 4019/4029 Version 3.08 or higher
- PostScript Versions 3.5 and 3.53

To find out the version number of a printer driver, do the following:

1. Open the Windows Control Panel and select Printers.
2. When Windows displays the list of printers that is installed on the system, highlight a printer in the list.
3. Choose Setup. (The Setup dialog box for the selected printer appears.)
4. Choose About to see information about the printer, including the version number of the driver.

Lotus 1-2-3 Release 4 is optimized for printing at 300 dots per inch (dpi). If you encounter problems when a print job contains many different fonts and you try to print it at 600 dpi, select the Printers icon in the Windows Control Panel and then check the Print True Type as Graphics check box in the printer's Setup Options or Setup Options Advanced dialog box.

Troubleshooting memory

If you have a problem getting enough memory when you are running 1-2-3 Release 3.1 under Windows 3.1, you may want to set the EMS KB rqd/limit. Use the SET command in Windows for 123MSIZE.

If the program's response time becomes slow, or if the cursor seems to drag, check which drive the temporary directory is located on. Lotus 1-2-3 may have run out of space and begun swapping to disk. To avoid this problem, make more room on the drive or use a drive with more space. Another approach is to try using SET 123VIRTSIZE=xxxx. (Here, the value xxxx is in kilobytes.) Try at least 2048K to start, and see whether performance improves.

You may encounter the following memory problems when you are using 1-2-3:

- **Problem:** Lotus 1-2-3 thinks that the computer has a math coprocessor and locks up whenever it tries to access the chip.

Solution: Load 1-2-3 by using the `-s` command switch to disable 1-2-3's coprocessor support (`1-2-3 -s`). Always use a lowercase *s*. Or go to the 1-2-3 program directory and type **COPY LTSSFP.DLD LTSHFP.DLD** to copy the software floating-point driver to the file that used to be the hardware floating-point driver.

■ **Problem:** You receive a General Protection Fault with the following message:

```
DOS/16M: General Protection Fault at 0228:1C5C in 123DOS.EXE

code=0000 ss=02ES es=0000

ax=0000 bx=266E cx=FFFF dx=0000 sp=C8B2 bp=C8BE si=0008 di=3F1C *EE

C:\RAJ3\RAJ\RAJ123>
```

Solution: One of your programs has a memory conflict with 1-2-3. You need to load the programs one at a time in order to find the culprit. Then remove that program.

■ **Problem:** You get a message that the WYSIWYG.LBR file cannot be found.

Solution: Check to make sure that this .LBR file is in the WYSIWYG directory. If it is, also check the Display Fonts directory and verify that a pointer such as the following exists for the WYSIWYG subdirectory:

```
C:\123R34\WYSIWYG
```

The Lotus @PV function calculates the present value of an annuity (equal payment on every period within the term), but not, for example, what $1000 was worth five years ago @ 5 percent compounded daily. In Lotus 1-2-3 Release 4, you can use the following formula to obtain the present value:

$$PV = FV/(1+i)^n$$

For future value, use this formula:

$$FV = PV*(1+i)^n$$

In this formula, i is periodic interest rate, and n is the number of periods.

Add-in files

Lotus installs some 20 .PLC and .DLD files with names such as ATLOGIC, ATFIN, ATBASE, MACRO and ll3<*name*>.DLD. These .PLC and .DLD files are library modules that are used with the Add-In Toolkit. An add-in won't run unless the appropriate add-in libraries that it needs are present. For example, the ATDATE.PLC file contains all the date and time procedures that include D360, Date, Datevalue, Day, Hour, Minute, Month, Now, Second, Time, Timevalue, Today, and Year. If you developed an add-in that uses any of these procedures or any of the add-ins that shipped with Lotus 1-2-3, then the ATDATE.PLC file needs to be there. For more information on the Add-In Toolkit, call Lotus Application Services at 800-223-1662.

■ **Problem:** Lotus doesn't recognize all the memory you actually have, and it is very slow.

Solution: Find these lines in the CONFIG.SYS file:

```
device=himem.sys
device=emm386.exe noems ram
```

MS-DOS 5 (or earlier) specifies `noems ram` and essentially shuts down the Windows memory manager, which 1-2-3 needs. Instead of specifying `noems ram`, edit the file to specify `ram` only. Or use MS-DOS 6.

Internal memory limits

Lotus 1-2-3 Release 4 sets a limit of 512 characters per cell. The amount of memory consumed depends on what those characters represent: labels, values, formulas, @functions, and so on. A ten-character label typically uses less memory than a ten-character formula.

Troubleshooting Excel 4 and Excel 5

This section provides methods for dealing with some of the problems that you can run into when you are using Excel 4 and Excel 5.

Troubleshooting Setup

When you run the Excel Setup program, you may have problems if a TSR is running or if you attempt to run more than one Setup program at a time.

Virus detectors

Many common Setup errors are initiated by virus checking TSR programs. Setup often fails simply because you have a virus protection utility running. Here is a sample of the kind of error messages that you may receive:

- `Application Execution Error`
- `Access to the specified device, path, file is denied.` (when you are trying to run Excel by using its Program Manager icon)
- `Not enough memory` or `Insufficient disk space`
- `Cannot access this file. Please verify security privileges on the network drive.` (when you are trying to run Excel from the File Manager)

Check the documentation that came with the antivirus utility and disable it. If Setup fails, trying to run Excel by using File Manager will usually not succeed.

Wired For Sound and other TSRs

TSRs, such as Wired For Sound, produce the following error message:

```
Setup has caused a General Protection Fault in module
USER.EXE at 001:AB65.
```

Disable Wired For Sound by removing it from the `Load=` line in the WIN.INI file and restarting Windows. Make sure that Wired For Sound is not in the start up group.

Retrying Setup

Retrying Setup can cause the following error message:

```
Can only run one copy of setup at a time.
```

Setup creates a directory called MS-SETUP.T in the root directory of the drive on which you are installing Excel. If Setup is interrupted, this directory will be left on the drive, and you will receive this Setup error message when you run Setup again. In order to run Setup without receiving the error message, locate the directory MS-SETUP.T and delete it. If a system stop or hang caused Setup to fail initially, you may want to try rebooting the machine with clean AUTOEXEC.BAT and CONFIG.SYS files. Also ensure that all Excel items are removed from the Windows 3.1 startup group and that the `Load=` and `Run=` lines in the WIN.INI file are blank.

Errors when running Excel

When you are running Excel, various errors may occur.

Saber hangs Setup

If you use the Saber Network Menu System shell (SMENU.EXE) instead of the Program Manager shell (PROGMAN.EXE), Setup may hang. You don't receive an error message. Saber Software's Saber Network Menu System for Windows 2.0 comes with the Saber LAN software package. The Saber Menu System shell has the filename SMENU.EXE, and it uses files with the .DAT file extension to identify program groups in much the same way that PROGMAN.EXE uses the .GRP extension to identify program groups. When you have the following line in the SYSTEM.INI file, you can't install Excel:

```
Shell=smenu.exe
```

Excel creates a file with the .GRP extension, and SMENU.EXE doesn't recognize this file extension, so the screen hangs. You need to comment out the Shell= line in the SYSTEM.INI file by placing a semicolon in front of the line. Add the following line immediately below the old Shell= line:

```
Shell=progman.exe
```

Save the SYSTEM.INI file, restart Windows, and run the Excel Setup program. When you finish installing Excel, remove the semicolon from the shell=smenu.exe line and remove the line shell=progman.exe from the SYSTEM.INI file. Save SYSTEM.INI and restart Windows. You can then use the Saber Menu shell.

Files not properly expanded

If you receive the following error message the first time you try to run Excel after installing it, the EXCEL.EXE file probably was not expanded properly:

```
Application Error: Excel has caused a segment load failure
in module excel.exe at xxxx:yyyy.
```

The EXCEL.EXE file is in the directory in which you installed Excel. Use the Windows File Manager to ensure that the file date and size match one of the following:

4/1/92 2740736

11/1/92 2766592

If the file date and size do not match these dates and sizes, delete EXCEL.EXE and reinstall Excel. When you reinstall it, you can skip installing all the other Excel files by choosing Custom Installation and selecting the Excel only option.

If the EXCEL.EXE file has the correct date and file size, reboot Excel in Windows and close down all other applications. In addition, clear the 32-Bit Access check box by going to the Windows Control Panel, clicking on the 386 Enhanced icon, selecting the Virtual Memory button, and choosing Change to clear the 32-Bit Access check box.

If you are using a third-party disk-compression utility, verify that the Windows swap file (temporary or permanent) is on the noncompressed drive. If you still receive the error, quit Windows. From DOS, fix the file allocation table by typing CHKDSK /F at the MS-DOS command prompt. If many lost clusters are reported, the hard drive may be fragmented and in need of optimization. You will have to use a hard drive utility, such as Norton Desktop, to optimize the drive. If the error persists, you will need to run diagnostic tests on the hard drive and controller.

Lotus 3-D .WK3 files are too large

You may open a Lotus 1-2-3 .WK1 or .WK3 file in Excel and receive one or both of the following messages:

```
Not enough Memory

Not enough system resources to display completely
```

In some cases, Excel may hang when you try to open Lotus 1-2-3 files that contain a large number of worksheets. Or Lotus .WK1 or .WK3 worksheets may contain an active cell table that includes a large number of blank cells. Check the active cell range on each worksheet by opening the worksheet and pressing End+Home. The last possible cell in Lotus is IV8192. If the lower-right cell is substantially beyond the range that contains data, delete the unnecessary cells.

Another possible cause of this problem may be the size and complexity of the Impress formatting file. Impress is an add-in that is built into Lotus 2.2 and later versions. It enables you to apply formatting, such as borders, shading, and fonts, to a worksheet. When you save a worksheet in Lotus, the formatting information is saved as a separate file with the same name as the worksheet, plus an .FMx extension. Rename the .FMx file and try opening the worksheet again.

The font size defaults to 1

In earlier versions of Excel, if you set the default font to be a TrueType font and did not include a font size, you received a `Not Enough Memory` message. If the font was set to a screen font or a printer font and the size was omitted, the font would default to a size of 1. In Excel Version 4, the error message doesn't occur when a TrueType (or other) font is specified. However, if you do not indicate a font size in the EXCEL4.INI file, the size will default to 1. Use the following syntax to specify a default font in the `[Microsoft Excel]` section of the EXCEL.INI file:

```
font=<font>,<size>
```

Tutorial error

If you run the Excel Tutorial and Feature Guide from a network and receive the following error message, the network drive where Excel is installed has Read-only privileges:

```
Cannot Access cbt.xlw
```

You can solve this problem by changing the current directory before you start the tutorial. Just choose File⇨Open and select a directory for which you have Write privileges. Or temporarily change the privileges to Read, Write, and Create for the Excel drive or directory until everyone has completed the Tutorial and Feature Guide. Be sure to make a backup copy of the files because anyone working on the server can make changes to these files.

On the other hand, you may prefer to copy the entire directory to the hard drive of the workstation that you want to use. After you have finished the Tutorial, just remove the directory from the workstation's hard drive.

If you move the tutorial files to a directory other than the Excel directory, be sure that you have Write privileges before running the tutorial because Excel will need to save current workbook settings. In order to run the Excel Version 4.0a tutorial when the tutorial files have been moved to a different directory, you need to add the following line to the `[Microsoft Excel]` section of the EXCEL4.INI file:

```
CBTLOCATION=<path to tutorial directory>
```

You need to enter *CBTLOCATION* in uppercase, as in the following example:

```
CBTLOCATION=F:\TUTORIAL\EXCEL
```

Change this line to represent the correct path to the SOLVER.XLA add-in file.

To default to a different directory

Excel normally starts up with the EXCEL directory active, but you may want to change this default to another directory. You can verify which default directory is current by choosing File⇨Open after you start Excel. The current directory is listed after "Directory is."

The following macro will open Excel in a specified default directory:

```
A1: DEFAULT_DIR
A2: =DIRECTORY("C:\USER")
A3: =RETURN()
```

Enter the macro into a macro sheet and select cell A1. Define this macro as an Auto Open macro by choosing Formula⇨Define Name, typing **AUTO OPEN** in the Name box, choosing the Command button, and clicking OK.

You also can save the macro as an add-in macro in the XLSTART directory by choosing File⇨ Save As⇨Options and then selecting Add-In from the list and clicking OK. For the filename, enter the path to the XLSTART directory, followed by the filename (for example, C:**\EXCEL\XLSTART\DEFLTDIR.XLA**). Documents saved in the XLSTART directory are automatically opened when Excel is started. Because this macro sheet is saved as an add-in macro (that is, like an Auto Open macro), it will open but be hidden. You can't even view it by using the Window Unhide command.

Still another method is to open a new macro sheet, choose File⇨Save As, and enter **C:\CHANGEDI.XLM** (or any valid path and filename) in the File Name box, and click on OK. Then enter the following macro onto the macro sheet:

```
A1: Auto_Open
A2: =DIRECTORY("C:\USER")
A3: =NEW()
A4: =RETURN()
```

The =DIRECTORY command sets the current drive to the path designated in the pathname. The =NEW command opens a blank worksheet. You can define this macro as an AutoOpen macro by selecting cell A1, choosing Formula⇨Define Name, choosing the Command button, and clicking OK.

Or go to the OPEN= statement in the [Microsoft Excel] section of the EXCEL4.INI file and use the /P option. This option specifies a directory to be used as the default directory from which documents are opened and to which documents are saved. Enter this switch to the right of the equal sign in the OPEN= statement.

Troubleshooting Excel printing

If you choose File⇨Page Setup and the dialog box fails to appear or Excel locks up, the default printer may be set to a corrupted printer driver or to a third-party driver that is incompatible with the COMMDLG.DLL file. You may have a similar problem when you choose Print or Print Preview. If a driver is incompatible with the COMMDLG.DLL file, Excel may momentarily stop, the Page Setup dialog box may fail to appear, or Excel may lock up. The only way to regain control is by using the infamous three-fingered salute: Ctrl+Alt+Delete.

Be sure that you have upgraded the old printer drivers to the Windows 3.1 version that is supplied by the Windows 3.1 Setup disks, the Windows Driver Library, or a third-party vendor. If you are already using the Windows 3.1 version of the driver, it may be corrupt. Remove it from the Control Panel, delete the associated .DRV file from the WINDOWS\SYSTEM subdirectory, and reinstall it.

Troubleshooting Excel memory

If you receive the `Not Enough Memory` message when you open a file or enter data, Excel may be hitting an internally set memory limit. Excel has two kinds of internal memory limits: cell table limits and heap space limits.

Exceeding cell table limits

Excel limits the number of rows that can contain data in each instance of Excel and the amount of memory that is allocated to each cell. The cumulative number of rows that can contain data on all open worksheets is 37,120. For each 16 rows of data, one selector is allocated to track rows. Each Excel session has a ceiling of 2,320 selectors.

If you open two spreadsheets that each contain the maximum number of rows, 16,384 per sheet, and you try to open another sheet with 5,000 rows of data, you will receive a `Not Enough Memory` message. You can, however, open another instance of Excel and then open a sheet with 5,000 rows.

Exceeding heap space limits

Excel allocates an 8-byte memory block for each cell that is used in a worksheet. If the information in a cell is too complex for an 8-byte block, Excel creates a pointer to a second memory space that is called the *heap space*.

The heap space contains formulas, formatting information, borders, fonts, defined names, and other non-cell-type data that includes embedded objects and pictures. Excel can use up to 16MB of available memory for heap space. Even if the machine has 16MB of RAM, if you open worksheets that contain many complex formulas, you can exceed the cell memory block limit and exhaust the 16MB heap space limit before you reach the row limit. Should this happen, reduce the number of fonts, simplify the formatting, cut down on the number of graphics or embedded objects, and use array formulas.

Troubleshooting Norton Desktop_____

This section can help you troubleshoot the problems that you may experience when you use Norton Desktop.

Installing Norton Desktop from Windows

Do not install Norton Desktop by double-clicking the Program Manager's DOS Prompt and shelling to DOS because the Norton Desktop install program launches Windows as part of the installation procedure. Instead, choose File⇨Run from the Program Manager's menu and type **A:INSTALL** (if the Setup disk is in drive A:). Or exit Windows and type **A:INSTALL** at the DOS command line.

Creating new Microsoft DOS 6 Anti-Virus checksums

After you have installed Norton Desktop for Windows, you can't run it if you are using Microsoft Anti-Virus (DOS 6) unless Microsoft Anti-Virus creates new checksums. You can tell that you are using Microsoft Anti-Virus if the load= line in the WIN.INI file says load=mwavtsr.exe and the AUTOEXEC.BAT file includes the command to run VSAFE. Follow these steps to create new checksums:

1. Run Microsoft Anti-Virus.

2. Press F8 to access the configuration options.

3. Check the Create New Checksums check box.

4. Click OK.

Showing Norton's hidden Anti-Virus icon

Just as you can hide or show the Norton Sleeper screen saver and Scheduler applet icons, you can hide or show Norton's Anti-Virus pop-up application icon. Icons normally appear at the bottom of the desktop when a running application is minimized. However, the Norton Anti-Virus pop-up application icon is hidden by default. To make it visible when Virus Intercept is running, do the following:

1. Double-click the Norton Anti-Virus Tool icon or choose Tools⇨Norton Anti-Virus.

2. From the Norton Anti-Virus menu, choose Options⇨Intercept.

3. Check the Hide Popup Icon check box.

4. Click OK.

 If you run Windows in standard mode and have 2MB of RAM or less, use NAV&.SYS/B as the Norton Anti-Virus device driver.

Installing Windows applications

When you load Norton Desktop, it (and not the Windows Program Manager) becomes the shell. However, some Windows applications are hard coded to look for the Program Manager or expect to find the Program Manager running. The Microsoft Productivity Pack, for example, always expects to find the Program Manager on the shell= line in the SYSTEM.INI file, and DBFast and AScent will not install properly unless the Program Manager is the shell. Some applications create Program Manager (.GRP) files and not Norton Desktop (.QAG) files or group items. Norton Desktop for Windows (in association with Windows 3.1) is known to affect Setup in the following applications: Adobe Illustrator, Aldus PageMaker 4.0, Central Point PC Tools 7.1, Computer Associates DBFast, CorelDRAW 2.0., Foresight Drafix-1 Windows CAD, Franklin Ascend, Informix Wingz, Microsoft Productivity Pack, Microsoft Windows SDK, Que RightWriter for Windows, Software Publishing Harvard Draw, WordPerfect for Windows, and TurboTax for Windows.

If you experience problems in installing applications when Norton Desktop is the shell, try running the Program Manager by choosing File⇨Run from the Norton Desktop menu, typing **PROGMAN,** and setting the Run Style to Minimized. After the Program Manager is running, try the installation again.

 You can create a Norton Desktop group from a Program Manager group by dragging the .GRP file from a drive window file pane and dropping it in a Norton Desktop group window. Drag it to the Quick Access group if you want to create a top-level group.

Using Norton Desktop with Norton Utilities

If you run both Norton Desktop for Windows and Norton Utilities 6.01 on the same machine, copy UNERASE.EXE from Norton Desktop's Fix-It Disk #1 over the copy in the Norton Utilities directory. This change is necessary because the UnErase in Norton Desktop works with SmartCan, but the UnErase in Norton Utilities does not.

In addition, use the SmartCan program that comes with Norton Desktop, rather than Erase Protect, which comes with Norton Utilities. Do not run two deletion-tracking programs at the same time.

Using fix-it disk utilities with compressed drives

Although Norton Disk Doctor is compatible with most compression products, including Stacker, SuperStor, and DoubleSpace (DOS 6 compression), use the diagnostic programs that come with the compression product before you run Norton Disk Doctor. Use Norton Disk Doctor only to correct the kinds of problems that you normally correct by using CHKDSK or some other DOS repair utility. Don't run SpeedDisk on a compressed drive. Use the defragmentation programs that came with your compression program to optimize compressed drives.

DOS Share and sharing violations

If you experience sharing violations when you are running Norton Desktop, add two parameters to the line that loads Share in the start-up files. This line may appear in either CONFIG.SYS (INSTALL=C:\DOS\SHARE.EXE) or in AUTOEXEC.BAT (C:\DOS\SHARE). In either case, add the following:

```
/L:60 /F:4096
```

These parameters increase the number of files that Share protects and should eliminate sharing violations.

Screen saver anomalies

Norton's Sleeper does not recognize the following screen savers: Intermission's Communique, and After Dark's Randomizer and Star Trek modules. If you have installed After Dark 2.0, you see After Dark Runner in the Sleeper list box. Choose After Dark Runner and then click Configure to launch After Dark 2.0. Make sure that the After Dark switch is turned on and then select the saver module that you want to use. Don't run Windows 3.1 savers with both a Sleeper password and a Microsoft password. Use only the Microsoft password.

SmartCan and Erase Protect

SmartCan is a memory-resident program that tracks deleted files. It is typically loaded from AUTOEXEC.BAT, and it copies deleted files to a hidden directory (called SmartCan) on the hard disk. SmartCan cannot access files which were saved to Trashcan by earlier versions of Norton Desktop. To recover files either from Trashcan or from SmartCan's hidden directory, use UnErase from Fix-It Disk #1.

Dealing with error messages and lockups

You may receive the `Disk Error while checking SmartCan` error message during bootup, experience a lockup with the message `Checking SmartCan on drive C:`, experience a lockup when you exit Norton Desktop, receive a Windows `System Error Reading/Writing to Drive C:` message, or receive an `Invalid command.com system halted` message.

If any of these things occur, you need to reboot the system from a DOS disk, type **C:** to change to drive C:, and type **CD \SMARTCAN** to change to the SMARTCAN subdirectory. Then type **DEL *.*** to delete all the files in that directory. Press Y when you see the prompt Are you sure?, remove the DOS disk from drive A, and reboot the computer. The problems should disappear. However, you will lose any deleted data files that are in the SmartCan file.

Troubleshooting Norton Backup

This section describes problems that you may have when you use Norton Backup and tells you how to solve them.

Upgrading from Norton Backup for DOS

Upgrading from Norton Backup for DOS to Norton Backup for Windows changes the Data Verification Setting. If data verification in the Setup file was set for Read-only in Norton Backup for DOS, be sure to check the settings in Norton Backup for Windows when you first load its Setup file. Because Norton Backup for Windows does not have the Read-only option, the setting defaults to Read and Compare. Change this setting if you prefer another option.

Incorrect floppy drives

If Norton Backup displays incorrect floppy disk drive types, select Floppy Configuration from the Configure screen and use the list boxes to correct the disk drive types. If this problem persists, check the computer's CMOS setup to make sure that the floppy drives are configured properly. You can check the CMOS setup by using the computer's Setup program.

Failing the compatibility test

DMA Operation is automatically set to Most Compatible. If your computer fails the compatibility test, run the test again to verify that you can make reliable backups by using the Most Compatible setting. After the DMA Operation is set to Most Compatible, you cannot change it manually. If you change your hardware, repeat the compatibility test. (*Note:* You can temporarily change the DMA Operation setting in the Compatibility Test dialog box by setting it to Fastest in the DMA Operation During Test list box.)

Using a 360K floppy disk in a 1.2MB drive

Norton Backup supports backups to 360K disks and to high-density (1.2MB) floppy drives. If you transfer files to a machine with a 360K drive, be sure to do compatibility testing between both machines. Before you start the backup, format the disks in the 360K drive and then choose the DOS Drive and Path in the Backup To list box and set the component size to 360K in the Advanced Options dialog box.

Error message: invalid drive specification

To ensure that access to floppy drives is not interrupted during the backup process, Norton hides other drives from your applications. As a result, programs that normally display a list of available drives do not show drives A: and B: during background operations. Avoid accessing floppy drives during the backup process. The normal use of drives will return after the backup is finished.

This restriction also applies to tape backups with no floppy drive controller.

Hardware incompatibilities

The following hardware is not compatible with Norton Backup:

- QIC 02 tape drives. These drives are not supported.

- COREtape Light QIC 80. Some Core International software versions are not compatible with Norton Backup. Verify that you can restore backups that are made with Core International software, and keep the Core International software available in case you need to restore old backups that were made with it.

- Iomega Accutrak. Norton Backup does not support Iomega Accutrak's Read mode.

- Maynard Archive. Some Maynard Archive 5240 drives are not compatible. Additionally, Norton Backup supports only tape drives that have serial numbers starting with BB or above. Serial numbers starting with AA or AB are not supported.

- Mountain 4000, 8000, and 4740(PS/2). If you install one of these drives, use it only as a drive B:. Or use a third connector cable.

- Wangtek QIC 3040F5 and 3080F5 and Tecmar QT40i. The jumpers for these drives are factory set for them to be used as drive B:. To configure the tape drive as the third device, follow the manufacturer's directions and change the jumper at the back of the tape drive. Note that Wangtek documentation refers to a unique setting for using Wangtek drives (3080F5) as a third device on Compaq machines. This setting does not work with Norton Backup. Use the phantom drive setting instead.

 Everex 60F tape drives are described as QIC 40-compatible. However, although tapes formatted by this machine are QIC 40-compatible, they are not QIC 117 interface-compatible.

Troubleshooting Quattro Pro 5

This section covers messages that you may see when you are using Quattro Pro 5 and describes ways of dealing with the problems that cause these messages.

Missing DLLs

When you install Quattro Pro 5, you may see several error messages.

Error message: QPSRV.DLL cannot be located

This message may appear if the Quattro Pro directory is not in the MS-DOS Path nor the start-up directory. Check the AUTOEXEC.BAT file to verify that the installation program added the Quattro Pro directory to the path. If you did not install Quattro Pro since you last rebooted, you need to add Quattro Pro to the path statement in the AUTOEXEC.BAT file. Reboot to make adjustments to the path statement take effect.

To change the start-up directory in Quattro Pro, first choose Property⇨Application⇨Startup. Then, in the Directory field, enter the Quattro Pro directory (for example, **C:\QPW**).

Error message: Cannot Find DLL *<DLL name>*

Quattro Pro uses files with the extension .DLL. These files contain parts of the program that have been broken out into Dynamic-Link Libraries (DLLs). Quattro Pro looks for .DLL files in the following directories, in this order:

- The Windows System directory (for example, C:\WINDOWS\SYSTEM)
- The Windows directory (for example, C:\WINDOWS)
- The current directory
- All directories in the MS-DOS path

Check to be sure that the missing DLL is in one of the directories that are searched. If not, copy this file from the installation disk.

Error message: Cannot Access Source Path

If you receive this message, you specified an invalid path when you were prompted for a disk and source path during Setup. If you have altered the source path to an invalid path, choose Cancel and exit the Setup program. Also be sure to delete any files that have been placed in Quattro Pro's C:\QPW directory and then reinstall Quattro Pro.

You also can get this message if you copied Quattro Pro's Setup from 3½-inch disks to 5¼-inch disks. If this is the case, copy all the files into a temporary directory on the hard drive and install Quattro Pro from the temporary directory.

Error message: Bad Table In Pack File *<filename>*

This message generally appears after the Cannot Access Source Path *PATH* message. You should exit Setup the first time Cannot Access Source Path *PATH* appears, delete any files installed in the Quattro Pro directory, and run the installation program again.

A conflict with memory-resident software or some device drivers also can cause the `Bad Table In Pack File <filename>` message to appear. Install the program from a temporary directory.

Error message: Invalid Serial Number

This message appears if you don't enter a serial number in the Setup's dialog box. Quattro Pro forces you to type in a serial number. The serial number is located on the front label of Disk #1. The format is *AA###A########*, where *A* is a letter and # is a number. The number has no spaces. LAN pack serial numbers are located on a card included in the Quattro Pro package.

Error message: Program Manager Did Not Respond. Group Quattro Pro for Windows Will Not Be Created

This error message means that Quattro Pro was unable to create a new program group. The installation program uses the Windows Program Manager to create a new program group, and it cannot create a new program group without the Program Manager. If you are using a different desktop (for example, Norton Desktop, hDC Powerlauncher, or PC Tools), change the desktop back to the Program Manager temporarily while you are installing Quattro Pro or manually create the group after you install it.

Error message: Bad Header in Pack File

Quattro Pro's Setup disk contains files that are unpacked (uncompressed) and combined into one file by the installation program. The first 64 characters of each of these files is a header that determines how the file should be unpacked. If you receive the `Bad Header in Pack File` message, the installation program was unable to create the combined file, or the first 64 characters of the file contained incorrect information. Setup cannot do its job if the hard drive contains a file with the same name as the combined file or if the hard drive has a bad sector. To avoid these problems, install Quattro Pro in an empty directory.

If you are installing from 5¼-inch disks that were made by copying 3½-inch installation disks (or vice versa), the `Bad Header in Pack File` message may appear because the installation program does not find the right files to combine. To avoid this problem, copy all the files into a temporary directory on the hard drive and install from there. When you are finished installing, delete the temporary directory.

Error message: Division By Zero

This message generally appears because of a hardware or memory conflict. Unload TSRs or other programs that may be running and install again. Run a disk evaluation program (such as CHKDSK) to check for errors on the hard drive.

Error message: BORINST Caused A General Protection Fault In SOUND.DRV

Some third-party programs that have attached .WAV sound files, such as Wired For Sound, cause problems with the Quattro Pro installation program, even when they are not running. This message appears because the application sends a notification to the user and tries to sound a default beep. A quick cure is to go to the Windows Control Panel and select Sound. Set the Default Beep to None instead of to a .WAV file.

Error message: Cannot lzexpand

This message generally indicates that a problem with the path statement prevents DOS from using the path. Be sure to include the drive letter designation for each directory that you include in the path statement. (For example, use C:\WINDOWS and not \WINDOWS.) The path statement may be too long. Make the Windows directory the first directory in the path. This message also can indicate a memory conflict. You can increase the environment space in the CONFIG.SYS file by increasing the /E parameter for the SHELL=COMMAND.COM statement to 2048 and by using SHARE /L:400. (The DOS SHARE command may be loaded from either the AUTOEXEC.BAT file or the CONFIG.SYS file.) Check the DOS documentation for information about using SHARE. You also may need to modify the WIN.INI file to eliminate programs that are loaded by using the LOAD= or RUN= lines.

The LZEXPAND.DLL file may be missing or corrupted. Verify that a file by that name is in the Windows System directory (C:\WINDOWS\SYSTEM). If you cannot decompress LZEXPAND with Setup, you may be able to directly decompress QPWINST.LZ by using EXPAND.EXE.

Error message: Cannot Read from QPWISNT.LZ

This message appears when Quattro Pro is installed from 5¼-inch disks that were created by copying 3½-inch disks or from 3½-inch disks that were created by copying 5¼-inch disks. Copy disks into a temporary directory on the hard drive and install from there. This message also appears when Setup cannot write to the Windows directory (for example, if disk space is insufficient). On a network, the installation program may not be able to write to the Windows directory if assigned rights are not sufficient. Verify that you have rights to the Windows directory.

Error message: Application Execution Error — Access to specified device, path, or file is denied

An Application Execution message may appear when a memory-resident program is installed that prevents other programs from modifying specific types of files. The virus protection programs VDEFEND and VSAFE are examples of this type of program. VDEFEND and VSAFE are installed in the system through the CONFIG.SYS file. VDEFEND.SYS comes with Central Point PC Tools 7.1; VSAFE comes with MS-DOS 6.

If you installed with VDEFEND or VSAFE active, delete the CHKLIST.CPS or CHKLIST.MS file from the Quattro Pro directory after completing the installation. VDEFEND creates the CHKLIST.CPS file in each directory from which an application is run when VDEFEND.SYS is loaded. Similarly, VSAFE creates the CHKLIST.MS file. To avoid deleting the CHKLIST.CPS file or the CHKLIST.MS file, remove VDEFEND.SYS or VSAFE.SYS from the CONFIG.SYS file before installing Quattro Pro. After Quattro Pro is installed, add VDEFEND or VSAFE back to the CONFIG.SYS file.

Error message: Cannot create install directory

Quattro Pro cannot create a directory because a file called QPW already exists. The installation is prevented from creating a directory of that name. Other causes of this message can include insufficient rights on a network.

Error message: Cannot find a function in DLL

The DLL is defective.

Error message: Application Error: PROGMAN caused segment load error in module PROGMAN.EXE at 0004:1141

This message may appear when you are installing Quattro Pro with Windows for Workgroups. You see it when you choose OK to proceed.

If you have proceeded this far, you have partially installed Quattro Pro. To complete the installation, delete the file SHELL.DDL in the Windows System directory (C:\WINDOWS\SYSTEM) and rename the SHELL.QPW file in the Windows System directory to SHELL.DDL. Exit Windows. Restart Windows. You now have an empty Quattro Pro for Windows program group. Add the program icons manually.

Network-related messages

You may see several messages when you are using Quattro Pro for Windows on a network.

Error message: Error Opening Network File

If a user does not have Write access to the directory that contains the network control file (QPW.NET), this message appears when the user loads Quattro Pro. To verify or change this file's location, run QWUPDATE.EXE, which is located in the same directory as Quattro Pro. The network control directory is on the third screen.

Error message: All User Counts Already Used

This message indicates that the number of Quattro Pro users on the network is equal to the number of issued serial numbers. A user needs to exit Quattro Pro before another user can use the program. If you get this message, use QWUPDATE.EXE to add more serial numbers.

The choices for Database Desktop and Table Query are dimmed on the menu.

If these choices are dimmed on Quattro Pro's Data menu, the lines WORKDIR= and PRIVDIR= are not in the [DBD] section of the WIN.INI file, or the WIN.INI file has no [DBD] section. WORKDIR can be shared or private. PRIVDIR must be accessible by only one user.

Error message: Net Init failed, cannot access lock file

Database Desktop creates a lock file to share database files on a network. This message means that the lock file cannot be opened. Check the location of the network control file directory by using ODAPICFG.EXE. The network control file should be in the same directory as PDOXUSERS.NET if users will be sharing files with Paradox 4.0 or Paradox for Windows. Otherwise, place the control file in the same location as the QPW.NET file. This message also can appear if the user does not have Create, Modify, and Write rights to the directory that contains the network control file (QPW.NET).

Error message: Could not initialize ODAPI: Generic Invalid Config param

This message appears while Database Desktop is loading on a Novell network if the user does not have Filescan (or Search on Netware 286) rights to the ODAPI directory but does have Read rights. Check the user's rights to the ODAPI directory. The user should have both Read and Filescan rights.

Error message: Cannot find ODAPI.DLL or Cannot find ODAPIQ.DLL

The ODAPI files are files used by Database Desktop. Either of these messages can occur if Windows cannot find the files. Verify that the ODAPI files are on the path and that the user has Read access to that directory.

Error message: Could not open the ODAPI.CFG file

If ODAPI.CFG cannot be accessed properly, this message may appear when ODAPICFG.EXE, the ODAPI configuration utility, is being loaded.

Each user's WIN.INI file indicates where Database Desktop looks for the ODAPI.CFG file. Make sure that the file is in the directory specified in the [ODAPI] section of the WIN.INI file where it states CONFIGFILE=.

The `CONFIGFILE` line in WIN.INI must specify both the path to ODAPI.CFG and the name of the file. Also, verify that the user has Read access to ODAPI.CFG.

The ODAPICFG.EXE program makes changes to the ODAPI.CFG file. If ODAPI.CFG cannot be updated, these changes will not be saved. The most common reason that ODAPI.CFG cannot be updated is that the user has only Read access to the file.

Error message: Could not initialize ODAPI. Cannot Open a System file

This message indicates that a user does not have Create access to WORKDIR. The user must have Create and Write access to this directory so that the DBDWORK.INI file can be created.

This message sometimes appears on a Novell network when a drive letter without a path is specified as the working directory. Using a drive letter followed by a backslash alone will not help because the root directory of a drive is not valid for the working directory. The .\ notation (to indicate the current directory on a drive) will work on mapped drives of Novell networks. Database Desktop automatically replaces the .\ with a full pathname.

Error message: Cannot find PXENGCFG.EXE or one of its components

PXENGCFG.EXE configures Quattro Pro for use with Paradox tables. This Windows message usually indicates that the user does not have rights to search the directory in which PXENGCFG.EXE is located.

Error message: Cannot Find DBD.EXE or one of its components

This message can appear when the system is loading Database Desktop. It often follows the message `Cannot find ODAPI.DLL`, which is caused by not having Read access to the ODAPI directory or by not having the ODAPI files in the path. Make sure that DBD.EXE is in the Quattro Pro directory.

Error message: Private Directory Already in Use

Any application that works with Paradox requires each user to have a private directory where temporary database files are created. Users also have a working directory where they store current data files. A private directory cannot be accessed by someone else who is using a Paradox-compatible program, nor can one directory double as both a working directory and a private directory. The working and private directories are specified in the [DBD] section of the WIN.INI file on the lines `PRIVDIR=` and `WORKDIR=`.

The message, `Private Directory Already in Use` appears if another user is accessing database files in a user's private directory. It also appears if another Paradox (or another application) that is running at the same time on the same machine is using the same private directory. Determine the location of the private directory by looking in the WIN.INI file and make certain that no other users are accessing files in that directory. Then delete any .LCK or .NET files in that directory. This will let Paradox know that no other users are actually using the private directory.

This message also appears if a user does not have sufficient rights to the private directory or if the location specified is a root directory. If a root directory was specified, name a subdirectory explicitly. The .\ notation (to indicate the current directory on a drive) will work on mapped drives of Novell networks. Database Desktop will automatically replace the .\ with a full pathname.

Another cause for this message is that no network control directory is specified in the ODAPI.CFG file and Quattro Pro is installed on a network drive. Use the ODAPICFG.EXE program to check the location of the network control directory. If multiple Paradox-compatible programs are on the network, they should all have the same network control directory.

This message also may appear if ODAPI.CFG is not in the directory specified in the `[ODAPI]` section of the WIN.INI file.

Error message: DBDWORK.INI could not be created

This message usually appears when you are exiting Database Desktop. The location of the file DBDWORK.INI is determined by the `WORKDIR=` line in the `[DBD]` section of the WIN.INI file. It usually indicates that the user does not have rights to the working directory. To resolve this situation, check the location of the working directory in the WIN.INI file. This message also can appear if DBDWORK.INI exists in that directory as Read-only, in which case you should remove the Read-only attribute.

Error message: Work Dir is invalid or undefined. Using Startup Dir

This message appears when the working directory specified on the `WORKDIR` line in the `[DBD]` section of the WIN.INI file is missing, and Database Desktop switches to the start-up directory. The start-up directory is the directory that contains the file DBD.EXE. Database Desktop will update the WIN.INI file to reflect this change. No change is necessary to make the program function. However, you may wish to change the working directory to the directory where you store your database files.

Error message: Could not update BWCC.DLL

If the file BWCC.DLL cannot be found, Database Desktop will place it in the network's shared Windows directory or in a user's WINDOWS\SYSTEM directory. The method used is to expand BWCC.LZ. If a user has insufficient rights to the Windows directory, Database Desktop will not be able to expand the file in the Windows directory, and the message, `Could not update bwcc.dll` appears.

This message also can appear if the Windows directory is a root directory, if the Novell MAP ROOT command was used to map the Windows directory, or if drives on a NETBIOS network are mapped to the name of the Windows directory. On a Novell network, use a MAP command to map the Windows directory.

Troubleshooting Microsoft Word 6

This section covers problems that you may have when you are using Microsoft Word 6 for Windows and tells you how to optimize both Windows and Word.

Troubleshooting error messages

You may see several error messages when you are using Microsoft Word 6.

Error message: DDE timed out. Continue waiting?

This message indicates that you used the Paste Link command to paste data into Microsoft Word from another application. The Paste Link process uses Windows' Dynamic Data Exchange (DDE) interprocess communications functionality to provide the link. This error message indicates that the application from which the data has been copied is taking too long to provide the data for the link. This error message often appears if the data has been copied from an Excel worksheet that draws data from several other worksheets. Word provides a WIN.INI setting that modifies the DDE time-out period. Place the following setting in the [Microsoft Word| section of the WIN.INI file:

```
[Microsoft Word|
DDETIMEOUT=n
```

Here, n is the number of seconds that you want Word to wait for DDE data from another application. The default value for n is 60.

Error message: Information file is not in current directory

If the Word Setup disk does not contain the WWORD20.INF file, this error message appears. Without the WWORD20.INF file, the setup process comes to a halt. You run the Word Setup program from a floppy disk drive by typing **SETUP** at the A:\> or B:\> prompt. To determine whether the WWORD20.INF file is on the Setup disk, type **DIR WWORD20.INF.** If the Setup disk does not contain the WWORD20.INF file, contact your dealer.

Error message: Cannot open existing NORMAL.DOT

Receiving this message may indicate that the computer does not have enough memory to open the NORMAL.DOT file. To remedy this situation, close all applications that you are not currently using and remove any memory-resident programs.

This message also appears if the NORMAL.DOT file is corrupted. Rename NORMAL.DOT and reload Word.

On a network, this same message may indicate that another user has logged onto the network and opened NORMAL.DOT. Wait until the file is free.

Finally, this message may indicate that NORMAL.DOT has been saved as a document file and is no longer a template. In this case, copy the file and rename it with a .DOT extension.

Error message: Word cannot save or create this file

Make sure that the disk is not write protected. This message may indicate that the file is in use by another user.

Error message: Word cannot open the document

To remedy this situation, close open documents to release file locks or increase the file locks parameter in the SHARE statement in AUTOEXEC.BAT or CONFIG.SYS. The recommended setting is SHARE /L:500 /F:5100. If you are using Windows for Workgroups 3.1 or 3.11, you should be using VSHARE.386, which loads in the SYSTEM.INI file. You do not need to load SHARE.EXE if you are using VSHARE.

Error message: Cannot save this document

If Word will not save files to a network server, either you do not have SHARE.EXE installed or the network software does not have file-locking capabilities. You will not be able to save to a network drive in Word for Windows 6 format if the server does not have Share or an equivalent file-locking utility installed. Make sure that the correct switches are set when you load Share. You need the following switches:

```
/L:500 /F:5100
```

Another possibility is that the documents have embedded objects in them. If the embedded objects have been edited in any way — such as cutting, copying, pasting, resizing, and so on — then the objects have become corrupted, and the only way to save the documents is to delete the objects. The bug that caused this problem is fixed in Word 6.0a, which was about to be released as this was being written.

Setup fails

Setup may fail if the computer uses any of the following:

- Compaticard
- American Megatrends Inc. (AMI) BIOS
- EMM386.EXE

Compaticard is a floppy disk controller that requires the CC4DRV.SYS driver in the CONFIG.SYS file. If you have a version of the CC4DRV.SYS driver that is earlier than Version 2.03 or a version of Micro Solutions' BIOS that is earlier than Version 1.05, contact Micro Solutions Inc., 815-756-3411, and update your driver.

General Protection Faults

Microsoft Word 6 can cause general protection faults (GPFs).

GPFs in using ToolsSpelling

If you run a macro that uses the ToolsSpelling command and the spelling checker flags a misspelled word in a document header or footer, a general protection fault (GPF) will occur after the spelling check is completed. The fault may occur as soon as you open the header or footer for viewing, or it may occur when you edit the header or footer. This problem is a bug in Word. To remedy this situation, run the macro by using the ToolsMacro command rather than the ToolsSpelling command. For example, use the ToolsMacro command, type **TOOLSSPELLING**, and choose Run.

GPFs in using Help files

If you receive a general protection fault while you are using Help, you may have a path statement that is over 128 characters long in the AUTOEXEC.BAT file. Decrease the length of the path statement. If you have upgraded from Word 2 and find that Help is not working, reduce the path length.

GPFs when using CorelDRAW clip art

If you receive a GP fault message in Word 6 when you are using CorelDRAW clip art, switch the video driver to a standard VGA video driver by using the

Windows Setup program in the Main program group. Also, switch the printer driver to the Generic/Text Only printer driver. Finally, if you use Word 2.0, exit Word and rename the WINWORD.INI file in the \WINWORD directory WINWORD.OLD. If you are using Word 6, exit Word and rename the WINWORD.OPT file WINWORD.OLD.

Changing the command string to eliminate GPFs

If you experience GPFs, check to see whether the command string in the Winword icon is C:\WINWORD\WINWORD.EXE /N. If you normally click the icon to start Word and then choose File⇨Find File, it will recall a previous search. If you then use the keyboard down-arrow key to look at the preview of each file in sequence, a GPF occurs.

The workaround is to remove the /N switch from the command string.

Seconds are not supported in the time field

The Word 6 *User's Guide* (page 826) incorrectly suggests that TimeFormat in the [Microsoft Word 2.0| section of the WIN.INI file will display the time with seconds:

```
timeformat=hh:mm:ss
```

This information is not correct. If you place ss in the TimeFormat entry, the {TIME} field will display ss, (for example, 10:00:ss AM). Word does not support the use of seconds in the {TIME} field.

Page spacing in Word 6

The Word 6 *User's Guide* (page 139) says, "Word also observes the spacing before a paragraph that follows a manual page break." This statement is incorrect. Word ignores *space before* when it is preceded by either a soft or a hard page break (except if the Page Break Before option is active).

Templates broken

Because of changes in the WordBasic syntax, you probably will not be able to use templates from earlier versions of Word (including Word 2) in Word 6. New versions of the sample templates that were included with Word 2.0 are available from Microsoft, and can be downloaded from the MSWORD Forum on CompuServe.

Spell-checking problems

If you have upgraded from Word 2 to Word 6 and find that the spell checker (or grammatical tools) do not work, use the Winword Setup program to remove the tools (including the spell checker) and reinstall them.

Eliminating crashes

If Word 6 crashes often, try these troubleshooting steps to isolate the problem:

1. Turn off the fast save options and the autosave options. If 32-Bit Disk Access is turned on, turn it off. (You access it by selecting 386 Enhanced in the Control Panel and then choosing Virtual Memory.)

2. Check the SMARTDrive settings. At the DOS prompt, type **SMARTDRV** to look at the settings. (Type **SMARTDRV /H** to bring up Help.) One other thing: Make sure that the TEMP variable that is set in AUTOEXEC.BAT is pointing to a valid directory (not a RAM drive) that has at least 8MB of free space.

3. Try using the Windows VGA driver.

4. Empty the Windows Startup group.

5. Open the WIN.INI file and make sure that the Load= and Run= lines are blank.

6. Open the SYSTEM.INI file and switch the Shell= line in the [boot] section so that it reads as follows:

   Shell=progman.exe

7. Select Printer in the Windows Control Panel and set Generic/Text Only as the default printer.

8. Clean out the AUTOEXEC.BAT and CONFIG.SYS files so that they contain only the essentials to run Windows and Word:

   CONFIG.SYS   *AUTOEXEC.BAT*

   files=60   path c:\;c:\dos;c:\windows

   buffers=30   prompt pg

   device=c:\[path]\himem.sys   set temp=c: stacks=9,256

         c:\dos\SHARE.EXE /L:500 /F: 5100

   If you use DoubleSpace, be sure to include the device drivers DBLSPACE.BIN and DBLSPACE.SYS (or the device drivers for any other disk-compression utility or special hardware that you are using).

9. With this configuration, run Windows in standard mode by typing **WIN /S** at the DOS prompt.

If the problem still occurs, look at other things, such as the CMOS setup, the BIOS, your Cirrus card, and other items that are related to hardware. If the problem is gone, return to the configuration that you started with, a few steps at a time, until you locate the problem.

Word 6.0a includes VSHARE.386, the virtual protected-mode version of SHARE that was introduced with Windows for Workgroups. If you're not running Windows for Workgroups, but you do have a 386 or better processor in your computer, you will benefit from using VSHARE.

Printing in Word 6

You may have some problems when you try to print in Microsoft Word 6 for Windows.

Adobe ATM font problems

Word may not print ATM fonts, even though they show up in the font selection box. This problem is a bug in Word. The workaround is to add ATM fonts one at a time, instead of using the ATM software to add them as a batch.

Using nonlisted font sizes

When you choose a scalable font (such as a TrueType font) in the font box, Word lists the following predefined sizes in the point-size box: 8, 9, 10, 11, 12, 14, 16, 18, 20, 22, 24, 26, 28, 36, 48, and 72. This list is the same as the lists that Excel 4.0 and Excel 5.0 use. You are not limited to these sizes, however. To keep the list from being too long, Word lists only the most commonly used sizes, but you can type any number from 1 to 1638 in the point-size box.

Making HP DeskJet print envelopes

Here's the problem: The HP DeskJet printer prints pages in reverse order. Using the Reverse Print Order option causes pages to be printed in the correct order. However, this feature doesn't work when you print envelopes by using the Create Envelope command.

To remedy this situation, modify the ToolsCreateEnvelope macro so that it clears the Reverse Printer Order option when you create an envelope and then select the option again after the envelope prints. To modify the ToolsCreate Envelope macro, add the following lines to the macro:

```
ToolsOptionsPrint.Reverse=0
ToolsOptionsPrint.Reverse=1
```

For example, you use the following:

```
Sub Main
ToolsOptionsPrint.Reverse = 0
Dim dlg As ToolsCreateEnvelope
GetCurValues dlg
x = Dialog(dlg)
If x = - 1 Then ToolsCreateEnvelope dlg
ToolsOptionsPrint.Reverse = 1
End Sub
```

Displaying raster fonts

Word may not display raster fonts, such as Terminal font, in the Ribbon Font Selection window. Word builds the font list for the Ribbon based on your printer selection. However, not all of the fonts installed on your system will print to any printer device. For example, Terminal font is a raster font and will not print to a HPPCL printer (LaserJet), so it will not be listed in the font list from the Word Ribbon.

Optimizing Windows for Word 6

Word 6 is larger than any previous version of Word. As a result, its performance may be slower. When you optimize the performance of Windows 3.1, you also optimize Word's performance. In other words, if you want to increase the performance of Word, you should first optimize Windows 3.1.

To optimize Windows 3.1, you need to optimize both the hardware and the software. The type and speed of the processor, the amount of memory, and the available hard disk space ultimately determine just how fast Word runs. Software factors, such as the type of memory that is required to run applications, also plays a role. The following suggestions can help you optimize both your hardware and software configurations for Word and other Windows-based applications that are running under Windows 3.1.

First, change the BitmapMemory and CacheSize in the WINWORD6.INI settings. To increase bitmap-redrawing speed and scrolling speed in Word, add the following two settings to the [Microsoft Word] section of the WINWORD6.INI file that is located in the WINDOWS directory:

```
BitMapMemory=
CacheSize=
```

The `BitMapMemory=` setting sets the amount of memory (in kilobytes) that is reserved for cache memory for bitmaps. Increasing this number increases the size of the bitmap cache that Word uses for redrawing pictures. The `BitMapMemory` setting should not exceed the amount of available free random-access memory (RAM). A setting of `1024` improves performance in Word (`256` is the default setting). Insert this command anywhere in the `[Microsoft Word]` section of WINWORD6.INI by using the following syntax:

```
[Microsoft Word]
BitMapMemory=xxxx
```

The `CacheSize=` setting sets the amount of memory (in kilobytes) that is reserved for cache memory for Word documents. The default value for the `CacheSize` command is `64` or `64K`. Increasing this setting (in multiples of 64K) improves scrolling speed, searching and replacing, the operation of the Go To command, and document load and save times. If the system has plenty of memory and you work with many large documents, consider setting the CacheSize to `256K` or `512K`. Insert the command anywhere in the `[Microsoft Word]` section of WINWORD6.INI by using the following syntax:

```
[Microsoft Word]
CacheSize=xxx
```

Troubleshooting Ami Pro 3.0

This section describes Ami Pro 3.0 error messages and video driver problems.

Troubleshooting error messages

You may see several error messages when you are using Ami Pro 3.0.

Error message: Incorrect version of Ami Pro detected

The AMIPRO.EXE file on 3½-inch, 720K media dates the files it copies when you run Setup. The Lotus Bonus Pack works only with AMIPRO.EXE files that have specific dates. If your Ami Pro Setup is on 3½-inch, 1.44MB media or 5¼-inch, 1.2MB media, you won't have this problem because AMIPRO.EXE is stored as a single file and copied to the hard drive with the original creation date.

You can't fix this problem by manually changing the date of the AMIPRO.EXE file that is located in the Ami Pro program subdirectory (usually C:\AMIPRO) because Windows doesn't let you change dates. You can, however, edit the file date in the LIST.TXT file in the Bonus Pack by following these steps:

1. Start Systems Engineer and locate the subdirectory where Ami Pro is installed (usually C:\AMIPRO). Find the AMIPRO.EXE file and copy the date to the right of the filename exactly as it appears.

2. Insert the Bonus Pack Disk 1 in a floppy drive and choose File⇨Open. In the File Name edit box type **x:\LIST.TXT.** (Substitute the correct drive for **x.** If the floppy disk drive is A:, then type **A:\LIST.TXT.**)

3. Locate the second line in the file. It reads as follows:

   `@;1313024;1993/06/07;487704;487785`

4. Change the date to match the date you copied from AMIPRO.EXE. If the file date is 1/15/94, change the line to read as follows:

   `@;1313024;1994/01/15;487704;487785`

5. Choose File⇨Exit and save the changes.

6. Restart the Bonus Pack.

Error message: The wrong version of Ami Pro is currently installed on your computer. To install options for Ami Pro, please first install Ami Pro.

You receive this error message whenever you want to add something to your original Ami Pro Setup and you choose Options Install. To remedy this situation, choose Custom Install, rather than Options Install. In Custom Install, select Ami Pro Basics (you must select this item) and then the option that you want to add.

Error message: Cannot create output file

Always install Ami Pro from the Windows Program Manager (*not* from the File Manager or from DOS). Ami Pro's Setup needs Windows. It copies and updates files in the Windows program directory by requesting locations from the Windows Program Directory. If Setup does not have a complete path (with a drive identifier), Setup can't locate the Windows program directory, and installation stops.

If you receive this message, the remedy is to make sure that the DOS path statement properly lists the location of the Windows program directory. To check the DOS path, exit Windows to the DOS prompt, type **PATH,** and press Enter. When you see the contents of the path on the screen, make sure that the complete path (a drive identifier, a colon, plus backslashes) to the Windows program directory is listed first in the path statement. C:\WINDOWS is a correct path; \WINDOWS is not.

If Windows is loaded with a batch file rather than with WIN.COM, check the batch file for a path statement. If the path is being reset with a batch file that loads Windows, the path statement in the batch file should correctly list the complete path to the Windows directory. If the path is being reset by any program after Windows is loaded, the path set by the program should list a correct path for the Windows program directory.

Make any necessary changes. You may need to edit the AUTOEXEC.BAT file, the batch file that loads Windows, or the path in any program that alters the path after Windows is loaded. After correcting the path, reboot and reload Windows. Click the DOS prompt icon from Windows to access the DOS prompt. Type **SET**, press Enter, and look for the variable `WINDIR=`. The path listed after the equal sign that follows `WINDIR` is the recognized path for the Windows program directory. If the directory name appears without a drive identifier (\WINDOWS, for example), or if it is incorrect in any other way, correct the path. Exit and return to the Windows Program Manager.

The `Cannot create output file` error message is also displayed when Ami Pro 3.0 is installed over a previous version of Ami Pro where program files are marked with the System attribute. If any existing Ami Pro program files have this attribute, the Ami Pro 3.0 installation cannot update them, and the error message displays. You need to check the attributes and rename them as archive files. To check and change attributes, follow these steps:

1. Start the Windows File Manager, choose View⇨By File Type, and click the selection box for Show Hidden / System Files.

2. Change to the drive and directory where the Ami Pro files are located (usually C:\AMIPRO). Choose View⇨Partial Details. Select File Attributes and click OK.

3. Scroll through the list of filenames, looking at the column on the right for files with the letters *S* or *HS*. These files are the System files that need to be changed.

4. Select a file with the letter *S (or HS)* in its name.

5. Select File⇨ Properties.

6. Select Attribute Archive by placing an *x* in the check box.

7. Click OK. The letter *A* will replace the letter *S*.

Error message: Not Enough Disk Space

This message can appear when you are installing over an existing copy of Ami Pro where the default document directory path under Tools⇨User Setup⇨Paths is set to a floppy drive. The message appears when you get to Disk 3 even though plenty of space is available on the hard drive. The problem is that Ami Pro tries to install the sample document, MERCURY.SAM, onto Disk 3 instead of onto the hard drive. The remedy is to restart Setup, and when you see the Overwriting Existing Paths screen, change the contents of the Document Directory edit box to a directory on the hard drive. Then continue with the installation.

Error message: Stack Fault Error in TSNI.EXE

This message occurs with video drivers such as the TS VGA Local Bus Card that uses the ET4000 640 x 480 x 16.7 video driver and the Diamond Speedstar 24 x 640 x 480 x 16 million video driver. To remedy this situation, change to the standard Windows VGA driver before installing Ami Pro. After the Ami Pro installation is complete, return to the original driver setting.

If you use a DOS-level driver, such as the one that is used with the Diamond Speedstar 24X video card, you need to remark out (REM) the lines for the driver in AUTOEXEC.BAT and CONFIG.SYS by placing a semicolon (;) in front of each of those lines. Review the documentation that came with the video card for the exact syntax of the line. Save the changes and reboot from the DOS prompt. Then change to a standard Windows VGA driver by following these steps:

1. From Windows, start Setup.

2. Choose Options⇨Change System Settings and then choose VGA.

3. Click OK and exit the dialog box. Exit Windows by pressing Alt+F4.

Restart Windows and install Ami Pro. When Setup is complete, remove REM from the video lines, and then go to Change System Settings and change the video driver back to its original setting. Reboot the computer so the AUTOEXEC.BAT and CONFIG.SYS video driver settings are recognized.

Error message: Cannot Find Specified File X6

This message sometimes occurs while the Tutorial is running. To remedy this situation, delete the Ami Pro program file, AMIVISD.INI, from the Windows directory. (AMIVISD.INI is automatically re-created in the Windows directory when Ami Pro is started again.) Follow these steps to delete the file:

1. Exit Ami Pro, open the Windows File Manager, and choose File⇨Delete.

2. Type **C:\WINDOWS\AMIVISD.INI** in the Delete edit box. If your path to Windows is different, type the correct path.

3. Click OK and start Ami Pro.

A new AMIVISD.INI file will automatically be created, and you can now run the Tutorial.

Error message: Cannot Find File PARADOX.NET. Is Share Loaded?

You may see this error message in Ami Pro when you are merging a Paradox file, even though Share is loaded and PARADOX.NET is in the root directory (that is, C:\). The remedy is to make sure that CONFIG.SYS contains the following lines:

```
Files=40 (at least)
Device=C:\Windows\EMM386.EXE
DOS=HIGH,UMB
Install=C:\DOS\SHARE.EXE
```

Loading SHARE.EXE through the CONFIG.SYS file, rather than through the AUTOEXEC.BAT file, is usually better. Whenever you change CONFIG.SYS, you need to reboot the computer after you save the changes. Be sure that 500K of conventional memory is available before you run Microsoft Windows. Exit Windows to the DOS prompt, type **CHKDSK,** and press Enter. The last line that appears on the screen should be XXXXXX bytes free, where XXXXXX is a number greater than (or equal to) 500000. If you don't have enough memory, remove some items from the CONFIG.SYS and AUTOEXEC.BAT files. Locate the PARADOX.NET file that is typically in the root of the hard drive (C:\ for example) and verify that the WIN.INI file contains a [Paradox Engine] section with a line reading NetNamePath=C:\ (or the correct path for the location of PARADOX.NET). If this section or line is missing or incorrect, remedy the situation and save the updated WIN.INI file. Exit and restart Windows. Run Ami Pro and run Merge again.

Error messages: Unable to print this document. Install the correct printer driver and try again and Cannot find printer driver. Formatting for the screen

Ami Pro displays these messages when you use the Windows Generic/Text printer driver to print. Windows applets (including Windows Write and Notepad) issue similar messages and will not print when the Generic/Text printer driver is selected. In order to use this driver, you need to disable Adobe Type Manager by following these steps:

1. From the Program Manager, run the ATM Control Panel.

2. Under ATM, select Off. Exit the ATM Control Panel.

3. Exit Windows and restart it to disable ATM.

Error message: Cannot open file for import/export

This error usually occurs when the user dictionary is located on a network drive and you try to edit it. When you open the file from a network, it is flagged as a Read-only file, and the ASCII filter that opens it doesn't change the file to Read/Write status properly. As a result, changes can't be saved and this error message is generated. To avoid this problem, move the user dictionary to a local drive by following these steps:

1. Exit Ami Pro, go to the Windows Program Manager, choose File⇨Run, and type **AMIPRO.INI.**

2. Go to the [AmiPro] section of the file and locate the line userdictionary=. If you can't find this line, carefully type it into the section. Set the line to your drive and directory. For example, type **USERDICTIONARY=C:\AMIPRO.**

3. Choose File⇨Exit and save the change.

When you start Ami Pro and choose Tools⇨Spell Check⇨Edit Dictionary, you will be able to edit (and save) the User Dictionary. This method creates a new user dictionary. If you want a user dictionary file that already exists, copy the file LTSUSER1.DIC to your drive and subdirectory.

Other Lotus applications, such as 1-2-3 Release 4 or Freelance Graphics, look to the LOTUS.INI file for their user dictionary information. Therefore, if you are running any of these applications, you need to edit the LOTUS.INI file.

Error message: TSNI.EXE caused a floating point stack underflow

This message occurs when the computer's CMOS Setup lists a math coprocessor when no math coprocessor is installed. You need to correct the CMOS setup. See the computer's manual for instructions or consult your dealer.

Error message: Unable to locate compressed file F:\AMIPRO\NODE\31LINFNT.CMZ

This message occurs when you install the Node Program on a network, after which the Node installation terminates. This problem is a bug, and you need a replacement set of 3½-inch disks from Lotus to install the Node Program properly.

You can continue to use 5¼-inch disks to install the Node Program by removing three lines from the SCRIPTN.INS file. However, if you use Ami Pro after installing Node without these three lines, you won't be able to use the LotusLineDraw font that translates line drawing in DisplayWrite files. If you import DisplayWrite files that contain line drawings, use the following method only as a stopgap measure:

1. From the Program Manager, move to the network drive that contains the Ami Pro Node subdirectory (usually drive F:) and select the Ami Pro Node subdirectory (usually \AMIPRO\NODE). Find SCRIPTN.INS.

2. Choose Search⇨ Find. In the Find What edit box type, **31LINFNT.CMZ.**

3. Choose Find Next and then choose Cancel. The complete line should read

```
31linfnt.cmz   <WINDOWS>
```

4. Press Home and then press the up-arrow key on the keyboard to position the insertion point on the line immediately above. This line should read as follows:

```
DECOMP
```

5. Press Shift and the down-arrow key four times to highlight the following three lines:

```
DECOMP
31linfnt.cmz  <WINDOWS>
BUILDFONT
```

6. Delete these three lines, exit, and save the changes.

7. Run the Ami Pro Node program at each computer from which Ami Pro is used. (*Note:* Do not use an ASCII text editor such as DOS Edit that converts tabs to spaces because the SCRIPTN.INS file needs tabs.) In a pinch, you can find both files — 31LINFNT.CMZ and SCRIPT.INS — in the Lotus Word Processing Division's bulletin board at 404-395-7707 or on the Lotus Word Processing forum on CompuServe. Download 301NOD.EXE, which contains both files.

8. To load the files, copy 301NOD.EXE onto a floppy disk and place the disk in floppy drive A: or B:. Double-click on 301NOD.EXE. When the file executes, it extracts the two files 31LINFNT.CMZ and SCRIPT.INS.

9. From the Windows File Manager, copy 31LINFNT.CMZ to the Ami Pro program Disk 3. Copy the file SCRIPT.INS to the Ami Pro program Disk 1.

10. Choose File⇨Exit and close the File Manager. Use the corrected disks to repeat the Node installation.

Error message: Invalid Argument

This message appears when you are saving a new cardfile database that was created by using DATAMAN.SMM if any field name length exceeds 25 characters. Field names cannot be longer than 15 characters because DATAMAN.SMM cannot display more than 15 characters in a field name.

Troubleshooting ATI video boards with Mach 32 video drivers

If you have this driver, find out what version it is by running the Mach 32 Control Panel. From Program Manager, choose File⇨Run. Type **M32PANEL.EXE.** The driver version is indicated at the bottom of the dialog box. *Note:* The ATI Mach 32 video driver is installed on Gateway computers and on other systems that have local bus video.

The ATI Mach 32 video driver has been reported to cause many problems, including making text characters drop out or cut off when printing; decompression errors, general protection faults when changing a frame to *transparent* or when importing a TIFF image, and Not Enough Memory error messages. Color problems include a disappearing cursor when running 32 million colors, changes that don't display when running 64K colors; incorrect screen colors for highlighted text in Ami Pro (menu items have the correct highlight color, but not shaded text), gray shading that does not print, incomplete display of two-column documents with a line between columns, open bullets that print filled with black, reverse type that does not print (even with the `HPLJClipping=1` and `TrueType as graphics` lines properly set), and system lockup when changing from Body Text to Bullet or from Bullet to Bullet1.

You can solve some color problems by switching to 256 colors or by changing the option in the ATI Setup to use a VGA palette, rather than a dithered color. If the screen locks up at 1024 x 768 x 256 when printing in Ami Print, try disabling the Ami Pro Print in Background feature. However, if you encounter these kinds of problems and the computer is manufactured by Gateway, call Gateway (800-248-2031) for an updated driver. Or call ATI (416-882-2626) for information on updated drivers. Alternatively, consider changing to the standard Windows VGA, SVGA, or 8514 driver.

Changing the HP LaserJet printer resolution

If your HP LaserJet printer renders the wrong resolution (75 or 150 dpi, rather than 300) in Ami Pro, you may be dealing with a problem in the Windows WIN.INI section. Follow these steps to correct the printer resolution information in WIN.INI:

1. Start System Engineer and find the WIN.INI file. Locate the `[hppcl,lptx]` for an HP LaserJet IIP or lower or `[hppcl5a,lptx]` for any of the HP LaserJet III level printers section. (*Note: x* indicates the parallel port number; *comx* indicates the serial port number.)

2. In this section, look for a line that reads as follows:

    `prtresfac=x`

    The *x* will be a number such as 0, 1, or 2. If you can't find this line, carefully type a line with a value of 0 for *x*. The line you insert should read as follows:

    `prtresfac=0`

3. Save the change, exit Windows even if the `prtresfac` line already exists in the printer section, and restart Windows.

Troubleshooting WordPerfect 6.0 Error Messages _____

This section describes how to deal with WordPerfect 6.0 error messages.

Setup/start-up error message: Not enough global memory

If you receive the message Not enough global memory when you are launching or working with WordPerfect 6 and you are on a network, the system may be trying to share the same WPCSET.BIF among several users. Try redirecting the files to another directory by using the /PI start-up option. Even if the problem is caused by something else, adding a /PI switch to the command line when you start WordPerfect and then deleting it may help you to work around the problem. You also can try renaming the WPCSET.BIF file or redirecting temporary files to another directory by using the /d-<directory> switch.

The memory message also occurs in cases where drive letters are variable. In other words, the client doesn't know which drive network users are going to use for WordPerfect. One day the drive may be F:, and another day the drive may be W: or X:. In this situation, the message Not Enough Global Memory [OK] displays on start-up, but clicking OK causes the program to execute normally. This is because Windows leapfrogs past the DOS environment variables at launch time and points to the drive for WordPerfect. The client, however, will have to enter the following in the properties for the WPWin 6.0 icon:

```
%DRIVE%:\WPWIN60\WPWIN.EXE /WPC-%DRIVE%:\WPC20
```

Error messages: WPWin Has Caused A GPF In Module DDEML.DLL, and Not Enough Global Memory To Perform The Requested Operation

An incorrect date stamp causes this problem. Receiving either of these error messages indicates that you need to copy the original Microsoft Windows DDEML.DLL (dated 03/13/92) onto your machines. Some companies licensed this file to ship with their own products and changed the date stamp of the file. WordPerfect changed the date stamp of the file to correspond to the Shared Code date (for example, 11/04/91 for English-US WPWin 5.1). The remedy is to copy the original DLL file onto your system. You can find it on WordPerfect 5.X disks. Or direct the public .BIF file to a local drive, start WordPerfect, and redirect the .BIF back to the network drive by using the /NI start-up option.

When you use the /NI option, you are not creating a .BIF file anywhere. The /NI option simply gives WordPerfect for Windows a different reference point. The same principle applies in the command line for the public .BIF file. The command line actually reads /NI=WP.

Troubleshooting WordPerfect 5.2

This section describes problems you may experience in using WordPerfect 5.2.

Display problems with Compaq's QVision

The QVision 7.23A graphics driver that ships with some Compaq computers may cause display problems in Print Preview and Reveal Codes. If you have this driver, upgrade to the QVision 7.25A graphics driver.

FaceLift error with Line Draw

If you are using FaceLift for Windows from Bitstream and a WordPerfect printer driver, characters in the Line Draw dialog box display incorrectly. Line Draw characters also display incorrectly when you edit a document in Draft Mode. (The characters do print correctly.)

The remedy is to insert the following line immediately below the Active= line in the [Typefaces] section of the WIN.INI file:

```
NoSubstVectFonts=1
```

Locate the FaceLift file called CACHEDMP.CCH in the Windows directory and delete it. Exit Windows and then restart it to make the changes take effect.

Close-Up requires updated keyboard driver

If you try to use Close-Up by Norton-Lambert and receive an application error when you launch WordPerfect, you need the updated keyboard driver. If you have a modem, you can download the driver from WordPerfect's Support Bulletin Board Service by dialing 801-225-4414. The BBS communications settings are 2400 bps, no parity, 8 data bits, and 1 stop bit. Download the file CUPKEYBD.DRV and copy it to the \WINDOWS\SYSTEM directory. Or contact Norton-Lambert.

Graphics print too dark

If graphics print too dark when you use a WordPerfect printer driver, add the following line to the WPWP.INI file:

```
[Settings]
WinDither=1
```

The default Windows printer will dither the graphic before the WordPerfect printer driver processes it, causing it to print lighter.

WordPerfect 5.2 doesn't convert Ami Pro 3.0 documents

WordPerfect 5.2 is not yet able to convert Ami Pro 3.0 files. In order to use an Ami Pro 3.0 file, save it to an earlier (Ami Pro 1.x or 2.x) format.

Troubleshooting Superbase

This section describes some of the problems that you may have when you use Superbase.

Dates are replaced by asterisks

In Superbase, the dates printed in a list report are replaced with two asterisks (**) when you import date information from a delimited ASCII file to an unformatted date field. This problem occurs because Professional File recognizes only data (including dates) as text format. If you enter a date format in the date field after importing the data, the format will affect only the new date information. Therefore, you need to put the date format in your form design before you import a delimited ASCII file.

Error message: This identifier isn't defined

This message occurs because Professional File does not calculate across pages. In other words, a formula references fields that are located only on one page.

Error message: Problem Diagnostic Error 364 (through 402)

Diagnostic errors 364 through 402 are all data file errors, and you can usually correct them by recovering your data file. To recover the file, use option 6 on the Main menu, followed by option 4 from the Select File menu.

Error message: Access to this file was denied

Professional File is a file-locking (not a record-locking) database application. As a result, only one person can use or update a file at one time. (However, two people can view or print from the same file at the same time.)

Troubleshooting Paradox

This section covers problems and error messages you may see when using Paradox.

Error message: File \win3_1\ could not be created

If an error message returns a filename like the one in this error message, you have not provided sufficient path information. Check the path and insert a drive name (that is, `C:\WIN3_1`).

Not enough memory

Most memory problems are caused by memory conflicts or device driver problems. Check the video driver. If you still can't load more than a few applications when Paradox is loaded (Paradox seems to take all your resources), or if you have to quit Paradox to load another application or to get another application to work properly, the following tips may help:

■ Load Paradox last.

■ Don't use a floating speedbar. Memory leakage is known to occur there.

■ Declare at least 100 files and don't keep a large SMARTDRV (512 is sufficient).

■ The following system setup is optimal:

For CONFIG.SYS, use `Files= 100` (or more)

For AUTOEXEC.BAT, use `Share /F:2048 /L:400`

If you are running DOS 6 with DoubleSpace and receive out of memory messages, set your files to 130–140.

Appendix C
WUGNET Windows Configuration Library

The following list of shareware and public domain tools represents Volume 1 of a set of six volumes that make up the *WUGNET Windows Configuration Library*. They comprise the following categories of utilities: screen savers, diagnostics, file enhancement utilities, communication, memory/resource, network management/administration, font utilities, disk management, icon/BMP tools, Program Manager add-ons and shells, and multimedia add-ons. To get to the WINUSER FORUM on CompuServe, which also is the online service for members of the Windows Users Group Network, type **GO WINUSER** at any ! prompt.

Unlike other online services, the actual shareware (program) authors and the online staff of the Windows Users Group Network maintain 24-hour support for these files over the CompuServe Information Network WINUSER FORUM. You can always count on the latest versions of these and other titles to be available on the WINUSER FORUM. We also recommend that you get the latest versions of these packages that may contain special offers for readers of *Windows 3.1 Configuration SECRETS*. Volume 1 of *WUGNET Windows Configuration Library* is available on 3 ½-inch disk media for $49.95 + $5.00 S/H. Contact WUGNET at Windows Users Group Network, 126 E. State St., Media, PA 19063. E-mail: CompuServe -76702,1023. Internet:76702.1023@CompuServe.Com. Tel. 215-565-1861. FAX 215-565-7106. Credit cards are accepted.

DF Lite for Windows v1.32

WDF.ZIP (Bytes: 101950)

This small utility makes an image of your 360K, 720K, 1.2MB, or 1.44MB diskette and places it in a file on your hard disk for later restore; makes multiple disk copies or sends a disk over the telephone via modem; restores 5 ¼-inch images to 3 ½-inch diskettes or visa versa; and makes copies of diskettes while doing other work within Windows.

Maintain INI files from the DOS command line

MAINTI.ZIP (Bytes: 15781)

MAINTINI is a small DOS-based program that enables you to modify any kind of
INI files from the DOS command line. It is useful for networks: just place it in the
login script. With the program, you can create new sections, add or modify keys
and values, delete keys and sections, and manage your SYSTEM.INI files
(device=. . . no problem). This program is email-ware.

Win Hex/ASCII Viewer with drag-and-drop

IVU141.ZIP (Bytes: 120192)

InfView 1.41. Windows ASCII/Hex File Viewer has a new drag-and-drop feature.
You can view multiple files of any size in ASCII/Hex/Raw/Text modes! The
COMPARE option lets you determine differences between multiple files in
viewer, and you can now load multiple files at once by using drag-and-drop and
Command line. Other available features are variable line length up to 1K,
formatted printing, Clipboard, disk and network search for files/words/charac-
ters with date and size qualifiers, file ID and execution, font and color selection,
hot keys, search list, bug fixes, and much more!

HEdit v1.2, Hexadecimal editor for binary files

HEDIT.ZIP (Bytes: 68580)

This is a hexadecimal editor for binary files with unlimited file size, drag-and-
drop, binary and text search, selectable fonts, Clipboard support, and multiple
document interface. A File Manager extension for file viewing/editing is included.

FM Applic 1.1c — applications menu for File Manager

FMAPLC.ZIP (Bytes: 142399)

At long last, the utility that Microsoft forgot to put into the File Manager is here!
FM Applic is a File Manager extension that provides you with an applications
menu and integrates virtually any Windows or DOS application with the File
Manager. You simply click the files and then the applications when File Manager starts. It has full WFWG Toolbar support and will "auto!oad" drag-and-drop
applications.

Whiskers for Shareware 3.1

W4S31.ZIP (Bytes: 111860)

WHISKERS IS BACK! Whiskers is the ultimate tool for programming all your mouse buttons, keyboard keys, and mouse button chords. Simply use the right button for the Enter key and the middle button for left double-click. Or be creative and use the 270+ standard Windows actions on the mouse buttons with combinations of Shift, Ctrl, and Alt. MouseTraps let you customize how the mouse and keyboard will work with each application. When unzipping, use the -d switch or turn on the Use directory names check box.

DGi's Tasker for Windows v1.1

TASKER.ZIP (Bytes: 178176)

Tasker is a small but very functional replacement for Task Manager and features drag-and-drop configuration, NeXT style button bar, launch menu with GUI editor, task and file management, clock/alarm and system resource display. Tasker is fully customizable and totally integrated with a complete help system, setup program, and a great 3D user interface.

Nest Groups in Program Manager

NESTGP.ZIP (Bytes: 4125)

NESTGRP.EXE (requires VBRUN300.DLL) is a new Windows program that lets you nest your Program Manager groups to better organize your programs and data.

Windows Commander English v1.12

WCM12E.ZIP (Bytes: 198413)

Windows Commander is the Windows version of Norton Commander for DOS. It has the same features, and the handling is similar to the DOS version. It has integrated unzip and is fast and simple to use. Just try it! This is the English version; a German version is available with the name WCM12D.ZIP.

Windows Commander German v1.12

WCM12D.ZIP (Bytes: 214015)

Windows Commander is the windows version of Norton Commander for DOS. It has the same features, and the handling is similar to the DOS version. It also has integrated unzip and is fast and simple to use. It can be used to replace the Program Manager and is shareware. This is the German version; an English version is available with the name WCM12E.ZIP.

Rosenthal WinLite — Windows 3.1 EXE file compressor

WINLIT.ZIP (Bytes: 241985)

Rosenthal WinLite compresses Windows programs to reduce their size. Programs compressed by Rosenthal WinLite are functionally identical to the originals, only smaller. For example, the 180K Solitaire game that comes with Windows compresses to 77K, or 43 percent. The smaller, more efficient programs save disk space, LAN overhead, and disk caching resources and discourage reverse engineering. The process is totally automatic and requires no additional drivers and no modification to the source code or linking.

WinDrop 1.1 — drag-and-drop launcher with hot keys

WDRP11.EXE (Bytes: 135190)

WinDrop is a drag-and-drop program launcher for Windows in the form of an icon bar. It has system wide hot keys and lots of features, including window position save, Clipboard doubler, clock, reminder, and CD player control, and it can stick to the File Manager. It can be used as full Program Manager replacement. The new version features EXE compilation and remote execution.

P.M. Group Launcher

GLAUNC.ZIP (Bytes: 71890)

The Windows 3.1 Launcher allows access to P.M. groups in a very compact display. The Launcher may be displayed horizontally or vertically, and available groups are selectable from a list, making setup a one-minute deal. The Launcher is for people who like to use Program Manager but don't like switching to the full-screen icon display. It is zipped, using 2.x. DDE. The source code is available by request.

File Watch 1.1b

FWATCH.ZIP (Bytes: 25876)

File Watch periodically scans your hard disk for the file(s) you specify and renames them to the location you choose. It is handy for shareware users who manually move files from a download directory to a more useful location. Stick it in the Startup group, run it minimized, and forget about it. File Watch does not interfere with ongoing downloads. It is fully functional and is uploaded and supported (for registered users) by the author. It requires VBRUN300.DLL.

Configuration Archiver for NDW 3.0

CFGZIP.ZIP (Bytes: 10955)

The NDW 3.0 script maker file (EXE and SM included) maintains a current compressed archive of files necessary to protect or reclaim your Windows and NDW configuration (.INI, .DAT, .BIN, .QAG, .GRP, .MNU, .SET, .BAT, and CONFIG.SYS). It uses SuperFind and NDW's built-in compression module. It keeps the current and most recent preceding configuration archives.

WaitNGo 1.0 — time-out boot launcher

WAITGO.EXE (Bytes: 10644)

Windows Wait and Go lets you run applications during Windows startup after confirmation or time-out. You can even select the application you want to run in Windows from your MS-DOS 6.0 boot menu.

ShowPar 1.1 — shows parameters of programs

SHOPAR.EXE (Bytes: 7956)

ShowPar is a small but useful utility that shows you various parameters that are passed when one application calls another, such as command line, default directory, show mode, and more. It can be used to check out whether you have configured your favorite program launcher correctly. Or you can use it during program development or to find out undocumented interactions between applications.

MySound 1.0 — sound assignment per application

MYSND.EXE (Bytes: 9539)

MySound allows you to replace boring default sounds with your favorite
Windows wave files (*.WAV) on a per application basis. You can also quiet any
overbeeped application.

FmView 1.0 — file contents viewer FM add-on

FVIEW1.EXE (Bytes: 122111)

FmView is a File Manager add-on. It tracks the selection in the File Manager and
displays the contents of the currently selected file. It automatically determines
the file format and selects an appropriate representation (such as .ZIP contents
file listing, WinWord as text, header of .EXE, binary as hex, .BMP as graphics).
Text files can be edited. You can use Incremental search to easily find text, even
in multiple files. It does the following: .TXT, .DOC, .WRI, .WMF, .BMP, .ARJ, .ZIP,
.LZH, .BAT, .COM, .EXE, .DRV, .DLL, 386, .PIF, C, H, .ASM, .ASS, .PAS, RC, .DEF,
.PCX, .OBJ, IC.

FmExtMan 1.0 — File Manager extension manager

FMXMAN.EXE (Bytes: 29824)

FmExtMan is a File Manager add-on. It allows you to add more than the four
add-on DLLs that File Manager limits you to. All top-level menus can be put into
one menu as submenus, so your File Manager menu is not clogged up.
FmExtMan has a dialog box that lets you change, reorder, install, and remove
File Manager extensions. You can quickly park and reinstate add-ons and toggle
between them, whether they show up in the menu bar or in a submenu. The
toolbar is supported.

DlgDrop 1.1 — drop files into edit fields and dial

DLGDRP.EXE (Bytes: 9088)

DlgDrop allows you to drag any file from the Windows File Manager and drop it
into a file dialog box or into any edit field in almost any dialog box. There is no
more unnecessary clicking through the directories in an open file dialog box
that you already see in your File Manager.

YEAH v3.5

YEAH.ZIP (Bytes: 194014)

YEAH is a replacement for the Program Manager. It also has a history and is always on top. It includes a built-in reminder and a startup of programs. It uses only 180K of memory. It drops the GIF/TIF BMP as wallpaper.

Outline Program Manager v1.0

OPM.ZIP (Bytes: 37581)

This little program is not a replacement for Program Manager — it is an enhancement, an alternate way of viewing your groups and launching programs. And it is FREE! It requires VBRUN300.DLL (not included).

Launcher with virtual desktops

LLAUNC (Bytes: 102979)

This is a Windows 3.1 program launcher. It sports a compact size, a virtual screen manager with integrated task switcher, drag and view/print (supply your own viewer), clock/alarm features, and the ability to load Program Manager groups. It is zipped w/2.x. Enjoy!

Easy Macro 2.0

EM20.ZIP (Bytes: 27768)

Easy Macro is a shareware Windows program that allows you to quickly and easily record and play back keystroke macros without leaving your application. Just put the program in your Startup group. Press F7 to begin recording; press F7 again to stop recording; and press F8 to play back your macro.

Directory Master v1.0

DM100.ZIP (Bytes: 149586)

Manage your disks and directories with this powerful, easy-to-use, fully configurable directory utility. It is similar to File Manager but much more user-friendly. You can copy, move, rename, launch applications, create directories, and more.

Too Cool Tool Cube 1.1 — now at 4° Kelvin!

CUBE3.ZIP (Bytes: 190114)

Too Cool Tool Cube now lowers the ambient temperature a few more degrees with improved file and icon browsing and more. TCTC is a program launcher with a difference! It provides multiple faces so that you can organize your tools into groups that make sense to you and still keep your workspace clean. Buttons are provided to rotate the cube to access the desired tool group. It also allows you to change icons for a program, launch uninstalled programs, and exit and restart Windows. It requires VBRUN300.DLL.

Application Timer 2.01

AT201.ZIP (Bytes: 37421)

Application Timer from Wintronix, Inc. is a Windows program that launches applications unattended on a user-definable schedule. It launches DOS or Windows programs. It can launch programs once, every minute, every 15 minutes, hourly, daily, weekly, monthly, and at month end. It can be used to automate operations such as data collection, modem communications, e-mail, long reports, intensive calculations, and so on. It can launch applications in normal, full screen, minimized, and background.

HideIt 1.2

HIDEIT.ZIP (Bytes: 94599)

This instantly makes any program invisible. For example, it makes Solitaire vanish before the boss catches you playing it and keeps prying eyes from seeing sensitive material. It has password protection (and no nags) and requires VBRUN300. It is guaranteed to reduce your productivity.

WinGo — Windows Startup with countdown

WINGO.ZIP (Bytes: 15889)

The WinGo program is a simple utility that starts Windows — or any other program — after a certain number of seconds. WinGo displays a few lines of text along with a countdown timer. When the countdown reaches zero, Windows starts. To abort WinGo, press the Esc key. If you don't want to wait for the countdown to finish, press the Enter key. This has been updated to add a countdown "tick."

WinFast Plus 1.3 — button bar program launcher

WINFST.ZIP (Bytes: 22192)

This allows fast access to applications under Windows and is a complete rewrite of WinFast. It has smaller, faster, and better setup tools and interface than the original. It lets you minimize groups on desktop (with any icon on your system). It is very quick.

DropPop v1.1 — desktop program launcher

DROP11.ZIP (Bytes: 102881)

DropPop works with Dropper (included in ZIP) to allow you to drop files from File Manager into the Windows desktop. Once dropped, the files appear as icons with raised borders. Clicking on the icons runs that program with lots of options available. DropPop extends Dropper to allow the desktop icons to be menus, each containing up to 26 more icons. You can choose any icon for each file, print or launch files, drop applications or documents, and more. Both programs are free!

Dial-It Pro desktop dialer

DIALIT.ZIP (Bytes: 229134)

Dial-It Pro v3.0 (DIALITPR.ZIP) has too many features to list, but some are as follows: it "grabs" and dials telephone numbers directly from text documents and other applications; it keeps a log with date, time, duration, number dialed, and recipient; its timer tells you the duration of the call; it has a memory dialer with 80-number storage; it auto redials on a busy signal; its modem can be disabled without exiting; it recognizes "vanity" numbers; and more. It requires VBRUN300.DLL.

TopGroup for Windows

TOPGRP.ZIP (Bytes: 131854)

TopGroup is a fast, low resources program launcher and alternative Windows shell. With a minimum of clicks, it launches files without navigating Program Manager's groups. TopGroup maintains a clean desktop by displaying a single group, which is always on top — the TopGroup icon. Click the icon to view a pop-up menu and run your programs with launch attributes configured to your preference. TopGroup's icon supports drag-and-drop from the File Manager. It uses online help, the Menu Builder utility, and a system resources monitor. It uses VBRUN300.DLL.

WizManager 1.5 File Manager add-on

WIZMGR.ZIP (Bytes: 351251)

There are many new features with WizManager v1.5 (for example, drag-and-drop to the button bar, set number of buttons displayed on the button bar, and so on). It is now fully compatible with WFW 3.11. WizManager is a great File Manager add-on that appends a powerful color button bar to the File Manager. It also appends a command line box to enter DOS commands, such as COPY and DEL, without leaving the File Manager. It includes many utilities, such as print directory, lock, scripts, customized menus, and so on. Try it!

SnapShot — screen-capture program for Windows

SNAPSH.ZIP (Bytes: 28951)

SnapShot is a screen capture program for Windows that works like a camera. After you load the film, your right mouse button becomes the shutter. You can take pictures of the entire screen, individual windows, or portions of windows. Pictures are transferable through the Clipboard. SnapShot is reviewed in PC/Computing's Guide to Shareware.

QuikDial Pro for Windows

QUIKDL.ZIP (Bytes: 171539)

This is an enhanced version of QuikDial 2.0 and is a low-resources speed-dialer for voice calls using the modem on your PC. With popular features, such as being always on top, minimizing on use, and having hot captions (dialing from the icons), QuikDial Pro also has a professional gray-scale interface with a button bar that displays icons for dialing, a scratch pad, settings and options, abort dialing, help, and exit, and settings for comm port, dial wait, enhanced interface, and more. It also has an alpha speed search facility and its directory accepts nearly 1000 entries. QuikDial uses VBRUN300.DLL.

Toolbar for MS-DOS Prompts

DOSBAR.ZIP (Bytes: 14276)

This adds a toolbar to MS-DOS prompts, facilitates the cut-and-paste feature, and even has a scroll back function! And best of all, it's freeware! It has an optional German language mode for international users.

MCLOCK v1.4

MCLO14.ZIP (Bytes: 47803)

This is an application for the Windows, NT environment (it needs VBRUN300.DLL). It is a clock with a chime pop-up and countdown timer tickler version 1.4. It also comes with a Window's help file. Shift-clicking any part of the pop-up activates the main window. The programmers fixed a bug in the restoration of Windows introduced in the preceding releases. MCLOCK is a Windows clock unlike the others because it's a little smarter and incorporates a chime feature that resurfaces on your desktop every time the chime period is reached.

MTIMER 1.1

MTIMER.ZIP (Bytes: 76969)

This is another Windows, NT application that provides you with a sophisticated timer. It features a large display that is visible from across the room. Each digit of the timer display is directly controllable, which means you have fast and precise control over setting the starting values. MTIMER also has intuitive controls and user-customizable tickler messages.

Enhanced version of VIEWER

MJYVIM.ZIP (Bytes: 12391)

Please see the narrative for MJYVIE.ZIP because this application is the same except for two improvements: the capability to multiselect files with a timer loop that displays each image in turn, and the capability to drag-and-drop the file straight into the image window. This is great for image rescaling, and if you press Alt+Print Screen, the image ends up in the Clipboard and can then be transferred into any other application that handles images.

StartUp v1.1: enhanced Windows startup

START1.ZIP (Bytes: 250177)

StartUp takes on the responsibility of the Window's 3.1 startup group and can manage up to 16 programs that can be started automatically or bypassed by pressing the Return key before a timer expires (60 seconds or less). It automatically recognizes programs in the WIN.INI load and run statements. This version corrects an installation problem and includes some minor fixes. It requires VBRUN300.DLL. It is shareware.

XFile v1.5

XFILE.ZIP (Bytes: 70223)

This multifunctional utility functions in various operating modes. Its file/directory modes include drag-and-drop deletion, attribute alteration, and renaming. It also supports time display, date display, resource gauge/monitor, and free memory monitor. Utilities include multiple alarms, program launcher, file finder, timed program execution, and miscellaneous system information.

NoteWare — the ultimate DOS and Windows notepad

NOTEWR.ZIP (Bytes: 114422)

NoteWare pops up at any time for you to write notes, capture screens, find information in notes, or to view files and directories. Mike Callahan says it is "by far the best TSR notepad I've seen." Run NoteWare as a TSR, as an icon in Windows, or pop it up over any DOS Window. It has a feature-packed editor and is great for screen capture, exporting, calendars, forms, and much more! v3.0A is compatible with SHARE.EXE. This 17K TSR can be loaded into high memory.

ThumbsUp v1.3a — graphics file browser

THUMBS.ZIP (Bytes: 386181)

The latest version of ThumbsUp is a fantastic graphics image and clip art browsing and catalog program that provides extensive viewing, thumbnailing, printing, and file organization. It supports .BMP, .DIB, .RLE, .WMF, .JPG (jfif), .ICO, .TTF, .PCX, .CDR, and .GIF files internally and can use MS graphics import filters to also handle .CGM, .TIF, .DXF, .DRW, .HGL, .EPS and many more. It requires Windows 3.1 and at least 386K. Try it and be amazed!

ThumbsUp v1.3a — graphics browser (description)

THUMBS.TXT/Asc(Bytes: 4321)

This file contains a description of THUMBS.ZIP, the latest version of ThumbsUp (see the preceding entry.)

LZEXP.DLL

LZEXP.ZIP (Bytes: 120292)

LZEXP.DLL is a Windows 3.1 File Manager add-in that allows you to use LZEXPAND.DLL (provided by Microsoft) to uncompress compressed Windows installation files rather than having to shell to DOS and run the DOS program's EXPAND.EXE. Use PKUNZIP.EXE v2.04 to unpack. This software is e-mailware!

Enhanced version of BMPVIEW (VIEWER.EXE)

MJYVIE.ZIP (Bytes: 10583)

This is a simple application that views .BMP, .ICO, .WMF, .DIB, and .RLE files. It needs no VBXs, so the zipped file is only 10K. This is a much better interface than BMPVIEW (my last project). This program gives you the capability to see just the image and has no buttons or caption to crowd your screen. It is a nice preview feature (thumbnail size or icon size). I know there are many programs around like this, but I think this one is worth a look. It needs VBRUN300.DLL, which is not included in a .ZIP file.

Another Button Bar 1.0a

TKBAR.ZIP (Bytes: 52453)

Another Button Bar v1.0a is one more in the heap of icon launchers. This one is ultra simple yet just as useful as the rest. It takes a Windows program group and turns it into a grid of icon buttons that reside on the Windows desktop. And it's freeware! It requires VBRUN300.DLL.

Find-It — the Ultimate DOS/Windows file locator

FINDIT.ZIP (Bytes: 90801)

Find-It v3.62 is the ultimate DOS and Windows file locator because it can find any file marked with any attribute located on any drive in any subdirectory marked with any attribute. After they're found, these files can be copied, moved, deleted, or processed with any compound batch command! It runs in the background (optional) and looks in ARC, ARJ, ZIP, LZH, DWC, PAK, and ZOO files. It also lists the file, date (using Windows date format), time, size, and directory (\parent file if contained in an ARCed file). It can also sort alphabetically to help find duplicates and provides online help.

*STARTUPSWAPPER DELUXE v2.01

SWAP20.ZIP (Bytes: 110911)

STARTUPSWAPPER DELUXE v2.01 changes the Windows startup screen. Each time you run Windows, you can be greeted with a different screen of your own choice or design or use your favorite one everyday. You can replace Microsoft's advertising with corporate logos, family photos, custom designs, and so on. You can also save disk space by using the RLE format as wallpaper. The program includes sample screens, help, and much more. It requires VBRUN200.DLL, Windows 3.1, and VGA or better. Register on CIS (GO SWREG), #1065. The shareware is from CheckBox Software Inc. 4,000+ CIS downloads!

PrintSwitch 2.1 — major update!

PSW21.ZIP (Bytes: 93083)

WinOnline Review said PrintSwitch "should be part of everyone's system." You can change your default Windows printer with just one click! It configures itself for your system and displays all installed printers. It shows the default selection and orientation when minimized; it offers quick access to printer setup; it toggles Windows Print Manager on and off; and it changes Print Manager priority and paper orientation. It requires VBRUN300.DLL, which is not included.

Capture It! v2.0

CAPT20.EXE (Bytes: 310144)

Capture It! v2.0 is one of the most popular screen capturing utilities in Japan. With its easy-to-use interface, it can capture any kind and shape of screen image and transfer it to files, Clipboards, printers, and so on. You can operate it at any time, with hot keys, even while other applications are running. It flexibly creates the prototype of images for other applications. Capture It! will surely improve your performance in the daily use of your computer! The self-extracting Archive/MS-WIN 3.1 is required.

Zip Manager v5.0 — no longer a shell

ZM5.ZIP (Bytes: 348552)

Zip Manager is no longer a shell! Version 5 has its own Windows-based ZMZIP and ZMUNZIP. Zip Manager creates 100 percent compatible 2.04 format ZIP files. Zip Manager works exactly like the Windows File Manager except that only Zip Manager offers you the switches available in PKZIP. It is a complete drag-and-drop server. ZMZIP'S speed and compression ratios will amaze you! This is a MUST HAVE program, the BEST archive management program!

K-Free v5.10 from Dragon's Eye software

KF510.ZIP (Bytes: 200220)

This is the latest release of the BEST free space monitoring application for Microsoft Windows. It keeps track of memory, disk space, and resources, has user-customizable alarms for those areas, and displays the time and date. K-Free has been reviewed in *PCWorld, Computer Shopper,* and *PC Magazine*. K-Free was featured in the High Five section of the March Nautilus CD. Try it today!

TrashMan 2.0a — a trash can for Windows 3.1

TRASHM.ZIP (Bytes: 63502)

This is the *Shareware Magazine* Editor's Choice award winner! TrashMan, the original and BEST drag-and-drop trash can for Windows 3.1, is back and better than ever. Simply drag your files or directories to TrashMan, and they'll be stored in the "trash" until you decide to restore or delete them. Choose from ten different sets of trash icons (including a recycling logo). You can associate WAV sound effects with different events. There is an easy to use toolbar and dozens of new improvements. The shareware is from CheckBox Software.

TOILET 1.1a — a drag-and-drop icon like Mac Trash

TOILET.ZIP (Bytes: 34241)

This is a drag-and-drop TOILET icon into which you can drag files from the File Manager application to be deleted. Files dropped into the TOILET icon are placed in a hidden directory, \DELETED.SYS, on the same drive. When the toilet is "flushed," all the files in \DELETED.SYS are purged from the drive. Files in the \DELETED.SYS directory may be undeleted before flushing. As an extra added bonus, the icons and sounds associated with dropping and flushing can be customized, as well as the window caption and DELETE.

WinShred 1.1

WSH11.ZIP (Bytes: 57626)

This is a quick way to delete files by drag-and-drop when you use the File Manager. WinShred simulates a paper shredder with sound and animation. It has settings for confirmation, on top, run as icon, screen position, and sound. It Requires VBRUN300.DLL, which is not included.

PAPERMAN — drag-and-drop wallpaper and image compressor

PAPR12.ZIP (Bytes: 100096)

PAPERMAN 1.2 is a drag-and-drop wallpaper utility that does more than change wallpaper. It also batch compresses .BMP files into .GIF, .JPG, or compressed .TIF files; it serves as a drag-and-drop image viewer for .BMP, .GIF, .TIF, .PCX, or .IPG mages; it quickly loads .BMP, .GIF, .TIF, .PCX, .TGA, and .JPG images as wallpaper; and it autocompresses wallpaper and Clipboard bitmaps into .GIF, .JPG, or COMP.TIF. The program saves time and disk space.

Visual Diff for Microsoft Windows

VDIFF.ZIP (Bytes: 358686)

Visual Diff for Microsoft Windows is a useful utility to compare two text files visually. Differences are shown in different colors (Deleted=red, Inserted=green, and Changed=blue). The two compared files are shown in two synchronized windows. File size is limited only by virtual memory. Lines may be up to 32K wide. An easy setup procedure provides fast installation.

Win Launch

WLAUNC.ZIP (Bytes: 52386)

Win Launch is no ordinary launch bar. It gives you the power to take control of your desktop away from Windows. It has an application database so that you can control startup position and size of you applications. It lets you control where the icon parking lot is and how it is filled. It lets you confine default startup applications. It does all that any other launch bar does plus more. It also has a selectable clock/date display and a selectable continuous resource monitor.

Win GDI — a GDI monitor

WINGDI.ZIP (Bytes: 19163)

Win GDI v1.2, with a minor bug fix, is uploaded by the author and requires Windows 3.1 or later. It is FREE! Win GDI gives a detailed listing of current GDI resources. The update speed can be adjusted. The GDI heap values can be marked at any time so that you can watch them change. Use it to check if other applications release all their resources because many do not.

WinCover Pix — additional WinCover bitmaps

WCVPIX.ZIP (Bytes: 185721)

WinCover includes 29 bitmap images in .BMP format for use with WinCover.

WinCover 3.1d

WCV31D.ZIP (Bytes: 260445)

Shareware Magazine said, "You should definitely have a look at WinCover." It prints great-looking fax cover sheets to your printer or fax modem. It maintains receiver and sender databases and history logs; it offers full support for bitmaps (non-PostScript required), full font support, drag-and-drop, WYSIWYG page setup, context sensitive help, and direct support for WinFax Pro 3.0. It is great for memos via your fax modem. It requires VBRUN300.DLL, which is not included.

INS & OUTS

INOUT1.ZIP (Bytes: 69348)

INS & OUTS is a collection of Windows enhancers. The enhancers bring life to the mundane, routine tasks in Windows, such as opening, closing, minimizing, and so on. This is the full working version of the first release of INS & OUTS. After you experience INS & OUTS, you will not be able to use Windows without it.

Win Groups — Program Manager group reader

GROUP.ZIP (Bytes: 18499)

Win Groups v1.1 and requires Windows 3.1 or later. It is FREE and has a minor bug fix. Win Groups is a utility that reads the Program Manager groups. It displays them alphabetically on small push buttons. When pushed, the groups items are shown and launched. Win Groups is attractively styled with minimal resources required and extreme ease of use.

ClipPrint Clipboard print/save utility

CLPRNT.ZIP (Bytes: 9793)

This utility allows you to print whatever is on the Windows Clipboard without having to open Notepad or Paintbrush. Graphics printing is done with a WYSIWYG display. It also saves Clipboard contents in the .TXT or .BMP format. It is handy to use as a screen capture/print utility. Requires VBRUN300.DLL.

SmilerShell 1.4 — Windows command line utility

SMI14.EXE (Bytes: 85539)

SmilerShell is the ultimate Windows command line. Unlike Program Manager's RUN command, it runs anything (DOS programs, Windows programs, DOS internal commands) and supports redirection. It has a built-in command line editor with history, search, cut/paste; aliases (type in or on Fn keys), and fast directory change (like Norton Chg Dir) across multiple drives. You can toggle between the current directory and the clock in the title bar. It has Windows memory/resources in the menu and much more. You need a Windows-hosted installer. It is ASP shareware. It also has a self-extracting archive. It is really nice to have. Register online with GO SWREG #1186.

sTOP tHAT! — a Windows keyboard enhancement

STOPTH.ZIP (Bytes: 53333)

sTOP tHAT is a Windows keyboard utility that allows the PC Caps Lock to behave in the same way as a typewriter. The PC Shift keys reverse the state of the Caps Lock, so that if the Caps Lock is on and you press the Shift key, yOUR TEXT WILL LOOK LIKE THIS. sTOP tHAT allows the Shift key to behave as it does on an IBM typewriter: A Shift key guarantees an uppercase character.

Findem v1.02

FINDEM.ZIP (Bytes: 93906)

Have you ever looked for files on your maze of drives and directories and not been able to find them? Findem is a Windows utility that searches your system for files that match the filename (including wild cards) that you enter. It lists all the locations of files that match the specs and outputs them to a window that you can cut to the Clipboard. It searches one or all your drives.

Win Change v2.2

WCHG22.ZIP (Bytes: 125099)

Win Change provides the ability to globally change text in .GRP, .INI, .PIF, and other file types. You can specify multiple change criteria and work across multiple drives, including network drives, and provide "back out" files in case a change goes awry. The new features include the capability to find files containing text strings and to find file types across multiple drives.

SuperBar 2.0 — add a toolbar to any Windows application

SPRBAR.ZIP (Bytes: 187775)

SuperBar is a program for creating user configurable toolbars. A toolbar contains a series of buttons, each assigned to an application's menu command or recorded macro. A toolbar can be added to any Windows application. SuperBar can be used to increase efficiency by placing commonly used menu commands or macros on a toolbar. SuperBar supports user-defined text and user-drawn icons for each button.

Windows Instant File Access 2.00

IFA200.ZIP (Bytes: 183272)

This utility has instant recall of files and directories and floating file lists of frequently used files and directories for each application. You can find files and text within files. It also has the capability to rename files and directories and to delete and create from within any application. This is a MUST HAVE utility.

FontSpec Pro v5.1 — font manager

FSP510.ZIP (Bytes: 213143)

FontSpec Pro is the ULTIMATE TrueType viewer/printer/installer. Easy access from other Windows applications makes using FontSpec a breeze. You can view all your fonts from 8 to 999 points and print professional-quality specimen sheets in single-column, two-column, or full sheets. You can preview and install fonts, manage them in font groups, and compare multiple fonts side by side. You can control just about everything. There are over 3500 copies distributed.

File Notes 1.0 — File Manager extension

FILNOT.ZIP (Bytes: 54103)

File Notes allows you to create and attach descriptive notes to files within File Manager. These notes are created and viewed from File Manager by using a new menu automatically added to File Manager. You can include an author, subject, and a lengthy comment in each note. You can access notes from common open and save as dialog boxes. File Notes includes a powerful search function for finding notes.

ExitWin 1.0

EXW10.ZIP (Bytes: 71220)

This is a very unusual, elegant, and functional exit to DOS utility with password protection. ExitWin places a free-floating EXIT sign on your desktop. It may be moved and locked in position by the user. It is configurable for Exit and Re-Start or Exit Only. It is always on top, and you use single-or double-click to exit, which requires confirmation. It uses .WAV file sound effects. ExitWin requires VBRUN300.DLL.

Mouse Odometer v2.0 by Toggle Booleans

ODOM20.ZIP (Bytes: 26649)

Two hundred miles and still clicking! What a mouse! Measure your mouse mileage with the original Mouse Odometer from Toggle Booleans. Version 2.0 now keeps track of different types of clicks and how many keystrokes your keyboard suffers and provides daily averages.

VidSwitch 1.4a

VSW14A.ZIP (Bytes: 51613)

If you frequently change your video resolution, you need VidSwitch. VidSwitch learns the settings for your various drivers and allows a quick change from one resolution to another. It is much simpler and quicker to use than using Windows setup. Requires VBRUN300.DLL. This version fixes the S3 chip problem.

SOLDIER BACKUP

SOLD.ZIP (Bytes: 19292)

Soldier Backup for Windows is very easy yet very powerful. After you've set up a script, Soldier Backup backs up only those files that have been modified. It comes complete with context-sensitive help and a brief tutorial and is better than anything else on the market.

ARCHIVER for Windows v3.1

AWIN.EXE (Bytes: 681193)

Version 3.1 of ARCHIVER is the easiest to use archive management shell available anywhere! It is simple to use with its point-and-shoot and drag-and-drop control screen and its "Smart File" system and user created syntax. It has arch/unarch, view/print, info, convert, self-extract, and more. It also has Auto VirusScan, program launch pad, file finder, auto directory create, full online help, and many significant new features. It supports .ZIP, .LHA, .ARJ, ARC-E, .ZOO, SCAN, VIRx, and Norton AV.

WinZip 5.0 — with built-in ZIP and UNZIP and drag-and-drop

WINZIP.ZIP (Bytes: 193281)

WinZip 5.0 is a Windows ZIP utility with built-in PKZIP. It is compatible with ZIP and UNZIP and brings the convenience of Windows to zipping. It features the drag-and-drop interface. It supports .ARJ, .LHA, and .ARC files plus most virus scanners. *CompuServe Magazine* (October, l993) calls it a "Top 10" Windows utility; *Inside Microsoft Windows* (August, l992) calls it a "hot product"; and *PC Computing* (March, l992) calls it the "Windows application of the month."

SnagIt 2.1 — a Windows screen-capture and print utility

SNAG21.EXE (Bytes: 111786)

SnagIt 2.1 is a full-featured utility that supports all Windows video modes and rastering printers. It is simple and easy to use and fully supports DDE (Dynamic Data Exchange) for integration with other applications. It has Windows .BMP and .TIF file output and printer and Clipboard output. It uses image scaling and color inverse.

RipBAR v4.2 — applications toolbar for Windows

RIPBAR.ZIP (Bytes: 182573)

RipBAR v4.2 is an applications-launching toolbar for Windows, where programs are just a click away. It displays memory and time/date information. It tracks applications' use of resources and memory and supports drag-and-drop and command-line launching. It includes the Exit tool, Run tool, Post-it style notes, application groups, hot key support, memory display as a gauge, and a built-in Task Manager. The bar is completely resizable. The new version includes the Print tool and support for documents on the bar.

Quick Screen Saver Switch

QSWTCH.EXE (Bytes: 79277)

This switch is a quick means of turning your screen saver on and off without going through the Control Panel and Desktop. Version 1.3 offers a choice of session or permanent (WIN.INI) switch. It is self-extracting to SWITCH.EXE.

just BUTTONS 1.01S

JB101S.ZIP (Bytes: 1359719)

just BUTTONS is a highly configurable general utility that uses panels of programmable buttons. Its functions include command line, memo, Control Panel applet, WinFile, and Talking Time. Dozens of other functions are available. Features include a toolbar, status line, drag-and-drop, scheduler, and embedding catalog. Buttons may have icons and/or text on their faces, passwords, process dropped files, annotations, and much more.

Handy Clock

HCLOCK.ZIP (Bytes: 78085)

Handy Clock is a resizable digital clock with four different typefaces suitable for various sizes of Handy Clock's window. It has the unique feature of never being an obstruction on the Windows Desktop because it moves out of the way on contact with the mouse cursor. Handy Clock has a 50-alarm setting capability, allows multiple time and date formats, and is configurable in various other ways.

WHAT I DID

WHATID.ZIP (Bytes: 486560)

This feature is a "safe" Windows 3.1 logger of each user's keystrokes and mouse clicks. Companies use this feature to record the utilization of the PC and the productivity of workers who are doing heavy data entry in Windows. All monitoring is unknown to the worker. Files are in Paradox format. You can create your own reports or use the two crystal reports included. Each window name and application name is stored along with the time, the mouse clicks, and the keystrokes. It is for multiusers and is network ready. It takes 50K and buffers I/O globally.

Time Log 1.5 for Windows (update)

TIMLOG.EXE (Bytes: 91146)

Time Log allows you to log, total, and print dates and the amount of time spent on any number of projects or dates. It is very user configurable. Features include a timer, audible alarm, and commandline options. It has pop-up, stay-on-top, and hide-icon capabilities and is fully functional. It comes with complete documentation and support. It requires Windows and VBRUN300.DLL.

RipSPACE v2.1 — disk analyzer for Windows

RIPSPA.ZIP (Bytes: 120749)

RipSPACE v2.1 is a disk space analyzer for Windows. It investigates disks and reports on the space used by directories. Reports can be printed, saved to disk, and customized in a number of useful ways. The new version supports better printing options, saves reports, and deals properly with shared volumes. It may also search a path instead of an entire disk.

Task Killer v1.2

KILL12.ZIP (Bytes: 117019)

Task Killer lists modules (EXEs and DLLs) in memory and terminates them or decrements their usage counts. It saves, prints, and compares module lists and finds from where DLLs or EXEs were executed. It has a 3-D MDI interface with the toolbar and online help. It is indispensable for programmers, network administrators, technical support, and power users. It helps you find out what's really going on in your system! Version 1.2 adds report options.

IcoShow v1.20 — Windows 3.1 icon manager

ICOSHO.ZIP (Bytes: 120041)

IcoShow for Windows 3.1 manages up to 16,384 icons within over 100 windows (directories) from icon files and libraries (EXE/DLL, NIL/ICL). It prints, copies, and moves icons (or all icons selected from a window), installs them into Program Manager, renames or edits icons one by one, and writes them to libraries (with more than 2700 icons in one library). IcoShow gives you full online help. New options have been added to this version.

People Savers 1.1 — religious screen savers

PSAVER.ZIP (Bytes: 59244)

People Savers are screen savers with a higher purpose: to provide a spiritual uplift to people. The Verse screen saver fades in Bible verses. The Cross screen saver shows a cross in varying colors and backgrounds. The Cross2 saver switches between a positive and negative cross image. The programs have password protection. You also need VBRUN300.DLL.

TrueType Garamond font

GARAMO.ZIP (Bytes: 33705)

This is a TrueType version of a Garamond font converted from the original Adobe Type 1 font.

Yet Another Clipboard Collector (YACC) for Windows

YACC.ZIP (Bytes: 27787)

Yet Another Clipboard Collector (YACC) is a Windows shareware utility that remembers the text that you copy or cut to the Windows Clipboard each time you copy or cut. YACC stores the text in a list box in the upper half of its window. When you click a selection in the list box, YACC displays the text in a more readable manner in the text box in the lower half of its window. YACC must be running for it to remember your text copies and cuts.

WallMan

WALMAN.ZIP (Bytes: 45556)

Look for upcoming articles in your favorite magazine on this product! Wallman is a great wallpaper manager for people who like to keep their wallpaper in directories other than the Windows directory. It locates the selected .BMP in other directories to use as wallpaper on Windows startup, thus eliminating the need to keep all those .BMPs in the Windows directory. Wallman can change your existing wallpaper, run a wallpaper show, or use the Preview feature to view your selections. This file requires VBRUN300.DLL.

Cool-Cool-Can v1.0 — the Windows Desktop Organizer

CCCAND.ZIP (Bytes: 354014)

Cool-Cool-Can is the Windows Desktop Organizer that helps you manage all your programs, program groups, and .ZIP files with a drag-and-drop interface. It features easy user interface, full drag-and-drop support, multiple graphics viewers (.BMP, .GIF, .PCX, .WPG, .ICO, and so on), built-in .ZIP support, quick access to applications, and smart buttons to instantly locate the file you need.

Stuffit by David Warren

STUFFT.ZIP (Bytes: 15502)

Stuffit is a Program Manager enhancement tool that launches applications and sends initial keystrokes. It is easier on your resources than Recorder macros. It is great for repetitive chores, such as starting WinChat and calling a coworker at the same time. It requires VBRUN200.DLL.

OutSide! by David Warren

OUTSID.ZIP (Bytes: 14421)

OutSide! is the perfect solution for those pesky DOS applications that misbehave in a Windows DOS session. You can launch a program from Windows but have it run "outside" of Windows with the full resources of the computer and return automatically to Windows when completed. It is ideal for high-resolution DOS games and sound applications that are less than ideal in a DOS box. It is the only safe way to launch CHKDSK/f from Windows and is great for other utilities as well. It requires VBRUN200.DLL.

MemWatch by David Warren

MEMWCH.ZIP (Bytes: 8804)

MemWatch is a little utility that displays available resources, the number of tasks running, and the net change up or down in system memory in real time, as programs run. It was originally written as a programming and debugging tool, but it is now a big help to anyone who is interested in how Windows uses memory or who wants to optimize his or her system. It requires VBRUN200.DLL.

David Warren's Utility Collection

DWUTIL.ZIP (Bytes: 113103)

By popular demand, this compressed file contains all of David Warren's utilities available separately elsewhere, including the following: NetSync, NetNews, DosSpooler, Logger, Kicker, NFC, COE, Stuffit, OutSide, and MemWatch. For full descriptions, see the individual listings in this library.

Chain of Events (COE)

COE.ZIP (Bytes: 6954)

You can use COE to hook all the other utilities together. It is a rather simple batch processor (runs programs only) but has an option to wait for each batch to complete before going on to the next one. It can also load but defer processing until a specific time. Together with Kicker and Stuffit, it offers some pretty surprising capabilities. It requires VBRUN200.DLL.

WinZip 5.0 — with built-in ZIP and UNZIP (beta)

WZBETA.ZIP (Bytes: 209222)

WinZip 5.0 is a beta test version; use with caution. (The latest production version is WinZip 4.1a, available as WINZIP.ZIP.) The preliminary beta test version includes built-in ZIP (in addition to the built-in unzipping in earlier versions) so that PKZIP is not needed for basic operations. Also new is the support for Windows-based virus scanners. All features in earlier versions (full drag-and-drop support, optional .ARC, .ARJ, and .LHA support, and so on) work in this version.

file updater

UPDT16.ZIP (Bytes: 11270)

This keeps the newest version of your data (and other) files always with you and on all computers you work on. The program compares the contents of selected directories (usually on floppy disks and the hard drive) and updates matching filenames by copying the newer one over the older one. You also have the option to copy nonduplicate files from one directory to the other. Selected directories and options can be saved to hard disk and retrieved again next time. It requires VBRUN300.DLL, which is not included.

Enhanced DOS for Windows (EDOS) — shareware v3.65-H

EDOS36.EXE (Bytes: 221394)

PC World Magazine calls this the "top Windows utility" (December, 1993, pp. 255, 263). It requires 386 enhanced mode. It runs text mode DOS applications up to 736K. It changes .PIF settings and titles or starts Windows applications from the DOS command line. Its features include Clipboard append/print/display, file drag-and-drop, special background task support, smart exiting with Alt+F4, and much more. You can load CONFIG.SYS device drivers in Windows or DOS virtual machines (in the registered version). It also disables dangerous commands. Jerry Pournelle of *Byte Magazine* (January, 1993) says to "be aware that EDOS does things Microsoft doesn't believe possible."

Plasma Clouds — screen saver for MS-Windows 3.1

PLASMA.ZIP (Bytes: 23808)

The Plasma Clouds screen saver creates some fantastic images on the screen of your computer. It uses color cycling over a randomly generated fractal image. Just copy the PLASMA.SCR file into your \WINDOWS directory and select Plasma Clouds in the Desktop dialog box of the Control Panel. This screen saver supports both Novell and MS Windows passwords. A 256 color video driver is required.

Crazy Balls screen saver for MS-Windows 3.1

BALL.ZIP (Bytes: 26112)

The Crazy Balls screen saver takes you into the amazing world of balls. Just copy BALL.SCR into your \WINDOWS directory and select Crazy Balls in the Desktop dialog box of the Control Panel. This screen saver supports both MS Windows and Novell passwords.

LaunchPad v1.01

LNCHPD.ZIP (Bytes: 57228)

LaunchPad is a task switcher, application launcher, and document manager for Windows 3.1. It has a user-configurable pop-up menu that can be accessed from anywhere in Windows and to which you can assign lists of commonly used applications and documents. Registration gets you free updates from CompuServe and support via CompuServe and paper mail.

Martinsen's Software PackIt! 1.11.04

PKT111.ZIP (Bytes: 86630)

This updated version fixes several bugs from previous versions. PackIt! is a powerful Windows front-end to Microsoft's Compress & Expand. Features include drag-and-drop from File Manager, internal drag-and-drop, fast Compression and expansion within Windows (without DOS Windows), and much more. This program is a MUST for any programmer. It requires VBRUN300.DLL and COMPRESS.EXE.

Martinsen's Software INI Manager 2.00.03

INIMAN.ZIP (Bytes: 73754)

This version fixes a problem with the command line feature that resulted in unexpected behavior.

WiDE — dialog box extenders v1.44

WDE144.ZIP (Bytes: 121904)

This facility adds file management buttons to File⇨Open and File⇨Save dialog boxes throughout Windows. It also applies that great 3-D sculpted look to most dialog boxes.

Program Manager minimizer v1.1

PMIN11.ZIP (Bytes: 35061)

This program minimizes the Program Manager and then runs your application. This program allows you to selectively minimize Program Manager as opposed to the Minimize On Use option. Version 1.1 now allows associated files to be run in addition to the standard executable files. It requires VBRUN300.DLL.

Focus Follower

FFLW10.ZIP (Bytes: 6400)

This little gadget makes whichever window is under your mouse pointer have the focus without coming to the front.

BackDesk Desktop Extenders v2.41

DESK24.ZIP (Bytes: 164413)

This file contains our very popular BigDesk virtual desktop (the original), which gives you up to 8 x 8 virtual screens that you can view through your physical screen and its companion BackMenu, the configurable pop-up cascading root menu that you configure with simple text files. Together, they form a simple and unbeatable way of using Windows without the Program Manager and (together with WiDE) without the File Manager. It also includes a DOS launcher for Windows programs.

WinMenu for single workstations

WMENU3.ZIP (Bytes: 92601)

WinMenu is a menu program for Windows 3.1 or above designed to help smooth the transition to the Windows environment by providing the functionality of a conventional menu. It is very easy to use and helps users gain confidence and control. The menu holds up to 1600 items. The mouse is optional. It is powerful enough to replace the Program Manager. It has a 20-day evaluation period. It has a great look and is loaded with functionality. It is written in C language and is a must see!

Martinsen's Software Beyond Windows Exit (BWE) 1.50.11

BWE.ZIP (Bytes: 26761)

This is a simple utility to provide a quick and easy way to exit windows and more. It is quite handy and includes the following features: you can exit Windows to the DOS prompt; you can restart Windows; you can drag-and-drop a program to BWE; the path and filename are automatically added to the Program Name text box; and you can exit, run the designated DOS program with indicated arguments, and then automatically restart Windows and reboot. This file requires VBRUN300.DLL.

BmpView — a bitmap viewer with some nice features

BMPVW.ZIP (Bytes: 86715)

This is a simple bitmap viewer that displays an image that hugs the forms client area with no title bar or control buttons to crowd your work space (it uses a right mouse toggle). The image can be resized instantly by resizing the form. Its features include an aspect ratio switch and an always-on-top switch. It saves the file's name, size, and place within your workspace after you exit the viewer so that the application can be placed in the startup group. It is able to grab, drag, and drop the whole image for easy placement. It runs in Windows 3.1 only and requires VBRUN300.DLL.

Draggin' Viewer v1.20S

DRAGGN.EXE (Bytes: 16566)

Draggin' Viewer (DV) is a drag-and-drop text and .PIF file viewer utility for Windows 3.1 or later. (Sorry, this application does not work with Windows 3.0 or earlier.) DV appears as an icon on the Desktop. First select one or more text, Windows Write, or .PIF filenames in the Windows File Manager. Then drag the names to the DV icon, and the files will be opened for viewing or editing in the Windows Notepad, Write, or the .PIF Editor, depending on the size and extension. This release adds the capability to launch the Windows File Manager at the same time.

Desktop Editor

DESKTO.ZIP (Bytes: 72385)

Desktop Editor is a Notepad replacement that allows you to open files of any length. It is easy to use, fun to explore, and, best of all, free.

DROPVIEW2 — a drag-and-drop multipage utility by SJHDesign

DROPV2.ZIP (Bytes: 131712)

DROPVIEW 2.01 is here! It is a drag-and-drop image editor that drags multiple .BMP, .GIF, .PCX, .TIF, .EPS, and JPEG files from the File Manager for viewing and editing. It supports all VESA true color video cards. You can cut, paste, merge, gray scale, dither, zoom, crop, scale, or load ANY image as wallpaper in one command. It has fast loading and handling of 24-bit images.

Catman 3.1 for Windows — a dedicated disk database

CAT31.ZIP (Bytes: 121387)

Catman is a dedicated database program to help you keep track of files stored on your floppy disks and is capable of scanning inside archives on these disks. Catman keeps track of the amount of free space available on each disk to help you make more efficient use of the disks. Catman can be used to find files on your hard disk even when they are inside archives, and it can help track down large files that take up space on your hard disk. Catman launches files and acts as a drag-and-drop server for nonarchived files on your hard drive.

WinBoot 1.0d — a Windows multireboot program

WBT1D!.ZIP (Bytes: 166321)

WinBoot is a multireboot program for Windows 3.1 with an updated program setup. It creates multiple AUTOEXEC.BAT and CONFIG.SYS files by using a unique editing screen and saves them to easy-to-use setup buttons. It has context-sensitive help and is fully compatible with all disk compression and caching programs. It requires VBRUN300.DLL.

App add-on giving selectable working directories

STAPP.ZIP (Bytes: 23946)

This is a front-end application for WinWord, Ami Pro, Excel, and so on, which allows you to set up an icon that you can select for the working directory you want to use at runtime.

WINMAP — a memory map for Windows

WMAP#.EXE (Bytes: 17922)

WinMap lists all the programs, DLLs, fonts, drivers, VBXs, and so on that are currently loaded. WinMap tells the user how much memory each of the loaded programs requires. WinMap is careware: You don't have to pay anything to the author for using it.

Win List — a list launcher

WLIST.ZIP (Bytes: 20633)

Win List is a utility that lets you drag-and-drop applications or associated files to it. You can then assign long descriptive names to the application. Double-click to run it. It is compact and easy to use.

Folders 4.0a — adds subgroups to Program Manager

FOLDER.ZIP (Bytes: 160835)

This new version of folders gives you the capability to create the equivalent of subgroups within Program Manager. You can organize your programs and data files by using groups and folders. Features include the capability to create folders within groups or folders, password protection, extensive drag-and-drop capability, the capability to launch multiple programs, the capability to display folders using icons, text, or buttons, and much more.

FileClip 4.0 for Windows

FILECL.ZIP (Bytes: 174738)

This is a powerful file and Clipboard manager that is ideal for both the novice and the power user. It has full drag-and-drop capability with a "trash can," printer, and floppy icons. It can also sort directories and filter or highlight filenames with color by type, size, age, and so on. The Clipboard stack maintains up to the last 100 cut/copies including graphics and allows almost unlimited undo capability. It supports the viewing of text and binary files, and the registered version also supports the viewing of graphics files.

Win GDI — GDI monitor

WGDI.ZIP (Bytes: 19093)

Win GDI gives a detailed listing of current GDI resources. The update speed can be adjusted. The GDI heap values can be marked at any time to watch for change. Use it to check whether applications release all there resources because many do not.

WinBoot 1.0 — a Windows multireboot program

WBOOT.ZIP (Bytes: 204859)

WinBoot v1.0c is an updated multireboot program. It creates multiple AUTOEXEC.BAT and CONFIG.SYS files by using a unique editing screen and saves them to easy-to-use setup buttons. It has context-sensitive help and is fully compatible with all disk-compression and caching programs. It requires VBRUN300.DLL.

Second Copy 4.01

SCP401.ZIP (Bytes: 138479)

This is the latest version of Second Copy, a shareware program that automatically copies important files for safekeeping. It periodically monitors your disk directories and makes a second copy of those files to another disk or network drive. It automatically updates these second copies when you make changes or additions to your original files. It works in the background. All you have to do is set it up once and forget about it because your important files will be saved twice. It works with any LAN drives and has a new 3-D capability. It needs PKZIP 2.x.

File-deletion security for Windows 3.x

GC0993.ZIP (Bytes: 94976)

This is a file-deletion program that is guaranteed to make any deleted file completely unrecoverable so that no form of disk scanner program can bring back the deleted data. You'll never have to worry again that someone is looking through your sensitive data.

Private Cryptographer

ENCRYP.ZIP (Bytes: 182483)

Protect your privacy! Private Cryptographer encrypts and decrypts files and Clipboard text. You can encrypt messages before sending e-mail. It is Incredibly easy to use with strong security. It requires VBRUN300.DLL. Version 1.14 adds a 7-bit ASCII option.

File DeDuplicator

DUPE14.ZIP (Bytes: 104877)

This searches across a disk or part of a disk or network for duplicate files. It finds duplicates by name, size, or contents. It can print reports and files and delete unwanted files.

ScreenSave Random Loader

SCRSAV.ZIP (Bytes: 1390)

SCR-ON.WBT is a Winbatch batch file that randomly selects one of your screen save scripts and loads it; SCR-OFF.WBT is a batch file that turns off your screen saver. Put SCR-ON.WBT in your startup group, and it will randomly load a new screen saver each time you start your Windows session. SCR-OFF.WBT can be used with a scheduler program to turn off your screen saver if it interferes with some other scheduled operation.

DisplayTest 1.5 — a display driver tester

DRVTST.ZIP (Bytes: 93249)

DisplayTest shows essential information about the display driver in use by Windows. The driver's filename and technology version are shown, along with the screen resolution and number of colors supported. It exercises the most common problems we have seen with display drivers. DisplayTest can also show a list of all modules loaded in Windows, along with their size, date, time, and pathname. The list can be sorted five different ways.

DOSFON 1.0 — fonts for DOS applications in a window

DOSFUN.ZIP (Bytes: 125570)

DOSFON 1.0 is a collection of fonts designed to improve the readability of DOS applications running in a window on Windows 3.0 or 3.1. Some Windows applications that like fixed width characters can also benefit by DOSFON.

Windows UnArchive v2.22

WUNA22.ZIP (Bytes: 147050)

Windows UnArchive v2.22 is an unzipper and unarchiver for Windows that doesn't need a DOS application to do the real work. It is easy to use and affordable. It has many features, including a "try out" feature for trying downloads, and the ability to read or run programs within archives. This release fixes the empty directory bug with PKZIP 2.04G and makes some speed improvements and some minor cosmetic changes.

Windows MS-DOS6 multiboot utility

WIN6UT.ZIP (Bytes: 10147)

Win6util allows you to use DOS 6's multiboot options with Windows.

Stroker for Windows

STROKE.ZIP (Bytes: 209533)

Stroker for Windows automates keystrokes into any Windows application. It differs from other similar programs because it has a timing option (delay in seconds) between keystrokes. It is great for automating applications, demonstrators, and training programs.

Note It — the Windows note taker

NOTE.EXE (Bytes: 28312)

Note It v1.7 is a simple little program which pops up on-screen to take notes. You enter the note, and it is saved in an ASCII file suitable for later importation into a database. It is perfect for those who can't remember what they did yesterday, much less last month. It is great as a personal electronic diary. It requires VBRUN300.DLL.

Byzans Task Manager

BTM-09.ZIP (Bytes: 90771)

The Byzans Task Manager (BTM) is a replacement task manager for MS Windows 3.1. BTM combines the functionality of the Windows Task List and Program Manager. Although BTM can theoretically be used as a Windows shell in place of the Program Manager, it is meant to complement and not replace the Windows Program Manager or any other shell that you may be using. BTM is available on demand at any moment during your Windows session. It is only a mouse click or Ctrl+Esc away. You have to search for it on your Desktop.

Bloating Directory Finder

BLOAT1.ZIP (Bytes: 198098)

This searches your disk, several disks, a network, or part of a disk and produces an ordered tree of the space taken up by each directory. It also displays the results as a pie chart or bar chart and contains facilities to delete, move, and archive unwanted files. The information provided by this program can be quite surprising.

Mouse Warp v2.0c by Toggle Booleans

WARP2C.ZIP (Bytes: 47386)

Mouse Warp is a multifunctional cursor-enhancement utility that has the following features: it changes both the arrow and hourglass cursors; it offers blinking cursors; it provides 100 percent keyboard mouse movement and selection; you can design your own cursor; you can use any Windows icon as a cursor; you can assign handy functions to unused mouse buttons; and (the original Mouse Warp feature) you can allow the cursor to wrap around the edges of the screen (great for trackball users). Version 2.0c fixes bugs in the button functions.

BYE v1.10

BYE_11.ZIP (Bytes: 19955)

BYE.EXE v1.10 allows you to exit Windows with a click (or two), even if DOS boxes are open. New options have been added.

Font Off — offload TrueType fonts

FOFF.EXE (Bytes: 67365)

Font Off v1.7 allows you to better manage your TrueType fonts in Windows. You can remove seldom-used fonts (or all fonts) and reload them as needed. Unlike other font managers, Font Off physically moves the font's files to another storage media. This not only makes Windows faster but frees up valuable disk space. It is perfect for those who now find themselves with several hundred fonts. It requires VBRUN300.DLL .

File Find — locate files on media

FFIND.EXE (Bytes: 24572)

File Find v3.0 is a Windows program that locates files on your hard drive or a directory tree by the characters in the name. For example, searching for *HQ* will find 1993HQ.WK1, HQPRES.SAM, NOTES.HQ1, and so on. It goes well beyond DOS wild cards. It requires VBRUN300.DLL.

Micro-View 3.1 File Viewer

MVIEW3.ZIP (Bytes: 44883)

Micro-View is an all-purpose file viewer for both text and graphics. It's also a "garbage" viewer, in that it loads binary files in the all mode and displays any ASCII characters that are evident. The graphics that are supported are .BMP, .ICO, and .WMF.

LHA (2.13) — archive and de-archive software

LHA213.EXE (Bytes: 44381)

LHA (2.13), the descendant of LHARC, is an archiving program that compresses better than PKZIP and also makes self-extracting files, such as LHA213.EXE. It has online help for the casual user and documentation for the advanced user. Just run LHA213.EXE, and out pops its contents. Its new features expand batch mode. It is free, not shareware.

ClipMate for Windows 2.09b — Clipboard enhancement

CLIPMT.ZIP (Bytes: 195835)

ClipMate remembers all items that you copy to the Windows Clipboard. You can view, edit, combine, and print Clipboard data. Data is saved to disk between sessions. The new release features support for most Clipboard formats, including Bitmap, Picture, RTF, OLE, and more! You can select items visually with the new Thumbnail view. The new PowerPaste feature eases pasting into your application. Advanced memory management lets you collect hundreds of items. It also fixes problems with Print Setup and Load On Demand.

Micro-TrashCan v2.0 freeware

MBTCAN.ZIP (Bytes: 39436)

TrashCan v2.0 is a revised animated file dumper for File Manager. It has on-top capabilities so that you can place it right inside File Manager. You can specify its animation speed and position it anywhere on the desktop. You also can save these parameters as default. In version 2.0, the TrashCan has been moved to the alley, and error handling for read-only, system, and hidden files has been added. It requires Windows 3.1 and VBRUN300.DLL.

Loco 2.0 GREP/WhereIs utility

LOCO2.ZIP (Bytes: 25600)

Loco is a file-search program that allows you to search a designated set of files (up to an entire drive) in order to locate the files in which the contents match your search request, which can consist of a single string or a string-based Boolean expression.

Task Killer v1.0

TKILLR.ZIP (Bytes: 107197)

Task Killer lists modules (EXEs and DLLs) in memory and terminates them or decrements their usage counts. It saves, prints, and compares module lists and finds from where DLLs or EXEs were executed. It has a 3-D MDI interface with toolbar and online help. It is indispensable for programmers, network administrators, technical support, and power users.

STOP v3.1 — quick exit for Windows

STOP.ZIP (Bytes: 5823)

STOP v3.1 is a new and enhanced version of the definitive quick exit utility for Microsoft Windows. STOP runs as an icon. You can set the options to always keep STOP on top of your open windows. You can choose to click once or to double-click to close all open Windows applications and exit back to DOS.

The Runner Utilities

RUNNER.ZIP (Bytes: 42583)

The Runner Utilities are four programs that make it easier to launch and manage Windows applications. TaskRunner is a powerful replacement for Windows' Task Manager that features hide/unhide, quick exit, quick reboot, and more. WinRunner controls window sizes. GroupRunner puts groups on groups in Program Manager. And RightClick calls TaskRunner with a single right mouse click. Comprehensive online help and wallpaper are included.

Finder — to manage all those windows

[100121,1520 FINDER.ZIP (Bytes: 16469)

Finder is a utility that helps you keep those windows under control. It is a bit like selecting a program on a Mac.

The Executor

EXECUT.ZIP (Bytes: 31718)

Executor configures any mouse action you want to reprogram to perform any action, including launching any application, operating system command, or batch file and even bringing up Task Manager. It handles up to six actions and three mouse buttons with click or double-click.

ArrowSmith

ASMITH.ZIP (Bytes: 36024)

ArrowSmith lets you change Windows' default mouse pointer and wait symbol (hourglass) to any one of 66 handcrafted cursors that are easier to see, easier to use, and more fun. You can change pointers interactively (in full-screen mode) or automatically (as part of your Windows startup). ArrowSmith uses zeroK (0K) and includes several left-handed cursors. It's a must for notebook users. Comprehensive online help is included.

WinDial

WDIAL.ZIP (Bytes: 55641)

WinDial is a program that databases names, addresses, and phone numbers (work and home) and also dials the number if a phone is hooked up to your modem. It is a nice little utility that interfaces easily. It requires VBRUN300.DLL, which is not included in the .ZIP file.

System Control for Windows

SYSCTL.ZIP (Bytes: 31964)

SysControl is a small program that reboots, restarts, or exits from Windows. This program is helpful mostly for restarting Windows after you make changes to .INI files. It interfaces nicely.

SPEECH RECOGNITION DEMO FOR WINDOWS

INCUBE.ZIP (Bytes: 170456)

IN CUBE voice command is a working speech recognition demo that gives the user voice commands for a dozen Windows desktop utilities. IN CUBE is a continuous word-spotting recognition system that runs on 386, 486, and up by using audio input data from any Windows-compatible audio board. All menus, dialog boxes, and help screens are included so that you get a good look at the product. (You just can't save any changes to the demo lexicon.) IN CUBE is used for Windows navigation, voice macro command input, and data collection.

NameTool v1.6

NT.EXE (Bytes: 235939)

NameTool is used to assign long descriptions (120 characters) to DOS filenames. With an interface somewhat like File Manager, you can see your long descriptions and open your data files by double-clicking on the filename. This version adds NameTool Lite, a less memory-intensive sibling that allows any application that supports DDE macros or scripts to access NameTool descriptions. This self-extracting ARJ file contains a fully functional version of both programs with complete documentation. Read NT.TXT for details before downloading.

Drag And View — viewers for Windows' File Manager

DRAGVU.ZIP (Bytes: 360930)

Drag And View v2.0, winner of the Shareware Industry Award as best new utility, adds drag-and-drop or menu interface for viewing files with Windows' File Manager. It allows you to view ASCII, Hex, Lotus, Q Pro, Q Pro Win, Excel, dBASE, FoxPro, Pdox, Pdox Win, MS Word, WinWord, Win Write, WordPerfect, Win WordPerfect, Ami Pro, MS Works, Q&A, WMF, BMP, PCX, ICO, TIF, GIF, ZIP, and LZH. It opens multiple windows, has search and goto functions, and features a quick button bar.

Twdyn — Windows screen-capture utility

TWDYN.ZIP (Bytes: 84953)

Twdyn allows you to capture portions of windows and put them in your Clipboard. The formats that are supported are TEXT and Windows METAFILE (graphics). Unlike bitmap formats, these may be processed normally in your applications. This utility is a full-featured copy.

Cardfile Conversion Utility

WINCRD.EXE (Bytes: 14976)

WINCRD is a DOS utility that converts Windows card file information to text files.

Russian Notepad Update

RUSPD2.ZIP (Bytes: 27905)

This file contains an updated font tile and an announcement of the new software for the Russian Notepad (see RUSPAD.ZIP).

Quick Note for Windows

QWKN16.ZIP (Bytes: 24907)

Quick Note is a notepad without a menu. It can be set to stay on top of your applications and retains its contents on exit. It is an edit area to quickly jot stuff down in or to copy stuff to as you move between applications. Notes can be stacked in a tree structure. It is best launched from the startup group for quickest access. It requires VBRUN300.DLL.

Objective Desktop 1.1c

ODESK.ZIP (Bytes: 380427)

This is an MS Windows Program and File Manager with a UNIX-style browser, full drag-and-drop server and host capabilities, .ZIP file support, and drag-and-drop printing. It includes such tools as Virtual Screen to make your desktop four times bigger, Smart Dialer with dialing directory, DigiPad (an electronic post pad with support for sound recording), Recycler for deleting files with drag-and-drop, and a clock/calendar button. It also allows you to save the size and location of launched applications windows. It has quick switching capabilities and a lot more.

METZ Lock 3.3 for Microsoft Windows

LOCK.ZIP (Bytes: 218253)

METZ Lock 3.3 is your key to Microsoft Windows security! You can use METZ Lock to protect your PC, prevent unauthorized use, and disable Ctrl+Alt+Del. You can customize the application to meet your security needs with its easy-to-use configuration options. Novell and Banyan Vines passwords are also supported. This self-extracting archive contains a fully functional evaluation version, including online help and installation. See the included METZLOCK.TXT for more details.

Runtime — a file required to run Visual Basic 3.0

VB300.ZIP (Bytes: 227982)

Runtime is required by Visual Basic 3.0 to run Windows shareware written in VB 3.0. It is a binary file that uncompresses with PKUNZIP 2.04, QuinZip 2.1, or its equivalent.

Swift Access v1.5 — working model

SWFT15.ZIP (Bytes: 48529)

Swift Access provides handy desktop icons representing your favorite Windows applications. The icons can be arranged in a button bar, or individual icons can be placed in specific locations. You have full control over program attributes, such as passing parameters, selecting working directories and the initial window state, and choosing icons from other programs and DLLs. There will be no more hunting around in the Program Manager just to find the Notepad. Drag and drop is supported and full online help is included.

Accuboard 1.1

ACUBO.ZIP (Bytes: 6756)

This is a Clipboard enhancer for text, only 8K. Its description is inside the ACUBO.TXT file.

Icon Manager v3.3 — complete icon management

ICM33.ZIP (Bytes: 148992)

This is the most comprehensive icon management utility! Version 3.3 adds multiple icon selection to ease moving and copying of icon groups. We've added the power to open all 4000+ icons in the famous ALLICON collection at one time! It saves loads of disk space and allows you to view full screens of icons. Simply click any icon to edit or install it to your desktop. Icon Manager establishes hot links with Paintbrush, Program Manager, and Norton Desktop for automated edit sessions and icon installations. It updates files and provides drag-and-drop between .ICO, .DLL, .EXE, and so on. It even has sound effects!

Font Print — prints font samples

FPRNT.EXE (Bytes: 24853)

Font Print is a simple but flexible program to print samples of your Windows fonts. You select the fonts, the output format, the character set, and so on and let Font Print do the rest. It works well with Font Off (another TARDIS product) for printing samples of fonts before off-loading them. It requires VBRUN300.DLL.

RE v2.0b — for virtual screens, runs, layouts

RE20B.ZIP (Bytes: 113519)

RE v2.0b is the first wide release for virtual screens with a new TaskList (Move, Kill, and so on). You can save a snapshot of running programs and reload later (with change, delete, add, and layouts). Quickmouse wraps your mouse pointer around the screen border. You have a Run application (with browse and a 15-item history). REStart/REBoot has four Quicklaunch buttons. It resources as text or as on-top percentage bars. It includes many more features. It needs VBRUN300.DLL.

WinAlarm — Windows pop-up alarm

WINALA.ZIP (Bytes: 37426)

WinAlarm is a single pop-up reminder utility for Windows. Type your own reminder message, and WinAlarm pops it up over any Windows application at the time you specify. WinAlarm also pops up wherever you want it to, alerting you with a flashing message bar, beeps, and a colorful screen so that you simply cannot miss it! WinAlarm requires VBRUN200.DLL.

ZIP Manager 4.0 upgrade

ZM4.ZIP (Bytes: 430116)

This upgrade supports PKZIP 1.10, 2.04, and ARJ. It works just like the Windows File Manager. It has complete drag-and-drop power to create new .ZIP and .ARJ files, add files, move files, and delete files. It drags files from one archive to another, and even from .ZIP to .ARJ files! It is compatible with DOS 6 and double-space drives. Now Norton Desktop, PC Tools, and XTree can create and open PKZIP 2.04 format compressed files thanks to ZIP Manager 4.0! It includes an Extension DLL that adds ZIP Manager to the File Manager.

GrabIt Pro — the top-rated screen-capture program

GRABPR.ZIP (Bytes: 164684)

GrabIt Pro is the upgrade to our popular and critically acclaimed GrabIt For Windows program. GrabIt Pro was designed for programmers, technical writers, and anyone who needs to quickly capture screens under Windows 3.1 You can capture an entire window, client area, the Desktop, or selected areas of any window. GrabIt Pro uses the multiple document interface so you can capture multiple images and review them before deciding which ones to save. GrabIt Pro saves screen shots in monochrome, 16-color, and 256-color bitmaps.

File Commander 2.0k — a File Manager extender

FC-20K.ZIP (Bytes: 281537)

File Commander takes the Windows 3.1's object-oriented File Manager and adds the powerful WIL program language (made famous in Command Post and WinBatch) with almost 200 functions. The result is a shell "with a difference." File Commander attaches itself to File Manager and adds up to four pull-down menus, each of which can have up to three levels of customizable submenus with up to 99 items. Version 2.0 adds a number of new functions, including greatly enhanced dialog boxes.

File List Printer (FLiP) v1.0

FLIP10.EXE (Bytes: 139264)

FLIP10.EXE is a self-extracting archive for File List Printer (FLiP) v1.0. FLiP is a productivity enhancement tool for the user who routinely prints multiple text (and binary) files. It is designed to automate the printing of files in a well-formatted, space-efficient manner. It will print up to four "pages" on a paper sheet, and it allows user-defined borders, descriptive headers and footers, and control over formatting.

Star2 — a very 3-D star field simulator

STAR2.ZIP (Bytes: 28182)

Star2 is a very realistic 3-D screen saver for Windows 3.1 that generates a star field simulation in which as many as 1000 stars at six brightness levels are displayed. A fast CPU with math coprocessor is recommended for large numbers of stars.

PopCal 3.0 freeware

POPCAL.ZIP (Bytes: 29318)

PopCal 3.0 (the bride of PopCal 2.0, a *Windows Magazine* top pick) now remembers its position on-screen and offers a choice of colors. PopCal 3.0 displays any date in any year between 1753 and 2077, with today's date highlighted. A Windows screen saver feature and a digital running clock make this an ideal desktop companion. It requires VBRUN200.DLL.

Exodus v1.2 — quick exit utility

EXOD.EXE (Bytes: 29293)

Exodus is a quick exiting utility with four exiting methods: Exit, which exits to DOS without the `Are you sure?` prompt of the Program Manager; Exit and Restart, which quickly restarts windows and is great for .INI changes; Exit and Reboot, which reboots the system and is great for CONFIG.SYS and AUTOEXEC.BAT; Exit, Run, and Restart, which clears memory of Windows completely and is great for graphical games and safe for CHKDSK /f *DDE support. It has command line support.

Talking Clock for Windows 3.1

TCLOCK.ZIP (Bytes: 266764)

Talking Clock v1.07 for Windows 3.1 displays the time and optionally announces the time every 15 minutes by using a Windows compatible sound card (such as SoundBlaster).

Stopwatch/Clock for Windows 3.1

SW.ZIP (Bytes: 13690)

Stopwatch/Clock v1.03 for Windows 3.1 is shareware.

Astronomy Clock for Windows 3.1

ACLOCK.ZIP (Bytes: 35944)

Astronomy Clock v1.13 for Windows 3.1 displays the current time in local mean time, universal time, local sidereal time, and Greenwich sidereal time format.

Work/Home File Synchronizer Utility

UPD8R.ZIP (Bytes: 75748)

In his June review of WinUpD8R v2.1 in *Windows Sources* magazine, Barry Simon states, "If you have two or more machines to keep in synch, you'll bless this program." WinUpD8R v3.0 keeps multiple PCs "UpD8ed" to the most current file versions by using floppy disks as the transfer medium. The major 3.0 upgrade adds a host of new features to WinUpD8R and a minor bug in the upload has been fixed (file stamp 5/21/93 3:01:00).

WMagic TOOLBARS-GRP ICONS-FAST

WMICON.EXE (Bytes: 130460)

Are you tired of the Program Manager shuffle? The solution is WindowMagic. It is THE productivity-enhancement tool for Program Manager. It includes color toolbars and tool groups, group and application icon customization, fantastic drag-and-drop icon management tools, a lightning fast launcher, and an enhanced exit. Edward Mendelson of Windows Sources says, "Adding WindowMagic moves you one step closer to an intuitive computing environment." You won't believe it's shareware!

TrashMan for Pen Windows! v2.0

TMPEN.ZIP (Bytes: 64128)

The original and BEST drag-and-drop trash can for Windows is now available in a special version for Microsoft's Windows for Pen Computing 3.1! You can drag files or directories to the trash icon, and they'll be stored (even after exiting and restarting TrashMan, Windows, or the PC itself) until you decide to restore or permanently delete them! You can associate .WAV sounds with different events! Choose from several different trash icons.

Index

Symbols

A

T

Notes

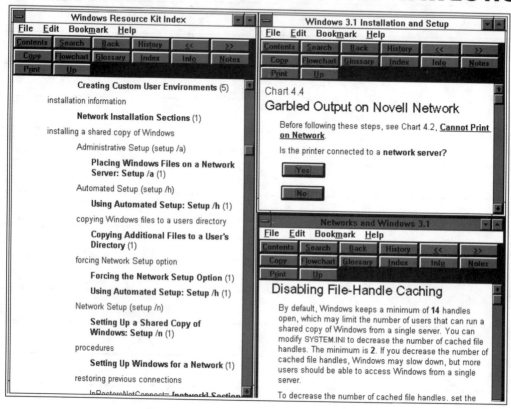

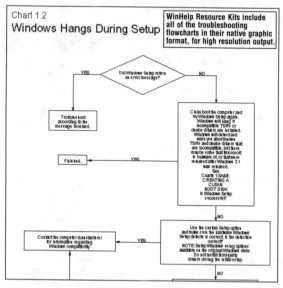

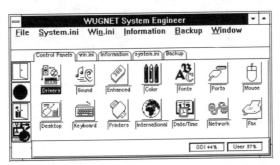

TIM HEFLIN
Manager, End-User Services
Microsoft, Inc.

Network Topology: Ethernet
Networking Protocol: TCP/IP
Host: DEC VAX

"DynaComm® is Microsoft's® choice for terminal emulation." It should be yours.

Evaluating terminal emulation software? Consider the one that Microsoft chose for communicating across their world-wide network. FutureSoft's DynaComm for Windows™ offers a single solution for PCs communicating across multi-platform networks to host computers.

DynaComm features:
- 16 Terminal emulation types for UNIX, DEC, Hewlett-Packard, IBM, Data General, and ViewData systems

- 19 Network interfaces including TCP/IP and IPX
- Powerful development tools for creating GUI front ends to host applications

800-989-8908
FutureSoft

12012 Wickchester Lane, Suite 600
Houston, Texas 77079-1222 USA
713.496.9400 • 713.496.1090 FAX
800.989.8908 Sales (USA)

Find out why over 6 million computer users love IDG'S ...FOR DUMMIES BOOKS!

"I laughed and learned..."
Arlene J. Peterson, Rapid City, South Dakota

DOS FOR DUMMIES,™ 2nd EDITION
by Dan Gookin

This fun and easy DOS primer has taught millions of readers how to learn DOS! A #1 bestseller for over 56 weeks!

ISBN: 1-878058-75-4
$16.95 USA/$21.95 Canada
£14.99 UK and Eire

 INTERNATIONAL BESTSELLER!

WINDOWS FOR DUMMIES™
by Andy Rathbone

Learn the Windows interface with this bestselling reference.

ISBN: 1-878058-61-4
$16.95 USA/$21.95 Canada
£14.99 UK and Eire

 #1 BESTSELLER!

THE INTERNET FOR DUMMIES™
by John Levine

Surf the Internet with this simple reference to command, service and linking basics. For DOS, Windows, UNIX, and Mac users.

ISBN: 1-56884-024-1
$19.95 USA/$26.95 Canada
£17.99 UK and Eire

 NATIONAL BESTSELLER!

PCs FOR DUMMIES,™ 2nd EDITION
by Dan Gookin & Andy Rathbone

This #1 bestselling reference is the perfect companion for the computer phobic.

ISBN: 1-56884-078-0
$16.95 USA/$21.95 Canada
£14.99 UK and Eire

 NATIONAL BESTSELLER!

MACs FOR DUMMIES,™ 2nd Edition
by David Pogue

The #1 Mac book, totally revised and updated. Get the most from your Mac!

#1 MAC BOOK

ISBN: 1-56884-051-9
$19.95 USA/$26.95 Canada
£17.99 UK and Eire

WORDPERFECT FOR DUMMIES™
by Dan Gookin

NATIONAL BESTSELLER!

Bestseller Dan Gookin teaches all the basics in this fun reference that covers WordPerfect 4.2 - 5.1.

ISBN: 1-878058-52-5
$16.95 USA/$21.95 Canada/£14.99 UK and Eire

UPGRADING AND FIXING PCs FOR DUMMIES™
by Andy Rathbone

Here's the complete, easy-to-follow reference for upgrading and repairing PCs yourself.

ISBN: 1-56884-002-0
$19.95 USA/$26.95 Canada

NATIONAL BESTSELLER!

WORD FOR WINDOWS FOR DUMMIES™
by Dan Gookin

Learn Word for Windows basics the fun and easy way. Covers Version 2.

ISBN: 1-878058-86-X
$16.95 USA/$21.95 Canada
£14.99 UK and Eire

 NATIONAL BESTSELLER!

WORDPERFECT 6 FOR DUMMIES™
by Dan Gookin

WordPerfect 6 commands and functions, presented in the friendly ...For Dummies style.

ISBN: 1-878058-77-0
$16.95 USA/$21.95 Canada
£14.99 UK and Eire

 NATIONAL BESTSELLER!

1-2-3 FOR DUMMIES™
by Greg Harvey

Spreadsheet guru Greg Harvey's fast and friendly reference covers 1-2-3 Releases 2 - 2.4.

ISBN: 1-878058-60-6
$16.95 USA/$21.95 Canada
£14.99 UK and Eire

 NATIONAL BESTSELLER!

EXCEL FOR DUMMIES,™ 2nd EDITION
by Greg Harvey

Updated, expanded—The easy-to-use reference to Excel 5 features and commands.

ISBN: 1-56884-050-0
$16.95 USA/$21.95 Canada
£14.99 UK and Eire

 NATIONAL BESTSELLER!

UNIX FOR DUMMIES™
by John R. Levine & Margaret Levine Young

NATIONAL BESTSELLER!

This enjoyable reference gets novice UNIX users up and running—fast.

ISBN: 1-878058-58-4
$19.95 USA/$26.95 Canada/   £17.99 UK and Eire

"DOS For Dummies is the ideal book for anyone who's just bought a PC and is too shy to ask friends stupid questions."

MTV, Computer Book of the Year,
United Kingdom

"This book allows me to get the answers to questions I am too embarrassed to ask."

Amanda Kelly, Doylestown, PA on Gookin and Rathbone's PCs For Dummies

"If it wasn't for this book, I would have turned in my computer for a stereo."

Experanza Andrade, Enfield, CT

CORELDRAW! FOR DUMMIES™
by Deke McClelland

This bestselling author leads designers through the drawing features of Versions 3 & 4.

ISBN: 1-56884-042-X
$19.95 USA/$26.95 Canada/17.99 UK & Eire

QUICKEN FOR WINDOWS FOR DUMMIES™
by Steve Nelson

Manage finances like a pro with Steve Nelson's friendly help. Covers Version 3.

ISBN: 1-56884-005-5
$16.95 USA/$21.95 Canada
£14.99 UK & Eire

NATIONAL BESTSELLER!

QUATTRO PRO FOR DOS FOR DUMMIES™
by John Walkenbach

This friendly guide makes Quattro Pro fun and easy and covers the basics of Version 5.

ISBN: 1-56884-023-3
$16.95 USA/$21.95 Canada/14.99 UK & Eire

MODEMS FOR DUMMIES™
by Tina Rathbone

Learn how to communicate with and get the most out of your modem — includes basics for DOS, Windows, and Mac users.

ISBN: 1-56884-001-2
$19.95 USA/$26.95 Canada
14.99 UK & Eire

1-2-3 FOR WINDOWS FOR DUMMIES™
by John Walkenbach

Learn the basics of 1-2-3 for Windows from this spreadsheet expert (covers release 4).

ISBN: 1-56884-052-7
$16.95 USA/$21.95 Canada/14.99 UK & Eire

NETWARE FOR DUMMIES™
by Ed Tittel & Denni Connor

Learn to install, use, and manage a NetWare network with this straightforward reference.

ISBN: 1-56884-003-9
$19.95 USA/$26.95 Canada/17.99 UK & Eire

OS/2 FOR DUMMIES™
by Andy Rathbone

This fun and easy OS/2 survival guide is perfect for beginning and intermediate users.

ISBN: 1-878058-76-2
$19.95 USA/$26.95 Canada/17.99 UK & Eire

QUICKEN FOR DOS FOR DUMMIES™
by Steve Nelson

Manage your own finances with this enjoyable reference that covers Version 7.

ISBN: 1-56884-006-3
$16.95 USA/$21.95 Canada/14.99 UK & Eire

WORD 6 FOR DOS FOR DUMMIES™
by Beth Slick

This friendly reference teaches novice Word users all the basics of Word 6 for DOS

ISBN: 1-56884-000-4
$16.95 USA/$21.95 Canada/14.99 UK & Eire

AMI PRO FOR DUMMIES™
by Jim Meade

Learn Ami Pro Version 3 with this friendly reference to the popular Lotus word processor.

ISBN: 1-56884-049-7
$16.95 USA/$21.95 Canada/14.99 UK & Eire

WORDPERFECT FOR WINDOWS FOR DUMMIES™
by Margaret Levine Young

Here's a fun and friendly reference that teaches novice users features and commands of WordPerfect For Windows Version 6.

ISBN: 1-56884-032-2
$16.95 USA/$21.95 Canada/14.99 UK & Eire

"I rely on your publication extensively to help me over stumbling blocks that are created by my lack of experience."

Fred Carney, Louisville, KY on
PC World DOS 6 Handbook

PC WORLD MICROSOFT ACCESS BIBLE
by Cary N. Prague & Michael R. Irwin

Easy-to-understand reference that covers the ins and outs of Access features and provides hundreds of tips, secrets and shortcuts for fast database development. Complete with disk of Access templates. Covers versions 1.0 & 1.1

ISBN: 1-878058-81-9
$39.95 USA/$52.95 Canada
£35.99 incl. VAT UK & Eire

PC WORLD WORD FOR WINDOWS 6 HANDBOOK
by Brent Heslop & David Angell

Details all the features of Word for Windows 6, from formatting to desktop publishing and graphics. A 3-in-1 value (tutorial, reference, and software) for users of all levels.

ISBN: 1-56884-054-3
$34.95 USA/$44.95 Canada
£29.99 incl. VAT UK & Eire

PC WORLD DOS 6 COMMAND REFERENCE AND PROBLEM SOLVER
by John Socha & Devra Hall

The only book that combines a DOS 6 Command Reference with a comprehensive Problem Solving Guide. Shows when, why and how to use the key features of DOS 6/6.2

ISBN: 1-56884-055-1
$24.95 USA/$32.95 Canada
£22.99 UK & Eire

QUARKXPRESS FOR WINDOWS DESIGNER HANDBOOK
by Barbara Assadi & Galen Gruman

ISBN: 1-878058-45-2
$29.95 USA/$39.95 Canada/£26.99 UK & Eire

PC WORLD WORDPERFECT 6 HANDBOOK
by Greg Harvey, author of IDG's bestselling 1-2-3 For Dummies

Here's the ultimate WordPerfect 6 tutorial and reference. Complete with handy templates, macros, and tools.

ISBN: 1-878058-80-0
$34.95 USA/$44.95 Canada
£29.99 incl. VAT UK & Eire

PC WORLD EXCEL 5 FOR WINDOWS HANDBOOK, 2nd EDITION
by John Walkenbach & Dave Maguiness

Covers all the latest Excel features, plus contains disk with examples of the spreadsheets referenced in the book, custom ToolBars, hot macros, and demos.

ISBN: 1-56884-056-X
$34.95 USA/$44.95 Canada /£29.99 incl. VAT UK & Eir

PC WORLD DOS 6 HANDBOOK, 2nd EDITION
by John Socha, Clint Hicks & Devra Hall

Includes the exciting new features of DOS 6, a 300+ page DOS command reference, plus a bonus disk of the Norto Commander Special Edition, and over a dozen DOS utilities.

ISBN: 1-878058-79-7
$34.95 USA/$44.95 Canada/£29.99 incl. VAT UK & Eire

OFFICIAL XTREE COMPANION, 3RD EDITION
by Beth Slick

ISBN: 1-878058-57-6
$19.95 USA/$26.95 Canada/£17.99 UK & Eire

For more information or to order by mail, call 1-800-762-2974. Call for a free catalog! For volume discounts and special orders, please call Tony Real, Special Sales, at 415-312-0644. For International sales and distribution information, please call our authorized distributors:

CANADA Macmillan Canada
416-293-8141

UNITED KINGDOM Transworld
44-81-231-6661

AUSTRALIA Woodslane Pty Ltd.
61-2-979-5944

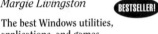

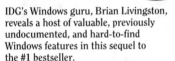

Order Form

Order Center: (800) 762-2974 (8 a.m.-5 p.m., PST, weekdays) or (415) 312-0650

For Fastest Service: Photocopy This Order Form and FAX it to: (415) 358-1260

Quantity	ISBN	Title	Price	Total

Shipping & Handling Charges

Subtotal	U.S.	Canada & International	International Air Mail
Up to $20.00	Add $3.00	Add $4.00	Add $10.00
$20.01-40.00	$4.00	$5.00	$20.00
$40.01-60.00	$5.00	$6.00	$25.00
$60.01-80.00	$6.00	$8.00	$35.00
Over $80.00	$7.00	$10.00	$50.00

In U.S. and Canada, shipping is UPS ground or equivalent.
For Rush shipping call (800) 762-2974.

Subtotal _____

CA residents add applicable sales tax _____

IN and MA residents add 5% sales tax _____

IL residents add 6.25% sales tax _____

RI residents add 7% sales tax _____

Shipping _____

Total _____

Ship to:

Name _____

Company _____

Address _____

City/State/Zip _____

Daytime Phone _____

Payment: ❏ Check to IDG Books (US Funds Only)   ❏ Visa   ❏ Mastercard   ❏ American Express

Card# _____ Exp._____ Signature_____

Please send this order form to: IDG Books, 155 Bovet Road, Suite 310, San Mateo, CA 94402.

Allow up to 3 weeks for delivery. Thank you!

IDG Books Worldwide License Agreement

By opening the accompanying disk package, you indicate that you have read and agree with the terms of this licensing agreement. If you disagree and do not want to be bound by the terms of this licensing agreement, return the book for refund to the source from which you purchased it.

The entire contents of these disks and the compilation of the software contained therein are copyrighted and protected by both U.S. copyright law and international copyright treaty provisions. The individual programs on these disks are copyrighted by the authors of each program respectively. Each program has its own use permissions and limitations. You may copy any or all of these programs to your computer system. To use each program, you must follow the individual requirements and restrictions detailed for each in the shareware section of this book. Do not use a program if you do not want to follow its licensing agreement. Absolutely none of the material on these disks or listed in this book may ever be distributed, in original or modified form, for commercial purposes.

Disclaimer and Copyright Notice

Warranty Notice: IDG Books Worldwide, Inc., warrants that the disks that accompany this book are free from defects in materials and workmanship for a period of 60 days from the date of purchase of this book. If IDG Books Worldwide receives notification within the warranty period of defects in material or workmanship, IDG Books Worldwide will replace the defective disks. The remedy for the breach of this warranty will be limited to replacement and will not encompass any other damages, including but not limited to loss of profit, and special, incidental, consequential, or other claims.

5¼", 1.2MB Disk Format Available. The enclosed disks are in 3½" 1.44MB, high-density format. If you have a different size drive, or a low-density drive, and you cannot arrange to transfer the data to the disk size you need, you can obtain the programs on 5¼" 1.2MB high-density disks or 5¼" 360K low-density disks by writing: IDG Books Worldwide, Attn: *InfoWorld Windows 3.1 Configuration SECRETS Disks,* IDG Books Worldwide, 155 Bovet Rd., Suite 310, San Mateo, CA 94402, or call 800-762-2974. Please specify the size of disk you need, and please allow 3 to 4 weeks for delivery.

Copyright Notice

Installation Instructions — Infoworld *Windows 3.1 Configuration SECRETS* Companion Disks

Before you install the contents of the companion disks, please read the Disclaimer and Copyright Notice on the preceding page. The companion disks contain tools and utilities that are described in the Disk Documentation section of this book.

The disks install automatically when you run the INSTALL.EXE file on the disks. You can choose to install the entire contents of each disk or selected groups of files from the disks. Additionally, you can specify the drive and directory to which you want to install the files. The default directory is C:\WCONFIG.

To use the automatic installation, follow these steps:

1. Insert disk 1 into the appropriate disk drive.

2. At the DOS prompt, log on to the drive containing the disk. (To log to drive A, for example, enter **A:**).

3. Type **INSTALL** and press Enter.

4. Choose one of the following options:

   Express setup   Installs all the files

   Custom setup   Enables you to select groups of files for installation

   Finished   Quit the installation program

   If you choose Express or Custom setup, you must select a drive to install to and press Enter.

5. To accept the default directory name, press Enter. Alternatively, type the name of the directory you want to install to and press Enter. (Install creates a directory if one does not exist.)

6. Choose Finished and press Enter.

   Note: After you are finished using the companion disks for installation, store them in a safe place.

IDG BOOKS WORLDWIDE REGISTRATION CARD

RETURN THIS REGISTRATION CARD FOR FREE CATALOG

Title of this book: Windows 3.1 Configuration SECRETS

My overall rating of this book: ❏ Very good [1] ❏ Good [2] ❏ Satisfactory [3] ❏ Fair [4] ❏ Poor [5]

How I first heard about this book:

❏ Found in bookstore; name: [6]   ❏ Book review: [7]

❏ Advertisement: [8]   ❏ Catalog: [9]

❏ Word of mouth; heard about book from friend, co-worker, etc.: [10]   ❏ Other: [11]

What I liked most about this book:

_____

_____

What I would change, add, delete, etc., in future editions of this book:

_____

_____

Other comments:

_____

Number of computer books I purchase in a year: ❏ 1 [12] ❏ 2-5 [13] ❏ 6-10 [14] ❏ More than 10 [15]

I would characterize my computer skills as: ❏ Beginner [16] ❏ Intermediate [17] ❏ Advanced [18] ❏ Professional [19]

I use ❏ DOS [20] ❏ Windows [21] ❏ OS/2 [22] ❏ Unix [23] ❏ Macintosh [24] ❏ Other: [25]_____
(please specify)

I would be interested in new books on the following subjects:
(please check all that apply, and use the spaces provided to identify specific software)

❏ Word processing: [26]   ❏ Spreadsheets: [27]

❏ Data bases: [28]   ❏ Desktop publishing: [29]

❏ File Utilities: [30]   ❏ Money management: [31]

❏ Networking: [32]   ❏ Programming languages: [33]

❏ Other: [34]

I use a PC at (please check all that apply): ❏ home [35] ❏ work [36] ❏ school [37] ❏ other: [38] _____

The disks I prefer to use are ❏ 5.25 [39] ❏ 3.5 [40] ❏ other: [41]_____

I have a CD ROM: ❏ yes [42] ❏ no [43]

I plan to buy or upgrade computer hardware this year: ❏ yes [44] ❏ no [45]

I plan to buy or upgrade computer software this year: ❏ yes [46] ❏ no [47]

Name: .   Business title: [48]   Type of Business: [49]

Address (❏ home [50] ❏ work [51]/Company name: _____)

Street/Suite# _____

City [52]/State [53]/Zipcode [54]: _____ Country [55] _____

❏ **I liked this book!** You may quote me by name in future
   IDG Books Worldwide promotional materials.

My daytime phone number is _____

IDG BOOKS

THE WORLD OF
COMPUTER
KNOWLEDGE

❏ YES!

Please keep me informed about IDG's World of Computer Knowledge.
Send me the latest IDG Books catalog.

COMPUTER
BOOK SERIES
FROM IDG